中国民政统计年鉴

（中国社会服务统计资料）

CHINA CIVIL AFFAIRS' STATISTICAL YEARBOOK

(Statistics of China Social Services)

2017

中华人民共和国民政部　编

Compiled by Ministry of Civil Affairs of the People's Republic of China

图书在版编目（CIP）数据

中国民政统计年鉴 ：中国社会服务统计资料. 2017 ：汉英对照 / 中华人民共和国民政部编. -- 北京 ：中国统计出版社，2017.8
ISBN 978-7-5037-8227-5

Ⅰ. ①中… Ⅱ. ①中… Ⅲ. ①民政事务－统计资料－中国－2017－年鉴－汉、英 Ⅳ. ①D632-66

中国版本图书馆CIP数据核字(2017)第174721号

中国民政统计年鉴－2017（中国社会服务统计资料）

作　　者/ 中华人民共和国民政部
责任编辑/ 李　冲
装帧设计/ 李雪燕
出版发行/ 中国统计出版社
通信地址/ 北京市丰台区西三环南路甲6号　　邮政编码/100073
电　　话/ 邮购 (010)63376909　　书店 (010)68783171
网　　址/ http://www.zgtjcbs.com/
印　　刷/ 河北鑫兆源印刷有限公司
排　　版/ 北京拓展诺美广告有限责任公司
经　　销/ 新华书店
开　　本/ 880×1230mm　　1/16
印　　张/ 43
字　　数/ 1400千字
版　　别/ 2017年8月第1版
版　　次/ 2017年8月第1次印刷
定　　价/ 280.00元

本书附同版本CD-ROM一张，光盘内容以书面文字为准。
如有印装错误，本社发行部负责调换。

《中国民政统计年鉴－2017》

（中国社会服务统计资料）

编委会和编辑出版人员

编者说明

《中国民政统计年鉴－2017》(中国社会服务统计资料)是一部反映2016年度中国社会服务发展的资料性年刊。2016年度社会服务统计资料是根据各省、自治区、直辖市以及计划单列市民政厅（局）报送的社会服务业统计年报及有关部门的报表编制而成。本书内容由六个部分组成：第一部分是专文，2016年社会服务发展统计公报；第二部分是社会服务主要数据图表；第三部分是社会服务综合统计资料；第四部分是社会服务历年统计资料；第五部分是社会服务当年分省统计资料；第六部分是附录，《中国民政统计年鉴－2016》勘误。本书对各级政府有关部门、从事社会服务研究和教学的人员，以及社会各界了解和研究社会服务发展状况、提高政府管理和决策水平，具有重要的参考价值。

书中涉及到的全国性统计数据均不包括香港特别行政区、澳门特别行政区和台湾省；表格中“－”符号表示数据不足本表最小计量单位；“空格”符号表示该项统计数据为零；“#”表示其中主要项。

本书凝聚了全国民政系统广大规划财务部门统计工作者和有关部门统计人员的辛勤汗水和工作成果。本书的编辑出版得到了各级领导和统计战线同仁们的热情支持和帮助。在此，向所有关心和支持该书出版发行的同志们表示衷心的谢意。

目　录

第一部分：专文

第二部分：社会服务主要数据图表

综合

社会工作

成员组织和其他社会服务

第三部分：社会服务综合统计资料

综合

社会工作

成员组织和其他社会服务

第四部分：社会服务历年统计资料

综合

社会工作

成员组织和其他社会服务

第五部分：社会服务当年分省统计资料

综合

行政区划和行政机关

社会服务总体情况

社会工作

提供住宿的社会服务活动

为老年人与残疾人提供住宿服务的机构

为智障与精神疾病人提供住宿服务的机构

为儿童提供住宿的社会服务机构

其他提供住宿的社会服务机构

不提供住宿的社会服务活动

为社区居民提供的服务

为老年人提供的服务

为残疾人提供的服务

为儿童提供的服务

为生活困难群众提供的服务

成员组织和其他社会服务

成员组织

自治组织

其他社会服务

婚姻服务

殡葬服务

其他

第六部分：附录

CONTENTS

Part 1: Feature Articles

Part 2: Primary Data and Figures of Social Services

I. Synthesis

II. Social Services

III. Member Organizations and Other Social Services

Part Three: Comprehensive Statistics of Social Services

I. Synthesis

II. Social Services

III. Member Organizations and Other Social Services

Part Four: Historical Statistics of Social Services

I. Synthesis

II. Social Services

III. Member Organizations and Other Social Services

Part Five: Provincial Statistics of Social Services in 2016

I. Synthesis

Administrative Divisions and Administrative Organs

Overall Situation of Social Service Industry

II. Social Services

Social Service Activities with Accommodation

Social Service Activities without Accommodation

III. Member Organizations and Other Social Services

Member Organizations

Other Social Services

Other Institutions

Part Six: Appendix

01

专文

2017

中华人民共和国
2016年社会服务发展统计公报

中华人民共和国民政部

2017年7月20日

2016年，全国民政系统认真贯彻党的十八大和十八届三中、四中、五中、六中全会精神，深入贯彻习近平总书记系列重要讲话精神，坚持稳中求进工作总基调，推进改革创新，加强法治建设，切实履行保障基本民生、加强和创新相关社会治理、支持国防和军队改革、提供相关基本公共服务职责，民政事业得到了新发展。

一、综合

截至2016年底，全国共有省级行政区划单位34个（其中直辖市4个、省23个、自治区5个、特别行政区2个），地级行政区划单位334个（其中地级市293个、地区8个、自治州30个、盟3个），县级行政区划单位2851个（其中市辖区954个、县级市360个、县1366个、自治县117个、旗49个、自治旗3个、特区1个、林区1个），乡级行政区划单位39862个，其中区公所2个、镇20883个、乡9731个、苏木152个、民族乡988个、民族苏木1个、街道8105个。

2016年，共联合检查省界13条，完成了总长度约为13629公里的省界联检任务。

图1　乡镇、街道变化情况

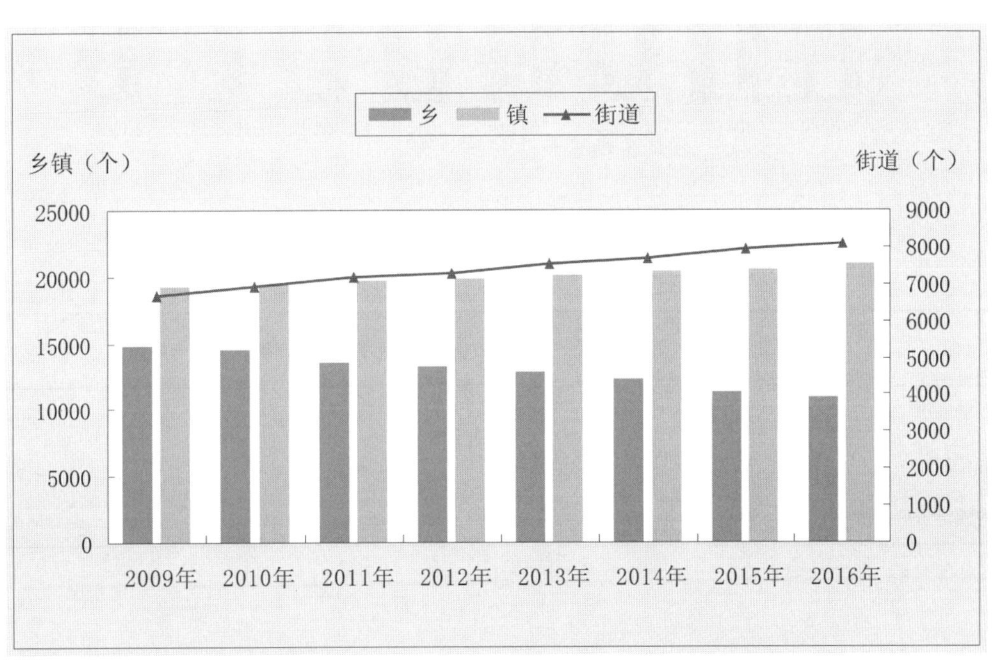

表 1 乡镇、街道变化情况

单位：个

指标	2009年	2010年	2011年	2012年	2013年	2014年	2015年	2016年
乡	14848	14571	13587	13281	12812	12282	11315	10872
镇	19322	19410	19683	19881	20117	20401	20515	20883
街道	6686	6923	7194	7282	7566	7696	7957	8105

截至2016年底，全国共有社会服务机构和设施174.5万个；职工总数1239.3万人，固定资产原价5393.6亿元；社会服务事业基本建设在建项目建设规模3050.9万平方米，全年实际完成投资总额245.8亿元；全国持证社会工作者共计28.8万人，其中社会工作师6.9万人，助理工作师21.9万人；全国社会服务事业费支出5440.2亿元，比上年增长10.4%，占国家财政支出比重为3.4%，其中中央财政向各地转移支付社会服务事业费2484.0亿元，比上年增长9.4%，占社会服务事业费比重为45.7%，同比下降0.4个百分点。

图2 社会服务基本情况

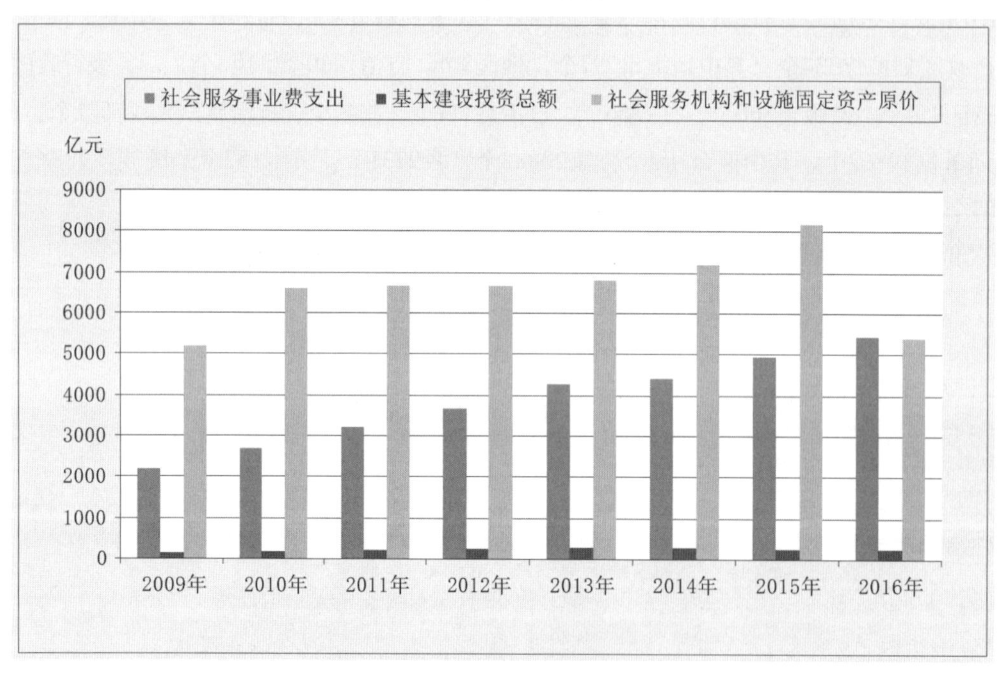

表2 社会服务基本情况

单位：亿元

指标	2009年	2010年	2011年	2012年	2013年	2014年	2015年	2016年
社会服务事业费支出	2181.9	2697.5	3229.1	3683.7	4276.5	4404.1	4926.4	5440.2
基本建设投资总额	157.0	183.0	218.5	235.0	292.8	282.2	239.9	245.8
社会服务机构固定资产原价	5198.0	6589.3	6676.7	6675.4	6810.2	7213.0	8183.1	5393.6

二、社会工作

（一）提供住宿的社会服务

截至2016年底，全国办理了注册登记手续的提供住宿的各类社会服务机构3.2万个，其中登记注册为事业单位的机构1.8万个，登记注册为民办非企业单位的1.2万个。机构内床位414.0万张，年末收留抚养人员241.0万人。

图3 社会服务机构床位

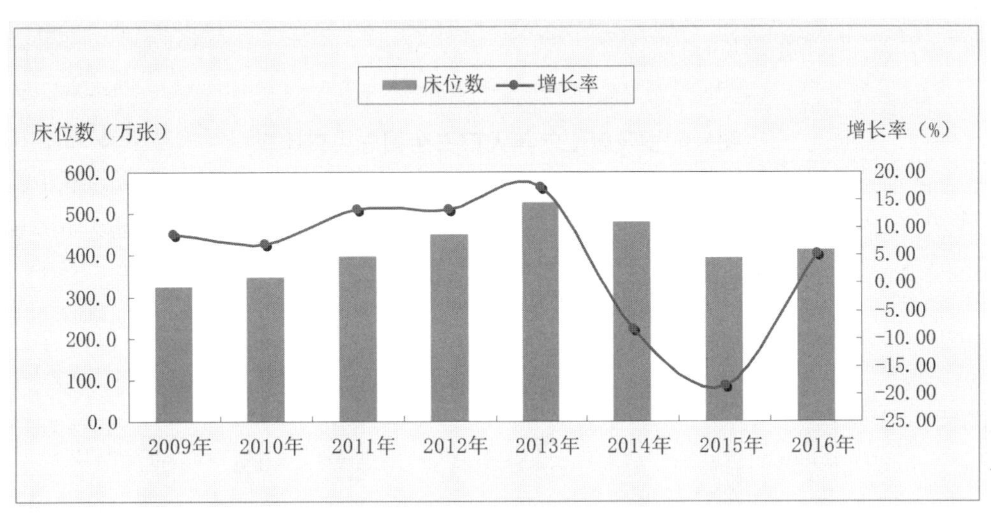

表3 社会服务机构床位

单位：万张、%

指标	2009年	2010年	2011年	2012年	2013年	2014年	2015年	2016年
床位数	326.5	349.6	396.4	449.3	526.7	482.3	393.2	414.0
增长率	8.72	7.08	13.39	13.35	17.23	−8.43	−18.47	5.29

注：自2014年起，调整社会服务机构的统计口径为在工商、编办和民政部门办理了注册登记手续的社会服务单位，原统计口径中未办理注册登记手续的社会服务单位，均已经调整到社会服务设施中。

1.提供住宿的养老服务。全国各类养老服务机构和设施14.0万个，比上年增长20.7 %，其中:注册登记的养老服务机构2.9万个，社区养老服务机构和设施3.5万个，社区互助型养老设施7.6万个；各类养老床位合计730.2万张，比上年增长8.6%（每千名老年人拥有养老床位31.6张，比上年增长4.3%），其中社区留宿和日间照料床位322.9万张。

2.提供住宿的精神卫生服务。全国民政部门管理的智障与精神疾病服务机构共有244个，床位8.4万张。其中社会福利医院（精神病院）150个，床位数5.3万张，年末收留抚养各类人员4.4万人；复退军人精神病院94个，床位数3.1万张，年末收留抚养各类人员2.5万人。

3.提供住宿的儿童福利和保护服务。全国共有儿童收养救助服务机构705个，床位10.0万张，年末收留抚养各类人员5.4万人。其中儿童福利机构465个，床位9.0万张；未成年人救助保护中心240个，床位1.0万张，全年共救助流浪乞讨未成年人5.2万人次。

4.其他提供住宿的社会服务。全国共有其他提供住宿的社会服务机构2371个，床位16.7万张。其中各类救助管理机构1736个，床位10.2万张，全年救助生活无着流浪乞讨人员328.3万人次（在站救助283.5万人次，站外救助44.7万人次）。军供站315个，其他提供住宿的机构320个。

（二）不提供住宿的社会服务

1.老龄服务。截至2016年底，全国60岁及以上老年人口23086万人，占总人口的16.7%，其中65岁及以上人口15003万人，占总人口的10.8%。全国共有老龄事业单位1828个，老年法律援助中心1.9万个，老年维权协调组织7.0万个，老年学校5.4万个、在校学习人员710.2万人，各类老年活动室35.9万个；享受高龄补贴的老年人2355.4万人，比上年增长9.3 %；享受护理补贴的老年人40.5万人，比上年增长52.8%；享受养老服务补贴的老年人282.9万人，比上年增长9.7%。

图4 60岁及以上老年人口占全国总人口比重

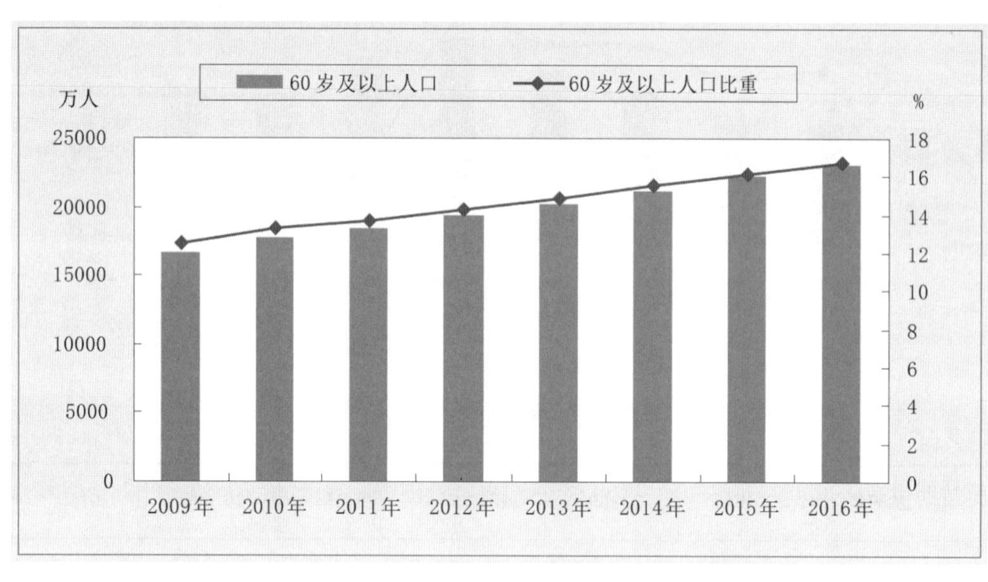

表4 60岁及以上老年人口占全国总人口比重

单位：万人、%

指标	2009年	2010年	2011年	2012年	2013年	2014年	2015年	2016年
60岁及以上人口	16714	17765	18499	19390	20243	21242	22200	23086
60岁及以上人口比重	12.5	13.26	13.7	14.3	14.9	15.5	16.1	16.7

2.儿童福利和收养登记。截至2016年底，全国共有孤儿46.0万人，其中集中供养孤儿8.8万人，社会散居孤儿37.3万人。2016年全国办理家庭收养登记1.9万件，其中：内地居民收养登记1.6万件，港澳台华侨收养登记131件，外国人收养登记2771件。

表5 家庭收养

单位：件、%

指标	2009年	2010年	2011年	2012年	2013年	2014年	2015年	2016年
家庭收养数	44260	34529	31424	27278	24460	22772	22348	18736
年增长率	4.8	−22.0	−9.0	−13.2	−10.3	−6.9	−1.9	−16.2

图5 家庭收养

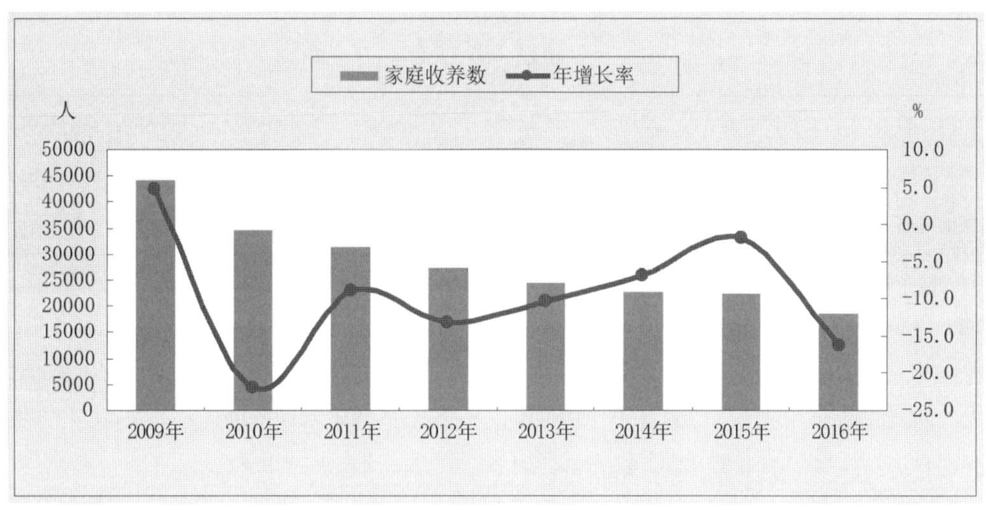

3.残疾人服务。2016年，困难残疾人生活补贴人数521.3万人，重度残疾人护理补贴人数500.1万人。截至2016年底,民政部门直属康复辅具机构25个，固定资产原价4.5亿元。

4.社会救助

截至2016年底，全国有城市低保对象855.3万户、1480.2万人。全年各级财政共支出城市低保资金687.9亿元。2016年全国城市低保平均标准494.6元/人•月，比上年增长9.6%。全国有农村低保对象2635.3万户、4586.5万人。全年各级财政共支出农村低保资金1014.5亿元。2016年全国农村低保平均标准3744.0元/人•年，比上年增长17.8%。

特困人员救助供养。截至2016年底，全国农村特困人员救助供养496.9万人，比上年减少3.9%。全年各级财政共支出农村特困人员救助供养资金228.9亿元，比上年增长9.0%。

临时救助。2016年临时救助累计救助850.7万人次，支出救助资金87.7亿元，平均救助水平1031.3元/人次，其中：救助非本地户籍对象24.4万人次。

图6 困难群众基本生活救助情况

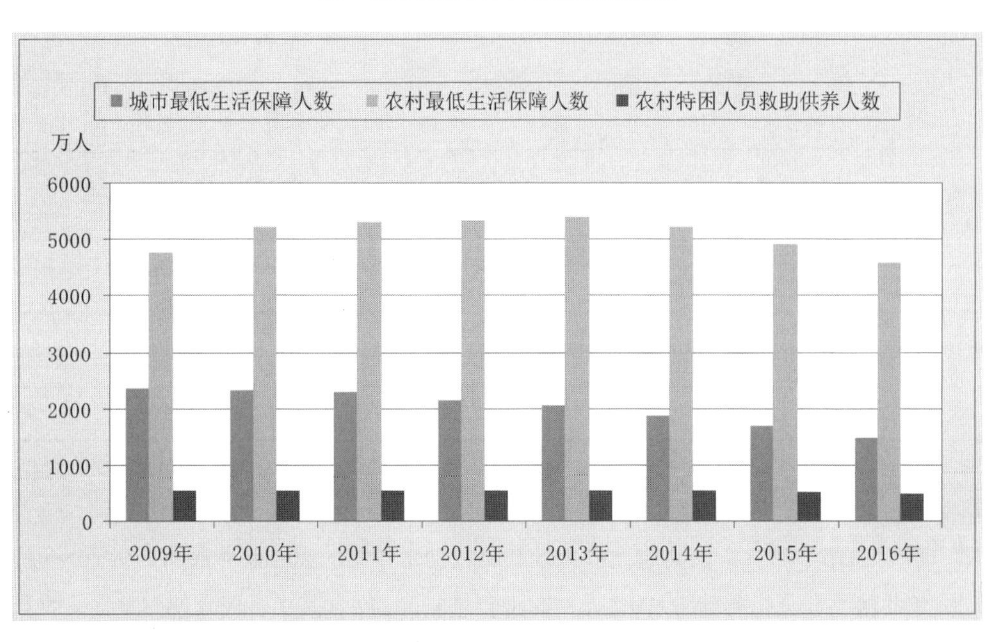

表6 困难群众基本生活救助情况

单位：万人

指标	2009年	2010年	2011年	2012年	2013年	2014年	2015年	2016年
城市最低生活保障人数	2345.6	2310.5	2276.8	2143.5	2064.2	1877.0	1701.0	1480.2
农村最低生活保障人数	4760.0	5214.0	5305.7	5344.5	5388.0	5207.2	4903.6	4586.5
农村特困人员救助供养人数	553.4	556.3	551	545.6	537.2	529.1	516.7	496.9

医疗救助。2016年资助参加基本医疗保险5560.4万人，支出资助参加基本医疗保险资金63.4亿元，资助参加基本医疗保险人均补助水平113.9元。2016年实施住院和门诊医疗救助2696.1万人次，支出资金232.7亿元，住院和门诊人次均救助水平分别为 1709.1元和190.0元。 2016年全年累计资助优抚对象409.2万人次，优抚医疗补助资金36.2亿元，人均补助水平885.5元。

5.防灾减灾救灾。2016年全国各类自然灾害共造成1.9亿人次不同程度受灾，因灾死亡失踪1706人，紧急转移安置910.1万人次；农作物受灾面积26220.7千公顷，其中绝收面积2902.2千公顷；倒塌房屋52.1万间，损坏房屋334.0万间；因灾直接经济损失5032.9亿元。国家减灾委、民政部共启动国家救灾应急响应22次，向各受灾省份累计下拨中央自然灾害生活补助资金79.1亿元（含中央冬春救灾资金57.1亿元），紧急调拨4.1万顶救灾帐篷、15万床棉被、1.6万件棉大衣、2.5万个睡袋、2.3万张折叠床等生活类中央救灾物资。

图7 因灾死亡（含失踪）人口

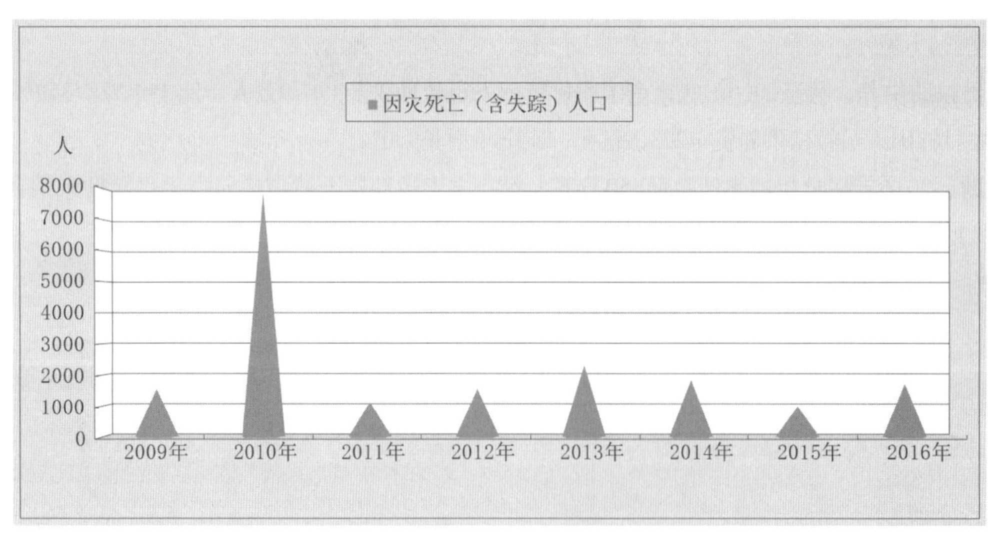

表7 因灾死亡（含失踪）人口

单位：人

指标	2009年	2010年	2011年	2012年	2013年	2014年	2015年	2016年
因灾死亡（含失踪）人口	1528	7844	1126	1530	2284	1818	967	1706

6.慈善事业

慈善捐赠。截至2016年底，全国共建立经常性社会捐助工作站、点和慈善超市2.9万个（其中：慈善超市8966个）。全年共接收社会捐赠款827.0亿元，比上年增长26.4%，其中：民政部门直接接收社会各界捐款40.3亿元，各类社会组织接收捐款786.7亿元。全年各地民政部门直接接收捐赠物资价值折合人民币7.4亿元，捐赠衣被6638.3万件。间接接收其他部门转入的捐赠物资折款1.4亿元，社会捐款5.9亿元，衣被488.0万件。全年有1165.8万人次困难群众受益。全年有931.0万人次在社会服务领域提供了2522.6万小时的志愿服务。

图8 接收社会捐款和衣被

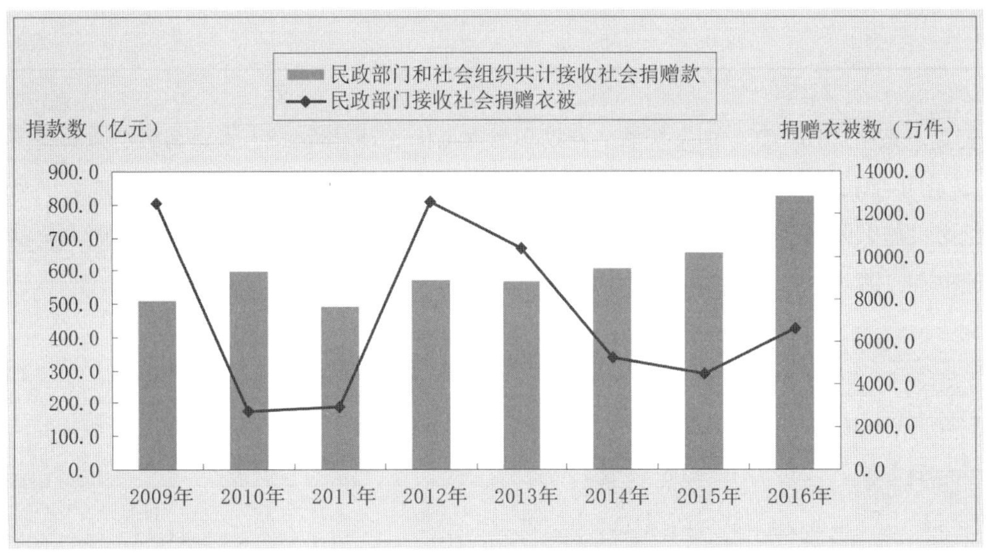

表8 接收社会捐款和衣被

单位：亿元、万件

指标	2009年	2010年	2011年	2012年	2013年	2014年	2015年	2016年
民政部门和社会组织共计接收社会捐赠款	507.2	596.8	490.1	572.5	566.4	604.4	654.5	827.0
民政部门接收社会捐赠衣被	12476.6	2750.2	2918.5	12538.2	10405.0	5244.5	4537.0	6638.3

福利彩票。2016年中国福利彩票销售2064.9亿元，比上年增加49.8亿元，增长2.5%。全年筹集福利彩票公益金591.5亿元，比上年增长4.9%。全年民政系统共支出彩票公益金268.3亿元，比上年减少20.6亿元，下降7.1%，其中用于抚恤7.1亿元，退役安置0.8亿元，社会福利172.9亿元，社会救助30.0亿元，自然灾害救助2.7亿元。

图9 福利彩票

销售额 年增长率

销售额（亿元） 年增长率（%）

2500.0 2000.0 1500.0 1000.0 500.0 0.0

35.0 30.0 25.0 20.0 15.0 10.0 5.0 0.0 -5.0

2009年 2010年 2011年 2012年 2013年 2014年 2015年 2016年

表9 福利彩票

单位：亿元、%

指标	2009年	2010年	2011年	2012年	2013年	2014年	2015年	2016年
销售额	756.0	968.0	1278.0	1510.3	1765.3	2059.7	2015.1	2064.9
年增长率	25.2	28.0	32.0	18.2	16.9	16.7	−2.2	2.5

7.优抚安置。截至2016年底，国家抚恤、补助各类重点优抚对象874.8万人。各级财政共支出抚恤事业费769.8亿元，比上年增长12.1%。全国共有注册登记的烈士纪念设施管理机构1109个，占地面积4167.4公顷，机构内烈士纪念设施0.9万处；零散烈士纪念设施1.2万处。2016年新增150人享受烈士待遇。全国共有军队离退休人员管理中心、活动中心293个，年末职工0.5万人，服务军队离退休人员37.5万人。

图10 国家抚恤、补助优抚对象

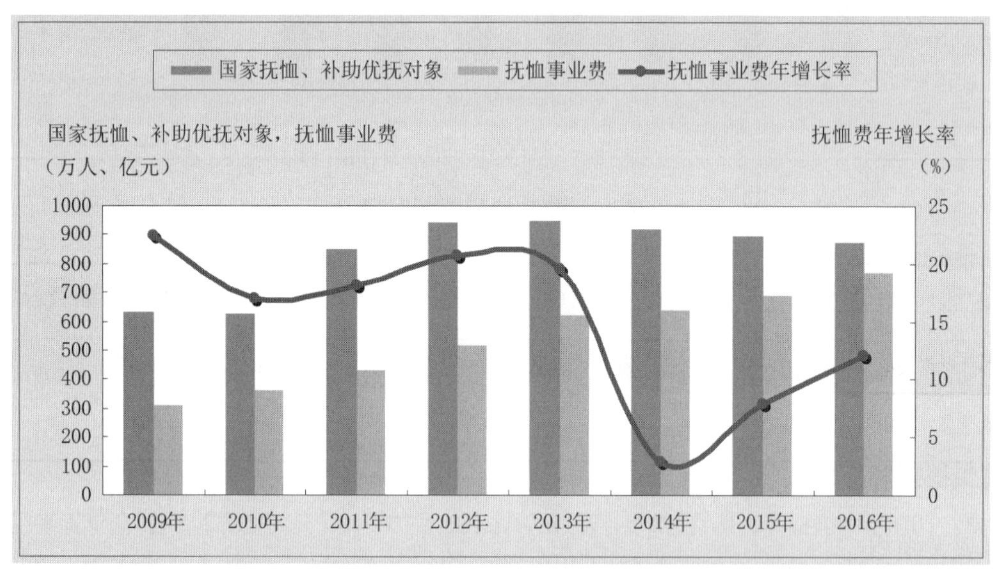

表10 国家抚恤、补助优抚对象

单位：万人、亿元、%

指标	2009年	2010年	2011年	2012年	2013年	2014年	2015年	2016年
国家抚恤、补助优抚对象	630.7	625.0	852.5	944.4	950.5	917.3	897.0	874.8
抚恤事业费	310.3	362.7	428.3	517.0	618.4	636.6	686.8	769.8
抚恤事业费年增长率	22.4	16.9	18.1	20.7	19.6	2.9	7.9	12.1

8.社区服务。截至2016年底，全国共有各类社区服务机构和设施38.6万个，其中社区服务指导中心809个（其中农村27个），社区服务中心2.3万个（其中农村0.8万个），社区服务站13.8万个（其中农村7.2万个），社区养老服务机构和设施3.5万个，比上年增长34.6%，互助型养老服务设施7.6万个，比上年增长22.6%，其他社区服务设施11.3万个，社区服务中心（站）覆盖率24.4%，其中城市社区服务中心（站）覆盖率79.3%，农村社区服务中心（站）覆盖率14.3%。城镇便民、利民服务网点8.7万个。社区志愿服务组织11.6万个。

图11 社区服务机构和设施

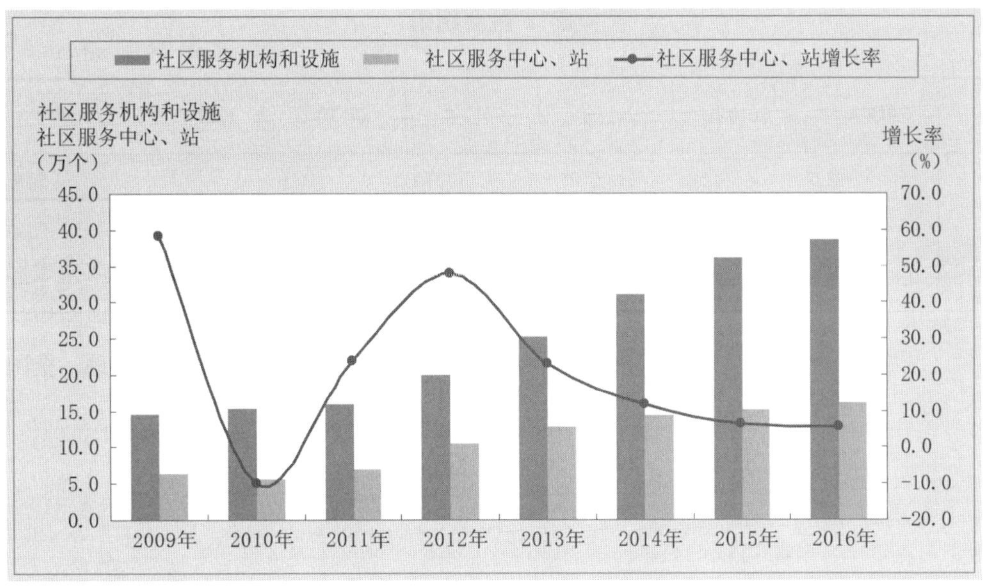

表11 社区服务机构和设施

单位：万个、%

指标	2009年	2010年	2011年	2012年	2013年	2014年	2015年	2016年
社区服务机构和设施	14.6	15.3	16.0	20.0	25.2	31.1	36.1	38.6
社区服务中心、站	6.3	5.7	7.1	10.4	12.8	14.3	15.2	16.1
社区服务中心、站增长率	58.4	−9.8	23.9	47.8	23.1	11.7	6.2	5.8

三、成员组织和其他社会服务

（一）成员组织

1.社会组织。截至2016年底，全国共有社会组织70.2万个，比上年增长6.0%；吸纳社会各类人员就业763.7万人，比上年增长3.9%。接收各类社会捐赠786.7亿元。全年共查处社会组织违法违规案件2363起，其中取缔非法社会组织16起，行政处罚2347起。

全国共有社会团体33.6万个，比上年增长2.3%。其中：工商服务业类3.8万个，科技研究类1.6万个，教育类1.0万个，卫生类0.9万个，社会服务类4.8万个，文化类3.5万个，体育类2.5万个，生态环境类0.6万个，法律类0.3万个，宗教类0.5万个，农业及农村发展类6.1万个，职业及从业组织类2.0万个，其他5.8万个。全年共查处社会团体违法违规案件1565起，其中取缔非法社会团体9起，行政处罚1556起。

全国共有各类基金会 5559 个，比上年增长 16.2%。其中：公募基金会 1730 个，非公募基金会 3791 个；民政部登记的基金会 245 个（其中：涉外基金会 9 个、境外基金会代表机构 29 个）。公募基金会和非公募基金会共接收社会各界捐赠 625.5 亿元。全年对基金会作出行政处罚 15 起。

全国共有民办非企业单位 36.1 万个，比上年增长 9.7%。其中：科技服务类 1.8 万个，生态环境类 444 个，教育类 19.9 万个，卫生类 2.5 万个，社会服务类 5.4 万个，文化类 1.8 万个，体育类 1.7 万个，法律类 617 个，工商业服务类 3459 个，宗教类 102 个，国际及其他涉外组织类 9 个，其他 2.4 万个。全年共查处民办非企业单位违法违纪案件 783 起，其中取缔非法民办非企业单位 7 起，行政处罚 776 起。

表12 社会组织

单位：万个

指标	2009年	2010年	2011年	2012年	2013年	2014年	2015年	2016年
社会团体	23.9	24.5	25.5	27.1	28.9	31.0	32.9	33.6
基金会(个)	1843	2200	2614	3029	3549	4117	4784	5559
民办非企业	19.0	19.8	20.4	22.5	25.5	29.2	32.9	36.1

图12 社会组织

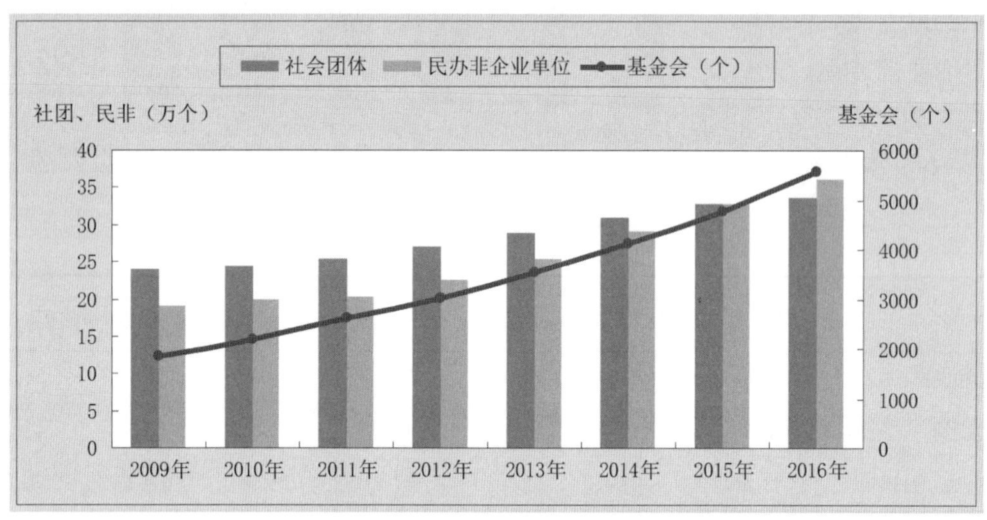

2.**自治组织**。截至2016年底，基层群众自治组织共计66.2万个。其中：村委会55.9万个，比上年下降3.8%，村民小组447.8万个，村委会成员225.3万人，比上年下降1.9%；居委会10.3万个，比上年增长3.3%，居民小组142.0万个，居委会成员54.0万人，比上年增长5.4%。全年共有9.7万个村（居）委会完成选举，参与选举的村（居）民登记数为1.7亿人，参与投票人数为0.9亿人。

图13 自治组织

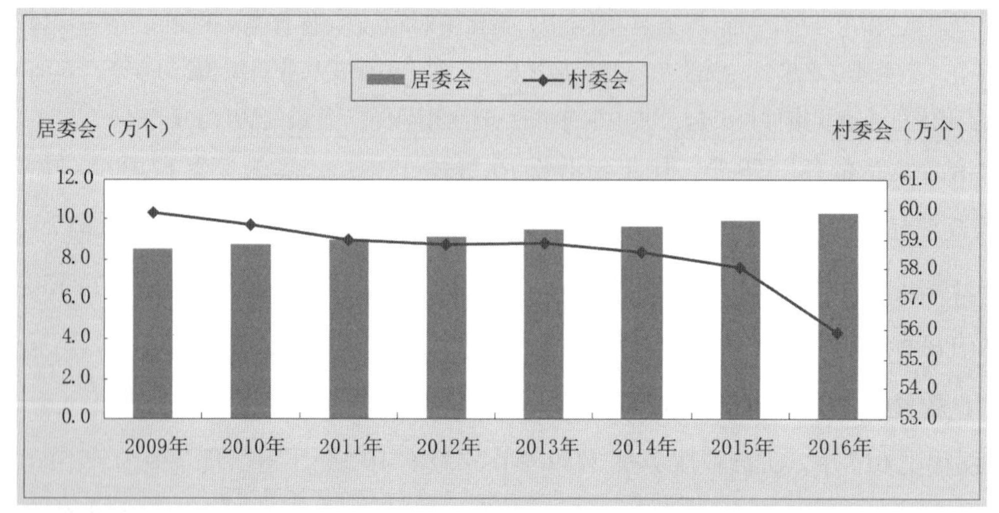

表13 自治组织

单位：万个

指标	2009年	2010年	2011年	2012年	2013年	2014年	2015年	2016年
居委会	8.5	8.7	8.9	9.1	9.5	9.7	10.0	10.3
村委会	59.9	59.5	59.0	58.8	58.9	58.5	58.1	55.9

（二）其他社会服务

1.婚姻登记服务。2016年全国共有事业单位性质的婚姻登记机构1393个，办理婚姻登记场所4863处。各级民政部门和婚姻登记机构共依法办理结婚登记1142.8万对，比上年下降6.7%，其中：涉外及华侨、港澳台居民登记结婚4.2万对。结婚率为8.3‰。2016年25—29岁办理结婚登记占结婚总人口比重最大，占38.2%。

2016年依法办理离婚手续的共有415.8万对，比上年增长8.3%，其中：民政部门登记离婚348.6万对，法院判决、调解离婚67.2万对。离婚率为3.0‰，比上年增加0.2个千分点。

图14 结婚率和离婚率

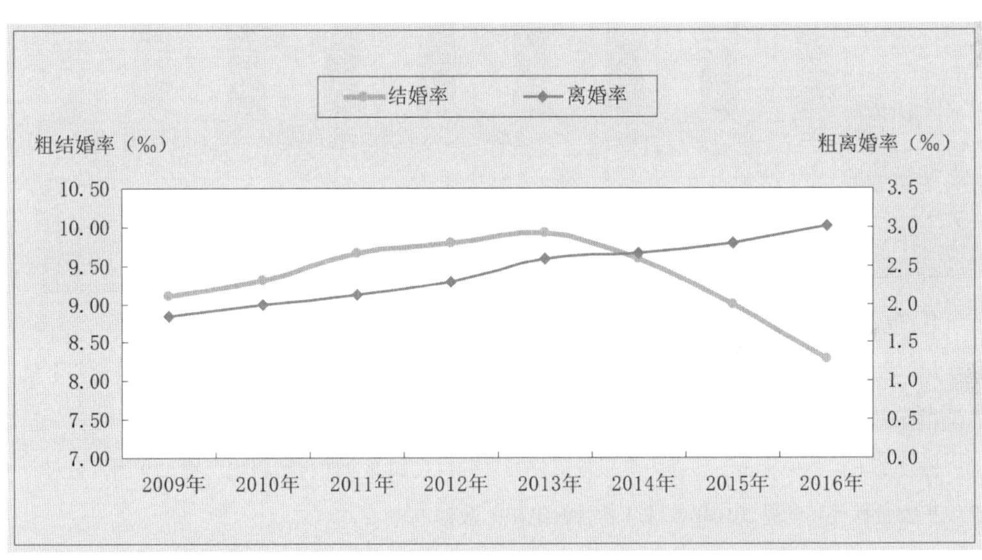

表14 结婚率和离婚率

单位：‰

指标	2009年	2010年	2011年	2012年	2013年	2014年	2015年	2016年
结婚率	9.10	9.30	9.67	9.80	9.92	9.58	9.00	8.3
离婚率	1.85	2.00	2.13	2.29	2.58	2.67	2.79	3.0

2.殡葬服务。截至2016年底，全国共有殡葬服务机构4166个，其中殡仪馆1775个，殡葬管理机构1005个，民政部门管理的公墓1386个。殡葬服务机构职工8.1万人，其中殡仪馆职工4.7万人。火化炉6206台，火化遗体471.8万具，火化率48.3%，比上年增加1.2个百分点。

表15 遗体火化情况

单位：万具、%

指标	2009年	2010年	2011年	2012年	2013年	2014年	2015年	2016年
遗体火化数	454.2	474.1	468.1	477.7	468.9	459.3	459.5	471.8
火化率	48.2	49.0	48.8	49.5	48.2	47.0	47.1	48.3

图15 遗体火化情况

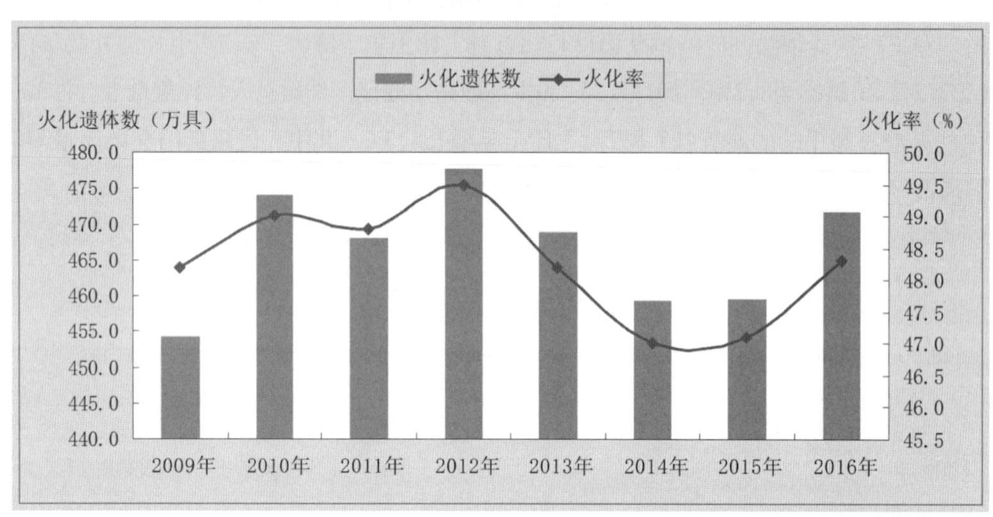

注释：

1. 图1中“乡”包含“民族乡、苏木和民族苏木”。
2. 自2016年起，民政部取消社会福利企业资质认定，不再统计社会福利企业情况指标，因此社会服务机构和设施固定资产原价指标出现较大降幅。
3. 财政部、民政部下拨中央资金不包含中央级救灾物资采购经费和部分拨付新疆生产建设兵团资金等。
4. 社会组织捐赠数据使用的是2016年完成年检社会组织的数据。
5. 离婚登记服务中法院判决、调解离婚数据来源于最高人民法院。
6. 本资料中的民政对象人数和机构数均为当年实际发生数和注册登记的法定机构数，与当年批准数、计划数和预算数不可比。
7. 本资料部分数据因四舍五入原因，存在分项数据与合计数据不等情况，由此产生的误差，均未作机械调整。
8. 各项统计数据均未包括香港特别行政区、澳门特别行政区和台湾省。
9. 结婚率、离婚率指标与2015年公报中粗结婚率、粗离婚率计算方法相同，含义一致。

Statistical Report of the People's Republic of China on the Development of Social Services in 2016

Ministry of Civil Affairs of
the People's Republic of China
July 20th, 2017

In 2016, the system of national civil affairs conscientiously implemented the guiding principles of the Eighteenth National Congress of the Communist Party of China and the Third, the Fourth, the Fifth, and the Sixth Plenary Session of the Eighteenth CPC Central Committee, thoroughly implemented the guiding principles of series of important speeches delivered by General Secretary Xi Jinping, adhered to the general work guideline of making progress while maintaining stability, pushed forward the reform and innovation, strengthened the construction of legal system, effectively fulfilled the responsibility to ensure the basic livelihood of the people, to strengthen and innovate relevant social governance, to support the reform of national defense and the armed forces, to provide the relevant basic public services. The civil administration has gained new development.

I. Synthesis

By the end of 2016, there were altogether 34 administrative areas at the provincial level in China (4 municipalities directly under the central government, 23 provinces, 5 autonomous regions and 2 special administrative regions), 334 administrative areas at the prefecture level (293 cities at the prefecture level, 8 prefectures, 30 autonomous prefectures and 3 leagues), 2,851 administrative areas at the county level (954 districts under the jurisdiction of cities, 360 cities at the county level, 1,366 counties, 117 autonomous counties, 49 banners, 3 autonomous banners, 1 special zone and 1 forestry district), 39,862 administrative areas at the township level (2 district public offices, 20,883 towns, 9,731 townships, 152 sumus, 988 ethnic townships, 1 ethnic sumu, 8,105 street communities).

In 2016, the joint inspections covered 13 provincial boundaries (13,629 kilometers).

Figure 1: Changes in Townships, Towns and Street Communities

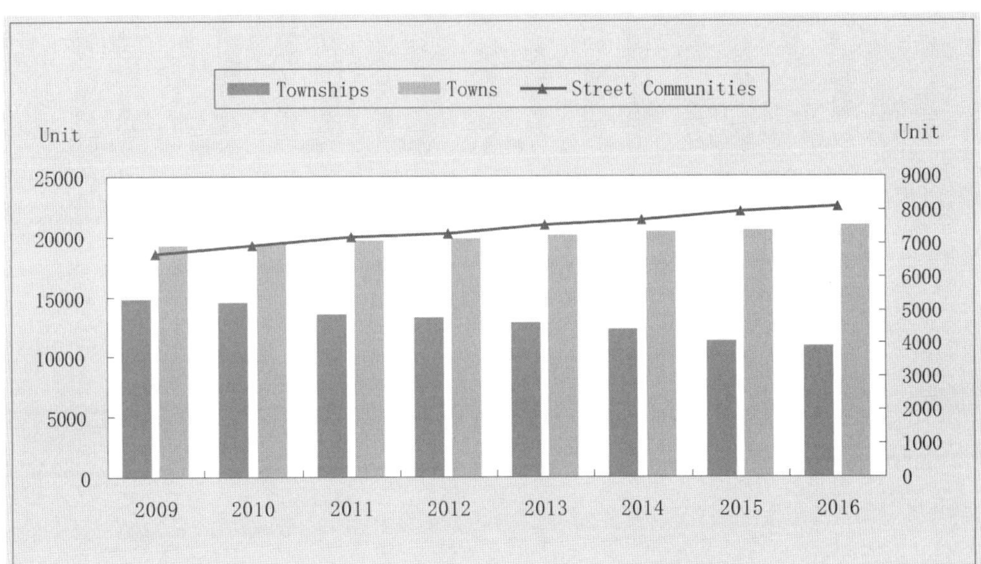

Table 1: Changes in Townships, Towns and Street Communities

Indicators	2009	2010	2011	2012	2013	2014	2015	2016
Townships (Unit)	14848	14571	13587	13281	12812	12282	11315	10872
Towns (Unit)	19322	19410	19683	19881	20117	20401	20515	20883
Street Communities (Unit)	6686	6923	7194	7282	7566	7696	7957	8105

By the end of 2016, there were 1.745 million various registered organizations and facilities on social services. The total number of staff was 12.393 million. The total fixed assets stood at 539.36 billion yuan. The area of construction projects for social services was 30,509,000 square meters and the total investment reached 24.58 billion yuan. The total number of National certified social workers is 288,000, 69,000 of them were social workers and 219,000 of them were assistant social workers. By the end of 2016, the total expenditure on social service industry reached 544.02 billion yuan, a rise of 10.4 percent over the previous year. The proportion of total expenditure on social service industry in the share of national financial expenditure was 3.4 percent. Thereinto, the transferred payment of the central government to social service industry amounted to 248.4 billion yuan, a rise of 9.4 percent over the previous year. It took up 45.7 percent of the total social service expenditure, a decrease of 0.4 percent over the previous year.

Figure 2: Basic Situation of Social Service Industry

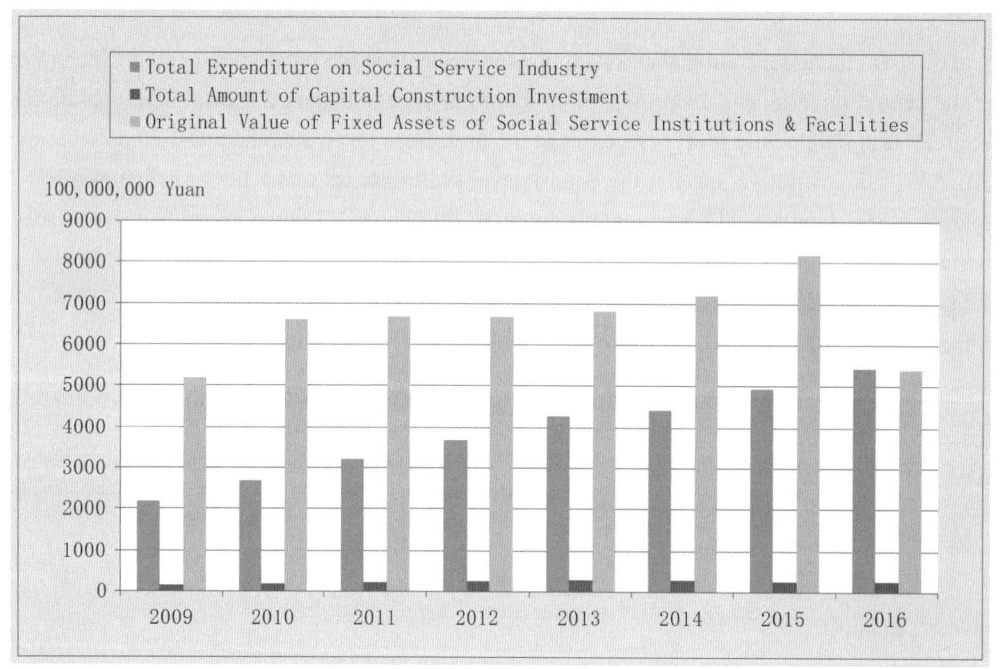

Table 2: Basic Situation of Social Service Industry

Indicators	2009	2010	2011	2012	2013	2014	2015	2016
Total Expenditure on Social Service Industry (100,000,000 Yuan)	2181.9	2697.5	3229.1	3683.7	4276.5	4404.1	4926.4	5440.2
Total Amount of Capital Construction Investment (100,000,000 Yuan)	157.0	183.0	218.5	235.0	292.8	282.2	239.9	245.8
Original Value of Fixed Assets of Social Service Institutions (100,000,000 Yuan)	5198.0	6589.3	6676.7	6675.4	6810.2	7213.0	8183.1	5393.6

II. Social Services

A. Social Services with Accommodation

By the end of 2016, there were 32 thousand social service institutions with accommodation which were registered. Thereinto, 18 thousand of them were public institutions, and 12 thousand of them were non-governmental and non-commercial enterprises. They offered 4.14 million beds and the number of adoptees reached 2.41 million.

Figure 3: Beds in Social Service Institutions

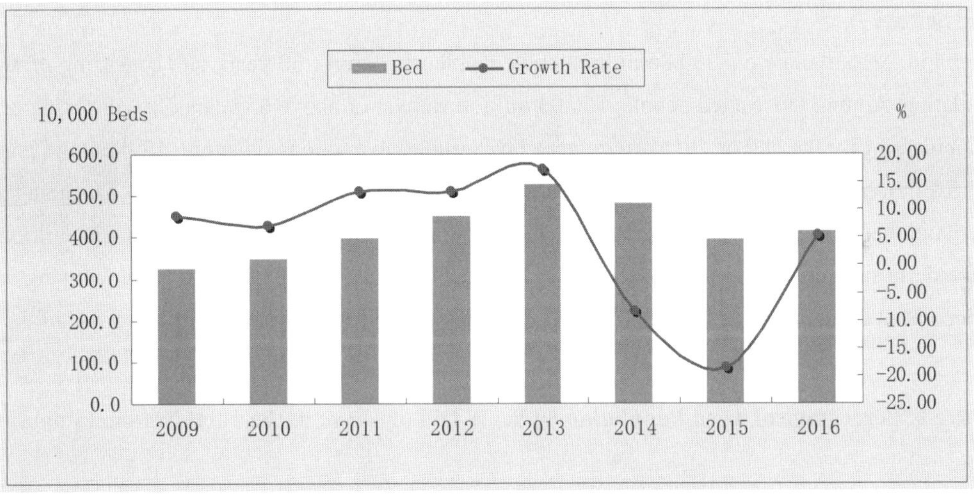

Table 3: Beds in Social Service Institutions

Indicators	2009	2010	2011	2012	2013	2014	2015	2016
Bed (10,000 Beds)	326.5	349.6	396.4	449.3	526.7	482.3	393.2	414.0
Growth Rate (%)	8.72	7.08	13.39	13.35	17.23	−8.43	−18.47	5.29

Note : From 2014, organizations on social services were those which were registered in bureau of industry and commerce, state commission office of public sectors reform and civil affairs departments. Facilities on social services were those which were not registered.

1. Social Services with Accommodation for the Aged

The number of welfare institutions and facilities for the aged was 140,000, a rise of 20.7 percent over the previous year. Thereinto, there were 29,000 welfare institutions for the aged which were registered, 35,000 community welfare institutions and facilities for the aged, 76,000 community mutual aid facilities for the aged. The number of all kinds of beds for aged people was 7.302 million, a rise of 8.6 percent over the previous year (the average number of beds per thousand seniors was 31.6, a rise of 4.3 percent in comparison with last year). Thereinto, 3.229 million beds were used for community accommodation and daytime care.

2. Service Agencies with Accommodation for Psychiatric Disorders

There were 244 service agencies for mental retardations and psychiatric disorders under the management of the civil affairs departments with 84 thousand beds. Thereinto, there were 150 social welfare homes (mental hospitals) with 53 thousand beds. By the end of 2016, 44 thousand people were adopted. There were 94 mental hospitals with 31 thousand beds for ex-servicemen and 25 thousand people were adopted by the end of the year.

3. Welfare and Protection Institutions with Accommodation and for the Children

By the end of the year, there were 705 adoption and relief institutions with 100 thousand beds for children, and 54 thousand children were adopted. Thereinto, there were 465 welfare institutions for children. They offered 90 thousand beds. There were 240 children relief and protection centers with 10 thousand beds. They received 52 thousand minor vagabonds (person-times) in the whole year.

4. Other Social Service Institutions with Accommodation Service

There were 2,371 other social service institutions with 167 thousand beds. Thereinto, there were 1,736 relief and management institutions with 102 thousand beds. In the whole year, they received 3.283 million street people (person-times) who had no means of support. Thereinto, 2.835 million (person-times) of those got in-shelter reliefs and 447 thousand (person-times) got out-shelter reliefs. There were 315 military depots for military supplies and 320 other institutions with accommodation.

B. Social Services without Accommodation

1. Aging Service

By the end of 2016, there were 230.86 million aged people at or above 60 years old, consisting of 16.7 percent of the total population. Among those aged people, 150.03 million were at or above 65 years old, consisting of 10.8 percent of the total population. By the end of 2016, there were 1,828 public institutions on aging, 19 thousand legal aid centers for the aged, 70 thousand rights safeguarding institutions for the aged, 54 thousand schools for the aged with 7.102 million students in these schools and 359 thousand activity rooms for the aged. There were 23.554 million aged people who received elderly subsidy, a rise of 9.3 percent over the previous year, 405 thousand received nursing care subsidy, a rise of 52.8 percent over the previous year, 2.829 million received elderly care service subsidy, a rise of 9.7 percent over the previous year.

Figure 4: Percentage of Aged Population 60 Years Old or above in the Total National Population

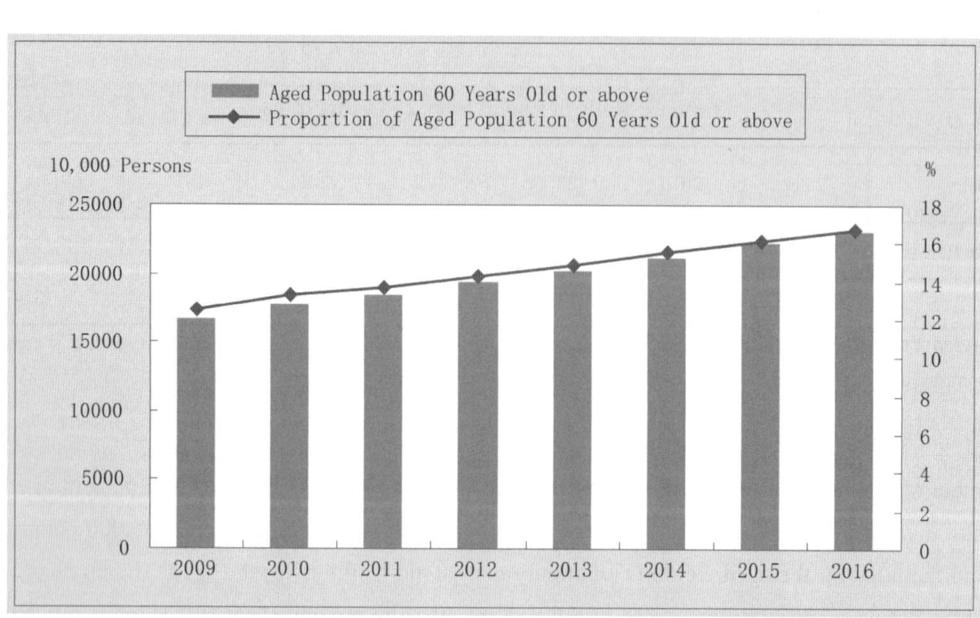

Table 4: Percentage of Aged Population 60 Years Old or above in the Total National Population

Indicators	2009	2010	2011	2012	2013	2014	2015	2016
Aged Population 60 Years Old or above (10,000 Persons)	16714	17765	18499	19390	20243	21242	22200	23086
Percentage of Aged Population 60 Years Old or above in the Total National Population (%)	12.5	13.26	13.7	14.3	14.9	15.5	16.1	16.7

2. Children Welfare and Adoption

By the end of 2016, there were 460 thousand orphans in China, of which 88 thousand orphans were collectively adopted, 373 thousand orphans scattered. In 2016, registered family adoptions totaled 19,000 cases. Thereinto, 16,000 cases were completed by mainland citizens, 131 cases were completed by overseas Chinese and residents in Hong Kong, Macao and Taiwan, 2,771 cases were completed by foreigners.

Figure 5: Children Adopted by Families

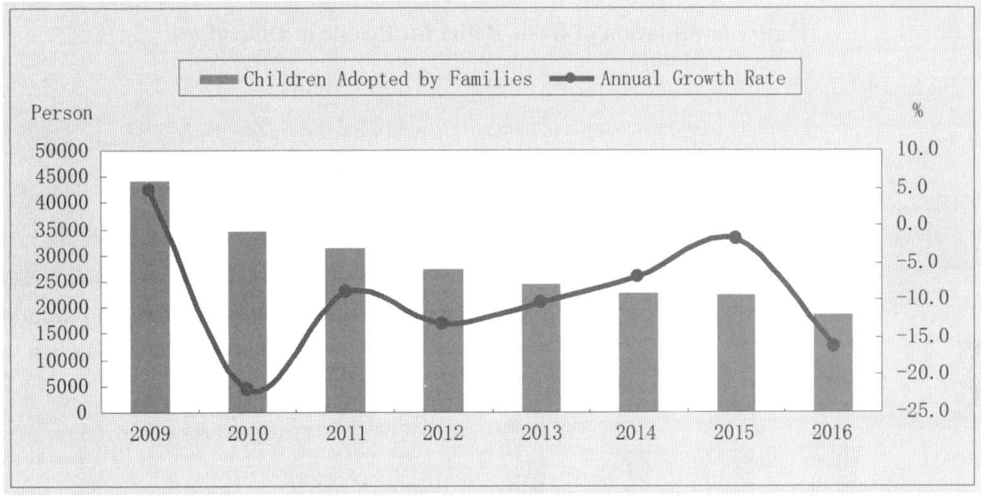

Table 5: Children Adopted by Families

Indicators	2009	2010	2011	2012	2013	2014	2015	2016
Children Adopted by Families (Person)	44260	34529	31424	27278	24460	22772	22348	18736
Annual Growth Rate (%)	4.8	−22.0	−9.0	−13.2	−10.3	−6.9	−1.9	−16.2

3. Agencies Providing Services for Disabled

In 2016, there were 5.213 million difficult disabled persons who received living subsidy, there were 5.001 million persons with severe disabilities who received nursing subsidy. By the end of 2016, there were 25 rehabilitation institutions with assistive equipment directly under the civil affairs departments, the total fixed assets stood at 450 million yuan.

4. Social Relief

- Minimum Life Guarantee

By the end of 2016, there were 8.553 million households or 14.802 million urban residents entitled to minimum living allowances in China. In 2016, the total fiscal expenditure on the urban minimum life guarantee reached 68.79 billion yuan, the average expenditure standard of urban minimum life guarantee was 494.6 yuan per person per month, a rise of 9.6 percent over the previous year. In 2016, there were 26.353 million households or 45.865 million rural residents entitled to minimum living allowances, the total fiscal expenditure on the rural minimum life guarantee reached 101.45 billion yuan, the average expenditure standard of rural minimum life guarantee was 3744.0 yuan per person per year, a rise of 17.8 percent over the previous year.

- Support of the Especially Poor Persons

By the end of 2016, there were 4.969 million especially poor persons who enjoyed government support in rural areas in China, a decrease of 3.9 percent over the previous year. The total fiscal expenditure on the support of the especially poor persons reached 22.89 billion yuan, a rise of 9.0 percent over the previous year.

- The Provisional Relief

In 2016, there were 8.507 million persons (times) that received provisional relief. Thereinto, according to the classification of the resident registration, 244 thousand persons (times) that received provisional relief belonged to non-local permanent residence. The total fiscal expenditure on the provisional relief reached 8.77 billion yuan, the average provisional relief standard was 1031.3 yuan per person (time).

Figure 6: Situation of Basic Relief for People in Difficulties

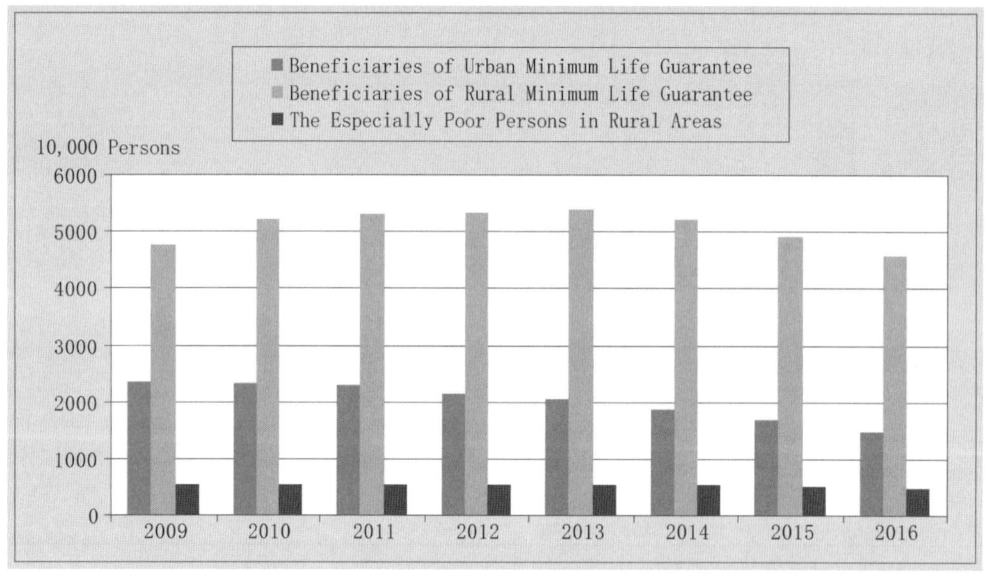

Table 6: Situation of Basic Relief for People in Difficulties

Indicators	2009	2010	2011	2012	2013	2014	2015	2016
Beneficiaries of Urban Minimum Life Guarantee (10,000 Persons)	2345.6	2310.5	2276.8	2143.5	2064.2	1877.0	1701.0	1480.2
Beneficiaries of Rural Minimum Life Guarantee (10,000 Persons)	4760.0	5214.0	5305.7	5344.5	5388.0	5207.2	4903.6	4586.5
Beneficiaries of Five Guarantees in Rural Areas (10,000 Persons)	553.4	556.3	551	545.6	537.2	529.1	516.7	496.9

- Medical Aid

In 2016, 55.604 million people received subsidized aid for medical insurance. The fund for subsidized aid for medical insurance was 6.34 billion yuan and the average expenditure was 113.9 yuan per person. There were 26.961 million people (person-times) of in-patients and out-patients that received medical aid. The total expenditure on medical aid was 23.27 billion yuan. The average expenditure for medical aid as in-patient and as out-patient was 1709.1 yuan and 190.0 yuan per person (time) respectively. In 2016, the number of people who were covered by state pension and preferential treatment program reached 4.092 million (person-times). The financial expenditure on medical subsidy totaled 3.62 billion yuan. The average expenditure was 885.5 yuan per person.

5. Disaster Prevention and Relief

In 2016, 190 million people (person-times) were influenced by various natural disasters. There were 1706 deaths and abscondences caused by disasters. There were 9.101 million people (person-times) who were transferred and resettled urgently. There were 26.2207 million hectares of farm crops hit by disasters, thereinto, 2.9022 million hectares of crops were demolished. Collapsed buildings reached 521 thousand and 3.340 million buildings were damaged. The direct economic loss which was caused by disasters stood at 503.29 billion yuan. The China National Commission for Disaster Reduction and the Ministry of Civil Affairs totally started disaster assistance emergency response for 22 times and allocated 7.91 billion yuan as central natural disaster relief funds (including 5.71 billion yuan set aside by the Central Government for disaster relief in winter and spring), 41 thousand tents, 150 thousand pieces of cotton-padded quilts, 16 thousand pieces of cotton-padded clothes, 25 thousand sleeping bags and 23 thousand folding beds.

Figure 7 : Deaths (Abscondences) Caused by Disasters

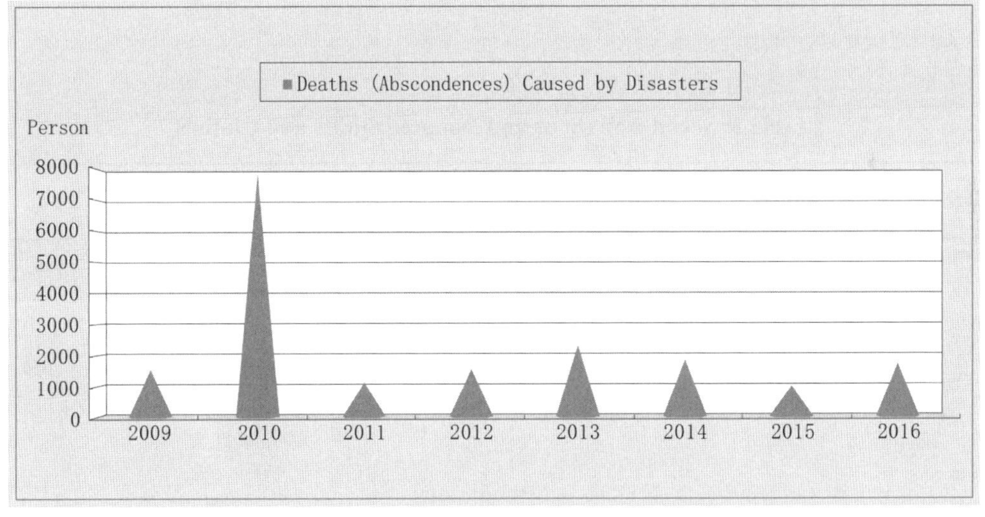

Table 7 : Deaths (Abscondences) Caused by Disasters

Indicators	2009	2010	2011	2012	2013	2014	2015	2016
Deaths (Abscondences) Caused by Disasters (Person)	1528	7844	1126	1530	2284	1818	967	1706

6. Social Charity

- Charitable Donations

By the end of 2016, there were 29 thousand regular workstations of social donations and charity supermarkets (8,966 of which were charity supermarkets). The total social donations reached 82.70 billion yuan, a rise of 26.4 percent over the previous year. Of this total, the civil affairs departments received direct donations of 4.03 billion yuan and social organizations received donations of 78.67 billion yuan. In 2016, the civil affairs departments received directly donated materials, valued at 740 million yuan. The donated quilts and clothes reached 66.383 million pieces. The indirect donated materials which were transferred from other departments were worth 0.14 billion yuan, and social donations of 0.59 billion yuan. There were also 4.880 million pieces of indirect-donated quilts and clothes. Over 11.658 million people (person-times) in difficulties benefited from the charitable donations. There were 9.310 million volunteers (person-times) who provided 25.226 million hours of social services in 2016.

Figure 8: Social Donations and Donated Quilts and Clothes

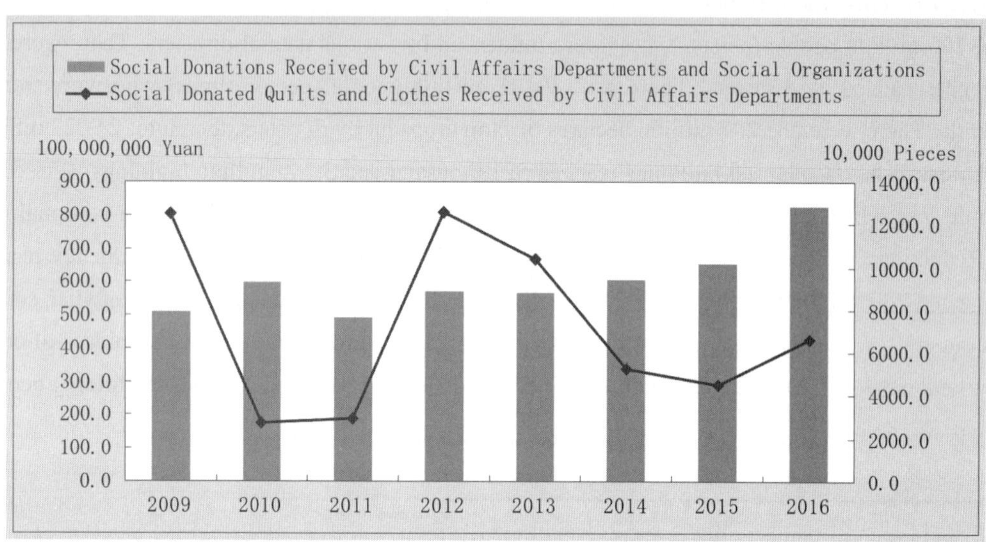

Table 8: Social Donations and Donated Quilts and Clothes

Indicators	2009	2010	2011	2012	2013	2014	2015	2016
Social Donations Received by Civil Affairs Departments and Social Organizations (100,000,000 Yuan)	507.2	596.8	490.1	572.5	566.4	604.4	654.5	827.0
Social Donated Quilts and Clothes by Civil Affairs Departments (10,000 Pieces)	12476.6	2750.2	2918.5	12538.2	10405.0	5244.5	4537.0	6638.3

- Welfare Lottery

In 2016, the sales of welfare lottery reached 206.49 billion yuan, an increase of 4.98 billion yuan over the previous year, a rise of 2.5 percent. The public lottery funds reached 59.15 billion yuan, a rise of 4.9 percent in comparison with last year. The expenditure of public lottery funds by the civil affairs departments totaled 26.83 billion yuan, a decrease of 2.06 billion yuan over the previous year, a decline of 7.1 percent. It included 710 million yuan on state pension, 80 million yuan on the placement of retired servicemen, 17.29 billion yuan on social welfare, 3 billion yuan on social relief, 270 million yuan on disaster relief.

Figure 9: Welfare Lottery

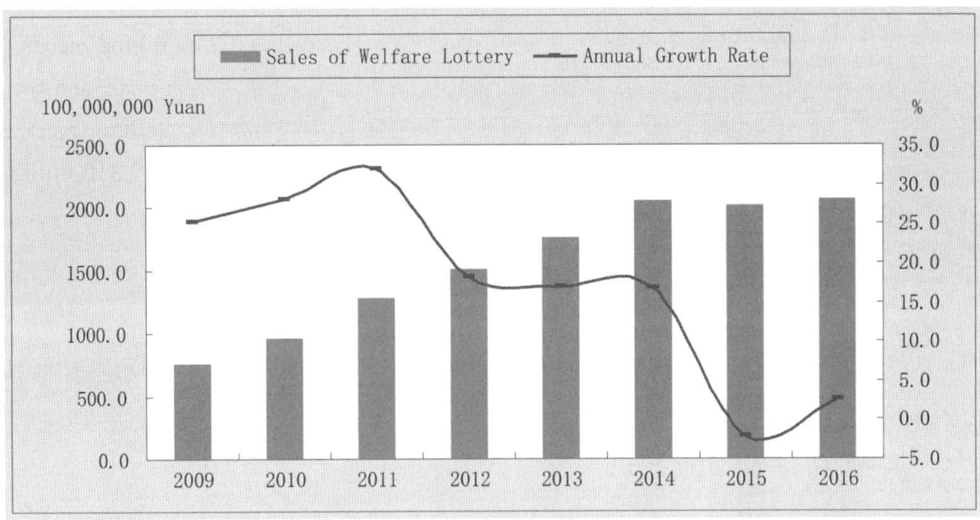

Table 9: Welfare Lottery

Indicators	2009	2010	2011	2012	2013	2014	2015	2016
Sales of Welfare Lottery (100,000,000 Yuan)	756.0	968.0	1278.0	1510.3	1765.3	2059.7	2015.1	2064.9
Annual Growth Rate (%)	25.2	28.0	32.0	18.2	16.9	16.7	−2.2	2.5

7. Preferential Treatment and Placement

By the end of 2016, there were 8.748 million people who were covered by state pension and preferential treatment program. The total operating expense on state pension reached 76.98 billion yuan, a rise of 12.1 percent over the previous year. In China, there were 1,109 registered management organizations of martyrs' monuments, taking up the space of 4,167.4 hectares. There were 9,000 martyrs' monuments which were within management organizations and there were 12,000 scattered monuments. In 2016, the government applied special treatment to the newly increased 150 martyrs. There were 293 management centers and activity centers with 5,000 employees, serving 375 thousand emeritus and retired personnel who were from troops.

Table 10: Beneficiaries of State Pension and Preferential Treatment

Indicators	2009	2010	2011	2012	2013	2014	2015	2016
Beneficiaries of State Pension and Preferential Treatment (10,000 Persons)	630.7	625.0	852.5	944.4	950.5	917.3	897.0	874.8
Operating Expense on State Pension (100,000,000 Yuan)	310.3	362.7	428.3	517.0	618.4	636.6	686.8	769.8
Annual Growth Rate of Operating Expense on State Pension (%)	22.4	16.9	18.1	20.7	19.6	2.9	7.9	12.1

Figure 10: Beneficiaries of State Pension and Preferential Treatment

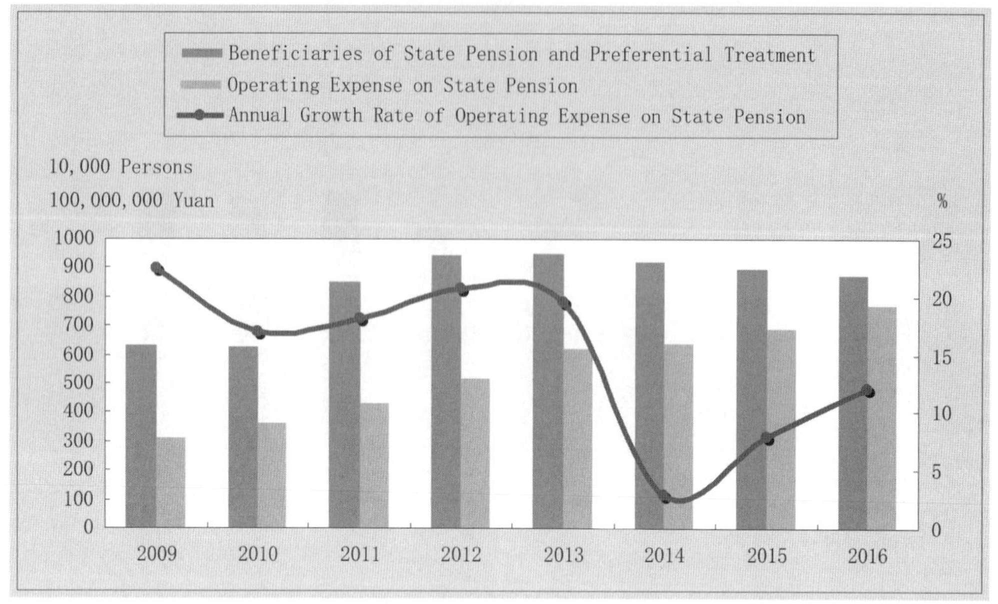

8. Community Services

By the end of 2016, there were 386 thousand community service institutions. Among these institutions, 809 were community service instruction centers (27 of them were in rural areas) and 23,000 were community service centers (8,000 of them were in rural areas). There were 138 thousand community service stations (72,000 of them were in rural areas). There were 35 thousand community welfare institutions and facilities for the aged, an increase of 34.6 percent over the previous year. There were 76,000 mutual aid service institutions for the aged, an increase of 22.6 percent over the previous year. There were 113 thousand other community service institutions. The coverage rate of community service centers (stations) was 24.4 percent. Thereinto, the coverage rate of community service centers (stations) in urban areas was 79.3 percent, the coverage rate of community service centers (stations) in rural areas was 14.3 percent. There were 87 thousand convenience stations and 116 thousand community organizations of volunteers in urban areas.

Table 11: Community Service Institutions and Facilities

Indicators	2009	2010	2011	2012	2013	2014	2015	2016
Community Service Institutions and Facilities (10,000 Units)	14.6	15.3	16.0	20.0	25.2	31.1	36.1	38.6
Community Service Centers and Stations (10,000 Units)	6.3	5.7	7.1	10.4	12.8	14.3	15.2	16.1
The growth rate of Community Service Stations (%)	58.4	−9.8	23.9	47.8	23.1	11.7	6.2	5.8

Figure 11: Community Service Institutions and Facilities

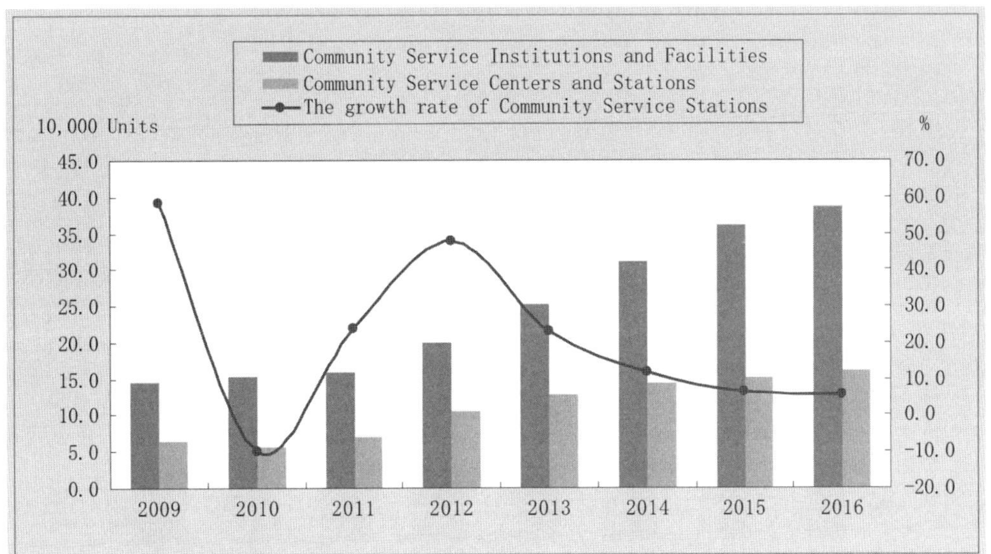

III. Member Organizations and Other Social Services

A. Member Organizations

1. Non-Government Organizations (NGOs)

By the end of 2016, there were altogether 702 thousand NGOs, an increase of 6.0 percent over that of the previous year. There were 7.637 million employees, an increase of 3.9 percent over the previous year. The NGOs received donations of 78.67 billion yuan. There were 2,363 law-breaking cases which concerned NGOs and were investigated and penalized. As a result, 16 illegal NGOs were banned and 2,347 administrative punishments took place.

There were 336 thousand social organizations, a growth of 2.3 percent over the previous year. Among these social organizations, 38,000 were engaged in industry and commercial services, 16,000 in science and technology services, 10,000 in education, 9,000 in health, 48,000 in social services, 35,000 in culture, 25,000 in sports, 6,000 in eco-environment, 3,000 in legal services, 5,000 in religion, 61,000 in agriculture and rural development, 20,000 in profession and 58,000 in other fields. In 2016, there were 1,565 law-breaking cases which concerned social organizations and were investigated and penalized. As a result, 9 illegal social organizations were banned and 1,556 administrative punishments took place.

In 2016, there were 5,559 foundations across the country, a rise of 16.2 percent over that of the previous year. Of this total, there were 1,730 public-raising foundations, 3,791 non-public raising foundations. There were 245 foundations registered in the Ministry of Civil Affairs, (thereinto, 9 foundations were concerning foreign affairs, 29 foundations were representative offices of overseas-based foundations). The public-raising foundations and non-public raising foundations totally received donations of 62.55 billion yuan. In 2016, 15 administrative punishments concerning foundations took place.

In 2016, there were altogether 361 thousand non-governmental and non-commercial enterprises, a rise of 9.7 percent over the previous year. Among these enterprises, there were 18,000 engaged in science and technology services, 444 in eco-environment, 199,000 in education, 25,000 in health, 54,000 in social services, 18,000 in culture, 17,000 in sports, 617 in legal services, 3,459 in industry and commercial services, 102 in religion, 9 in international and other overseas affairs, 24,000 in other fields. In 2016, there were 783 law-breaking and discipline violation cases which concerned non-governmental and non-commercial enterprises and were investigated and penalized. As a result, 7 illegal non-governmental and non-commercial enterprises were banned, and 776 administrative punishments took place.

Figure 12: Non-Governmental Organizations

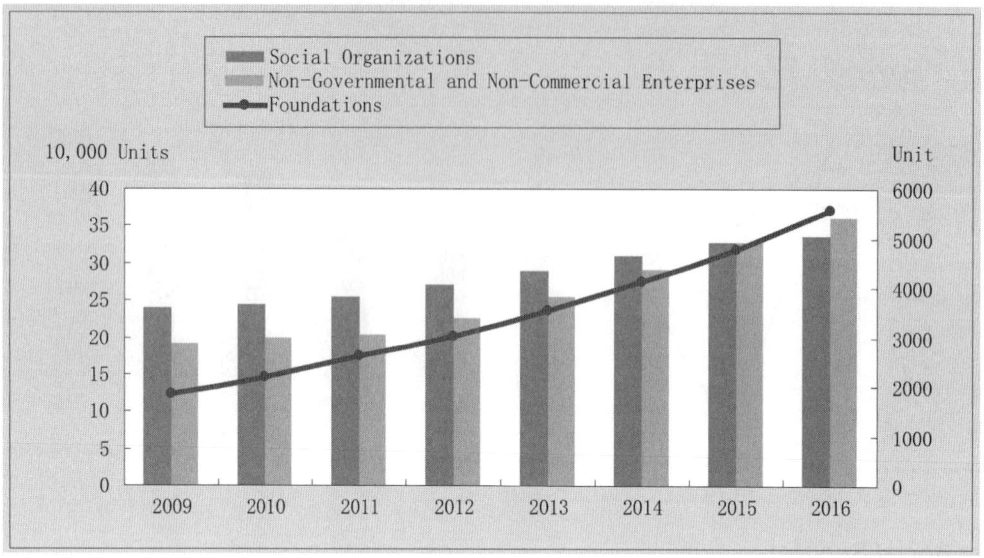

Table 12: Non-Governmental Organizations

Indicators	2009	2010	2011	2012	2013	2014	2015	2016
Social Organizations (10,000 Units)	23.9	24.5	25.5	27.1	28.9	31.0	32.9	33.6
Foundations(Unit)	1843	2200	2614	3029	3549	4117	4784	5559
Non- Governmental and Non-Commercial Enterprises (10,000 Units)	19.0	19.8	20.4	22.5	25.5	29.2	32.9	36.1

2. Self-Governing Organizations

By the end of 2016, self-governing organizations at the grass-roots totaled 662 thousand. Of this total, there were 559 thousand village committees, a decline of 3.8 percent over that of the previous year. The number of village groups was 4.478 million. There were 2.253 million members in the village committees, a decline of 1.9 percent over that of the previous year. There were 103,000 community neighborhood committees, a rise of 3.3 percent over that of the previous year. There were 1.420 million neighborhood groups. There were 540 thousand members of neighborhood committees, a rise of 5.4 percent over that in the previous year. In 2016, elections in 97 thousand neighborhood committees and village committees were completed. The registered number of residents and villagers who participated in the elections was 170 million. The number of voters was 90 million.

Table 13: Self-Governing Organizations

Indicators	2009	2010	2011	2012	2013	2014	2015	2016
Community Neighborhood Committees (10,000 Units)	8.5	8.7	8.9	9.1	9.5	9.7	10.0	10.3
Village Committees (10,000 Units)	59.9	59.5	59.0	58.8	58.9	58.5	58.1	55.9

Figure13: Self-Governing Organizations

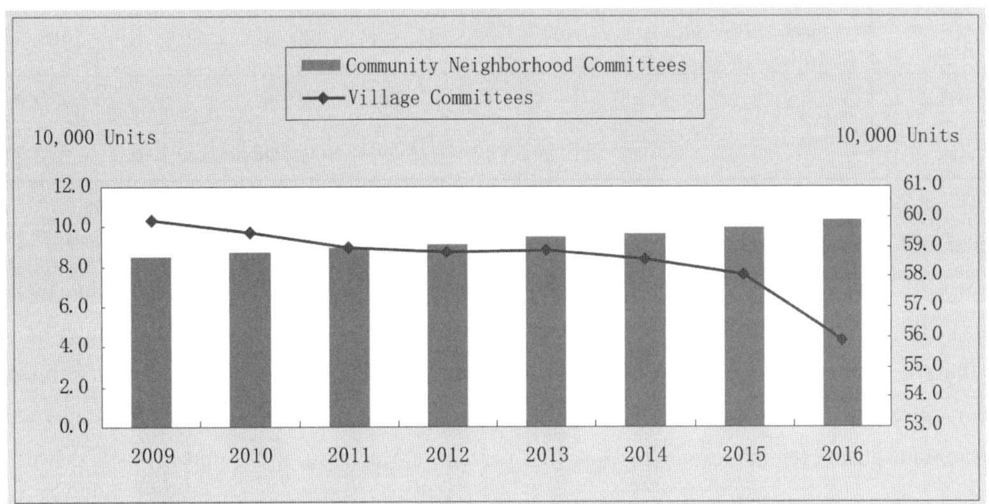

B. Other Social Services

1. Marriage Service

In 2016, there were 1,393 service institutions of marriage registration (qualified as public institutions) and 4,863 service offices of marriage registration in China. The number of people that registered their marriage through civil affairs departments or marriage registration institutions reached 11.428 million couples, a decline of 6.7 percent over the previous year. Of this total, there were 42 thousand couples concerning foreigners, overseas Chinese and residents of Hong Kong, Macau and Taiwan. The marriage rate was 8.3 per thousand. The proportion of people ranged from 25 to 29 years old accounted for 38.2 percent of all registered for marriage, taking the lead among other age groups.

In 2016, there were 4.158 million couples handling divorce, which was an increase of 8.3 percent over the previous year. Of this total, 3.486 million couples were registered through the civil affairs departments and those who divorced through courts were 672 thousand couples. The divorce rate was 3.0 per thousand, which was an increase of 0.2 per thousand over that in 2015.

Figure 14: Crude Nuptiality and Divorce Rate

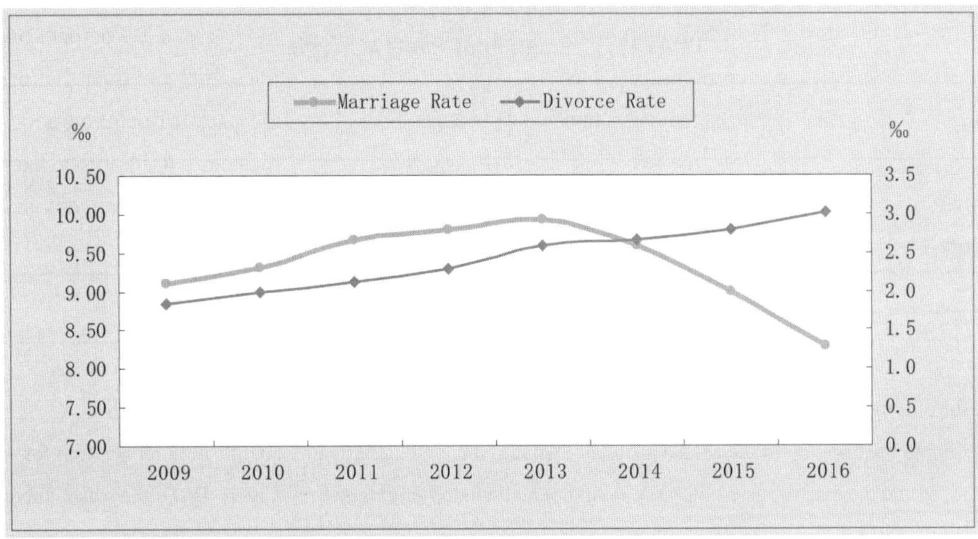

Table 14: Crude Nuptiality and Divorce Rate

Indicators	2009	2010	2011	2012	2013	2014	2015	2016
Crude Nuptiality (‰)	9.10	9.30	9.67	9.80	9.92	9.58	9.00	8.3
Crude Divorce Rate (‰)	1.85	2.00	2.13	2.29	2.58	2.67	2.79	3.0

2. Funeral and Interment

By the end of 2016, there were 4,166 funeral and interment service institutions. Of this total, there were 1,775 funeral parlors, 1,005 funeral management organizations. There were 1,386 public cemeteries under the management of the civil affairs departments. There were 81 thousand employees in the funeral and interment service institutions. Among these institutions, 47 thousand people worked for funeral parlors. There were 6,206 cremators, which cremated 4.718 million remains. The cremation rate stood at 48.3 percent, an increase of 1.2 percent over that of the previous year.

Figure 15: Cremation of Funeral Service

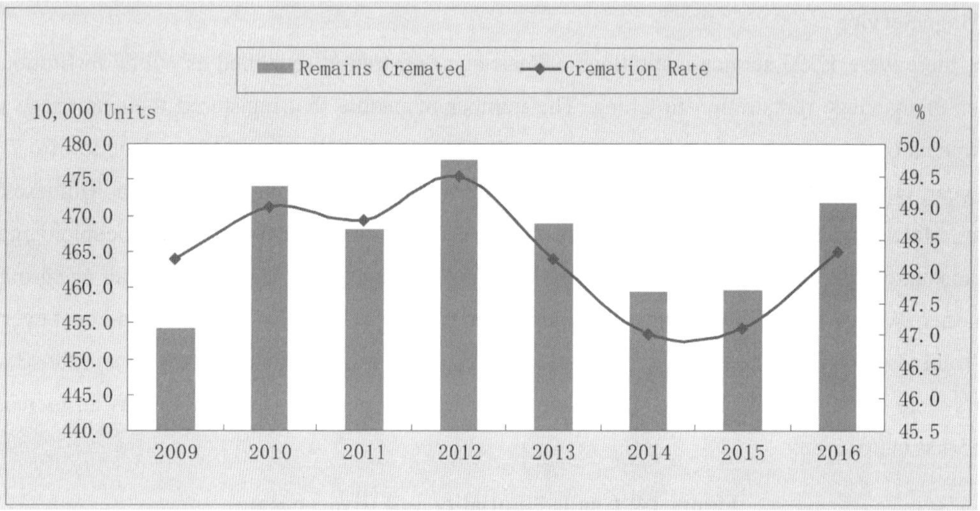

Table 15: Cremation of Funeral Service

Indicators	2009	2010	2011	2012	2013	2014	2015	2016
Remains Cremated (10,000 Units)	454.2	474.1	468.1	477.7	468.9	459.3	459.5	471.8
Cremation Rate(%)	48.2	49.0	48.8	49.5	48.2	47.0	47.1	48.3

Notes:

[1] Townships in figure 1 include ethnic townships, sumus and ethnic sumus.

[2] According to the decision of the Ministry of Civil Affairs, there will be no more qualification recognition for social welfare enterprises and the data of these enterprises will not be included from the year of 2016. That's the reason there is a larger decline in the indicator of original value of fixed assets of social service institutions & facilities.

[3] The funds allocated by the Ministry of Finance and the Ministry of Civil Affairs do not include the purchasing funds for relief material at the level of central government and part of the funds that the central government allocated to Xinjiang

Production and Construction Corps.

[4] Donation data of the Non-Government Organizations used were collected from those NGOs that passed the annual inspections in 2016.

[5] The statistics of judicial decisions and mediate divorces recorded in the divorce registration service were provided by the Supreme People's Court.

[6] In this report, the numbers of people (objects of service of civil affairs departments) are actual ones. The numbers of institutions were collected from the registered and legal institutions. These numbers are not comparable with the approved numbers, the planned numbers and the budgeted numbers.

[7] For part of the data in this report, the itemized figures may not match the totalized ones due to round-off errors and no mechanical adjustments were made for mending the errors.

[8] Statistics of Hong Kong SAR, Macao SAR and Taiwan Province were not included into the report.

[9] The indicators of marriage rate & devorce rate share the same calculation methods and meanings with those of the crude nuptiality and divorce rate in Report of 2015.

02

社会服务主要数据图表

2017

图1-1 市、区、县

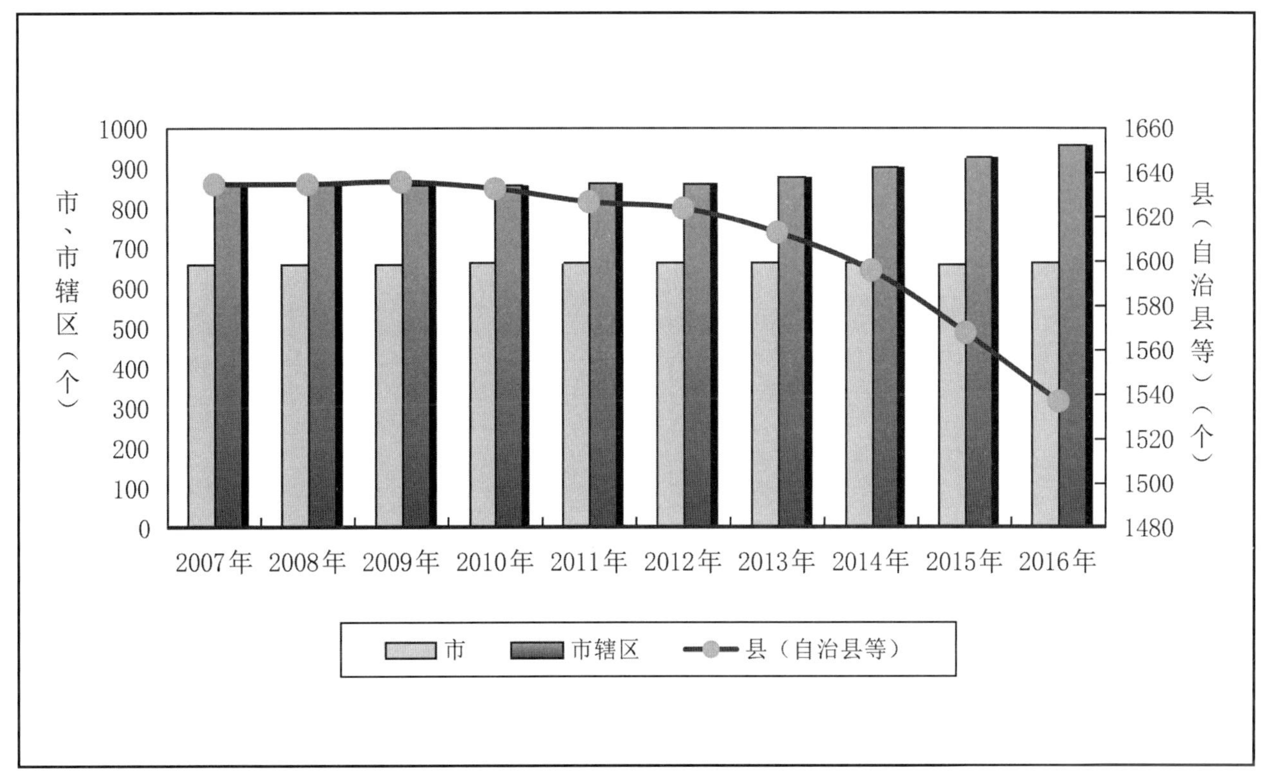

单位：个

指 标	2007年	2008年	2009年	2010年	2011年	2012年	2013年	2014年	2015年	2016年
市	655	655	654	657	657	657	658	658	656	657
市辖区	856	856	855	853	857	860	872	897	921	954
县（自治县等）	1635	1635	1636	1633	1627	1624	1613	1596	1568	1537

注：市含直辖市、地级市及县级市。

图1–2　乡镇与街道

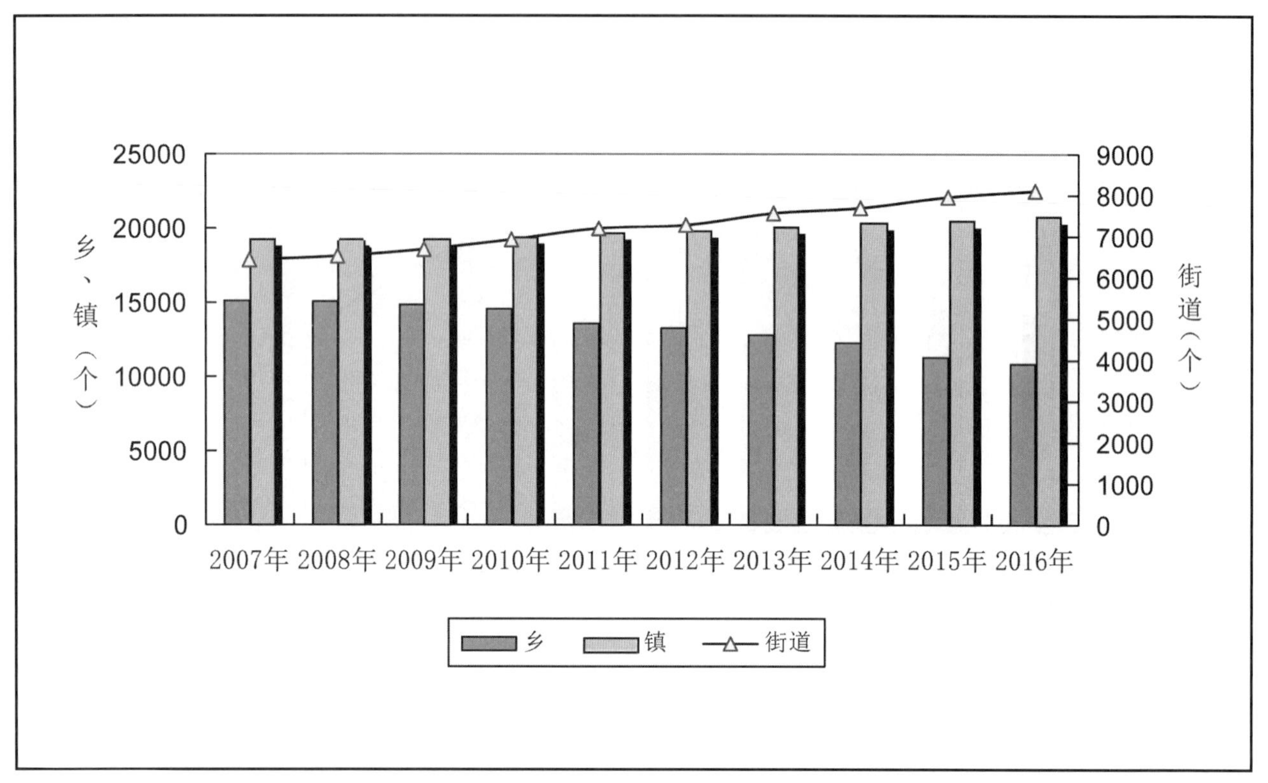

单位：个

指　标	2007年	2008年	2009年	2010年	2011年	2012年	2013年	2014年	2015年	2016年
乡	15120	15067	14848	14571	13587	13281	12812	12282	11315	10872
镇	19249	19234	19322	19410	19683	19881	20117	20401	20515	20883
街道	6434	6524	6686	6923	7194	7282	7566	7696	7957	8105

图1-3　60岁及以上老年人口占全国总人口比重

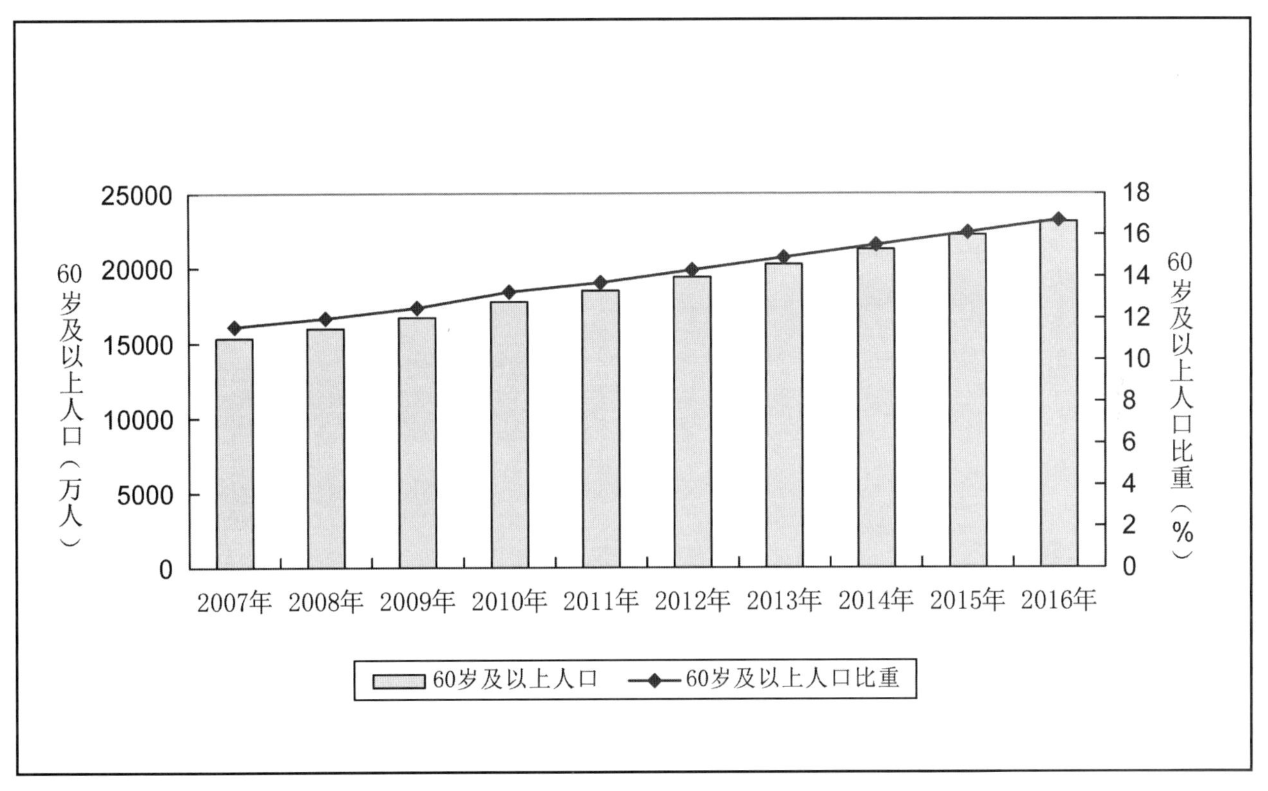

单位：万人、%

指　标	2007年	2008年	2009年	2010年	2011年	2012年	2013年	2014年	2015年	2016年
60岁及以上人口	15340	15989	16714	17765	18499	19390	20243	21242	22200	23086
60岁及以上人口比重	11.6	12	12.5	13.26	13.7	14.3	14.9	15.5	16.1	16.7

注：本表数据来源于国家统计局。

图1-4　人口年龄结构

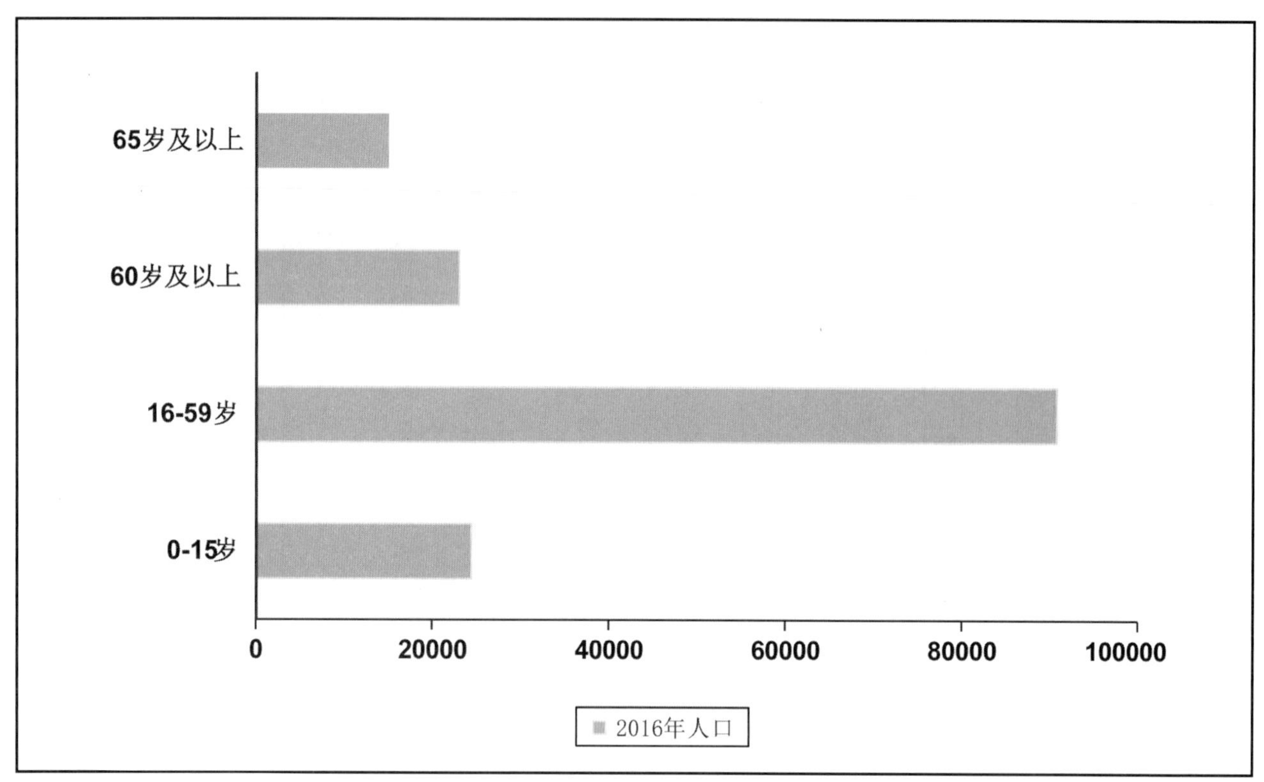

单位：万人、%

指　标	0-15岁	16-59岁	60岁及以上	65岁及以上
2016年人口	24438	90747	23086	15003
不同年龄段人口比重	17.7	65.6	16.7	10.8
比2015年增减百分点	0	-0.7	0.6	0.3

注：本表数据来源于国家统计局。

图1-5 社会服务对象占全国总人口比重

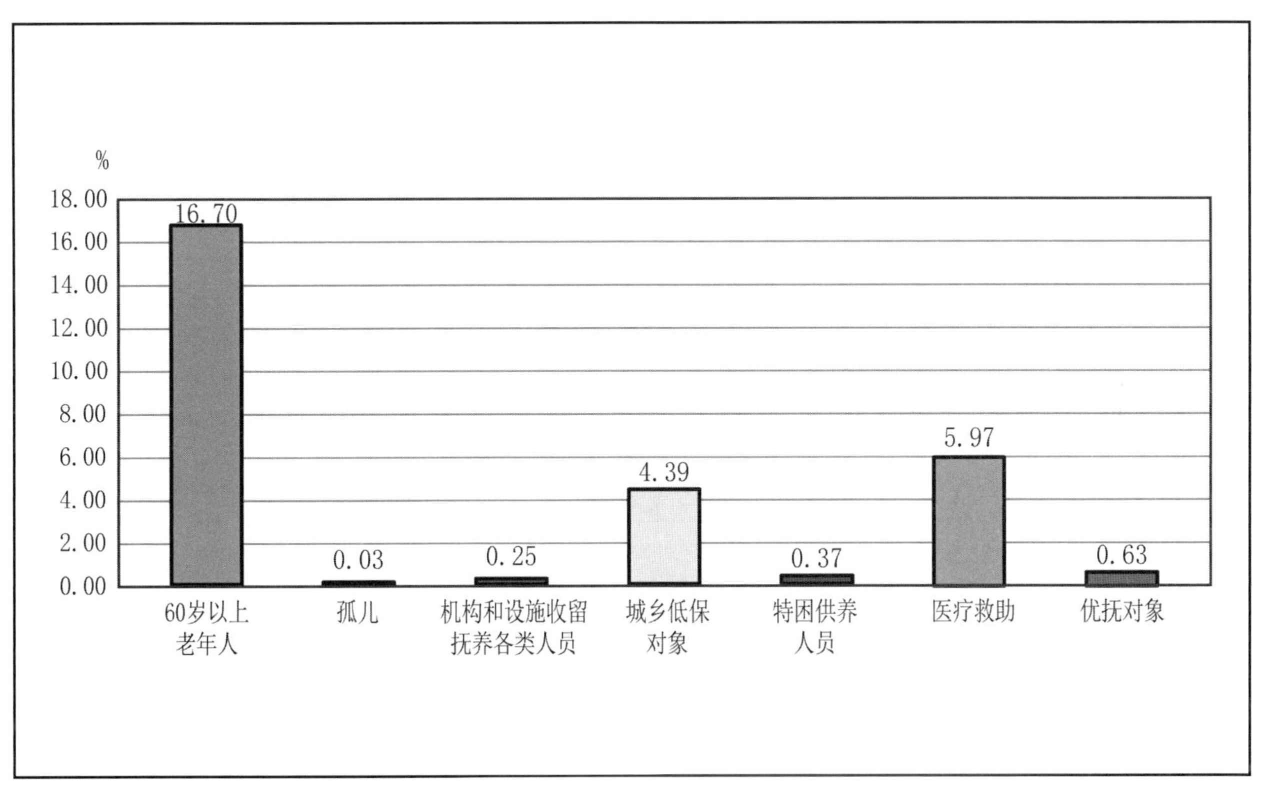

单位：万人、%

指　标	2016年	比　重
全国总人口	138271	100.0
社会服务对象	40120.8	29.02
#60岁以上老年人	23086	16.70
#孤儿	46.0	0.03
#机构和设施收留抚养各类人员	344.2	0.25
#城乡低保对象	6066.7	4.39
#特困供养人员	505.9	0.37
#医疗救助	8256.5	5.97
#优抚对象	874.8	0.63

注：医疗救助为人次数。

图1-6　社会服务机构和设施职工

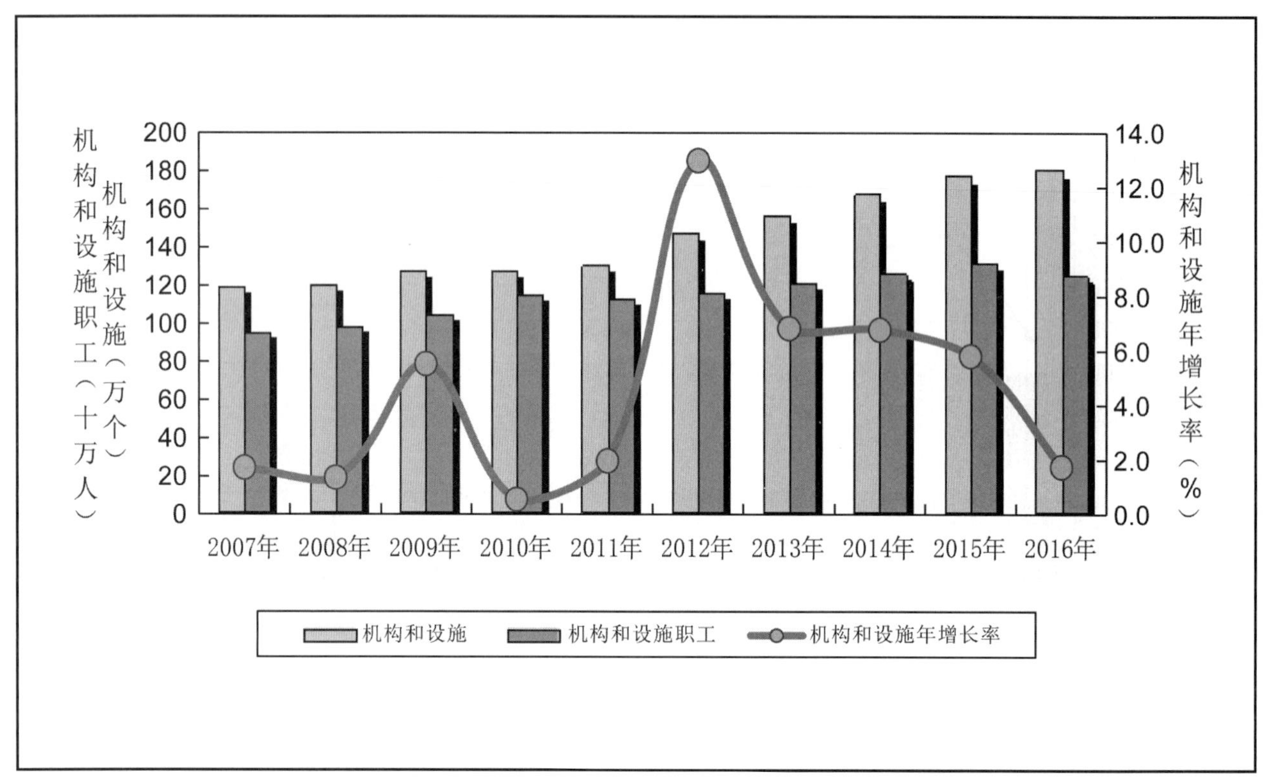

单位：万个、%、十万人

指　标	2007年	2008年	2009年	2010年	2011年	2012年	2013年	2014年	2015年	2016年
机构和设施	118	119.6	126.2	126.9	129.4	146.2	156.2	166.8	176.5	174.5
机构和设施职工	93.8	96.7	103.8	113.8	112.1	114.7	119.8	125.1	130.9	123.9
机构和设施年增长率	1.7	1.4	5.5	0.6	2.0	13.0	6.8	6.8	5.8	-1.1

注：为避免重复，社会服务机构和设施总数中剔除了在民政部门登记的社会工作类和其他社会服务类机构。

图1-7　社会服务机构和设施固定资产原价

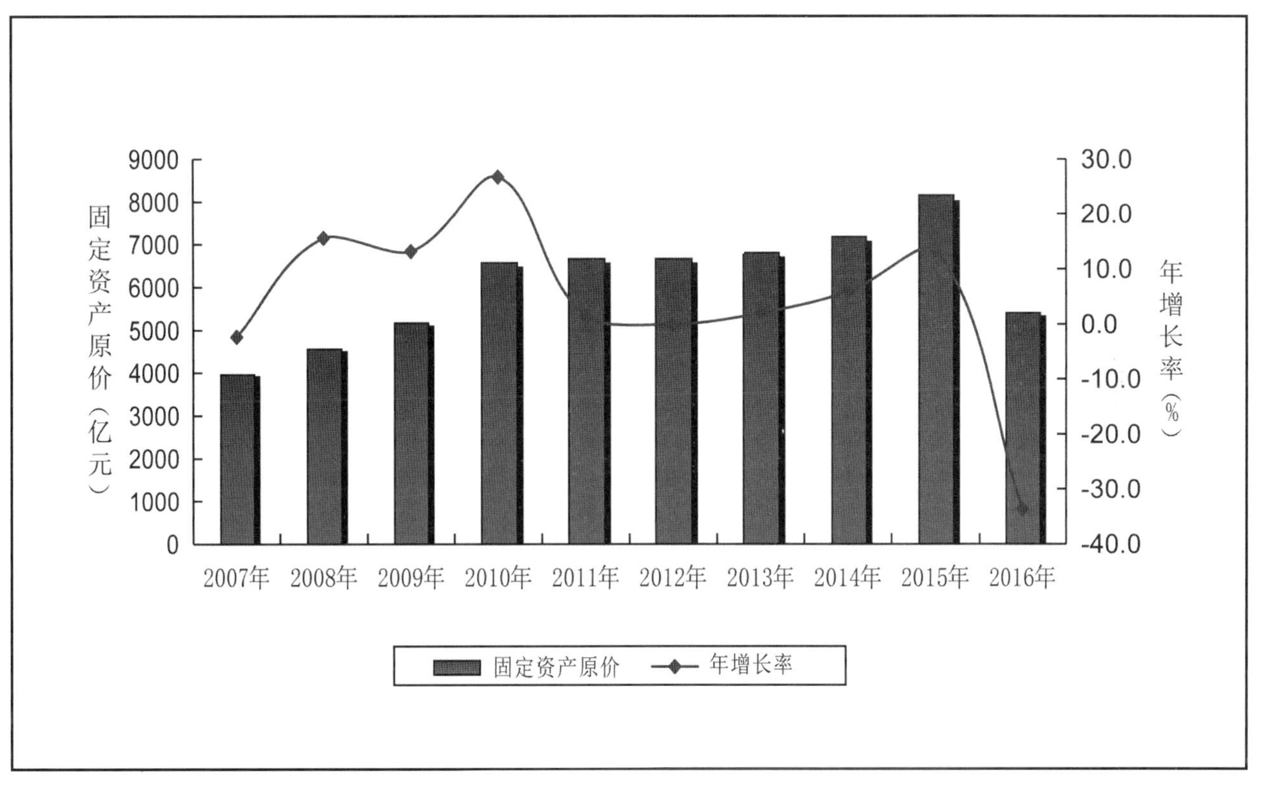

单位：亿元、%

指　标	2007年	2008年	2009年	2010年	2011年	2012年	2013年	2014年	2015年	2016年
固定资产原价	3973	4592.8	5198	6589.3	6676.7	6675.4	6810.2	7213.0	8183.1	5393.6
年增长率	-2.3	15.6	13.2	26.8	1.3	0.0	2.0	5.9	13.4	-33.6

注：自2016年起，民政部取消社会福利企业资质认定，不再统计社会福利企业情况指标，因此社会服务机构和设施固定资产原价指标出现较大降幅。

图1-8　社会服务事业费支出

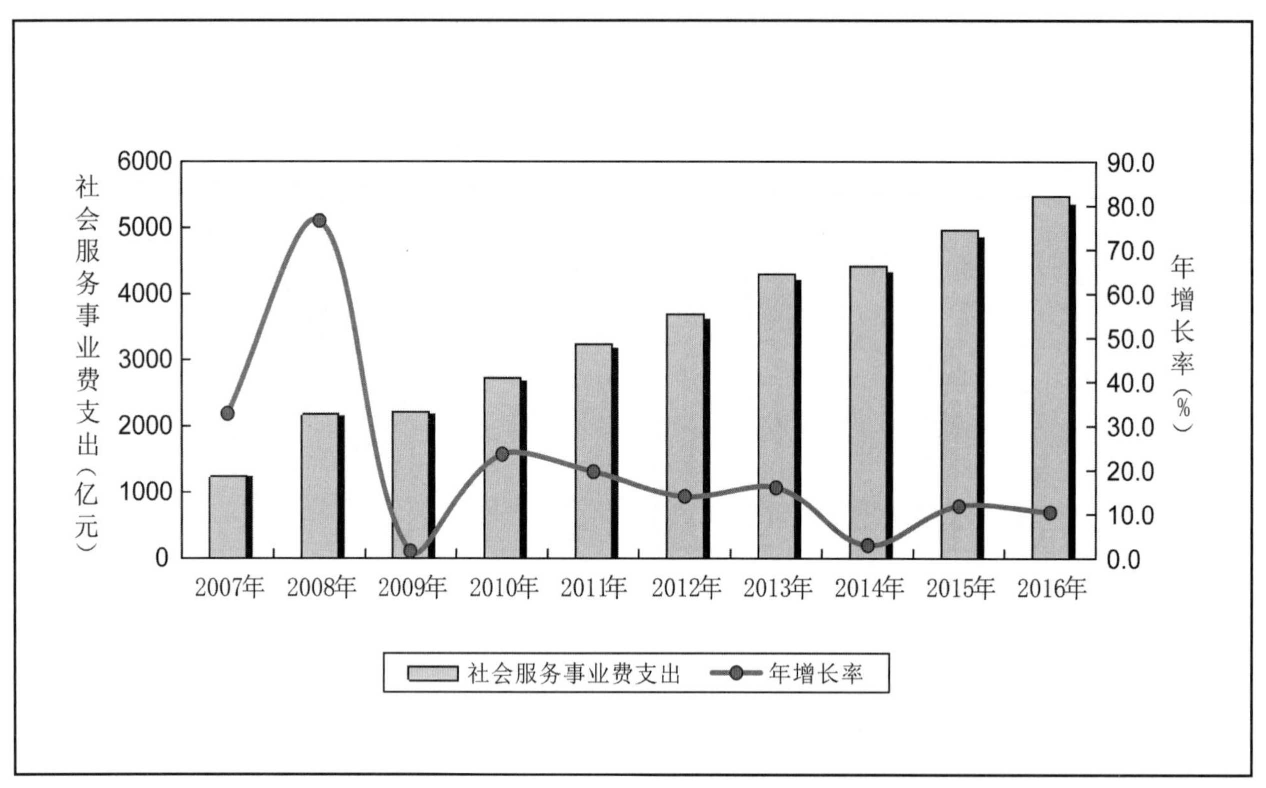

单位：亿元、%

指　标	2007年	2008年	2009年	2010年	2011年	2012年	2013年	2014年	2015年	2016年
社会服务事业费支出	1215.5	2146.5	2181.9	2697.5	3229.1	3683.7	4276.5	4404.1	4926.4	5440.2
年增长率	32.8	76.6	1.6	23.6	19.7	14.1	16.1	3.0	11.9	10.4

图1-9　社会服务事业费支出占国家财政支出的比重

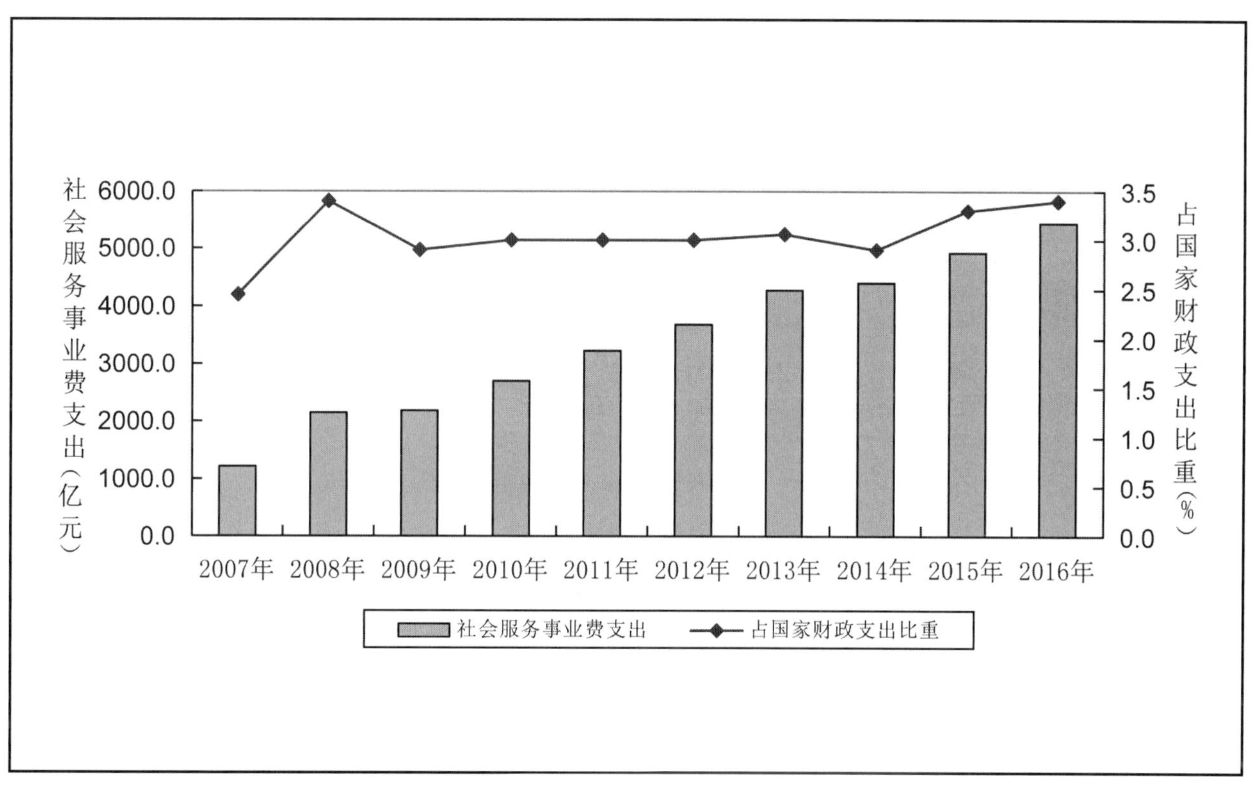

单位：亿元、%

指　标	2007年	2008年	2009年	2010年	2011年	2012年	2013年	2014年	2015年	2016年
社会服务事业费支出	1215.5	2146.5	2181.9	2697.5	3229.1	3683.7	4276.5	4404.1	4926.4	5440.2
占国家财政支出比重	2.5	3.4	2.9	3.0	3.0	3.0	3.1	2.9	3.3	3.4

图1-10 按用项分社会服务事业费

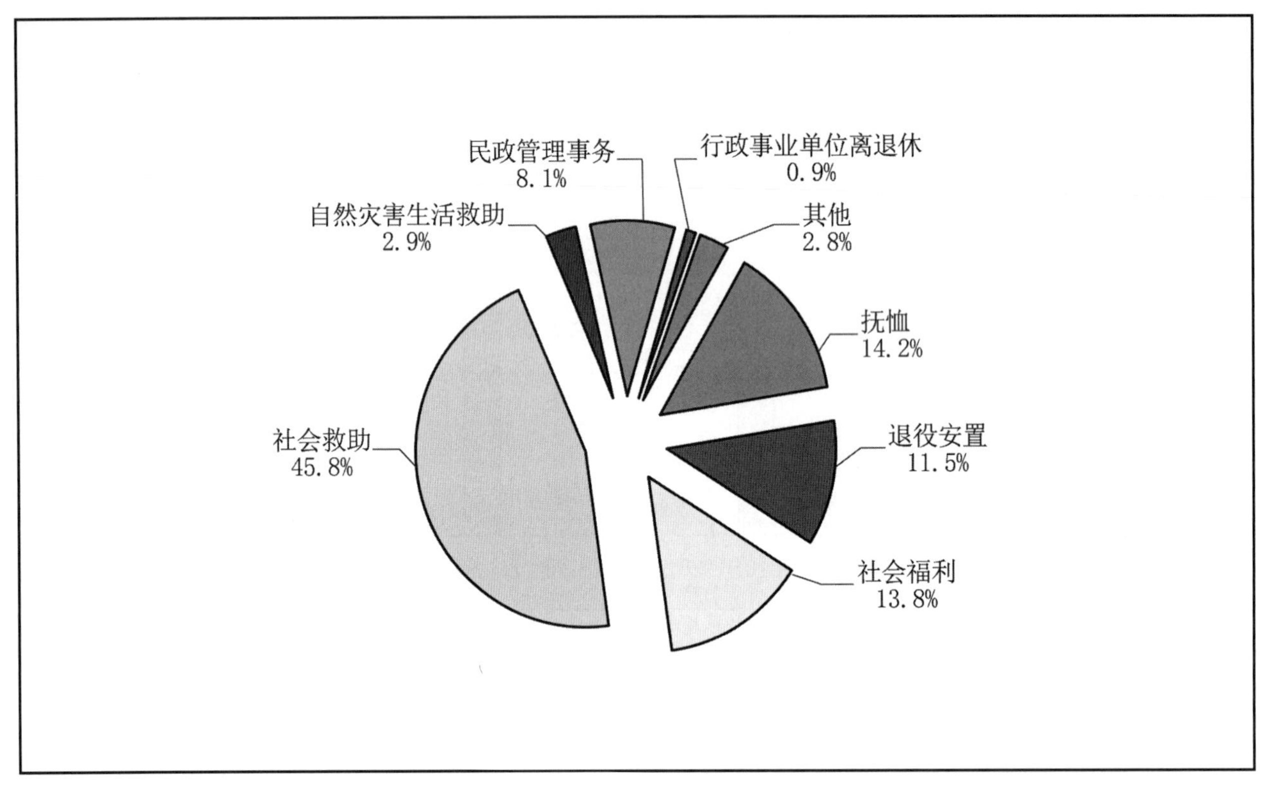

单位：亿元、%

指 标	社会服务事业费	抚恤	退役安置	社会福利	社会救助	自然灾害生活救助	民政管理事务	行政事业单位离退休	其他
金 额	5440.2	769.8	625.6	753.4	2492.8	156.1	441.7	48.4	152.2
比 重	100.0	14.2	11.5	13.8	45.8	2.9	8.1	0.9	2.8

图1-11 中央转移支付社会服务事业费

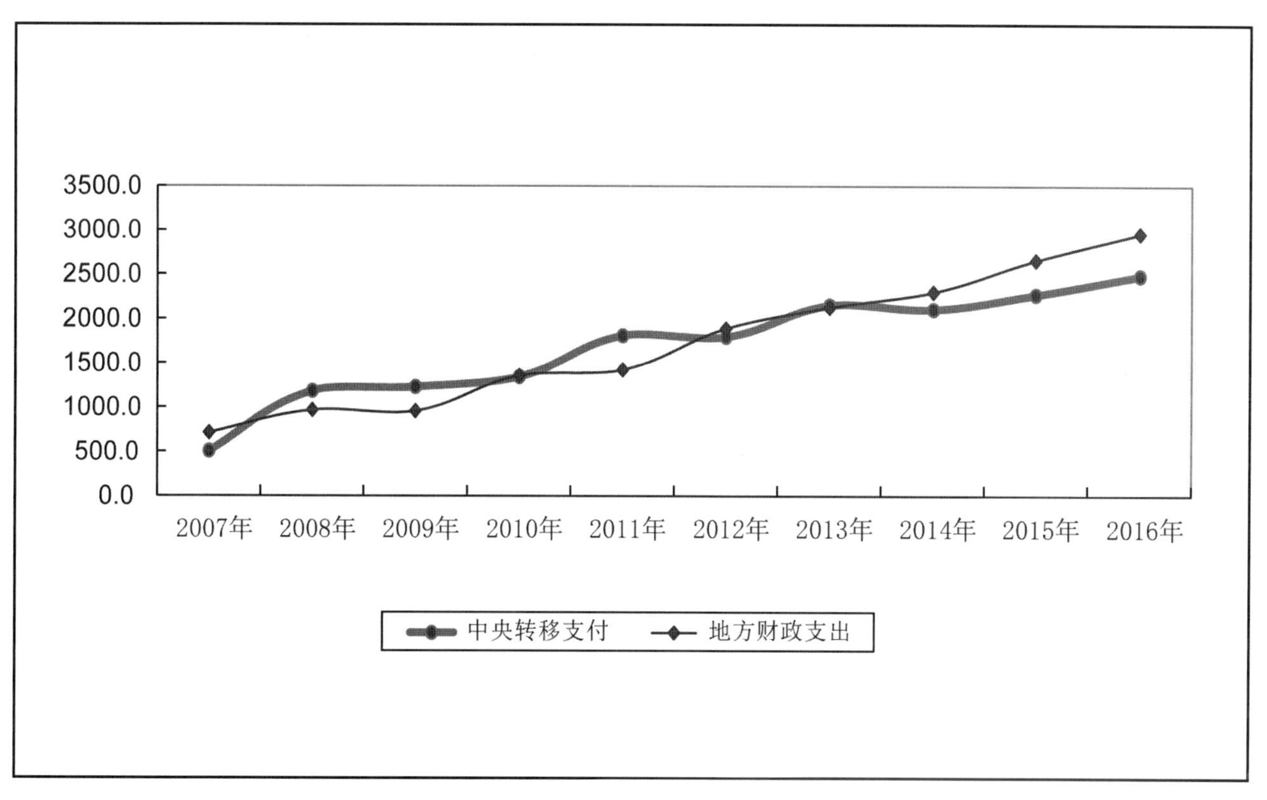

单位：亿元、%

指　标	2007年	2008年	2009年	2010年	2011年	2012年	2013年	2014年	2015年	2016年
社会服务事业费支出	1215.5	2146.5	2181.9	2697.5	3229.1	3683.7	4276.5	4404.1	4926.4	5440.2
#中央转移支付	504.4	1181.1	1227.0	1342.4	1808.0	1794.6	2149.7	2105.0	2270.3	2484.0
地方财政支出	711.1	965.4	954.9	1355.1	1421.1	1889.1	2126.8	2299.1	2656.1	2956.2
中央转移支付比重	42.6	55.0	56.2	49.8	56.0	48.7	50.3	47.8	46.1	45.7

图1-12 社会服务基本建设投资

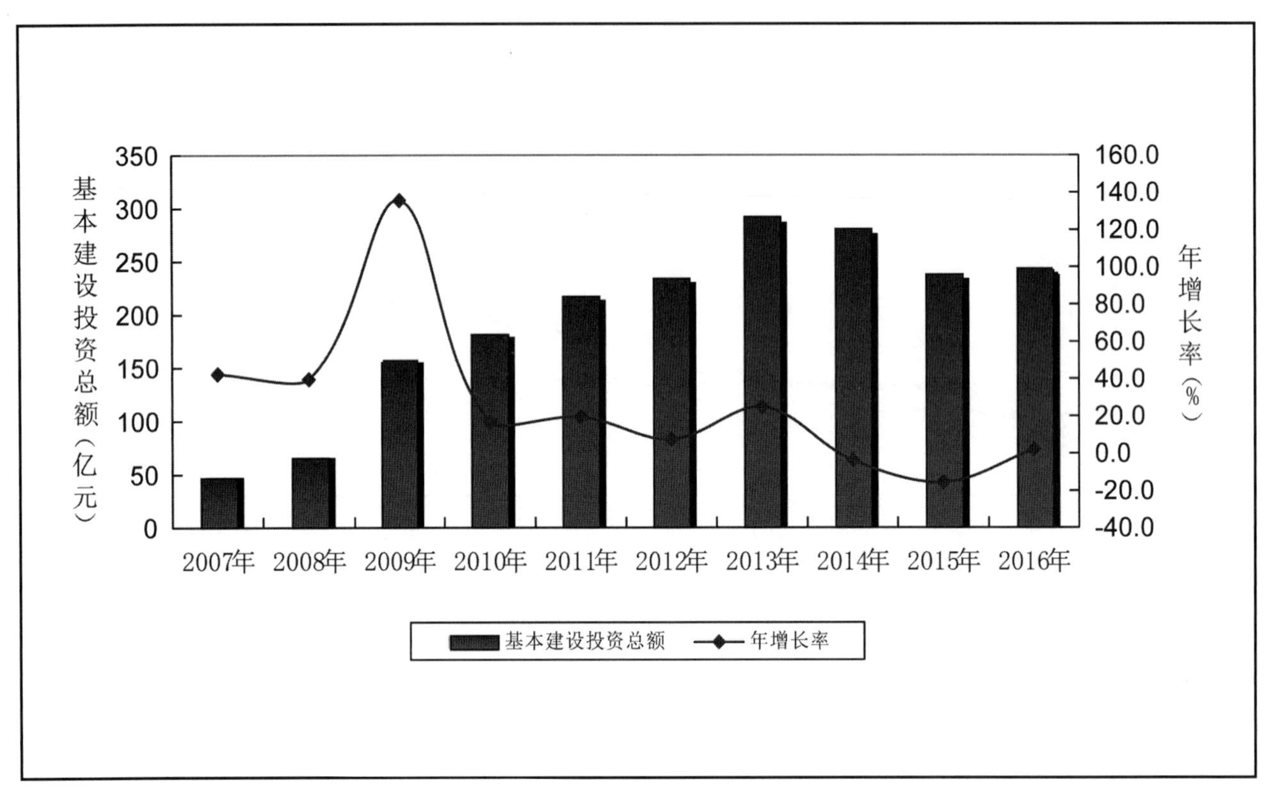

单位：亿元、%

指　标	2007年	2008年	2009年	2010年	2011年	2012年	2013年	2014年	2015年	2016年
基本建设投资总额	47.7	66.6	157	183	218.5	234.7	292.8	282.2	238.5	245.8
年增长率	42.4	39.6	135.7	16.6	19.4	7.4	24.8	-3.6	-15.5	2.5

图1-13　预算内基本建设支出和中央转移支付情况

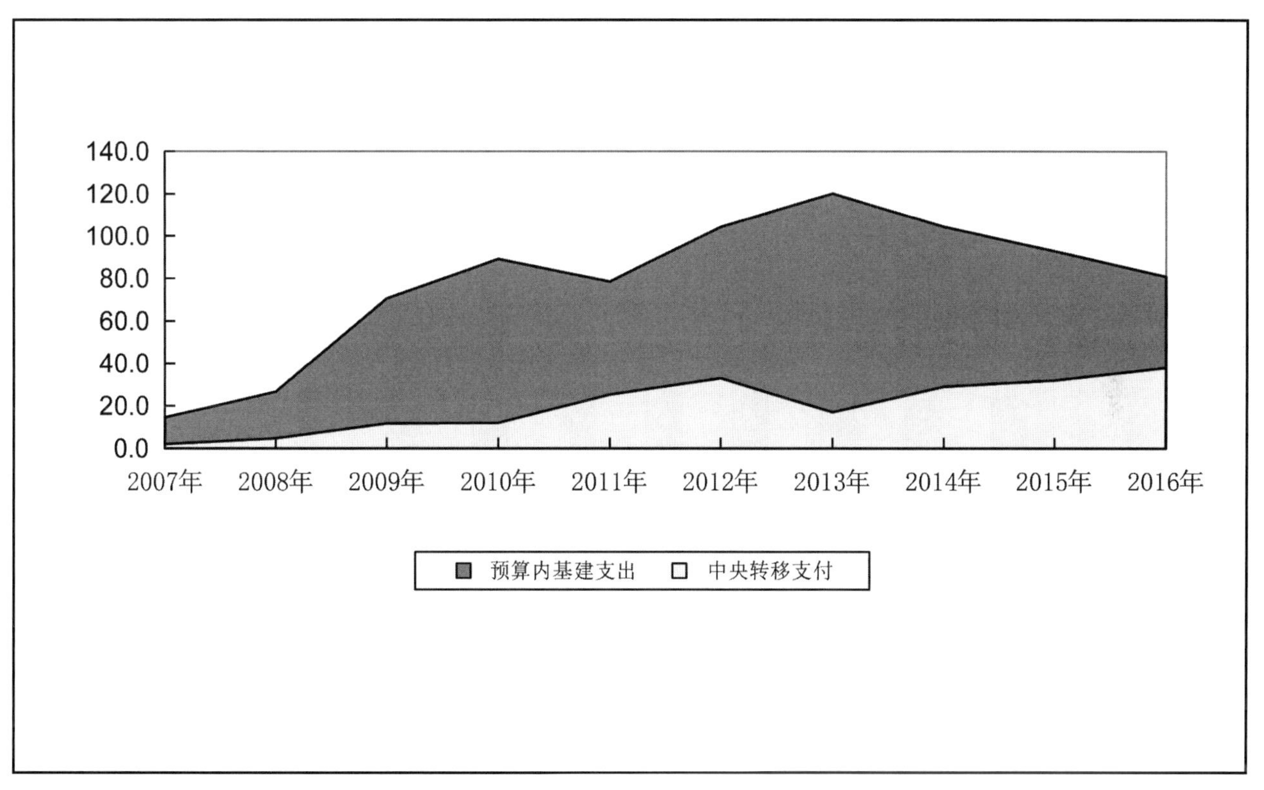

单位：亿元、%

指　标	2007年	2008年	2009年	2010年	2011年	2012年	2013年	2014年	2015年	2016年
社会服务事业费支出	1215.5	2146.5	2181.9	2697.5	3229.1	3683.7	4276.5	4404.1	4926.4	5440.2
预算内基建支出	14.5	26.6	70.6	89.1	78.5	104.2	120.1	104.3	92.8	84.4
中央转移支付	2.0	4.7	11.7	12.0	25.3	33.0	17.0	29.0	32.0	38.0

图2-1　社会服务床位数

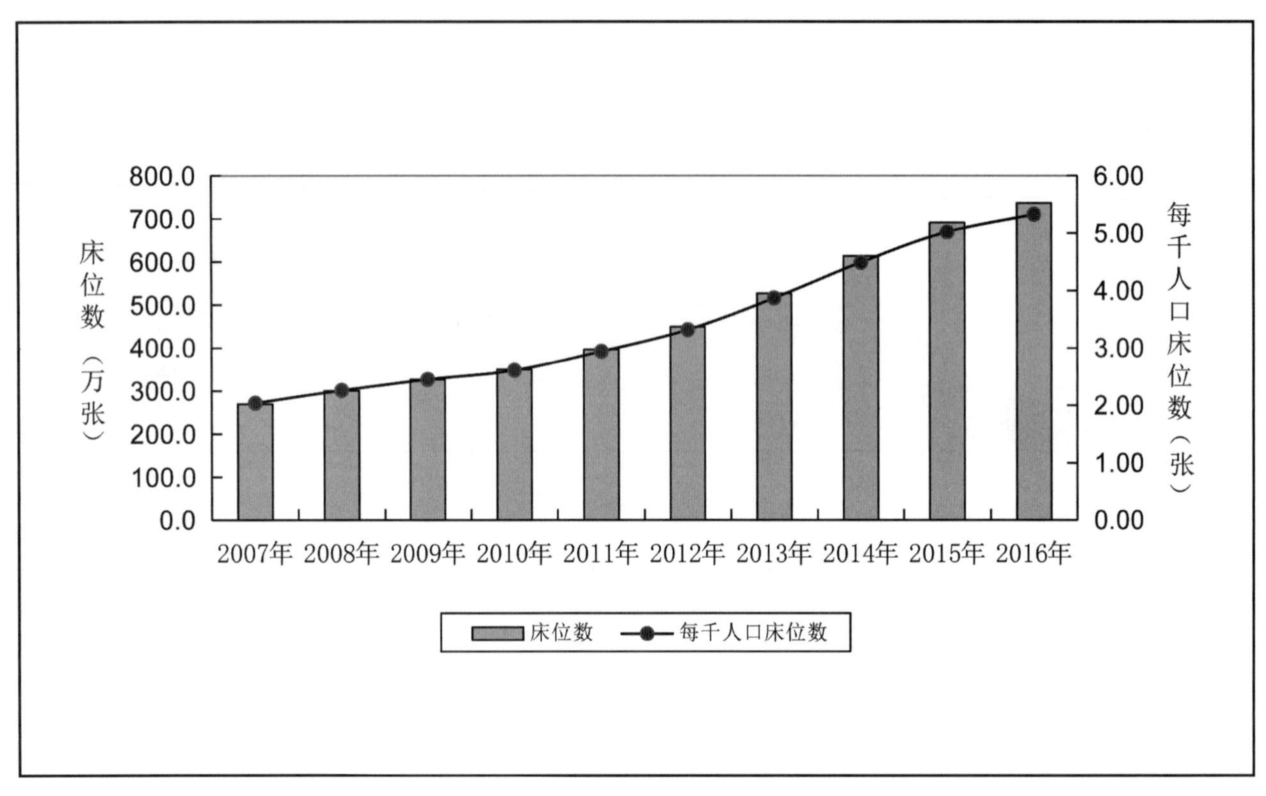

单位：万张、张

指　标	2007年	2008年	2009年	2010年	2011年	2012年	2013年	2014年	2015年	2016年
床位数	269.6	300.3	326.5	349.6	396.4	449.3	526.7	613.5	691.3	771.2
每千人口床位数	2.04	2.26	2.45	2.61	2.94	3.32	3.87	4.49	5.02	5.50

图2-2　养老服务床位数

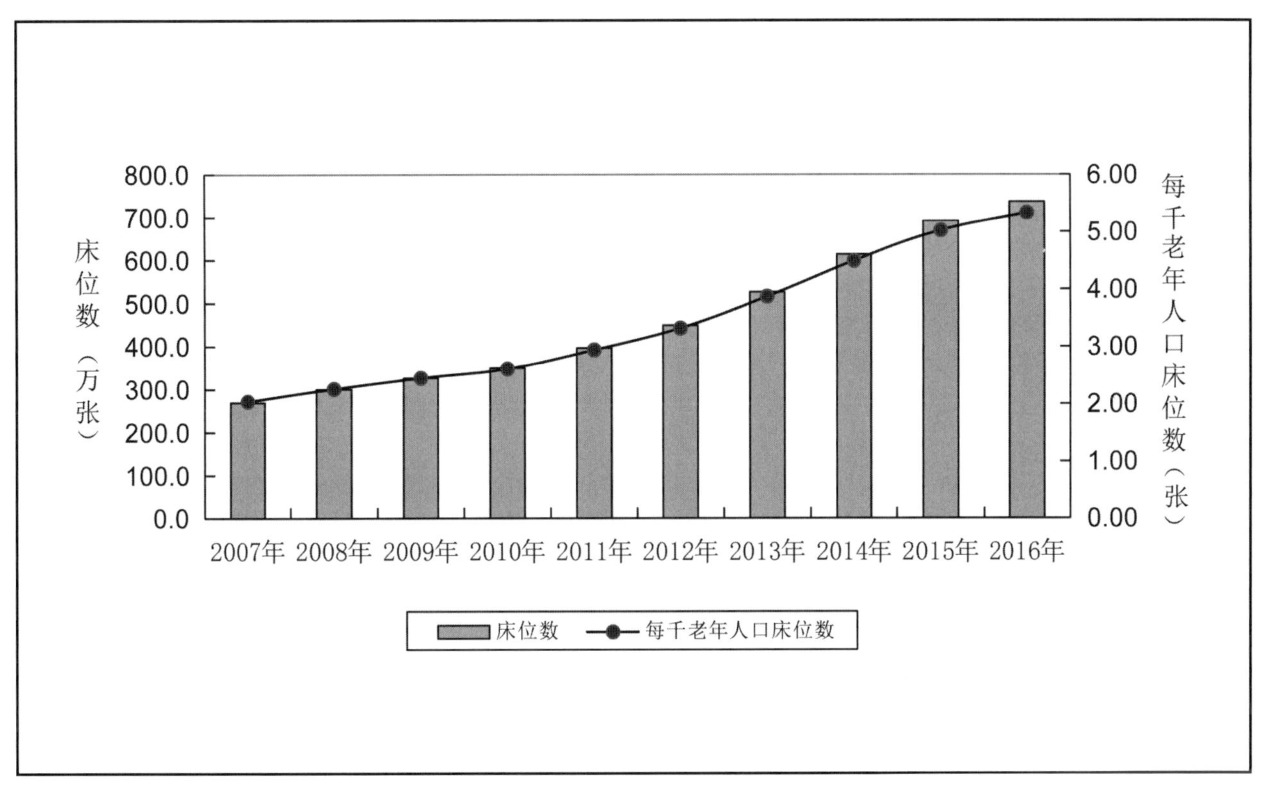

单位：万张、%、张

指　标	2007年	2008年	2009年	2010年	2011年	2012年	2013年	2014年	2015年	2016年
床位数	242.9	267.4	293.5	316.1	369.2	416.5	493.7	577.7	672.7	730.2
增长率	35.2	10.1	9.8	7.7	16.8	12.8	18.5	17.0	16.4	8.5
每千老年人口养老床位数	15.83	16.72	17.56	17.79	19.96	21.48	24.39	27.2	30.3	31.6

图2-3　智障和精神疾病服务床位数

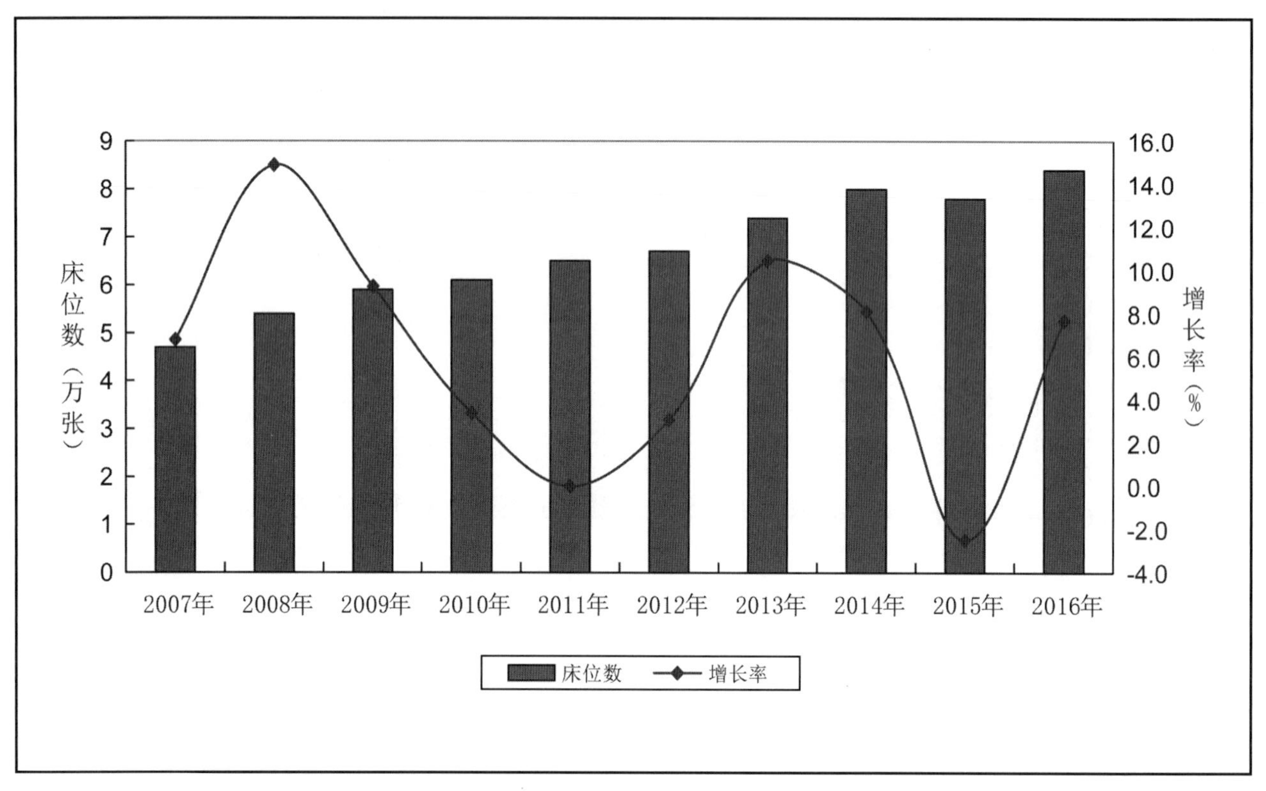

单位：万张、%

指　标	2007年	2008年	2009年	2010年	2011年	2012年	2013年	2014年	2015年	2016年
床位数	4.7	5.4	5.9	6.1	6.5	6.7	7.4	8.0	7.8	8.4
增长率	6.8	14.9	9.3	3.4	6.6	3.1	10.4	8.1	-2.5	7.7

图2-4　儿童服务床位数

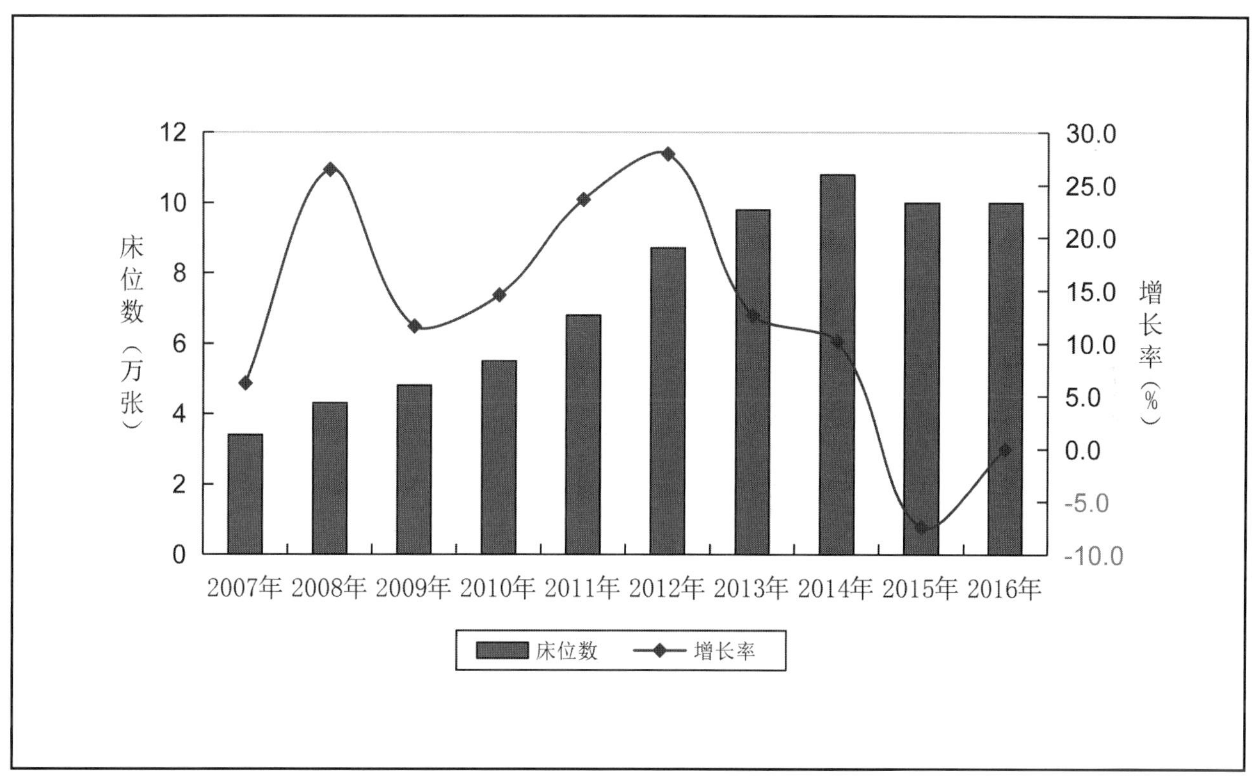

单位：万张、%

指　标	2007年	2008年	2009年	2010年	2011年	2012年	2013年	2014年	2015年	2016年
床位数	3.4	4.3	4.8	5.5	6.8	8.7	9.8	10.8	10.0	10.0
增长率	6.2	26.5	11.6	14.6	23.6	27.9	12.6	10.2	-7.4	0.0

图2-5　老年人福利

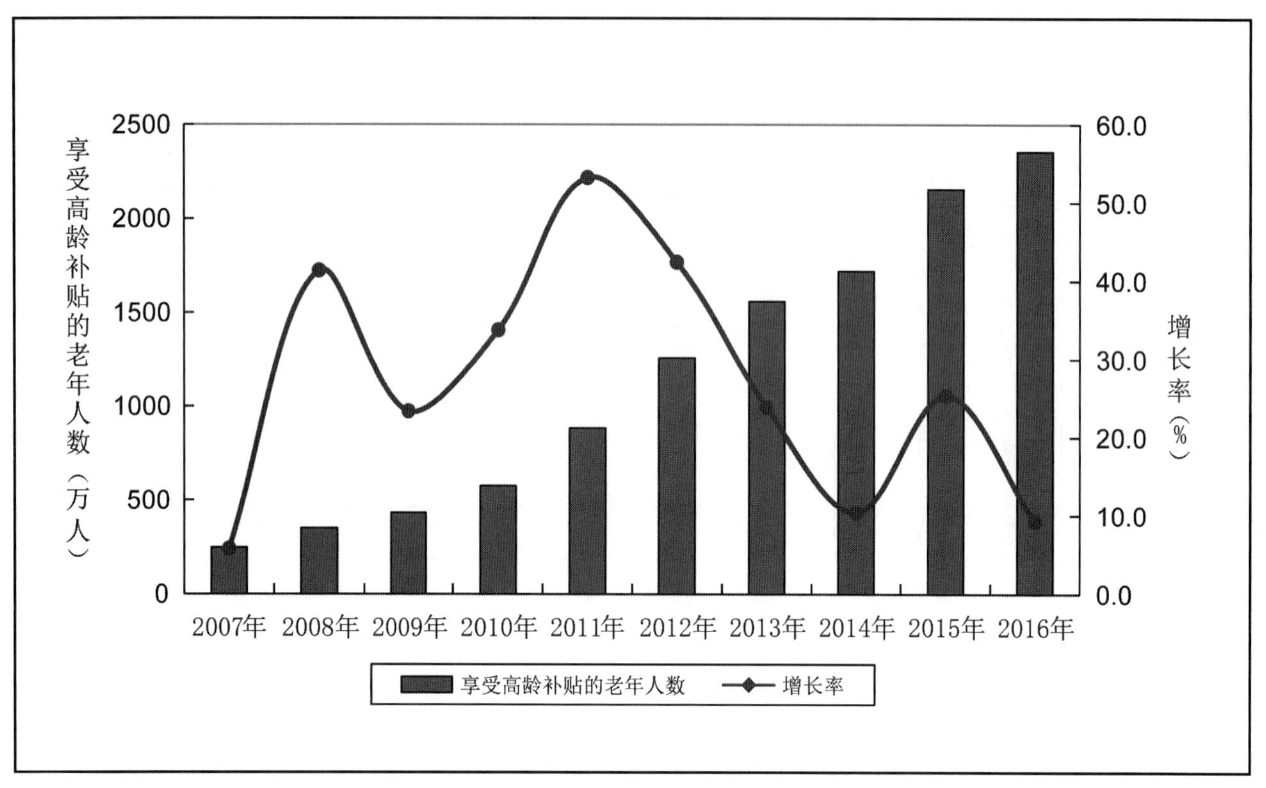

单位：万人、%

指　标	2007年	2008年	2009年	2010年	2011年	2012年	2013年	2014年	2015年	2016年
享受高龄补贴的老年人数	247.1	349.3	430.9	576.4	883.1	1257.7	1557.9	1719.6	2155.1	2355.4
增长率	5.8	41.4	23.4	33.8	53.2	42.4	23.9	10.4	25.3	9.3

图2-6　家庭收养

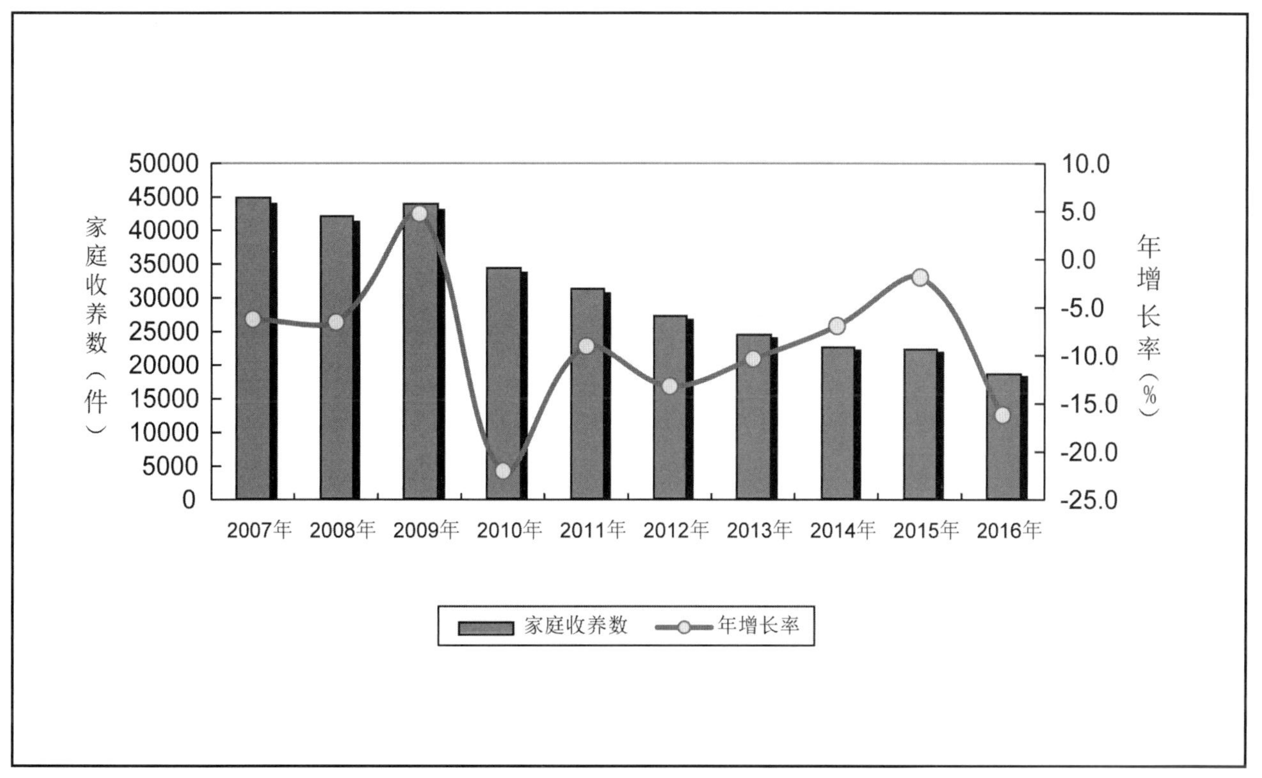

单位：件、%

指　标	2007年	2008年	2009年	2010年	2011年	2012年	2013年	2014年	2015年	2016年
家庭收养数	45192	42250	44260	34529	31424	27278	24460	22772	22348	18736
年增长率	-6.2	-6.5	4.8	-22.0	-9.0	-13.2	-10.3	-6.9	-1.9	-16.2

图2-7 城市最低生活保障

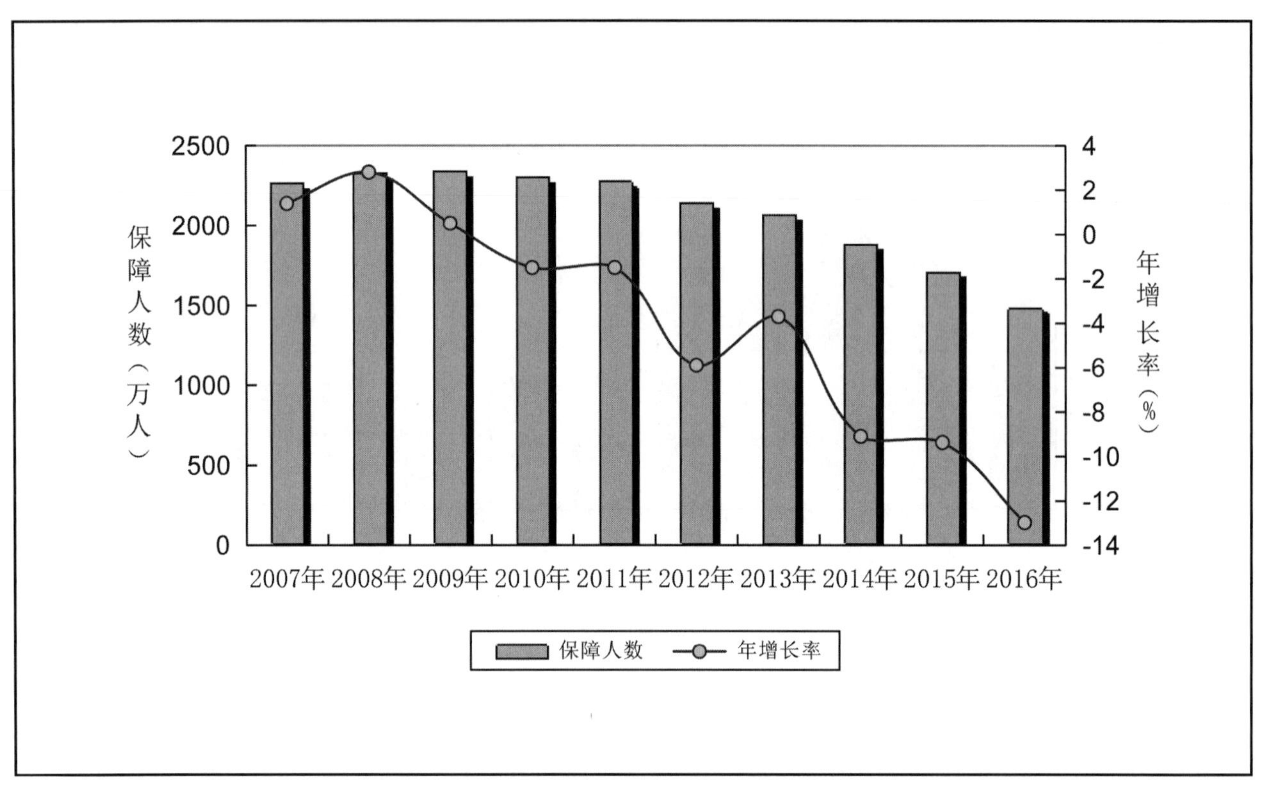

单位：万人、%

指　标	2007年	2008年	2009年	2010年	2011年	2012年	2013年	2014年	2015年	2016年
保障人数	2272.1	2334.8	2345.6	2310.5	2276.8	2143.5	2064.2	1877	1701.1	1480.2
年增长率	1.4	2.8	0.5	-1.5	-1.5	-5.9	-3.7	-9.1	-9.4	-13.0

图2-8　城市低保平均标准

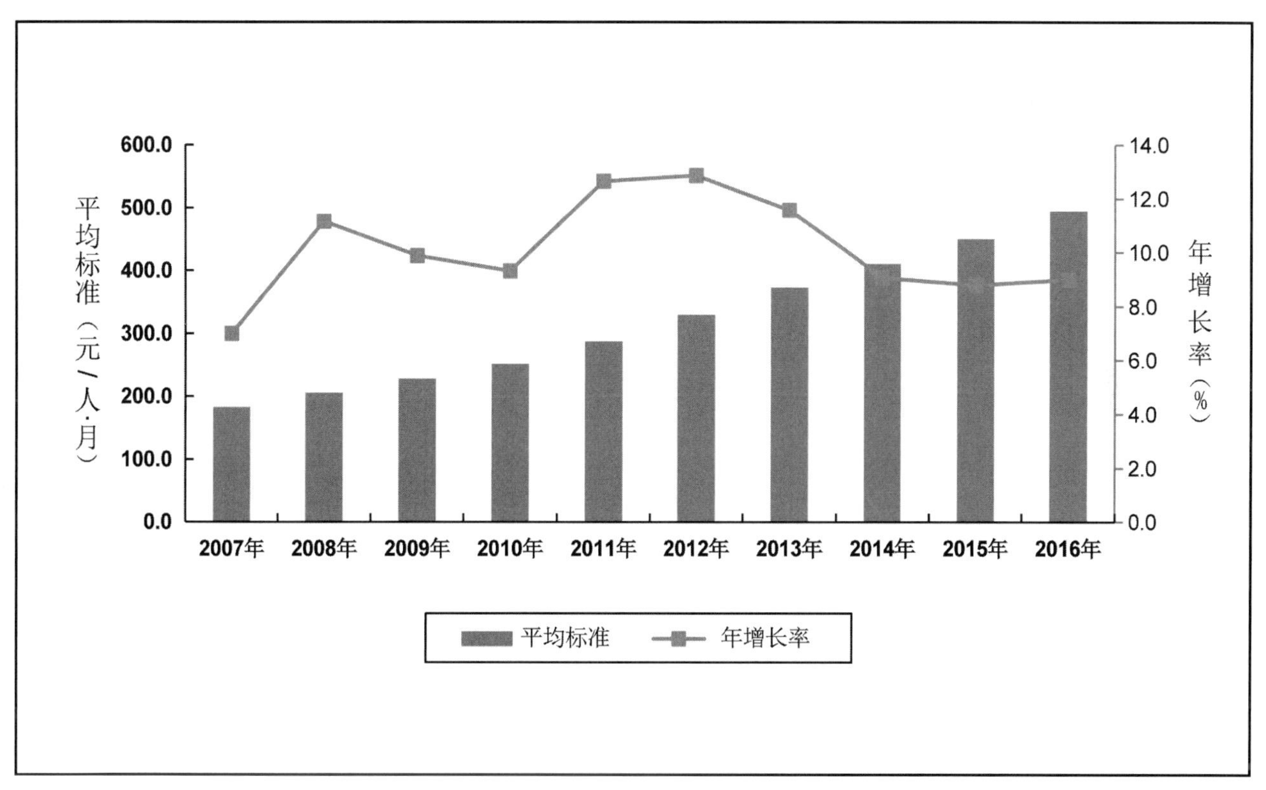

单位：元/人·月

指　标	2007年	2008年	2009年	2010年	2011年	2012年	2013年	2014年	2015年	2016年
平均标准	182.4	205.3	227.8	251.2	287.6	330.1	373.3	410.5	450.1	494.6
年增长率	7.0	11.2	9.9	9.3	12.7	12.9	11.6	9.1	8.8	9.0

图2-9 分省城市低保平均标准

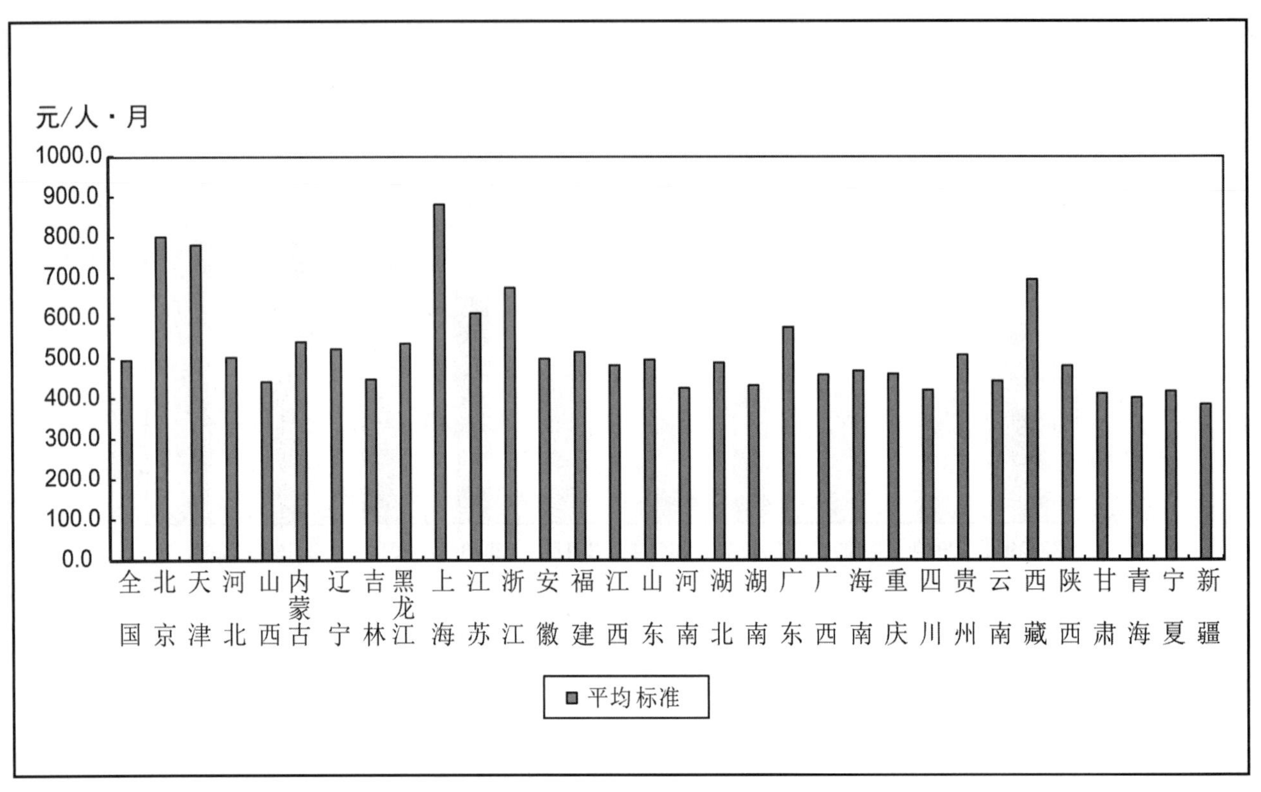

单位：元/人·月

地区	平均标准	地区	平均标准	地区	平均标准	地区	平均标准
全国	**494.6**	黑龙江	535.9	河南	425.1	贵州	507.3
北京	800.0	上海	880.0	湖北	487.9	云南	442.2
天津	780.0	江苏	610.8	湖南	431.3	西藏	693.5
河北	501.2	浙江	673.7	广东	576.2	陕西	479.5
山西	441.1	安徽	497.1	广西	457.6	甘肃	410.9
内蒙古	540.2	福建	514.8	海南	467.0	青海	400.8
辽宁	522.8	江西	480.8	重庆	459.6	宁夏	416.4
吉林	446.9	山东	494.9	四川	419.5	新疆	383.9

图2-10 农村最低生活保障

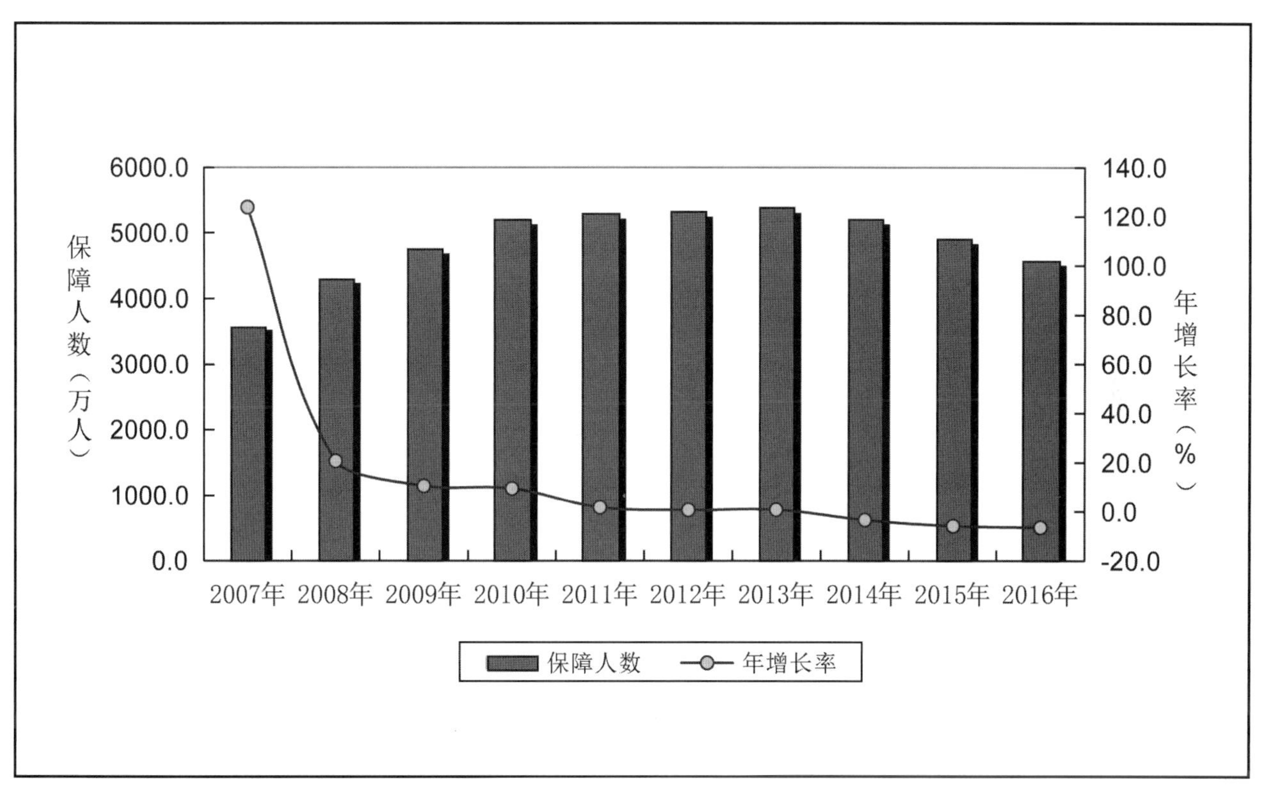

单位：万人、%

指　标	2007年	2008年	2009年	2010年	2011年	2012年	2013年	2014年	2015年	2016年
保障人数	3566.3	4305.5	4760.0	5214.0	5305.7	5344.5	5388.0	5207.2	4903.6	4586.5
年增长率	123.9	20.7	10.6	9.5	1.8	0.7	0.8	-3.4	-5.8	-6.5

图2-11　农村低保平均标准

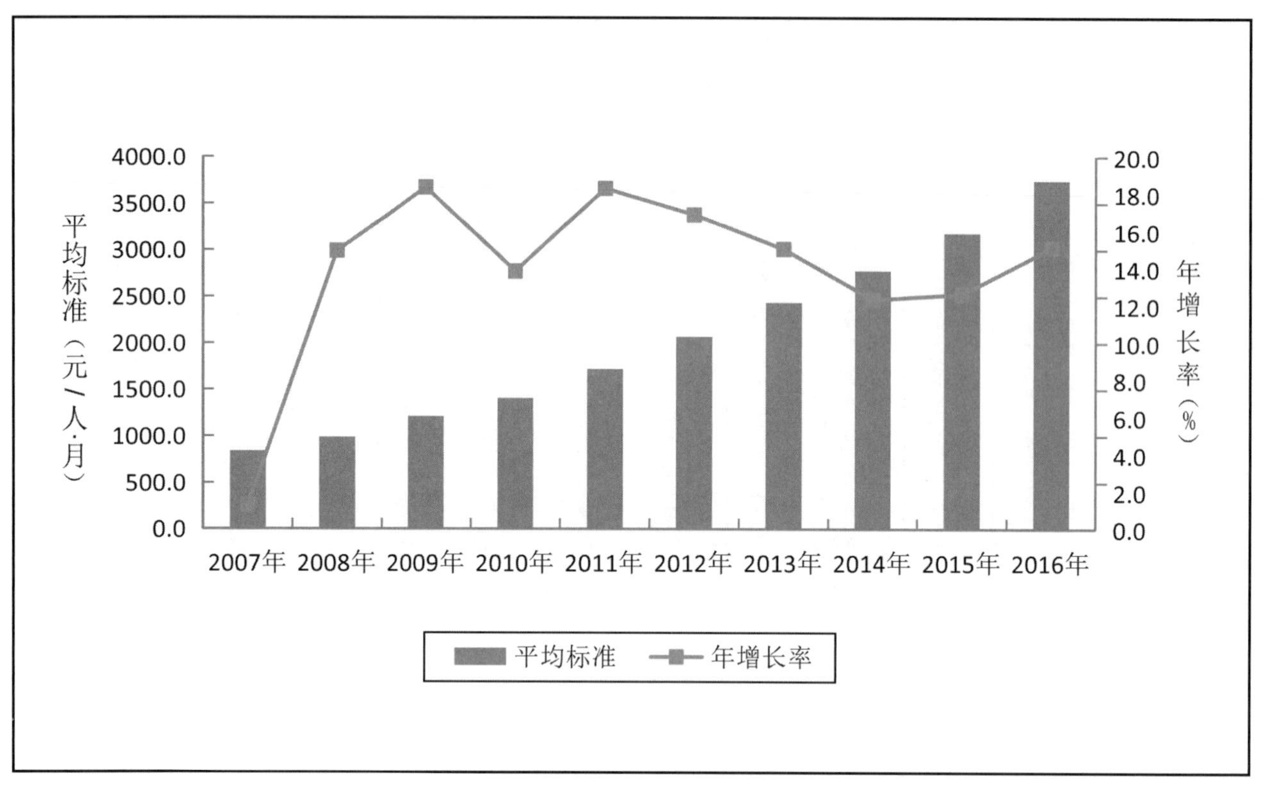

单位：元/人·年

指　标	2007年	2008年	2009年	2010年	2011年	2012年	2013年	2014年	2015年	2016年
平均标准	840.0	987.6	1209.6	1404.0	1718.4	2067.8	2433.9	2776.6	3178.2	3744.0
年增长率	1.3	14.9	18.4	13.8	18.3	16.9	15.0	12.3	12.6	15.1

图2-12　分省农村低保平均标准

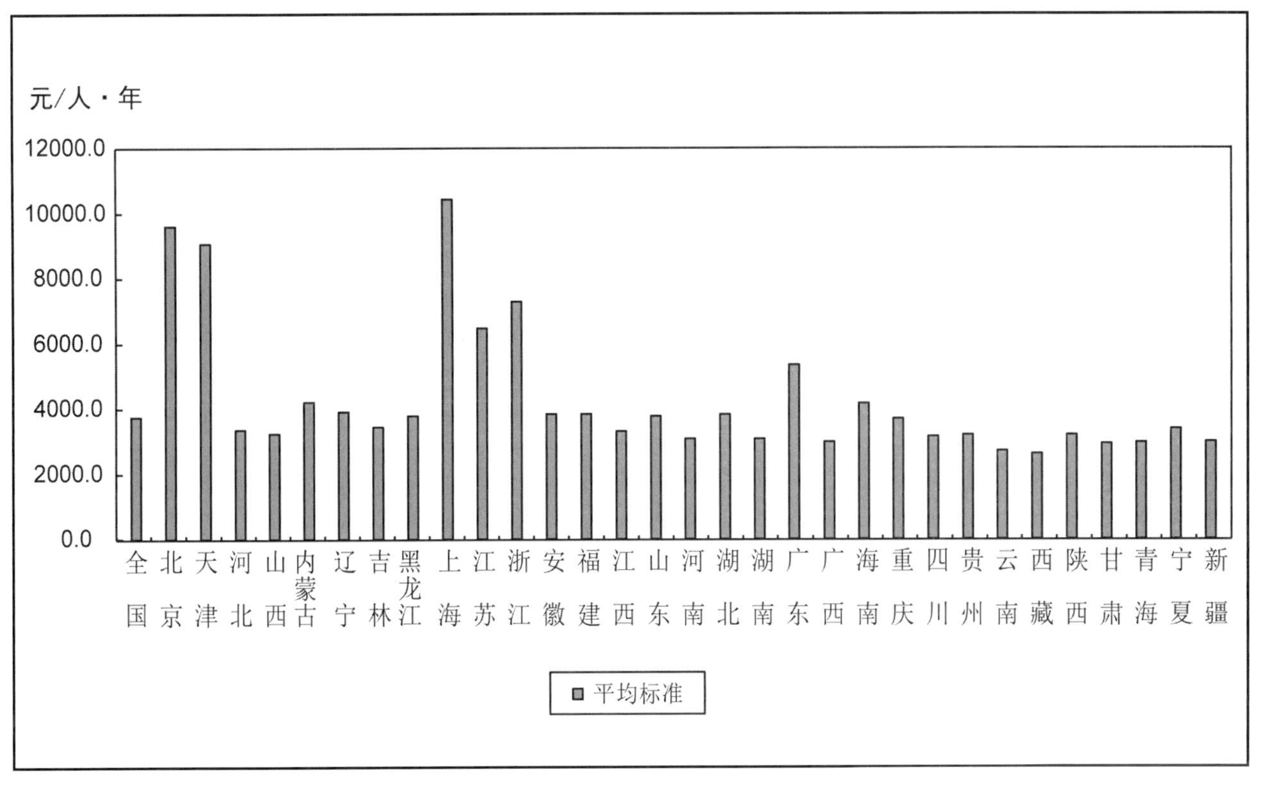

单位：元/人·年

地　区	平均标准	地　区	平均标准	地　区	平均标准	地　区	平均标准
全　国	**3744.0**	黑龙江	3787.1	河　南	3084.4	贵　州	3201.8
北　京	9600.0	上　海	10440.0	湖　北	3828.8	云　南	2710.7
天　津	9060.0	江　苏	6480.9	湖　南	3082.0	西　藏	2621.5
河　北	3359.0	浙　江	7292.4	广　东	5342.7	陕　西	3203.3
山　西	3246.6	安　徽	3840.4	广　西	2985.3	甘　肃	2932.9
内蒙古	4212.0	福　建	3841.4	海　南	4163.5	青　海	2970.0
辽　宁	3914.9	江　西	3314.9	重　庆	3694.9	宁　夏	3388.9
吉　林	3444.9	山　东	3777.8	四　川	3154.6	新　疆	2994.2

图2-13　农村特困人员救助供养

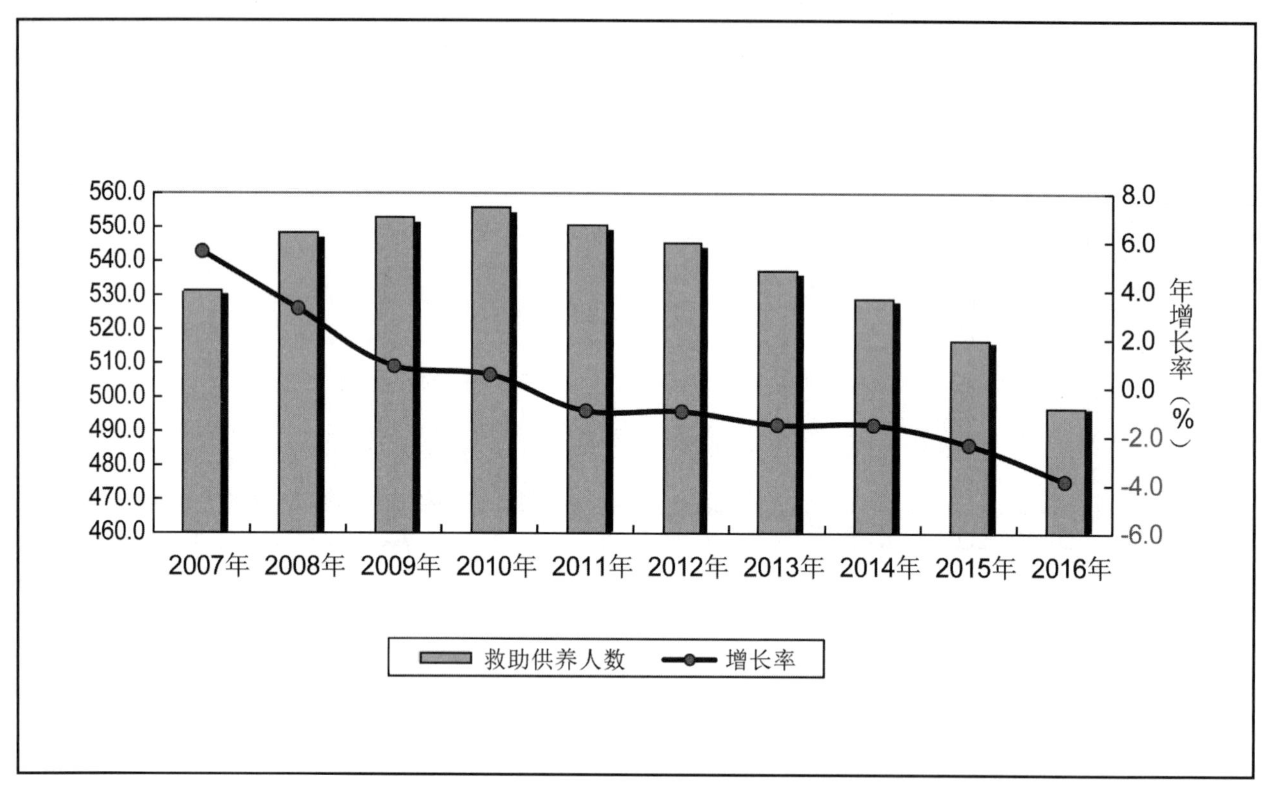

单位：万人、%

指　标	2007年	2008年	2009年	2010年	2011年	2012年	2013年	2014年	2015年	2016年
救助供养人数	531.3	548.6	553.4	556.3	551.0	545.6	537.3	529.1	516.7	496.9
增长率	5.6	3.3	0.9	0.5	-1.0	-1.0	-1.5	-1.5	-2.3	-3.9

图2-14　社会捐赠

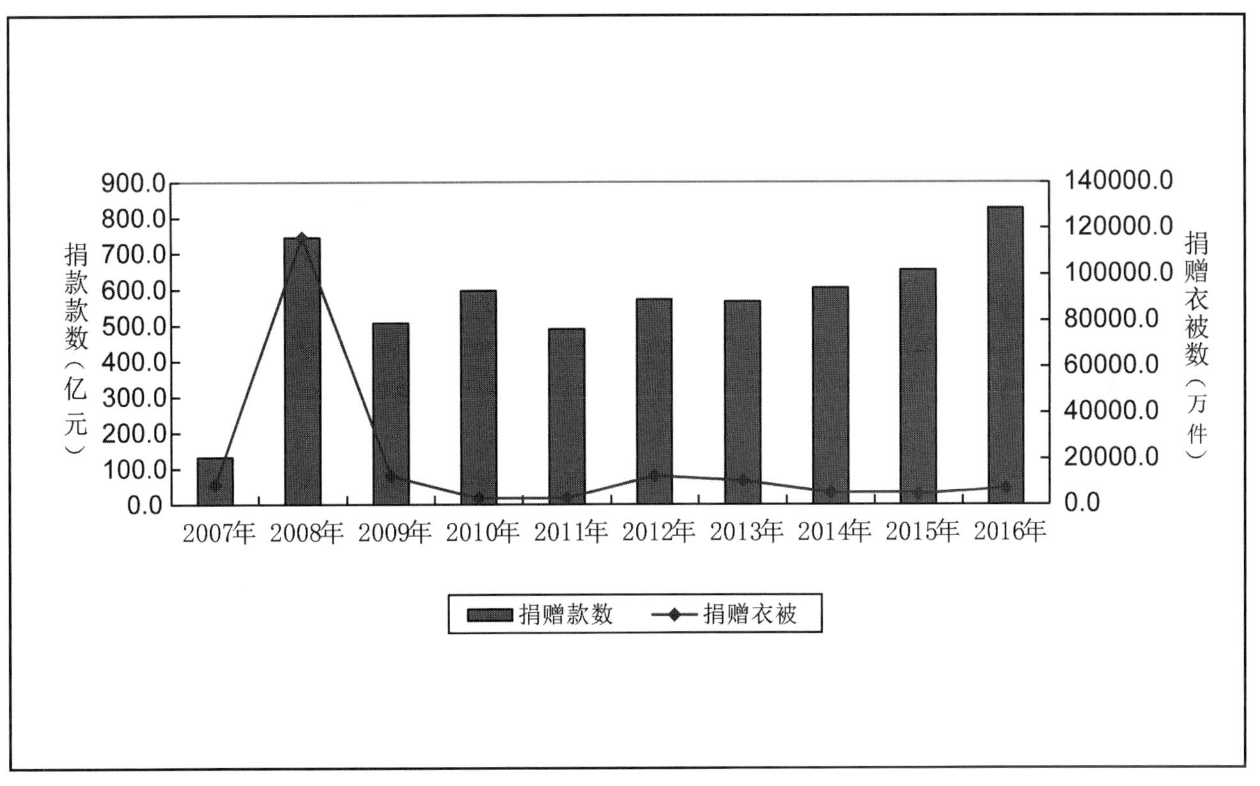

单位：亿元、万件

指　标	2007年	2008年	2009年	2010年	2011年	2012年	2013年	2014年	2015年	2016年
捐赠款数	132.8	744.5	507.2	596.8	490.1	572.5	566.4	604.4	654.5	827.0
捐赠衣被	8756.8	115816.3	12476.6	2750.2	2918.5	12538.2	10405.0	5244.5	4537.0	7126.3

注：捐赠款为民政部门和社会组织接收的合计数。

图2-15　福利彩票

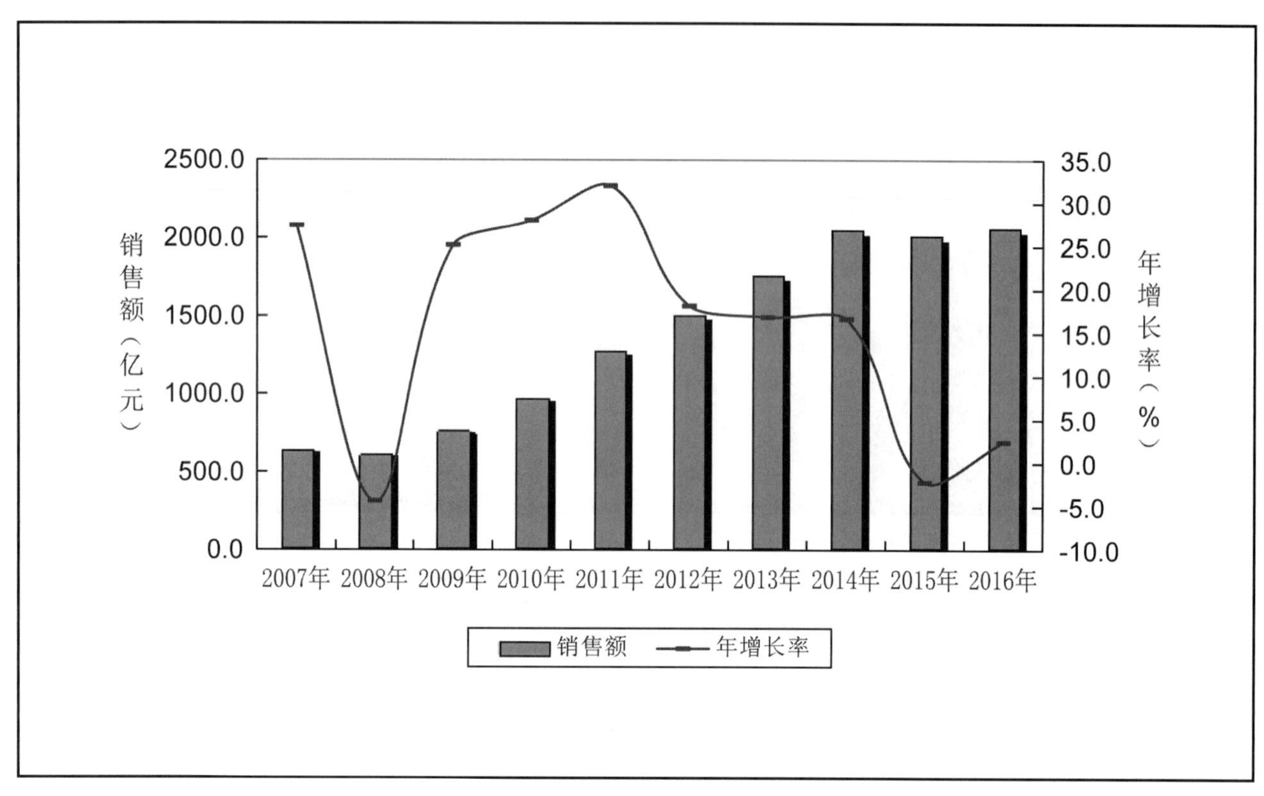

单位：亿元、%

指　标	2007年	2008年	2009年	2010年	2011年	2012年	2013年	2014年	2015年	2016年
销售额	631.6	604.0	756.0	968.0	1278.0	1510.3	1765.3	2059.7	2015.1	2064.9
年增长率	27.4	−4.4	25.2	28.0	32.0	18.2	16.9	16.7	−2.2	2.5

图2-16 国家抚恤、补助优抚对象

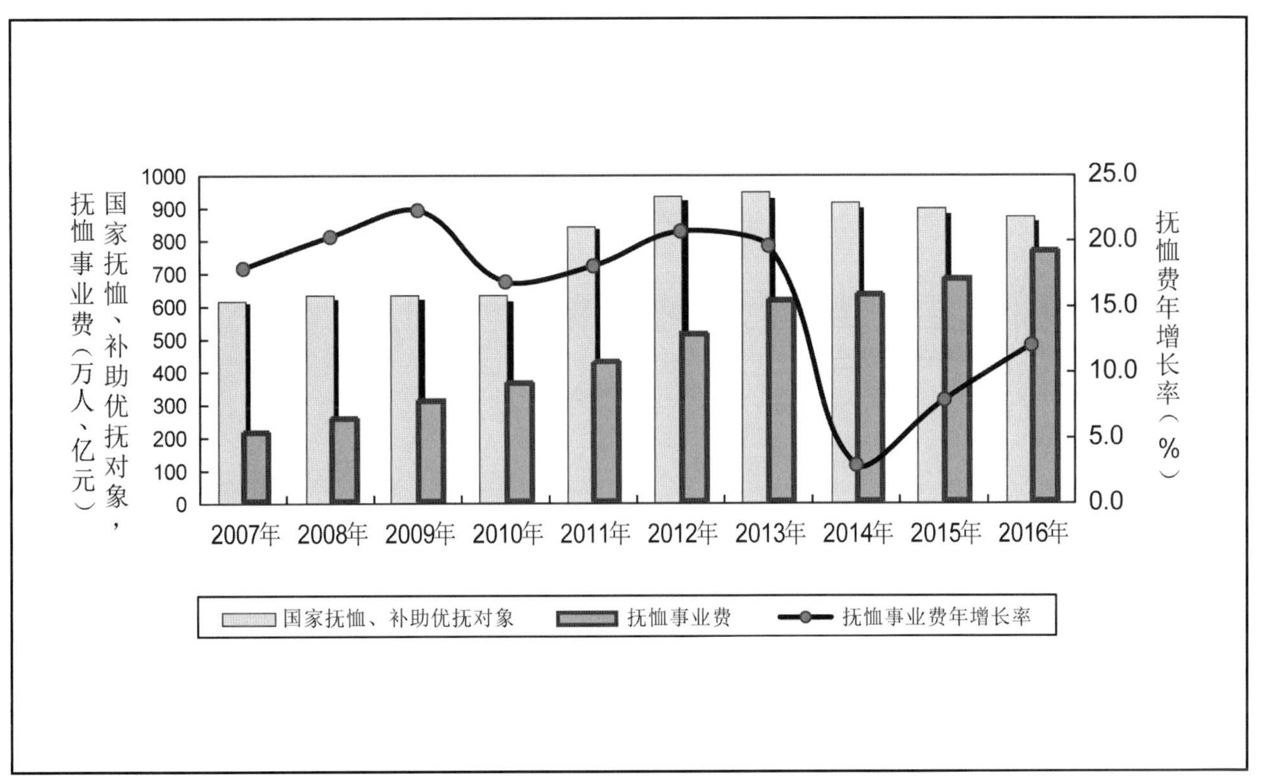

单位：万人、亿元、%

指　标	2007年	2008年	2009年	2010年	2011年	2012年	2013年	2014年	2015年	2016年
国家抚恤、补助优抚对象	622.4	633.2	630.7	625	852.5	944.4	950.5	917.3	897.0	874.8
抚恤事业费	210.8	253.6	310.3	362.7	428.3	517	618.4	636.6	686.8	769.8
抚恤事业费年增长率	17.9	20.3	22.4	16.9	18.1	20.7	19.6	2.9	7.9	12.1

图2-17　优抚对象分类

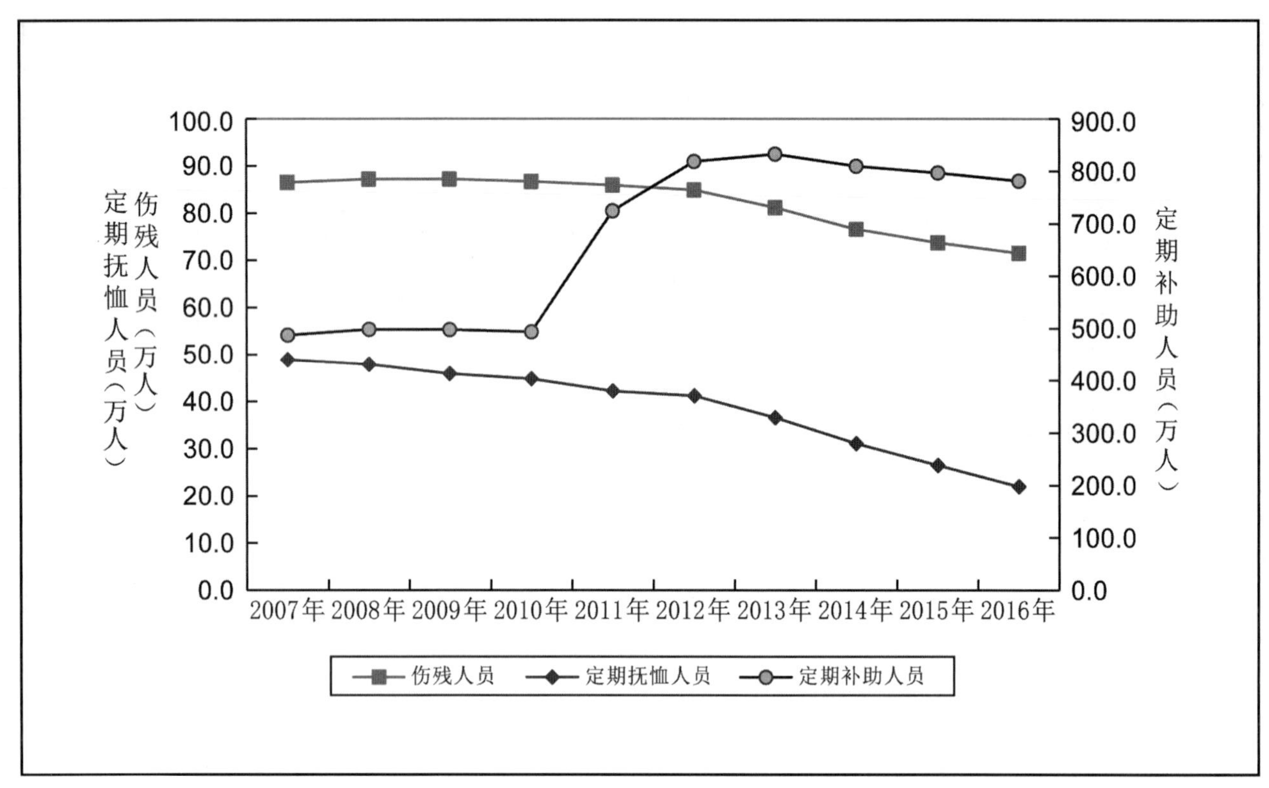

单位：万人

指　标	2007年	2008年	2009年	2010年	2011年	2012年	2013年	2014年	2015年	2016年
伤残人员	86.5	87.2	87.2	86.7	85.9	84.9	81.2	76.6	73.7	71.5
定期抚恤人员	48.9	47.9	45.9	44.8	42.2	41.2	36.6	31.1	26.5	22.0
定期补助人员	487.1	498.2	497.7	493.5	724.4	818.4	832.6	809.6	796.8	781.3

图2-18　接收军休干部、军休职工

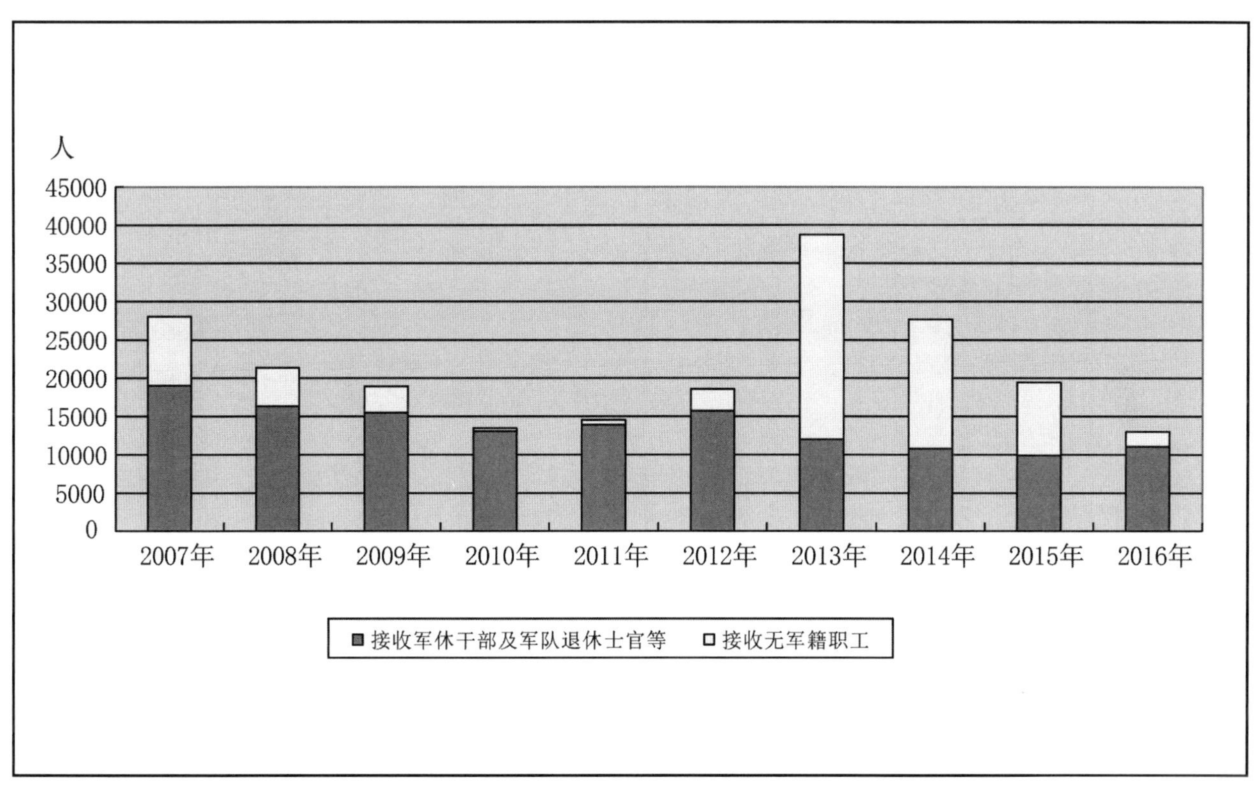

单位：人

指　标	2007年	2008年	2009年	2010年	2011年	2012年	2013年	2014年	2015年	2016年
接收军休干部及军队退休士官等	18997	16331	15492	13070	13901	15723	11997	10791	9921	9094
接收无军籍职工	9061	5047	3412	381	629	2847	26709	16908	9508	1959

图2-19 烈士纪念建筑物管理机构和藏品量

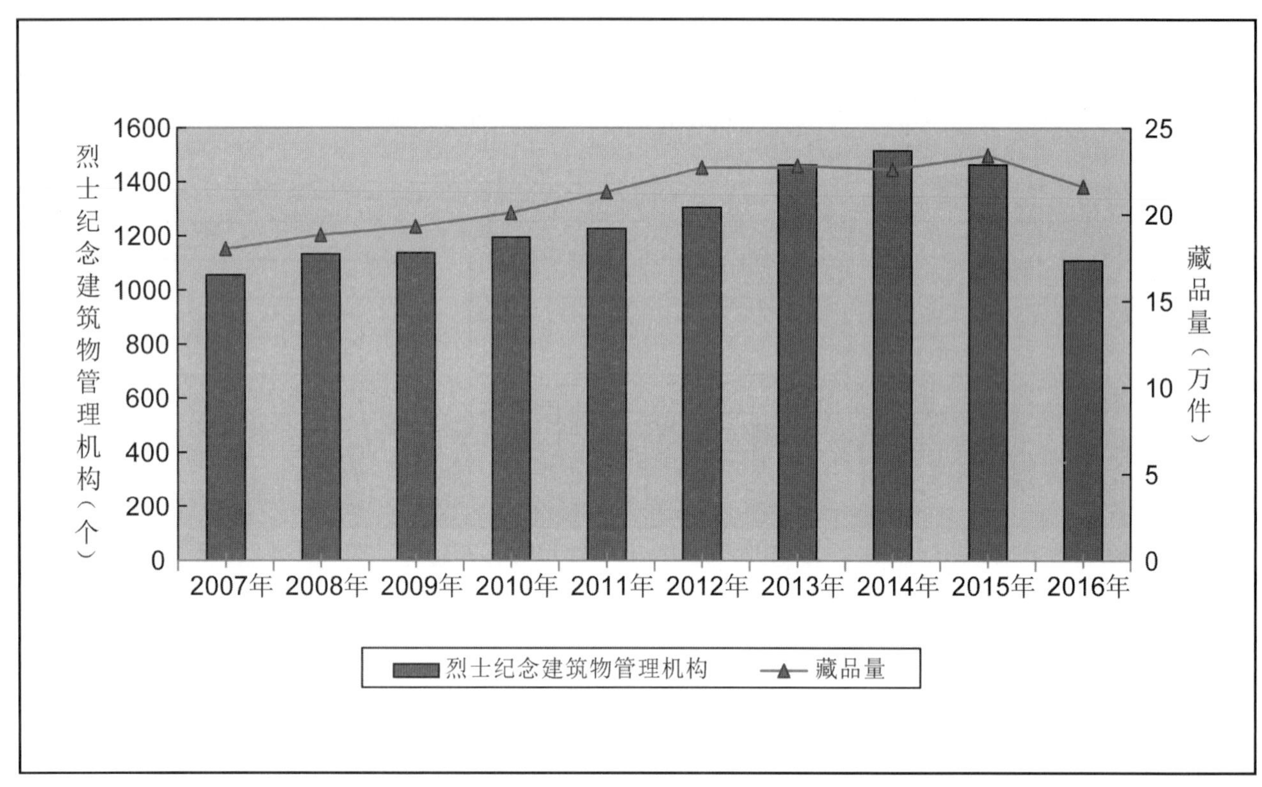

单位：个、万件

指　标	2007年	2008年	2009年	2010年	2011年	2012年	2013年	2014年	2015年	2016年
烈士纪念建筑物管理机构	1056	1133	1137	1195	1227	1306	1463	1516	1464	1109
藏品量	18	18.8	19.3	20.1	21.3	22.7	22.8	22.6	23.4	21.6

图2-20 烈士褒扬和零散烈士纪念设施

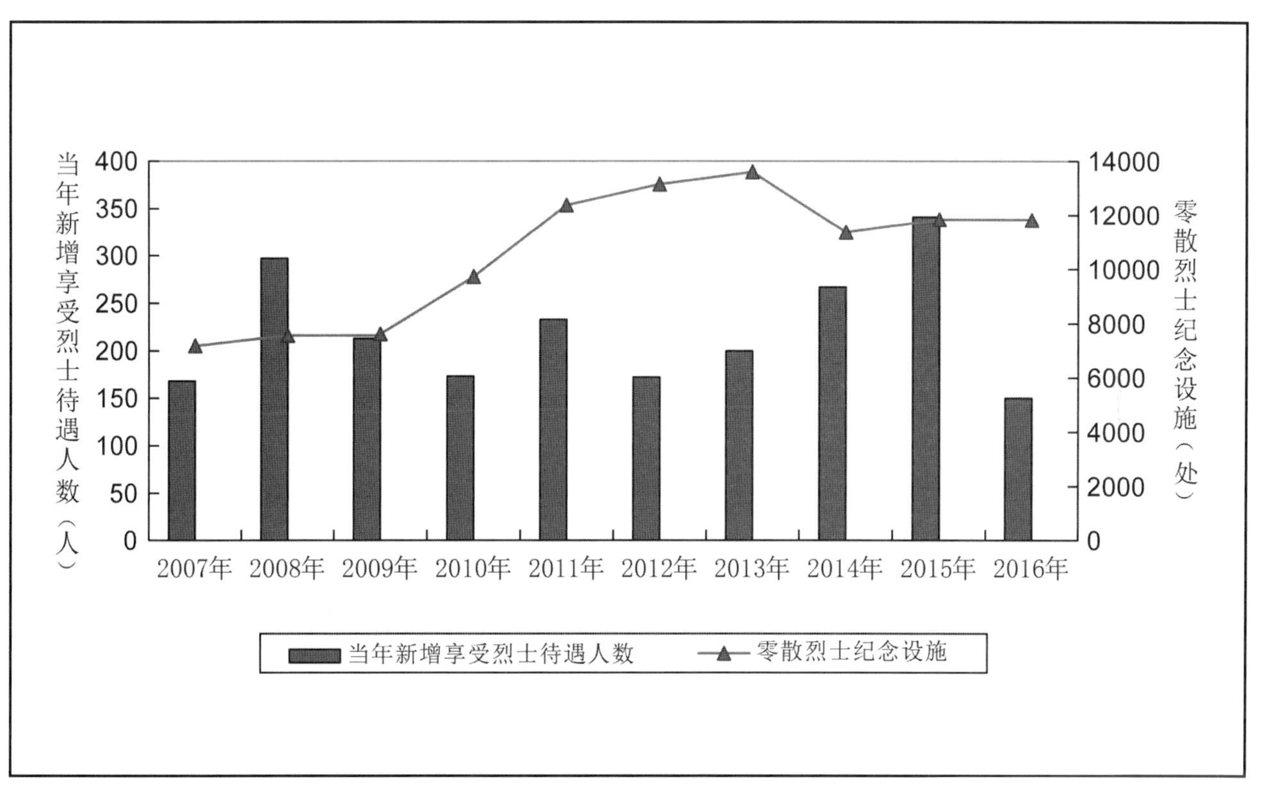

单位：人、处

指　标	2007年	2008年	2009年	2010年	2011年	2012年	2013年	2014年	2015年	2016年
当年新增享受烈士待遇人数	168	297	213	173	233	172	200	267	341	150
零散烈士纪念设施	7186	7569	7622	9729	12378	13151	13601	11365	11838	11815

图2-21　因灾死亡失踪人口

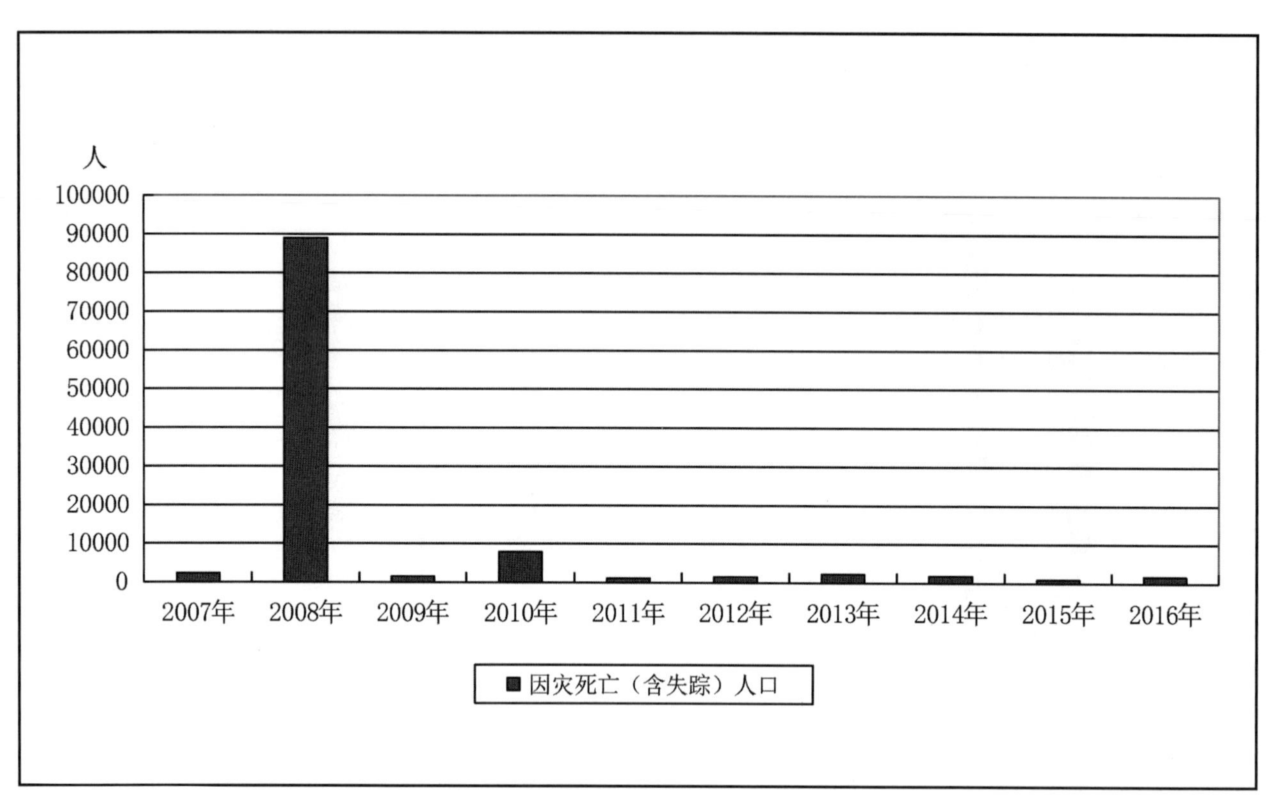

单位：人

指　标	2007年	2008年	2009年	2010年	2011年	2012年	2013年	2014年	2015年	2016年
因灾死亡(含失踪)人口	2325	88928	1528	7844	1126	1530	2284	1818	967	1706

图2-22　受灾人口

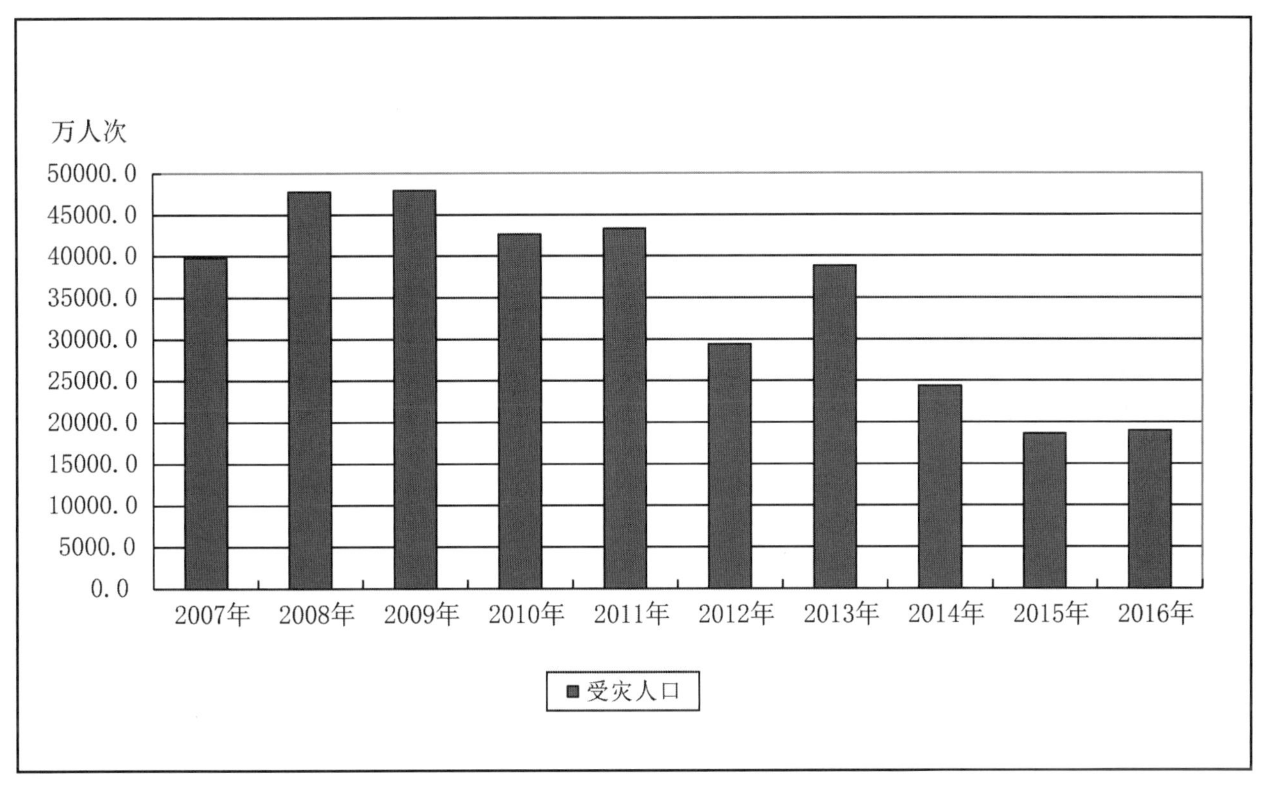

单位：万人次

指　标	2007年	2008年	2009年	2010年	2011年	2012年	2013年	2014年	2015年	2016年
受灾人口	39777.9	47795.0	47933.5	42610.2	43290.0	29421.7	38818.7	24353.7	18620.3	18911.7

图2-23 社区服务机构和设施

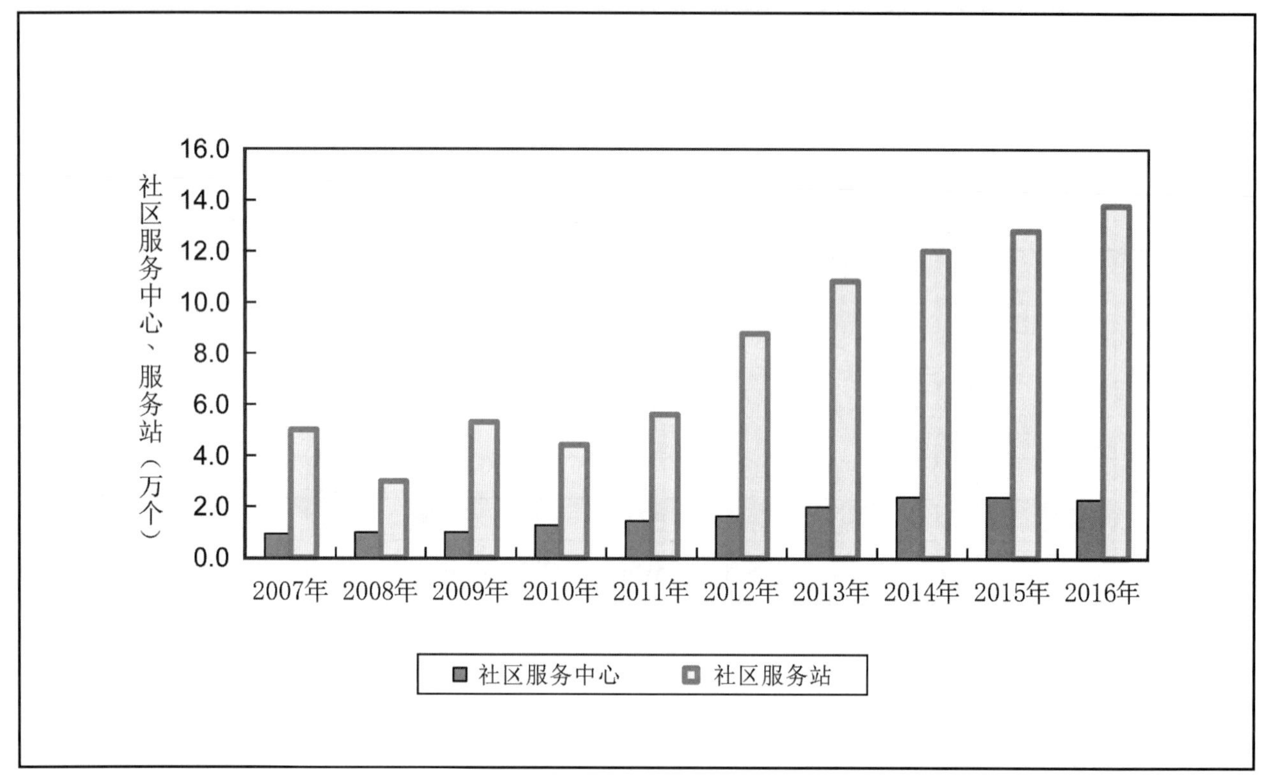

单位：万个

指　标	2007年	2008年	2009年	2010年	2011年	2012年	2013年	2014年	2015年	2016年
社区服务机构和设施	12.9	14.6	14.6	15.3	16.0	20.0	25.2	31.1	36.1	38.6
#社区服务中心	0.9	1.0	1.0	1.3	1.4	1.6	2.0	2.4	2.4	2.3
社区服务站	5.0	3.0	5.3	4.4	5.6	8.8	10.8	12.0	12.8	13.8

注：2014年以后社区服务中心中含社区服务指导中心。

图2-24　社区服务中心（站）覆盖率

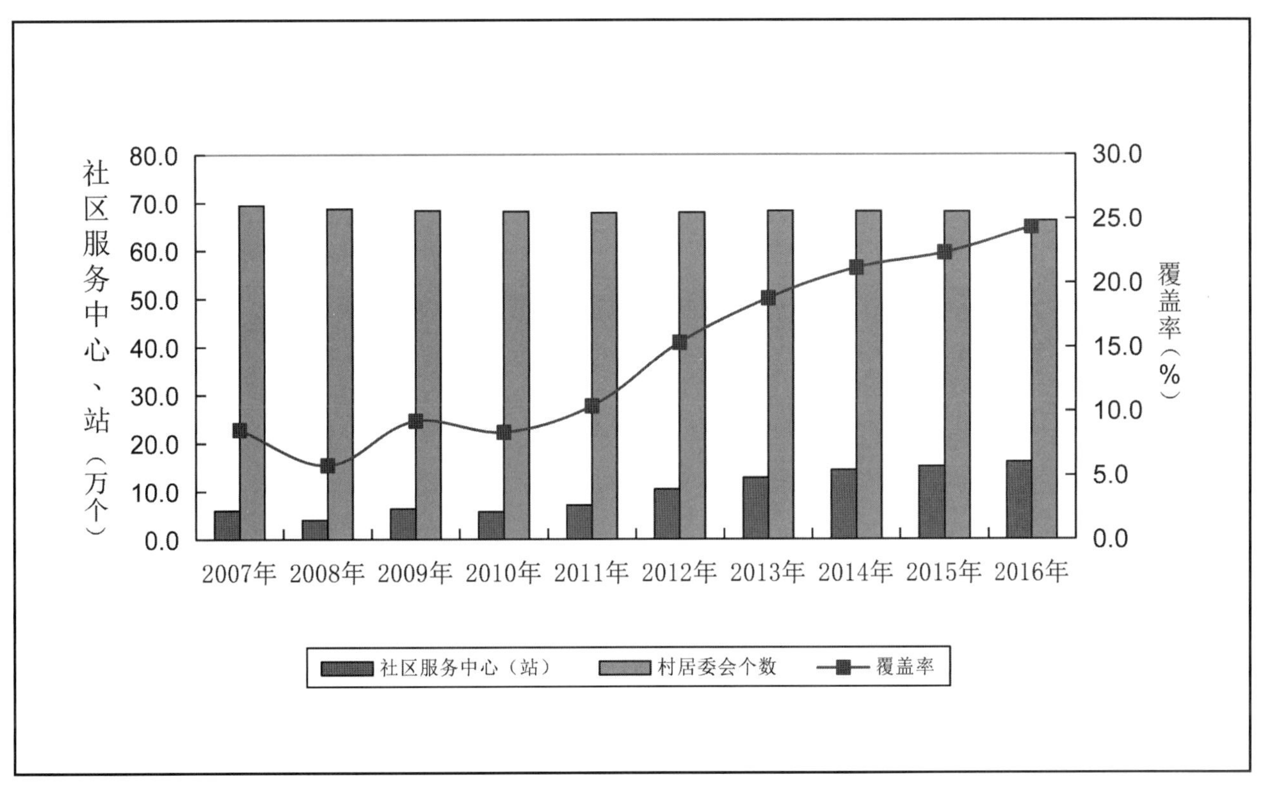

单位：万个、%

指　标	2007年	2008年	2009年	2010年	2011年	2012年	2013年	2014年	2015年	2016年
社区服务中心（站）	5.9	4.0	6.3	5.7	7.1	10.4	12.8	14.4	15.2	16.1
村居委会个数	69.5	68.8	68.4	68.2	67.9	68.0	68.3	68.2	68.1	66.2
覆盖率	8.6	5.8	9.2	8.4	10.4	15.3	18.8	21.1	22.3	24.3

图3-1　社会组织

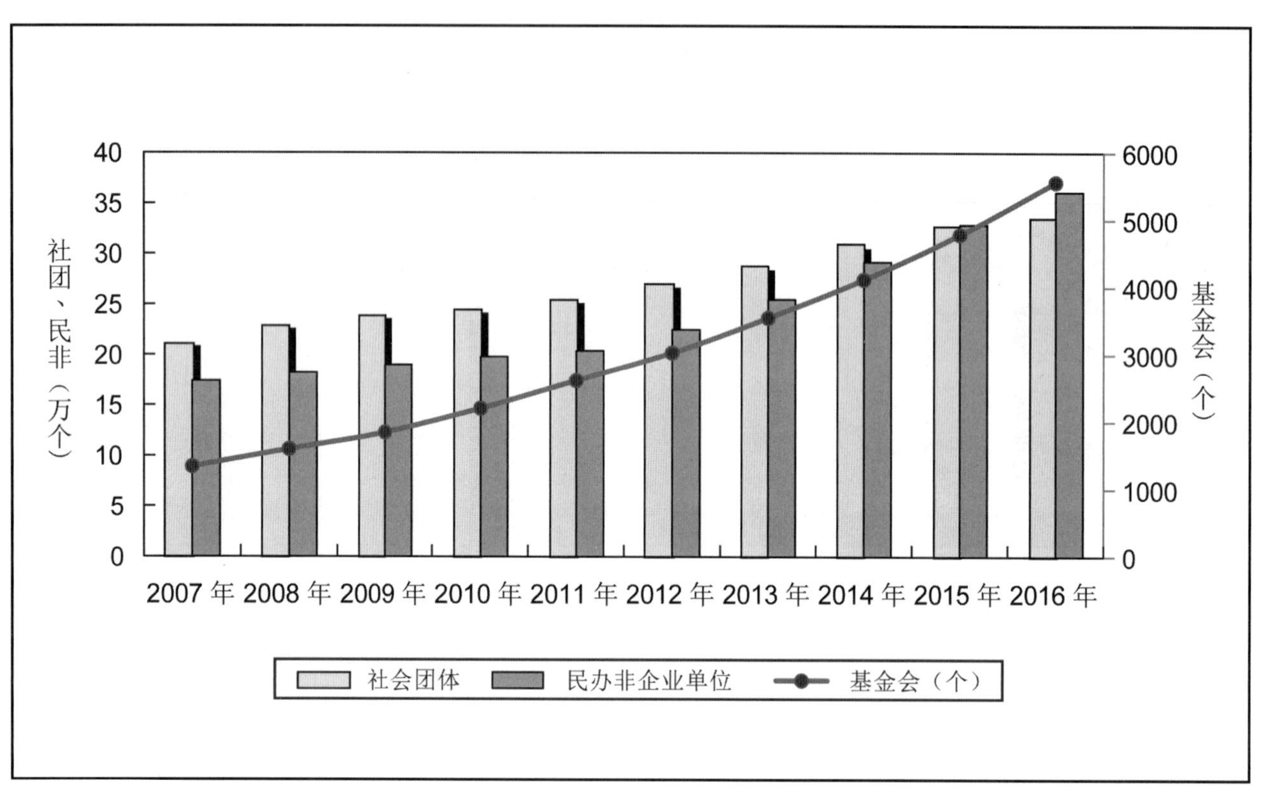

单位：万个

指　标	2007年	2008年	2009年	2010年	2011年	2012年	2013年	2014年	2015年	2016年
社会组织	38.7	41.4	43.1	44.6	46.2	49.9	54.7	60.6	66.2	70.2
社会团体	21.2	23	23.9	24.5	25.5	27.1	28.9	31	32.9	33.6
基金会(个)	1340	1597	1843	2200	2614	3029	3549	4117	4784	5559
民办非企业单位	17.4	18.2	19	19.8	20.4	22.5	25.5	29.2	32.9	36.1

图3-2 自治组织

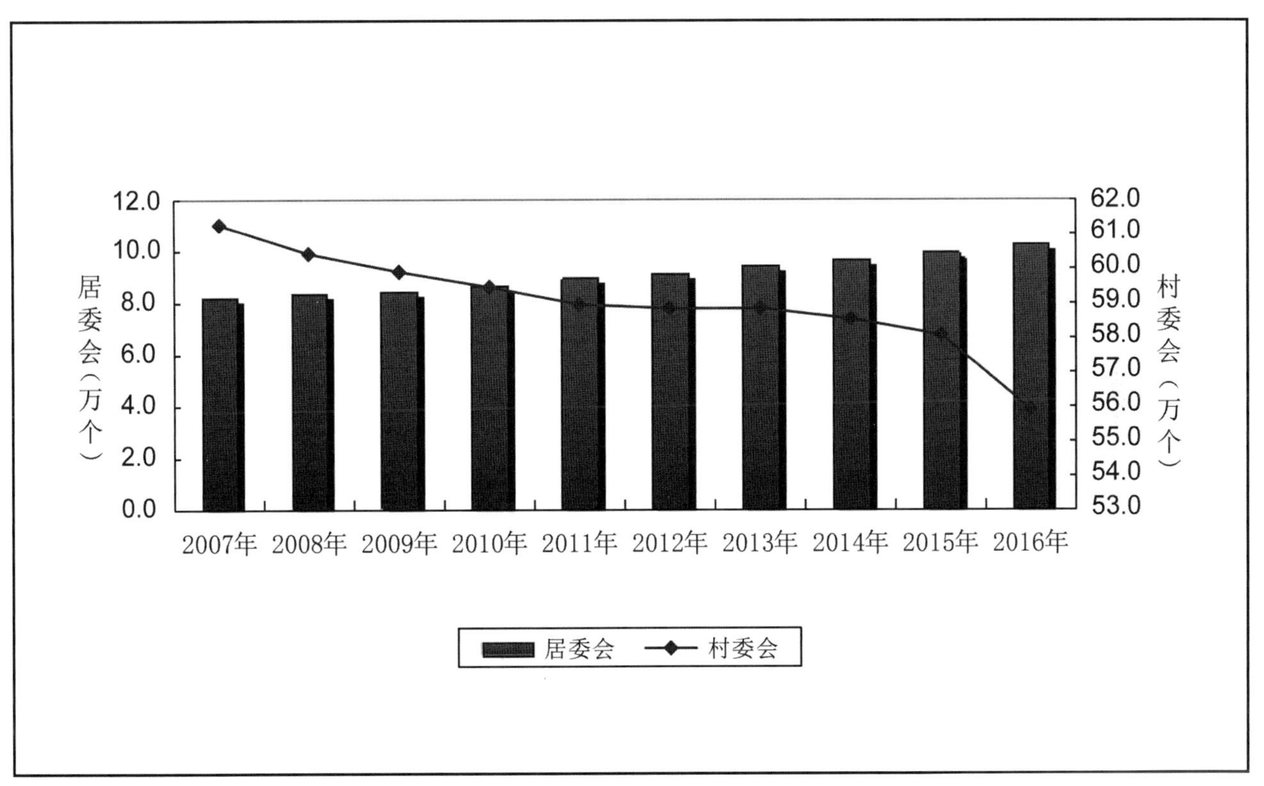

单位：万个

指　标	2007年	2008年	2009年	2010年	2011年	2012年	2013年	2014年	2015年	2016年
自治组织	69.5	68.8	68.4	68.2	67.9	68.0	68.3	68.2	68.1	66.2
居委会	8.2	8.3	8.5	8.7	8.9	9.1	9.5	9.7	10.0	10.3
村委会	61.3	60.4	59.9	59.5	59.0	58.8	58.9	58.5	58.1	55.9

图3-3 结婚登记

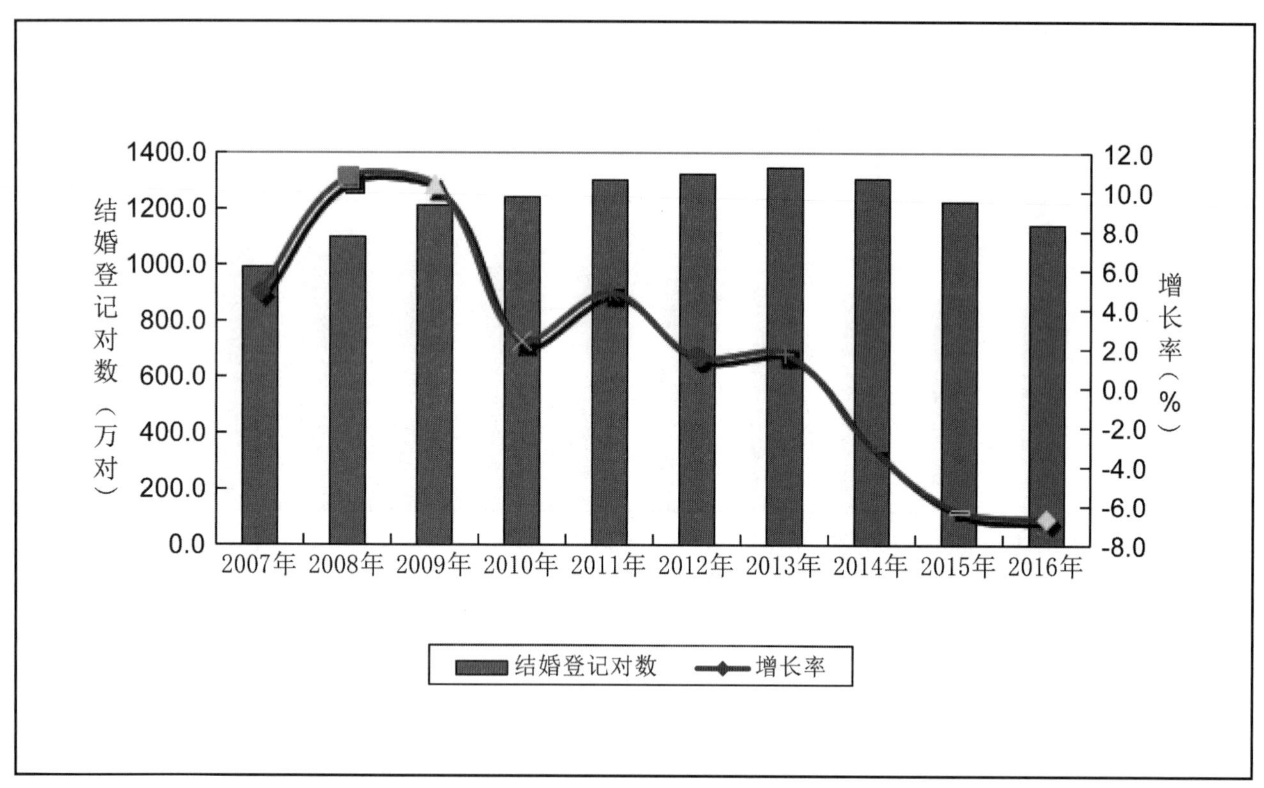

单位：万对、%

指　标	2007年	2008年	2009年	2010年	2011年	2012年	2013年	2014年	2015年	2016年
结婚登记对数	991.4	1098.3	1212.2	1241.0	1302.4	1323.6	1346.9	1306.7	1224.7	1142.8
年增长率	4.9	10.8	10.4	2.4	4.9	1.6	1.8	-3.0	-6.3	-6.7

图3-4　分年龄组结婚登记

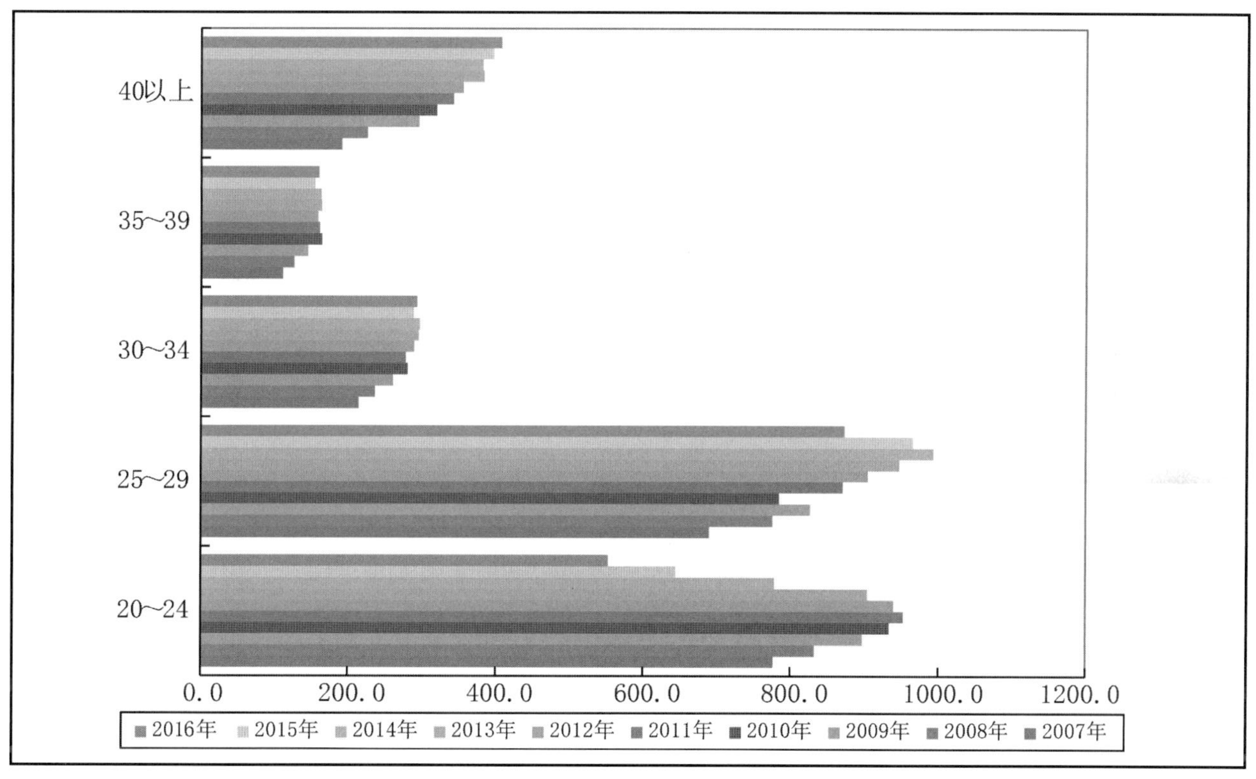

单位：万人

年　份	20～24岁	25～29岁	30～34岁	35～39岁	40岁及以上
2007	776.7	689.5	214.0	110.9	191.6
2008	832.3	775.7	236.1	126.5	226.2
2009	896.7	826.4	260.3	145.4	295.5
2010	933.4	784.6	279.9	164.5	319.6
2011	953.0	870.2	277.6	161.5	342.4
2012	939.6	904.1	289.0	158.9	355.6
2013	903.4	947.5	295.1	164.3	383.5
2014	778.2	993.1	296.5	163.5	382.2
2015	643.9	965.7	288.1	155.3	396.4
2016	552.3	872.2	293.0	160.6	407.3

图3-5 结婚率和离婚率

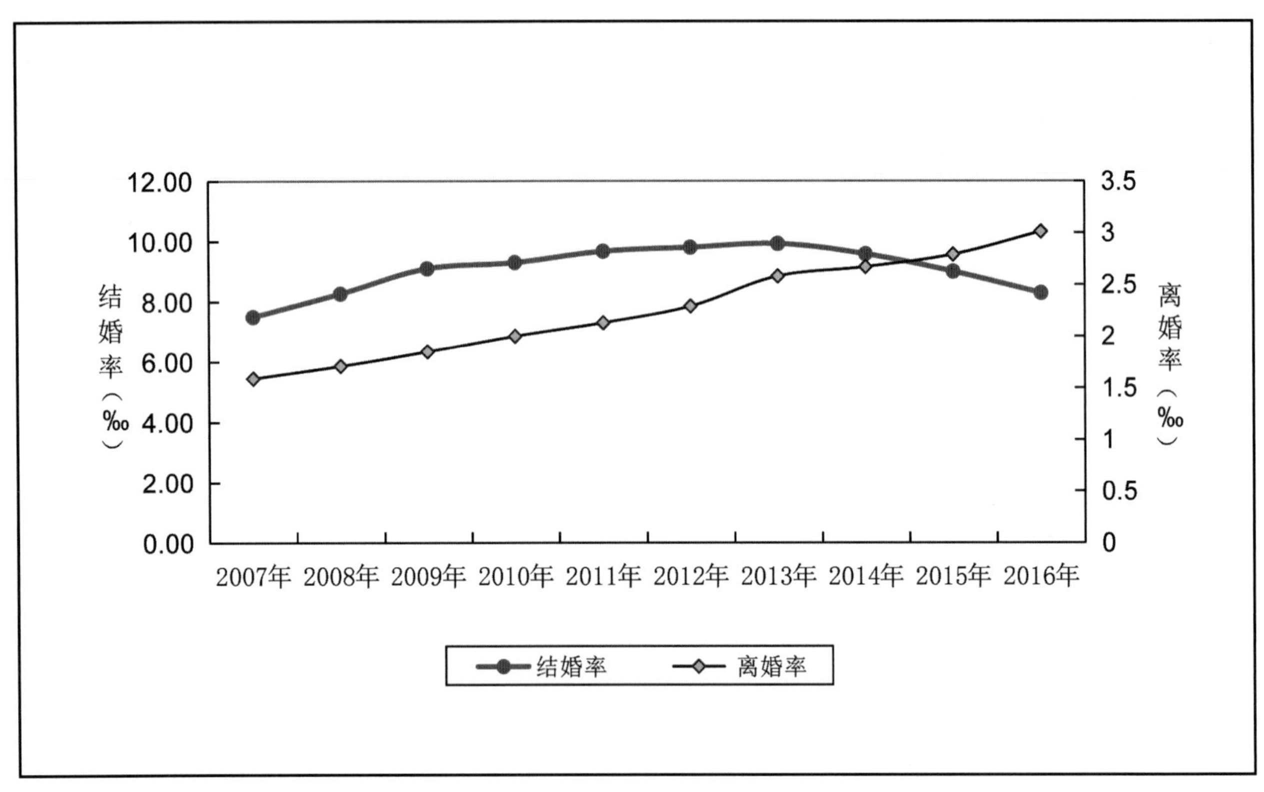

单位：‰

指　标	2007年	2008年	2009年	2010年	2011年	2012年	2013年	2014年	2015年	2016年
结婚率	7.50	8.27	9.10	9.30	9.67	9.80	9.92	9.58	9.00	8.29
离婚率	1.59	1.71	1.85	2	2.13	2.29	2.58	2.67	2.79	3.01

注：结（离）婚率计算方法：结（离）婚对数除以当期人口平均数。

图3-6 民政部门和法院办理离婚

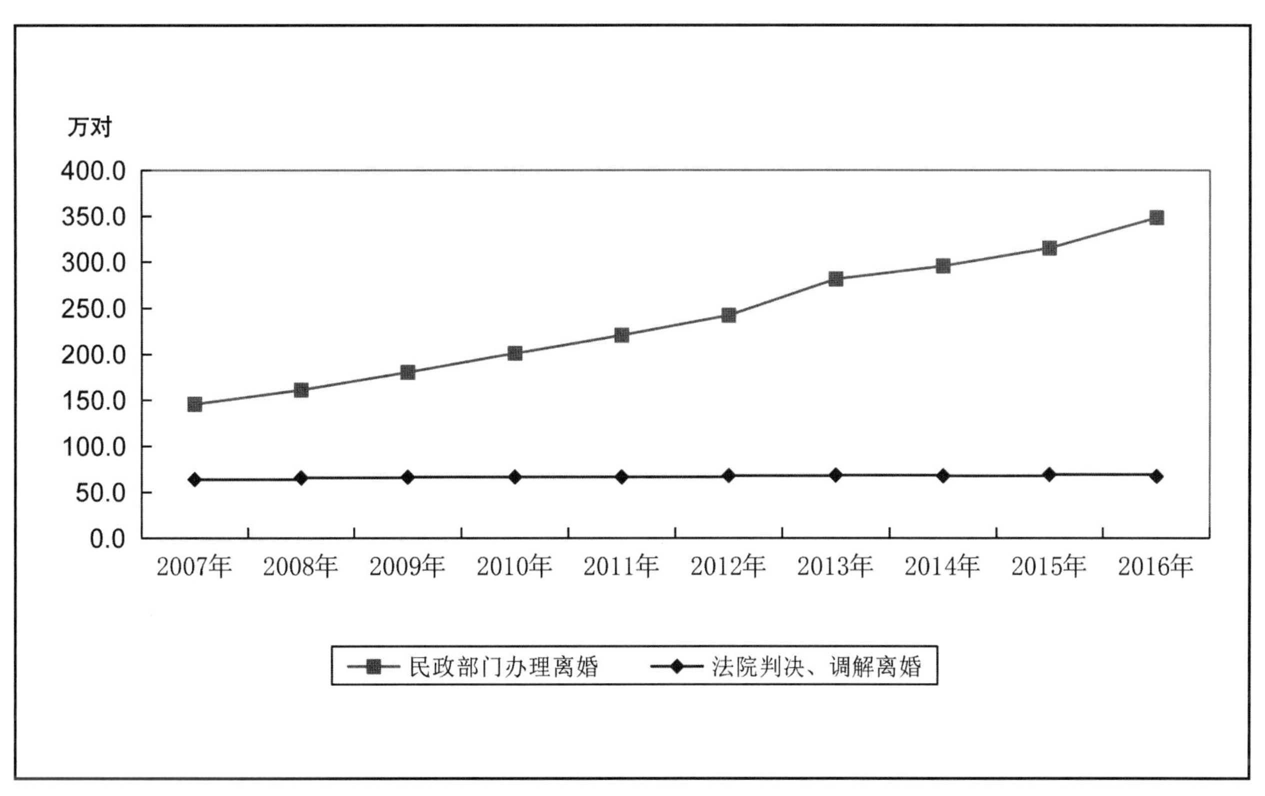

单位：万对

指 标	2007年	2008年	2009年	2010年	2011年	2012年	2013年	2014年	2015年	2016年
离婚对数	209.8	226.9	246.8	267.8	287.4	310.4	350.0	363.6	384.1	415.2
民政部门办理离婚	145.7	161.0	180.2	201.0	220.7	242.3	281.5	295.7	314.9	348.0
法院判决、调解离婚	64.1	65.9	66.6	66.8	66.7	68.1	68.5	67.9	69.3	67.2

图3-7　火化遗体

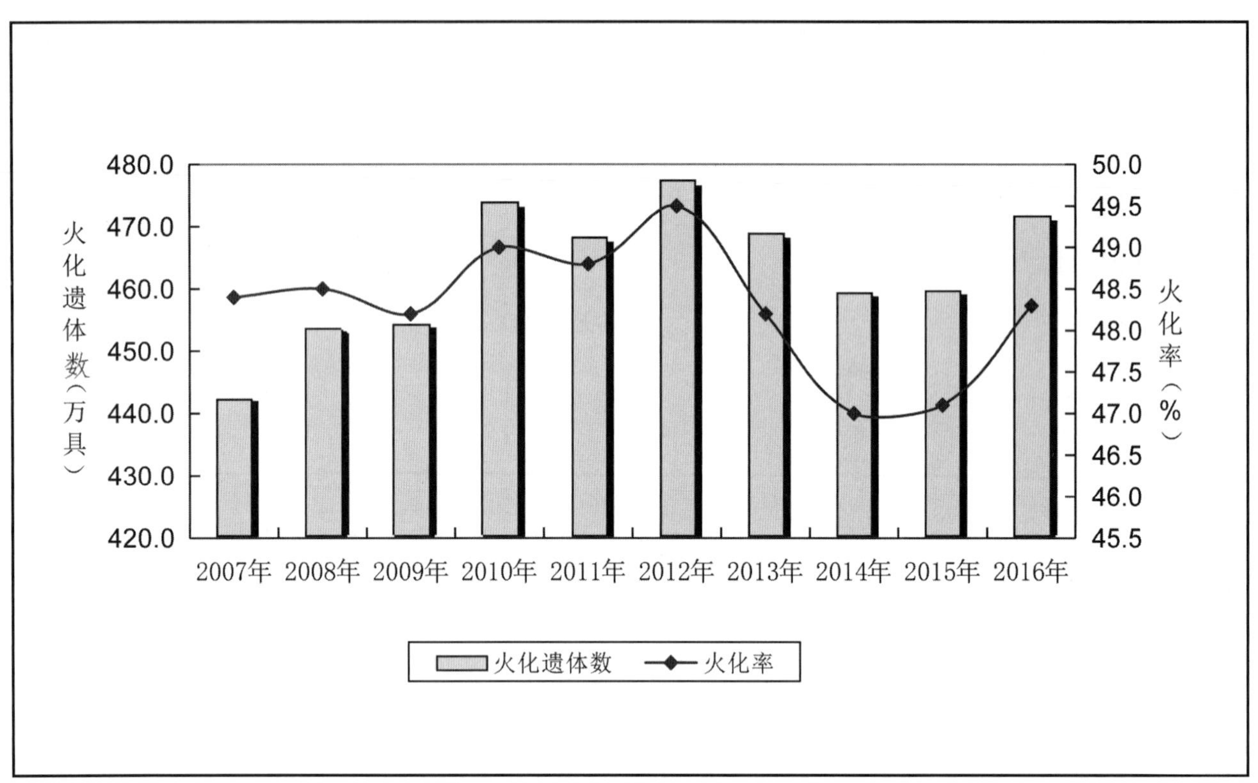

单位：万具、%

指　标	2007年	2008年	2009年	2010年	2011年	2012年	2013年	2014年	2015年	2016年
火化遗体数	442.1	453.4	454.2	474.1	468.1	477.7	468.9	459.3	459.5	471.8
火化率	48.4	48.5	48.2	49.0	48.8	49.5	48.2	47.0	47.1	48.3

03

社会服务综合统计资料

2017

A-1-1 “七五”—“十三五”时期社会服务发展速度

单位：%

指　标	“七五”时期平均增长速度	“八五”时期平均增长速度	“九五”时期平均增长速度	“十五”时期平均每年增长速度	“十一五”时期平均增长速度	“十二五”时期平均增长速度	“十三五”时期前一年平均增长速度
一、综合							
行政区划							
镇	5.7	7.7	3.0	-0.8	-0.1	1.1	1.8
乡	-11.6	-7.8	-4.7	-7.2	-1.8	-4.9	-3.9
60岁及以上老年人口					4.3	4.6	4.0
事业费支出	11.9	14.8	17.3	25.6	30.3	12.8	10.4
固定资产原价	20.8	22.5	53.1	9.9	16.3	4.4	-34.1
二、社会工作							
社会服务床位	9.7	4.6	3.0	7.7	13.8	14.6	5.2
# 养老床位				5.0	15.3	16.3	6.1
智障和精神疾病床位				10.0	8.8	6.7	6.3
儿童床位				11.7	11.5	21.2	0.0
家庭收养				-2.0	-7.5	-8.9	-16.2
福利彩票		54.5	14.6	29.4	18.7	15.8	2.5
城市最低生活保障				40.9	0.7	-5.9	-13.0
优抚对象	8.5	1.1	-0.3	0.8	6.3	7.5	-2.5
社区服务中心			8.0	5.6	8.2	13.7	-4.2
三、成员组织和其他社会服务							
社会组织		75.5	-3.2	15.8	6.9	8.2	6.0
社会团体				5.6	7.5	6.1	2.3
基金会					17.7	16.8	16.3
民办非企业单位				45.5	6.1	10.7	9.7
自治组织							
村民委员会	1.1	-6.9	-4.7	-3.0	-1.1	-0.5	-3.8
社区居委会	4.1	2.5	-0.6	-5.9	1.7	2.8	3.3
婚姻							
办理结婚登记	2.7	-0.4	-0.2	-0.6	8.6	-0.3	-6.7
办理离婚登记	11.7	5.7	2.8	8.0	8.5	7.5	8.3
殡葬							
火化遗体数	5.3	5.5	7.3	3.8	1	-0.6	2.7

A-1-2 社会服务发展主要指标预期值

指　标	单　位	2017年预期值	2020年预期值	2030年预期值	2050年预期值
一、综合					
行政区划					
镇	万个	2.1	2.2	2.4	2.9
乡	万个	1.0	0.9	0.6	0.3
人口	百万人	1387.7	1403.9	1459.2	1576.5
60岁及以上老年人口	万人	23905.8	26543.9	37627.7	75612.0
事业费支出	亿元	5881.1	7431.1	16206.2	77079.4
固定资产原价	亿元	5168.4	4547.8	2968.9	1265.3
二、社会工作					
社会服务床位	万张	851.3	1171.6	3397.7	28574.8
# 养老床位	万张	817.0	1144.2	3516.9	33224.9
智障和精神疾病床位	万张	8.8	10.1	15.8	39.1
儿童床位	万张	10.3	11.2	14.8	25.8
家庭收养	万件	1.8	1.4	0.7	0.2
福利彩票	亿元	2198.2	2652.0	4957.2	17321.4
城市最低生活保障	万人	1374.5	1100.7	524.9	119.4
优抚对象	万人	861.5	822.8	706.0	519.8
社区服务中心	万个	2.5	3.1	6.5	28.1
三、成员组织和其他社会服务					
社会组织	万个	75.2	92.2	182.6	715.1
社会团体	万个	35.1	39.9	61.3	145.0
基金会	万个	0.6	0.9	3.0	34.5
民办非企业单位	万个	39.7	52.7	135.6	898.9
自治组织					
村民委员会	万个	55.3	53.7	48.5	39.6
社区居委会	万个	10.6	11.4	14.6	23.9
婚姻					
办理结婚登记	万对	1109.7	1016.1	757.5	420.9
办理离婚登记	万对	440.8	525.4	942.7	3035.5
殡葬					
火化遗体数	万具	470.6	467.1	455.7	433.6

注：发展速度为“十三五”时期平均增长速度。

A-1-3 2012-2016年社会服务发展主要指标数据

指　标	单　位	2012年	2013年	2014年	2015年	2016年
一、综合						
乡镇级行政区划						
镇	个	19881	20117	20401	20515	20883
乡	个	13281	12812	12282	11315	10872
# 民族乡	个	1064	1035	1020	991	989
街道办事处	个	7282	7566	7696	7957	8105
区公所	个	2	2	2	2	2
社会服务基本情况						
机构和设施	万个	136.7	156.2	166.8	176.5	174.5
职工人数	万人	1144.7	1197.6	1251.0	1308.9	1239.3
固定资产原价	亿元	6675.4	6810.2	7213.0	8183.1	5393.6
基本建设投资	亿元	234.7	292.8	282.2	239.9	245.8
# 预算内投资	亿元	104.2	120.1	104.3	92.8	84.4
# 公益金投资	亿元	51.1	64.7	57.5	61.7	68.4
预算内基本建设投资占事业费比重	%	2.8	2.8	2.4	1.9	1.5
公益金基本建设投资占公益金支出的比重	%	32.1	33.1	24.9	21.4	25.5
事业费	亿元	3683.7	4276.5	4404.1	4926.4	5440.2
# 抚恤	亿元	517.0	618.4	636.6	686.8	769.8
退役安置	亿元	372.1	435.3	456.8	582.7	625.6
社会福利	亿元	319.5	397.6	480.9	562.8	753.4
社会救助	亿元	1866.1	2172.4	2197.5	2347.4	2492.8
自然灾害生活救助	亿元	163.4	178.7	124.4	148.5	156.1
民政管理事务	亿元	248.4	296.7	308.3	399.6	441.7
行政事业单位离退休	亿元	39.0	43.6	44.2	50.1	48.4
其他	亿元	158.3	133.9	155.3	148.5	152.2
# 公益金支出	亿元	159.0	195.5	231.3	288.9	268.3
中央转移支付的事业费占全国总事业费比重	%	48.7	50.3	47.8	46.1	45.7
全国总事业费占财政支出的比重	%	3.0	3.1	2.9	3.3	3.4
二、社会工作						
提供住宿的社会服务						
机构数	万个	4.8	4.6	3.7	3.1	3.2
机构和设施各类床位数	万张	449.4	526.7	613.5	732.9	771.2
# 养老机构和设施床位数	万张	416.5	493.7	577.8	672.7	730.2
机构和设施收养人数	万人	309.5	322.5	336.8	319.9	348.9
每千人口社会服务床位数	张	3.3	3.9	4.5	5.3	5.5
每千老年人口养老床位数	张	21.5	24.4	27.2	30.3	31.6

A−1−3续表1

指　标	单　位	2012年	2013年	2014年	2015年	2016年
不提供住宿的社会服务						
机构和设施数	万个	13.3	27.7	33.4	38.2	39.1
老龄人口						
60岁及以上老年人口	万人	19390	20243	21242	22200	23086
占全国总人口	%	14.3	14.9	15.5	16.1	16.7
儿童						
孤儿数	万人	57.0	54.9	52.5	50.2	46.0
家庭收养	万人	2.7	2.4	2.3	2.2	1.9
流浪儿童救助	万人次	15.2	18.4	17.0	16.7	16.7
社会救助						
最低生活保障						
城市最低生活保障人数	万人	2143.5	2064.2	1877.0	1701.1	1480.2
城市最低生活保障户数	万户	1114.9	1097.2	1026.1	957.4	855.3
城市最低生活保障平均标准	元/人・月	330.1	373.3	410.5	451.1	494.6
农村最低生活保障人数	万人	5344.5	5388.0	5207.2	4903.6	4586.5
农村最低生活保障户数	万户	2814.9	2931.1	2943.6	2846.2	2635.3
农村最低生活保障平均标准	元/人・年	2067.8	2433.9	2776.6	3177.6	3744.0
特困人员救助供养						
农村特困人员救助供养	万人	545.6	537.3	529.1	516.7	496.9
城市特困人员救助供养	万人	9.8	8.6	7.6	6.8	9.1
医疗救助						
直接医疗救助	万人次	2173.7	2126.4	2395.3	2518.9	2696.1
资助参加基本医疗保险	万人	5877.5	6358.8	6723.7	6213.0	5560.4
生活无着人员救助						
生活无着人员救助	万人次	276.6	348.5	351.7	375.2	333.8
为弱势群体筹集资金的活动						
民政部门接收捐赠款数	亿元	101.7	107.6	79.6	44.2	40.3
民政部门接收捐赠衣被数	亿件	1.3	1.0	0.5	0.5	0.7
民政部门接收捐赠其他物资价值	亿元	6.3	8.7	8.0	5.2	7.4
受益人次数	万人次	1325.0	1246.0	1694.9	1838.4	1165.8
社会捐赠接收站、点数	万个	3.1	3.1	3.2	3.0	2.9
销售福利彩票	亿元	1510.3	1765.3	2059.7	2015.1	2064.9
筹集公益金	亿元	449.4	510.7	585.7	563.8	591.5

A-1-3续表2

指　标	单　位	2012年	2013年	2014年	2015年	2016年
优抚安置						
国家抚恤、补助各类优抚对象	万人	944.4	950.5	917.3	897.0	874.8
接收军队离退休人员人数	万人	1.9	3.9	2.8	1.9	1.1
社区服务						
社区服务机构和设施	万个	20.0	25.2	31.1	36.1	38.6
# 社区服务中心	个	16306	19904	24006	24138	23493
社区服务站	个	87931	108377	120188	128083	137533
社区服务中心（站）覆盖率	%	15.3	18.8	21.1	22.5	24.4
便民利民网点数	万个	39.7	35.9	30.9	24.9	8.9
自然灾害情况						
受灾人口	万人次	29421.7	38818.7	24353.7	18620.3	18911.7
因灾死亡（含失踪）人口	人	1530	2284	1818	967	1706
直接经济损失	亿元	4185.5	5808.4	3373.8	2704.1	5032.9
三、成员组织和其他社会服务						
社会组织	万个	49.9	54.7	60.6	66.2	70.2
社会团体	万个	27.1	28.9	31.0	32.9	33.6
基金会	个	3029	3549	4117	4784	5559
民办非企业	万个	22.5	25.5	29.2	32.9	36.1
社会组织接收捐款数	亿元	470.8	458.8	524.8	610.3	786.7
自治组织	万个	67.9	68.3	68.2	68.1	66.2
村委会	万个	58.8	58.9	58.5	58.1	55.9
居委会	万个	9.1	9.5	9.7	10.0	10.3
婚姻服务						
结婚登记	万对	1323.6	1346.9	1306.7	1224.7	1142.8
# 涉外及华侨、港澳台	万对	5.3	5.5	4.7	4.1	4.2
结婚率	‰	9.8	9.9	9.6	9.0	8.3
离婚登记	万对	310.4	350.0	363.7	384.1	415.8
离婚率	‰	2.3	2.6	2.7	2.8	3.0
殡葬服务						
火化遗体数	万具	477.7	468.9	459.3	459.5	471.8
火化率	%	49.5	48.2	47.0	47.1	48.3

A-1-4 社会服务发展主要数据与上年比较

指　标	单　位	2016年	2015年	比上年增长(%)
一、综合				
行政区划				
镇	个	20883	20515	1.8
乡	个	10872	11315	-3.9
# 民族乡	个	989	991	-0.2
街道办事处	个	8105	7957	1.9
区公所	个	2	2	0.0
老龄人口				
60岁及以上老年人口	万人	23086	22200	4.0
占全国总人口	%	16.7	16.1	0.6(百分点)
65岁及以上老年人口	万人	15003	14386	4.3
占全国总人口	%	10.8	10.5	0.3(百分点)
资产				
社会服务事业费总支出	亿元	5440.2	4926.4	10.4
# 抚恤	亿元	769.8	686.8	12.1
退役安置	亿元	625.6	582.7	7.4
社会福利	亿元	753.4	562.8	33.9
社会救助	亿元	2492.8	2347.4	6.2
自然灾害生活救助	亿元	156.1	148.5	5.1
民政管理事务	亿元	441.7	399.6	10.5
行政事业单位离退休	亿元	48.4	50.1	-3.4
其他	亿元	152.2	148.5	2.5
基本建设支出	亿元	245. 8	239.9	2. 5
固定资产原价	亿元	5393.6	8183.1	-34.1
二、社会工作				
提供住宿的社会服务机构				
单位数	万个	3.2	3.1	3.2
床位数	万张	414.0	393.2	5.3
收养人数	万人	236.3	231.7	2.0
每千人口社会服务床位数	张	5.5	5.3	3.8

A−1−4续表1

指　标	单　位	2016年	2015年	比上年增长(%)
社会救助				
城市低保				
城市最低生活保障人数	万人	1480.2	1701.1	-13.0
城市最低生活保障户数	万户	855.3	957.4	-10.7
城市最低生活保障平均标准	元/人·月	494.6	451.1	9.6
农村低保				
农村最低生活保障人数	万人	4586.5	4903.6	-6.5
农村最低生活保障户数	万户	2635.3	2846.2	-7.4
农村最低生活保障平均标准	元/人·年	3744.0	3177.6	17.8
特困人员救助供养				
农村特困人员救助供养	万人	496.9	516.7	-3.8
城市特困人员救助供养	万人	9.1	6.8	33.8
医疗救助				
直接医疗救助	万人次	2696.1	2518.9	7.0
资助参加基本医疗保险	万人	5560.4	6213.0	-10.5
儿童收养				
家庭收养	万人	1.9	2.2	-13.6
福利彩票				
销售福利彩票	亿元	2064.9	2015.1	2.5
筹集公益金	亿元	591.5	563.8	4.9
优抚安置				
国家抚恤、补助各类优抚对象	万人	874.8	897.0	-2.5
接收军队离退休人员人数	万人	1.1	1.9	-42.1
社会捐赠				
社会捐赠款数	亿元	40.3	44.2	-8.8
捐赠衣被总数	亿件	0.7	0.5	40.0
捐赠其他物资价值	亿元	7.4	5.2	42.3
受益人次数	万人次	1165.8	1838.4	-36.6
社会捐赠接收站、点数	万个	2.9	3.0	-3.3

A-1-4续表2

指　标	单　位	2016年	2015年	比上年增长(%)
社区服务机构和设施				
社区服务机构和设施总数	个	386186	360956	7.0
社区服务指导中心	个	809	863	-6.3
社区服务中心	个	23493	24138	-2.7
社区服务站	个	137533	128083	7.4
社区养老机构和设施	个	34924	26067	34.0
社区互助型养老设施	个	76374	62027	23.1
其他	个	113053	119778	-5.6
社区服务中心（站）覆盖率	%	24.4	22.5	8.6(百分点)
便民利民网点	个	8.7	24.9	-65.1
三、成员组织和其他社会服务				
社会组织				
社会组织总数	万个	70.2	66.2	6.0
社会团体	万个	33.6	32.9	2.1
基金会	个	5559	4784	16.2
民办非企业	万个	36.1	32.9	10.1
自治组织				
村委会	万个	55.9	58.1	-3.8
居委会	万个	10.3	10.0	3.0
婚姻				
结婚登记	万对	1142.8	1224.7	-6.7
# 涉外及华侨、港澳台	万对	4.2	4.1	2.4
结婚率	‰	8.3	9.0	-0.7(千分点)
离婚登记	万对	415.8	384.1	8.3
离婚率	‰	3.0	2.8	0.1(千分点)
殡葬				
火化遗体数	万具	471.8	459.5	2.7
火化率	%	48.3	47.1	1.2(百分点)

A-1-5 行政区划与上年比较

单位：个

指　标	2016年	2015年	比上年增长(%)
地级行政区划合计	**334**	**334**	**-**
# 地级市	293	291	0.7
地区	8	10	-20.0
自治州	30	30	-
盟	3	3	-
县级行政区划合计	**2851**	**2850**	**-**
# 市辖区	954	921	3.6
县级市	360	361	-0.3
县	1366	1397	-2.2
自治县	117	117	-
旗	49	49	-
自治旗	3	3	-
特区	1	1	-
林区	1	1	-
乡镇、街道级行政区划合计	**39862**	**39789**	**0.2**
# 镇	20883	20515	1.8
乡	10872	11315	-3.9
苏木	152	152	-
民族乡	989	990	-0.1
民族苏木	1	1	-
街道办事处	8105	7957	1.9
区公所	2	2	-

A-1-6 社会服务机构和设施与上年比较

单位：个

指　标	2016年	2015年	比上年增长(%)
社会服务	**1745498**	**1750443**	**2.6**
一、社会工作	**423348**	**398811**	**6.2**
提供住宿的社会服务机构	**31912**	**31187**	**2.3**
老年人与残疾人服务机构	**28592**	**27752**	**3.0**
城市养老服务机构	8891	7656	16.1
农村养老服务机构	15398	15587	-1.2
社会福利院	1604	1717	-6.6
光荣院	1040	1106	-6.0
荣誉军人康复医院	44	46	-4.3
复员军人疗养院	38	36	5.6
军休所	1577	1604	-1.7
智障与精神疾病服务机构	**244**	**242**	**0.8**
社会福利医院	150	151	-0.7
复退军人精神病院	94	91	3.3
儿童收养救助服务机构	**705**	**753**	**-6.4**
儿童福利机构	465	478	-2.7
未成年人救助保护中心	240	275	-12.7
其他提供住宿的服务机构	**2371**	**2440**	**-2.8**
生活无着人员救助管理站	1736	1766	-1.7
军供站	315	320	-1.6
其他提供住宿的机构	320	354	-9.6

A-1-6续表

单位：个

指　标	2016年	2015年	比上年增长(%)
不提供住宿的社会服务机构	**391436**	**367624**	**6.5**
老龄机构	1828	2280	-19.8
民政部门直属康复辅具机构	25	24	4.2
救助低保服务机构	949	965	-1.7
救灾储备机构	258	776	-66.8
福利彩票发行机构	788	861	-8.5
军队离退休人员管理中心	269	271	-0.7
军队离退休人员活动中心	24	27	-11.1
烈士纪念建筑物管理机构	1109	1464	-24.2
社区服务机构和设施	386186	360956	7.0
二、成员组织和其他社会服务	**1370442**	**1349554**	**1.5**
成员组织	**1364883**	**1342960**	**1.6**
社会组织	**702405**	**662425**	**6.0**
社会团体	335932	328500	2.3
基金会	5559	4784	16.2
民办非企业	360914	329141	9.7
自治组织	662478	680535	-2.7
居委会	103292	99679	3.6
村委会	559186	580856	-3.7
其他社会服务	**5559**	**6594**	**-15.7**
婚姻服务机构	**1393**	**2064**	**6.9**
殡葬服务机构	**4166**	**4530**	**-8.0**
殡仪馆	1775	1821	-2.5
公墓	1386	1567	-11.6
殡葬管理机构	1005	1127	-10.8
三、其他事业单位	**1987**	**2078**	**-4.4**
行政机关	**3490**	**3482**	**0.2**

A-1-7 社会服务机构和设施职工与上年比较

单位：万人

指　标	2016年	2015年	比上年增长(%)
社会服务	**1239.3**	**1197.8**	**3.5**
一、社会工作	**185.6**	**170.8**	**8.7**
提供住宿的社会服务机构	**41.0**	**38.4**	**6.5**
老年人与残疾人服务机构	**33.9**	**31.8**	**6.3**
城市养老服务机构	15.0	13.2	13.6
农村养老服务机构	11.2	10.9	2.8
社会福利院	4.3	4.3	0.0
光荣院	0.9	0.9	0.0
荣誉军人康复医院	0.6	0.6	0.0
复员军人疗养院	0.3	0.3	0.0
军休所	1.5	1.6	-6.3
智障与精神疾病服务机构	**2.8**	**2.5**	**12.0**
社会福利医院	1.5	1.4	-
复退军人精神病院	1.3	1.1	18.2
儿童收养救助服务机构	**1.5**	**1.4**	**7.1**
儿童福利机构	1.3	1.2	8.3
未成年人救助保护中心	0.2	0.2	-
其他提供住宿的服务机构	**2.8**	**2.7**	**3.7**
生活无着人员救助管理站	1.7	1.7	0.0
军供站	0.5	0.5	-
其他提供住宿的机构	0.6	0.5	20.0

A−1−7续表

单位：万人

指　标	2016年	2015年	比上年增长(%)
不提供住宿的社会服务机构	**144.7**	**132.4**	**9.3**
老龄机构	0.8	0.9	-11.1
民政部门直属康复辅具机构	0.1	0.2	950.0
救助低保服务机构	0.8	0.8	-
救灾储备单位	0.1	0.2	-50.0
福利彩票发行机构	1.2	1.2	-
军队离退休人员管理中心	0.4	0.4	-
军队离退休人员活动中心	0.1	0.1	-
烈士纪念建筑物管理机构	0.9	1.0	-
社区服务机构和设施	140.3	127.6	9.9
二、成员组织和其他社会服务	**1052.0**	**1025.2**	**2.6**
成员组织	**1043.0**	**1015.7**	**2.7**
社会组织	**763.7**	**734.8**	**3.9**
社会团体	396.0	390.2	1.5
基金会	3.1	2.5	23.9
民办非企业	364.6	342.1	6.6
自治组织	**279.3**	**280.9**	**-0.6**
居委会	54.0	51.2	5.4
村委会	225.3	229.7	-1.9
其他社会服务	**9.0**	**9.5**	**-5.3**
婚姻服务机构	**0.9**	**1.0**	**-13.2**
殡葬服务机构	**8.1**	**8.5**	**-4.7**
殡仪馆	4.7	4.7	0.6
公墓	2.6	2.7	-4.7
殡葬管理机构	0.8	1.0	-18.0
三、其他事业单位	**1.6**	**1.8**	**-11.1**
行政机关	**9.6**	**9.5**	**0.9**

A-1-8 社会服务机构和设施中社会工作师人员情况

单位：人

指 标	社会工作师			助理社会工作师		
	2016年	2015年	比上年增长(%)	2016年	2015年	比上年增长(%)
社会服务	**55115**	**44480**	**23.9**	**81709**	**59065**	**38.3**
一、社会工作	**18015**	**12931**	**39.3**	**30385**	**19588**	**55.0**
提供住宿的社会服务机构	**5676**	**4422**	**28.4**	**6840**	**4624**	**47.9**
老年人与残疾人服务机构	**3969**	**3009**	**31.9**	**5191**	**3363**	**54.4**
城市养老服务机构	1128	905	24.6	1958	1345	45.6
农村养老服务机构	833	396	110.4	1296	401	223.2
社会福利院	1208	1020	18.4	1246	1108	12.5
光荣院	143	135	5.9	168	118	42.4
荣誉军人康复医院	76	65	16.9	41	40	2.5
复员军人疗养院	83	69	20.3	45	30	50.0
军休所	498	419	18.9	437	321	36.1
智障与精神疾病服务机构	**298**	**246**	**21.1**	**382**	**238**	**60.5**
社会福利医院	150	139	7.9	191	123	55.3
复退军人精神病院	148	107	38.3	191	115	66.1
儿童收养救助服务机构	**651**	**543**	**19.9**	**508**	**398**	**27.6**
儿童福利机构	589	492	19.7	448	344	30.2
未成年人救助保护中心	62	51	21.6	60	54	11.1
其他提供住宿的服务机构	**758**	**663**	**14.3**	**759**	**625**	**21.4**
生活无着人员救助管理站	604	535	12.9	530	490	8.2
军供站	61	51	19.6	66	54	22.2
其他提供住宿的机构	93	77	20.8	163	81	101.2

A-1-8续表

单位：人

指　标	社会工作师			助理社会工作师		
	2016年	2015年	比上年增长(%)	2016年	2015年	比上年增长(%)
不提供住宿的社会服务机构	**12339**	**8470**	**45.7**	**23545**	**14964**	**57.3**
老龄机构	129	141	-8.5	87	102	-14.7
民政部门直属康复辅具机构	33	-	-	33	-	-
救助低保服务机构	173	155	11.6	163	140	16.4
救灾储备单位	38	40	-5.0	19	40	-52.5
福利彩票发行机构	153	125	22.4	178	184	-3.3
军队离退休人员管理中心	119	110	8.2	116	84	38.1
军队离退休人员活动中心	7	4	75.0	6	4	50.0
烈士纪念建筑物管理机构	204	183	11.5	132	115	14.8
社区服务机构和设施	11483	7712	48.9	22811	14295	59.6
二、成员组织和其他社会服务	**36606**	**31141**	**17.5**	**50962**	**39193**	**27.7**
成员组织	**35666**	**30385**	**17.4**	**50045**	**38342**	**30.5**
社会组织	**27126**	**24206**	**12.1**	**27824**	**21509**	**29.4**
社会团体	13751	12050	14.1	8741	8298	5.3
基金会	186	233	-20.2	466	343	35.9
民办非企业	13189	11923	10.6	18617	12868	44.7
自治组织	**8540**	**6179**	**38.2**	**22221**	**16833**	**32.0**
居委会	7268	557	1204.8	18787	1700	1005.1
村委会	1272	5622	-77.4	3434	15133	-77.3
其他社会服务	**940**	**756**	**24.3**	**917**	**851**	**7.8**
婚姻服务机构	**204**	**205**	**-0.5**	**173**	**194**	**-10.8**
殡葬服务机构	**736**	**551**	**33.6**	**744**	**657**	**13.2**
殡仪馆	308	278	10.8	456	404	12.9
公墓	290	137	111.7	187	166	12.7
殡葬管理机构	138	136	1.5	101	87	16.1
三、其他事业单位	**494**	**408**	**21.1**	**362**	**284**	**27.5**
行政机关	**1964**	**1787**	**9.9**	**1819**	**1630**	**11.6**

A-1-9 性别统计情况

指 标	职工总数（人）	#女性	女性占比（%）	比上年增长（百分点）
社会服务	**12392884**	**3904051**	**31.5**	**-**
一、社会工作	**1856741**	**765938**	**41.3**	**3.3**
提供住宿的社会服务机构	**409713**	**232549**	**56.8**	**0.7**
老年人与残疾人服务机构	**338793**	**195552**	**57.7**	**0.9**
城市养老服务机构	150465	96471	64.1	0.7
农村养老服务机构	112246	55990	49.9	0.4
社会福利院	42634	26660	62.5	0.6
光荣院	9308	4381	47.1	-0.5
荣誉军人康复医院	5916	3394	57.4	2.7
复员军人疗养院	3029	1674	55.3	-0.9
军休所	15195	6982	45.9	1.0
智障与精神疾病服务机构	**28095**	**16260**	**57.9**	**-1.5**
社会福利医院	15079	8902	59.0	1.0
复退军人精神病院	13016	7358	56.5	-4.5
儿童收养救助服务机构	**14466**	**9683**	**66.9**	**2.4**
儿童福利机构	12770	8977	70.3	1.9
未成年人救助保护中心	1696	706	41.6	3.5
其他提供住宿的服务机构	**28359**	**11054**	**39.0**	**-0.7**
生活无着人员救助管理站	17344	5982	34.5	0.4
军供站	4977	1953	39.2	0.3
其他提供住宿的机构	6038	3119	51.7	-8.6

A−1−9续表

指　标	职工总数（人）	#女性	女性占比（%）	比上年增长（百分点）
不提供住宿的社会服务机构	**1447028**	**533389**	**36.9**	**1.8**
老龄机构	8400	3707	44.1	0.3
民政部门直属康复辅具机构	1425	463	32.5	-0.5
救助低保服务机构	8005	3589	44.8	-
救灾储备单位	1258	414	32.9	1.3
福利彩票发行机构	11858	5222	44.0	1.3
军队离退休人员管理中心	3848	1741	45.2	0.6
军队离退休人员活动中心	400	176	44.0	3.2
烈士纪念建筑物管理机构	9020	3654	40.5	1.2
社区服务机构和设施	1402814	514423	36.7	-
二、成员组织和其他社会服务	**10519946**	**3130623**	**29.8**	**-**
成员组织	**10429986**	**3101106**	**29.7**	**-**
社会组织	**7636579**	**2330770**	**30.5**	**-**
社会团体	3959949	909587	23.0	-0.4
基金会	30876	9101	29.5	0.5
民办非企业	3645754	1412082	38.7	0.1
自治组织	**2793407**	**770336**	**27.6**	**-0.1**
居委会	540226	263024	48.7	-0.5
村委会	2253181	507312	22.5	-0.4
其他社会服务	**89960**	**29517**	**32.8**	**-**
婚姻服务机构	**8502**	**5629**	**66.2**	**1.3**
殡葬服务机构	**81458**	**23888**	**29.3**	**0.5**
殡仪馆	46682	12179	26.1	0.2
公墓	26314	9455	35.9	1.4
殡葬管理机构	8462	2254	26.6	0.1
三、其他事业单位	**16197**	**7490**	**46.2**	**0.6**
行政机关	**96369**	**32272**	**33.5**	**0.6**

A-1-10 社会服务机构固定资产原价与上年比较

单位：亿元

指　标	2016年	2015年	比上年增长(%)
社会服务	**5393.6**	**6408.8**	**-15.8**
一、社会工作	**1238.6**	**1117.9**	**10.8**
提供住宿的社会服务机构	**966.4**	**868.2**	**11.3**
老年人与残疾人服务机构	**795.4**	**726.0**	**9.6**
城市养老服务机构	309.8	260.6	18.9
农村养老服务机构	256.9	243.9	5.3
社会福利院	133.5	131.3	1.7
光荣院	19.2	18.3	4.9
荣誉军人康复医院	26.0	23.2	12.1
复员军人疗养院	12.8	11.9	7.6
军休所	37.4	36.8	1.6
智障与精神疾病服务机构	**59.6**	**49.1**	**21.4**
社会福利医院	33.0	26.9	22.7
复退军人精神病院	26.6	22.2	19.8
儿童收养救助服务机构	**44.0**	**37.6**	**16.8**
儿童福利机构	42.0	35.5	18.3
未成年人救助保护中心	1.9	2.1	-9.5
其他提供住宿的服务机构	**67.3**	**55.5**	**21.3**
生活无着人员救助管理站	33.1	31.6	4.7
军供站	18.8	15.8	19.0
其他提供住宿的机构	15.4	8.1	90.1

A-1-10续表

单位：亿元

指　标	2016年	2015年	比上年增长(%)
不提供住宿的社会服务机构	**272.0**	**249.7**	**8.9**
老龄机构	8.1	8.3	-2.4
民政部门直属康复辅具机构	4.5	4.6	-2.2
救助低保服务机构	2.8	1.6	75.0
救灾储备单位	11.3	11.8	-4.2
福利彩票发行机构	91.5	76.0	20.4
军队离退休人员管理中心	19.4	17.2	12.8
军队离退休人员活动中心	8.8	7.2	22.2
烈士纪念建筑物管理机构	53.8	52.6	2.3
社区服务机构和设施	71.8	70.4	2.0
二、成员组织和其他社会服务	**4100.7**	**5242.4**	**-21.8**
成员组织	**3807.3**	**4950.4**	**-23.1**
社会组织	**2740.0**	**2311.1**	**18.6**
社会团体	349.2	379.6	-8.0
基金会	72.3	35.8	102.0
民办非企业	2318.5	1895.7	22.3
自治组织	1067.3	2639.3	-59.6
居委会	161.4	485.5	-66.8
村委会	905.9	2153.8	-57.9
其他社会服务	**293.4**	**292.0**	**0.5**
婚姻服务机构	**7.9**	**8.0**	**-1.3**
殡葬服务机构	**285.4**	**284.0**	**0.5**
殡仪馆	186.9	174.8	6.9
公墓	82.3	87.4	-5.8
殡葬管理机构	16.3	21.1	-22.7
三、其他事业单位	**54.4**	**48.5**	**12.2**
行政机关	**192.4**	**251.5**	**-23.5**

A-1-11 基本建设投资与上年比较

单位：亿元、万平方米

指　标	2016年	2015年	比上年增长(%)
计划总投资	**824.8**	**882.9**	**-6.6**
本年计划投资	**208.9**	**217.2**	**-3.8**
社会工作	160.7	161.4	-0.5
提供住宿的社会服务机构	133.9	128.9	3.9
老年人与残疾人服务机构	111.9	107.4	4.2
智障与精神疾病服务机构	9.4	9.7	-2.9
儿童收养救助服务机构	9.3	8.4	10.7
其他提供住宿的服务机构	3.3	3.4	-2.3
不提供住宿的社会服务机构	26.8	32.5	-17.8
其他社会服务机构	33.0	36.3	-9.1
其他	15.3	19.5	-21.5
开工累计完成投资	**428.7**	**450.2**	**-4.8**
本年实际完成投资	**245.8**	**239.9**	**2.5**
社会工作	188.4	184.3	2.2
提供住宿的社会服务机构	158.4	147.4	7.6
老年人与残疾人服务机构	136.8	123.8	10.5
智障与精神疾病服务机构	9.0	9.5	-4.8
儿童收养救助服务机构	10.5	10.4	0.5
其他提供住宿的服务机构	2.2	3.6	-39.4
不提供住宿的社会服务机构	30.0	36.9	-18.8
其他社会服务机构	36.0	40.3	-10.7
其他	21.3	15.3	39.2
国家预算内投资	84.4	92.8	-9.1
国内贷款	2.7	4.7	-42.8
利用外资	-	0.8	-
福利彩票公益金	68.4	61.7	10.9
其他	90.3	79.9	13.0
本年完工项目规模	**1243.2**	**1048.4**	**18.6**

A-1-12 社会服务事业费与上年比较

单位：亿元

指　标	2016年	2015年	比上年增长(%)
社会服务事业费合计	**5440.2**	**4926.4**	**10.4**
占国家财政支出比重（%）	3.4	3.3	0.1(百分点)
# 中央转移支付的事业费	2484.0	2270.3	9.4
占社会服务事业费的比重（%）	45.7	46.1	-0.4
# 国家预算内基本建设投资	84. 4	92.8	-9. 1
# 公益金支出	268.3	288.9	-7.1
按支出性质分			
抚恤	769.8	686.8	12.1
退役安置	625.6	582.7	7.4
社会福利	753.4	562.8	33.9
社会救助	2492.8	2347.4	6.2
# 最低生活保障	1702.4	1650.8	3.1
临时救助	131.1	106.2	23.4
特困人员救助供养	237.3	214.9	10.4
其他社会救助	89.6	71.8	24.8
医疗救助	332.3	303.7	9.4
自然灾害生活救助	156.1	148.5	5.1
民政管理事务	441.7	399.6	10.5
行政事业单位离退休	48.4	50.1	-3.4
其他	152.2	148.5	2.5

A-1-13 中央财政转移支付的社会服务事业费与上年比较

单位：亿元

指　标	2016年	2015年	比上年增长(%)
中央财政转移支付的社会服务事业费合计	**2484.0**	**2270.3**	**9.4**
# 抚恤	390.9	350.0	11.7
退役安置	384.7	352.9	9.0
社会福利	54.0	73.0	-26.0
社会救助	1568.1	1391.6	12.7
# 最低生活保障	1341.5	1166.7	15.0
临时救助	28.7	41.0	-30.0
医疗救助	177.9	163.9	8.5
生活无着人员救助	20.0	20.0	-
自然灾害生活救助	79.1	94.6	-16.4
民政管理事务	7.3	8.1	-9.9
# 预算内基本建设投资	38.0	32.0	18.8
# 养老服务	28.0	28.0	-
殡葬服务	5.0	-	-
儿童和精神疾病服务	5.0	2.0	150.0
# 公益金支出	52.6	68.4	-23.1

A-1-14 按支出形式分类的社会服务事业费支出情况

单位：亿元

指　标	2016年	2015年	占全部(%)	比上年增长额	比上年增长(%)
总计	**5440.2**	**4926.4**	**100.0**	**115.0**	**2.3**
直接发放	**4298.4**	**3918.8**	**85.3**	**379.7**	**9.7**
按标准发放和报销	3239.9	2959.7	64.3	280.2	9.5
发放数	3175.5	2904.0	63.0	271.5	9.4
定期发放	3138.6	2874.2	62.3	264.4	9.2
军队干部离休金	33.7	41.5	0.7	-7.8	-18.8
军队干部退休金	277.0	214.0	5.5	63.0	29.5
军队无军籍退休金	65.4	58.9	1.3	6.5	11.1
地方干部、人员退休金、退职金	10.7	12.2	0.2	-1.5	-12.4
离休、退休、退职金小计	386.8	326.6	7.7	60.2	18.5
烈属和牺牲病故定期抚恤金	35.9	34.9	0.7	1.0	3.0
伤残抚恤金	135.5	123.0	2.7	12.5	10.1
在乡退伍红军老战士生活费	-	0.1	-	-	-48.6
红军失散人员补助费	0.4	0.7	-	-0.2	-36.3
复员退伍军人定期定量补助费	176.1	162.0	3.5	14.1	8.7
“参战”退伍军人补助费	76.5	64.8	1.5	11.7	18.0
“涉核”退伍军人补助费	12.0	10.2	0.2	1.8	17.9
抚恤、补助费小计	436.4	395.6	8.7	40.8	10.3
军队离休干部遗属、退休人员遗属定期定量补助费	2.9	2.7	0.1	0.2	8.0
农村特困救助供养救济费	228.9	209.9	4.5	19.0	9.1
农村最低生活保障金	980.2	893.5	19.4	86.8	9.7
城市最低生活保障金	687.9	719.3	13.7	-31.4	-4.4
其他社会救助	89.6	71.8	1.8	17.8	24.8
定期定量救济费小计	1989.6	1897.2	39.5	92.4	4.9
分散安置伤残军人护理费	3.3	3.2	0.1	0.1	4.0
军队离休、退休人员护理费	5.0	4.1	0.1	0.9	20.9
儿童福利支出	56.3	54.8	1.1	1.4	2.6
老年人福利	261.2	192.7	5.2	68.5	35.5
非定期发放	36.9	29.8	0.7	7.1	23.8
烈士和牺牲病故人员一次性抚恤金	31.9	25.8	0.6	6.1	23.6
企事业退休人员一次性抚恤金	0.8	0.7	-	0.1	11.0
离休、退休干部死亡丧葬补助费	4.2	3.3	0.1	0.9	28.1
城市最低生活保障对象临时补助	27.7	39.5	0.6	-11.8	-29.8
农村最低生活保障对象临时补助	34.3	38.1	0.7	-3.8	-9.9
报销数	64.4	55.7	1.3	8.7	15.6
伤残补助费	7.6	7.0	0.2	0.6	8.3
离休、退休干部其他费用	56.8	48.7	1.1	8.1	16.6

A−1−14续表

单位：亿元

指　标	2016年	2015年	占全部(%)	比上年增减额	比上年增长(%)
临时性发放	1058.5	959.0	21.0	99.5	10.4
烈军属复员退伍军人临时补助费	287.6	253.7	5.7	33.8	13.3
退伍军人建房补助费	2.3	2.1	0.1	0.2	10.7
义务兵优待金	147.0	128.4	2.9	18.5	14.4
退役士兵自谋职业金	87.9	95.7	1.7	-7.9	-8.2
城镇退役士兵生活补助	16.8	17.6	0.3	-0.8	-4.4
优抚对象临时补助费小计	541.5	497.6	10.7	43.9	8.8
灾民生活救济费	96.9	92.1	1.9	4.9	5.3
医疗救助	332.3	303.7	6.6	28.7	9.4
其他对象临时救助	87.7	65.7	1.7	22.0	33.5
单位拨款	**406.8**	**352.2**	**8.1**	**54.6**	**15.5**
民政部门举办事业单位经费	333.5	287.9	6.6	45.7	15.9
优抚事业单位	67.0	47.5	1.3	19.4	40.9
荣誉军人康复医院	14.1	8.0	0.3	6.1	76.4
复员军人慢性病疗养院	4.2	3.6	0.1	0.6	15.1
复员退伍军人精神病院	13.2	10.4	0.3	2.8	27.4
光荣院	8.4	8.6	0.2	-0.1	-1.5
烈士纪念建筑物管理机构	18.2	9.2	0.4	8.9	96.8
其他优抚事业单位	8.8	7.7	0.2	1.1	14.5
社会福利事业单位	129.8	106.4	2.6	23.4	22.0
社会福利院	73.6	56.0	1.5	17.6	31.5
儿童福利院	17.6	15.7	0.4	1.9	11.9
精神病人福利院	19.9	18.1	0.4	1.8	10.1
流浪乞讨人员救助站	18.7	16.7	0.4	2.1	12.5
军队离退休干部管理机构	52.2	66.5	1.0	-14.3	-21.5
殡葬事业单位	84.6	67.5	1.7	17.1	25.4
火葬场	34.0	29.0	0.7	5.0	17.3
其他殡葬事业单位	50.6	38.5	1.0	12.1	31.5
集体办事业单位补贴	47.7	45.5	1.0	2.2	4.7
优抚事业单位	0.3	0.1	-	0.2	133.2
社会福利事业单位	47.4	45.4	0.9	2.0	4.4
生产单位拨款	4.2	3.6	0.1	0.6	17.3
假肢厂、站	3.1	1.0	0.1	2.0	201.8
安置农场	1.2	2.6	-	-1.4	-54.6
灾民紧急抢救、转移、安置费	8.9	8.5	0.2	0.5	5.3
救灾储备	12.4	6.7	0.3	5.7	85.3
其他支出	**735.0**	**655.5**	**13.5**	**79.4**	**12.1**

A-1-15 按支出性质分类的社会服务事业费支出情况

单位：亿元

指 标	2016年	2015年	占全部(%)	比上年增长额	比上年增长(%)
总计	**5440.2**	**4926.4**	**100.0**	**513.7**	**10.4**
优待抚恤支出合计	**769.8**	**686.8**	**14.2**	**83.1**	**12.1**
死亡抚恤	74.1	65.3	1.4	8.9	13.6
伤残抚恤	143.1	130.0	2.6	13.0	10.0
在乡复员、退伍军人生活补助	265.1	237.7	4.9	27.3	11.5
优抚事业单位	67.3	63.0	1.2	4.3	6.8
义务兵优待金	147.0	128.4	2.7	18.5	14.4
其他优抚支出	73.3	62.3	1.4	11.0	17.7
退役安置	**625.6**	**582.7**	**11.5**	**42.9**	**7.4**
退伍军人安置	122.2	131.0	2.3	-8.8	-6.7
军队移交政府的离退休人员安置	432.9	363.1	8.0	69.9	19.2
军队移交政府离退休干部管理机构	52.2	66.5	1.0	-14.3	-21.5
其他退役安置支出	18.4	22.2	0.3	-3.8	-17.1
社会福利	**753.4**	**562.8**	**13.9**	**190.7**	**33.9**
儿童福利	56.3	54.8	1.0	1.4	2.6
老年人福利	261.2	192.7	4.8	68.5	35.5
假肢矫形	73.2	2.5	1.3	70.7	2860.6
殡葬	84.6	67.5	1.6	17.1	25.4
社会福利事业单位	159.6	137.8	2.9	21.9	15.9
其他社会福利支出	118.5	107.5	2.2	11.0	10.3
社会救助	**2492.8**	**2347.4**	**45.8**	**145.4**	**6.2**
最低生活保障	1702.4	1650.8	31.3	51.6	3.1
城市最低生活保障	687.9	719.3	12.7	-31.4	-4.4
农村最低生活保障	1014.5	931.5	18.7	83.0	8.9

A-1-15续表

单位：亿元

指　标	2016年	2015年	占全部(%)	比上年增减额	比上年增长(%)
其他社会救助	85.7	71.8	1.6	13.9	19.3
医疗救助	332.3	303.7	6.1	28.7	9.4
资助参加基本医疗保险	63.4	36.8	1.2	26.6	72.4
直接医疗救助	232.7	214.6	4.3	18.2	8.5
优抚对象医疗补助	36.2	34.6	0.7	1.6	4.7
自然灾害生活救助	**156.1**	**148.5**	**2.9**	**7.6**	**5.1**
生活救济费	96.9	92.1	1.8	4.9	5.3
紧急抢救、安置、转移灾民支出	8.9	8.5	0.2	0.5	5.3
救灾储备	11.1	6.7	0.2	4.4	65.7
自然灾害灾后重建补助	26.9	30.4	0.5	-3.4	-11.3
其他救助	10.9	10.9	0.2	-0.1	-0.5
民政管理事务	**441.7**	**399.6**	**8.1**	**42.1**	**10.5**
行政运行	112.5	94.8	2.1	17.7	18.7
一般行政管理事务	18.3	19.1	0.3	-0.8	-4.2
机关服务	3.0	2.3	0.1	0.7	29.1
拥军优属	23.5	22.6	0.4	0.9	3.8
老龄事务	27.0	33.5	0.5	-6.5	-19.4
民间组织管理	8.9	7.8	0.2	1.1	14.2
行政区划和地名管理	15.2	12.1	0.3	3.2	26.3
基层政权和社区建设	122.6	105.9	2.3	16.7	15.7
部队供应	6.0	5.0	0.1	1.0	19.6
其他民政管理事务支出	104.7	96.5	1.9	8.2	8.5
行政事业单位离退休	**48.4**	**50.1**	**0.9**	**-1.7**	**-3.4**
地方离退休人员经费	12.2	13.5	0.2	-1.3	-9.6
行政单位离退休	19.2	20.1	0.4	-0.9	-4.6
事业单位离退休	13.7	13.5	0.3	0.2	1.5
离退休人员管理机构	0.4	0.4	0.0	0.1	18.6
其他行政事业单位离退休支出	2.9	2.7	0.1	0.3	9.4
其他	**152.2**	**148.5**	**2.8**	**3.7**	**2.5**

A-2-1 社会工作类机构财务状况

单位：万元

指　标	2016年	2015年	比上年增长(%)
执行企业会计制度单位情况			
存货	208115.9	-	-
固定资产原价	14824934.5	18045518.1	-17.85
累计折旧	270252.5	-	-
# 本年折旧	1235099.3	1723915.5	-28.35
资产总计	1575889.9	-	-
负债合计	995629.7	-	-
营业收入	36283415.9	43959557	-17.46
营业成本	17054615.6	20234453.5	-15.71
营业税金及附加	515830.7	640889.6	-19.51
销售费用	1267102.8	1746581.9	-27.45
管理费用	1734008.6	2090815.4	-17.07
# 税金	193479.6	250320.4	-22.71
差旅费	56678.9	83073.9	-31.77
财务费用	1474942.8	1555403.3	-5.17
# 利息支出	1163735.6	1190935.8	-2.28
资产减值损失	12994.4	-	-
公允价值变动收益	5579.1	4261.2	30.93
投资收益	21684.3	56915.5	-61.90
营业利润	1001572.5	1211099	-17.30
营业外收入	277082.1	298479.5	-7.17
# 政府补助	75940.7	91860.8	-17.33
应付职工薪酬	2777680.5	3253550.4	-14.63
本年应交增值税	40584.8	-	-

A-2-1续表

单位：万元

指　标	2016年	2015年	比上年增长(%)
执行行政事业单位会计制度填报			
存货	46697.9	-	-
固定资产原价	8239795.6	8376074.4	-1.6
资产总计	3199632.2	-	-
负债合计	2152103.4	-	-
本年收入合计	8345082.1	8051375.2	3.6
# 事业收入	3428344	3205999.7	6.9
经营收入	131130.2	135331.5	-3.1
本年支出合计	8042032	7452602.4	7.9
# 工资福利支出	1565527.5	1392427.5	12.4
商品和服务支出	1568041.4	1447749.9	8.3
# 取暖费	43642.7	45050.7	-3.1
差旅费	21850.6	19219.2	13.7
因公出国（境）费用	397.1	837.2	-52.6
劳务费	120608.7	112327.7	7.4
工会经费	11332.8	8952.3	26.6
福利费	22632.8	20271.4	11.6
对个人和家庭的补助	2822386.9	2726659.6	3.5
# 抚恤金	35822.3	29890.4	19.8
生活补助	475931.7	406016.2	17.2
救济费	158816.5	138773.2	14.4
助学金	1993.1	1560.5	27.7
奖励金	17121.6	11236	52.4
生产补贴	785.9	537	46.4
经营支出	84112.3	66925.7	25.7
销售税金	7424.5	4792.4	54.9
执行民间非营利组织单位会计制度填报			
存货	3254.9	-	-
固定资产原价	3773841.2	2500456.1	50.9
资产总计	395981.1	-	-
负债合计	199600.4	-	-
本年收入合计	1501377.5	1130226.3	32.8
# 捐赠收入	61191.9	42860.9	42.8
会费收入	57438.3	51509.5	11.5
本年费用合计	1309953.5	965823.9	35.6
# 业务活动成本	757183.2	512054.1	47.9
# 人员费用	296386.9	206067.1	43.8
日常费用	127554.5	101833.4	25.3
固定资产折旧	76740.1	57570.8	33.3
税费	7899.3	3650.7	116.4
管理费用	373227.6	345206.3	8.1
# 人员费用	170544.3	150299.1	13.5
日常费用	68631	61732.5	11.2
固定资产折旧	36381	30675.8	18.6
税费	13470.4	13057.6	3.2
净资产变动额	48669.7	31737.2	53.4

A-2-2 提供住宿的社会服务机构和社区养老情况与上年比较

指 标	机构与设施数（个）			职工人数（万人）		
	2016年	2015年	比上年增长(%)	2016年	2015年	比上年增长(%)
机构和设施合计	**418098**	**392128**	**6.6**	**181.2**	**166.0**	**9.2**
机构合计	**31912**	**31172**	**2.4**	**40.9**	**38.4**	**6.6**
养老机构和设施	**414778**	**388708**	**6.7**	**174.1**	**159.4**	**9.2**
机构类	**28592**	**27752**	**3.0**	**33.9**	**31.8**	**6.3**
城市养老服务机构	8891	7656	16.1	15.0	13.2	13.4
农村养老服务机构	15398	15587	-1.2	11.2	10.9	2.4
社会福利院	1604	1717	-6.6	4.3	4.3	-
光荣院	1040	1106	-6.0	0.9	0.9	-4.3
荣誉军人康复医院	44	46	-4.3	0.6	0.6	7.8
复员军人疗养院	38	36	5.6	0.3	0.3	13.7
军休所	1577	1604	-1.7	1.5	1.6	-3.7
社区机构和设施类	**386186**	**360956**	**7.0**	**140.3**	**127.6**	**9.9**
社区养老机构和设施	34924	26067	34.0	15.6	12.2	28.1
社区互助型养老设施	76374	62027	23.1	14.8	12.4	19.0
其他	274888	272862	0.7	109.9	103.0	6.7
智障与精神疾病服务机构	**244**	**242**	**0.8**	**2.8**	**2.5**	**12.0**
社会福利医院	150	151	-0.7	1.5	1.4	7.1
复退军人精神病院	94	91	3.3	1.3	1.1	18.2
儿童收养救助服务机构	**705**	**753**	**-6.4**	**1.5**	**1.4**	**7.1**
儿童福利院	465	478	-2.7	1.3	1.2	8.3
流浪儿童救助保护中心	240	275	-12.7	0.2	0.2	-
其他提供住宿的服务机构	**2371**	**2425**	**-2.2**	**2.8**	**2.7**	**3.7**
生活无着人员救助管理站	1736	1766	-1.7	1.7	1.7	-
军供站	315	320	-1.6	0.5	0.5	-
其他	320	339	-5.6	0.6	0.5	20.0

A–2–2续表

指　标	床位数（万张）			收留抚养救助人数（万人）		
	2016年	2015年	比上年增长（%）	2016年	2015年	比上年增长（%）
机构和设施（含在建）合计	**771.2**	**732.9**	**5.2**	**344.2**	**326.2**	**5.5**
机构合计	**414.0**	**393.1**	**5.3**	**236.3**	**231.7**	**2.0**
养老机构和设施	**730.2**	**672.7**	**8.5**	**327.6**	**295.7**	**10.8**
机构类	**378.8**	**358.2**	**5.7**	**219.8**	**214.8**	**2.3**
城市养老服务机构	135.9	116.4	16.8	68.1	59.6	14.2
农村养老服务机构	179.9	177.1	1.6	113.2	115.2	-1.7
社会福利院	37.1	37.7	-1.7	20.0	21.1	-5.2
光荣院	7.5	7.6	-1.8	4.2	4.3	-3.3
荣誉军人康复医院	1.1	1.0	9.4	0.6	0.6	-
复员军人疗养院	0.7	0.7	-	0.4	0.4	-
军休所（万户）	16.5	17.6	-6.2	13.3	13.6	-2.2
社区机构和设施类	**322.8**	**298.1**	**8.3**	**107.9**	**94.5**	**14.2**
社区养老机构和设施	153.5	134.2	14.4	59.2	55.7	6.3
社区互助型养老设施	77.1	70.7	9.1	26.0	21.1	23.2
其他社区机构和设施	92.2	93.2	-1.1	22.7	17.7	28.2
智障与精神疾病服务机构	**8.4**	**7.9**	**6.3**	**6.9**	**6.4**	**7.8**
社会福利医院	5.3	4.9	8.2	4.4	4.0	10.0
复退军人精神病院	3.1	3.0	3.3	2.5	2.4	4.2
儿童收养救助服务机构	**10.0**	**10.0**	**-**	**5.5**	**5.6**	**-1.8**
儿童福利院	9.0	8.9	1.1	5.3	5.5	-3.6
流浪儿童救助保护中心	1.0	1.1	-9.1	0.2	0.1	100.0
其他提供住宿的服务机构	**16.7**	**17.0**	**-1.8**	**4.2**	**4.9**	**-14.3**
生活无着人员救助管理站	10.2	10.3	-1.0	2.7	3.4	-20.6
军供站	3.7	3.8	-2.6	-	-	-
其他	2.8	2.9	-3.4	1.5	1.5	-
在建机构和设施	**34.3**	**41.7**	**-17.7**			
在建养老机构和设施	28.6	34.0	-15.9			
其他在建机构和设施	5.7	7.7	-26.0			

A-2-3 家庭收养与上年比较

单位：人、件

指　标	2016年	2015年	比上年增长(%)
孤儿数	**460450**	**502105**	**-8.3**
集中供养孤儿	87502	91712	-4.6
社会散居孤儿	372948	410393	-9.1
家庭收养服务			
收养登记合计(件)	18736	22348	-16.2
中国公民收养登记	15965	19406	-17.7
# 香港居民	77	105	-26.7
澳门居民	3	3	-
台湾居民	26	42	-38.1
华侨	25	29	-13.8
外国人收养登记	2771	2942	-5.8
被收养人合计（人）	18736	22363	-16.2
# 女性	12586	14751	-14.7
残疾儿童	2554	3290	-22.4
社会福利机构抚养的儿童	8884	10704	-17.0
# 被外国人收养	2490	2804	-11.2
社会孤儿	4696	5645	-16.8
# 被外国人收养	244	7	3385.7
近亲属抚养人数	1076	1143	-5.9
# 被外国人收养	7	113	-93.8
生父母有特殊困难无力抚养人数	601	539	11.5
# 被外国人收养	8	9	-11.1
其他	3479	4332	-19.7
# 被外国人收养	22	-	-

A-2-4 社会救助与上年比较

指　标	单位	2016年	2015年	比上年增长(%)
社会救助总人数	**万人**	**16083.0**	**17746.4**	**-9.4**
城市最低生活保障人数	万人	1480.2	1701.1	-13.0
# 女性	万人	643.6	727.1	-11.5
残疾人	万人	156.5	165.7	-5.6
# 重度残疾人	万人	7.6	-	-
# 老年人	万人	258.0	293.5	-12.1
# 成年人	万人	950.9	-	-
在职人员	万人	22.7	31.1	-27.0
灵活就业	万人	304.4	377.3	-19.3
登记失业	万人	252.9	264.1	-4.2
无就业条件	万人	370.9	394.0	-5.9
# 未成年人	万人	271.4	341.0	-20.4
城市最低生活保障户数	万户	855.3	957.4	-10.7
城市最低生活保障资金支出	亿元	687.9	719.3	-4.4
城市最低生活保障平均标准	元/人·月	494.6	451.1	9.6
农村最低生活保障人数	万人	4586.5	4903.6	-6.5
农村最低生活保障户数	万户	2635.3	2846.2	-7.4
农村最低生活保障费	亿元	1014.5	931.5	8.9
农村最低生活保障平均标准	元/人·年	3744.0	3177.6	17.8
特困人员救助供养				
农村特困人员救助供养人数	万人	496.9	516.8	-3.9
城市特困人员救助供养人数	万人	9.1	6.8	33.8
传统救济人数	**万人**	**60.2**	**63.8**	**-5.6**
临时救助	**万人次**	**850.7**	**655.4**	**29.8**
医疗救助				
直接救助人次数	万人次	2696.1	2518.9	7.0
资助参加基本医疗保险人数	万人	5560.4	6213.0	-10.5
生活无着人员救助	万人次	**333.8**	**375.2**	**-11.0**

注：社会救助总人数是救助人数和人次数的合计。

A-2-5 分省城市最低生活保障平均标准与上年比较

单位：元/人·月

地 区	2016年	2015年	比上年增长(%)
全 国	**494.6**	**451.1**	**9.6**
北 京	800.0	710.0	12.7
天 津	780.0	705.0	10.6
河 北	501.2	441.4	13.5
山 西	441.1	413.2	6.8
内蒙古	540.2	508.0	6.3
辽 宁	522.8	493.5	5.9
吉 林	446.9	401.6	11.3
黑龙江	535.9	506.4	5.8
上 海	880.0	790.0	11.4
江 苏	610.8	581.7	5.0
浙 江	673.7	640.5	5.2
安 徽	497.1	455.0	9.2
福 建	514.8	478.1	7.7
江 西	480.8	452.0	6.4
山 东	494.9	470.1	5.3
河 南	425.1	374.1	13.6
湖 北	487.9	447.1	9.1
湖 南	431.3	359.8	19.9
广 东	576.2	513.8	12.1
广 西	457.6	404.4	13.2
海 南	467.0	466.8	0.0
重 庆	459.6	419.1	9.7
四 川	419.5	367.0	14.3
贵 州	507.3	453.4	11.9
云 南	442.2	395.9	11.7
西 藏	693.5	591.3	17.3
陕 西	479.5	460.7	4.1
甘 肃	410.9	378.1	8.7
青 海	400.8	370.4	8.2
宁 夏	416.4	361.8	15.1
新 疆	383.9	349.2	9.9

A-2-6 社会捐赠与上年比较

指　标	单位	2016年	2015年	比上年增长(%)
社会捐赠合计	**万元**	**8343384.9**	**6597061.4**	**26.5**
直接接收捐赠情况				
捐赠款数额	万元	402815.1	442029.5	-8.9
捐赠衣被合计	万件	6638.3	4537.0	46.3
捐赠其他物资价值	万元	73795.0	52408.2	40.8
间接接收捐赠情况				
捐赠款数额	万元	58645.3	42562.3	37.8
捐赠衣被合计	万件	488.0	172.5	182.9
捐赠其他物资价值	万元	14483.2	6164.4	134.9
受益人次数	万人次	1165.8	1838.4	-36.6
社会捐赠接收工作站、点数	个	28904	30362	-4.8
# 社会捐赠接收工作站数	个	12899	12810	0.7
慈善超市数	个	8966	9654	-7.1
各类社会组织接收捐赠	**万元**	**7866774.8**	**6102623.7**	**28.9**

注：由于社会组织年检工作滞后于年报汇总工作，社会组织捐赠数据为2015年数据。

A-2-7 自然灾害与上年比较

指　标	单位	2016年	2015年	比上年增长(%)
农作物受灾情况				
受灾	千公顷	26220.7	21769.8	20.4
绝收	千公顷	2902.2	2232.7	30.0
旱灾				
受灾	千公顷	9872.7	10609.7	-6.9
绝收	千公顷	1018.3	1046.1	-2.7
洪涝（含山体滑坡和泥石流）				
受灾	千公顷	8531.4	5620.2	51.8
绝收	千公顷	1297.3	659.5	96.7
风雹				
受灾	千公顷	2908.0	2918.0	-0.3
绝收	千公顷	268.8	309.1	-13.0
台风				
受灾	千公顷	2023.5	1721.1	17.6
绝收	千公顷	145.1	181.5	-20.1
地震				
受灾	千公顷	0.1	0.5	-80.0
绝收	千公顷	-	-	-
雪灾、低温冷冻				
受灾	千公顷	2885.0	900.3	220.4
绝收	千公顷	172.7	36.5	373.2
人口受灾情况				
受灾	万人次	18911.7	18620.3	1.6
死亡人口（含失踪）	人	1706.0	967.0	76.4
紧急转移人口	万人次	910.1	644.4	41.2
损失情况				
倒塌房屋	万间	52.1	24.8	110.1
损坏房屋	万间	334.0	49.2	578.9
直接经济损失	亿元	5032.9	2704.1	86.1

A-2-8 国家优抚、补助对象与上年比较

单位：人

指　标	2016年	2015年	比上年增长(%)
优抚对象人数	**8748016**	**8970288**	**-2.5**
抚恤	934549	1001843	-6.7
烈士家属	124950	160948	-22.4
因公牺牲	38725	43711	-11.4
病故军人家属	55899	60316	-7.3
伤残人员	714975	736868	-3.0
补助	7813467	7968445	-1.9
在乡退伍红军老战士	55	177	-68.9
在乡西路军红军老战士	50	64	-21.9
红军失散人员	2060	3708	-44.4
在乡复员军人	636698	792440	-19.7
带病回乡退伍军人	1127704	1183750	-4.7
60岁以上农村籍退伍军人	4055748	3924604	3.3
参战退役人员	1362905	1409601	-3.3
参试退役人员	179705	184840	-2.8
部分60周岁以上烈士（含错杀被平反）人员子女	239617	241257	-0.7
其他补助人数	208925	228004	-8.4
本年接收和安置复员干部数	**4065**	**288**	**1311.5**
本年新增享受烈士待遇人数	**150**	**341**	**-56.0**
零散烈士纪念设施	**11815**	**11838**	**-0.2**
优待			
优待优抚对象（万户）	304.4	317.0	-4.0
# 军属（万户）	82.6	85.8	-3.7
优待金（亿元）	171.3	193.0	-11.2
# 军属（亿元）	84.1	76.6	9.8

A–2–9 社区服务与上年比较

单位：个、张、%

指 标	2016年	2015年	比上年增长(%)
社区服务机构和设施总数	**386186**	**360956**	**7.0**
社区服务指导中心	809	863	-6.3
社区服务中心	23493	24138	-2.7
社区服务站	137533	128083	7.4
社区养老机构和设施	34924	26067	34.0
社区互助型养老设施	76374	62027	23.1
其他机构和设施	113053	119778	-5.6
社区服务中心（站）覆盖率	**24.4**	**22.5**	**8.6**
便民利民网点数（万个）	**8.7**	**24.9**	**-65.1**
社区养老床位数	**3228448**	**2981379**	**8.3**
日间照料床位	1415600	1212564	16.7
留宿照料床位	1812848	1768815	2.5
社区服务志愿者组织数（万个）	**11.6**	**9.6**	**20.8**

A-3-1 社会组织财务状况

单位：万元

指 标	2016年	2015年	比上年增长(%)
执行民间非营利组织单位会计制度填报			
存货	4792499.90	-	-
固定资产原价	27399933.5	22833898.0	20.0
资产总计	16085347.0	-	-
负债合计	2856450.7	-	-
本年收入合计	27476139.0	28774009.2	-4.5
# 捐赠收入	7866774.8	6102623.7	28.9
会费收入	2432366.5	2420408.6	0.5
本年费用合计	26327743.4	23608642.7	11.5
# 业务活动成本	16432860.8	11099752.6	48.0
# 人员费用	4396524.8	3942515.4	11.5
日常费用	2358708.8	2033252.6	16.0
固定资产折旧	1071211.0	912313.7	17.4
税费	171699.1	165658.6	3.6
管理费用	5522615.1	5181971.0	6.6
# 人员费用	2025134.4	1865588.3	8.6
日常费用	747405.1	670059.8	11.5
固定资产折旧	369165.6	301515.2	22.4
税费	83405.3	85545.4	-2.5
净资产变动额	9191404.9	8552726.4	7.5

A-3-2 社会组织分类情况与上年比较

单位：个

指　标	2016年	2015年	比上年增长(%)
社会组织合计	**702405**	**662425**	**6.0**
社会团体	**335932**	**328500**	**2.3**
按活动区域分			
中央级	1985	1974	0.6
省级	30493	29233	4.3
地级	82554	80220	2.9
县级	220900	217073	1.8
基金会	**5559**	**4784**	**16.2**
按性质分类			
公募性	1730	1548	11.8
非公募性	3791	3198	18.5
涉外基金会	9	9	-
境外代表机构	29	29	-
民办非企业	**360914**	**329141**	**9.7**
按性质分类			
法人	291207	260479	11.8
合伙	8679	8791	-1.3
个体	61028	59871	1.9

A-3-3 自治组织财务状况

单位：万元

指　标	2016年	2015年	比上年增长(%)
执行企业会计制度单位填报			
存货	21902.4	-	-
固定资产原价	2163749.6	2727337.9	-20.7
累计折旧	112359.7	-	-
# 本年折旧	80067.4	148945.1	-46.2
资产总计	1758348.8	-	-
负债合计	906661.0	-	-
营业收入	532835.1	1580476.7	-66.3
营业成本	379103.6	1108891.8	-65.8
营业税金及附加	12758.3	21022.0	-39.3
销售费用	19085.9	29720.1	-35.8
管理费用	177520.0	265244.6	-33.1
# 税金	1886.1	4821.0	-60.9
差旅费	169.4	305.4	-44.5
财务费用	-30033.4	-13441.4	123.4
# 利息支出	-32435.9	-24942.3	30.0
资产减值损失	-	-	-
公允价值变动收益	29.2	-1020.7	-102.9
投资收益	38705.8	64131.6	-39.6
营业利润	17234.2	62691.9	-72.5
营业外收入	127014.2	168935.6	-24.8
其中：政府补助	44015.8	61798.3	-28.8
应付职工薪酬	59352.3	95143.3	-37.6
本年应交增值税	-	-	-
执行事业单位会计制度填报			
存货	1890.0	-	-
固定资产原价	3357236.3	21189913.5	-84.2
资产总计	234845.7	-	-
负债合计	93998.7	-	-
本年收入合计	1743008.3	7817047.8	-77.7
# 事业收入	293901.1	2174753.8	-86.5
经营收入	199377.9	665861.9	-70.1

A-3-3续表

单位：万元

指　标	2016年	2015年	比上年增长(%)
本年支出合计	1533918.8	6997608.0	-78.1
# 工资福利支出	341067.1	2009732.5	-83.0
商品和服务支出	266692.3	1810948.1	-85.3
# 取暖费	4114.7	52962.9	-92.2
差旅费	4730.2	66494.3	-92.9
因公出国（境）费用	6.5	1147.1	-99.4
劳务费	17757.8	169461.7	-89.5
工会经费	5728.2	15370.4	-62.7
福利费	42406.5	154715.4	-72.6
对个人和家庭的补助	92897.1	306354.5	-69.7
# 抚恤金	1092.2	3661.0	-70.2
生活补助	49489.8	89784.9	-44.9
救济费	738.5	6988.6	-89.4
助学金	2513.7	8384.0	-70.0
奖励金	5388.7	5940.4	-9.3
生产补贴	812.5	8966.8	-90.9
经营支出	12731.6	51954.6	-75.5
销售税金	1134.3	9922.7	-88.6
执行民间非营利组织单位会计制度填报			
存货	1333.6	-	-
固定资产原价	5151909.7	2476078.9	108.1
资产总计	8245.4	-	-
负债合计	6121.8	-	-
本年收入合计	486741.3	891636.6	-45.4
# 捐赠收入	5869.7	24917.2	-76.4
会费收入	29351.5	96592.1	-69.6
本年费用合计	233974.5	804695.1	-70.9
# 业务活动成本	102658.5	453388.1	-77.4
# 人员费用	40519.7	143659.8	-71.8
日常费用	19701.5	79205.2	-75.1
固定资产折旧	18835.1	78485.3	-76.0
税费	1068.6	8987.0	-88.1
管理费用	69491.4	225951.1	-69.2
# 人员费用	22533.3	83409.4	-73.0
日常费用	10085.8	44670.9	-77.4
固定资产折旧	9972.8	20543.1	-51.5
税费	278.9	5719.9	-95.1
净资产变动额	12153.6	89227.2	-86.4

A-3-4 自治组织主要指标与上年比较

单位：个、人

指　标	2016年	2015年	比上年增长(%)
城市			
社区居委会	103292	99679	3.6
居民小组	1420344	1347274	5.4
居民委员会成员人数	540226	512196	5.5
#女性	263024	251946	4.4
居委会选举情况			
当年完成选举的居委会数	20263	29970	-32.4
当年完成选举的居委会选民登记总数	50762592	62635078	-19.0
#本届登记选民数	30212168	52699497	-42.7
参加投票人数	23555010	40804184	-42.3
农村			
村民委员会	559186	580856	-3.7
村民小组	4478489	4691632	-4.5
村民委员会成员人数	2253181	2297061	-1.9
#女性	507312	525741	-3.5
村委会选举情况			
当年完成选举的村委会数	77011	134675	-42.8
当年完成选举的村委会选民登记总数	120575159	149455947	-19.3
#本届登记选民数	73754381	134197410	-45.0
参加投票人数	64400407	118633157	-45.7

A-3-5 其他社会服务机构财务状况

单位：万元

指　标	2016年	2015年	比上年增长(%)
执行企业会计制度单位填报			
存货	67433.9	-	-
固定资产原价	966064.0	970507.7	-0.5
累计折旧	69245.7	-	-
其中：本年折旧	76941.6	81492.1	-5.6
资产总计	562115.4	-	-
负债合计	299123.9	-	-
营业收入	1085109.8	1074715.6	1.0
营业成本	237169.8	242462.5	-2.2
营业税金及附加	9577.3	12084.7	-20.7
销售费用	88278.0	90090.1	-2.0
管理费用	181509.1	179853.9	0.9
其中：税金	6493.5	4683.3	38.7
差旅费	1717.8	1659.6	3.5
财务费用	6298.7	6562.6	-4.0
其中：利息支出	525.5	796.1	-34.0
资产减值损失	810.0	-	-
公允价值变动收益	360.0	-	-
投资收益	2139.4	2919.0	-26.7
营业利润	215804.0	218696.8	-1.3
营业外收入	65772.4	-	-
其中：政府补助	2849.5	-	-
应付职工薪酬	90390.2	94422.6	-4.3
本年应交增值税	3381.4	-	-

A-3-5续表

单位：万元

指　标	2016年	2015年	比上年增长(%)
执行事业单位会计制度填报			
存货	21668.9	-	-
固定资产原价	1894378.9	1884846.3	0.5
资产总计	700456.3	-	-
负债合计	143940.7	-	-
本年收入合计	1512340.8	1378451.0	9.7
其中：事业收入	760368.6	697503.5	9.0
经营收入	297468.2	286039.9	4.0
本年支出合计	1398034.8	1322894.3	5.7
其中：工资福利支出	388071.4	360530.6	7.6
商品和服务支出	515176.1	512347.7	0.6
其中：取暖费	6041.1	6736.0	-10.3
差旅费	4627.3	4336.9	6.7
因公出国（境）费用	34.5	47.7	-27.7
劳务费	42211.6	39521.2	6.8
工会经费	2975.0	2638.0	12.8
福利费	7032.0	7131.4	-1.4
对个人和家庭的补助	70208.9	65120.1	7.8
其中：抚恤金	537.6	889.2	-39.5
生活补助	4894.2	4434.0	10.4
救济费	755.1	433.3	74.3
助学金	108.1	90.1	20.0
奖励金	1386.1	1733.5	-20.0
生产补贴	427.1	411.1	3.9
经营支出	156029.4	152914.6	2.0
销售税金	3581.0	4190.0	-14.5
执行民间非营利组织单位会计制度填报			
存货	495.9	-	-
固定资产原价	72605.2	64594.5	12.4
资产总计	15237.8	-	-
负债合计	11577.4	-	-
本年收入合计	22245.0	16510.0	34.7
其中：捐赠收入	487.0	400.8	21.5
会费收入	2552.0	553.0	361.5
本年费用合计	20400.3	11523.0	77.0
其中：业务活动成本	13228.6	6778.6	95.2
其中：人员费用	3047.6	2142.6	42.2
日常费用	4994.2	2465.2	102.6
固定资产折旧	3175.9	1063.3	198.7
税费	214.1	219.5	-2.5
管理费用	5749.3	3250.2	76.9
其中：人员费用	2923.4	1208.4	141.9
日常费用	1348.1	715.4	88.4
固定资产折旧	664.2	367.3	80.8
税费	60.1	27.8	116.2
净资产变动额	15552.1	882.2	1662.9

A-3-6 其他社会服务主要指标与上年比较

指　标	单位	2016年	2015年	比上年增长(%)
婚姻服务				
事业单位性质的婚姻登记机构	个	1393	2064	-32.5
办理婚姻登记业务的处数	处	4863	5714	-14.9
结婚登记	对	11428216	12247056	-6.7
内地居民登记结婚对数	对	11386050	12205888	-6.7
初婚人数	人	19132566	21089700	-9.3
再婚人数	人	3723866	3404412	9.4
# 女性	人	1950215	1772263	10.0
恢复结婚	对	473905	398527	18.9
涉外及华侨、港澳台居民登记结婚	对	42166	41168	2.4
结婚率	‰	8.3	9.0	-0.7(千分点)
离婚登记	对	4158211	3841407	8.2
民政部门办理离婚对数	对	3486257	3148779	10.7
内地居民办理离婚	对	3479942	3142542	10.7
华侨、港澳台居民登记离婚	对	6315	6237	1.3
法院判决、调解离婚件数	件	671954	692628	-3.0
离婚率	‰	3.0	2.8	0.2(千分点)
殡葬服务				
殡葬服务机构	个	4166	4530	-8.0
火化炉数	台	6206	6063	2.4
全年火化遗体数	具	4718141	4595065	2.7
火化率	%	48.3	47.1	1.2(百分点)
穴位数	个	15570132	15811006	-1.5
安葬数	具	10907556	10379760	5.1

04

社会服务历年统计资料

2017

B-1-1 县及以上行政区划

单位：个

年份	省级	地级（不含地级市）	县级（不含县级市、市辖区）	市	#地级	#县级	市辖区	县级合计
1978	30	212	2153	193	98	92	408	2653
1979	30	211	2153	216	104	109	428	2690
1980	30	211	2151	223	107	113	511	2775
1981	30	208	2144	233	108	122	514	2780
1982	30	210	2140	245	112	130	527	2797
1983	30	178	2091	289	144	142	552	2785
1984	30	175	2069	300	147	150	595	2814
1985	30	165	2046	324	162	159	621	2826
1986	30	159	2017	353	166	184	629	2830
1987	30	156	1986	381	170	208	632	2826
1988	31	151	1936	434	183	248	647	2831
1989	31	151	1919	450	185	262	648	2829
1990	31	151	1903	467	185	279	651	2833
1991	31	151	1894	479	187	289	650	2833
1992	31	148	1848	517	191	323	662	2833
1993	31	139	1795	570	196	371	669	2835
1994	31	127	1735	622	206	413	697	2845
1995	31	124	1716	640	210	427	706	2849
1996	31	117	1696	666	218	445	717	2858
1997	33	110	1693	668	222	442	727	2862
1998	33	104	1689	668	227	437	737	2863
1999	34	95	1682	667	236	427	749	2858
2000	34	74	1674	663	259	400	787	2861
2001	34	67	1660	662	265	393	808	2861
2002	34	57	1649	660	275	381	830	2860
2003	34	51	1642	660	282	374	845	2861
2004	34	50	1636	661	283	374	852	2862
2005	34	50	1636	661	283	374	852	2862
2006	34	50	1635	656	283	369	856	2860
2007	34	50	1635	655	283	368	856	2859
2008	34	50	1635	655	283	368	856	2859
2009	34	50	1636	654	283	367	855	2858
2010	34	50	1633	657	283	370	853	2856
2011	34	48	1627	657	284	369	857	2853
2012	34	48	1624	657	285	368	860	2852
2013	34	47	1613	658	286	368	872	2853
2014	34	45	1596	653	288	361	897	2854
2015	34	43	1568	656	291	361	921	2850
2016	34	41	1537	657	293	360	954	2851

B-1-2 乡镇级行政区划

单位：个

年 份	乡镇级	镇	乡	#民族乡	街道办事处	区公所
1978	6195	2173				4022
1979	10424	2361			4444	3619
1980						
1981	11434	2678			4965	3791
1982						
1983	49695	2968	35514		5304	5909
1984	106439	7186	85290		5844	8119
1985	104900	9140	82450	3144	5402	7908
1986	83954	10718	61353	2936	5718	6165
1987	81025	11103	58739	3020	5680	5503
1988	65345	11481	45195	1571	5099	3570
1989	65419	11873	44624	1755	5420	3502
1990	65188	12084	44397	1980	5269	3438
1991	63391	12455	42654	1403	5186	3096
1992	54830	14539	33827	1348	5233	1231
1993	54863	15805	32445	1351	5470	1143
1994	54605	16702	31463	1322	5372	1068
1995	53360	17532	29502	1330	5596	730
1996	51336	18171	27056	1383	5565	544
1997	50967	18925	25966	1545	5678	398
1998	50999	19216	25712	1517	5732	339
1999	50750	19756	24745	1222	5904	345
2000	51024	20312	24555	1356	5902	255
2001	46369	20358	20012	1165	5972	27
2002	44822	20600	18640	1162	5516	66
2003	44067	20226	18064	1149	5751	26
2004	43275	19892	17534	1127	5829	20
2005	41636	19522	15951	1093	6152	11
2006	41040	19369	15306	1089	6355	10
2007	40813	19249	15120	1094	6434	10
2008	40828	19234	15067	1097	6524	3
2009	40858	19322	14848	1098	6686	2
2010	40906	19410	14571	1096	6923	2
2011	40466	19683	13587	1086	7194	2
2012	40446	19881	13281	1064	7282	2
2013	40497	20117	12812	1035	7566	2
2014	40381	20401	12282	1020	7696	2
2015	39789	20515	11315	991	7957	2
2016	39862	20883	10872	989	8105	2

B-1-3 全国人口情况

单位：万人、%

年份	总人口	城镇	乡村	农村贫困人口	65岁及以上老年人口	65岁及以上人口比重	60岁及以上老年人口	60岁及以上人口比重	出生人口	死亡人口	当年净增人口
1978	96259	17245	79014	25000							
1979	97542	18495	79047								1283
1980	98705	19140	79565								1163
1981	100072	20171	79901								1367
1982	101654	21480	80174		4991	4.9					1469
1983	103008	22274	80734								954
1984	104357	24017	80340	12800							
1985	105851	25094	80757	12500							1164
1986	107507	26366	81141	13100							1476
1987	109300	27674	81626	12200	5968	5.4					1500
1988	111026	28661	82365	9600							1541
1989	112704	29540	83164	10200							1577
1990	114333	30195	84138	8500	6368	5.6			2391	762	1629
1991	115823	31203	84260						2258	768	1490
1992	117171	32175	84996	8000					2119	771	1348
1993	118517	33173	85344						2126	780	1346
1994	119850	34169	85681	7000					2104	771	1333
1995	121121	35174	85947	6540	7510	6.2			2063	792	1271
1996	122389	37304	85085		7833	6.4			2067	799	1268
1997	123626	39449	84177	4962	8085	6.5			2038	801	1237
1998	124761	41608	83153	4210	8359	6.7			1942	807	1135
1999	125786	43748	82038	3412	8679	6.9			1834	809	1025
2000	126743	45906	80837	3209	8821	7.0			1771	814	957
2001	127627	48064	79563	2927	9062	7.1			1702	818	884
2002	128453	50212	78241	2820	9377	7.3			1647	821	826
2003	129227	52376	76851	2900	9692	7.5			1599	825	774
2004	129988	54283	75705	2610	9857	7.6			1593	832	761
2005	130756	56212	74544	2365	10055	7.7	14408	11	1617	849	768
2006	131448	57706	73742	2148	10419	7.9	14901	11.3	1584	892	692
2007	132129	59379	72750	4320	10636	8.1	15340	11.6	1594	913	681
2008	132802	60667	72135	4007	10956	8.3	15989	12	1608	935	673
2009	133450	62186	71288	3597	11309	8.5	16714	12.5	1615	943	672
2010	134091	66558	67415	2688	11883.2	8.9	17765	13.3	1596	953	642
2011	134735	69079	65656	12238	12288	9.1	18499	13.7	1604	960	644
2012	135404	71182	64222	9899	12714	9.4	19390	14.3	1635	966	669
2013	136072	73111	62961	8249	13161	9.7	20243	14.9	1640	972	668
2014	136782	74916	61866	7017	13755	10.1	21242	15.5	1687	977	710
2015	137462	77116	60346	5575	14386	10.5	22200	16.1	1655	975	680
2016	138271	79298	58973	4335	79298	10.8	23086	16.7	1786	977	809

注：本表资料来源于国家统计局。

B-1-4 社会服务机构和设施（按登记类型分类）

单位：万个

年 份	合 计	事业单位及设施合计	事业单位	企业性质机构	社会组织	社会服务类	自治组织	行政机关
1978	1.1	1.1		0.1				
1979	1.3	1.2		0.1				
1980	1.4	1.3		0.1				
1981	1.5	1.3		0.2				
1982	1.7	1.6		0.2				
1983	40.2	1.9		0.6			37.7	
1984	103.6	2.6		0.7			100.3	
1985	107.7	3.3		1.5			103.0	
1986	101.2	3.9		2.0			95.3	
1987	100.1	4.2		2.8			93.2	
1988	106.7	4.3		4.0	0.4		97.8	
1989	111.8	4.4		4.2	0.5		102.8	
1990	119.8	4.5		4.2	1.1		110.0	
1991	129.2	4.7		4.4	8.3		111.9	
1992	136.1	4.8		5.0	15.5		110.8	
1993	139.7	5.3		5.7	16.8		112.0	
1994	140.3	5.2		6.0	17.4		111.7	
1995	133.7	5.2		6.0	18.1		104.4	
1996	133.9	5.3		5.9	18.5		104.2	
1997	131.4	5.3		5.6	18.1		102.4	
1998	122.2	5.4		5.1	16.6		95.2	
1999	115.7	5.4		4.5	14.3		91.6	
2000	109.5	6.1		4.1	15.3		84.0	
2001	109.8	5.7		3.8	21.1		79.2	0.6
2002	110.5	5.8		3.6	24.5		76.7	0.5
2003	109.9	5.8		3.4	26.7		74.0	0.4
2004	111.1	6.7		3.2	28.9		72.2	0.4
2005	112.6	6.6		3.1	32.0		70.9	0.4
2006	115.7	6.7		3.0	35.4		70.5	0.4
2007	117.7	7.0		2.5	38.7		69.5	0.3
2008	119.2	6.6		2.4	41.4		68.8	0.4
2009	125.9	12.1		2.3	43.1		68.4	0.3
2010	126.6	11.6		2.2	44.6	6.3	68.2	0.3
2011	129.4	13.1		2.2	46.2	6.6	67.9	0.3
2012	146.2	26.3		2	49.9	7.5	68	0.3
2013	156.2	31.4	2.6	1.8	54.7	8.0	68.3	0.3
2014	166.5	36.0	2.9	1.7	60.6	8.8	68.2	0.3
2015	176.5	40.7	3.1	1.5	66.2	9.9	68.1	0.3
2016	174.5	37.9	3.1	0.1	70.2	10.4	66.2	0.3

B-1-5 社会服务机构和设施（按国民经济行业分类）

单位：万个

年 份	合 计	社会工作	成员组织			其他社会服务	其他事业单位	行政机关
				社会组织	自治组织			
1978	1.1	0.8				0.3		
1979	1.3	1.0				0.3		
1980	1.4	1.1				0.3		
1981	1.5	1.2				0.3		
1982	1.7	1.4				0.3		
1983	40.2	2.2	37.7		37.7	0.3		
1984	103.6	3.0	100.3		100.3	0.3		
1985	107.7	4.5	103.0		103.0	0.3		
1986	101.2	5.6	95.3		95.3	0.3		
1987	100.1	6.6	93.2		93.2	0.3		
1988	106.7	8.1	98.3	0.4	97.8	0.3		
1989	111.8	8.3	103.3	0.5	102.8	0.3		
1990	119.8	8.4	111.1	1.1	110.0	0.3		
1991	129.2	8.7	120.2	8.3	111.9	0.3		
1992	136.1	9.5	126.3	15.5	110.8	0.3		
1993	139.7	10.7	128.7	16.8	112.0	0.3		
1994	140.3	10.9	129.1	17.4	111.7	0.3		
1995	133.6	10.9	122.4	18.1	104.4	0.3		
1996	133.9	10.9	122.7	18.5	104.2	0.3		
1997	131.4	10.6	120.5	18.1	102.4	0.3		
1998	122.2	10.2	111.8	16.6	95.2	0.3		
1999	115.7	9.5	105.9	14.3	91.6	0.3		
2000	109.5	9.8	99.3	15.3	84.0	0.3		
2001	109.8	9.2	100.3	21.1	79.2	0.3		0.6
2002	110.5	9.1	101.2	24.5	76.7	0.3		0.5
2003	109.9	8.9	100.7	26.7	74.0	0.3		0.4
2004	111.1	9.6	101.1	28.9	72.2	0.3		0.4
2005	112.6	9.5	102.9	32.0	70.9	0.3		0.4
2006	115.7	9.2	105.9	35.4	70.5	0.5		0.4
2007	117.7	9.0	108.2	38.7	69.5	0.5		0.3
2008	119.2	8.4	110.2	41.4	68.8	0.6		0.4
2009	125.9	13.8	111.5	43.1	68.4	0.6		0.3
2010	126.6	13.2	112.8	44.6	68.2	0.6		0.3
2011	129.4	14.6	114.1	46.2	67.9	0.7		0.3
2012	146.2	27.5	117.9	49.9	68	0.6	0.2	0.3
2013	156.1	32.3	123.0	54.7	68.3	0.6	0.2	0.3
2014	166.8	37.1	128.8	60.6	68.2	0.7	0.2	0.3
2015	176.5	41.3	134.3	66.2	68.1	0.7	0.2	0.3
2016	174.5	42.3	136.4	70.2	66.2	0.6	0.2	0.3

注：2012年开始社会工作中包含其他社区服务设施。

B-1-6 社会服务机构和设施职工

单位：万人

年份	合计							行政机关	乡、镇民政助理员
		社会工作	成员组织	社会组织	自治组织	其他社会服务	其他事业单位		
1978	19.7	19.7							
1979	21.9	21.9							
1980	25.3	25.3							
1981	27.8	27.8							
1982	29.1	29.1							
1983	41.5	41.5							
1984	48.0	48.0							
1985	497.9	83.4	414.5		414.5				
1986	506.2	104.1	402.1		402.1				
1987	529.1	132.2	396.9		396.9				
1988	569.6	166.9	402.7		402.7				
1989	587.5	171.5	416.0		416.0				
1990	631.8	179.3	452.5		452.5				
1991	661.2	192.7	468.5		468.5				
1992	691.3	213.9	477.4		477.4				
1993	733.9	230.0	503.9		503.9				
1994	749.6	243.1	506.5		506.5				
1995	694.2	245.7	448.5		448.5				
1996	676.0	229.2	446.8		446.8				
1997	666.8	238.2	428.6		428.6			14.3	
1998	634.4	225.0	409.4		409.4			14.8	
1999	615.1	213.7	401.4		401.4			14.8	5.9
2000	566.8	203.4	363.4		363.4			13.5	5.7
2001	565.2	202.4	362.8		362.8			12.1	4.6
2002	526.2	192.4	333.8		333.8			11.2	4.1
2003	551.8	193.0	358.8		358.8			10.8	3.7
2004	532.4	197.8	334.6		334.6			11.3	3.9
2005	500.6	189.5	311.1		311.1			8.4	5.5
2006	895.5	183.0	712.5	425.2	287.3			8.3	4.6
2007	930.0	190.4	739.6	456.9	282.7			8.4	4.7
2008	958.7	206.9	751.8	475.8	276.0			8.7	4.5
2009	1029.3	207.5	821.8	544.7	277.1			8.8	4.7
2010	1129.5	234.0	895.5	618.2	277.3			8.9	5.0
2011	1120.8	235.7	876.6	599.3	277.3	8.5		9.0	4.9
2012	1144.7	241.4	892.5	613.3	279.2	8.6	2.2	9.3	5.2
2013	1197.6	269.2	917.3	636.6	280.7	9.1	2.0	9.4	5.2
2014	1250.9	277.3	962.5	682.3	280.2	9.3	1.9	9.5	5.4
2015	1308.9	281.9	1015.7	734.8	280.9	9.5	1.8	9.5	5.3
2016	1239.3	185.7	1043.0	763.7	279.3	9	1.6	9.6	5.3

注：合计数不含行政机关人员和乡镇助理员。

B-1-7 社会工作师

单位：人

年　份	报考人数	考试通过人数	社会服务行业在业人数	社会工作	成员组织	其他社会服务	其他事业单位	行政机关
2008	77698	4192	2858	1496	1191	171		286
2009	46015	4227	6602	3809	2544	249		758
2010	25547	2664	8979	5176	3473	330		922
2011	25500	2338	10750	5165	5247	338		854
2012	34245	6104	17101	6276	10056	443	326	1114
2013	48287	11658	21917	8014	12994	560	349	1280
2014	62881	7427	25782	10252	14442	681	407	1475
2015	79535	13155	45248	13699	30385	756	408	1787
2016	88974	17772	55115	18015	35666	940	494	1964

B-1-8 助理社会工作师

单位：人

年　份	报考人数	考试通过人数	社会服务行业在业人数	社会工作	成员组织	其他社会服务	其他事业单位	行政机关
2008	60139	20648	16965	4727	11840	398		609
2009	38204	6611	23297	5530	17388	379		798
2010	46047	5428	23731	6724	16517	490		969
2011	54515	8068	28663	10686	17419	558		963
2012	92621	23846	36436	11998	23513	645	280	1163
2013	121937	27300	43301	15471	26871	694	265	1264
2014	144813	28431	50770	18295	31381	803	291	1404
2015	196965	34274	59043	20902	37006	851	284	1630
2016	210267	64638	81709	30385	50045	917	362	1819

B-1-9 社会服务职业技能人员情况

单位：人

年 份	合格总人数	养老护理员	假肢类技能人员	孤残儿童护理员	灾害信息员	殡葬类技能人员
2007	114		21			93
2008	1027		139			888
2009	3575	24	302	23	1397	1829
2010	16809	171	252	196	14554	1636
2011	33240	1538	164	1270	27842	2426
2012	34931	4220	219	2590	25608	2294
2013	17612	4072	193	2216	8989	2142
2014	13246	5934	338	2093	2765	2116
2015	12871	8127	268	1570	791	2115
2016	12144	8528	393	1117	-	2106

说明：1.以上数据为民政部职业技能鉴定指导中心及分布在全国31个省、自治区、直辖市76个鉴定站鉴定人数和竞赛晋级人数（不含地方自行组织的鉴定人数）。

2.殡葬类职业包括：殡仪服务员（初中高技师4个级别）、遗体接运工（初中高3个级别）、遗体防腐师（初中高技师高级技师5个级别）、遗体整容师（初中高技师高级技师5个级别）、遗体火化师（初中高技师高级技师5个级别）、墓地管理员（初中高技师4个级别）。

3.假肢类职业包括：假肢师（初中高技师高级技师5个级别）、矫形器师（初中高技师高级技师5个级别）。

B-1-10 历年性别情况统计

单位：万人、人次

年 份	城市最低生活保障人数	其中：女	农村最低生活保障人数	其中：女	农村特困人员集中救助供养人数	其中：女	本年在站救助人次数	其中：女
1996	84.9							
1997	87.9							
1998	184.1							
1999	256.9							
2000	402.6							
2001	1170.7		304.6					
2002	2064.7		407.8					
2003	2246.8		367.1				634528	
2004	2205.0		488.0				820254	
2005	2234.2	592.4	825.0	235.1			1196305	209632
2006	2240.1	787.5	1593.1	455.1			1295506	221164
2007	2272.1	922.5	3566.3	1169.2	531.3	137.5	1544492	281987
2008	2334.8	947.7	4305.5	1337.0	548.6	127.5	1573484	269609
2009	2345.6	961.4	4760.0	1502.4	553.4	123.9	1680532	281387
2010	2310.5	943.4	5214.0	1673.4	556.3	120.7	1719008	314866
2011	2276.8	920.2	5305.7	1700.6	551.0	115.6	2409701	373103
2012	2143.5	889.9	5344.5	1814.5	545.6	109.4	2765761	383262
2013	2064.2	867.0	5388.0	1866.5	537.3	102.0	3479536	609333
2014	1877.0	792.4	5207.2	1826.4	529.1	94.1	2953359	568551
2015	1701.1	727.1	4903.6	1795.0	516.7	87.2	3233912	608786
2016	1480.2	643.6	4586.5	1774.2	496.9	76.2	2886925	467503

B-1-10续表

单位：万人

年份	社团负责人数	其中：女	基金会负责人数（人）	其中：女	民办非企业单位负责人数	其中：女	居委会主任数	其中：女	村委会主任数	其中：女
1996										
1997										
1998										
1999	47.6	6.0			0.9	0.2				
2000	45.4	6.1			3.2	0.7				
2001	43.3	5.7			10.1	3.6				
2002	45.5	6.1			14.4	5.1				
2003	51.8	6.2			16.6	5.8				
2004	56.0	6.6			19.1	6.5				
2005	64.0	6.9	2940	450	23.1	7.0				
2006	36.4	7.0	3014	738	20.9	6.5				
2007	39.2	7.9	3113	925	25.9	7.4	8.2	3.7	61.1	9.1
2008	49.5	10.2	3231	600	30.6	8.9	7.8	3.4	57.6	5.9
2009	49.4	9.4	3856	637	31.1	9.6	7.8	3.4	56.3	6.2
2010	56.9	9.1	4797	1019	35.7	10.1	8.1	3.5	56.3	5.9
2011	59.4	8.2	6257	1388	33.6	11.0	8.0	3.5	54.5	6.1
2012	61.6	9.1	6896	1167	35.9	11.9	9.1	3.8	58.7	6.9
2013	61.0	10.0	7331	1429	37.7	12.6	9.4	3.9	58.7	7.0
2014	63.9	10.7	8952	1687	41.3	13.9	9.6	3.9	58.4	7.2
2015	66.3	12.2	12491	2852	48.4	16.0	9.9	4.1	57.9	6.7
2016	73.8	12.7	11902	2504	51.6	18.0	10.3	4.1	55.8	5.9

B-1-11 社会服务机构固定资产原价

单位：亿元

年 份	合计	社会工作				其他社会服务	其他事业单位	行政机关
			成员组织					
				社会组织	自治组织			
1978								
1979								
1980								
1981								
1982								
1983	13.0	13.0						
1984	14.9	14.9						
1985	20.1	20.1						
1986	24.2	24.2						
1987	28.7	28.7						
1988	40.8	40.8						
1989	44.1	44.1						
1990	51.7	51.7						
1991	63.6	63.6						
1992	75.6	75.6						
1993	100.3	100.3						
1994	119.0	119.0						
1995	142.6	142.6						
1996	168.1	168.1						
1997	211.5	211.5						
1998	962.4	962.4						
1999	1017.3	1017.3						
2000	1199.3	1199.3						
2001	1317.0	1317.0						
2002	1394.9	1394.9						
2003	1644.3	1644.3						
2004	1755.6	1755.6						62.8
2005	3032.9	1858.0	1174.9		1174.9			64.9
2006	3972.4	2103.0	1869.4	423.0	1446.4			94.3
2007	3840.2	1934.3	1905.9	682.0	1223.9			132.8
2008	4459.9	2186.8	2273.1	805.8	1467.3			132.9
2009	5078.8	2326.4	2752.4	1030.0	1722.4			119.2
2010	6467.5	2671.9	3795.6	1864.1	1931.5			121.8
2011	6705.6	2790.4	3684.2	1885.0	1799.2	231.0		284.2
2012	6675.4	2898.9	3477.7	1425.4	2052.3	251.8	47.0	344.1
2013	6810.2	3030.7	3465.7	1496.6	1969.1	267.0	46.8	185.4
2014	7212.9	3273.0	3609.3	1560.6	2048.6	283.8	46.8	169.3
2015	8183.1	2892.2	4950.4	2311.1	2639.3	292.0	48.5	251.5
2016	5393.6	1238.6	3807.3	2740.0	1067.3	293.3	54.4	192.4

B-1-12 历年国家财政支出和社会服务事业费支出情况

单位：亿元

年　份	国家财政支出	社会服务事业费支出	占财政支出%	年　份	国家财政支出	社会服务事业费支出	占财政支出%
1950	68.04	1.32	1.94	1984	1701.02	24.24	1.43
1951	122.32	1.37	1.12	1985	2004.25	29.58	1.48
1952	175.78	2.83	1.61	**“七五”时期**	**12865.67**	**208.49**	**1.62**
1953	220.50	3.55	1.61	1986	2204.91	34.41	1.56
1954	280.93	6.04	2.15	1987	2262.18	35.93	1.59
1955	474.29	4.98	1.05	1988	2491.21	39.56	1.59
“一五”时期	**1367.89**	**25.99**	**1.90**	1989	2823.78	46.65	1.65
1956	536.79	5.69	1.06	1990	3083.59	51.94	1.68
1957	303.43	5.31	1.75	**“八五”时期**	**24387.46**	**386.59**	**1.59**
1958	408.75	3.27	0.80	1991	3386.62	62.54	1.85
1959	553.09	4.48	0.81	1992	3742.20	63.71	1.70
1960	652.25	7.24	1.11	1993	4642.30	69.87	1.51
“二五”时期	**3760.99**	**53.03**	**1.41**	1994	5792.62	87.02	1.50
1961	367.66	9.89	2.69	1995	6823.72	103.45	1.52
1962	305.33	7.45	2.44	**“九五”时期**	**57043.46**	**840.90**	**1.47**
1963	339.15	8.75	2.58	1996	7937.55	121.15	1.53
1964	398.77	16.15	4.05	1997	9233.56	133.52	1.45
1965	467.10	10.79	2.31	1998	10798.18	161.84	1.50
“三五”时期	**2523.24**	**35.83**	**1.42**	1999	13187.67	194.70	1.48
1966	540.49	8.81	1.63	2000	15886.50	229.69	1.45
1967	441.40	8.21	1.86	**“十五”时期**	**127800.69**	**2471.74**	**1.93**
1968	359.62	5.61	1.56	2001	18902.58	284.75	1.51
1969	525.20	6.67	1.27	2002	22053.15	392.27	1.78
1970	646.53	6.53	1.01	2003	24649.95	498.92	2.02
“四五”时期	**3924.37**	**46.70**	**1.19**	2004	28486.89	577.39	2.03
1971	734.41	6.83	0.93	2005	33708.12	718.41	2.13
1972	768.87	8.15	1.06	**“十一五”时期**	**317654.99**	**9156.70**	**2.88**
1973	810.57	9.97	1.23	2006	40213.16	915.35	2.28
1974	792.98	9.04	1.14	2007	49565.40	1215.49	2.45
1975	820.00	12.71	1.55	2008	62427.03	2146.45	3.44
“五五”时期	**5198.77**	**84.22**	**1.62**	2009	75874.00	2181.90	2.88
1976	804.48	16.17	2.01	2010	89575.40	2697.51	3.01
1977	842.27	18.53	2.20	**“十二五”时期**	**676383.92**	**20529.88**	**3.04**
1978	1122.09	13.71	1.22	2011	108929.67	3229.14	2.96
1979	1281.79	18.33	1.43	2012	125712.25	3683.74	2.93
1980	1228.83	17.48	1.42	2013	139744.00	4276.50	3.06
“六五”时期	**7483.18**	**113.85**	**1.52**	2014	151662.00	4414.10	2.91
1981	1138.41	19.23	1.69	2015	150336.00	4926.40	3.28
1982	1229.98	19.19	1.56	**“十三五”时期**	**160351.34**	**5440.15**	**3.39**
1983	1409.52	21.61	1.53	2016	160351.34	5440.15	3.39

B-1-13 按用项分社会服务事业费

单位：亿元

年份	社会服务事业费	抚恤费	离休费	社会福利及其他社会救济费	最低生活保障事业费	自然灾害救济费	退休费	其他社会服务事业费
1978	13.7	2.8		4.4		4.2	2.3	
1979	18.4	3.5		5.2		6.8	2.9	
1980	17.5	4.4		5.2		4.5	3.4	
“六五”时期	**114.2**	**27.3**	**0.9**	**32.1**		**35.2**	**16.8**	**1.7**
1981	19.2	4.4		5.1		6.3	3.4	
1982	19.6	4.8		5.1		6.0	3.5	
1983	21.6	5.3		6.5		6.4	3.4	
1984	24.2	6.1	0.2	8.0		6.9	3.0	
1985	29.6	6.7	0.7	7.4		9.6	3.5	1.7
“七五”时期	**208.4**	**59.2**	**11.4**	**46.7**		**56.4**	**22.0**	**12.8**
1986	34.4	8.4	1.2	8.3		10.7	3.8	1.9
1987	35.9	9.6	1.8	8.6		9.9	4.1	2
1988	39.6	11	2.3	9		10.4	4.3	2.5
1989	46.6	14	2.9	10		12.3	4.6	2.9
1990	51.9	16.2	3.2	10.8		13.1	5.2	3.5
“八五”时期	**386.6**	**107.8**	**23.2**	**75.6**		**94.1**	**45.5**	**40.5**
1991	62.5	16.8	3.6	11.7		20.9	5.4	4.2
1992	63.7	18	4.2	12.4		17.1	6.6	5.4
1993	69.9	20.1	3.6	14.5		14.9	8.3	8.4
1994	87	24.4	5.5	17.3		17.7	12.1	10.1
1995	103.5	28.5	6.3	19.7		23.5	13.1	12.4

年份	社会服务事业费	抚恤费	军队离退休、退职费	社会福利及其他社会救济费	最低生活保障事业费	自然灾害救济费	地方离、退休人员费	其他社会服务事业费
“九五”时期	**840.9**	**220.6**	**76.9**	**201.8**	**48.7**	**171.5**	**58.0**	**112.2**
1996	121.2	31.9	6.2	22.8	3	30.8	13.9	15.5
1997	133.5	36.1	12.4	27.1	2.9	28.7	10.3	19
1998	161.8	39.4	15.2	34	7.1	41.2	10.9	21.3
1999	194.7	49.7	18.4	52.5	13.8	35.6	11.2	27.2
2000	229.7	63.5	24.7	65.4	21.9	35.2	11.7	29.2

B−1−13续表

单位：亿元

年 份	社会服务事业费	抚恤	退役安置	社会福利	社会救助	城市低保及其他城市社会救济	农村低保及其他农村社会救济	医疗救助	自然灾害生活救助	离退休人员经费	其他
“十五”时期	**2471.8**	**479.8**	**302.7**	**444.7**		**668**	**127.6**	**11**	**247.6**	**66.9**	**273.7**
2001	284.8	69.5	31.2	90.6		41.6			41	13	39.5
2002	392.3	74.7	49.5	167.5		108.7			40	13.2	47.3
2003	498.9	87.9	59	78.9	153.1	153.1			52.9	13.1	54
2004	577.4	104.1	74.1	52.1	223.6	172.7	47.7	3.2	51.1	13.9	58.5
2005	718.4	143.6	88.9	55.6	279.6	191.9	79.9	7.8	62.6	13.7	74.4
“十一五”时期	**9156.8**	**1316.2**	**956**	**490**	**3673.6**	**1941.7**	**1710.7**	**436.1**	**1205**	**125.7**	**975.4**
2006	915.4	178.8	115.7	65.3	372	224.2	126.6	21.2	79	14	90.6
2007	1215.5	210.8	165	87.6	509.7	277.4	189.8	42.5	79.8	24.8	137.8
2008	2146.5	253.6	180.6	103.1	806.7	393.4	326.8	86.5	609.8	26.5	166.2
2009	2181.9	310.3	225.7	124.1	1098.1	482.1	487.9	128.1	199.2	30	194.5
2010	2697.5	362.7	269	109.9	1302	564.6	579.6	157.8	237.2	30.4	386.3

年 份	社会服务事业费	抚恤	退役安置	社会福利	社会救助	城乡低保	其他社会救助	医疗救助	自然灾害生活救助	民政管理事务	行政事业单位离退休	其他
“十二五”时期	**20520**	**2887.1**	**2149.2**	**1993.1**	**10349.7**	**7586.3**	**1471.4**	**1292**	**743.7**	**1496.1**	**212.2**	**688.9**
2011	3229.2	428.3	302.3	232.2	1766.3	1327.6	222.4	216.3	128.7	220.8	35.3	115.3
2012	3683.8	517	372.1	319.5	1866.1	1392.3	243.2	230.6	163.4	248.5	39	158.2
2013	4276.5	618.4	435.3	397.6	2172.4	1623.6	291.4	257.4	178.7	296.7	43.6	133.8
2014	4404.1	636.6	456.8	481	2197.5	1592.0	321.5	284.0	124.4	330.5	44.2	133.1
2015	4926.4	686.8	582.7	562.8	2347.4	1650.8	392.9	303.7	148.5	399.6	50.1	148.5
“十三五”时期	**5440.2**	**769.8**	**625.6**	**753.4**	**2492.8**	**1702.4**	**458.0**	**332.3**	**156.1**	**441.7**	**48.4**	**152.2**
2016	5440.2	769.8	625.6	753.4	2492.8	1702.4	458.0	332.3	156.1	441.7	48.4	152.2

B-1-14 中央转移支付社会服务事业费

单位：万元

年份	合计	中央级社会服务事业费	中央专项转移支付	抚恤、退休、救济费	救灾	社会福利救济事业费	其他
1978	11	11					
1979	44	44					
1980	103	103					
“六五”时期	**335594**	**1108**	**334486**	**63306**	**270745**	**220**	**215**
1981	138	138					
1982	74120	78	74042	14247	59795		
1983	74368	163	74205	14205	60000		
1984	78872	286	78586	18586	60000		

年份	合计	中央级社会服务事业费	中央专项转移支付	抚恤	安置	救灾	社会福利救济事业费	其他
1985	108096	443	107653	9698	6570	90950	220	215
“七五”时期	**778310**	**9267**	**769043**	**148718**	**105230**	**512500**		
1986	132802	2526	130276	16396	9285	102000		
1987	133877	2742	131135	21726	19409	90000		
1988	158355	1297	157058	24110	21948	111000		
1989	174374	1185	173189	43206	26483	103500		
1990	178902	1517	177385	43280	28105	106000		
“八五”时期	**1488090**	**15897**	**1472193**	**328272**	**315101**	**828820**		
1991	309432	1792	307640	49010	34210	224420		
1992	209360	3217	206143	52156	40587	113400		
1993	238083	3108	234975	60494	53481	121000		
1994	353831	4077	349754	79084	90670	180000		
1995	377384	3703	373681	87528	96153	190000		
“九五”时期	**2943934**	**104302**	**2839632**	**749824**	**773058**	**1122750**	**190000**	**4000**
1996	426354	6371	419983	102394	102589	215000		
1997	455309	5954	449355	110430	114925	220000		4000
1998	568049	50783	517266	120000	149516	247750		

B-1-14续表

单位：亿元

年 份	合 计	中央级社会服务事业费	中央专项转移支付	抚恤	安置	救灾	低保	临时救助	医疗救助	福利	其他
1999	62.8	1.2	61.6	18.0	17.6	22.0	4.0				
2000	86.6	2.9	83.7	23.7	23.0	22.0	15.0				
“十五”时期	**1004.3**	**11.9**	**992.4**	**212.1**	**217.3**	**170.1**	**373.1**		**12.0**		**7.9**
2001	109.6	1.4	108.2	26.3	28.7	30.2	23.0				
2002	140.2	1.8	138.4	31.6	37.0	24.3	45.5				
2003	213.6	1.8	211.8	37.1	39.2	40.5	92.0		3.0		0.1
2004	227.7	3.9	223.8	40.7	47.4	32.0	100.6		3.0		0.1
2005	313.2	2.9	310.3	76.4	65.0	43.1	112.0		6.0		7.7
“十一五”时期	**4761.3**	**89.3**	**4658.9**	**767.6**	**699.9**	**856.1**	**1941.6**		**319.6**		**74.2**
2006	406.8	2.8	404.0	111.7	73.9	49.4	136.0		14.3		18.7
2007	523.1	5.6	504.4	110.9	117.4	49.9	189.9		36.3		0.1
2008	1207.7	26.6	1181.1	142.1	142.9	478.4	363.1		54.5		0.1
2009	1232.5	5.5	1227.0	187.3	160.2	174.7	620		84.5		0.3
2010	1391.2	48.8	1342.4	215.6	205.5	103.7	632.6		130		55
“十二五”时期	**10189.2**	**61.5**	**10127.7**	**1668.5**	**1390.9**	**489.5**	**5312.0**	**73.0**	**785.6**	**258.0**	**150.2**
2011	1817.4	9.4	1808.0	277.4	206.4	84	1004.7		150	25.2	60.3
2012	1804.6	10	1794.6	333.3	265.4	112.7	870.5		150	42	20.7
2013	2163.5	13.7	2149.8	369.8	277.4	101.9	1168.8		156.7	54.4	20.8
2014	2117.8	12.8	2105.0	338	288.8	96.3	1101.3	32	165	63.4	20.2
2015	2285.9	15.6	2270.3	350	352.9	94.6	1166.7	41	163.9	73	28.2
“十三五”时期	**2500.6**	**16.6**	**2484.0**	**390.9**	**384.7**	**79.1**	**1341.5**	**28.7**	**177.9**	**54.0**	**27.3**
2016	2500.6	16.6	2484.0	390.9	384.7	79.1	1341.5	28.7	177.9	54.0	27.3

B-1-15 彩票公益金支出

单位：亿元

年 份	合计	抚恤	退役安置	社会福利	低保及其他社会救济	医疗救助	自然灾害生活救助	其他
2003								
2004								
2005								
“十一五”时期	**485.3**	**17.6**	**6**	**204.9**	**26.2**	**48.8**		**175.6**
2006	52.6	2.6	1	24.1	3.3			21.6
2007	77.6	3	0.9	35.5	4.3			33.9
2008	119.2	3.7	1.3	44.9	7.2	17.5		38.5
2009	113.4	3.4	1.2	49.3	5.9	15.5		38
2010	122.5	4.9	1.6	51.1	5.5	15.8		43.6
“十二五”时期	**1002.6**	**30.5**	**2.6**	**596.4**	**42.7**	**90.4**	**8.8**	**206.7**
2011	127.9	4.8	0.4	61.4	7.4	16.3	0.8	36.6
2012	159.0	5.4	0.5	92.2	7.3	16.8	1.3	35.6
2013	195.5	7.5	0.6	117.1	8.7	17.5	2.6	41.5
2014	231.3	5.9	0.9	143.6	10.0	19.1	2.2	49.4
2015	288.9	6.9	0.2	182.1	9.3	20.7	1.9	43.6
“十三五”时期	**268.3**	**7.1**	**0.8**	**172.9**	**10.4**	**19.6**	**2.7**	**54.7**
2016	268.3	7.1	0.8	172.9	10.4	19.6	2.7	54.7

B-1-16 中央彩票公益金使用情况

单位：亿元

年 份	合 计	中央级	转移支付						
				养老	残疾人	儿童	社会公益	医疗救助	居家和社区养老服务改革试点
“十五”时期	**14.91**		**14.91**	**0.70**		**2.06**	**0.15**	**12.0**	
2001									
2002									
2003	3.00		3.00					3.0	
2004	5.91		5.91	0.70		2.06	0.15	3.0	
2005	6.00		6.00					6.0	
“十一五”时期	**112.29**	**2.47**	**109.82**	**21.64**		**16.37**	**1.81**	**70.0**	
2006	14.03	0.10	13.93	1.59		3.24	0.10	9.0	
2007	16.98	0.88	16.10	1.53		1.24	0.33	13.0	
2008	28.14	0.10	28.04	4.79		6.67	0.58	16.0	
2009	26.61	0.09	26.52	7.79		2.05	0.68	16.0	
2010	26.53	1.30	25.23	5.94		3.17	0.12	16.0	
“十二五”时期	**220.81**	**8.20**	**212.61**	**75.83**	**25.34**	**22.88**	**8.56**	**80.0**	
2011	30.03	1.30	28.73	7.86		3.48	1.39	16.0	
2012	35.98	2.30	33.68	10.67	0.99	4.35	1.67	16.0	
2013	48.71	1.80	46.91	22.16	1.98	5.08	1.69	16.0	
2014	35.95	1.10	34.85	10.20	2.97	3.97	1.71	16.0	
2015	70.14	1.70	68.44	24.94	19.40	6.00	2.10	16.0	
“十三五”时期	**54.37**	**1.78**	**52.59**	**13.11**	**3.00**	**5.98**	**2.50**	**18.0**	**10.0**
2016	54.37	1.78	52.59	13.11	3.00	5.98	2.50	18.0	10.0

B-1-17 社会服务事业基本建设投资（按投资来源分）

单位：亿元、万平方米

年　份	计划总投资	本年完成投资	国家投资	国内贷款	自　筹	福利彩票公益金	其　他	本年完工项目个数
1989	5.8	2.0	0.7	0.1	0.8		0.2	
1990	6.9	2.4	0.8	0.1	1.0		0.3	
“八五”时期	**63.4**	**27.6**	**10.3**	**1.2**	**13.4**		**2.8**	
1991	7.0	3.0	1.0	0.1	1.5		0.3	
1992	7.3	3.2	1.0	0.1	1.9		0.4	
1993	12.8	5.6	1.4	0.2	3.4		0.7	
1994	15.5	6.2	2.3	0.5	2.9		0.6	
1995	20.9	9.6	4.6	0.3	3.8		0.9	
“九五”时期	**237.9**	**89.8**	**21.3**	**5.9**	**54.3**	**6.8**	**8.3**	**2793**
1996	29.8	10.1	2.1	0.4	6.4		1.1	
1997	35.7	13.8	2.7	0.8	8.6		1.6	
1998	41.0	16.6	2.8	0.8	11.1		1.9	
1999	63.2	24.7	6.0	2.3	14.6	3.5	1.8	1456
2000	68.2	24.7	7.7	1.6	13.6	3.3	1.9	1337
“十五”时期	**376.9**	**151.7**	**47.9**	**8.8**	**78.4**	**21.0**	**16.6**	**22117**
2001	77.5	30.8	10.4	2.2	15.1	3.6	3.1	1360
2002	88.7	30.1	9.5	1.4	15.9	3.3	3.3	3659
2003	87.3	30.0	9.9	1.7	15.1	3.5	3.3	3867
2004	89.7	29.2	8.9	2.4	14.4	4.7	3.5	8982
2005	33.8	31.6	9.1	1.0	17.9	5.8	3.5	4249
“十一五”时期	**485.6**	**487.8**	**210.7**	**12.4**	**148.8**	**96.8**	**82.3**	**62453**
2006	34.8	33.5	9.9	0.9	19.9	8.4	2.5	3626
2007	47.6	47.7	14.5	3.0	26.9	13.0	2.9	2446
2008	63.5	66.6	26.6	1.9	34.6	16.5	3.2	3906
2009	166.5	157.0	70.6	3.7	67.4	26.6	15.3	6457

年　份	本年计划总投资	本年完成投资	国家投资	国内贷款	利用外资	福利彩票公益金	其　他	本年完工项目规模
2010	173.2	183.0	89.1	2.9	0.2	32.3	58.5	46018
“十二五”时期	**1234.7**	**1268.1**	**499.9**	**19.6**	**5.8**	**288.3**	**454.5**	**38309.3**
2011	217.3	218.5	78.5	6.2	0.5	53.4	79.9	4533
2012	222.3	234.7	104.2	3.8	1.1	51	74.6	6095
2013	311.9	292.8	120.1	1.4	1.7	64.7	104.8	15328
2014	266	282.2	104.3	3.5	1.7	57.5	115.3	11355
2015	217.2	239.9	92.8	4.7	0.8	61.7	79.9	1048.4
“十三五”时期	**208.9**	**245.8**	**84.4**	**2.7**	**-**	**68.4**	**90.3**	**1243**
2016	208.9	245.8	84.4	2.7	-	68.4	90.3	1243

注：2015年后，本年完工项目个数指标更改为本年完工项目规模，单位为万平方米。

B-1-18 国家对社会服务事业基本建设投资(按项目分)

单位：亿元

年 份	国家预算内基本建设投资	优抚安置单位	社区服务设施	收养性福利机构	殡仪	救助	其他
1989	0.7						0.7
1990	0.8			0.2	0.1		0.5
“八五”时期	**10.3**	**4.2**		**1.4**	**1.1**	**0.2**	**3.4**
1991	1.0	0.1		0.2	0.1		0.6
1992	1.0			0.2			0.8
1993	1.4			0.2	0.4		0.8
1994	2.3	1.2		0.3	0.3		0.5
1995	4.6	2.9		0.5	0.3	0.2	0.7
“九五”时期	**21.3**	**2.0**	**1.6**	**6.6**	**6.5**		**4.6**
1996	2.1	0.1		0.5	0.5		1.0
1997	2.7			0.7	1.1		0.9
1998	2.8	0.2		1.8	0.8		
1999	6.0	0.9	0.6	1.5	1.7		1.3
2000	7.7	0.8	1.0	2.1	2.4		1.4
“十五”时期	**47.9**	**5.0**	**9.4**	**14.3**	**9.2**		**10.0**
2001	10.4	0.7	1.5	3.1	2.1		3.0
2002	9.5	0.7	2.1	2.8	1.9		2.0
2003	9.9	1.2	2.4	3.3	1.5		1.5
2004	9.0	1.1	2.3	2.5	1.1		2.0
2005	9.1	1.3	1.1	2.6	2.6		1.5
“十一五”时期	**210.8**	**27.8**	**31.5**	**85.2**	**19.2**	**8.1**	**39.0**
2006	9.9	1.8	0.8	3.9	1.4	0.3	1.6
2007	14.5	2.5	0.9	6.5	2.4	0.4	1.8
2008	26.6	8.2	1.9	8.5	3.7	1.1	3.2
2009	70.6	7.4	14.0	30.1	5.7	2.5	11.0
2010	89.2	7.9	13.9	36.2	6.0	3.8	21.4
“十二五”时期	**499.9**	**20.8**	**29.4**	**277.3**	**12.9**	**63.5**	**95.9**
2011	78.5	9.5	11.1	31.1	5.8	3.8	17.2
2012	104.2	11.3	18.3	45.1	7.1	6.1	16.2

年 份	国家预算内基本建设投资	提供住宿的社会服务机构	为老年人与残疾人提供服务的机构	为智障与精神病提供服务的机构	为儿童提供收养救助服务的机构	不提供住宿的社会服务机构	其他
2013	120.1	76.2	66.5	3.2	4.6	22.2	21.7
2014	104.3	66.4	58.1	2.7	4.5	16.2	21.7
2015	92.8	58.5	51.6	2.2	4.0	15.2	19.1
“十三五”时期	**84.4**	**54.0**	**46.7**	**2.3**	**4.1**	**10.0**	**20.4**
2016	84.4	54.0	46.7	2.3	4.1	10.0	20.4

B-1-19 中央预算内

年份	项目合计（个）	投资合计	本级情况				养老	
			本级项目数	本级投资	地方项目小计	补助地方投资小计	项目数	资金额
1990		0.1		0.1				
“八五”时期		**0.2**		**0.2**				
1991		0.2		0.2				
“十五”时期	**24**	**0.8**	**24**	**0.8**				
2001	3	0.3	3	0.3				
2002	10	0.2	10	0.2				
2003	6	0.1	6	0.1				
2004	3	0.1	3	0.1				
2005	2	0.1	2	0.1				
“十一五”时期	**2088**	**35.9**	**18**	**5.5**	**2070**	**30.37**	**189**	**5.0**
2006	2	0.2	2	0.2				
2007	218	2.8	5	0.8	213	2.0		
2008	575	6.8	3	2.1	572	4.7		
2009	774	13.0	4	1.3	770	11.7	63	2.0
2010	519	13.1	4	1.1	515	12.0	126	3
“十二五”时期	**1874**	**143.2**	**51**	**6.9**	**1856**	**136.3**	**1364**	**108.0**
2011	433	26.0	4	0.7	429	25.3	338	9
2012	699	33.3	7	0.31	692	33.0	669	31
2013	742	17.2	7	0.21	735	17.0	357	15

年　份	建设规模	投资合计	本级情况				养老	
			建设规模	本级投资	建设规模	补助地方投资小计	建设规模	资金额
2014	385.5	30.3	7.6	1.3	377.9	29.0	330.0	25.0
2015	368.4	36.4	25.4	4.4	343.0	32.0	302.0	28.0
“十三五”时期	**329.5**	**39.3**	**32.2**	**1.3**	**297.3**	**38.0**	**206.4**	**28.0**
2016	329.5	39.3	32.2	1.3	297.3	38.0	206.4	28.0

基本建设投资情况

单位：亿元、个、万平方米

地方情况									
精神卫生		儿童		流浪		社区		烈建	
项目数	资金额	项目数	资金额	项目数	资金额	项目数	资金额	项目数	资金额
26	**4.4**	**134**	**5.0**	**254**	**5.0**	**1334**	**6.0**	**133**	**5.0**
		15	0.5	28	0.8	170	0.7		
		32	1.3	65	1.4	475	2.0		
		33	1.3	78	1.4	463	2.0	133	5.0
26	4.37	54	1.9	83	1.4	226	1.3		
131	**20.3**		**0.0**		**4.0**	**401**	**4.0**		
91	16.3								
						23	2		
						378	2		

地方情况					
儿童和精神病人		社会事务		社区	
建设规模	资金额	建设规模	资金额	建设规模	资金额
22.3	2.0			25.6	2.0
17.5	2.0			23.5	2.0
44.7	**5.0**	**46.2**	**5.0**		
44.7	5.0	46.2	5.0		

B-2-1 提供住宿的社会服务机构

单位：个

年　份	单位数	老年及残疾人	智障和精神疾病	儿童	其他	#救助管理站	#军供站
1978	8571	8365	139	67			
1979	8988	8801	135	52			
1980	9669	9460	150	59			
1981	10031	9813	155	63			
1982	12275	12046	165	64			
1983	15807	15582	165	60			
1984	22796	22566	167	63			
1985	29100	28852	161	59	28		
1986	35008	34750	166	58	34		
1987	37372	37109	170	60	33		
1988	39030	38767	173	62	28		
1989	39743	39472	180	64	27		
1990	40583	40340	181	62			
1991	42264	42013	188	63			
1992	43319	43063	189	67			
1993	43681	43375	190	67	49		
1994	43240	42911	188	73	68		
1995	43074	42735	190	77	72		
1996	42829	42518	155	84	72		
1997	42385	42027	192	91	75		
1998	42131	41755	195	105	76		
1999	40430	40030	191	110	99		
2000	40491	39321	201	126	843		
2001	38785	38106	200	160	319		
2002	38200	37591	200	178	231		
2003	37294	36224	205	192	1587		
2004	38593	37880	211	208	1320		
2005	42487	40641	226	224	1396		
2006	43187	40964	219	249	1755		
2007	44958	42713	234	269	1742		
2008	41099	38674	244	290	1891		
2009	43944	39671	266	419	3588		
2010	44482	39904	251	480	3847		
2011	45973	42828	251	638	2256	1547	327
2012	48078	44304	257	724	2793	1770	328
2013	45977	42475	261	803	2438	1891	325
2014	36810	33044	254	890	2622	1949	327
2015	31187	27753	242	753	2439	1766	320
2016	31912	28592	244	705	2371	1736	315

B-2-2 提供住宿的社会服务机构床位

单位：万张

年　份	床位数合计	老年及残疾人床位	智障和精神疾病床位	儿童床位	其他床位	#救助管理站	#军供站	每千人口拥有社会服务床位数	每千老年人口拥有养老床位数
1978	16.3	15.7	0.6					0.17	
1979	22.6	20.1	2.1	0.4				0.23	
1980	24.2	21.3	2.4	0.5				0.25	
1981	25.3	22.2	2.5	0.6				0.25	
1982	28.2	24.8	2.8	0.6				0.28	
1983	32.4	29.0	2.8	0.6				0.31	
1984	42.5	39.0	2.9	0.6				0.41	
1985	49.1	45.7	2.9	0.5	0.2			0.46	
1986	58.7	55.0	3.1	0.6	0.3			0.55	
1987	64.9	61.0	3.3	0.6	0.3			0.59	
1988	69.5	65.5	3.4	0.6	0.2			0.63	
1989	73.8	69.5	3.6	0.7	0.2			0.65	
1990	78.0	73.5	3.7	0.8				0.68	
1991	82.8	78.3	3.8	0.7				0.71	
1992	89.8	85.2	3.8	0.8				0.77	
1993	92.7	87.8	4.0	0.9	0.4			0.78	
1994	95.5	90.6	4.0	0.9	0.5			0.80	
1995	97.6	92.5	4.0	1.1	0.6			0.81	
1996	100.8	95.6	4.0	1.2	0.6			0.82	
1997	103.1	97.8	4.0	1.3	0.6			0.83	
1998	105.8	100.2	4.1	1.5	0.6			0.85	
1999	108.9	102.4	4.1	1.6	0.8			0.87	
2000	113.0	104.5	4.1	1.8	2.6			0.89	
2001	140.7	114.6	4.2	2.3	19.6			1.10	
2002	141.5	114.9	4.3	2.5	19.8			1.10	
2003	142.9	120.6	4.5	2.7	15.1			1.11	
2004	157.2	139.5	4.5	3.0	10.2			1.21	
2005	180.7	158.1	4.4	3.2	15.0			1.38	10.97
2006	204.5	179.6	4.4	3.2	17.3			1.56	12.05
2007	269.6	242.9	4.7	3.4	18.6			2.04	15.83
2008	300.3	267.4	5.4	4.3	23.2			2.26	16.72
2009	326.5	293.5	5.9	4.8	22.3			2.45	17.56
2010	349.6	316.1	6.1	5.5	21.9			2.61	17.79
2011	396.4	369.2	6.5	6.8	13.9	7.1	3.8	2.94	19.96
2012	449.3	416.5	6.7	8.7	17.4	9.0	3.8	3.32	21.48
2013	462.4	429.5	7.4	9.8	15.7	9.7	3.7	3.87	24.39
2014	426.0	390.2	8.0	10.8	17.0	9.9	3.7	4.49	27.20
2015	393.2	358.2	7.9	10.0	17.1	10.3	3.8	5.30	30.30
2016	414.0	378.8	8.4	10.0	16.7	10.2	3.7	5.54	31.60

B-2-3 提供住宿的社会服务机构收养人员情况

单位：万人

年 份	总人数	老年及残疾人	智障和精神疾病人	儿童	其他
1978	16.3	14.0	1.9	0.4	
1979	18.6	16.3	1.9	0.4	
1980	19.1	16.7	2.0	0.4	
1981	19.7	17.0	2.2	0.5	
1982	22.5	19.7	2.3	0.5	
1983	25.9	23.0	2.4	0.5	
1984	34.1	31.0	2.6	0.5	
1985	40.8	37.5	2.6	0.5	0.2
1986	47.4	43.9	2.8	0.5	0.2
1987	51.8	48.2	2.9	0.5	0.2
1988	54.8	51.1	3.0	0.6	0.1
1989	56.9	53.0	3.1	0.6	0.2
1990	59.9	56.1	3.2	0.6	
1991	64.6	60.8	3.2	0.6	
1992	69.6	65.6	3.3	0.7	
1993	72.4	68.0	3.4	0.7	0.3
1994	73.6	69.2	3.3	0.8	0.3
1995	74.7	70.1	3.2	1.0	0.4
1996	76.9	72.3	3.1	1.1	0.4
1997	78.5	73.7	3.2	1.2	0.4
1998	80.0	74.9	3.2	1.4	0.5
1999	82.7	77.6	3.2	1.4	0.5
2000	85.4	78.6	3.2	1.8	1.8
2001	88.5	82.0	3.3	2.1	1.1
2002	91.6	85.0	3.4	2.2	1.0
2003	96.5	89.1	3.5	2.5	1.4
2004	110.9	103.9	3.6	2.8	0.6
2005	123.6	116.2	3.7	2.9	0.8
2006	147.0	138.5	3.8	3.2	1.5
2007	200.0	191.3	4.1	3.0	1.6
2008	240.0	211.5	4.5	3.4	20.6
2009	256.0	227.5	5.0	3.7	19.8
2010	278.2	247.0	5.3	4.2	21.7
2011	293.4	279.7	5.5	4.6	3.6
2012	309.5	293.6	5.8	5.4	4.7
2013	322.5	307.4	6.0	5.6	3.5
2014	337.0	320.4	6.5	5.9	4.2
2015	231.7	214.8	6.4	5.6	4.9
2016	236.3	219.8	6.9	5.5	4.2

B-2-4 按城乡分类的提供住宿的社会服务机构情况

年份	单位数（个）	城市	农村	床位数（万张）	城市	农村	收养人数（万人）	城市	农村
1978	8571	728	7843	16.3	0.1	16.2	16.3	5.7	10.6
1979	8988	1518	7470	22.6	6.4	16.2	18.6	8	10.6
1980	9669	1407	8262	24.2	7.1	17.1	19.1	7.9	11.2
1981	10031	1487	8544	25.3	7.4	17.9	19.7	8.2	11.5
1982	12275	1689	10586	28.2	7.6	20.6	22.5	8.7	13.8
1983	15807	1760	14047	32.4	7.7	24.7	25.9	9	16.9
1984	22796	1925	20871	42.5	8.5	34	34.1	10	24.1
1985	29100	5478	23622	49.1	18.2	30.9	40.8	14.6	26.2
1986	35008	8330	26678	58.7	23.6	35.1	47.4	18.9	28.5
1987	37372	9358	28014	64.9	25.8	39.1	51.8	20.5	31.3
1988	39030	10498	28532	69.5	28.4	41.1	54.8	22.3	32.5
1989	39743	10118	29625	73.8	28.7	45.1	56.9	22.3	34.6
1990	40583	12697	27886	78	34.5	43.5	59.9	26.8	33.1
1991	42264	13197	29067	82.8	36.7	46.1	64.6	28.5	36.1
1992	43319	16847	26472	89.8	44.6	45.2	69.6	34.5	35.1
1993	43681	17400	26281	92.7	47	45.7	72.4	37.2	35.2
1994	43240	18035	25205	95.5	50	45.5	73.6	39.1	34.5
年份	单位数（个）	国有社会福利院	社会办敬老院	床位数（万张）	国有社会福利院	社会办敬老院	收养人数（万人）	国有社会福利院	社会办敬老院
1995	43074	11184	31890	97.6	18.6	79	74.7	14.4	60.3
1996	42829	11216	31613	100.8	19.2	81.6	76.9	14.8	62.1
1997	42385	10417	31968	103.1	19.9	83.2	78.5	15.4	63.1
1998	42131	9895	32236	105.8	21	84.8	80	16.1	63.9
1999	40430	3086	37344	108.9	23.6	85.3	82.7	17.9	64.8
年份	单位数（个）	城市	农村	床位数（万张）	城市	农村	收养人数（万人）	城市	农村
2000	40491	14915	25576	113.0	57.4	55.6	85.4	42.6	42.8
2001	38785	12135	26650	140.7	72.3	68.4	88.5	39.6	48.9
2002	38200	12503	25697	141.5	75.3	66.2	91.6	42.2	49.4
2003	37294	12951	24343	142.9	75.3	67.6	96.5	46.1	50.4
2004	38593	12151	26442	157.2	79.7	77.5	110.9	51.5	59.4
2005	42487	12806	29681	180.7	91.2	89.5	123.6	55.7	67.9
2006	43187	11814	31373	204.5	90.9	113.6	147.0	55.0	92.0
2007	44958	10274	34684	269.6	89.8	179.8	200.0	43.9	149.3
2008	41099	10731	30368	300.3	107.2	193.1	240.0	79.5	160.5
2009	43944	12658	31286	326.5	117.7	208.8	256.0	83.0	173.0
2010	44482	13010	31472	349.6	124.7	224.9	278.2	95.7	182.5
2011	45973	13833	32140	396.4	154.5	241.9	293.4	100.9	192.5
2012	48078	15291	32787	449.3	188.3	261	309.5	109.5	200.0
2013	45977	15730	30247	462.4	189.6	272.8	322.5	121.3	201.2
2014	36810	16549	20261	426.0	206.4	219.6	334.0	127.6	155.7
2015	31187	15600	15587	393.2	216.1	177.1	236.3	121.1	115.2
2016	31912	16514	15398	414.0	234.1	179.9	236.3	123.1	113.2

B-2-5 老年人和残疾人福利

单位：万人

年 份	老年福利			残疾人补贴	
	享受高龄补贴的老年人数	享受护理补贴的老年人数	享受养老服务补贴的老年人数	困难残疾人生活补贴人数	重度残疾人护理补贴人数
2004					
2005					
2006	233.5				
2007	247.1				
2008	349.3				
2009	430.9				
2010	576.4				
2011	883.1				
2012	1257.7				
2013	1557.9	11.7	101.9		
2014	1719.6	20.0	154.7		
2015	2155.1	26.5	257.9		
2016	2355.4	40.5	282.9	521.3	500.0

B-2-6 孤儿和收养

单位：件、人

年份	孤儿数	收养登记总数	中国公民收养登记	外国公民收养登记	被收养人合计	福利机构抚养的儿童	被中国公民收养	被外国人收养
1996		18896	14804	4092	20389	2201		
1997		21548	17193	4355	21548	975		
1998		26498	20611	5887	26498	677		
1999		38074	31916	6158	38019	1670	31882	6137
2000		55802	49037	6765	56191	1847	49500	6691
2001		44706	36089	8617	45844	1908	37200	8644
2002		45336	35372	9964	47860	2404	37642	10218
2003		54159	44884	9275	54159	3427	44884	9275
2004		52603	40084	12519	55572	3189	44708	10864
2005		49506	35470	14036	50921	3564	38057	12864
2006		48178	38393	9785	49148	2867	39424	9724
2007		45192	36893	8299	46047	1146	37790	8257
2008	67921	42550	37009	5541	44115	1846	38617	5498
2009	127599	44260	39801	4459	44359	1605	39964	4395
2010	252110	34529	29618	4911	34473	1878	29978	4495
2011	509695	31424	27579	3845	31329	1679	28117	3212
2012	570075	27278	23157	4121	27310	1760	23189	4121
2013	548845	24460	21230	3230	24491	9657	21261	3230
2014	525179	22772	19885	2887	22876	10336	20055	2821
2015	502105	22348	19406	2942	22363	10704	19430	2933
2016	460450	18736	15965	2771	18736	8884	15965	2771

注：2012年以前福利机构抚养的儿童是孤儿，2013年以后含弃婴。

B-2-7 城市社会救济和城市最低生活保障

单位：万人

年份	城市传统救济总人数	城市传统定救人数	城市精简退职老职工人数		
				享受40%人数	定量救济人数
1979	33.6	23.7	9.9		
1980	32.9	22.9	10		
1981	31.5	21.5	10		
1982	34.7	21.4	13.3		
1983	47.1	22.6	24.5		
1984	207.4	160.6	46.8	25.3	
1985	30.0	18.2	11.8	6.4	5.4
1986	49.0	35.6	13.4	7.1	6.3
1987	29.8	16.2	13.6	7.2	6.4
1988	32.9	17.6	15.3	7.7	7.6
1989	30.5	16.2	14.3	7.1	7.2
1990	41.8	16.4	25.4	16.4	9.0
1991	33.7	16.1	17.6	8.5	9.0
1992	39.5	19.2	20.3	9.7	10.6
1993	24.6	13.8	10.8	5	5.8
1994	23.0	12.4	10.6	4.9	5.7
1995	109.0	55.2	53.8	23.9	29.9
1996	120.1	66.5	53.6	23.6	30.0

年份	城市最低生活保障人数	在职人员	下岗人员	退休人员	失业人员	“三无”人员	其他人员
1996	84.9						
1997	87.9						
1998	184.1						
1999	256.9						
2000	402.6						
2001	1170.7						
2002	2064.7	186.8	554.5	90.8	358.3	91.9	783.1
2003	2246.8	179.3	518.4	90.7	409	99.9	949.3
2004	2205	141	468.9	73.1	423.1	95.4	1003.5
2005	2234.2	114.1	430.7	61.3	410.1	95.8	1122.1
2006	2240.1	97.6	350	53.2	420.8	93.1	1225.3

年份	城市最低生活保障人数	残疾人	三无人员	老年人	成年人				未成年人
					在职人员	灵活就业	登记失业	未登记失业	
2007	2272.1	161.0	125.8	298.4	93.9	343.8	627.2	364.3	544.6
2008	2334.8	169.1	106.9	316.7	82.2	381.7	564.3	402.2	587.7
2009	2345.6	181.0	94.1	333.5	79.0	432.2	510.2	410.9	579.8
2010	2310.5	180.7	89.3	338.6	68.2	432.4	492.8	420.0	558.5
2011	2276.8	184.1	80.3	346.9	61.5	429.7	472.5	426.7	539.5
2012	2143.5	174.5	64.9	339.3	49.6	459.3	400.4	422.1	472.8
2013	2064.2	169.2	58.0	330.3	45.1	462.1	365.5	416.8	444.5
2014	1877.0	161.1	50.0	315.8	37.5	425.8	312.5	398.7	386.7
2015	1701.1	165.7	43.8	293.5	31.1	377.3	264.1	394.0	341.0
2016	1480.2	156.5		258.0	22.7	304.4	252.9	370.9	271.4

注：1984年的精简退职老职工人数含农村的数据。

B-2-8 农村社会救济和农村最低生活保障

单位：万人、万户

年份	农村社会救济总人数	农村定期定量救济人数	农村精简退职老职工人数	享受40%人数	定量救济人数
1979	6847.6	*6837.7*	*9.9*		
1980	4651.8	*4641.8*	*10*		
1981	4265.1	*4255.1*	*10*		
1982	4270.7	*4257.4*	*13.3*		
1983	3526.7	*3502.2*	*24.5*		
1984	3842.7	*3795.9*	*46.8*	*25.3*	
1985	116.7	75.1	41.6	18.1	23.5
1986	103	63.1	39.9	18.1	21.7
1987	92.2	53.2	39	17.7	21.3
1988	93	54.1	38.9	17.6	21.4
1989	75.7	35.0	40.7	18.3	22.3
1990	100.2	46.7	53.5	23.6	29.9
1991	97	43.8	53.2	23.5	29.8
1992	97.5	45.6	51.9	23.3	28.6
1993	80.1	36.3	43.8	19.5	24.3
1994	82.1	38.5	43.6	19.2	24.3
1995	98.3	55.2	43.1	19	24.1
1996	109.2	66.5	42.7	18.6	24.1
1997	104.5	51.4	53.1	23.2	29.8
1998	120.5	65.6	54.9	24.9	30
1999	107.1	55.6	51.5	22.5	28.7
2000	112.2	62.5	49.7	22.1	27.6
2001	130.5	80.7	49.8	21.3	27.8
2002	138.7	*90*	48.7	20.9	27.8

年份	农村困难群众救助总人数	农村最低生活保障人数	农村特困户救助人数	农村困难群众救助总户数	农村最低生活保障户数	困难户	其他	农村特困户救助户数	困难户	其他	农村特困供养户数	农村传统救济人数
2001	385.3	304.6	80.7									
2002	497.8	407.8	*90.0*	156.7	156.7							
2003	1160.5	367.1	793.4	632.8	146.5	114.5	32	282.1	192.7	89.3	204.2	
2004	1402.1	488	914.1	780.8	197.9	165.2	33.6	317.1	260.4	56.6	265.8	
2005	1891.8	825	1066.8	1061	356.5	298.8	57.7	354.8	290.4	64.4	349.7	
2006	2987.8	1593.1	775.8	1606.3	777.2			325.8			503.3	115.6

年份	农村救助总人数	农村最低生活保障人数	农村特困人员集中供养人数	农村特困分散供养	传统救济人数
2007	4172.6	3566.3	138.0	393.3	75.0
2008	4926.3	4305.5	155.6	393.0	72.2
2009	5375.6	4760.0	171.8	381.6	62.2
2010	5829.8	5214.0	177.4	378.9	59.5
2011	5925.4	5305.7	184.5	366.5	68.7
2012	5969.7	5344.5	185.3	360.3	79.6
2013	5998.3	5388.0	183.5	353.8	73.0
2014	5810.8	5207.2	174.3	354.8	74.5
2015	5484.1	4903.6	162.3	354.4	63.8
2016	5143.6	4586.5	139.7	357.2	60.2

注：1984年以前含应保未保的农村救济人数。

B-2-9 最低生活保障平均标准和医疗救助

单位：元/人·月、元/人·年、万人次、万人

年 份	城市最低生活保障平均标准	农村最低生活保障平均标准	民政部门资助参加城市医疗保险人数	民政部门资助参加农村合作医疗人数	民政部门直接医疗救助人次数		
						住院救助	门诊救助
2004	152.0			552.6	121.1		
2005	156.0			654.9	199.6		
2006	169.6	850.8		1317.1	201.3		
2007	182.4	840.0		2517.3	819.1		
2008	205.3	987.6	642.6	3432.4	1203.1		
2009	227.8	1210.1	1095.9	4059.1	1140.4		
2010	251.2	1404.0	1461.2	4615.4	1479.3		
2011	287.6	1718.4	1549.8	4825.3	2144		
2012	330.1	2067.8	1387.1	4490.4	2173.7	1141.4	1032.3
2013	373.3	2433.9	1490.1	4868.7	2126.4	1074.0	1052.4
2014	410.5	2776.6	1702.0	5021.7	2395.3	1106.6	1288.7

年 份	城市最低生活保障平均标准	农村最低生活保障平均标准	民政部门资助参加基本医疗保障人数	民政部门直接医疗救助人次		
					住院救助	门诊救助
2015	451.1	3177.6	6213.0	2515.9	1204.3	1311.6
2016	494.6	3744	5560.4	2696.1	1194.9	1501.2

B-2-10 城市生活无着人员救助

年　份	救助站（个）	未成年人救助保护中心（个）	生活无着人员救助总数（人次）	# 未成年人救助总数	救助类单位床位总数（张）	# 未成年人救助保护中心床位
1978	783					
1979	845					
1980	665					
1981	598					
1982	610					
1983	615					
1984	628					
1985	636					
1986	647					
1987	639					
1988	644					
1989	669					
1990	666					
1991	691					
1992	692					
1993	719					
1994	712					
1995	722					
1996	720					
1997	728					
1998	742					
1999	800					
2000	857					
2001	838					
2002	861					
2003	864		634528	60257		
2004	977		820254	104455	47086	
2005	1079	40	1196305	120487	45603	1849
2006	1189	50	1295506	129337	45661	1133
2007	1261	90	1544492	159989	46800	3621
2008	1334	88	1573484	155794	50642	3543
2009	1372	116	1680532	167283	51049	3670
2010	1448	145	1719008	146329	55562	5221
2011	1547	241	2409701	178705	71109	8165
2012	1770	261	2765761	152070	99901	10038
2013	1891	274	3484727	183802	108360	11499
2014	1949	345	3474544	128033	110806	11584
2015	1766	275	3752106	166723	113402	10682
2016	1736	240	3338221	167029	112944	10473

B-2-11 社会捐赠

单位：亿元、亿件

年 份	社会捐赠款物合计	社会捐赠款	民政部门	各类社会组织	社会捐赠其他物资折款	接收社会捐赠衣被数量
1997	14.0	4.2			9.9	0.9
1998	113.2	50.2	50.2		63.0	2.9
1999	17.8	6.9	5.0	2.0	10.8	0.6
2000	16.3	9.3	5.4	3.9	7.0	0.8
2001	20.0	11.7	7.6	4.1	8.3	1.3
2002	20.8	19.0	11.1	7.9	1.8	2.3
2003	43.4	41.0	29.2	11.9	2.4	2.0
2004	35.1	34.0	17.1	16.9	1.2	0.9
2005	61.9	60.3	31.3	29.0	1.6	1.0
2006	89.5	83.1	43.0	40.1	6.4	0.7
2007	148.3	132.8	50.9	81.9	15.6	0.9
2008	764.1	744.5	479.3	265.2	19.6	11.6
2009	485.9	483.7	66.5	417.2	2.2	1.2
2010	601.7	596.8	179.8	417.0	4.9	0.3
2011	494.9	490.1	96.6	393.5	4.8	0.3
2012	578.8	572.5	101.7	470.8	6.3	1.3
2013	575.1	566.4	107.6	458.8	8.7	1.0
2014	612.4	604.4	79.6	524.9	8.0	0.5
2015	659.7	654.5	44.2	610.3	5.2	0.5
2016	834.4	827.0	40.3	786.7	7.4	0.7

B-2-12 中国福利彩票销售

年 份	福利彩票发行单位（个）	福利彩票销售额（亿元）	提取公益金（亿元）	公益金支出（亿元）
“六五”时期				
1981				
1982				
1983				
1984				
1985				
“七五”时期		**14.2**	**4.6**	
1986				
1987		0.2	0.1	
1988		3.8	1.2	
1989		3.8	1.3	
1990		6.5	2.0	
“八五”时期		**115.2**	**34.3**	
1991		7.7	2.5	
1992		13.8	4.1	
1993		18.4	5.5	
1994		18.0	5.3	
1995		57.3	16.9	
“九五”时期		**358.7**	**103.5**	**72.7**
1996		64.8	19.1	
1997		36.4	10.1	
1998		63.2	19.6	14.1
1999	1169	104.4	30.5	19.9
2000	1253	89.9	24.2	38.7
“十五”时期		**1145.2**	**377.1**	**161.9**
2001	1185	139.6	41.9	19.7
2002	1121	168.0	52.3	25.5
2003	1145	200.1	67.2	30.6
2004	1128	226.4	79.4	33.8
2005	1113	411.2	136.3	52.3
“十一五”时期		**3455.3**	**1127.4**	**484.0**
2006	989	495.7	168.8	52.6
2007	985	631.6	211.0	77.6
2008	999	604.0	205.4	119.2
2009	988	756.0	243.4	113.4
2010	993	968.0	298.8	121.2
“十二五”时期		**8628.7**	**2491.6**	**1002.6**
2011	974	1278.0	382.0	127.9
2012	955	1510.3	449.4	159
2013	940	1765.3	510.7	195.5
2014	893	2060.0	585.7	231.3
2015	861	2015.1	563.8	288.9
“十三五”时期		**2064.9**	**591.5**	**268.3**
2016	788	2064.9	591.5	268.3

B-2-13 定期抚恤优抚对象

单位：人

年份	抚恤补助总人数（万人）	定期抚恤人数	烈属	牺牲、病故军人家属	伤残人员（万人）
1978	205.9				73.4
1979	173.6				75.6
1980	222.4				78.6
1981	233.6				79.6
1982	240.8	590104	541516	48588	81.6
1983	251.2	577791	526826	50965	83.0
1984	267.3	585403	536523	48880	84.4
1985	283.3	518566	440000	78566	85.3
1986	339.8	533245	446209	87036	86.5
1987	366.3	548063	453480	94583	88.0
1988	378.5	537472	429271	108201	88.7
1989	411.7	525134	422656	102478	89.1
1990	425.7	516638	407276	109362	87.4
1991	434.8	614945	504462	110483	87.5
1992	433.7	602163	492457	109706	87.6
1993	441.2	495994	383924	112070	88.3
1994	442.0	487256	372850	114406	88.5
1995	448.8	486250	370685	115565	88.8
1996	447.0	484270	366216	118054	89.3
1997	448.3	480464	362086	118378	89.5
1998	447.0	473901	357492	116409	89.2
1999	445.1	458079	336587	121492	88.7
2000	442.4	448276	325116	123160	88.1

年份	抚恤补助总人数（万人）	定期抚恤人数	烈属	牺牲军人家属	病故军人家属	伤残人员（万人）
2001	450.7	480852	348521	60081	72250	85.5
2002	459.0	480466	341109	63953	75404	85.8
2003	464.9	488820	345141	65303	78376	86.0
2004	462.0	485733	339817	65695	80221	85.6
2005	460.3	492517	349253	63603	79661	84.5
2006	462.6	491320	346089	64248	80983	86.0
2007	622.4	488675	342101	64478	82096	86.5
2008	633.2	478880	332390	65001	81489	87.2
2009	630.7	458578	317675	62304	78599	87.2
2010	625.0	447824	307587	62338	77899	86.7
2011	852.5	422439	286449	60534	75456	85.9
2012	944.4	411711	277712	59478	74521	84.9
2013	950.5	366400	240375	55734	70291	81.2
2014	917.3	311210	197955	48179	65076	76.6
2015	897.0	264975	160948	43711	60316	73.7
2016	874.8	219574	124950	38725	55899	71.5

B-2-14 定期补助优抚对象

单位：人

年份	定期补助总人数	红军老战士合计	在乡红军老战士	西路军	红军失散人员	在乡复员军人	带病回乡退伍军人	60岁及以上农村籍退伍军人	其他
1978	9251	9251	9251						
1979	7872	7872	7872						
1980	6922	6922	6922						
1981	6567	6567	6567						
1982	1002181	6383	6383			859055	136743		
1983	1104586	6142	6142			952993	145451		
1984	1243633	6159	6159			1081350	156124		
1985	1461180	6329	6329			1185502	183129		86220
1986	1999872	6315	6315			1673990	210445		109122
1987	2230873	7466	7466			1833402	241290		148715
1988	2360462	7415	7415			1950641	247009		155397
1989	2715258	6628	6628			2272639	283075		152916
1990	2866579	7514	7514			2373873	305045		180147
1991	2939074	7015	7015			2419453	346021		166585
1992	2975175	6599	6599			2402869	373989		191718
1993	2947209	113728	5531	2997	105200	2424984	408497		
1994	2963965	112054	5058	2430	104566	2424435	427476		
1995	2987751	108484	4659	2318	101507	2423191	456076		
1996	3018047	115317	4480	2303	108534	2421517	481213		
1997	3037367	122115	4195	2214	115706	2396017	519235		
1998	3033826	118245	3996	2157	112092	2367266	548315		
1999	3056727	111096	3687	2106	105303	2363466	582165		
2000	3057257	105632	3326	1997	100309	2320739	630886		
2001	3170877	98345	3325	1889	93131	2246954	782802		42776
2002	3251971	94848	3136	1691	90021	2274657	882090		376
2003	3300232	90767	2893	1610	86264	2262264	919349		27852
2004	3277914	87521	2701	1454	83366	2214467	950428		25498
2005	3265797	79639	2681	1370	75588	2145421	977424		63313
2006	3274059	71707	2417	1220	68070	2064713	1072684		64955
2007	4870800	66220	2049	966	63205	1988977	1134414		1681189
2008	4981893	49198	1622	440	47136	1920235	1193622		1818838
2009	4976839	42945	1351	322	41272	1809019	1219752		1905123
2010	4935399	38630	1226	273	37131	1703396	1265664		1927709
2011	7243706	30309	911	190	29208	1587006	1321786	2373772	1930833
2012	8183693	26882	757	164	25961	1474790	1324325	3210986	2146710
2013	8326336	19740	647	117	18976	1260945	1306479	3566766	2172406
2014	8095950	11697	341	87	11269	993204	1242020	3748039	2100990
2015	7968445	3949	177	64	3708	792440	1183750	3924604	2063702
2016	7813467	2165	55	50	2060	636698	1127704	4055748	1991152

B-2-15 接收军队离退休、退职人员

单位：人

年　份	合　计	军队离退休干部	地方(含军队职工)人员
1980			
1981			
1982	21993	801	21192
1983	20038	1507	18531

年　份	合　计	军队离退休干部	#离　休	地方人员	军队职工
1984	9916	1873	117	6228	1815
1985	12429	6137	3327	4472	1820
1986	29260	21564	15598	4236	3460
1987	14146	10035	6224	1719	2392
1988	6050	4242	2329	1287	521
1989	4858	3441	1530	994	423
1990	6214	4988	2573	1008	218
1991	6558	5568	2703	806	184
1992	4420	3551	1516	693	176
1993	5578	916	283	543	4318
1994	5773	1016	447	566	4190
1995	3531	1056	323	476	1999
1996	9346	3210	371	282	5854
1997	6311	3246	401	230	2835
1998	8156	5868	785	691	1597

年　份	合　计	军队离退休干部	地方离退休干部	军队无军籍职工
1999	12380	9464	305	2611
2000	15238	10197	219	4822
2001	13738	6236	373	7129

年　份	合　计	军队离退休干部(含地方)	#离　休	军队退休士官	军队无军籍职工
2002	14428	3640		161	10627
2003	11057	5055	143	140	6312
2004	10794	8884	200	90	1820

年　份	合　计	军队离退休干部	#离　休	地方离退休干部	#离　休	军队退休士官	军队无军籍职工
2005	18512	17280	223	136	14	192	904
2006	31968	20794	259	673	85	365	10136
2007	28058	18534	258	303	23	160	9061
2008	21378	15829	78	205	15	297	5047
2009	18904	13836	143	348	5	1308	3412
2010	13451	11775	148	183	4	1112	381
2011	14530	12355	140	141	8	1405	629
2012	18570	14341	416	335	45	1047	2847
2013	38762	10927	108	500	29	570	26709
2014	27699	10067	246	221	9	503	16908
2015	19429	9102	600	409	81	410	9508
2016	11053	8080	209	549	49	465	1959

B-2-16 烈士褒扬和优待

年份	烈士纪念建筑物管理机构（个）	本年新增享受烈士待遇的人数（人）	零散烈士纪念设施（个）	优待优抚对象户数（户）	#优待军属户数	优待总金额（万元）	#固定优待军属总额
1978			5347				
1979			3779			20393	
1980			2825			31459	
1981			2915			47255	
1982	965	8601	3592	4730756		58750	
1983	928	11024	3826	4387292		59588	
1984	786	8478	3953	4102419		62263	
1985	579	5887	3716	3567165	2884906	71655	577018
1986	582	11758	3871	3355694	2710272	75243	62205
1987	587	10644	4121	3223550	2562036	80915	66321
1988	632	9035	4236	3225253	2477699	87160	71735
1989	637	3960	4466	3086285	2423418	92169	77764
1990	632	3067	6065	2941486	2522476	99535	86739
1991	630	1556	6474	2967881	2540714	106354	93069
1992	684	1338	6957	2967002	2535037	116573	102008
1993	696	1467	6956	3009163	2470099	131555	113330
1994	718	1215	7279	3027420	2462671	155627	133070
1995	715	1277	7067	3051322	2476261	194379	166414
1996	740	1187	7020	3040439	2449077	251798	217527
1997	737	888	7048	3334000	2427586	321741	261865
1998	752	749	7322	3250395	2415838	356413	292305
1999	774	616	7252	3818210	2380675	402998	305386
2000	795	468	7427	3855797	2282584	469054	363675
2001	845	460	7802	3973085	2086464	385859	275456
2002	873	403	8051	4130817	1929011	374819	251854
2003	918	461	7781	3962425	1672205	391581	239410
2004	938	316	7425	3632630	1430630	418499	267458
2005	989	314	7483	3393218	1224036	379631	213968
2006	1072	265	7414	3220933	1183674	421010	224354
2007	1056	168	7186	3277318	1145223	454090	233479
2008	1133	297	7569	3301682	1108878	666011	267750
2009	1137	213	7622	3280522	1190816	751065	297448
2010	1195	173	9729	3308766	1169833	671536	340382
2011	1227	233	12378	3330859	1050918	968175	555402
2012	1306	172	13151	3471611	1008477	1121135	520520
2013	1463	200	13601	3402629	958255	1351368	646023
2014	1516	267	11365	3354536	883066	1510252	693201
2015	1464	341	11838	3170333	858330	1929548	766241
2016	1109	150	11815	3043916	826332	1713322	841350

注：2011年由于部分省份指标理解错误，数据有调整。

B-2-17 自然灾害情况

年　份	受灾人口（万人次）	因灾死亡人口（含失踪）（人）	紧急转移人口（万人）	直接经济损失（亿元）	倒塌房屋（万间）	农作物受灾面积（万公顷）
1978		4965			73.1	4844
1979		6962			152.1	3937
1980		6821			137.3	5003
1981	26710.0	7422			261.5	3979
1982	22900.7	7935			320.3	3313
1983	22439.0	10952		260.9	345.4	3471
1984	20894.0	6927			274.7	3189
1985	26446.0	4394	290.5	410.4	224.9	4437
1986	29928.0	5410	345.8		209.7	4714
1987	23512.0	5495	348.0	326.3	180.0	4207
1988	36169.0	7306	582.9		258.0	5087
1989	34569.0	5952	365.3	525.0	194.1	4699
1990	29348.0	7338	579.2	616.0	247.4	3847
1991	41941.0	7315	1308.5	1215.1	581.5	5547
1992	37174.0	5741	303.6	853.9	196.6	5133
1993	37541.0	6125	307.7	933.2	271.6	4867
1994	43799.0	8549	1054.0	1876.0	512.1	5504
1995	24215.0	5561	1064.0	1863.0	439.3	4587
1996	32305.0	7273	1216.0	2882.0	809.0	5975
1997	47886.0	3212	511.3	1975.0	288.0	5343
1998	35216.0	5511	2082.4	3007.4	821.4	2229
1999	35319.0	2966	664.8	1962.4	174.5	4998
2000	45652.3	3014	467.1	2045.3	147.3	5469
2001	37255.9	2583	211.1	1942.0	92.2	5215
2002	37841.8	2840	471.8	1717.4	175.7	4711.9
2003	49745.9	2259	707.3	1884.2	343.0	5438.6
2004	33920.6	2250	563.2	1602.3	155.0	3710.6
2005	40653.7	2475	1570.3	2042.1	226.4	3881.8
2006	43453.3	3186	1384.5	2528.1	193.3	4109.1
2007	39777.9	2325	1499.1	2363.0	146.7	4899.3
2008	47795.0	88928	2682.2	11752.4	1097.7	3999.0
2009	47933.5	1528	709.9	2523.7	83.8	4721.4
2010	42610.2	7844	1858.4	5339.9	273.3	3742.6
2011	43290.0	1126	939.4	3096.4	93.5	3247.1
2012	29421.7	1530	1109.6	4185.5	90.6	2496.2
2013	38818.7	2284	1215.0	5808.4	87.5	3135.0
2014	24353.7	1818	601.7	3373.8	45.0	2489.1
2015	18620.3	967	644.4	2704.1	24.8	2176.9
2016	18911.7	1706	910.1	5032.9	52.1	2622.1

B-2-18 社区服务机构和设施

单位：个

年份	城乡各类社区服务机构和设施合计	社区服务中心	其他社区服务机构	便民利民网点
1988	69699		69699	
1989	71357		71357	
1990	84757		84757	
1991	89918		89918	
1992	112171		112171	
1993	92946	3711	89235	169503
1994	98679	4034	94645	204229
1995	115175	4380	110795	234024
1996	132309	5055	127254	259201
1997	138366	5113	133253	307226
1998	154196	6154	148042	345075
1999	164962	7623	157339	405740
2000	187888	6444	181444	451567
2001	201758	6179	195579	539544
2002	206743	7898	198845	622986
2003	203945	7520	196425	668418
2004	205926	7804	198122	703760
2005	203275	8479	194796	664764
2006	160007	8565	151442	457896

年份	城乡各类社区服务机构和设施合计	社区指导中心	社区服务中心	社区服务站	其他社区服务机构	便民利民网点
2007	134852		9319	50116	75417	892656
2008	146322		9873	30021	106428	748684
2009	146341		10003	53170	83168	692625
2010	152941		12720	44237	95984	539136
2011	160352		14391	56156	89805	452868
2012	200162	809	15497	87931	95925	397222
2013	251939	890	19014	108377	123658	358518

年份	城乡各类社区服务机构和设施合计	社区指导中心	社区服务中心	社区服务站	社区养老机构和设施	互助型养老设施
2014	310652	918	23088	120188	18927	40357
2015	360956	863	24138	128083	26067	62027
2016	386186	809	23493	137533	34924	76374

B-3-1 社会组织

单位：个

年份	社会组织合计	社会团体	基金会	民办非企业
1978				
1979				
1980				
1981				
1982				
1983				
1984				
1985				
1986				
1987				
1988	4446	4446		
1989	4544	4544		
1990	10855	10855		
1991	82814	82814		
1992	154502	154502		
1993	167506	167506		
1994	174060	174060		
1995	180583	180583		
1996	184821	184821		
1997	181318	181318		
1998	165600	165600		
1999	142665	136764		5901
2000	153322	130668		22654
2001	210939	128805		82134
2002	244509	133297		111212
2003	266612	141167	954	124491
2004	289432	153359	892	135181
2005	319762	171150	975	147637
2006	354393	191946	1144	161303
2007	386916	211661	1340	173915
2008	413660	229681	1597	182382
2009	431069	238747	1843	190479
2010	445631	245256	2200	198175
2011	461971	254969	2614	204388
2012	499268	271131	3029	225108
2013	547245	289026	3549	254670
2014	606048	309736	4117	292195
2015	662425	328500	4784	329141
2016	702405	335932	5559	360914

注：2001年以前的基金会含在社会团体内。

B-3-2 自治组织

年　份	自治组织合计（万个）	居民委员会（个）	居民小组（万个）	居民委员会成员（万人）	村民委员会（万个）	村民小组（万个）	村民委员会成员（万人）
1978							
1979		46810					
1980							
1981		57169					
1982							
1983	37.7	65519			31.2		
1984	100.3	75609			92.7		
1985	103.0	80943		34.9	94.9		379.6
1986	95.3	86824		36.2	86.6		365.9
1987	93.2	86799		37.0	84.5		359.9
1988	97.8	95684		36.1	88.3		366.6
1989	102.8	93691		36.6	93.4		379.4
1990	110.0	98814		43.1	100.1		409.4
1991	111.9	100347		44.1	101.9		424.4
1992	110.8	104136		46.5	100.4		430.9
1993	112.0	107173		47.9	101.3		456.0
1994	111.7	110112		48.0	100.7		458.5
1995	104.4	111860		48.0	93.2		400.5
1996	104.2	113690		49.3	92.8		397.5
1997	102.4	117915	108.3	49.8	90.6	535.8	378.8
1998	95.2	119042	117.2	50.8	83.3	537.1	358.6
1999	91.6	114815	124.7	50.1	80.1	555.7	351.3
2000	84.0	108424	127.2	48.4	73.2	553.4	315.0
2001	79.2	91893	125.9	46.4	70.0	541.9	316.4
2002	76.7	86087	124.4	39.6	68.1	528.6	294.2
2003	74.1	77431	122.2	39.7	66.3	519.2	319.1
2004	72.2	77884	129.6	42.5	64.4	507.9	292.1
2005	70.9	79947	123.3	45.4	62.9	490.5	265.7
2006	70.4	80717	123.5	44.3	62.4	453.3	243.0
2007	69.5	82006	122.3	41.6	61.3	466.9	241.1
2008	68.8	83413	128.7	42.2	60.4	480.9	233.9
2009	68.4	84689	129.5	43.1	59.9	480.5	234.0
2010	68.2	87057	130.7	43.9	59.5	479.1	233.4
2011	67.9	89480	134.0	45.4	59.0	476.4	231.9
2012	68.0	91153	133.5	46.9	58.8	469.4	232.3
2013	68.3	94620	135.7	48.4	58.9	466.4	232.3
2014	68.2	96693	135.8	49.7	58.5	470.4	230.5
2015	68.1	96679	134.7	51.2	58.1	469.2	229.7
2016	66.2	103292	142.0	54.0	55.9	447.8	225.3

B-3-3 结婚

年 份	结婚登记总数（万对）	内地居民登记结婚数（万对）	涉外华侨港澳台登记结婚数（万对）	结婚登记人数（万人）
1978	597.8	597.8		
1979	637.1	636.3	0.8	
1980	720.9	719.8	1.1	
1981	1041.7	1040.3	1.4	
1982	836.9	835.5	1.4	
1983	765.4	764.2	1.3	
1984	784.8	783.4	1.4	
1985	831.3	829.1	2.2	
1986	884.0	882.3	1.7	
1987	926.7	924.7	2.0	
1988	899.2	897.2	2.0	
1989	937.2	935.2	2.0	
1990	951.1	948.7	2.4	
1991	953.6	951.0	2.6	
1992	957.5	954.5	3.0	
1993	915.4	912.2	3.3	
1994	932.4	929.0	3.4	
1995	934.1	929.7	4.4	
1996	938.7	934.0	4.7	1877.4
1997	914.1	909.1	5.1	1828.3
1998	891.7	886.7	5.0	1783.4
1999	885.3	879.9	5.4	1770.6
2000	848.5	842.0	6.5	1697.0
2001	805.0	797.1	7.9	1610.0
2002	786	778.8	7.3	1572.0
2003	811.4	803.5	7.8	1622.8
2004	867.2	860.8	6.4	1734.4
2005	823.1	816.6	6.4	1646.2
2006	945	938.2	6.8	1890.0
2007	991.4	986.3	5.1	1982.8
2008	1098.3	1093.2	5.1	2196.6
2009	1212.4	1207.5	4.9	2424.8
2010	1241	1236.1	4.9	2482.0
2011	1302.4	1297.5	4.9	2604.8
2012	1323.6	1318.3	5.3	2647.2
2013	1346.9	1341.4	5.5	2693.8
2014	1306.7	1302.0	4.7	2613.5
2015	1224.7	1220.6	4.1	2449.4
2016	1142.8	1138.6	4.2	2285.6

结婚率计算方法：

$$\text{结婚率}=\frac{\text{登记结婚人数}}{\text{（当年期初人口数+当年期末人口数）}/2}\times 1000‰$$

登记

初婚人数（万人）	再婚人数（万人）	#女（万人）	#恢复结婚（对）	结婚率（‰）
				6.2
				6.7
				7.3
				10.4
				8.3
				7.5
				7.5
				7.9
				8.2
				8.6
				8.3
				8.4
				8.2
				8.3
				8.3
				7.8
				7.8
				7.7
1781.7	86.2	41.1	48044	7.7
1726.0	92.2	46.3	62752	7.4
1675.4	97.9	49.8	69160	7.2
1659.4	100.5	50.0	57815	7.1
1581.4	102.6	50.8	56324	6.7
1481.7	112.5	58.0	63442	6.3
1440.3	117.2	60.2	68081	6.1
1483.9	123.3	60.7	68204	6.3
1569.6	152.0	77.1	84799	6.7
1483.0	163.1	74.3	115003	6.3
1705.6	184.4	86.7	107113	7.2
1779.7	203.1	97.3	138967	7.5
1972.5	224.1	108.0	162244	8.3
2168.8	256.0	124.7	181162	9.1
2200.9	281.1	138.8	190356	9.3
2309.9	294.9	146.5	209781	9.7
2361.2	286.0	145.8	229607	9.8
2386.0	307.9	156.5	298766	9.9
2286.8	326.7	168.7	348285	9.6
2109.0	340.4	177.2	398527	9.0
1913.3	372.4	195.0	473905	8.3

B-3-4 离婚登记

年 份	离婚总数（万对）	民政部门登记离婚数（万对）	内地居民登记离婚数（万对）	涉外华侨港澳台登记离婚数（对）	法院部门判决、调解离婚数（万件）	离婚率（‰）
1978	28.5	17.0	17		11.5	0.18
1979	31.9	19.3	19.3	82	12.6	0.33
1980	34.1	18.0	18	330	16.1	0.35
1981	38.9	18.7	18.7	46	20.2	0.39
1982	42.8	21.1	21.1	116	21.7	0.42
1983	41.8	19.7	19.7	126	22.1	0.42
1984	45.4	19.9	19.9	110	25.5	0.40
1985	45.8	19.6	19.6	108	26.2	0.44
1986	50.6	21.4	21.4	205	29.2	0.47
1987	58.1	23.6	23.6	220	34.5	0.55
1988	65.5	26.4	26.4	310	39.1	0.60
1989	75.3	28.8	28.7	518	46.5	0.68
1990	80.0	30.1	30	602	49.9	0.69
1991	83.1	30.1	30	588	53	0.72
1992	85.0	31.6	31.5	833	53.4	0.74
1993	91.0	33.6	33.5	968	57.4	0.77
1994	98.2	35.5	35.4	737	62.7	0.82
1995	105.6	36.8	36.7	813	68.8	0.88
1996	113.4	39.4	39.3	1175	74	0.93
1997	119.9	44.0	43.9	1385	75.9	0.97
1998	119.2	46.6	46.5	948	72.6	0.96
1999	120.2	47.8	47.7	975	72.4	0.96
2000	121.3	48.9	48.8	1075	72.4	0.96
2001	125.0	52.8	52.5	2856	72.2	0.98
2002	117.7	57.3	56.8	5221	60.4	0.90
2003	133.0	69	68.7	3333	64	1.05
2004	166.5	104.6	104.0	5830	61.9	1.28
2005	178.5	118.4	117.5	8267	60.1	1.37
2006	191.3	129.1	128.3	8414	62.2	1.46
2007	209.8	145.7	144.8	8852	64.1	1.59
2008	226.9	161.0	160.0	9470	65.9	1.71
2009	246.8	180.2	179.6	5608	66.6	1.85
2010	267.8	201.0	200.4	5783	66.8	2.00
2011	287.4	220.7	220.2	5761	66.7	2.13
2012	310.4	242.3	241.7	6161	68.1	2.29
2013	350.0	281.5	280.9	6538	68.5	2.58
2014	363.9	295.7	295.1	6714	67.9	2.67
2015	384.3	314.9	314.3	6237	69.3	2.79
2016	415.8	348.6	348.0	6315	67.2	3.01

离婚率计算方法：

$$离婚率=\frac{离婚人数}{（当年期初人口数+当年期末人口数）/2}\times 1000‰$$

B-3-5 殡葬服务

年　份	殡仪馆（个）	公墓（个）	殡葬管理机构（个）	火化炉数（台）	火化遗体数（万具）	火化率（%）
1978				1712	117.5	
1979				2300	102.1	
1980				2510	98.7	
1981				2586	85.4	
1982				2622	96.2	
1983				2622	108.0	
1984				2686	128.2	
1985	9	24	122	2729	155.2	
1986	5	25	143	2745	155.5	26.2
1987	6	29	195	2752	162.0	27.0
1988	14	37	219	2729	180.9	29.5
1989	17	50	217	2768	182.3	30.1
1990	1260	73	211	2795	201.3	31.5
1991	1283	84	234	2714	215.6	34.0
1992	1288	88	228	2852	242.6	31.2
1993	1264	136	296	2891	247.6	31.6
1994	1272	163	284	2882	257.1	33.4
1995	1281	209	302	2927	262.7	33.2
1996	1283	256	313	3005	282.7	35.2
1997	1289	359	340	2959	295.0	36.8
1998	1310	425	374	3157	319.7	39.6
1999	1318	624	402	3340	336.4	41.5
2000	1363	692	466	3565	373.7	46.0
2001	1415	757	540	4299	386.7	47.3
2002	1486	854	542	3945	415.2	50.6
2003	1515	855	599	4159	434.9	52.7
2004	1549	937	633	4792	436.9	52.5
2005	1594	1009	681	5037	450.2	53.0
2006	1635	1109	805	5649	430.2	48.2
2007	1708	1162	799	4838	442.1	48.4
2008	1692	1209	853	4789	453.4	48.5
2009	1729	1266	901	5123	454.2	48.2
2010	1724	1308	919	5229	474.1	49.0
2011	1745	1406	952	5209	468.1	48.8
2012	1782	1597	978	5539	477.7	49.5
2013	1784	1535	1063	5743	468.9	48.2
2014	1801	1617	1141	5908	459.3	47.0
2015	1821	1582	1127	6063	459.5	47.1
2016	1775	1386	1005	6206	471.8	48.3

注：斜体下划线数据经过修正。1989年以前部分数据统计不完全。

05

社会服务当年分省统计资料

2017

C-1-1 省级行政区划

地 区	面积（万平方千米）	省级合计（个）	直辖市	省	自治区	特别行政区
全 国	**960**	**34**	**4**	**23**	**5**	**2**
北 京	1.68	1	1			
天 津	1.1	1	1			
河 北	19	1		1		
山 西	15	1		1		
内蒙古	110	1			1	
辽 宁	15	1		1		
吉 林	18	1		1		
黑龙江	46	1		1		
上 海	0.58	1	1			
江 苏	10	1		1		
浙 江	10	1		1		
安 徽	13	1		1		
福 建	12	1		1		
江 西	16	1		1		
山 东	15	1		1		
河 南	16	1		1		
湖 北	18	1		1		
湖 南	21	1		1		
广 东	18	1		1		
广 西	23	1			1	
海 南	3.4	1		1		
重 庆	8.23	1	1			
四 川	48	1		1		
贵 州	17	1		1		
云 南	38	1		1		
西 藏	120	1			1	
陕 西	19	1		1		
甘 肃	39	1		1		
青 海	72	1		1		
宁 夏	6.6	1			1	
新 疆	160	1			1	
香 港		1				1
澳 门		1				1
台 湾		1		1		

C-1-2 地级与县级行政区划

单位：个

地 区	地级合计	地级市	地区	自治州	盟	县级合计	市辖区	县级市	县	自治县	旗	自治旗	特区	林区
全 国	**334**	**293**	**8**	**30**	**3**	**2851**	**954**	**360**	**1366**	**117**	**49**	**3**	**1**	**1**
北 京						16	16							
天 津						16	16							
河 北	11	11				168	47	19	96	6				
山 西	11	11				119	23	11	85					
内蒙古	12	9			3	103	23	11	17		49	3		
辽 宁	14	14				100	59	16	17	8				
吉 林	9	8		1		60	21	20	16	3				
黑龙江	13	12	1			128	65	19	43	1				
上 海						16	16							
江 苏	13	13				96	55	21	20					
浙 江	11	11				89	36	19	33	1				
安 徽	16	16				105	44	6	55					
福 建	9	9				85	28	13	44					
江 西	11	11				100	24	11	65					
山 东	17	17				137	54	27	56					
河 南	17	17				158	52	21	85					
湖 北	13	12		1		103	39	24	37	2				1
湖 南	14	13		1		122	35	16	64	7				
广 东	21	21				121	64	20	34	3				
广 西	14	14				111	40	7	52	12				
海 南	4	4				23	8	5	4	6				
重 庆						38	26		8	4				
四 川	21	18		3		183	52	16	111	4				
贵 州	9	6		3		88	15	7	54	11			1	
云 南	16	8		8		129	16	15	69	29				
西 藏	7	5	2			74	6		68					
陕 西	10	10				107	29	3	75					
甘 肃	14	12		2		86	17	4	58	7				
青 海	8	2		6		43	6	3	27	7				
宁 夏	5	5				22	9	2	11					
新 疆	14	4	5	5		105	13	24	62	6				

C-1-3 乡镇级行政区划

单位：个

地 区	乡镇级合计	镇	乡	#民族乡	街道办事处	区公所
全 国	**39862**	**20883**	**10872**	**989**	**8105**	**2**
北 京	331	143	38	5	150	
天 津	245	124	3	1	118	
河 北	2255	1107	845	49	302	1
山 西	1398	564	632		202	
内蒙古	1014	503	272	18	239	
辽 宁	1531	642	212	56	677	
吉 林	910	428	182	28	300	
黑龙江	1197	521	365	52	311	
上 海	214	107	2		105	
江 苏	1287	763	69	1	455	
浙 江	1378	655	274	14	449	
安 徽	1488	953	289	9	246	
福 建	1105	638	288	19	179	
江 西	1555	824	579	8	152	
山 东	1826	1106	73		647	
河 南	2435	1120	682	12	633	
湖 北	1234	759	168	10	307	
湖 南	1929	1135	401	83	393	
广 东	1600	1128	11	7	461	
广 西	1246	788	330	59	128	
海 南	218	175	21		22	
重 庆	1028	622	190	14	216	
四 川	4633	2105	2182	98	346	
贵 州	1379	832	326	193	221	
云 南	1389	681	545	140	163	
西 藏	697	140	545	9	12	
陕 西	1295	988	23		284	
甘 肃	1352	741	487	34	124	
青 海	399	140	225	28	34	
宁 夏	237	102	90		45	
新 疆	1057	349	523	42	184	1

C-1-4 民政部门

地 区	单位数	年末职工人数		受教育程度		职业资
			女性	大学专科	大学本科及以上	助理社会工作师
全 国	**3490**	**96369**	**32272**	**36678**	**42915**	**1819**
中央级	1	372	112	8	364	
北 京	18	1112	505	152	910	8
天 津	18	591	171	142	393	
河 北	194	6353	2357	2286	2183	124
山 西	131	2601	844	1122	1041	41
内蒙古	117	3235	1081	1381	1455	7
辽 宁	121	2961	965	1024	1721	21
吉 林	70	1277	280	365	582	6
黑龙江	151	2571	935	1081	1205	58
上 海	18	668	282	105	542	67
江 苏	118	3475	996	962	2193	262
浙 江	103	2613	725	895	1454	26
安 徽	121	2723	818	1029	1343	129
福 建	96	1761	387	646	747	14
江 西	117	3150	955	1094	1084	33
山 东	179	6516	2097	2377	3266	183
河 南	183	8197	3022	3474	2712	113
湖 北	120	4211	1421	1900	1651	43
湖 南	145	6735	2322	2421	2588	121
广 东	145	4244	1373	1477	2210	140
广 西	127	2282	732	905	1106	10
海 南	23	674	177	308	251	21
重 庆	41	1188	395	378	750	8
四 川	209	5545	1943	2318	2322	91
贵 州	100	3437	1121	1525	1436	15
云 南	148	4491	1509	1843	1895	26
西 藏	82	1143	528	482	474	44
陕 西	118	3811	1111	1616	1442	24
甘 肃	101	3179	962	1143	1248	98
青 海	55	891	311	315	375	22
宁 夏	28	763	278	258	423	44
新 疆	292	3599	1557	1646	1549	20

行政机构

单位：个、人、人次、时

格水平	年龄结构				志愿服务	
社会工作师	35岁及以下	36岁至45岁	46岁至55岁	56岁及以上	志愿者服务人次数	志愿服务时间
1964	**24532**	**35195**	**29523**	**7119**	**225112**	**476035.0**
	133	126	69	44		
22	281	355	398	78	172	172.0
	123	177	223	68	550	1350.0
114	1837	2331	1839	346	2650	6501.0
28	667	913	862	159	454	1142.0
16	861	1167	981	226	2339	2975.0
31	665	971	1038	287	630	1225.0
22	138	596	444	99		
46	623	966	851	131	324	552.0
83	132	181	245	110	536	1122.0
285	573	1193	1325	384	40502	79945.6
68	460	774	1074	305	78761	104576.0
114	502	1052	933	236	29260	86374.0
54	300	566	704	191	747	3073.0
30	605	1247	1010	288	3265	9095.0
253	2088	2394	1726	308		
136	2777	2980	1901	539	786	2782.0
56	792	1369	1462	588	1637	5222.0
101	1982	2565	1701	487	12562	45982.0
140	993	1490	1435	326	3757	11468.0
25	290	725	1029	238	93	
4	173	228	214	59	5	8.0
32	252	344	480	112	1882	5888.0
73	1368	2198	1641	338	22271	50925.4
9	878	1407	956	196	10097	31241.0
26	908	1708	1594	281	1490	2290.0
3	617	392	122	12		
66	1080	1352	1104	275	7188	14321.0
71	1035	1165	805	174	795	1924.0
11	230	391	232	38	134	342.0
32	158	319	249	37	52	104.0
13	1011	1553	876	159	2173	5435.0

C-1-4续表

地区	职工按行政级别分				乡、镇、街道民政助理员
	中央级	省级	地级	县级	
全　国	**372**	**3819**	**13916**	**78262**	**51722**
中央级	372				
北　京		235		877	718
天　津		131		460	316
河　北		114	679	5560	2849
山　西		96	387	2118	1407
内蒙古		82	483	2670	1636
辽　宁		96	746	2119	950
吉　林		119	290	868	185
黑龙江			614	1957	404
上　海		172		496	353
江　苏		172	663	2640	1680
浙　江		135	419	2059	1622
安　徽		111	507	2105	1965
福　建		115	298	1348	1419
江　西		80	378	2692	782
山　东		145	851	5520	5415
河　南		144	779	7274	2226
湖　北		101	561	3549	1400
湖　南		186	763	5786	4679
广　东		138	1013	3093	916
广　西		110	428	1744	2892
海　南		76	106	492	284
重　庆		189		999	3017
四　川		128	747	4670	4434
贵　州		138	415	2884	2417
云　南		142	633	3716	1466
西　藏		116	259	768	28
陕　西		141	485	3185	3483
甘　肃			664	2515	1799
青　海		105	151	635	402
宁　夏		92	121	550	165
新　疆		210	476	2913	413

单位：人、万元

行政单位会计制度财务指标			
固定资产原价	本年收入合计	本年支出合计	收支结余
1924106.0	**9564506.5**	**9265699.7**	**2694396.2**
84149.2	150890.8	153813.0	22099.6
43695.5	580802.8	563448.5	123967.0
15113.7	233693.6	222006.9	17433.6
82869.8	513709.6	507750.6	130567.3
51824.7	167411.0	176497.9	57273.3
62842.9	77162.3	76655.4	37304.2
60854.4	175985.8	188074.7	51454.1
27716.4	83823.7	74087.7	21783.4
29808.7	117569.2	112405.0	26180.6
36579.7	661197.4	649165.1	129011.2
77200.4	482850.4	475447.2	161297.3
56357.2	789508.9	777627.5	241425.6
69907.8	271761.4	267960.1	92611.0
33612.7	345168.5	361012.3	95981.5
39027.6	68885.3	68301.6	26970.3
94940.8	341854.0	345797.7	147963.6
41564.4	214061.7	209158.9	61351.8
103819.2	185275.9	178584.6	90858.1
66407.3	507430.7	506821.7	211127.7
137082.5	838931.6	836214.4	228385.6
98874.5	438803.7	436176.6	96388.9
10717.7	161419.1	148602.8	9143.2
47177.7	137051.4	115790.6	46968.0
83879.0	348933.5	341908.8	142673.9
64579.3	281524.0	248462.1	69529.3
98206.3	399588.6	390282.5	102615.0
44804.2	30076.6	25975.4	7704.1
54477.5	235350.5	229086.3	88242.1
29419.9	107237.6	100685.2	20084.0
48922.6	118281.9	118965.1	24605.7
27494.7	240387.1	112374.4	16521.3
100177.7	257877.9	246559.1	94873.9

C-1-5 社会服务

地 区	机构和设施数	按登记类型分				
		工商登记	编制登记	民政登记	自治组织	设施和多牌子机构
全 国	**1745498**	**1185**	**31215**	**702405**	**662478**	**348215**
中央级	2370		31	2339		
北 京	29198	19	815	10754	6995	10615
天 津	13487	5	150	5062	5371	2899
河 北	112383	7	927	20916	53054	37479
山 西	49519	18	853	13004	30459	5185
内蒙古	31859	30	674	13664	13412	4079
辽 宁	44549	41	949	21039	15767	6753
吉 林	24540	42	1250	10669	11202	1377
黑龙江	30648	19	604	14401	12820	2804
上 海	23379	60	293	14181	5843	3002
江 苏	125750	78	1810	84094	21556	18212
浙 江	108910	89	1289	47536	31987	28009
安 徽	52205	37	666	25708	17978	7816
福 建	49207	34	592	26154	16739	5688
江 西	42170	8	2297	15813	20484	3568
山 东	152209	36	1250	45963	80948	24012
河 南	87028	31	1398	29328	51574	4697
湖 北	73972	55	2122	28498	29454	13843
湖 南	75150	39	2301	30361	29193	13256
广 东	153151	109	1879	59455	26436	65272
广 西	54410	31	762	23928	16207	13482
海 南	11783	10	63	6293	3061	2356
重 庆	35449	58	701	16199	11123	7368
四 川	115444	141	3128	39448	53068	19659
贵 州	54739	61	1258	11848	18388	23184
云 南	40519	27	643	22552	14299	2998
西 藏	6189		21	627	5467	74
陕 西	51138	34	826	20758	22884	6636
甘 肃	50004	24	539	22763	17386	9292
青 海	9946	10	73	3658	4622	1583
宁 夏	9752	19	179	5751	2789	1014
新 疆	24441	13	872	9641	11912	2003

总表

单位：个、人

按行业分类分				年末职工人数		按登记类型分	
*社会工作	*成员组织	*其他社会服务	其他事业单位		女性	工商登记	编制登记
423348	**1364883**	**5559**	**1987**	**12392884**	**3904051**	**31813**	**362266**
2	2339		29	39612	17466		1733
12643	17749	63	73	271115	106245	807	13871
3282	10433	41	21	86681	42383	246	3374
38906	73970	219	35	692226	238056	226	16378
6240	43463	119	77	304004	91425	500	9893
5013	27076	159	21	190279	63803	589	7609
8994	36806	510	105	338819	132777	866	14962
3347	21871	199	26	136942	47040	1918	15236
4290	27221	172	27	253801	94186	291	11515
6880	20024	90	40	296462	91091	3301	8640
42837	105650	330	68	919078	274693	1784	24490
32049	79523	274	156	638340	207165	1696	14298
9542	43686	192	25	412407	120948	489	9614
6360	42893	162	48	377674	92195	1324	6114
5460	36297	182	392	307891	86125	85	13696
28195	126911	267	52	862358	252126	471	19404
6379	80902	268	126	524159	159417	829	19877
16301	57952	254	84	526406	174351	1074	23502
15647	59554	257	97	445256	152905	956	19348
68480	85891	302	37	978408	348388	4122	26155
14304	40135	154	73	467392	118465	777	10057
2667	9354	19	8	86488	26815	490	1167
8656	27322	160	21	264051	114630	1459	6774
24209	92516	371	135	859214	285500	2294	22849
24520	30236	136	76	382973	98978	2475	10851
3740	36851	171	29	558637	193927	446	5921
93	6094	2		39782	10234		346
7865	43642	161	39	421812	115628	1276	9928
9941	40149	126	31	338372	54937	480	5154
1660	8280	21	3	50183	12192	79	980
1404	8540	69	8	102990	26122	280	1883
3442	21553	109	25	219072	53838	183	6647

*注：为了便于各行业统计需要，在成员组织类（社会组织登记）中有50279家也在社会工作类和其他社会服务类行业中活动并统计，故行业分类合计数会有重复。

C－1－5续表1

地　区	按登记类型分		受教育程度		职业资格水平	
	民政登记	设施	大学专科人数	大学本科及以上人数	助理社会工作师人数	社会工作师人数
全　国	**8021788**	**3976158**	**1968057**	**1401444**	**81709**	**55115**
中央级	37879		321	29238	603	8809
北　京	182962	73475	53950	117150	7003	3113
天　津	47266	35795	21908	22693	2047	649
河　北	405351	270271	58381	37804	2303	2686
山　西	153026	140585	46028	17353	1188	1265
内蒙古	113658	68423	42473	19449	1312	820
辽　宁	210514	112477	72763	50318	2706	1599
吉　林	74768	44557	23531	8612	1455	1064
黑龙江	166407	75588	33755	16374	1342	1057
上　海	241137	43384	80196	28114	2440	3718
江　苏	691921	200883	170234	110531	11558	4619
浙　江	421357	200989	126350	76714	5055	2999
安　徽	287887	114417	79828	53572	3734	1344
福　建	278635	91601	38643	30923	1589	1221
江　西	201657	92453	34641	13164	1498	451
山　东	412393	430090	171052	113442	6365	2744
河　南	262526	240927	79326	43948	1625	1012
湖　北	336843	164987	95131	40896	1789	957
湖　南	272485	152221	88529	53302	1781	1650
广　东	625125	323006	183007	166769	12127	6074
广　西	352450	104108	52417	32095	1413	988
海　南	57378	27453	11058	8126	65	132
重　庆	174187	81631	59735	51599	4009	2272
四　川	563211	270796	105591	99587	2854	1527
贵　州	184651	184910	56592	50437	395	265
云　南	466910	85360	48861	32302	784	300
西　藏	12664	26772	2379	1623	27	9
陕　西	296082	114526	51336	29139	1123	702
甘　肃	242288	90450	32839	16745	590	365
青　海	25079	24045	6166	2158	135	120
宁　夏	83384	17443	9794	7993	187	129
新　疆	139707	72535	31242	19274	607	455

单位：人、人次、时

年龄结构				志愿服务	
35岁及以下人数	36岁至45岁人数	46岁至55岁人数	56岁及以上人数	志愿者服务人次数	志愿服务时间
3775135	**4734011**	**2823059**	**1060482**	**9310415**	**25226309.1**
10948	14970	8680	5014		
70253	73347	107629	19886	4565922	13098904.6
22660	28955	27316	7750	75668	134425.0
177443	321302	150617	42864	54499	203503.5
93768	107993	73077	29166	16554	60994.2
58439	71247	45655	14893	30395	71154.0
94769	123132	73602	47316	73018	108146.0
31259	75533	23265	6885	23290	46578.0
86085	97146	53256	17314	195553	586128.0
88732	99162	73889	34679	61147	185929.0
256846	339067	235292	87873	628848	1602503.5
189007	240718	138429	70192	375905	858245.0
119856	161633	99056	31856	216948	544293.0
94071	128267	97697	57589	135053	370391.0
96047	134218	57915	19711	7440	21490.7
254248	362269	192386	53455	978500	2315301.5
180141	201047	104457	38514	12120	29081.0
175616	180743	133362	36685	26167	46906.0
157012	173601	87421	27150	59476	178914.0
408472	320111	185299	64526	90557	293225.3
119558	174522	122873	50438	6686	17643.0
27138	36262	17777	5311	18455	31824.0
96760	86920	58328	22043	879039	2111589.3
277869	340658	158153	82534	256784	811770.0
112421	157841	85012	27699	381041	1001731.5
160040	196193	121333	81071	12964	51537.0
10288	14730	9465	5299	24	65.0
111379	149646	125589	35198	56023	157764.0
95062	126504	97183	19623	4622	7964.0
13657	22800	10371	3351	5467	11379.0
24740	60284	13929	4012	5131	9262.0
60551	113190	34746	10585	57119	257667.0

C-1-5续表2

地 区	企业会计制度财务指标			
	固定资产原价	营业收入	费用合计	营业利润
全 国	**3519631.3**	**1679364.4**	**469806**	**229812**
中央级	13537.6	17960	7752.9	5.5
北 京	1880616.4	593062.1	184918.8	34400.6
天 津	6598.2	5996.9	1695.4	2485.8
河 北	5886.2	4898.6	3291	302.5
山 西	26243.2	3145.1	1512.1	512.1
内蒙古	27482.2	5729.4	3907.2	676.7
辽 宁	42797	26823.3	13997.5	2633.3
吉 林	37013.3	2645.1	1058.7	57
黑龙江	35074.4	10945.1	6333.6	911.5
上 海	301790.8	486512.9	80487	118153.7
江 苏	274959	63869.6	13711.8	33169.5
浙 江	131782.9	56322.2	15750.6	10176.2
安 徽	22000.1	12180.3	4101.5	1623.2
福 建	62779.9	23588.8	11537.8	1122.1
江 西	20004	4458.1	1661	326.8
山 东	24146.9	6127.3	3258.8	776.1
河 南	21424.1	8785.2	3844	876.1
湖 北	32014.5	20172.1	8517.4	2267
湖 南	55655.9	8625.5	4074.2	518.8
广 东	105958.4	48418.3	17215.5	4944.3
广 西	41166.7	81057.5	10123.1	2871.7
海 南	19165.7	5401.5	4329.2	1527.7
重 庆	55762.3	28152.2	11611.5	2877.6
四 川	104247.6	61847.5	21269.2	4554.5
贵 州	81182.2	50494.5	21348.7	4397
云 南	17385.5	6235.5	1935.1	915
西 藏	5537.2			
陕 西	18924.5	24036.8	8888.4	1335.1
甘 肃	7295.6	7236.5	1113.2	1513.2
青 海	4554.3	30	30	
宁 夏	12422.5	1411.7	249.4	1.8
新 疆	24222.2	3194.8	281.4	46.2

单位：万元

事业单位会计制度财务指标			民间非营利组织会计制度财务指标		
固定资产原价	本年收入合计	本年支出合计	固定资产原价	本年收入合计	本年费用合计
14006196.4	**11467117.3**	**10795019.9**	**36409996.6**	**23372909.8**	**21103484**
169605.3	284352.8	174424.1	887180.2	4663525.9	3982226.7
1008289.9	1355923.4	1335509.9	3657527.8	1066855.2	1070018.9
183845.9	211729.8	181495	167049.8	157807.9	207240.5
448061.6	434255.1	405944.6	1673510.3	532154.7	572769
489996.3	232348.1	221317.8	430325.6	163480.3	176687.8
248592.6	162881.4	163646.5	195460.6	72036.4	72771.6
476428.6	481215.5	538888.6	373040.2	648063.4	464973.1
255403.3	144115.3	137657.2	48236.8	32196	27211.2
309762	149622	136133.2	338148.6	114422.3	90176.9
571089.7	700705.6	554022.4	1112593.2	2918964.9	2694064.3
1373189.3	891113.5	795937.4	3060145.5	2705284.1	2402950.7
886195	611846.1	535071.2	2326481.4	1464673.2	1188314.6
265533.2	187050.8	178376.9	1464962.5	543264.7	534031.2
147601.1	202583.2	188069.9	364322.2	170406.4	192584.3
372442.2	175278.8	170199.2	393865	259521.7	260484.8
629107.4	723623.8	727647.6	1321801.8	955275.2	966611
297601.9	299846	305367.2	650025.1	227421.4	215993.6
804129.2	539745.8	520630.9	745974.1	387352.8	372842.2
587728.4	397738.2	359875.6	677618.3	1006679.1	547901.9
1564034.1	1213144.5	1157797.4	10611259.7	2034756.2	1886958.4
252871.3	198796.8	194268.5	215990.9	98442.1	84947.6
53227.4	64069.6	62811.5	121095.4	290823	59775.5
220713.1	251489.9	230798.3	789838.7	545370.8	451691.7
750000.1	422558	431855.9	2171459.6	1610150.1	1715825.6
243906.2	132759.7	127422.4	218155.8	206938.3	215336
521368.6	236041.4	220054.4	687784.5	243664.1	275404.3
33364.7	12448.8	12249.8	13668.2	3113.7	2575.8
343037.3	379442.6	377928.6	1197903.1	122985.8	177732.2
152788.9	124940.5	119674.8	185745.7	27879	31348
34785.9	28953.2	30707.9	58465	14831.9	20489.7
61301.8	47986.8	35299.2	88051.1	42176.7	93697.8
250194.1	168510.3	163936	162309.9	42392.5	47847.1

C-1-6 社会服务发展

地 区	社会服务综合指数（%）	每万人口社会服务机构和设施数（个/万人）	每万人口社会服务职工人数（人/万人）	每百万人口社工助工师（人/百万人）	每千人口固定资产原价（万元/千人）
全 国	**100.0**	**12.6**	**89.6**	**20.8**	**39.0**
北 京	230.5	13.4	124.8	115.4	301.3
天 津	118.8	8.6	55.5	42.0	22.9
河 北	83.2	15.0	92.7	6.1	28.5
山 西	68.6	13.4	82.6	8.5	25.7
内蒙古	99.9	12.6	75.5	8.0	18.7
辽 宁	102.5	10.2	77.4	24.7	20.4
吉 林	81.7	9.0	50.1	21.5	12.5
黑龙江	88.4	8.1	66.8	11.8	18.0
上 海	151.5	9.7	122.5	60.2	82.1
江 苏	154.7	15.7	114.9	47.0	58.9
浙 江	150.6	19.5	114.2	40.2	59.8
安 徽	103.3	8.4	66.6	12.1	28.3
福 建	101.7	12.7	97.5	23.5	14.8
江 西	69.9	9.2	67.0	6.9	17.1
山 东	99.3	15.3	86.7	13.0	19.9
河 南	69.4	9.1	55.0	6.0	10.2
湖 北	106.4	12.6	89.4	13.5	26.9
湖 南	93.9	11.0	65.3	9.0	19.4
广 东	131.5	13.9	89.0	53.8	111.7
广 西	83.3	11.2	96.6	7.3	10.5
海 南	86.8	12.8	94.3	4.5	21.1
重 庆	106.3	11.6	86.6	18.6	35.0
四 川	97.8	14.0	104.0	12.6	36.6
贵 州	104.1	15.4	107.7	3.2	15.3
云 南	90.8	8.5	117.1	5.8	25.7
西 藏	12.3	18.7	120.4	0.8	15.9
陕 西	99.8	13.4	110.6	26.3	40.9
甘 肃	84.9	19.2	129.6	5.7	13.3
青 海	47.6	16.8	84.6	6.1	16.5
宁 夏	95.3	14.4	152.6	13.6	24.0
新 疆	69.2	10.2	91.4	10.1	18.2

综合指数

社会服务事业费占财政支出的比重(‰)	每千人口社会服务事业费(万元/千人)	每百万人口乡镇街道数(个/百万人)	万人口社会服务床位(张/万人)	千老年人口养老床位(张/千人)	每十万人口孤儿数(人/十万人)	每百万人口家庭收养数(件/百万人)
33.9	**39.3**	**28.8**	**55.4**	**31.6**	**33.3**	**13.6**
39.9	117.8	15.2	71.8	38.2	9.5	6.4
24.2	57.3	15.7	43.2	23.1	5.2	4.0
35.0	28.3	30.2	61.8	35.0	22.1	3.4
37.7	35.1	38.0	33.2	22.2	34.9	6.6
31.0	55.6	40.2	92.6	58.3	20.6	7.8
40.3	42.2	35.0	52.2	22.9	16.5	4.2
29.0	38.1	33.3	51.2	25.6	18.7	0.8
36.1	40.2	31.5	54.9	27.3	19.2	1.8
22.1	63.3	8.8	60.5	28.9	7.5	12.6
28.8	35.9	16.1	83.4	40.3	20.6	21.5
27.2	34.0	24.7	101.7	56.3	7.6	44.4
35.7	31.8	24.0	61.3	35.2	44.0	11.9
24.4	26.9	28.5	37.9	23.2	14.2	27.8
37.2	37.4	33.9	46.4	30.2	46.5	6.2
34.8	30.7	18.4	71.8	38.5	17.5	19.9
33.1	25.9	25.5	39.1	23.5	35.7	7.5
37.7	41.2	21.0	61.5	33.0	32.8	11.8
42.9	39.8	28.3	41.4	21.8	54.6	10.3
22.7	27.8	14.5	35.5	28.2	32.6	13.1
35.5	32.6	25.8	38.8	25.6	45.2	36.3
21.8	32.8	23.8	22.6	18.0	16.9	9.4
32.5	42.6	33.7	64.7	29.3	17.7	8.1
43.5	42.2	56.1	68.9	31.4	35.0	12.1
37.6	45.1	38.8	57.1	36.8	56.9	7.1
46.8	49.2	29.1	29.9	21.6	50.7	26.3
14.9	71.3	210.9	38.8	14.2	180.5	3.9
46.0	53.0	34.0	44.5	25.5	30.3	10.2
51.8	62.5	51.8	56.0	34.4	72.1	3.3
32.3	83.0	67.2	47.1	38.4	265.7	8.3
33.5	62.4	35.1	52.7	40.7	98.5	5.5
33.7	58.2	44.1	33.4	26.6	92.1	10.4

C-1-6续表

地 区	每万人口流浪救助人次数（人次/万人）	城市低保平均标准（十元/人·月）	农村低保平均标准（十元/人·月）	每万人口优抚对象人数（人/万人）	每千人口福利彩票销售（万元/千人）
全 国	**24.1**	**49.5**	**31.2**	**63.3**	**14.9**
北 京	151	80	80	20.7	21.7
天 津	8.4	78	75.5	29.6	24.4
河 北	11.9	50.1	28	77.9	8.4
山 西	36.9	44.1	27.1	48.7	11.9
内蒙古	19.6	54	35.1	19.9	23
辽 宁	14.6	52.3	32.6	48.8	25
吉 林	9.5	44.7	28.7	44.2	13.1
黑龙江	7.8	53.6	31.6	30.6	13.3
上 海	10	88	87	16.3	18.6
江 苏	17.5	61.1	54	58.7	18.6
浙 江	13	67.4	60.8	54.9	27.1
安 徽	20.8	49.7	32	74	11
福 建	15.5	51.5	32	48	12.9
江 西	14.9	48.1	27.6	64.1	6.5
山 东	10.3	49.5	31.5	84.6	14.8
河 南	17.7	42.5	25.7	77.4	6.9
湖 北	41.5	48.8	31.9	75	17.2
湖 南	96.7	43.1	25.7	116.4	12.5
广 东	19.2	57.6	44.5	38.4	19.2
广 西	20.6	45.8	24.9	59.8	9.9
海 南	11.3	46.7	34.7	28.8	18.2
重 庆	14.3	46	30.8	83.1	14.7
四 川	20.9	42	26.3	102.4	10.3
贵 州	26.7	50.7	26.7	64.3	7.6
云 南	14.6	44.2	22.6	67.5	15.3
西 藏	18.5	69.4	21.8	10	47.8
陕 西	28.8	47.9	26.7	64.9	22.6
甘 肃	10.2	41.1	24.4	48.5	17.3
青 海	22	40.1	24.8	24.2	25.9
宁 夏	18.5	41.6	28.2	18.5	25.4
新 疆	26.1	38.4	25	14.1	17.5

社区服务中心（站）覆盖率(%)	每十万人口社会组织(个/十万人)	每十万人口村居委会个数(个/十万人)	每万人口结婚对数(对/万人)	每万人口离婚对数(对/万人)	火化率(%)
24.4	**50.8**	**47.9**	**82.7**	**30.1**	**48.3**
95.0	49.5	32.2	76.5	48.7	89.7
40.8	32.4	34.4	62.8	41.8	81.0
4.9	28.0	71.0	73.9	29.5	38.7
8.2	35.3	82.7	81.5	20.8	11.6
13.9	54.2	53.2	78.7	39.0	49.6
29.7	48.1	36.0	71.4	36.6	97.0
15.2	39.0	41.0	81.0	47.3	65.5
15.5	37.9	33.7	80.6	49.3	65.0
52.3	58.6	24.1	51.7	34.1	100.0
85.5	105.1	26.9	89.5	32.7	93.5
47.3	85.0	57.2	65.6	26.3	100.0
24.6	41.5	29.0	115.1	35.1	75.8
19.2	67.5	43.2	81.2	24.9	84.6
7.2	34.4	44.6	65.8	22.2	28.6
13.8	46.2	81.4	67.4	25.6	87.7
3.1	30.8	54.1	101.7	29.1	20.5
17.1	48.4	50.0	87.3	31.1	54.3
14.8	44.5	42.8	73.2	28.4	18.9
83.1	54.1	24.0	71.5	19.3	98.2
10.4	49.5	33.5	81.4	23.3	28.7
76.9	68.6	33.4	85.3	18.1	6.0
24.2	53.1	36.5	91.4	45.6	35.0
20.2	47.7	64.2	88.0	35.9	37.6
107.1	33.3	51.7	127.5	34.0	37.6
10.8	47.3	30.0	93.5	25.0	22.2
0.0	19.0	165.4	90.9	10.5	5.6
13.0	54.4	60.0	87.2	26.6	24.4
15.6	87.2	66.6	83.9	19.3	11.7
10.3	61.6	77.9	103.1	25.6	19.0
29.8	85.2	41.3	91.9	29.0	12.1
17.9	40.2	49.7	89.3	39.0	18.9

C-1-7 社会工作师、助理

地 区	社会工作师和助理社会工作师累计合格人数	社会工作师		
		累计合格人数	当年考试通过人数	当年报考人数
全 国	**288185**	**69391**	**17772**	**88974**
北 京	25082	6188	1125	4787
天 津	6566	1431	429	1667
河 北	4566	1674	351	1411
山 西	3143	1164	297	1792
内蒙古	2012	656	253	2038
辽 宁	10823	2665	712	3722
吉 林	5882	1281	396	2306
黑龙江	4495	1198	294	1554
上 海	14569	3789	908	6719
江 苏	37590	8419	2034	8058
浙 江	22456	6886	1754	8060
安 徽	7517	1892	465	2235
福 建	9109	2602	735	3137
江 西	3151	758	147	777
山 东	12943	4502	1283	7047
河 南	5734	1685	348	1710
湖 北	7954	1450	429	2503
湖 南	6172	1540	375	2296
广 东	59224	11330	2746	13836
广 西	3545	746	161	880
海 南	410	91	20	92
重 庆	5683	1456	477	2154
四 川	10412	2058	547	3012
贵 州	1147	203	62	495
云 南	2766	648	213	1161
西 藏	25	6	1	8
陕 西	10014	1730	839	2333
甘 肃	1484	338	105	808
青 海	360	71	12	144
宁 夏	920	216	67	581
新 疆	2431	718	187	1651

社工师人员情况

单位：人

	助理社会工作师			
当年实考人数	累计合格人数	当年考试通过人数	当年报考人数	当年实考人数
69640	**218794**	**64638**	**210267**	**166915**
3949	18894	3234	10650	9072
1504	5135	1397	4127	3568
1207	2892	569	1468	1263
1479	1979	709	2149	1785
1527	1356	581	2082	1674
3140	8158	3118	11240	9145
1847	4601	1301	6707	5247
1254	3297	744	2858	2350
4568	10780	4249	17069	12003
6589	29171	7726	23800	19503
6214	15570	4568	12380	9974
1737	5625	1446	4389	3412
2454	6507	1851	5379	4329
590	2393	516	1691	1337
4876	8441	2582	7865	6078
1443	4049	932	2491	2158
2101	6504	2075	7210	5970
1630	4632	1326	4842	3647
10894	47894	13754	44053	33726
705	2799	710	2244	1891
81	319	91	362	315
1748	4227	1612	5552	4446
2435	8354	2934	10269	8359
320	944	267	1281	898
887	2118	702	2583	1974
7	19	7	62	37
2036	8284	4107	7449	6362
574	1146	399	1415	1120
98	289	58	389	292
482	704	410	1904	1693
1264	1713	663	4307	3287

C-1-8 社会服务职业

地 区	累计鉴定合格人数	2016年鉴定合格人数	养老护理员		假肢类技能人员	
			累计鉴定合格人数	2016年鉴定合格人数	累计鉴定合格人数	2016年鉴定合格人数
全 国	**145569**	**12144**	**32614**	**8528**	**2289**	**393**
中央级	10389	2664	4805	1865	785	190
北 京	12785	128	238		58	
天 津	751	20	144		2	
河 北	1391	307	897	263	10	
山 西	3195	391	1324	336		
内蒙古	2433	149	379		21	
辽 宁	2725	43	346		128	
吉 林	3414	388	575	388	5	
黑龙江	3425	171	565	102	4	
上 海	2823	118	85	77	211	41
江 苏	3551	219	147	49	222	24
浙 江	31712	140	122	69	104	24
安 徽	2267		182		24	
福 建	2603	160	1078	127	9	1
江 西	2681	87	69		33	9
山 东	7141	1337	2219	1129	127	40
河 南	6844	708	3548	471	73	10
湖 北	2636	45	360		23	
湖 南	5471	390	124		28	1
广 东	9523	1436	5823	1162	168	30
广 西	3247	722	1853	593	123	11
海 南	438	127	303	114		
重 庆	4612	446	347	330	39	
四 川	6636	1130	4623	955	2	1
贵 州	2613	89	383	89	8	
云 南	3029	184	189	42	23	
西 藏	205	12	128			
陕 西	671		73			
甘 肃	1074	29	201		45	11
青 海	421	98	310	56		
宁 夏	3691	191	674	171		
新 疆	1172	215	500	140	14	

说明：1.以上数据为民政部职业技能鉴定指导中心及分布在全国31个省、自治区、直辖市76个鉴定站鉴定人数和竞赛晋级人数（不含地方自行组织的鉴定人数）。

2.殡葬类职业包括：殡仪服务员（初中高技师4个级别）、遗体接运工（初中高3个级别）、遗体防腐师（初中高技师高级技师5个级别）、遗体整容师（初中高技师高级技师5个级别）、遗体火化师（初中高技师高级技师5个级别）、墓地管理员（初中高技师4个级别）。

3.假肢类职业包括：假肢师（初中高技师高级技师5个级别）、矫形器师（初中高技师高级技师5个级别）。

技能人员情况

单位：人

孤残儿童护理员		灾害信息员		殡葬类技能人员	
累计鉴定合格人数	2016年鉴定合格人数	累计鉴定合格人数	2016年鉴定合格人数	累计鉴定合格人数	2016年鉴定合格人数
11075	**1117**	**81946**		**17645**	**2106**
1350	240	1005		2444	369
230	26	10651		1608	102
129	20	246		230	
346	44	11		127	
378	55	1493			
462	92	1145		426	57
219		1573		459	43
168		2666			
214		2440		202	69
96		2420		11	
499		1869		814	146
363		30671		452	47
176		1498		387	
116	28	1396		4	4
467	58	1840		272	20
454		3052		1289	168
1010	227	2041		172	
347	45	1691		215	
368	22	2157		2794	367
849	141	1238		1445	103
387	50	177		707	68
97	13	30		8	
174		3058		994	116
397	14	1245		369	160
299		1603		320	
296		1517		1004	142
49				28	12
591		7			
128		479		221	18
106	42	5			
128		2611		278	20
182		111		365	75

C-1-9 1952-2016年社会服务

地 区	1952年	1953年	1954年	1955年	1956年	1957年
全 国	**28265**	**35484**	**60390**	**49842**	**56906**	**53119**
中央级	6	443	20619	8736	270	85
北 京	198	237	276	247	584	302
天 津	208	315	131	157	217	240
河 北	2849	4558	4764	4526	9681	6640
山 西	1253	1398	1531	1373	2096	1953
内蒙古	912	370	306	364	625	417
辽 宁	611	1434	1392	1298	1638	1339
吉 林	346	595	880	856	1331	1610
黑龙江	640	831	912	952	1442	1336
上 海	550	306	411	729	1121	1073
江 苏	1980	1993	2051	3003	4052	5051
浙 江	398	426	505	757	1430	988
安 徽	2051	4061	3382	3453	4748	4306
福 建	828	732	789	933	1473	866
江 西	1519	1040	1368	2253	1889	1802
山 东	2624	3993	5082	3975	3664	5261
河 南	1440	2745	2307	2494	4360	5539
湖 北	2719	1058	2765	2664	1306	1505
湖 南	1255	1089	3381	2205	2259	2177
广 东	1762	1454	1270	1407	2725	2729
广 西	516	645	735	700	1414	1589
海 南						
重 庆						
四 川	1583	2035	2052	2646	3570	2606
贵 州	368	686	633	567	618	494
云 南	630	695	875	740	908	599
西 藏			43	207	91	
陕 西	519	1023	984	1135	1794	1250
甘 肃	390	1074	675	1171	1083	871
青 海	52	134	140	154	281	237
宁 夏						
新 疆	58	114	131	140	236	254

事业费支出情况

单位：万元

1958年	1959年	1960年	1961年	1962年	1963年	1964年
32693	**44786**	**72444**	**98912**	**74475**	**87533**	**161510**
82	192	262	39			31
376	751	824	658	542	638	816
194						
2494	4148	5070	10807	5780	15681	31433
2279	1656	2659	2896	2556	2640	2361
505	873	525	785	1468	1124	1360
1098	1249	4475	4392	3933	3467	3382
1126	764	1055	1271	1660	2138	2235
948	782	991	1485	2151	2362	2796
464	475	471	422	539	874	1074
2617	2956	4843	4107	4873	7282	11070
672	874	857	1414	1597	1166	1152
1642	3169	3161	4704	3530	5431	10567
823	4141	2823	2798	1493	1687	1394
1717	1691	2179	3224	3168	2273	3081
3795	4494	8141	11332	6963	7201	11079
2990	2672	10271	11417	8107	10099	48554
1210	2466	4428	4569	3767	3468	3319
1344	967	1690	4299	2697	2834	4522
1223	2982	4608	3475	2830	3146	3056
582	903	997	2687	1505	2125	4006
1982	2583	6315	9758	5918	4227	4,495
331	613	750	2390	1429	1792	1,808
514	675	880	1692	773	1250	1,494
2	1	25	48	117		133
588	1109	1113	1530	1422	1640	1,918
539	681	1778	4522	2464	2988	2,310
164	447	576	1028	1005		465
92	239	428	303	365		378
300	233	249	860	1823		1,212

C-1-9续表1

地区	1965年	1966年	1967年	1968年	1969年	1970年
全国	**107869**	**88112**	**81887**	**56154**	**66683**	**65349**
中央级	2325	454	534	308	11	
北京	1047	914	939	868	820	895
天津			473	439	572	405
河北	18545	12395	6983	4443	5333	2054
山西	2899	4447	2692	2478	2579	4777
内蒙古	1440	2182	2401	1194	842	891
辽宁	2942	2572	2781	2473	3542	2867
吉林	1798	1704	1745	1579	1890	1837
黑龙江	2611	2548	2169	1775	2355	2247
上海	1220	1472	1654	1410	1359	1442
江苏	5506	7298	5400	3756	3839	4191
浙江	1351	1142	1366	1486	1481	1496
安徽	3347	4119	6861	4025	4246	5547
福建	1463	1673	1738	1727	1922	1463
江西	1989	2145	2318	1637	1924	2047
山东	15807	9458	9844	5878	7622	6442
河南	17841	9303	8611	4105	6983	4947
湖北	2790	2579	3177	2651	3509	4197
湖南	2482	2141	2562	1848	2019	1668
广东	2664	2454	2644	2046	2639	2734
广西	1983	1997	2541	1641	1607	1555
海南						
重庆						
四川	5179	4774	4067	3374	3439	3678
贵州	1726	1730	1926	1224	1314	1646
云南	1596	1772	1412	807	1018	2460
西藏	192	374			96	100
陕西	3137	3623	1874	1477	1733	1778
甘肃	1611	1161	1963	671	989	952
青海	695	409	185	190	246	207
宁夏	284	272	287	200	238	242
新疆	1399	1000	740	444	516	584

单位：万元

1971年	1972年	1973年	1974年	1975年	1976年	1977年
68269	**81549**	**99675**	**90406**	**127082**	**161690**	**185288**
		8	10			
974	1192	1506	1284	1461	1742	3068
407	546	762	937	881	933	13670
3591	5482	8727	5925	5960	7041	36568
4563	4025	4696	3587	3420	4111	4813
649	1020	1914	1575	1559	2502	1873
3922	4574	5590	3902	18731	14705	7427
1968	1753	2174	2500	2448	2834	3677
2317	2768	3701	3884	3701	4176	5463
1554	1676	1885	2088	2263	2469	2581
4969	7368	6988	7258	8001	7719	8031
1517	2399	2103	1973	1984	2424	2641
3365	4639	4625	3981	5828	15690	6300
1481	1721	2142	2150	1991	2432	2826
2357	2357	4039	3220	2964	3606	3981
9034	8801	8110	8601	10417	9746	10599
4699	4799	5474	4190	24152	40056	21437
3116	3462	4747	3487	4471	5463	5160
1602	2272	3321	2580	2942	3442	3550
2410	2800	4041	5051	3836	4884	5546
1827	1713	1597	1669	1653	1963	2355
4518	5615	6780	5936	6061	9037	12602
1535	2116	3574	1955	2352	2748	3296
1454	1746	1509	2245	2242	3428	3783
104	173	228	195	206	289	270
2099	2415	3435	2986	2579	3174	4575
968	2206	3421	4183	2603	2240	5485
291	366	311	342	521	407	514
354	810	1369	1813	600	1150	1780
651	727	896	909	1255	1279	1417

C-1-9续表2

地 区	1978年	1979年	1980年	1981年	1982年	1983年
全 国	**137135**	**183279**	**174769**	**192267**	**191874**	**216116**
中央级	11	44	103	138	78	163
北 京	1990	2238	2802	3167	3416	4063
天 津	1061	1482	1474	1670	1669	2194
河 北	11605	9140	11165	13597	10179	9692
山 西	5437	8154	6749	7893	7854	7015
内蒙古	2040	5922	5714	6218	5135	7379
辽 宁	6103	5607	6671	8073	10591	11727
吉 林	3869	3477	4482	4970	4951	6300
黑龙江	5545	5149	5370	6562	8,005	9,546
上 海	2777	3290	3375	3381	3215	3170
江 苏	9208	10019	11269	12914	11991	14750
浙 江	2853	3475	3703	3897	4070	4808
安 徽	6756	13263	9385	9550	7521	12093
福 建	2730	3272	3625	4268	4773	5506
江 西	3953	8610	6289	5309	6183	7093
山 东	12292	15169	16327	14126	18998	17811
河 南	14140	19495	12007	10921	12862	15216
湖 北	6149	9597	9265	12458	7956	10798
湖 南	4380	6747	7026	8924	7546	10428
广 东	5435	8146	8337	7767	9550	9035
广 西	2073	4019	3213	3674	3897	4779
海 南						
重 庆						
四 川	8511	12722	12063	15429	14542	13943
贵 州	2740	4767	4123	4718	4354	5211
云 南	2948	3478	4172	4599	4231	5251
西 藏	379	1366	1704	1208	1,151	1,357
陕 西	4834	5780	5390	8198	6271	5820
甘 肃	4030	5204	4801	4338	5778	4902
青 海	696	853	862	915	1068	1270
宁 夏	1090	1040	1385	1118	1819	2329
新 疆	1500	1754	1918	2267	2220	2467

单位：万元

1984年	1985年	1986年	1987年	1988年	1989年	1990年
242371	**295841**	**344064**	**359278**	**395646**	**466492**	**519383**
286	443	2526	2742	1297	1185	1517
4904	5719	7287	8906	11355	12805	14738
3101	3583	4113	4531	5209	5861	6585
12427	16654	16581	20578	24272	26484	32162
7924	10683	10193	11833	13977	15845	15976
7909	9030	11684	10867	11254	10975	13510
11741	18341	22112	18104	19595	22233	26318
5952	8391	13570	14016	10692	11439	14155
8782	10119	13791	13686	14205	15127	15982
3540	4467	5503	5603	3965	4741	5364
16403	16254	20586	21208	23816	27647	33150
6480	8174	10211	12353	16113	18710	21111
14059	14340	13524	12942	14854	16444	19755
5601	8298	7657	9238	10332	11213	13935
8360	8364	9768	11546	13240	15076	15791
17413	22757	22496	29017	31890	39382	44965
13710	18456	20939	2260	21784	26566	24275
10760	11860	14581	14846	17804	20704	21092
10373	12357	15013	15167	19110	22384	24981
12337	14516	15526	17076	16675	20206	21863
6382	9438	9634	9054	9757	11955	11313
				2338	3659	3366
17823	20667	24973	25524	28123	32186	36228
5833	9182	8657	9092	9408	11568	12079
7025	10137	13752	12712	14934	31640	33901
1821	1391	1789	1828	1795	2116	2909
6313	7545	8586	9299	10602	12277	13688
8983	6541	7655	7238	8346	7681	8813
1674	1918	2134	1837	1750	1802	2086
1497	1826	1990	1780	2609	1805	2000
2958	4395	4768	4896	4549	4776	5775

C−1−9续表3

地 区	1991年	1992年	1993年	1994年	1995年	1996年
全 国	**625359**	**637097**	**698708**	**870194**	**1034502**	**1211500**
中央级	1792	3217	3108	4077	3703	6371
北 京	16249	19073	26105	36146	44073	54012
天 津	7176	8173	9218	11970	15023	17254
河 北	30785	33344	38161	48303	58804	74364
山 西	17378	19264	19515	22995	31008	37882
内蒙古	13449	14250	15314	18378	20470	26012
辽 宁	26380	29561	32903	44239	60067	59580
吉 林	14619	16553	18461	24648	30876	31416
黑龙江	18411	19734	19377	26195	28798	30459
上 海	6270	7742	10368	15557	19773	23984
江 苏	50604	48290	47590	59349	69907	80163
浙 江	22094	22124	26924	40044	43610	50852
安 徽	80611	39002	26982	26883	37348	43979
福 建	15070	18423	20141	25502	31904	34498
江 西	16915	21249	21410	23815	30354	33883
山 东	46744	52525	62616	71995	76826	88009
河 南	27675	31304	34498	44163	52458	59353
湖 北	23318	23677	28918	39148	40291	50385
湖 南	23436	24712	29096	35093	42680	53778
广 东	25022	29602	43983	53653	64806	75354
广 西	12728	14317	16760	30480	28730	36280
海 南	3843	4270	4630	6163	7210	8828
重 庆						
四 川	39004	42563	49037	59629	70257	77059
贵 州	11043	11761	15154	15641	20528	26419
云 南	38725	41026	30502	31529	36916	46048
西 藏	3499	2647	2598	5304	4466	5228
陕 西	13412	16805	20107	20404	26336	32108
甘 肃	9124	11256	12186	13897	17748	21484
青 海	2036	2387	2965	3454	4342	6473
宁 夏	2206	2456	2464	3244	3458	4279
新 疆	5741	5790	7617	8297	11732	15706

单位：万元

1997年	1998年	1999年	2000年	2001年	2002年	2003年
1335202	**1618445**	**1946843**	**2296954**	**2847548**	**3922695**	**4989171.8**
5954	50783	11856	29338	13965	18467	18027.2
61184	74406	97748	150746	196540	233429	303795.3
19738	20952	20611	30547	41580	58202	62682.2
71151	79064	88202	113381	125698	153525	185640.8
37150	39519	45466	56815	71776	105897	124002.5
26773	35484	35659	44674	55328	70606	99367.7
65370	74946	85394	131675	180547	227704	279736.9
33928	52337	53311	51153	76026	118392	166702.2
33020	55977	60566	61753	80658	177852	167487.2
30860	37336	54151	87021	121538	167719	222539.6
93383	108862	121349	159691	170800	205763	256062.6
60657	65733	88269	97755	124023	159432	189645.4
50559	56473	72895	72568	89476	138918	208605.9
46134	49421	50996	67797	68897	85353	94060.8
35962	47177	45334	49521	57966	92013	149217.2
101613	112960	131746	159315	180470	233918	283989.3
64155	68311	80338	102698	117574	159157	221712.8
58511	85285	75622	113381	122382	167653	229233.85
48234	54533	73272	80343	104818	158443	210815.4
88748	96993	112133	144461	198362	278022	341821.0
28944	30995	31950	35135	49819	82929	109901.0
8274	9472	10818	13568	15372	18032	24304.1
25048	35054	51123	55934	70571	117114	125112.4
63016	72283	89492	105249	139493	194774	244374.4
27866	27126	30834	36085	51264	67973	82093.5
52043	53384	63169	78944	98782	115945	150814.0
6987	11749	6824	9920	14979	15358	17912.7
31702	25791	43230	54365	72136	103474	147038.8
20366	20554	26371	35251	42851	58315	75346.0
8088	8669	23784	16159	19790	24812	36616.0
4397	5442	8651	13775	21289	28724	30448.1
25387	22690	55676	56940	52768	104762	130065.0

C-1-9续表4

地 区	2004年	2005年	2006年	2007年	2008年	2009年
全 国	**5773906.5**	**7184146**	**9153527**	**12154874**	**21464484**	**21819430.2**
中央级	39289.8	37423	27907	32841	263213	55240.2
北 京	327957	370918	450229	575756	575302	745435.4
天 津	71091.4	92462	121917	149046	196893	244982.6
河 北	216769.6	283480	356510	488387	678036	843485.2
山 西	147569.6	192257	236469	339210	457567	562518.4
内蒙古	126236.7	141727	187147	283105	420111	575897.9
辽 宁	304551.2	368476	437608	575209	724799	887386.5
吉 林	182133.4	218688	284676	341920	470519	642777.6
黑龙江	193823.3	222865	376619	478896	643011	800947.6
上 海	228764.3	282196	316864	406118	515828	557187.9
江 苏	309196	419996	502744	632560	811832	996449.2
浙 江	294720.4	354320	415110	508925	610800	704117.9
安 徽	195411.9	250782	312519	490974	659432	804010.6
福 建	139539.3	157015	226313	247500	282403	322487.9
江 西	176371.5	225667	340990	434664	596019	693704.1
山 东	311522.3	408419	526836	715079	885720	1122739
河 南	251438.9	337872	425038	598726	785189	1035342.8
湖 北	270653.4	345556	440298	514067	748412	897367.7
湖 南	252891.5	326694	422998	521304	771404	997685.9
广 东	386221.4	483430	635940	720130	834465	1021108.9
广 西	113722.5	156841	175928	247212	410162	492763.3
海 南	27949.8	38103	49003	65929	96527	142315.6
重 庆	145713	174682	216847	307697	435014	514479.6
四 川	302566.3	376043	500440	734868	4848630	2289514.1
贵 州	102696.6	151257	181266	264299	443051	560108.4
云 南	183854.7	202346	228950	420914	687354	930167.6
西 藏	23199.7	22574	30224	38363	69982	82169.4
陕 西	149120.1	186935	244342	365358	849627	867024.3
甘 肃	91876.1	111530	149598	226791	1063855	577204.8
青 海	39139.1	47402	51844	81455	123508	189659.7
宁 夏	34071.3	35346	57593	79705	110375	143479.2
新 疆	133844.4	160847	222762	267867	395446	519670.9

单位：万元

2010年	2011年	2012年	2013年	2014年	2015年	2016年
26975149.0	**32291356.0**	**36837379.4**	**42765370.8**	**44041244.2**	**49264448.4**	**54401503.4**
488035.9	93505.4	100110.8	137419.9	128646.0	155949.2	165749.1
982144.3	1031493.0	1260515.9	1555734.8	1600353.6	2220633.5	2558934.6
313824.7	375011.5	444250.9	552118.0	591814.0	769084.9	895069.9
969269.1	1244217.3	1438698.1	1672465.7	1653297.9	1805161.2	2115331.3
634004.6	876097.5	936468.5	1130400.3	1144649.5	1201392.7	1291517.7
768526.2	968084.5	1127395.6	1236610.0	1409253.2	1410121.9	1400524.5
1066504.6	1347428.2	1567755.2	1672890.8	1694087.8	1844543.3	1845473.1
750632.3	801698.3	765275.0	986245.5	942015.8	1057440.4	1041251.7
854398.8	1050480.9	1152380.1	1589618.1	1373441.2	1504605.0	1526756.7
572521.7	662862.5	727872.8	832211.6	857287.8	966471.0	1532275.2
1265312.3	1711513.8	1970955.5	2335259.9	2460508.3	2605552.1	2872252.8
884859.5	1061597.3	1253870.2	1428845.7	1502557.1	1674651.1	1899440.0
971558.4	1263090.4	1421837.3	1601142.2	1699609.2	1812233.9	1970515.8
422187.8	503195.6	614533.8	729824.6	775607.4	903162.9	1041706.7
847650.9	986614.7	1075144.7	1224409.1	1472214.2	1571857.7	1717261.4
1437374.8	1691804.7	2183629.3	2502270.9	2706751.9	2871388.9	3048812.9
1230796.6	1586875.1	1740800.2	2097496.0	2054924.0	2292633.2	2469598.6
1082788.8	1408483.1	1531263.7	1849392.5	1852790.6	2269799.1	2423266.1
1165255.4	1545645.5	2003252.4	1996276.3	2085354.4	2305544.2	2716411.4
1154286.9	1480652.6	1668953.2	1981669.0	2237116.3	2595187.3	3056715.3
731162.4	971372.9	1173997.1	1292515.6	1391271.4	1492923.0	1577969.5
190264.1	223849.3	240254.6	254400.4	287775.5	296623.7	300733.3
674873.3	783120.4	907587.4	999446.7	1027739.5	1146517.8	1299701.7
2408738.2	2168767.6	2375722.4	2880631.2	2917857.6	3152459.5	3486433.8
728242.8	1116447.6	1248670.9	1341494.8	1391678.3	1472311.4	1602657.5
1224026.2	1432131.1	1730472.3	1845730.7	1979476.0	2310934.8	2348845.7
85017.8	130279.7	155073.7	156074.8	136789.5	175034.3	235821.1
1139380.6	1356364.3	1424205.1	1838401.7	1679000.3	1847868.8	2020674.1
740624.8	1000902.5	1051754.7	1299304.5	1214834.5	1367615.6	1631306.1
330701.5	359785.5	341516.9	377594.3	381598.0	462567.9	492304.9
161335.6	195226.4	220055.6	266258.2	264662.5	409809.1	420877.6
698848.1	862756.8	983105.5	1101217.0	1126280.9	1292369.0	1395313.3

C-1-10 社会服务事业费

地 区	合计	抚恤合计	财社[2016]47号	财社[2016]46号	
			追减宾团抚恤补助资金	优抚对象抚恤补助资金	老党员生活补贴
全 国	**24840219**	**3909271**	**-1010**	**1760551**	**5245**
北 京	845090	29095		13202	47
天 津	199107	30088		10098	28
河 北	1110045	225025		107850	1513
山 西	731938	104754		49190	596
内蒙古	654149	38750		16456	69
辽 宁	978915	83359		35561	69
吉 林	695346	69374		27918	52
黑龙江	907266	63206		25800	81
上 海	179323	17479		8214	1
江 苏	624278	178711		81760	552
浙 江	283335	86429		41053	109
安 徽	1000620	182573		86673	49
福 建	330103	62336		27585	7
江 西	909581	147099		68408	3
山 东	1225791	368166		129863	1644
河 南	1451856	301275		144201	235
湖 北	1240647	218763		97667	10
湖 南	1517625	398827		191902	11
广 东	546927	129526		61764	9
广 西	909081	108994		52311	
海 南	191247	16673		7844	12
重 庆	593059	125565		53764	5
四 川	1815207	402332		185215	15
贵 州	1124294	109588		52430	3
云 南	1306158	164195		74988	12
西 藏	148655	5107		1032	
陕 西	986501	131386		59486	96
甘 肃	1028623	53763		24744	13
青 海	305300	10722		3961	1
宁 夏	217999	8546		3755	1
新 疆	766554	37798		15856	2
兵 团	15599	-233	-1010		

中央专项拨款对账单

单位：万元

财社[2016]68号	财社[2016]70号	财社〔2016〕63号	财社〔2016〕147号	财社〔2016〕141号	
优抚事业单位补助资金	兵团优抚事业单位抚恤资金	烈士褒扬	一次性生活补助金	抚恤提标(优抚对象抚恤补助金)	抚恤提标(老党员生活补助)
72075	**715**	**23048**	**1777**	**129382**	**387**
644		341	1	805	4
628		8481		593	2
4344		579	1	7930	110
2775		410	9	3675	34
1694		507	4	1092	5
1880		433	3	2553	5
2410		87	1	2196	3
2652		796	4	2038	5
234		87		515	
1904		507	2	5944	44
1650		312	35	2995	8
2878		574	161	5944	4
2017		254	64	2453	0
4263		508	634	5786	0
4803		826		12042	124
3372		840	194	10392	23
3623		427	49	8882	2
4274		719	37	13349	1
2937		225	8	3624	1
2525		174	158	3378	
732		81	9	648	1
1664		87		3746	
3646		1064	270	13091	1
2966		286	7	3242	
2267		621	2	4818	1
652		260		159	
3189		168	115	4202	8
1478		260	6	1777	1
1051				289	
919			2	240	
2004		3134	1	984	
	715				

C-1-10续表1

地　区	财社[2016]140号	财社[2015]198号	财社[2015]199号	财社[2016]3号	财社[2016]4号
	抚恤提标	提前下达2016年优抚对象补助资金(第一批)	提前下达2015年优抚对象补助资金(第二批)老党员	墓地维修和烈属接待	墓地维修和烈属接待
全　国	**62**	**1905712**	**10327**	**500**	**500**
北　京		13951	100		
天　津		10201	57		
河　北		99737	2961		
山　西		47321	744		
内蒙古		18793	130		
辽　宁		42688	167		
吉　林		36614	93		
黑龙江		31678	152		
上　海		8426	2		
江　苏		86836	1162		
浙　江		40067	200		
安　徽		86188	102		
福　建		29944	12		
江　西		67490	7		
山　东		215521	3343		
河　南		141346	672		
湖　北		108050	53		
湖　南		188513	21		
广　东		60944	14		
广　西		49944	4	500	
海　南		7318	28		
重　庆		66286	13		
四　川		199001	29		
贵　州		50650	4		
云　南		80965	21		500
西　藏		3004			
陕　西		63929	193		
甘　肃		25456	28		
青　海		5419	1		
宁　夏		3626	3		
新　疆		15806	11		
兵　团	62				

单位：万元

退役安置合计	财社[2015]200号	财社[2015]201号	财社[2016]65号		
	军休人员，无军籍退休职工、生活补助	工作人员、车辆经费、退休职工服务管理经费	退役安置补助资金（第一批，退役士兵职业教育和技能培训）	退役安置补助资金（第一批，转业士官待分配期间管理教育补助）	退役安置补助资金（第一批，一级至四级分散供养残疾退役士兵购建房补助）
3847307	**1926103**	**72968**	**64754**	**515**	**1710**
782244	367433	14063	136	6	60
91852	46770	1592	176	3	10
202255	106786	4343	3212	37	80
64559	35080	1279	1301	11	40
42840	21986	1115	951	14	20
357793	189579	6811	1422	21	60
77698	40331	1704	981	10	40
65136	32158	1514	2331	5	40
128791	61987	2402	218	3	
211486	105503	3998	4883	15	100
78329	38810	1532	1930	18	50
56779	26663	1208	3973	10	120
61033	30938	1246	1500	11	90
33562	16467	648	2863	26	20
308323	159087	5294	4549	42	200
118357	57618	2372	5811	35	150
140354	72374	2528	4337	23	90
90304	43582	1755	4846	55	120
157363	79283	2730	2316	13	50
36736	17551	823	2077	11	30
21087	9883	451	402	4	
64099	32428	1104	1403	6	50
165677	83252	3037	4549	40	120
24356	11422	539	1881	15	10
99914	53033	2139	1801	27	
17788	8367	219	86	5	10
170557	87658	3116	1805	32	90
66361	33828	1387	1714	14	20
19745	9815	363	273	1	
11953	5722	252	558	1	
79976	40709	1404	469	1	40

C-1-10续表2

地 区	财社[2016]61号	财社[2016]62号	财社[2016]69号	社会福利合计
	退役安置补助资金（第三批，离退休人员服务管理）	退役安置补助资金（第二批，军休人员）	2016年退役安置补助资金（第四批，军休干部管理机构用房）	
全 国	**47606**	**1601462**	**132189**	**193925**
北 京	9282	324749	66515	481
天 津	1018	39293	2990	208
河 北	2757	82844	2196	5655
山 西	840	25084	924	5050
内蒙古	720	17613	421	3320
辽 宁	4290	151307	4303	1933
吉 林	1126	32196	1310	1914
黑龙江	924	27250	914	2769
上 海	1633	55222	7326	472
江 苏	2716	89489	4782	4282
浙 江	1026	33791	1172	1160
安 徽	811	22909	1085	9913
福 建	858	25112	1278	1458
江 西	430	12561	547	8338
山 东	3468	129575	6108	4212
河 南	1543	48279	2549	15439
湖 北	1711	56181	3110	8796
湖 南	1152	37765	1029	14856
广 东	1868	64114	6989	9323
广 西	558	14641	1045	11458
海 南	308	8651	1388	703
重 庆	716	27035	1357	5385
四 川	1976	69416	3287	14497
贵 州	345	9829	315	10343
云 南	1366	39403	2145	11369
西 藏	144	8540	417	2820
陕 西	2038	72255	3563	6007
甘 肃	833	27480	1085	9881
青 海	176	8667	450	7816
宁 夏	156	4945	319	3308
新 疆	817	35266	1270	10759
兵 团				

单位：万元

财社[2016]59号	财社[2015]202号	社会救助合计	城乡低保及临时救助小计	财社[2016]71号
2016年下达孤儿基本生活保障资金	提前下达2016孤儿基本生活保障资金			低保、特困人员救助供养、临时救助支出
70373	**123552**	**15679851**	**13701298**	**5247506**
158	323	22870	6932	3200
80	128	71104	63185	29162
2248	3407	609260	536423	237762
1739	3311	510297	450876	189291
1322	1998		465442	169216
		522385		
811	1122	511253	467250	155750
715	1199	521395	455090	151697
1063	1706	742412	659866	219955
176	296	22783	17160	7920
1623	2659	194500	158100	72969
415	745	94826	75434	34816
3987	5926	688645	600175	231515
521	937	164463	141855	65471
1885	6453	657200	569185	245683
1669	2543	514993	448616	207053
5373	10066	976181	863204	287735
2749	6047	786305	695861	231954
5309	9547	932354	798210	323023
3285	6038	232119	188170	86848
4632	6826	729064	647919	290982
238	465	139141	111337	51386
1804	3581	377845	316104	105369
5694	8803	1175086	1004081	334693
4052	6291	916599	825934	275311
4389	6980	982491	882609	346538
1128	1692	107466	83525	38550
2256	3751	641723	558117	186039
3654	6227	841520	753288	312732
3102	4714	236735	197786	91285
1269	2039	176505	145724	67257
3027	7732	580224	513840	196344
		107		

C-1-10续表3

地 区	财社[2015]233号		城乡医疗救助小计	城乡医疗
	2016年救助补助资金预算指标下达(低保补助资金)	2016年救助补助资金预算指标下达(临时救助补助资金)		本次下达小计
全 国	**8167211**	**286581**	**1541323**	**547681**
北 京		3732	2401	853
天 津	29987	4036	3572	1271
河 北	288646	10015	58086	25574
山 西	252771	8814	48416	21189
内蒙古	287512	8714	50893	19254
辽 宁	303098	8402	32443	11541
吉 林	295026	8367	58055	18871
黑龙江	428705	11206	74424	24191
上 海		9240	2309	822
江 苏	75130	10001	16226	5772
浙 江	32240	8378	7879	2802
安 徽	357783	10877	67760	23350
福 建	69126	7258	12803	4554
江 西	312107	11395	73805	23990
山 东	229349	12214	33861	
				12045
河 南	563710	11759	85409	27762
湖 北	452979	10928	65075	21153
湖 南	463523	11664	92813	30168
广 东	91661	9661	16020	5698
广 西	346463	10474	68438	28702
海 南	53290	6661	23328	11082
重 庆	202021	8714	48956	20982
四 川	656159	13229	134324	43661
贵 州	540908	9715	77388	25154
云 南	525363	10708	86121	27993
西 藏	38461	6514	22479	
				10678
陕 西	361695	10383	70581	22942
甘 肃	429759	10797	82488	26812
青 海	98494	8007	35626	15475
宁 夏	71597	6870	28658	13614
新 疆	309648	7848	60686	19726
兵 团				

单位：万元

财社[2016]72号		财社[2015] 223号	流浪乞讨救助小计	财社[2016]60号	财社[2015]209号
救助补助资金		提前下达城乡医疗救助补助资金预算指标		流浪乞讨人员救助资金本次下达	提前下达2016年流浪乞讨救助补助预算指标
一般公共预算资金	彩票公益金				
367681	**180000**	**993642**	**199986**	**59995**	**139991**
573	280	1548	11584	5346	6238
854	417	2301	1200	364	836
18791	6783	32512	3895	4	3891
15535	5654	27227	5177	977	4200
13311	5943	31639	2660		2660
7752	3789	20902	5688	2625	3063
12091	6780	39184	3089	460	2629
15500	8691	50233	3133	783	2350
552	270	1487	2074	568	1506
3877	1895	10454	8698	1974	6724
1882	920	5077	5520	1818	3702
15437	7913	44410	9261	1977	7284
3059	1495	8249	4752	1778	2974
15371	8619	49815	6605	2215	4390
		21816	10713	4944	5769
8091	3954				
17788	9974	57647	12089	4944	7145
13553	7600	43922	12502	602	11900
19329	10839	62645	20444	7346	13098
3827	1871	10322	17303	7986	9317
20710	7992	39736	6515	215	6300
8358	2724	12246	2350	1014	1336
15265	5717	27974	4486	2070	2416
27972	15689	90663	16210	3646	12564
16116	9038	52234	6500	2731	3769
17936	10057	58128	3942	1508	2434
		11801	422		422
8053	2625				
14699	8243	47639	5188	397	4791
17179	9633	55676	2714	699	2015
11314	4161	20151	1383		1383
10267	3347	15044	715	15	700
12639	7087	40960	3174	989	2185

C-1-10续表4

地 区	优抚医疗小计	财社[2016]53号	财社[2016]42号	财社[2015]204号
		优抚对象医疗补助资金	兵团对象优抚医疗补助	提前下达2015年优抚对象医疗补助资金预算指标
全 国	**237244**	**94880**	**107**	**142257**
北 京	1953	796		1157
天 津	3147	1277		1870
河 北	10856	4193		6663
山 西	5828	2415		3413
内蒙古	3390	1355		2035
辽 宁	5872	2343		3529
吉 林	5161	1922		3239
黑龙江	4989	1869		3120
上 海	1240	507		733
江 苏	11476	4623		6853
浙 江	5993	2477		3516
安 徽	11449	4666		6783
福 建	5053	2013		3040
江 西	7605	2772		4833
山 东	21803	7801		14002
河 南	15479	6181		9298
湖 北	12867	4937		7930
湖 南	20887	9344		11543
广 东	10626	4598		6028
广 西	6192	2503		3689
海 南	2126	888		1238
重 庆	8299	3162		5137
四 川	20471	8651		11820
贵 州	6777	2663		4114
云 南	9819	3984		5835
西 藏	1040	396		644
陕 西	7837	2918		4919
甘 肃	3030	1201		1829
青 海	1940	789		1151
宁 夏	1408	590		818
新 疆	2524	1046		1478
兵 团	107		107	

单位：万元

自然灾害生活救助合计	财社[2016]14号	财社[2016]33号	财社[2016]74号	财社[2016]79号	财社[2016]80号
	下达2016年中央自然灾害生活补助资金	救灾	救灾	救灾	救灾
790601	**7101**	**2000**	**10000**	**58700**	**800**
49	49				
391	391				
51000					
33800				4000	
36200					
10017	617				
13200					
19266	666				
0					
14400			10000		
6000					
47476	276			4700	
33058	258	2000			
48500				10700	
7300					
23735	635				
69371	471			6600	
58711	411			9000	
6000					
9679	179				
8900					
12700					
35509	609				
53700				11700	
33513	513				
4964	64				
25199	599				
41649	349				
17602	402				
11400					
44512	612			12000	
12800					800

C-1-10续表5

地 区	财社[2016]95号	财社[2016]112号	财社[2016]116号	财社[2016]117号	财社[2016]129号
	救灾	救灾	救灾	救灾	救灾
全 国	**56000**	**7500**	**25000**	**15000**	**6000**
北 京					
天 津					
河 北			25000		
山 西				6000	
内蒙古					6000
辽 宁					
吉 林					
黑龙江					
上 海					
江 苏					
浙 江					
安 徽	18000				
福 建		7500			
江 西					
山 东					
河 南				9000	
湖 北	20000				
湖 南	11000				
广 东					
广 西					
海 南					
重 庆					
四 川					
贵 州	7000				
云 南					
西 藏					
陕 西					
甘 肃					
青 海					
宁 夏					
新 疆					
兵 团					

单位：万元

财社[2016]138号	财社[2016]139号	财社[2016]152号	财社[2016]203号	财社[2016]204号	民政管理事务合计（地名普查）财社[2016]15号
救灾	救灾	救灾	冬春救济	冬春救济	
6000	**22000**	**4000**	**558500**	**12000**	**73368**
					611
					563
			26000		3444
			23800		2782
			30200		3048
			9400		1996
			13200		1596
			18600		3052
					597
			4400		1726
	4000		2000		1509
			24500		2349
	18000		5300		1914
			37800		2674
			7300		
					2228
			14100		3065
			42300		2453
			38300		2923
			6000		1713
			9500		3220
		4000	4900		934
			12700		1555
			34900		4131
			35000		3074
			33000		3573
			4900		3162
			24600		2987
6000			35300		3215
			17200		2601
			11400		1577
			31900		3096
				12000	

C-1-10续表6

地　区	彩票公益金合计	财社[2016]110号			
		老年人福利	残疾人福利	儿童福利	社会公益
全　国	**345896**	**2000**	**450**	**380**	**95**
北　京	9740				
天　津	4901				
河　北	13406				
山　西	10696				
内蒙古	7606				
辽　宁	12564				
吉　林	10169				
黑龙江	11425				
上　海	9201				
江　苏	19173				
浙　江	15082				
安　徽	12885				
福　建	5841				
江　西	12208				
山　东	20569				
河　南	13804				
湖　北	14605				
湖　南	19650				
广　东	10883				
广　西	9930				
海　南	3809				
重　庆	5910				
四　川	17975				
贵　州	6634				
云　南	11103				
西　藏	7348				
陕　西	8642				
甘　肃	12234				
青　海	10079				
宁　夏	4710				
新　疆	10189				
兵　团	2925	2000	450	380	95

单位：万元

财社[2016]111号	财社[2016]111号			财社[2016]197号
老年人福利	残疾人福利	儿童福利	社会公益	居家和社区养老服务改革试点
129072	**29550**	**59444**	**24905**	**100000**
1494	1091	1752	509	4894
1259	110	390	331	2811
6072	1027	1690	790	3827
3498	728	1558	971	3941
3512	1617	1737	740	
4175	616	1615	996	5162
3306	395	1738	642	4088
4180	785	1525	760	4175
1835	1100	201	327	5738
6271	1582	2379	906	8035
4481	544	1457	604	7996
6420	652	1274	912	3627
2887	523	1706	725	
4594	1609	1570	884	3551
7620	822	2683	1063	8381
6887	1944	3996	977	
5244	1619	2165	902	4675
6470	1733	2994	1141	7312
4516	724	1504	778	3361
4692	1669	2556	1013	
2323	170	620	696	
3820	260	1023	807	
8056	1094	2493	1209	5123
3783	559	1469	823	
3785	785	1921	866	3746
2470	488	3626	764	
3753	1646	2282	961	
3618	553	1874	779	5410
2571	1296	1434	631	4147
2515	191	1402	602	
2965	1618	4810	796	

C-1-11 社会服务

地 区	收入合计	上年结余	本年收入合计	本年实际支出
全 国	**58808470.6**	**3382117.9**	**55426352.7**	**54401503.4**
中央级	323404.7	68794.9	254609.8	165749.1
北 京	3049234.4	425980.4	2623254	2558934.6
天 津	1055974.7	151382.6	904592.1	895069.9
河 北	2283428.2	116258.7	2167169.5	2115331.3
山 西	1526695.6	158481.9	1368213.7	1291517.7
内蒙古	1556557.2	95012.2	1461545	1400524.5
辽 宁	1892242.7	28934	1863308.7	1845473.1
吉 林	1059535.6	16717.7	1042817.9	1041251.7
黑龙江	1547118.4	20883.4	1526235	1526756.7
上 海	1724294.7	197498.2	1526796.5	1532275.2
江 苏	2917962	43149.7	2874812.3	2872252.8
浙 江	2015620.7	94203.4	1921417.3	1899440
安 徽	1978753.7	9015.8	1969737.9	1970515.8
福 建	1179431.2	107906.2	1071525	1041706.7
江 西	1718069.4	111.4	1717958	1717261.4
山 东	3056256.5	8651	3047605.5	3048812.9
河 南	2575697.1	65374.9	2510322.2	2469598.6
湖 北	2732479.2	45090.2	2687389	2423266.1
湖 南	2751678.2	38783.4	2712894.8	2716411.4
广 东	3183990.2	83958.9	3100031.3	3056715.3
广 西	1839496.2	212067	1627429.2	1577969.5
海 南	463888.2	117559.5	346328.7	300733.3
重 庆	1410380.5	89556.3	1320824.2	1299701.7
四 川	3705685.9	206172.7	3499513.2	3486433.8
贵 州	2160583.1	458051.3	1702531.8	1602657.5
云 南	2532940.9	174866.7	2358074.2	2348845.7
西 藏	257410.3	12410.2	245000.1	235821.1
陕 西	2106494.6	95324.5	2011170.1	2020674.1
甘 肃	1732787.9	75138.9	1657649	1631306.1
青 海	504149.4	3881.1	500268.3	492304.9
宁 夏	534403.3	100110.2	434293.1	420877.6
新 疆	1431825.9	60790.6	1371035.3	1395313.3

事业费收支简表

单位：万元

收支结余	用事业基金弥补收支差额	结余分配	年末净结余
4406967.2	**127269.5**	**216107**	**4318129.7**
157655.6	432.3	1927	156160.9
490299.8	5622.7	12000.2	483922.3
160904.8	2162.3	5846.6	157220.5
168096.9	3695.4	5134.8	166657.5
235177.9	479.7	559.5	235098.1
156032.7	8075.5	8075.5	156032.7
46769.6	1990.9	347.1	48413.4
18283.9	3950.6	3116.6	19117.9
20361.7	856.2	543.3	20674.6
192019.5	741	8454	184306.5
45709.2	1101.7	4127.1	42683.8
116180.7	0.2	11010.2	105170.7
8237.9	18.8	1734.4	6522.3
137724.5	1431.3	3416.2	135739.6
808			808
7443.6	75.1	275.1	7243.6
106098.5		963.2	105135.3
309213.1	12717.4	17793.5	304137
35266.8	375.8	535	35107.6
127274.9	1382.4	22204.2	106453.1
261526.7	9480.5	15042.7	255964.5
163154.9	20233.5	28038.3	155350.1
110678.8	7554.7	10406.2	107827.3
219252.1	9359.7	10877.8	217734
557925.6	230	772	557383.6
184095.2	8550.4	18526.3	174119.3
21589.2	17545.4	20489.2	18645.4
85820.5	6159.9	316.5	91663.9
101481.8			101481.8
11844.5			11844.5
113525.7	3046.1	3574.5	112997.3
36512.6			36512.6

C-1-12 社会服务事业费

地 区	收入合计	上年结余合计	抚恤	退役安置	社会福利
全 国	**58808470.6**	**3382117.9**	**281558.0**	**589807.8**	**662362.5**
中央级	323404.7	68794.9	511.3		10400.0
北 京	3049234.4	425980.4	17601.1	311098.8	33054.2
天 津	1055974.7	151382.6	5640.7	14431.7	55573.0
河 北	2283428.2	116258.7	14485.7	22772.2	26985.1
山 西	1526695.6	158481.9	17879.9	14406.6	28520.0
内蒙古	1556557.2	95012.2	8755.1	8622.1	16135.6
辽 宁	1892242.7	28934.0	842.4	10554.5	1361.6
吉 林	1059535.6	16717.7	1968.9	1250.6	580.6
黑龙江	1547118.4	20883.4	984.7	1293.8	2128.2
上 海	1724294.7	197498.2	8452.3	44569.9	45943.7
江 苏	2917962.0	43149.7	1598.1	2014.1	24407.9
浙 江	2015620.7	94203.4	14688.6	8704.0	23042.3
安 徽	1978753.7	9015.8	544.6	308.2	2514.2
福 建	1179431.2	107906.2	11287.2	18967.9	33671.4
江 西	1718069.4	111.4			
山 东	3056256.5	8651.0	4238.7	39.5	48.5
河 南	2575697.1	65374.9	3156.5	3796.0	8783.1
湖 北	2732479.2	45090.2	493.0	21061.1	11371.0
湖 南	2751678.2	38783.4	1763.1	368.5	102.2
广 东	3183990.2	83958.9	9161.2	12810.1	19121.2
广 西	1839496.2	212067.0	37397.5	14313.4	54476.4
海 南	463888.2	117559.5	9026.3	12465.5	24197.6
重 庆	1410380.5	89556.3	4599.0	3413.3	27425.1
四 川	3705685.9	206172.7	10906.7	11447.0	72110.5
贵 州	2160583.1	458051.3	42459.3	14761.2	65922.4
云 南	2532940.9	174866.7	32289.1	14585.4	16658.6
西 藏	257410.3	12410.2	207.3	44.8	504.1
陕 西	2106494.6	95324.5	7366.1	5473.9	12501.1
甘 肃	1732787.9	75138.9	3395.8	8174.4	14747.5
青 海	504149.4	3881.1	631.8		684.8
宁 夏	534403.3	100110.2	1350.0	2901.7	6130.4
新 疆	1431825.9	60790.6	7876.0	5157.6	23260.2

收支明细表

单位：万元

社会救助	自然灾害生活救助	民政管理事务	行政事业单位离退休	其他款项用于民政支出
1015912.9	**184013.9**	**325289.3**	**8800.2**	**314373.3**
		22424.9	13.7	35445.0
21463.4	20.0	21636.4	295.2	20811.3
27298.8	911.3	45839.2	231.7	1456.2
28092.9	10819.7	12614.3	93.4	395.4
81438.0	5959.1	5068.0	12.8	5197.5
25413.4	5891.2	22958.3	26.9	7209.6
1226.3	3188.8	3371.1	185.4	8203.9
11432.5	388.0	1097.1		
13132.9	390.8	2540.1		412.9
44643.5	1000.0	34977.3	403.9	17507.6
2637.2	2181.8	4663.7	6.6	5640.3
20947.9	6666.8	16989.7	919.6	2244.5
4869.4	409.3	166.3		203.8
16258.6	4862.6	16116.5	868.7	5873.3
111.4				
31.2		4293.1		
45113.9	97.2	773.8		3654.4
7998.2	230.0	2331.9		1605.0
5863.2	241.6	257.4		30187.4
23771.1	2395.1	9207.4	735.8	6757.0
52266.5	19924.1	13524.8	59.1	20105.2
45093.5	3225.7	13439.4	137.4	9974.1
36812.0	6708.1	7026.1	7.9	3564.8
61004.4	27426.5	6913.6	109.4	16254.6
268011.3	37525.2	18252.4	77.2	11042.3
41795.8	19174.7	18215.1	466.4	31681.6
767.3	8491.4	1339.1		1056.2
63341.8	2632.7	3493.6	1.3	514.0
20109.1	4331.8	3676.0	27.3	20677.0
2564.5				
25349.1	8177.4	6648.7	4119.3	45433.6
17053.8	743.0	5434.0	1.2	1264.8

C-1-12续表1

地 区	本年收入合计	抚恤	退役安置	社会福利
全 国	**55426352.7**	**7705669.5**	**6170371.9**	**7788253.5**
中央级	254609.8	761.5		17104.0
北 京	2623254.0	148339.1	1243676.9	465614.7
天 津	904592.1	98175.7	119834.2	156308.2
河 北	2167169.5	430403.5	344946.4	255331.6
山 西	1368213.7	241778.0	100015.7	128635.6
内蒙古	1461545.0	99747.4	87007.2	202752.3
辽 宁	1863308.7	203727.4	466119.5	156000.7
吉 林	1042817.9	136340.2	87323.0	91184.0
黑龙江	1526235.0	161943.7	84452.5	133403.9
上 海	1526796.5	109533.2	204454.4	614162.0
江 苏	2874812.3	482430.9	424210.5	540222.2
浙 江	1921417.3	318173.0	162353.3	476359.1
安 徽	1969737.9	317086.2	156600.3	250140.1
福 建	1071525.0	150691.4	110392.0	221245.3
江 西	1717958.0	252861.3	60636.2	111738.2
山 东	3047605.5	778464.8	449727.3	407845.8
河 南	2510322.2	510645.9	204940.7	245003.9
湖 北	2687389.0	394769.4	203587.6	246241.1
湖 南	2712894.8	528411.7	145299.4	318746.2
广 东	3100031.3	425018.1	306943.1	563928.3
广 西	1627429.2	224053.4	67679.0	243821.3
海 南	346328.7	30907.4	21834.7	71637.1
重 庆	1320824.2	195194.2	105654.4	171997.6
四 川	3499513.2	592397.4	303434.4	450425.4
贵 州	1702531.8	166529.7	47930.0	189774.1
云 南	2358074.2	250302.5	139429.2	148520.2
西 藏	245000.1	11192.5	19746.0	26308.5
陕 西	2011170.1	281907.3	253479.8	344589.2
甘 肃	1657649.0	68153.4	102807.6	173184.9
青 海	500268.3	17738.1	33156.3	105980.4
宁 夏	434293.1	15848.5	11724.1	30180.2
新 疆	1371035.3	62142.7	100976.2	229867.4

单位：万元

社会救助	自然灾害生活救助	民政管理事务	行政事业单位离退休	其他款项用于民政支出
25573756.0	**1597835.6**	**4483340.8**	**479913.1**	**1627212.3**
	13500.0	140914.5	5867.2	76462.6
216219.0	2364.7	322702.0	61158.2	163179.4
283041.7	1996.6	228096.4	3270.8	13868.5
881695.6	102029.4	110325.0	30984.5	11453.5
744427.2	49096.2	67832.4	8232.5	28196.1
875741.4	59157.2	68284.6	16473.7	52381.2
736759.0	21521.4	209909.3	20964.5	48306.9
600108.2	27642.2	65353.0	7675.1	27192.2
1035522.0	36967.3	51642.1	14681.3	7622.2
392255.9		159779.2	5804.9	40806.9
936041.7	60406.2	269982.0	27323.5	134195.3
618123.5	35512.9	240312.5	16118.9	54464.1
1056257.8	71805.6	78682.5	18042.3	21123.1
365115.4	65530.1	100134.4	18753.5	39662.9
1124202.5	58411.4	60244.2	10739.4	39124.8
1075942.7	15695.1	233123.4	14901.2	71905.2
1288900.0	48698.5	132781.8	22833.7	56517.7
1437505.3	148590.6	190979.2	22290.5	43425.3
1404128.5	106227.4	144544.3	7684.2	57853.1
1132890.1	36397.9	361477.1	54630.8	218745.9
863989.0	42898.9	139285.6	17010.1	28691.9
133135.6	10657.4	41385.2	2430.5	34340.8
656421.7	36433.6	124479.2	13416.9	17226.6
1773541.8	64182.6	243897.9	16777.9	54855.8
1048106.4	107532.6	127036.8	1640.8	13981.4
1443653.4	71789.2	178306.1	16073.0	110000.6
115255.3	35899.7	15676.3	1125.1	19796.7
881131.9	46843.4	176441.0	7627.0	19150.5
1148903.0	83809.0	54675.1	6060.6	20055.4
249182.0	27808.9	41978.6	1302.6	23121.4
252002.8	17930.2	40122.0	3419.2	63066.1
803555.6	90499.4	62957.1	4598.7	16438.2

C-1-12续表2

地 区	本年实际支出	抚恤	退役安置	社会福利
全 国	**54401503.4**	**7698352.6**	**6256423.7**	**7534094.3**
中央级	165749.1	584.3		17827.9
北 京	2558934.6	145638.5	1316380.3	331694.5
天 津	895069.9	96839.2	122872.7	129640.2
河 北	2115331.3	430666.7	339278.4	248756.5
山 西	1291517.7	240703.0	104696.7	123380.1
内蒙古	1400524.5	103537.7	87493.9	192802.7
辽 宁	1845473.1	203995.9	460946.4	156576.3
吉 林	1041251.7	137186.9	88277.6	90798.9
黑龙江	1526756.7	160175.6	83920.1	133153.9
上 海	1532275.2	106832.7	223506.0	602473.9
江 苏	2872252.8	484846.6	424085.1	544463.0
浙 江	1899440.0	315497.4	161075.9	464686.4
安 徽	1970515.8	313670.7	156509.5	249740.0
福 建	1041706.7	150920.2	106477.9	223292.3
江 西	1717261.4	252649.1	60569.5	111851.9
山 东	3048812.9	780669.4	449727.8	407359.0
河 南	2469598.6	511927.7	203503.7	241360.7
湖 北	2423266.1	393859.8	209618.7	245194.6
湖 南	2716411.4	527889.7	142988.7	312310.0
广 东	3056715.3	420549.1	305113.2	553255.2
广 西	1577969.5	222955.5	66387.4	239413.6
海 南	300733.3	29796.5	26820.1	60620.7
重 庆	1299701.7	195891.2	108441.2	163857.2
四 川	3486433.8	604649.8	294417.6	442223.4
贵 州	1602657.5	167913.4	43866.0	167888.8
云 南	2348845.7	238661.0	139410.7	147924.1
西 藏	235821.1	9870.3	19274.8	24255.8
陕 西	2020674.1	284958.7	260844.0	351300.3
甘 肃	1631306.1	69182.8	105733.7	162454.3
青 海	492304.9	18293.7	33115.0	111559.9
宁 夏	420877.6	15664.4	10962.8	30427.4
新 疆	1395313.3	61875.1	100108.3	251550.8

单位：万元

社会救助	自然灾害生活救助	民政管理事务	行政事业单位离退休	其他款项用于民政支出
24927885.6	**1560797.1**	**4417368.7**	**484177.0**	**1522404.4**
	11959.1	72228.7	5833.9	57315.2
218281.9	2166.6	297806.9	60704.6	186261.3
292388.2	798.7	242725.5	3380.4	6425.0
855761.2	95409.7	110438.9	30949.2	4070.7
688572.8	46600.5	66761.7	8241.4	12561.5
814018.7	57931.2	78838.3	17677.1	48224.9
727376.8	20020.9	212865.3	21643.3	42048.2
601284.6	23818.9	70844.9	7965.0	21074.9
1036529.0	37201.1	53285.8	14681.3	7809.9
390198.3	300.0	165587.6	5664.3	37712.4
936682.6	60223.8	270477.0	27933.7	123541.0
616995.4	36151.4	237512.6	16207.4	51313.5
1061699.3	71623.3	78991.8	18101.2	20180.0
347573.2	60913.0	97015.3	18164.1	37350.7
1124268.8	58311.4	60095.8	10739.4	38775.5
1072954.8	15721.1	235775.8	14901.2	71703.8
1256623.7	46546.4	134205.9	22859.2	52571.3
1173591.3	146886.5	191293.5	22263.1	40558.6
1397503.5	106185.3	148386.3	7833.6	73314.3
1121026.4	37413.5	370399.6	55450.5	193507.8
809762.8	48649.3	135101.3	17083.8	38615.8
121598.5	5613.3	34771.5	2431.0	19081.7
651651.5	30766.1	117203.0	13364.2	18527.3
1757959.3	81102.8	238083.4	19253.2	48744.3
995539.8	91384.8	120923.4	1680.9	13460.4
1441506.2	79518.5	182361.2	16597.2	102866.8
115777.4	29310.7	17863.3	1107.1	18361.7
880291.8	43353.5	176337.7	7617.3	15970.8
1126099.3	81603.2	52041.4	6149.2	28042.2
240288.6	28085.3	44203.7	1368.7	15390.0
240725.2	16352.0	34512.9	2342.1	69890.8
813354.7	88875.2	68428.7	3988.4	7132.1

C-1-12续表3

地 区	收支结余			用事业基金弥补收支差额	结余分配
		事业结余	经营结余		
全 国	**4406967.2**	**4386343.0**	**20624.2**	**127269.5**	**216107.0**
中央级	157655.6	157655.6		432.3	1927.0
北 京	490299.8	492189.2	-1889.4	5622.7	12000.2
天 津	160904.8	159415.4	1489.4	2162.3	5846.6
河 北	168096.9	168096.9		3695.4	5134.8
山 西	235177.9	235182.1	-4.2	479.7	559.5
内蒙古	156032.7	155423.9	608.8	8075.5	8075.5
辽 宁	46769.6	47297.2	-527.6	1990.9	347.1
吉 林	18283.9	18283.9		3950.6	3116.6
黑龙江	20361.7	20361.7		856.2	543.3
上 海	192019.5	194891.0	-2871.5	741.0	8454.0
江 苏	45709.2	45469.4	239.8	1101.7	4127.1
浙 江	116180.7	116396.4	-215.7	0.2	11010.2
安 徽	8237.9	8237.9		18.8	1734.4
福 建	137724.5	136518.7	1205.8	1431.3	3416.2
江 西	808.0	808.0			
山 东	7443.6	7443.6		75.1	275.1
河 南	106098.5	106098.5			963.2
湖 北	309213.1	302427.8	6785.3	12717.4	17793.5
湖 南	35266.8	35998.1	-731.3	375.8	535.0
广 东	127274.9	127116.2	158.7	1382.4	22204.2
广 西	261526.7	258598.3	2928.4	9480.5	15042.7
海 南	163154.9	163155.1	-0.2	20233.5	28038.3
重 庆	110678.8	110325.9	352.9	7554.7	10406.2
四 川	219252.1	219156.8	95.3	9359.7	10877.8
贵 州	557925.6	546256.0	11669.6	230.0	772.0
云 南	184095.2	182807.6	1287.6	8550.4	18526.3
西 藏	21589.2	21589.2		17545.4	20489.2
陕 西	85820.5	85778.0	42.5	6159.9	316.5
甘 肃	101481.8	101481.8			
青 海	11844.5	11844.5			
宁 夏	113525.7	113525.7		3046.1	3574.5
新 疆	36512.6	36512.6			

单位：万元

转入事业基金	其他	年末结转及结余	抚恤	退役安置	社会福利
129054.8	**87052.2**	**4318129.7**	**295652.3**	**529523.9**	**868719.3**
1724.3	202.7	156160.9	688.5		9676.1
6488.8	5511.4	483922.3	20508.8	238512.5	150389.9
4608.8	1237.8	157220.5	7666.8	10455.7	80346.3
4436.2	698.6	166657.5	13470.7	31585.0	32026.7
446.8	112.7	235098.1	24786.7	20111.3	32277.4
8075.5		156032.7	6625.3	8636.2	19267.7
170.8	176.3	48413.4	1201.9	19281.3	1910.2
3116.6		19117.9	1134.5	396.4	1857.8
543.3		20674.6	2399.8	1237.5	3179.6
5744.1	2709.9	184306.5	10707.4	24013.9	49624.2
2855.3	1271.8	42683.8	627.6	2733.0	28326.1
9058.6	1951.6	105170.7	17316.1	8679.9	30181.8
1463.4	271.0	6522.3	415.7	460.6	570.5
3416.2		135739.6	10620.7	22341.5	31065.0
		808.0		100.0	270.2
200.0	75.1	7243.6	1902.1	39.0	546.3
963.2		105135.3	3450.5	5176.4	18285.1
6348.4	11445.1	304137.0	1705.9	18238.3	8300.3
574.7	-39.7	35107.6	4899.3	1983.4	2939.5
9085.3	13118.9	106453.1	8059.8	8159.2	24318.2
4220.1	10822.6	255964.5	34056.7	16143.3	59034.0
17252.0	10786.3	155350.1	10781.0	16026.8	29439.4
9315.6	1090.6	107827.3	4548.1	893.7	31607.3
1705.3	9172.5	217734.0	14224.0	20642.4	66914.9
693.2	78.8	557383.6	41087.1	18516.3	87654.6
8980.6	9545.7	174119.3	35797.4	14863.0	15059.2
17251.2	3238.0	18645.4	905.3	111.4	470.4
316.5		91663.9	4461.2	3770.2	8283.2
		101481.8	2111.1	5738.6	25467.9
		11844.5	142.7	1.4	1512.4
	3574.5	112997.3	1409.4	3906.2	9061.8
		36512.6	7940.2	6769.5	8855.3

C-1-12续表4

地 区	社会救助	自然灾害生活救助	民政管理事务	行政事业单位离退休	其他款项用于民政支出
全 国	**1589286.9**	**210042.4**	**412461.5**	**7068.3**	**405375.1**
中央级		1540.9	79281.4	68.7	64905.3
北 京	18305.0	218.0	34689.4	998.1	20300.6
天 津	17927.9	2109.2	36946.9	61.9	1705.8
河 北	56571.1	14468.6	14960.1	252.8	3322.5
山 西	137341.0	8454.8	6249.0	3.9	5874.0
内蒙古	43268.4	9210.3	7965.1	397.4	60662.3
辽 宁	11635.8	2081.6	4407.1	147.9	7747.6
吉 林	9612.8	4744.9	711.4		660.1
黑龙江	12194.4	304.7	1076.6		282.0
上 海	47527.6	700.0	30867.8	360.4	20505.2
江 苏	1583.5	2182.2	4748.4	28.8	2454.2
浙 江	22899.5	5887.0	16833.7	846.2	2526.5
安 徽	2007.3	310.9	2583.1	3.9	170.3
福 建	34693.4	10075.6	17893.6	1471.0	7578.8
江 西	437.8				
山 东	3008.1		1746.7		1.4
河 南	71223.5	2218.5	996.6	179.4	3605.3
湖 北	268755.7	2060.2	2662.4	4.0	2410.2
湖 南	11234.5	716.0	1607.5		11727.4
广 东	37149.6	1728.0	12030.9	632.3	14375.1
广 西	103932.5	13941.4	17096.3	61.5	11698.8
海 南	48987.4	7605.9	10149.3	70.7	32289.6
重 庆	45021.5	7123.7	15861.6	4.8	2766.6
四 川	69605.8	9988.4	22158.6	93.4	14106.5
贵 州	320577.9	53725.6	24543.7	37.1	11241.3
云 南	48389.4	10783.4	16876.2	136.3	32214.4
西 藏	795.5	14610.1	929.1		823.6
陕 西	61666.6	6107.6	4590.2	11.0	2773.9
甘 肃	32183.7	5563.8	6292.9	19.8	24104.0
青 海	9860.7	170.3	111.1		45.9
宁 夏	34462.0	9325.6	13758.6	1083.8	39989.9
新 疆	6427.0	2085.2	1836.2	93.2	2506.0

单位：万元

本年收入来源情况补充表	财政拨款	上级补助收入	事业费收入	经营收入	附属单位上缴收入
55426352.7	**54076516.2**	**110044.1**	**366154.0**	**111234.3**	**3641.7**
254609.8	225508.0				
2623254.0	2308360.2	36605.7	28791.7	9213.1	3550.0
904592.1	868739.5		11372.8	17917.7	
2167169.5	2153562.2	1647.3	9217.7	210.6	8.8
1368213.7	1344270.1	897.5	5357.1	3752.5	
1461545.0	1461419.4		110.0		
1863308.7	1843518.7	5127.2	9856.1	927.6	
1042817.9	1042817.9				
1526235.0	1522624.1	4.7	1285.5	27.6	
1526796.5	1364255.8	343.3	26911.7	2118.3	
2874812.3	2837218.2	366.2	14023.4	1309.0	
1921417.3	1827323.3	4622.3	42096.7	11878.5	
1969737.9	1962880.9	4091.3	341.5	290.0	6.9
1071525.0	1047033.5	5960.5	5012.5	549.0	
1717958.0	1717958.0				
3047605.5	3034045.1	10424.7			
2510322.2	2505517.4	326.2	330.0		
2687389.0	2657392.1	1464.2	10057.2	12949.2	
2712894.8	2629351.5	12543.7	41770.1	11709.2	76.0
3100031.3	2932627.3	1912.0	77859.0	19468.9	
1627429.2	1586689.5	1579.5	25244.8	6910.4	
346328.7	345502.6				
1320824.2	1278379.4		22720.7	1529.5	
3499513.2	3409275.3	7180.1	22947.3		
1702531.8	1689876.6		1552.3	7795.7	
2358074.2	2324847.9	14625.5	6975.9	2168.5	
245000.1	245000.1				
2011170.1	1972446.8			509.0	
1657649.0	1638509.7	322.2			
500268.3	500268.3				
434293.1	431475.3				
1371035.3	1367821.5		2320.0		

C-1-12续表5

地区	其他收入	本年支出情况补充表	基本支出	项目支出	上缴上级支出
全国	**758762.4**	**22735437.7**	**5204926.1**	**17415717.1**	**15007.9**
中央级	29101.8	165749.1	40975.2	120862.5	
北京	236733.3	2558934.6	369016.4	2177718.0	32.1
天津	6562.1	508862.8	182599.9	309834.6	
河北	2522.9	1045943.8	263358.2	782444.4	136.2
山西	13936.5	1270972.7	212956.9	1055856.1	
内蒙古	15.6	641090.0	338520.0	300139.9	
辽宁	3879.1	404072.3	94079.0	307005.9	
吉林		96651.4	21428.1	75223.3	
黑龙江	2293.1	243381.2	113340.2	130041.0	
上海	133167.4	851175.4	95345.4	753250.3	1166.1
江苏	21895.5	1056295.1	246450.8	807672.5	
浙江	35496.5	1201824.6	188843.7	1005065.7	
安徽	2127.3	295851.1	109058.8	186495.4	
福建	12969.5	1041706.7	123309.0	918291.7	
江西		199730.1	84326.5	110586.8	
山东	3135.7	921834.9	260204.9	659754.4	
河南	4148.6	372457.1	255327.7	117121.4	
湖北	5526.3	399514.0	73571.1	317872.1	
湖南	17444.3	180865.7	34674.9	134047.1	
广东	68164.1	1464193.7	330234.6	1127714.6	1971.2
广西	7005.0	939814.0	159979.3	776402.6	809.0
海南	826.1	181016.9	21336.5	158490.7	451.2
重庆	18194.6	1299701.7	218738.3	1080963.4	
四川	60110.5	1632835.8	186600.0	1442286.0	
贵州	3307.2	1602657.5	415741.9	1180665.8	
云南	9456.4	726476.4	299962.7	422234.5	1925.9
西藏					
陕西	38214.3	748130.2	201389.0	537836.5	8438.2
甘肃	18817.1	394548.8	206829.4	187417.5	78.0
青海		35079.3	3499.0	31580.3	
宁夏	2817.8	139689.0	12811.3	126877.7	
新疆	893.8	114381.8	40417.4	73964.4	

单位：万元

经营支出	对附属单位补助支出	行政事业性收费	婚姻登记收费	收养登记收费	殡葬收费
88458.8	**11327.8**	**305642.7**	**9214.7**	**371.6**	**296056.4**
3911.4					
9965.7	2202.4	18331.3		4.6	18326.7
16428.3		6371.1	141.6		6229.5
	5.0	10736.2	2.0	3.1	10731.1
2159.7		16836.2	317.1	6.4	16512.7
1054.4	1375.7	10834.0	95.4	0.8	10737.8
2987.4		6153.1			6153.1
		1342.3	114.3	1.0	1227.0
		7908.1	90.1	0.5	7817.5
1413.6					
2171.8		17016.8			17016.8
7915.2		13098.7		34.3	13064.4
290.0	6.9	15575.1	888.2	10.8	14676.1
	106.0	19548.1	213.2	22.8	19312.1
	4816.8				
	1875.6	16316.5	471.6	133.9	15711.0
	8.0	6087.6	962.9	4.5	5120.2
8070.8		30389.6	263.7	4.2	30121.7
12143.7		1033.4	628.3	11.4	393.7
4142.4	130.9	16998.8	682.7	26.5	16289.6
2623.1		18574.4	769.8	36.9	17767.7
738.5		2.0	2.0		
		769.0	760.1	8.9	
3373.2	576.6	36033.6	1245.5	24.8	34763.3
6249.8		4082.7	457.9	4.5	3620.3
2353.3		2482.4	474.7	21.2	1986.5
466.5		1571.7	117.9	5.6	1448.2
	223.9	7689.2	244.6	1.6	7443.0
		109.7	98.5	0.2	11.0
		102.5	12.5	0.5	89.5
		19648.6	160.1	2.6	19485.9

C-1-13 社会服务事业费

地区	预算指标			中央
	2016年	2015年	增长(%)	2016年
全 国	**54227752.3**	**49749705.7**	**9.0**	**24925600.9**
中央级	225508.0	162275.6	39.0	225508.0
北 京	2302953.1	1933909.2	19.1	844939.0
天 津	867424.2	841748.4	3.1	198544.0
河 北	2155865.3	1821618.6	18.3	1110045.0
山 西	1374236.3	1249590.2	10.0	731938.0
内蒙古	1428900.8	1427487.8	0.1	654149.0
辽 宁	1953631.3	1809406.2	8.0	978915.0
吉 林	1192802.9	1129292.7	5.6	695198.0
黑龙江	1531901.1	1519390.0	0.8	907266.0
上 海	1385697.7	1171982.6	18.2	21236.9
江 苏	2879429.9	2582318.3	11.5	624278.0
浙 江	1847983.0	1664446.4	11.0	283335.0
安 徽	1977183.7	1802709.5	9.7	1000620.0
福 建	1047510.8	901048.7	16.3	330103.0
江 西	1722219.0	1570132.1	9.7	909581.0
山 东	3046273.1	2824994.4	7.8	1225791.0
河 南	2488786.5	2240757.3	11.1	1451856.0
湖 北	2546205.7	2352767.5	8.2	1240647.0
湖 南	2530834.7	2327130.3	8.8	1517625.0
广 东	2939661.9	2557435.2	14.9	546927.0
广 西	1673906.7	1485762.4	12.7	909081.0
海 南	395931.8	347546.4	13.9	191247.0
重 庆	1267556.0	1406014.3	-9.8	593059.0
四 川	3403427.4	3181029.2	7.0	1815207.0
贵 州	1701048.0	1567198.2	8.5	1124294.0
云 南	2332690.9	2285288.3	2.1	1306158.0
西 藏	255469.5	274419.5	-6.9	148655.0
陕 西	2036485.8	1862287.4	9.4	1003400.0
甘 肃	1615413.3	1376628.3	17.3	1028623.0
青 海	507496.1	481697.7	5.4	305300.0
宁 夏	421114.2	431753.8	-2.5	217999.0
新 疆	1172203.6	1159639.2	1.1	784076.0

当年预算安排简表

单位：万元

安排预算指标		地方安排预算指标		
2015年	增长(%)	2016年	2015年	增长(%)
22849095.0	**9.1**	**29302151.4**	**26900610.7**	**8.9**
162275.6	39.0	0.0		
748326.0	12.9	1458014.1	1185583.2	23.0
167167.0	18.8	668880.2	674581.4	-0.8
930476.0	19.3	1045820.3	891142.6	17.4
635019.0	15.3	642298.3	614571.2	4.5
613624.0	6.6	774751.8	813863.8	-4.8
939043.0	4.2	974716.3	870363.2	12.0
674728.0	3.0	497604.9	454564.7	9.5
872969.0	3.9	624635.1	646421.0	-3.4
152312.0	-86.1	1364460.8	1019670.6	33.8
547874.0	13.9	2255151.9	2034444.3	10.8
255400.0	10.9	1564648.0	1409046.4	11.0
884261.0	13.2	976563.7	918448.5	6.3
288401.0	14.5	717407.8	612647.7	17.1
784245.0	16.0	812638.0	785887.1	3.4
1139291.0	7.6	1820482.1	1685703.4	8.0
1360291.0	6.7	1036930.5	880466.3	17.8
1162586.0	6.7	1305558.7	1190181.5	9.7
1319227.0	15.0	1013209.7	1007903.3	0.5
485110.0	12.7	2392734.9	2072325.2	15.5
774902.0	17.3	764825.7	710860.4	7.6
155352.0	23.1	204684.8	192194.4	6.5
574243.0	3.3	674497.0	831771.3	-18.9
1754442.0	3.5	1588220.4	1426587.2	11.3
1073927.0	4.7	576754.0	493271.2	16.9
1195370.0	9.3	1026532.9	1089918.3	-5.8
154501.0	-3.8	106814.5	119918.5	-10.9
929812.0	7.9	1033085.8	932475.4	10.8
930116.0	10.6	586790.3	446512.3	31.4
258961.0	17.9	202196.1	222736.7	-9.2
185017.0	17.8	203115.2	246736.8	-17.7
739826.4	6.0	388127.6	419812.8	-7.5

C-1-14 社会服务事业费

地　区	全国预算安排合计	中央安排合计	全省安排合计	省　级	市　级	县级及以下	抚　恤	中央安排
全　国	**54227752.3**	**24925600.9**	**29302151.4**	**9432591.8**	**4781923.0**	**15087636.6**	**7604752.7**	**3899304.5**
中央级	225508.0	225508.0					761.5	761.5
北　京	2302953.1	844939.0	1458014.1	519858.7		938155.4	147693.4	28944.0
天　津	867424.2	198544.0	668880.2	122748.0		546132.2	94342.9	30088.0
河　北	2155865.3	1110045.0	1045820.3	434840.5	182122.4	428857.4	418005.8	225025.0
山　西	1374236.3	731938.0	642298.3	198532.1	191125.3	252640.9	242350.1	104754.0
内蒙古	1428900.8	654149.0	774751.8	295952.4	159988.0	318811.4	96470.9	38750.0
辽　宁	1953631.3	978915.0	974716.3	170422.5	367807.3	436486.5	207365.6	83359.0
吉　林	1192802.9	695198.0	497604.9	172810.4	91662.5	233132.0	148987.5	73977.0
黑龙江	1531901.1	907266.0	624635.1	280975.0	104560.3	239099.8	164177.9	63206.0
上　海	1385697.7	21236.9	1364460.8	144004.4		1220456.4	108442.9	237.0
江　苏	2879429.9	624278.0	2255151.9	459839.1	290236.5	1505076.3	488656.2	178711.0
浙　江	1847983.0	283335.0	1564648.0	291339.8	173612.0	1099696.2	283402.6	86429.0
安　徽	1977183.7	1000620.0	976563.7	170397.5	170082.5	636083.7	316330.5	182573.0
福　建	1047510.8	330103.0	717407.8	195282.9	162219.2	359905.7	149692.2	62336.0
江　西	1722219.0	909581.0	812638.0	294964.8	65943.6	451729.6	252583.7	147099.0
山　东	3046273.1	1225791.0	1820482.1	480545.0	439561.7	900375.4	779848.4	368166.0
河　南	2488786.5	1451856.0	1036930.5	336816.1	197248.9	502865.5	508645.5	301275.0
湖　北	2546205.7	1240647.0	1305558.7	459134.7	249368.0	597056.0	380380.5	218763.0
湖　南	2530834.7	1517625.0	1013209.7	429582.1	152250.2	431377.4	510936.2	398827.0
广　东	2939661.9	546927.0	2392734.9	853891.7	592009.2	946834.0	415864.9	129526.0
广　西	1673906.7	909081.0	764825.7	302765.6	164301.5	297758.6	199737.1	108994.0
海　南	395931.8	191247.0	204684.8	50768.5	31180.5	122735.8	35014.4	18799.0
重　庆	1267556.0	593059.0	674497.0	375942.0		298555.0	197021.5	125565.0
四　川	3403427.4	1815207.0	1588220.4	397629.2	243716.9	946874.3	579055.0	402332.0
贵　州	1701048.0	1124294.0	576754.0	184912.7	122192.1	269649.2	166873.1	109588.0
云　南	2332690.9	1306158.0	1026532.9	433825.8	210171.4	382535.7	252279.4	164195.0
西　藏	255469.5	148655.0	106814.5	21444.2	30317.0	55053.3	10301.9	5107.0
陕　西	2036485.8	1003400.0	1033085.8	532981.5	247306.9	252797.4	289036.3	131089.0
甘　肃	1615413.3	1028623.0	586790.3	414184.0	73475.9	99130.4	68560.6	53763.0
青　海	507496.1	305300.0	202196.1	95623.4	9505.5	97067.2	18308.0	10722.0
宁　夏	421114.2	217999.0	203115.2	129014.0	22482.9	51618.3	15487.1	8546.0
新　疆	1172203.6	784076.0	388127.6	181563.2	37474.8	169089.6	58139.1	37798.0

当年预算安排明细表

单位：万元

全省安排	省　级	市　级	县级及以下	退役安置	中央安排	全省安排	省　级
3705448.2	**968378.9**	**389862.2**	**2347207.1**	**6184124.2**	**3733579.9**	**2450544.3**	**640286.4**
118749.4	104.1		118645.3	1093994.4	782244.0	311750.4	196000.4
64254.9	6627.1		57627.8	117049.8	91852.0	25197.8	231.5
192980.8	76554.5	22674.1	93752.2	340361.9	202255.0	138106.9	48029.3
137596.1	15455.9	34439.5	87700.7	101795.5	64559.0	37236.5	15711.1
57720.9	8646.0	4052.1	45022.8	88072.3	42840.0	45232.3	5740.0
124006.6	14031.2	30417.5	79557.9	540196.1	357793.0	182403.1	10479.2
75010.5	34901.7	884.9	39223.9	135175.0	78108.0	57067.0	8119.6
100971.9	72543.9	4636.8	23791.2	87615.1	65136.0	22479.1	4760.9
108205.9	8863.7		99342.2	214088.9	14653.9	199435.0	8916.0
309945.2	67827.5	19027.3	223090.4	461201.6	211486.0	249715.6	41391.0
196973.6	18447.5	7719.8	170806.3	168430.1	78329.0	90101.1	1808.5
133757.5	18754.8	12370.1	102632.6	155966.1	56779.0	99187.1	7083.7
87356.2	20247.0	10986.1	56123.1	103839.6	61033.0	42806.6	4804.7
105484.7	53173.3	3065.8	49245.6	60635.9	33562.0	27073.9	11047.7
411682.4	70314.8	66582.2	274785.4	450393.3	308323.0	142070.3	29962.0
207370.5	42718.8	18006.7	146645.0	203333.1	118357.0	84976.1	14072.4
161617.5	43095.7	24379.8	94142.0	201148.4	140354.0	60794.4	13983.0
112109.2	43916.8	19586.3	48606.1	135129.3	90304.0	44825.3	15880.3
286338.9	74897.1	53679.1	157762.7	291925.9	157363.0	134562.9	25309.8
90743.1	38872.2	3657.3	48213.6	67353.4	36736.0	30617.4	10348.2
16215.4	1575.1	2367.5	12272.8	42362.2	21087.0	21275.2	3144.9
71456.5	32154.6		39301.9	108409.2	64099.0	44310.2	19585.2
176723.0	35033.5	15487.4	126202.1	277461.9	165677.0	111784.9	20321.9
57285.1	11260.6	8929.2	37095.3	47364.9	24356.0	23008.9	3360.3
88084.4	33076.8	10196.1	44811.5	137609.1	99914.0	37695.1	4823.6
5194.9	866.2	2272.8	2055.9	30107.6	17788.0	12319.6	602.0
157947.3	105060.0	10672.5	42214.8	237990.4	170557.0	67433.4	43236.1
14797.6	5066.2	1478.1	8253.3	120888.5	66361.0	54527.5	43401.0
7586.0	3668.5	213.7	3703.8	42776.0	19745.0	23031.0	18800.0
6941.1	1030.6	1280.0	4630.5	21517.1	11953.0	9564.1	3914.3
20341.1	9593.2	799.5	9948.4	99931.6	79976.0	19955.6	5417.8

C-1-14续表1

地 区	市级	县级及以下	社会福利	中央安排	全省安排	省级	市级	县级及以下
全 国	**534862.2**	**1275395.7**	**7285352.5**	**555509.6**	**6729842.9**	**2249052.8**	**1454073.7**	**3026716.4**
中央级			17104.0	17104.0				
北 京		115750.0	404546.6	10221.0	394325.6	200792.3		193533.3
天 津		24966.3	128806.8	5109.0	123697.8	56139.8		67558.0
河 北	45009.4	45068.2	237354.6	19061.0	218293.6	56800.0	50018.9	111474.7
山 西	7671.7	13853.7	127157.4	15746.0	111411.4	30995.5	56762.5	23653.4
内蒙古	5007.6	34484.7	236453.5	10926.0	225527.5	139319.5	33293.5	52914.5
辽 宁	132904.1	39019.8	144301.8	14497.0	129804.8	8959.0	72585.5	48260.3
吉 林	39911.3	9036.1	98084.7	12083.0	86001.7	31173.6	25867.6	28960.5
黑龙江	6574.7	11143.5	132841.6	14194.0	118647.6	37247.9	46847.7	34552.0
上 海		190519.0	522820.0	5456.6	517363.4	66320.6		451042.8
江 苏	29050.6	179274.0	527890.3	23455.0	504435.3	105362.2	123434.9	275638.2
浙 江	23551.1	64741.5	483308.5	16242.0	467066.5	127429.3	51339.7	288297.5
安 徽	21788.2	70315.2	219146.4	22798.0	196348.4	39605.9	58579.1	98163.4
福 建	12505.2	25496.7	207883.2	7299.0	200584.2	79768.4	50444.3	70371.5
江 西	2723.4	13302.8	112109.0	20546.0	91563.0	15301.8	15107.7	61153.5
山 东	35638.7	76469.6	417151.5	24781.0	392370.5	128037.8	107085.7	157247.0
河 南	38902.6	32001.1	265846.4	29243.0	236603.4	88921.1	69059.0	78623.3
湖 北	21136.5	25674.9	215522.6	14605.0	200917.6	18928.0	64346.9	117642.7
湖 南	9269.9	19675.1	290166.2	34506.0	255660.2	154353.4	35024.2	66282.6
广 东	16166.4	93086.7	502743.0	19428.0	483315.0	88022.3	180445.1	214847.6
广 西	13578.4	6690.8	238168.9	21388.0	216780.9	91865.2	60533.3	64382.4
海 南	12265.5	5864.8	72345.9	5848.0	66497.9	25337.8	2085.9	39074.2
重 庆		24725.0	147499.1	11295.0	136204.1	50172.7	0.0	86031.4
四 川	8092.1	83370.9	441673.6	32472.0	409201.6	160789.9	96180.3	152231.4
贵 州	6112.7	13535.9	170870.2	16977.0	153893.2	60684.5	38522.6	54686.1
云 南	14845.3	18026.2	141163.2	22472.0	118691.2	31189.7	40010.1	47491.4
西 藏	10617.0	1100.6	26193.1	10590.0	15603.1	3801.0	6904.0	4898.1
陕 西	13177.2	11020.1	351036.2	14649.0	336387.2	173803.1	101860.6	60723.5
甘 肃	4682.1	6444.4	159643.1	22115.0	137528.1	87424.3	35571.9	14531.9
青 海	10.8	4220.2	91743.4	17895.0	73848.4	49077.5	1503.0	23267.9
宁 夏	2862.1	2787.7	25029.4	8018.0	17011.4	5723.8	5477.2	5810.4
新 疆	807.6	13730.2	128748.3	34490.0	94258.3	35704.9	25182.5	33370.9

单位：万元

社会救助	中央安排合计	全省安排合计	省级	市级	县级及以下	城市最低生活保障	中央安排	全省安排
25743965.8	**15654512.4**	**10089453.4**	**4279776.5**	**951299.4**	**4858377.5**	**12085548.6**	**8829587.5**	**3255961.1**
208012.4	22870.0	185142.4	19033.6		166108.8	77805.8		77805.8
281715.8	71104.0	210611.8	42252.8		168359.0	128915.8	59149.0	69766.8
896953.2	609260.0	287693.2	190445.6	27184.9	70062.7	512082.2	353824.0	158258.2
771009.4	510297.0	260712.4	124071.0	59433.4	77208.0	607383.7	450876.0	156507.7
847140.3	522385.0	324755.3	130451.0	77189.5	117114.8	628212.4	465442.0	162770.4
777155.5	511253.0	265902.5	72916.0	61248.2	131738.3	598283.8	472938.0	125345.8
677307.8	513145.0	164162.8	60387.0	2962.0	100813.8	562390.4	455090.0	107300.4
1049869.2	742412.0	307457.2	139888.6	22334.1	145234.5	740892.9	582672.0	158220.9
357248.7	889.4	356359.3	15809.8		340549.5	123868.0		123868.0
939462.0	194500.0	744962.0	194886.0	24419.3	525656.7	173244.5	22517.0	150727.5
604848.7	94826.0	510022.7	131055.7	26469.4	352497.6	179452.2	32240.0	147212.2
1095139.4	688645.0	406494.4	71850.0	45707.0	288937.4	293394.5	242785.0	50609.5
371461.2	164463.0	206998.2	55486.7	32719.1	118792.4	51346.2	32014.0	19332.2
1123364.7	657200.0	466164.7	167075.9	25868.6	273220.2	413367.9	293041.0	120326.9
1075947.8	514993.0	560954.8	226989.4	113112.5	220852.9	168468.6	100000.0	68468.6
1288919.5	976181.0	312738.5	151704.9	21762.6	139271.0	942349.7	863204.0	79145.7
1374103.0	795101.0	579002.0	333161.0	62109.4	183731.6	874442.8	684933.0	189509.8
1362470.2	932354.0	430116.2	192831.1	44812.2	192472.9	983682.1	798210.0	185472.1
1142372.4	232119.0	910253.4	586722.1	58733.5	264797.8	196747.2		196747.2
947894.8	729064.0	218830.8	133407.4	12589.6	72833.8	132448.0	7024.2	125423.8
171920.8	135679.0	36241.8	5126.0	2807.8	28308.0	118630.3	112351.0	6279.3
642174.4	377845.0	264329.4	229481.9		34847.5	157456.1	154350.0	3106.1
1762808.7	1175086.0	587722.7	142455.9	60130.1	385136.7	505679.3	396341.0	109338.3
1073656.2	916599.0	157057.2	60759.6	29151.4	67146.2	168291.0	135318.8	32972.2
1440398.4	982491.0	457907.4	252433.1	67248.8	138225.5	785685.1	529565.0	256120.1
136495.1	107044.0	29451.1		4322.1	25129.0	32083.9	22297.0	9786.9
901641.9	641723.0	259918.9	137552.7	50837.8	71528.4	218849.5	185422.0	33427.5
1152342.8	841520.0	310822.8	250343.3	15157.1	45322.4	949393.3	753288.0	196105.3
274086.3	236735.0	37351.3	5789.0	588.4	30973.9	101937.5	94889.0	7048.5
249170.6	176505.0	72665.6	52814.6	860.0	18991.0	60193.2	38189.5	22003.7
746874.6	580224.0	166650.6	102594.8	1540.6	62515.2	598570.7	491617.0	106953.7

C−1−14续表2

地 区	省级	市级	县级及以下	农村最低生活保障	中央安排	全省安排	省级	市级
全 国	**1774950.9**	**296759.5**	**1184250.7**	**6341853.0**	**3988563.6**	**2353289.4**	**884816.1**	**243559.1**
中央级								
北 京			77805.8	38516.8		38516.8		
天 津			69766.8	51109.8		51109.8		
河 北	132000.0	11786.9	14471.3	18977.2		18977.2		2336.8
山 西	110109.0	27978.1	18420.6	26435.6		26435.6		7890.0
内蒙古	120902.0	24373.5	17494.9	68242.6		68242.6		26781.7
辽 宁	65516.0	23726.8	36103.0	41583.8		41583.8		15635.5
吉 林	55087.0	25.0	52188.4	17779.6		17779.6		0.0
黑龙江	72420.0	13087.8	72713.1	40202.9		40202.9		2968.0
上 海			123868.0	20544.9		20544.9		
江 苏	33016.0	5108.5	112603.0	387814.2	109582.0	278232.2	133652.0	648.0
浙 江	90505.0	3528.8	53178.4	154042.4		154042.4		1974.2
安 徽	6655.0	10165.0	33789.5	408559.6	308998.0	99561.6	46585.0	15210.5
福 建		4279.6	15052.6	130429.6	79276.0	51153.6		9300.7
江 西	1269.3	7845.2	111212.4	385359.4	259866.0	125493.4	35678.0	1854.7
山 东	26146.6	15723.5	26598.5	548440.8	348616.0	199824.8	75588.7	53422.6
河 南	66544.0	1699.0	10902.7	25529.2		25529.2		5180.7
湖 北	111676.0	36820.9	41012.9	264749.8		264749.8	220000.0	2200.3
湖 南	120704.0	28673.0	36095.1	58003.8		58003.8		7650.2
广 东	128847.2	13982.1	53917.9	432913.3	174369.0	258544.3	172934.7	13434.0
广 西	120278.2	2070.2	3075.4	476920.7	471912.2	5008.5	9.8	396.6
海 南	3500.0	110.0	2669.3	7907.9		7907.9		90.0
重 庆	2101.0		1005.1	200425.5	142471.0	57954.5	54072.8	
四 川	23677.4	12463.0	73197.9	731416.5	594511.0	136905.5	35516.1	25674.8
贵 州	15000.0	6621.2	11351.0	675811.9	615752.3	60059.6	22500.0	13754.4
云 南	199009.3	23969.2	33141.6	479753.8	353044.0	126709.8	47635.0	27652.3
西 藏		2844.4	6942.5	44067.0	33803.0	10264.0		
陕 西	2795.0	17803.9	12828.6	359487.1	311285.0	48202.1	16106.0	9314.5
甘 肃	171552.0	1823.0	22730.3	7194.9		7194.9		44.9
青 海	82.0		6966.5	102665.0	94890.0	7775.0	61.0	
宁 夏	13106.9	4.8	8892.0	121813.7	90188.1	31625.6	24477.0	38.1
新 疆	82452.0	246.1	24255.6	15153.7		15153.7		105.6

单位：万元

县级及以下	其他社会救助	中央安排	全省安排				医疗救助	中央安排
				省级	市级	县级及以下		
1224914.2	**3941728.5**	**1068737.3**	**2872991.2**	**916023.9**	**269662.1**	**1687305.2**	**3374835.7**	**1767624.0**
38516.8	61979.5	18516.0	43463.5	16324.2		27139.3	29710.3	4354.0
51109.8	54110.5	5236.0	48874.5	1392.1		47482.4	47579.7	6719.0
16640.4	249810.8	186494.0	63316.8	36560.0	9003.6	17753.2	116083.0	68942.0
18545.6	53490.4	5177.0	48313.4	100.0	14519.9	33693.5	83699.7	54244.0
41460.9	59694.2	2660.0	57034.2	1841.0	12947.5	42245.7	90991.1	54283.0
25948.3	64482.5		64482.5	1400.0	13387.6	49694.9	72805.4	38315.0
17779.6	22541.7		22541.7		2937.0	19604.7	74596.1	58055.0
37234.9	118318.4	80327.0	37991.4	12734.6	3976.5	21280.3	150455.0	79413.0
20544.9	177373.8	889.4	176484.4	15592.5		160891.9	35462.0	
143932.2	228766.1	34699.0	194067.1	5118.0	14319.6	174629.5	149637.2	27702.0
152068.2	155696.8	48714.0	106982.8	13466.4	15194.8	78321.6	115657.3	13872.0
37766.1	228450.3	57653.0	170797.3	7260.0	14552.7	148984.6	164735.0	79209.0
41852.9	91552.1	35317.0	56235.1	4878.3	8510.2	42846.6	98133.3	17856.0
87960.7	153076.9	22883.0	130193.9	99917.4	12030.2	18246.3	171560.5	81410.0
70813.5	183987.7	10713.0	173274.7	88405.1	27481.3	57388.3	175050.7	55664.0
20348.5	193402.8	12089.0	181313.8	80060.9	12361.9	88891.0	127637.8	100888.0
42549.5	120149.6	32226.0	87923.6	600.0	15964.5	71359.1	114760.8	77942.0
50353.6	164856.1	20444.0	144412.1	63135.1	4444.5	76832.5	155928.2	113700.0
72175.6	253279.9	31104.0	222175.9	107239.9	22448.8	92487.2	259432.0	26646.0
4602.1	244923.7	175497.6	69426.1	1419.6	7923.5	60083.0	93602.4	74630.0
7817.9	15355.1		15355.1		1876.4	13478.7	30027.5	23328.0
3881.7	161658.7	23769.0	137889.7	120454.4		17435.3	122634.1	57255.0
75714.6	280072.4	29439.0	250633.4	48842.4	11653.8	190137.2	245640.5	154795.0
23805.2	121747.4	81362.9	40384.5	12212.0	5964.3	22208.2	107805.9	84165.0
51422.5	55134.8	3942.0	51192.8	1288.3	4534.7	45369.8	119824.7	95940.0
10264.0	31849.0	27425.0	4424.0		781.4	3642.6	28495.2	23519.0
22781.6	187395.6	66598.0	120797.6	78554.2	17297.4	24946.0	135909.7	78418.0
7150.0	100085.3	2714.0	97371.3	73489.0	12969.6	10912.7	95669.3	85518.0
7714.0	22965.9	9390.0	13575.9	646.0	588.4	12341.5	46517.9	37566.0
7110.5	32921.0	18061.4	14859.6	12449.7	803.1	1606.8	34242.7	30066.0
15048.1	52599.5	25397.0	27202.5	10642.8	1188.9	15370.8	80550.7	63210.0

C-1-14续表3

地 区	全省安排				自然灾害生活救助	中央安排	全省安排	
		省级	市级	县级及以下				省级
全 国	**1607211.7**	**703985.6**	**141318.7**	**761907.4**	**1399007.8**	**791301.0**	**607706.8**	**309209.0**
中央级								
北 京	25356.3	2709.4		22646.9	2364.7	49.0	2315.7	1951.8
天 津	40860.7	40860.7			1996.6	391.0	1605.6	1262.0
河 北	47141.0	21885.6	4057.6	21197.8	110884.0	51000.0	59884.0	39126.7
山 西	29455.7	13862.0	9045.4	6548.3	42413.1	33800.0	8613.1	4300.0
内蒙古	36708.1	7708.0	13086.8	15913.3	49091.4	36200.0	12891.4	3000.0
辽 宁	34490.4	6000.0	8498.3	19992.1	17273.2	10017.0	7256.2	2326.7
吉 林	16541.1	5300.0		11241.1	33900.5	13200.0	20700.5	11266.5
黑龙江	71042.0	54734.0	2301.8	14006.2	23140.8	19266.0	3874.8	2838.9
上 海	35462.0	217.3		35244.7				
江 苏	121935.2	23100.0	4343.2	94492.0	60660.5	14400.0	46260.5	18093.1
浙 江	101785.3	27084.3	5771.6	68929.4	28489.8	6000.0	22489.8	
安 徽	85526.0	11350.0	5778.8	68397.2	72033.4	47476.0	24557.4	15343.7
福 建	80277.3	50608.4	10628.6	19040.3	61422.3	33058.0	28364.3	14100.0
江 西	90150.5	30211.2	4138.5	55800.8	63654.4	48500.0	15154.4	5000.0
山 东	119386.7	36849.0	16485.1	66052.6	14477.1	7300.0	7177.1	1500.0
河 南	26749.8	5100.0	2521.0	19128.8	35024.0	23735.0	11289.0	7824.3
湖 北	36818.8	885.0	7123.7	28810.1	140019.8	69371.0	70648.8	6700.0
湖 南	42228.2	8992.0	4044.5	29191.7	74945.1	58711.0	16234.1	11989.0
广 东	232786.0	177700.3	8868.6	46217.1	36903.6	6000.0	30903.6	24485.4
广 西	18972.4	11699.8	2199.3	5073.3	30657.0	9679.0	20978.0	13498.2
海 南	6699.5	1626.0	731.4	4342.1	18832.5	8900.0	9932.5	7617.0
重 庆	65379.1	52853.7		12525.4	29538.9	12700.0	16838.9	14320.1
四 川	90845.5	34420.0	10338.5	46087.0	60207.0	35509.0	24698.0	13528.4
贵 州	23640.9	11047.6	2811.5	9781.8	104162.2	53700.0	50462.2	30238.0
云 南	23884.7	4500.5	11092.6	8291.6	59026.8	33513.0	25513.8	14957.6
西 藏	4976.2		696.3	4279.9	20061.2	4964.0	15097.2	10910.0
陕 西	57491.7	40097.5	6422.0	10972.2	42492.4	25199.0	17293.4	5088.0
甘 肃	10151.3	5302.3	319.6	4529.4	50540.2	41649.0	8891.2	6500.0
青 海	8951.9	5000.0		3951.9	29193.3	17602.0	11591.3	9702.7
宁 夏	4176.7	2781.0	14.0	1381.7	18052.7	11400.0	6652.7	5488.9
新 疆	17340.7	9500.0		7840.7	54049.3	44512.0	9537.3	6252.0

单位：万元

市级	县级及以下	民政管理事务	中央安排	全省安排	省级	市级	县级及以下
71463.3	**227034.5**	**4274906.8**	**204353.7**	**4070553.1**	**588329.2**	**944533.6**	**2537690.3**
		129990.7	129990.7				
	363.9	298086.4	611.0	297475.4	99733.1		197742.3
	343.6	227753.6		227753.6	13579.8		214173.8
8096.6	12660.7	111202.3	3444.0	107758.3	16754.3	20043.9	70960.1
2271.5	2041.6	67499.0	2782.0	64717.0	4397.6	23512.5	36806.9
5850.0	4041.4	66921.1	3048.0	63873.1	7817.0	16125.4	39930.7
1734.9	3194.6	159559.0	1996.0	157563.0	4048.1	42450.8	111064.1
12.3	9421.7	71198.8	4685.0	66513.8	14682.5	14497.1	37334.2
	1035.9	51953.0	3052.0	48901.0	15201.9	15624.6	18074.5
		153921.6		153921.6	35179.0		118742.6
3300.5	24866.9	266197.1	1726.0	264471.1	28468.2	48074.1	187928.8
6743.4	15746.4	216443.6	1509.0	214934.6	10354.3	47591.6	156988.7
442.0	8771.7	80315.1	2349.0	77966.1	12070.3	21533.4	44362.4
5222.1	9042.2	96303.2	1914.0	94389.2	19876.5	23691.8	50820.9
2851.0	7303.4	59731.0	2674.0	57057.0	9983.4	12510.7	34562.9
2473.6	3203.5	232844.7	2228.0	230616.7	17487.4	77202.3	135927.0
1479.6	1985.1	129236.2	3065.0	126171.2	7205.6	34616.7	84348.9
5255.9	58692.9	175621.3	2453.0	173168.3	13267.0	66909.5	92991.8
1041.0	3204.1	130830.8	2923.0	127907.8	10183.5	32741.8	84982.5
1871.5	4546.7	350020.2	1713.0	348307.2	19672.2	174716.2	153918.8
935.7	6544.1	145493.2	3220.0	142273.2	13752.7	52793.9	75726.6
397.5	1918.0	32087.8		32087.8	6312.9	4035.0	21739.9
	2518.8	114193.7	1555.0	112638.7	24610.9		88027.8
1773.4	9396.2	236202.7	4131.0	232071.7	22126.2	49365.3	160580.2
5311.7	14912.5	124079.2	3074.0	121005.2	18319.5	29407.5	73278.2
5240.8	5315.4	176366.9	3573.0	172793.9	37927.0	43385.5	91481.4
1061.9	3125.3	14666.0	3162.0	11504.0	5265.0	3183.6	3055.4
7127.9	5077.5	183009.5	2987.0	180022.5	66069.1	58532.9	55420.5
507.7	1883.5	38156.4	3215.0	34941.4	7770.4	10504.7	16666.3
140.0	1748.6	41720.0	2601.0	39119.0	7316.0	6174.0	25629.0
320.8	843.0	35623.4	1577.0	34046.4	9679.3	9071.3	15295.8
	3285.3	57679.3	3096.0	54583.3	9218.5	6237.5	39127.3

C-1-14续表4

地区	行政事业单位离退休	中央安排	全省安排	省级	市级	县级及以下
全国	**470442.1**	**5741.0**	**464701.1**	**57197.7**	**105519.7**	**301983.7**
中央级	5741.0	5741.0				
北京	61158.0		61158.0	630.2		60527.8
天津	3270.8		3270.8			3270.8
河北	30503.0		30503.0	7116.0	4893.5	18493.5
山西	8333.6		8333.6	827.0	2994.9	4511.7
内蒙古	17378.5		17378.5	978.9	6496.3	9903.3
辽宁	20481.0		20481.0	3020.8	6600.9	10859.3
吉林	7454.4		7454.4	798.9	2122.0	4533.5
黑龙江	14681.3		14681.3	8492.9	3905.5	2282.9
上海	5804.9		5804.9	1713.7		4091.2
江苏	26133.5		26133.5	1195.8	4545.4	20392.3
浙江	16015.4		16015.4	1001.6	4668.9	10344.9
安徽	18018.3		18018.3	2389.7	4656.3	10972.3
福建	18465.5		18465.5	999.6	3626.2	13839.7
江西	10739.4		10739.4	2200.0	2101.2	6438.2
山东	14901.2		14901.2	5086.2	3430.8	6384.2
河南	22824.2		22824.2	3868.4	6635.3	12320.5
湖北	17321.8		17321.8		3881.0	13440.8
湖南	7405.2		7405.2		1252.6	6152.6
广东	52242.0		52242.0	4665.6	25042.4	22534.0
广西	17158.5		17158.5	359.8	4376.7	12422.0
海南	2355.8		2355.8	612.0	168.6	1575.2
重庆	13409.0		13409.0	3838.9		9570.1
四川	16888.9		16888.9	3189.0	3282.2	10417.7
贵州	1630.6		1630.6			1630.6
云南	16072.6		16072.6	727.6	2168.9	13176.1
西藏	1756.7		1756.7		1047.9	708.8
陕西	7393.6		7393.6	10.7	2654.9	4728.0
甘肃	6060.6		6060.6	1131.4	1766.4	3162.8
青海	1302.6		1302.6	863.7	301.8	137.1
宁夏	2941.5		2941.5	1479.3	616.0	846.2
新疆	4598.7		4598.7		2283.1	2315.6

单位：万元

其他款项用于民政支出	中央安排	全省安排			
			省级	市级	县级及以下
1265200.4	**81298.8**	**1183901.6**	**340361.3**	**330308.9**	**513231.4**
58410.8	58410.8				
87097.2		87097.2	1613.2		85484.0
12487.9		12487.9	2655.0		9832.9
10600.5		10600.5	14.1	4201.1	6385.3
13678.2		13678.2	2774.0	4039.3	6864.9
27372.8		27372.8		11973.6	15399.2
87299.1		87299.1	54641.5	19865.4	12792.2
20694.2		20694.2	11480.6	5405.3	3808.3
7622.2		7622.2		4636.9	2985.3
23370.7		23370.7	7201.6		16169.1
109228.7		109228.7	2615.3	38384.4	68229.0
47044.3		47044.3	1242.9	5528.1	40273.3
20234.5		20234.5	3299.4	5006.4	11928.7
38443.6		38443.6		23024.4	15419.2
39400.9		39400.9	31182.7	1715.2	6503.0
60709.1		60709.1	1167.4	34035.9	25505.8
34957.6		34957.6	20500.6	6786.4	7670.6
42088.3		42088.3	30000.0	1349.0	10739.3
18951.7		18951.7	428.0	8522.2	10001.5
147589.9	778.0	146811.9	30117.2	81355.0	35339.7
27443.8		27443.8	661.9	15836.6	10945.3
21012.4	934.0	20078.4	1042.8	7052.7	11982.9
15310.2		15310.2	1777.7		13532.5
29129.6		29129.6	184.4	9406.1	19539.1
12411.6		12411.6	290.2	4757.0	7364.4
109774.5		109774.5	58690.4	27075.9	24008.2
15887.9		15887.9		907.7	14980.2
23885.5	17196.0	6689.5	2161.8	2443.1	2084.6
19221.1		19221.1	12547.4	3807.9	2865.8
8366.5		8366.5	406.0	573.8	7386.7
53292.4		53292.4	48883.2	1995.5	2413.7
22182.7	3980.0	18202.7	12782.0	624.0	4796.7

C-1-15 社会服务事业费预算

地 区	本年预算指标合计	上年结转预算指标	本级财政安排预算指标	本年上级下达预算指标	本年下达所属地方预算指标	本年抚恤预算指标
全 国	**57013005.5**	**2937063.9**	**54227752.3**	**80645807.5**	**80797618.2**	**7751431.3**
中央级	225508.0		24925600.9		24700092.9	761.5
北 京	2321120.2	18167.1	1458014.1	1876247.2	1031308.2	148654.1
天 津	880973.4	13549.2	668880.2	388605.6	190061.6	97712.4
河 北	2278310.0	124840.0	1045820.3	3977602.1	2869952.4	428398.6
山 西	1500849.9	126613.6	642298.3	2555847.6	1823909.6	252564.4
内蒙古	1564728.1	110506.9	774751.8	2576612.1	1897142.7	103763.9
辽 宁	1945496.0	84267.2	974716.3	2875075.9	1988563.4	202065.0
吉 林	1046514.4	3071.0	497604.9	1404697.4	858858.9	138332.5
黑龙江	1537237.2	26175.1	624635.1	3390609.2	2504182.2	162539.5
上 海	1387806.3	13291.0	1364460.8	178726.0	168671.5	108205.9
江 苏	3054916.5	212486.8	2255151.9	2459044.4	1871766.6	494160.0
浙 江	1909607.4	75815.4	1564648.0	854976.0	585832.0	298579.2
安 徽	2005089.6	27905.9	976563.7	2232992.3	1232372.3	319718.2
福 建	1122997.4	77469.9	717407.8	1290741.6	962621.9	155346.1
江 西	1755758.0	33539.1	812638.0	3220491.3	2310910.4	252861.3
山 东	3086849.6	36177.1	1820482.1	4539898.3	3309707.9	779976.9
河 南	2556182.6	67401.8	1036930.5	4840536.1	3388685.8	511312.4
湖 北	2862295.5	320924.8	1305558.7	3191072.5	1955260.5	383286.7
湖 南	2643903.3	58488.8	1013209.7	5260110.9	3687906.1	530414.3
广 东	3019446.1	81049.7	2392734.9	3405210.8	2859549.3	423176.2
广 西	1848569.8	179142.0	764825.7	2406565.8	1501963.7	221850.1
海 南	425958.7	96559.7	204684.8	348870.6	224156.4	35838.5
重 庆	1659518.0	391962.0	674497.0	1521711.0	928652.0	198006.9
四 川	3498202.1	94654.4	1588220.4	6217092.2	4401764.9	581964.2
贵 州	1908806.9	207758.9	576754.0	3714839.8	2590545.8	177026.3
云 南	2363083.5	30392.6	1026532.9	4835817.8	3529659.8	256191.1
西 藏	382807.6	46152.5	106814.5	300371.2	70530.6	16589.6
陕 西	2156340.0	158349.3	1033085.8	4038527.9	3073623.0	305955.5
甘 肃	1671880.6	80316.5	586790.3	2435993.2	1431219.4	68937.8
青 海	517678.5	959.4	202196.1	997816.5	683293.5	17771.2
宁 夏	482805.2	61691.0	203115.2	521803.9	303804.9	16598.7
新 疆	1391765.1	77385.2	388127.6	2787300.3	1861048.0	62872.3

指标收入结余情况表

单位：万元

上年结转预算指标	本级财政安排预算指标	本年上级下达预算指标	本年下达所属地方预算指标	本年退役安置预算指标	上年结转预算指标	本级财政安排预算指标
157136.3	**7604752.7**	**12281329.8**	**12291787.5**	**6146311.7**	**189871.4**	**6184124.2**
	3899304.5		3898543.0			3733579.9
960.7	118749.4	52414.1	23470.1	1093994.4		311750.4
3369.5	64254.9	60571.0	30483.0	122703.0	5653.2	25197.8
11750.3	192980.8	779570.5	555903.0	351811.4	11445.5	138106.9
10214.3	137596.1	331948.1	227194.1	104773.1	2977.6	37236.5
5064.8	57720.9	137190.8	96212.6	90353.0	4411.7	45232.3
1261.5	124006.6	264068.8	187271.9	479481.8	13380.5	182403.1
	75010.5	169572.1	106250.1	88514.6		57067.0
383.9	100971.9	332123.2	270939.5	85026.6	428.1	22479.1
	108205.9	17479.0	17479.0	213209.0	6653.0	199435.0
10196.5	309945.2	613163.7	439145.4	453492.5	19228.6	249715.6
9461.6	196973.6	204734.4	112590.4	161853.7	2551.7	90101.1
3387.6	133757.5	377079.3	194506.2	157969.9	2004.2	99187.1
5908.7	87356.2	231806.6	169725.4	113894.1	10786.4	42806.6
278.4	105484.7	520892.3	373794.1	60636.2		27073.9
188.6	411682.4	1213540.5	845434.6	454867.7	4474.5	142070.3
1170.7	207370.5	972884.0	670112.8	205106.4	1668.8	84976.1
3236.2	161617.5	511685.1	293252.1	199821.4	1349.0	60794.4
4614.5	112109.2	1241013.9	827323.3	132294.3	1491.8	44825.3
7311.4	286338.9	553967.2	424441.3	328331.5	36405.4	134562.9
22113.0	90743.1	292807.4	183813.4	72640.5	5294.9	30617.4
6480.0	16215.4	33435.1	20292.0	49993.6	10243.6	21275.2
985.4	71456.5	282602.0	157037.0	109735.9	1326.7	44310.2
2922.9	176723.0	1273637.0	871318.7	288130.3	10861.3	111784.9
10153.2	57285.1	350143.3	240555.3	48917.6	1552.7	23008.9
3911.7	88084.4	563294.7	399099.7	139135.9	1526.8	37695.1
5221.3	5194.9	11318.6	5145.2	32267.6	12438.1	12319.6
24758.3	157947.3	589150.4	465900.5	244742.2	13912.8	67433.4
541.2	14797.6	111737.0	58138.0	105115.0	5909.5	54527.5
	7586.0	36183.1	25997.9	33744.8		23031.0
780.2	6941.1	18454.0	9576.6	22845.9	1895.0	9564.1
509.9	20341.1	132862.6	90841.3	100907.8		19955.6

C−1−15续表1

地 区			本年社会福利预算指标			
	本年上级下达预算指标	本年下达所属地方预算指标		上年结转预算指标	本级财政安排预算指标	本年上级下达预算指标
全 国	**9057077.6**	**9284761.5**	**7736848.2**	**489269.4**	**7285352.5**	**4613401.8**
中央级		3733579.9	17104.0		555509.6	
北 京	1639169.8	856925.8	419298.2	14751.3	394325.6	140956.4
天 津	183651.0	91799.0	130375.0	1568.2	123697.8	9142.9
河 北	549230.5	346971.5	269110.6	25004.4	218293.6	185563.5
山 西	160615.6	96056.6	142758.2	15600.8	111411.4	97855.3
内蒙古	95400.3	54691.3	235138.6	27669.1	225527.5	222054.9
辽 宁	805707.0	522008.8	150822.5	1837.0	129804.8	84484.7
吉 林	114923.1	83475.5	91729.0	1.1	86001.7	47993.1
黑龙江	146213.5	84094.1	131472.7	361.0	118647.6	59082.4
上 海	128791.0	121670.0	526934.9	6638.0	517363.4	9673.0
江 苏	593084.9	408536.6	529325.9	17670.9	504435.3	207711.0
浙 江	153451.5	84250.6	470094.5	32113.9	467066.5	109180.1
安 徽	128883.9	72105.3	257940.5	8098.0	196348.4	129461.2
福 建	150452.0	90150.9	239633.7	32772.6	200584.2	109138.4
江 西	91569.3	58007.0	111738.2	92.3	91563.0	78633.4
山 东	793872.3	485549.4	419846.8	3233.9	392370.5	366898.3
河 南	293989.5	175528.0	248856.7	4087.3	236603.4	190081.2
湖 北	321062.1	183384.1	233304.6	2530.7	200917.6	88885.5
湖 南	246930.7	160953.5	274181.6	13103.4	255660.2	317712.9
广 东	483107.3	325744.1	512093.1	9350.1	483315.0	272434.3
广 西	87759.9	51031.7	309617.5	71650.2	216780.9	147298.1
海 南	34136.8	15662.0	75675.0	21066.5	66497.9	18371.7
重 庆	147572.0	83473.0	158845.3	11346.2	136204.1	46951.2
四 川	499365.9	333881.8	474938.4	38173.4	409201.6	416093.3
贵 州	71640.8	47284.8	203538.2	32668.0	153893.2	130395.2
云 南	289680.9	189766.9	143907.5	2744.3	118691.2	144434.9
西 藏	25287.9	17778.0	30586.9	3533.8	15603.1	21596.9
陕 西	465022.3	301626.3	369760.5	20790.3	336387.2	429108.5
甘 肃	131559.0	86881.0	173035.4	15248.3	137528.1	129470.4
青 海	58638.6	47924.8	114285.9	35.7	73848.4	149484.3
宁 夏	26851.7	15464.9	30085.3	5573.3	17011.4	16471.3
新 疆	139456.5	58504.3	240813.0	49955.4	94258.3	236783.5

单位：万元

本年下达所属地方预算指标	本年社会救助预算指标	上年结转预算指标	本级财政安排预算指标	本年上级下达预算指标	本年下达所属地方预算指标
4651175.5	**27246573.5**	**1552702.6**	**25743965.8**	**50282920.5**	**50333015.4**
538405.6			15654512.4		15654512.4
130735.1	210292.0	2279.9	185142.4	42595.1	19725.4
4033.9	283438.8	1723.0	210611.8	134849.7	63745.7
159750.9	951038.4	60340.0	287693.2	2206345.5	1603340.3
82109.3	849766.8	78757.4	260712.4	1831438.1	1321141.1
240112.9	879404.5	23364.5	324755.3	1895899.3	1364614.6
65304.0	810682.8	63623.2	265902.5	1573721.4	1092564.3
42266.9	599130.8	2758.1	164162.8	1015076.3	582866.4
46618.3	1046363.9	8484.6	307457.2	2746560.0	2016137.9
6739.5	356359.3		356359.3	22783.0	22783.0
200491.3	1086722.4	153000.4	744962.0	907082.4	718322.4
138266.0	636815.3	17029.4	510022.7	347509.2	237746.0
75967.1	1073550.2	10593.4	406494.4	1472452.3	815989.9
102861.5	382216.7	10857.7	206998.2	621842.1	457481.3
58550.5	1124202.5	611.4	466164.7	2314282.9	1656856.5
342655.9	1095315.3	14795.9	560954.8	2096127.9	1576563.3
181915.2	1321809.0	31306.3	312738.5	3218695.7	2240931.5
59029.2	1670218.3	300808.6	579002.0	2033143.4	1242735.7
312294.9	1407808.2	6945.2	430116.2	3128122.4	2157375.6
253006.3	1164449.6	23342.7	910253.4	1877367.9	1646514.4
126111.7	982486.1	38548.3	218830.8	1811785.0	1086678.0
30261.1	172984.4	36265.9	36241.8	240956.5	140479.8
35656.2	1001017.7	358843.3	264329.4	982932.8	605087.8
388529.9	1780565.1	20519.6	587722.7	3846767.7	2674444.9
113418.2	1207763.2	134107.0	157057.2	2891827.0	1975228.0
121962.9	1453844.2	13445.8	457907.4	3510310.3	2527819.3
10146.9	224779.8	17961.4	29451.1	204820.8	27453.5
416525.5	964180.3	77969.1	259918.9	2260482.3	1634190.0
109211.4	1174816.2	23241.6	310822.8	1931912.8	1091161.0
109082.5	256849.5	923.7	37351.3	679611.9	461037.4
8970.7	268588.1	19924.1	72665.6	405014.1	229015.7
140184.2	809114.1	331.1	166650.6	2030604.7	1388472.3

C-1-15续表2

地 区	本年城市最低生活保障预算指标	上年结转预算指标	本级财政安排预算指标	本年上级下达预算指标	本年下达所属地方预算指标	本年农村最低生活保障预算指标	上年结转预算指标
全 国	**8424500.6**	**645505.5**	**12085548.6**	**20902817.4**	**25209370.9**	**10550484.0**	**637795.4**
中央级			8829587.5		8829587.5		
北 京	77835.9		77805.8	30.1		38816.0	
天 津	115404.2	640.8	69766.8	104145.6	59149.0	66278.7	1016.5
河 北	396141.4	34609.5	158258.2	1110401.9	907128.2	197366.1	17598.9
山 西	365800.0	43577.5	156507.7	1030501.7	864786.9	277074.1	20314.0
内蒙古	331196.7	13251.0	162770.4	1030838.1	875662.8	331370.8	3467.4
辽 宁	427096.0	49979.8	125345.8	1102422.8	850652.4	207069.1	11302.1
吉 林	323490.4	2143.0	107300.4	730486.8	516439.8	158609.0	35.6
黑龙江	514128.5	1456.3	158220.9	1589679.2	1235227.9	262806.4	492.9
上 海	123868.0		123868.0			20544.9	
江 苏	174649.3	1200.9	150727.5	133180.4	110459.5	530152.8	145226.6
浙 江	73299.9	2424.9	147212.2	48037.8	124375.0	289437.8	7434.8
安 徽	273970.4	5475.1	50609.5	492986.0	275100.2	431554.9	2376.2
福 建	52534.3	1646.4	19332.2	100232.3	68676.6	132722.0	767.4
江 西	424098.3	111.4	120326.9	1068824.6	765164.6	376316.9	
山 东	153443.9	4134.8	68468.6	347957.2	267116.7	568338.1	4196.7
河 南	346828.2	14927.7	79145.7	1511717.0	1258962.2	634936.9	11727.6
湖 北	542376.0	124065.3	189509.8	1110149.3	881348.4	584721.9	123335.4
湖 南	448638.1	6389.9	185472.1	1697572.7	1440796.6	485436.5	
广 东	198445.7	1698.5	196747.2	267182.7	267182.7	441717.2	8803.9
广 西	140971.5	8523.4	125423.8	196856.5	189832.2	490299.7	13379.0
海 南	64149.5	19682.0	6279.3	153184.0	114995.8	53301.6	11435.7
重 庆	380086.8	222630.7	3106.1	310801.0	156451.0	301737.5	101312.0
四 川	688790.3	9279.4	109338.3	1720888.0	1150715.4	556806.7	7230.8
贵 州	193942.9	25651.9	32972.2	442011.6	306692.8	766392.1	90580.2
云 南	446808.6	3847.9	256120.1	1415046.4	1228205.8	749878.5	6999.5
西 藏	53992.8	2289.8	9786.9	41916.1		72652.5	846.4
陕 西	242371.1	27475.6	33427.5	592176.0	410708.0	388940.6	34629.1
甘 肃	347763.9	8991.1	196105.3	1067507.5	924840.0	611711.8	7816.8
青 海	100944.4		7048.5	286741.3	192845.4	78315.8	
宁 夏	67795.1	9072.7	22003.7	88015.1	51296.4	127843.1	5469.9
新 疆	333638.5	328.2	106953.7	1111327.7	884971.1	317334.0	

单位：万元

本级财政安排预算指标	本年上级下达预算指标	本年下达所属地方预算指标	本年其他社会救济预算指标	上年结转预算指标	本级财政安排预算指标	本年上级下达预算指标	本年下达所属地方预算指标
6341853.0	**17752046.5**	**14181210.9**	**4736948.9**	**156739.5**	**3941728.5**	**5475589.0**	**4837108.1**
3988563.6		3988563.6			1068737.3		1068737.3
38516.8	299.2		64767.0	2001.9	43463.5	31963.6	12662.0
51109.8	14152.4		54176.2	65.7	48874.5	9832.7	4596.7
18977.2	229501.8	68711.8	237522.4	4885.4	63316.8	613967.7	444647.5
26435.6	468539.0	238214.5	115603.1	7787.9	48313.4	132234.0	72732.2
68242.6	537752.3	278091.5	123810.5	4303.8	57034.2	137160.6	74688.1
41583.8	285861.2	131678.0	103869.8	444.6	64482.5	69117.7	30175.0
17779.6	142780.1	1986.3	50299.7	163.1	22541.7	27964.6	369.7
40202.9	510946.2	288835.6	115947.1	598.2	37991.4	267870.4	190512.9
20544.9			176484.4		176484.4	19234.0	19234.0
278232.2	555192.0	448498.0	232689.5	5408.9	194067.1	101733.5	68520.0
154042.4	130367.6	2407.0	149736.4	3658.0	106982.8	106303.3	67207.7
99561.6	701694.0	372076.9	202830.4	2282.1	170797.3	102598.7	72847.7
51153.6	248653.7	167852.7	96976.8	6561.7	56235.1	114405.9	80225.9
125493.4	669132.3	418308.8	152315.7	500.0	130193.9	271085.9	249464.1
199824.8	1266148.6	901832.0	196883.6	4618.8	173274.7	230249.5	211259.4
25529.2	1179851.0	582170.9	210555.2	4332.3	181313.8	211585.7	186676.6
264749.8	426438.8	229802.1	373988.7	33400.5	87923.6	296927.0	44262.4
58003.8	605568.4	178135.7	309074.1	555.3	144412.1	435483.0	271376.3
258544.3	881948.4	707579.4	260885.5	6700.0	222175.9	292703.1	260693.5
5008.5	1028636.7	556724.5	254297.7	13331.1	69426.1	401802.0	230261.5
7907.9	34446.0	488.0	30400.7	3174.6	15355.1	11913.0	42.0
57954.5	244214.8	101743.8	179917.0	18258.3	137889.7	262351.9	238582.9
136905.5	1394692.4	982022.0	289931.3	2859.5	250633.4	197743.2	161304.8
60059.6	1905172.3	1289420.0	132005.6	10258.2	40384.5	269022.9	187660.0
126709.8	1625820.5	1009651.3	134123.9	831.0	51192.8	165348.7	83248.6
10264.0	61542.1		39718.1	248.4	4424.0	35148.2	102.5
48202.1	981318.4	675209.0	194918.5	10015.1	120797.6	368679.5	304573.7
7194.9	596700.1		118419.9	5154.2	97371.3	92097.4	76203.0
7775.0	232881.8	162341.0	31071.2	923.7	13575.9	42024.2	25452.6
31625.6	205366.2	114618.6	37456.7	3417.2	14859.6	49433.6	30253.7
15153.7	586428.2	284247.9	66272.2		27202.5	107603.5	68533.8

C-1-15续表3

地 区	本年医疗救助预算指标	上年结转预算指标	本级财政安排预算指标	本年上级下达预算指标	本年下达所属地方预算指标
全 国	**3534640.0**	**112662.2**	**3374835.7**	**6152467.6**	**6105325.5**
中央级			1767624.0		1767624.0
北 京	28873.1	278.0	25356.3	10302.2	7063.4
天 津	47579.7		40860.7	6719.0	
河 北	120008.5	3246.2	47141.0	252474.1	182852.8
山 西	91289.6	7078.0	29455.7	200163.4	145407.5
内蒙古	93026.5	2342.3	36708.1	190148.3	136172.2
辽 宁	72647.9	1896.7	34490.4	116319.7	80058.9
吉 林	66731.7	416.4	16541.1	113844.8	64070.6
黑龙江	153481.9	5937.2	71042.0	378064.2	301561.5
上 海	35462.0		35462.0	3549.0	3549.0
江 苏	149230.8	1164.0	121935.2	116976.5	90844.9
浙 江	124341.2	3511.7	101785.3	62800.5	43756.3
安 徽	165194.5	460.0	85526.0	175173.6	95965.1
福 建	99983.6	1882.2	80277.3	158550.2	140726.1
江 西	171471.6		90150.5	305240.1	223919.0
山 东	176649.7	1845.6	119386.7	251772.6	196355.2
河 南	129488.7	318.7	26749.8	315542.0	213121.8
湖 北	169131.7	20007.4	36818.8	199628.3	87322.8
湖 南	164659.5		42228.2	389498.3	267067.0
广 东	263401.2	6140.3	232786.0	435533.7	411058.8
广 西	96917.2	3314.8	18972.4	184489.8	109859.8
海 南	25132.6	1973.6	6699.5	41413.5	24954.0
重 庆	139276.4	16642.3	65379.1	165565.1	108310.1
四 川	245036.8	1149.9	90845.5	533444.1	380402.7
贵 州	115422.6	7616.7	23640.9	275620.2	191455.2
云 南	123033.2	1767.4	23884.7	304094.7	206713.6
西 藏	58416.4	14576.8	4976.2	66214.4	27351.0
陕 西	137950.1	5849.3	57491.7	318308.4	243699.3
甘 肃	96920.6	1279.5	10151.3	175607.8	90118.0
青 海	46518.1		8951.9	117964.6	80398.4
宁 夏	35493.2	1964.3	4176.7	62199.2	32847.0
新 疆	91869.4	2.9	17340.7	225245.3	150719.5

单位：万元

本年自然灾害生活救助预算指标	上年结转预算指标	本级财政安排预算指标	本年上级下达预算指标	本年下达所属地方预算指标
1772542.2	**354427.8**	**1399007.8**	**2786785.0**	**2767678.4**
13500.0		791301.0		777801.0
2364.7		2315.7	500.8	451.8
1996.6		1605.6	391.0	
124444.9	14338.0	59884.0	231232.8	181009.9
59978.4	17565.3	8613.1	116289.5	82489.5
74840.5	25740.1	12891.4	137627.4	101418.4
23446.8	3011.4	7256.2	36624.8	23445.6
27965.2	234.9	20700.5	35906.2	28876.4
38125.9	16472.0	3874.8	92266.2	74487.1
61232.2	1089.7	46260.5	74789.0	60907.0
39991.2	6470.4	22489.8	18781.0	7750.0
73454.7	1423.3	24557.4	108823.9	61349.9
74592.0	13174.7	28364.3	130854.3	97801.3
96211.4	32557.0	15154.4	141717.0	93217.0
17165.1	2556.8	7177.1	25979.2	18548.0
50087.7	15021.7	11289.0	110146.3	86369.3
148900.1	9326.3	70648.8	152433.9	83508.9
107978.5	30229.2	16234.1	248623.0	187107.8
38665.2	1761.6	30903.6	64769.1	58769.1
56613.5	25956.4	20978.0	27765.3	18086.2
18173.3	7830.4	9932.5	16777.9	16367.5
45206.2	15667.3	16838.9	46687.0	33987.0
72054.3	11847.3	24698.0	118144.7	82635.7
124401.3	20239.1	50462.2	222702.8	169002.8
64541.2	5514.4	25513.8	121168.7	87655.7
40714.5	6472.2	15097.2	25912.4	6767.3
48122.5	6442.9	17293.4	85595.4	61209.2
85060.5	34779.3	8891.2	122903.0	81513.0
28171.3	0.0	11591.3	36343.0	19763.0
20320.0	2267.3	6652.7	27290.0	15890.0
94222.5	26438.8	9537.3	207739.4	149493.0

C-1-15续表4

地　区	本年民政管理事务预算指标	上年结转预算指标	本级财政安排预算指标	本年上级下达预算指标	本年下达所属地方预算指标	本年行政事业单位离退休预算指标	上年结转预算指标
全　国	**4434200.9**	**75620.7**	**4274906.8**	**1022773.9**	**939100.5**	**473389.4**	**473.2**
中央级	129990.7		204353.7		74363.0	5741.0	
北　京	298086.4		297475.4	611.0		61158.2	0.2
天　津	228988.9	1235.3	227753.6			3270.8	
河　北	111493.6	1661.8	107758.3	25050.3	22976.8	30622.0	
山　西	68555.5	1056.5	64717.0	17701.0	14919.0	8333.6	
内蒙古	78784.3	5737.5	63873.1	27702.8	18529.1	17378.5	
辽　宁	209211.9	1101.4	157563.0	92719.0	42171.5	20964.4	
吉　林	65975.0	76.9	66513.8	14269.3	14885.0	7675.1	
黑龙江	51405.1	45.5	48901.0	14363.9	11905.3	14681.3	
上　海	153921.6		153921.6			5804.9	
江　苏	267630.6	1174.4	264471.1	31242.2	29257.1	27466.1	15.6
浙　江	233766.1	6239.8	214934.6	17813.7	5222.0	16037.3	21.9
安　徽	79738.7	87.3	77966.1	13798.9	12113.6	18018.3	
福　建	97770.7	1574.4	94389.2	34053.7	32246.6	18751.9	286.4
江　西	60244.2		57057.0	15181.8	11994.6	10739.4	
山　东	233239.4	153.8	230616.7	41154.2	38685.3	14901.2	
河　南	133075.8	234.4	126171.2	28037.8	21367.6	22824.2	
湖　北	177609.8	1961.5	173168.3	61662.5	59182.5	17364.9	0.1
湖　南	146327.2	1991.8	127907.8	47289.7	30862.1	7594.2	83.0
广　东	350796.6	776.4	348307.2	91444.3	89731.3	52242.0	
广　西	151904.5	6723.9	142273.2	38845.1	35937.7	17163.8	5.3
海　南	38494.5	6169.7	32087.8	397.0	160.0	2376.0	20.2
重　庆	115789.9	1596.2	112638.7	14750.0	13195.0	13416.9	7.9
四　川	245823.4	9392.9	232071.7	43706.5	39347.7	16888.9	
贵　州	131162.8	7083.6	121005.2	46837.6	43763.6	1663.2	32.6
云　南	177896.2	1529.3	172793.9	89912.3	86339.3	16072.6	
西　藏	16735.6	525.7	11504.0	7287.9	2582.0	1127.1	
陕　西	193020.1	12010.1	180022.5	157671.2	156683.7	7627.0	
甘　肃	38666.9	209.5	34941.4	7831.0	4315.0	6060.6	
青　海	42154.2		39119.0	13544.4	10509.2	1302.6	
宁　夏	42937.7	5271.1	34046.4	10608.2	6988.0	3452.1	
新　疆	63003.0		54583.3	17286.6	8866.9	4669.3	

单位：万元

本级财政安排预算指标	本年上级下达预算指标	本年下达所属地方预算指标	本年其他款项用于民政支出预算指标	上年结转预算指标	本级财政安排预算指标	本年上级下达预算指标	本年下达所属地方预算指标
470442.1	**3222.5**	**748.4**	**1451708.3**	**117562.5**	**1265200.4**	**598296.4**	**529351.0**
5741.0			58410.8		81298.8		22888.0
61158.0			87272.2	175.0	87097.2		
3270.8			12487.9		12487.9		
30503.0	119.0		11390.5	300.0	10600.5	490.0	
8333.6			14119.9	441.7	13678.2		
17378.5			85064.8	18519.2	27372.8	60736.6	21563.8
20481.0	483.4		48820.8	52.2	87299.1	17266.8	55797.3
7454.4	220.7		27192.2		20694.2	6736.6	238.6
14681.3			7622.2		7622.2		
5804.9			23370.7		23370.7		
26133.5	1317.0		134886.8	10110.7	109228.7	30654.2	15106.8
16015.4			52470.1	1926.7	47044.3	3506.1	7.0
18018.3			24699.1	2312.1	20234.5	2492.8	340.3
18465.5			40792.2	2109.0	38443.6	12594.5	12354.9
10739.4			39124.8		39400.9	58214.6	58490.7
14901.2			71537.2	10773.6	60709.1	2325.9	2271.4
22824.2			63110.4	13912.6	34957.6	26701.6	12461.4
17321.8	43.0		31789.7	1712.4	42088.3	22157.0	34168.0
7405.2	106.0		37305.0	29.9	18951.7	30312.3	11988.9
52242.0			149691.9	2102.1	146811.9	62120.7	61342.8
17158.5			36293.8	8850.0	27443.8	305.0	305.0
2355.8			32423.4	8483.4	20078.4	4795.6	934.0
13409.0			17499.2	2189.0	15310.2	216.0	216.0
16888.9			37837.5	937.0	29129.6	19377.1	11606.2
1630.6			14334.3	1922.7	12411.6	1293.1	1293.1
16072.6	90.7	90.7	111494.8	1720.3	109774.5	116925.3	116925.3
1756.7	28.1	657.7	20006.5		15887.9	4118.6	
7393.6	233.4		22931.9	2465.8	6689.5	51264.4	37487.8
6060.6			20188.2	387.1	19221.1	580.0	
1302.6			23399.0		8366.5	24011.2	8978.7
2941.5	510.6		77977.4	25980.0	53292.4	16604.0	17899.0
4598.7	70.6		16163.1	150.0	18202.7	22496.4	24686.0

C-1-15续表5

地 区	本年财政拨款	抚恤	退役安置	社会福利
全 国	**54092101.4**	**7597896.8**	**5891213.2**	**7313955.2**
中央级	225508.0	761.5		17104.0
北 京	2308360.2	148248.3	1092797.5	410095.7
天 津	868739.5	96980.7	117509.4	125745.7
河 北	2153562.2	421091.3	343884.0	255010.5
山 西	1344270.1	240973.2	96427.8	124970.3
内蒙古	1461419.4	99747.4	87007.2	202752.3
辽 宁	1843518.7	199834.4	465154.2	148001.3
吉 林	1042817.9	136340.2	87323.0	91184.0
黑龙江	1522624.1	161530.9	84096.5	131416.1
上 海	1364255.8	108205.9	199230.0	517363.4
江 苏	2837218.2	481887.7	420450.6	517582.5
浙 江	1827323.3	289204.7	159530.5	428973.3
安 徽	1962880.9	312672.0	156597.6	249613.1
福 建	1047033.5	149649.2	102403.0	213511.6
江 西	1717958.0	252861.3	60636.2	111738.2
山 东	3034045.1	778464.8	449727.3	407845.8
河 南	2505517.4	510645.9	204666.2	243630.8
湖 北	2657392.1	385622.3	202211.6	231449.5
湖 南	2629351.5	528411.7	132067.3	270039.8
广 东	2932627.3	417426.5	293781.5	502996.1
广 西	1586689.5	201690.9	63991.8	234975.6
海 南	345502.6	30859.2	21834.7	71637.1
重 庆	1278379.4	194962.3	105599.4	142484.6
四 川	3409275.3	577258.9	270745.3	434586.0
贵 州	1689876.6	166334.7	45867.8	179773.6
云 南	2324847.9	249346.9	137054.1	139262.9
西 藏	245000.1	11192.5	19746.0	26308.5
陕 西	1972446.8	281907.3	222725.6	340242.2
甘 肃	1638509.7	68114.5	102589.4	171612.4
青 海	500268.3	17738.1	33156.3	105980.4
宁 夏	431475.3	15275.0	11597.5	30119.5
新 疆	1383406.7	62656.6	100803.9	235948.4

单位：万元

社会救助	自然灾害 生活救助	民政管理 事务	行政事业 单位离退休	其他款项 用于民政支出
25505227.7	**1576719.6**	**4367319.1**	**476586.6**	**1363183.2**
	13500.0	129990.7	5741.0	58410.8
208337.2	2364.7	298086.4	61158.2	87272.2
282826.1	1996.6	227922.3	3270.8	12487.9
879571.4	102018.9	110092.6	30503.0	11390.5
744374.9	49096.2	67539.9	8232.5	12655.3
875741.4	59157.2	68284.6	16473.7	52255.6
733067.6	21432.2	207268.1	20963.8	47797.1
600108.2	27642.2	65353.0	7675.1	27192.2
1035141.9	36893.9	51241.3	14681.3	7622.2
356359.3		153921.6	5804.9	23370.7
932954.8	60345.2	267404.2	27323.5	129269.7
617506.4	35400.2	229188.8	15942.3	51577.1
1056257.8	70344.6	78265.3	18007.4	21123.1
363208.4	65034.2	95939.8	18733.6	38553.7
1124202.5	58411.4	60244.2	10739.4	39124.8
1073497.9	15695.1	233123.4	14901.2	60789.6
1288727.5	48698.5	132752.3	22824.2	53572.0
1437187.3	146046.6	189159.0	22290.5	43425.3
1404078.5	106227.4	143655.5	7596.2	37275.1
1131065.7	36397.9	350077.3	52242.0	148640.3
859587.5	42847.1	138511.1	17010.1	28075.4
132412.3	10657.4	41335.9	2430.5	34335.5
655874.4	36357.4	112915.8	13416.9	16768.6
1769958.7	64171.3	239169.2	16777.9	36608.0
1048054.5	107366.6	126915.9	1640.8	13922.7
1441133.9	57019.1	176232.8	16072.6	108725.6
115255.3	35899.7	15676.3	1125.1	19796.7
881129.6	44842.5	175521.6	7627.0	18451.0
1148310.9	83557.0	38309.5	6060.6	19955.4
249182.0	27808.9	41978.6	1302.6	23121.4
251900.3	17930.2	38234.1	3419.2	62999.5
808213.5	91559.4	63008.0	4598.7	16618.2

C-1-15续表6

地 区	本年预算指标结余	抚恤	退役安置	社会福利
全 国	**2920904.1**	**153534.5**	**255098.5**	**422893.0**
中央级				
北 京	12760.0	405.8	1196.9	9202.5
天 津	12233.9	731.7	5193.6	4629.3
河 北	124747.8	7307.3	7927.4	14100.1
山 西	156579.8	11591.2	8345.3	17787.9
内蒙古	103308.7	4016.5	3345.8	32386.3
辽 宁	101977.3	2230.6	14327.6	2821.2
吉 林	3696.5	1992.3	1191.6	545.0
黑龙江	14613.1	1008.6	930.1	56.6
上 海	23550.5		13979.0	9571.5
江 苏	217698.3	12272.3	33041.9	11743.4
浙 江	82284.1	9374.5	2323.2	41121.2
安 徽	42208.7	7046.2	1372.3	8327.4
福 建	75963.9	5696.9	11491.1	26122.1
江 西	37800.0			
山 东	52804.5	1512.1	5140.4	12001.0
河 南	50665.2	666.5	440.2	5225.9
湖 北	204903.4	-2335.6	-2390.2	1855.1
湖 南	14551.8	2002.6	227.0	4141.8
广 东	86818.8	5749.7	34550.0	9097.0
广 西	261880.3	20159.2	8648.7	74641.9
海 南	80456.1	4979.3	28158.9	4037.9
重 庆	381138.6	3044.6	4136.5	16360.7
四 川	88926.8	4705.3	17385.0	40352.4
贵 州	218930.3	10691.6	3049.8	23764.6
云 南	38235.6	6844.2	2081.8	4644.6
西 藏	137807.5	5397.1	12521.6	4278.4
陕 西	183893.2	24048.2	22016.6	29518.3
甘 肃	33370.9	823.3	2525.6	1423.0
青 海	17410.2	33.1	588.5	8305.5
宁 夏	51329.9	1323.7	11248.4	-34.2
新 疆	8358.4	215.7	103.9	4864.6

单位：万元

社会救助	自然灾害生活救助	民政管理事务	行政事业单位离退休	其他款项用于民政支出
1741345.8	**195822.6**	**66881.8**	**-3197.2**	**88525.1**
1954.8				
612.7		1066.6		
71467.0	22426.0	1401.0	119.0	
105391.9	10882.2	1015.6	101.1	1464.6
3663.1	15683.3	10499.7	904.8	32809.2
77615.2	2014.6	1943.8	0.6	1023.7
-977.4	323.0	622.0		
11222.0	1232.0	163.8		
153767.6	887.0	226.4	142.6	5617.1
19308.9	4591.0	4577.3	95.0	893.0
17292.4	3110.1	1473.4	10.9	3576.0
19008.3	9557.8	1830.9	18.3	2238.5
	37800.0			
21817.4	1470.0	116.0		10747.6
33081.5	1389.2	323.5		9538.4
233031.0	2853.5	-11549.2	-4925.6	-11635.6
3729.7	1751.1	2671.7	-2.0	29.9
33383.9	2267.3	719.3	0.0	1051.6
122898.6	13766.4	13393.4	153.7	8218.4
40572.1	7515.9	-2841.4	-54.5	-1912.1
345143.3	8848.8	2874.1		730.6
10606.4	7883.0	6654.2	111.0	1229.5
159708.7	17034.7	4246.9	22.4	411.6
12710.3	7522.1	1663.4		2769.2
109524.5	4814.8	1059.3	2.0	209.8
83050.7	3280.0	17498.5		4480.9
26505.3	1503.5	357.4		232.8
7667.5	362.4	175.6		277.6
16687.8	2389.8	4703.6	32.9	14977.9
900.6	2663.1	-5.0	70.6	-455.1

C-1-16 社会服务事业费

地区	社会服务事业费总支出	抚恤	死亡抚恤	一次性抚恤金	定期抚恤金	其他	伤残抚恤
全　国	**54401503.4**	**7698352.6**	**741460.3**	**318622.9**	**359051.2**	**63786.2**	**1430601.7**
中央级	165749.1	584.3					
北　京	2558934.6	145638.5	61539.5	52373.6	3068.0	6097.9	20812.5
天　津	895069.9	96839.2	16150.7	6219.8	2112.6	7818.3	16351.1
河　北	2115331.3	430666.7	32974.8	14273.1	18074.5	627.2	82787.7
山　西	1291517.7	240703.0	15606.5	5830.8	8770.3	1005.4	38641.3
内蒙古	1400524.5	103537.7	8627.4	4613.4	2859.0	1155.0	19789.4
辽　宁	1845473.1	203995.9	30748.1	16845.6	10575.6	3326.9	47242.5
吉　林	1041251.7	137186.9	12318.5	5106.0	6363.8	848.7	35444.8
黑龙江	1526756.7	160175.6	11808.4	4621.0	6653.5	533.9	25382.8
上　海	1532275.2	106832.7	17306.1	9267.8	6485.5	1552.8	19229.2
江　苏	2872252.8	484846.6	48514.0	20672.6	21379.0	6462.4	107000.8
浙　江	1899440.0	315497.4	20616.6	7806.1	11537.6	1272.9	46871.0
安　徽	1970515.8	313670.7	18015.9	5545.7	11569.3	900.9	54320.2
福　建	1041706.7	150920.2	17377.5	5725.0	11191.4	461.1	20947.0
江　西	1717261.4	252649.1	41839.8	7396.1	28758.3	5685.4	36224.5
山　东	3048812.9	780669.4	58145.3	21564.0	34085.8	2495.5	222002.6
河　南	2469598.6	511927.7	28521.5	9342.6	18742.0	436.9	106355.4
湖　北	2423266.1	393859.8	43903.8	9512.3	33093.2	1298.3	56356.1
湖　南	2716411.4	527889.7	62683.8	27686.8	27494.3	7502.7	109019.6
广　东	3056715.3	420549.1	30947.9	18211.9	12373.3	362.7	46815.7
广　西	1577969.5	222955.5	10378.3	3041.0	7241.1	96.2	18757.3
海　南	300733.3	29796.5	4708.0	1153.5	3453.6	100.9	5256.5
重　庆	1299701.7	195891.2	17928.6	6678.6	7403.1	3846.9	39077.1
四　川	3486433.8	604649.8	49860.8	16454.3	31104.6	2301.9	115723.7
贵　州	1602657.5	167913.4	11951.1	6435.9	4306.6	1208.6	23308.4
云　南	2348845.7	238661.0	20014.5	9983.8	8606.5	1424.2	35570.7
西　藏	235821.1	9870.3	4545.2	652.1	1920.6	1972.5	2754.8
陕　西	2020674.1	284958.7	22481.2	9515.5	11246.5	1719.2	37233.0
甘　肃	1631306.1	69182.8	7056.6	3377.5	3235.7	443.4	17315.4
青　海	492304.9	18293.7	2507.8	1615.5	796.0	96.3	3443.0
宁　夏	420877.6	15664.4	2749.9	1057.5	1690.0	2.4	3865.6
新　疆	1,395,313.3	61,875.1	9,632.2	6,043.5	2,859.9	728.8	16,702.0

总体支出情况

单位：万元

伤残抚恤金	在乡伤残抚恤金	在职保健金	伤残补助费	分散安置残疾军人护理费	在乡复员、退伍军人生活补助	在乡复退军人定期定量补助费	在乡红军老战士定期定量补助费	红军失散人员定期定量补助费
1354526.7	**1034947.6**	**319579.1**	**76075.0**	**33344.6**	**2650561.8**	**1760993.5**	**496.2**	**4361.8**
19617.4	11944.9	7672.5	1195.1	521.5	11939.4	8348.9	5.0	
14833.6	8004.9	6828.7	1517.5	507.1	28134.5	19889.9		
79948.7	74105.4	5843.3	2839.0	1169.4	150168.0	108791.2		
37313.6	23529.2	13784.4	1327.7	774.1	49333.0	40059.9	18.4	2.0
17822.1	9474.0	8348.1	1967.3	135.7	19010.4	17809.2	15.7	
46049.8	32279.4	13770.4	1192.7	532.3	45860.7	39634.3		
34611.4	27665.6	6945.8	833.4	491.4	26460.7	23813.7	7.3	
24703.1	18626.7	6076.4	679.7	211.4	37494.1	34301.8	4.2	4.4
17654.7		17654.7	1574.5	299.0	13046.5	9387.5		
99044.3	79043.0	20001.3	7956.5	4572.0	130423.0	103228.6		1.7
43685.9	29972.7	13713.2	3185.1	729.9	87308.8	67787.8		66.8
52572.9	39059.0	13513.9	1747.3	983.4	130907.9	105734.8		340.8
19822.4	16390.7	3431.7	1124.6	407.1	48746.2	25775.5		200.9
34335.5	31847.1	2488.4	1889.0	878.6	101977.6	68547.8	29.2	1965.2
210327.1	152548.9	57778.2	11675.5	8365.3	207577.7	161029.3		
103088.7	76503.1	26585.6	3266.7	1772.3	185799.3	121710.0	8.7	294.7
52651.3	46114.4	6536.9	3704.8	776.0	141056.8	99539.2	4.3	103.3
101438.1	83503.7	17934.4	7581.5	2265.0	214737.5	134660.3	4.6	316.0
44192.8	34754.2	9438.6	2622.9	672.4	211383.8	89906.6		7.4
17846.9	15599.9	2247.0	910.4	191.1	94409.9	36520.6		367.6
4965.0	4859.3	105.7	291.5	15.4	8176.4	4469.1		17.0
36469.0	26151.4	10317.6	2608.1	1714.2	97994.9	67248.9		
109962.8	93728.3	16234.5	5760.9	3538.9	293049.4	205967.7	170.6	462.9
21828.8	17145.0	4683.8	1479.6	530.9	81639.0	39577.7	6.7	10.4
32267.5	21758.8	10508.7	3303.2	296.4	91273.3	37632.8		6.8
2734.3	2723.6	10.7	20.5		538.0	486.6	44.0	
35945.0	29531.2	6413.8	1288.0	476.3	90237.3	55643.5	119.1	186.2
16145.9	11235.6	4910.3	1169.5	314.7	27137.9	14513.8	21.6	3.8
2992.9	2405.2	587.7	450.1	8.0	3384.6	2340.3		
3841.1	3816.1	25.0	24.5	15.3	3740.2	2916.1	24.6	1.9
15,814.1	10,626.3	5,187.8	887.9	179.5	17,615.0	13,720.1	12.2	2.0

C-1-16续表1

地　区	“参战”退伍军人生活补助	“涉核”退伍军人生活补助	优抚事业单位	烈士纪念建筑物管理维修经费	荣誉军人康复医院经费	复员军人疗养院经费
全　国	**764980.3**	**119730.0**	**672884.0**	**181817.9**	**141199.0**	**41913.6**
中央级			584.3	584.3		
北　京	2698.6	886.9	10222.7	4817.9		
天　津	8176.5	68.1	12172.9	2011.6		1044.0
河　北	28990.4	12386.4	64748.4	16832.4	10875.8	4460.1
山　西	5340.3	3912.4	48428.9	10037.9	2097.9	5976.3
内蒙古	1070.5	115.0	10116.6	2386.6	741.1	31.4
辽　宁	3536.3	2690.1	16838.7	3670.0	1911.9	3981.7
吉　林	1805.7	834.0	12208.3	1900.8	4903.9	
黑龙江	2793.6	390.1	11628.1	2446.0	4373.1	26.6
上　海	2969.5	689.5	13363.1	8404.0	1890.4	
江　苏	23066.1	4126.6	30590.9	15010.9	2121.6	2258.4
浙　江	17725.3	1728.9	40523.9	6191.2	29554.6	
安　徽	17840.6	6991.7	23765.9	12192.9	3506.4	
福　建	22452.3	317.5	8264.5	2971.4	29.0	
江　西	29416.7	2018.7	19255.9	4005.7	10537.1	96.0
山　东	38198.1	8350.3	79291.3	22351.8	15952.0	16291.7
河　南	49210.2	14575.7	25945.1	7083.6	5277.8	1342.8
湖　北	36528.4	4881.6	40479.3	6039.0	3602.8	61.2
湖　南	71709.2	8047.4	41790.2	9567.3	1047.8	80.0
广　东	115512.1	5957.7	28896.4	10192.7	748.8	3635.8
广　西	54600.1	2921.6	32545.9	8255.7	3780.6	380.8
海　南	3421.4	268.9	2799.0	1046.2		
重　庆	26593.8	4152.2	6165.3	1392.6	1621.0	
四　川	73152.5	13295.7	47046.2	5003.8	26424.1	190.6
贵　州	41897.1	147.1	8502.0	3056.0	1949.8	23.0
云　南	53613.2	20.5	5032.0	1543.8	1274.5	
西　藏	7.4		367.7	21.7	300.0	
陕　西	22255.2	12033.3	18263.0	5012.7	5449.4	2033.2
甘　肃	8083.7	4515.0	5149.6	3728.0	590.1	
青　海	475.2	569.1	1297.0	436.9		
宁　夏	577.6	220.0	631.9	626.4		
新　疆	1,262.7	2,618.0	5969.0	2996.1	637.5	

单位：万元

复退军人精神病院经费	光荣院经费	其他优抚事业单位经费	集体办优抚事业单位补助费	义务兵优待金	其他优抚支出	临时补助
132124.9	**84495.9**	**88240.1**	**3092.6**	**1469530.5**	**733314.3**	**70006.3**
	4216.0	1188.8		21090.5	20033.9	2144.4
2360.0	3384.8	3372.5		12001.6	12028.4	2759.1
8163.2	10117.3	14299.6		86287.1	13700.7	379.2
14057.4	8442.0	7817.4		70590.1	18103.2	539.1
2210.9	3008.2	1738.4		35285.4	10708.5	1.3
467.1	5158.0	1650.0		44662.6	18643.3	723.6
500.5	2482.3	2420.8		41630.5	9124.1	2111.0
614.7	1535.0	2472.4	160.3	67742.0	6120.2	1760.9
105.9		2962.8		35475.3	8412.5	644.2
4321.1	777.0	6101.9		87650.0	80667.9	3622.4
2527.6	588.6	1661.9		90771.4	29405.7	4176.7
3234.7	3220.6	1473.3	138.0	58084.8	28576.0	1537.9
713.2	2837.9	1650.0	63.0	38341.5	17243.5	723.8
10.0	3580.9	914.2	112.0	32837.0	20514.3	2485.2
21278.4	1427.3	1975.1	15.0	135494.0	78158.5	165.0
6661.9	2505.7	2882.3	191.0	131587.2	33719.2	1760.8
22332.5	6655.3	1788.5		83013.9	29049.9	3654.7
5144.8	10065.6	15379.7	505.0	54797.9	44860.7	8279.7
9623.5	2892.4	1768.2	35.0	54084.9	48420.4	14181.1
16638.4	1894.4	1596.0		44016.9	22847.2	1555.3
	494.3	1244.4	14.1	2618.7	6237.9	439.5
300.0	1731.3	1120.4		20145.1	14580.2	2026.7
8300.2	2626.0	3505.5	996.0	71967.5	27002.2	4088.7
	2378.5	966.9	127.8	19455.7	23057.2	726.6
183.6	100.0	1930.1		16155.2	70615.3	4052.8
		46.0		863.2	801.4	42.0
1445.9	1783.9	1902.5	635.4	90071.8	26672.4	3353.6
781.5	5.0	45.0		7273.0	5250.3	182.6
		860.1		3308.3	4353.0	198.9
	5.5			3679.9	996.9	12.5
147.9	582.1	1505.4	100.0	8547.5	3409.4	1677.0

C-1-16续表2

地　区	退役安置	退伍军人安置	一次性建房补助费	退役士兵自谋职业金	城镇退役士兵生活补助	军队移交政府的离退休人员安置	军队离休干部离休金	军队退休干部退休金
全　国	**6256423.7**	**1221663.9**	**22743.3**	**878685.3**	**168487.2**	**4329360.9**	**337153.6**	**2769874.3**
中央级								
北　京	1316380.3	28564.4	50.1	28340.8	82.5	1085589.2	23386.1	746297.8
天　津	122872.7	15994.2		13453.6	65.0	94710.8	5298.3	53480.6
河　北	339278.4	85820.8	2777.5	45551.4	20256.4	229042.5	21250.7	153217.2
山　西	104696.7	20411.0	39.5	8267.7	7257.2	72225.9	8636.2	43908.0
内蒙古	87493.9	37083.8	650.9	18889.4	10991.0	39022.1	5199.5	25359.0
辽　宁	460946.4	42248.6	829.2	25264.0	4043.1	388330.7	40538.6	264259.8
吉　林	88277.6	11819.0	1804.8	6002.0	3079.7	64147.9	4020.8	43913.9
黑龙江	83920.1	34303.7	2982.7	18590.5	3198.8	45256.0	3420.3	25387.8
上　海	223506.0	34065.2	5.0	22533.4	7469.1	151340.9	6525.0	84898.5
江　苏	424085.1	130125.4	1909.0	111851.6	9545.9	257227.6	20428.9	176247.8
浙　江	161075.9	55333.0	916.8	38901.1	7841.1	83464.3	11628.2	52271.1
安　徽	156509.5	83998.9	951.9	70951.1	8790.6	58615.0	8570.0	34299.3
福　建	106477.9	34371.4	121.8	28621.0	3840.4	59026.2	7701.9	42277.8
江　西	60569.5	22801.2	51.2	15096.7	5741.6	29239.3	6598.3	11518.2
山　东	449727.8	101139.2	712.1	74670.6	10544.6	310123.7	37024.0	191399.6
河　南	203503.7	50365.0	509.5	27026.7	14137.6	123947.0	14326.6	81842.0
湖　北	209618.7	38174.7	468.0	26714.0	5309.5	151551.0	16845.4	86907.1
湖　南	142988.7	30955.1	1038.2	13647.9	9324.8	92801.3	10545.4	43502.3
广　东	305113.2	100042.8	626.6	92560.2	3714.1	168627.5	14674.0	96786.5
广　西	66387.4	16770.8	693.3	11087.1	1629.1	39125.9	2775.3	24578.2
海　南	26820.1	6143.0	255.8	4097.2	934.0	15621.6	584.9	8202.4
重　庆	108441.2	34771.6	154.0	32867.1	427.2	65127.9	3252.1	42364.4
四　川	294417.6	84573.8	1521.1	69602.0	5340.8	179916.3	13918.5	128458.1
贵　州	43866.0	14391.6	546.6	9607.2	2576.5	25150.9	2386.9	13973.3
云　南	139410.7	20373.0	234.8	13889.4	3114.8	104629.1	5079.4	52324.5
西　藏	19274.8	1245.5	20.0	374.0	112.9	17276.7		13870.7
陕　西	260844.0	33371.1	986.9	16890.7	11267.5	207937.1	16694.4	137602.8
甘　肃	105733.7	22896.9	896.0	11049.4	6517.8	64385.6	3762.7	39960.7
青　海	33115.0	7229.5	139.1	3949.3	36.3	23639.5	672.0	11301.4
宁　夏	10962.8	8111.3		6322.2	567.9	1921.1	208.3	594.1
新　疆	100108.3	14168.4	850.9	12016.0	729.4	80340.3	21200.9	38869.4

单位：万元

军队无军籍职工退休金	军队离退休人员其他费用						军队移交政府离退休干部管理机构	其他退役安置支出
		死亡丧葬费	护理费	遗属生活困难补助费	定期定量补助费	其他费用		
654182.5	**568150.5**	**42011.3**	**49755.2**	**28792.0**	**14630.2**	**447592.0**	**521505.2**	**179795.0**
136716.4	179188.9	3039.6	7374.3	2242.9	161.3	166532.1	199873.4	2362.1
11894.5	24037.4	928.5	1560.0	185.1	103.4	21363.8	11369.4	798.5
30021.6	24553.0	2853.3	2534.8	2892.7	1217.6	16272.2	21862.3	2552.8
10926.5	8755.2	843.8	1924.3	1834.8	861.3	4152.3	6697.0	5463.7
5750.1	2713.5	451.3	437.0	467.9	128.9	1357.3	5233.1	6154.9
51950.6	31581.7	5602.3	6466.2	2226.5	1218.6	17286.7	24744.5	5622.6
13505.4	2707.8	394.4	26.0	80.8	33.8	2206.6	5357.2	6953.5
9376.7	7071.2	257.8	431.3	279.6	84.5	6102.5	2706.0	2034.5
26782.9	33134.5	1131.5	2562.1	87.9	75.1	29353.0	33418.4	4708.1
36069.6	24481.3	5264.8	2414.3	1429.9	655.7	15372.3	22440.1	14309.1
14062.2	5502.8	551.5	886.2	454.5	296.9	3610.6	14471.4	7400.9
6329.0	9416.7	937.0	1042.8	882.0	360.6	6554.9	8034.1	5861.5
5368.3	3678.2	806.5	950.9	371.6	168.9	1549.2	7298.7	1872.0
5552.8	5570.0	170.6	322.7	251.1	90.9	4825.6	5183.2	3345.8
37539.6	44160.5	5599.9	8854.4	4085.9	2964.5	25620.3	23746.1	14718.8
14982.8	12795.6	2135.2	1511.8	1312.2	576.2	7836.4	17799.1	11391.6
29932.2	17866.3	1364.4	883.6	1100.4	569.9	14517.9	12724.4	7168.6
21641.4	17112.2	1625.7	996.9	1019.5	256.5	13470.1	13180.0	6052.3
45925.5	11241.5	1547.2	757.7	324.9	110.8	8611.7	16150.6	18789.9
6068.0	5704.4	540.5	585.6	2247.4	2108.9	2330.9	6313.3	6336.7
5252.8	1581.5	32.8	192.6	86.1	31.3	1270.0	4257.5	798.0
11302.6	8208.8	933.5	897.3	286.0	166.6	6092.0	6638.6	1921.9
23821.7	13718.0	2204.6	1924.5	978.0	613.9	8610.9	13888.0	15629.8
4005.0	4785.7	482.2	333.5	199.6	103.0	3770.4	2610.8	1712.7
17054.9	30170.3	570.8	883.7	757.4	363.6	27958.4	8097.2	5830.6
3328.4	77.6					77.6	319.3	433.3
27452.0	26187.9	886.4	608.2	1150.6	704.8	23542.7	12105.2	7441.9
15023.6	5638.6	413.4	2186.9	821.2	184.3	2217.1	10774.0	7565.2
10399.5	1266.6	61.7	4.2	171.2	4.0	1029.5	446.3	1799.7
983.0	135.7	22.0	8.4	10.2	10.2	95.1	679.5	250.9
15162.9	5107.1	358.1	193.0	554.1	404.2	4001.9	3086.5	2513.1

C-1-16续表3

地 区	社会福利	儿童福利	孤儿生活补助	老年人福利	高龄补贴	护理补贴	养老服务补贴
全 国	**54401503.4**	**7698352.6**	**741460.3**	**318622.9**	**359051.2**	**63786.2**	**1430601.7**
中央级	165749.1	584.3					
北 京	2558934.6	145638.5	61539.5	52373.6	3068.0	6097.9	20812.5
天 津	895069.9	96839.2	16150.7	6219.8	2112.6	7818.3	16351.1
河 北	2115331.3	430666.7	32974.8	14273.1	18074.5	627.2	82787.7
山 西	1291517.7	240703.0	15606.5	5830.8	8770.3	1005.4	38641.3
内蒙古	1400524.5	103537.7	8627.4	4613.4	2859.0	1155.0	19789.4
辽 宁	1845473.1	203995.9	30748.1	16845.6	10575.6	3326.9	47242.5
吉 林	1041251.7	137186.9	12318.5	5106.0	6363.8	848.7	35444.8
黑龙江	1526756.7	160175.6	11808.4	4621.0	6653.5	533.9	25382.8
上 海	1532275.2	106832.7	17306.1	9267.8	6485.5	1552.8	19229.2
江 苏	2872252.8	484846.6	48514.0	20672.6	21379.0	6462.4	107000.8
浙 江	1899440.0	315497.4	20616.6	7806.1	11537.6	1272.9	46871.0
安 徽	1970515.8	313670.7	18015.9	5545.7	11569.3	900.9	54320.2
福 建	1041706.7	150920.2	17377.5	5725.0	11191.4	461.1	20947.0
江 西	1717261.4	252649.1	41839.8	7396.1	28758.3	5685.4	36224.5
山 东	3048812.9	780669.4	58145.3	21564.0	34085.8	2495.5	222002.6
河 南	2469598.6	511927.7	28521.5	9342.6	18742.0	436.9	106355.4
湖 北	2423266.1	393859.8	43903.8	9512.3	33093.2	1298.3	56356.1
湖 南	2716411.4	527889.7	62683.8	27686.8	27494.3	7502.7	109019.6
广 东	3056715.3	420549.1	30947.9	18211.9	12373.3	362.7	46815.7
广 西	1577969.5	222955.5	10378.3	3041.0	7241.1	96.2	18757.3
海 南	300733.3	29796.5	4708.0	1153.5	3453.6	100.9	5256.5
重 庆	1299701.7	195891.2	17928.6	6678.6	7403.1	3846.9	39077.1
四 川	3486433.8	604649.8	49860.8	16454.3	31104.6	2301.9	115723.7
贵 州	1602657.5	167913.4	11951.1	6435.9	4306.6	1208.6	23308.4
云 南	2348845.7	238661.0	20014.5	9983.8	8606.5	1424.2	35570.7
西 藏	235821.1	9870.3	4545.2	652.1	1920.6	1972.5	2754.8
陕 西	2020674.1	284958.7	22481.2	9515.5	11246.5	1719.2	37233.0
甘 肃	1631306.1	69182.8	7056.6	3377.5	3235.7	443.4	17315.4
青 海	492304.9	18293.7	2507.8	1615.5	796.0	96.3	3443.0
宁 夏	420877.6	15664.4	2749.9	1057.5	1690.0	2.4	3865.6
新 疆	1,395,313.3	61,875.1	9,632.2	6,043.5	2,859.9	728.8	16,702.0

单位：万元

残疾人福利	假肢厂(站)专项拨款	其他经费	困难残疾人生活补贴	重度残疾人护理补贴	殡葬	补贴火化场经费	补贴殡葬类单位经费
731613.5	**30571.5**	**31460.7**	**353588.7**	**315992.6**	**845964.6**	**339863.6**	**506101.0**
3959.2		2054.7	1870.9	33.6	31178.1	12116.6	19061.5
23510.3		1490.9	11280.7	10738.7	32658.3	1123.0	31535.3
44845.8	350.0	202.6	23773.1	20520.1	34351.5	11267.7	23083.8
9221.1	400.0	175.0	8480.6	165.5	19988.9	17746.6	2242.3
6062.0		363.2	2183.8	3515.0	14124.6	2884.7	11239.9
24116.4		516.7	13410.1	10189.6	37299.3	20635.3	16664.0
18674.2		229.0	7795.7	10649.5	19600.5	2870.4	16730.1
17620.6		502.0	8169.2	8949.4	16610.5	4006.7	12603.8
					1501.8		1501.8
38171.2		1019.4	27906.2	9245.6	74643.0	34201.3	40441.7
22094.3		8406.5	10971.4	2716.4	89413.2	37678.8	51734.4
32374.0	142.0	56.1	1293.0	30882.9	32036.3	17513.7	14522.6
44718.3		1942.0	18805.1	23971.2	21750.1	14940.6	6809.5
7760.2	847.7	10.0	4276.1	2626.4	7165.6	4031.2	3134.4
78414.9		389.1	38736.1	39289.7	22997.8	13516.5	9481.3
26206.7	3775.0	1467.9	11987.6	8976.2	22590.1	12928.1	9662.0
33898.4	4784.3	679.8	11517.4	16916.9	38565.0	4997.8	33567.2
72358.5	474.4	5299.3	35538.6	31046.2	35189.8	6940.4	28249.4
27468.8	2036.0	1358.6	8258.9	15815.3	86727.8	22303.1	64424.7
31467.4	3162.4	165.1	12084.2	16055.7	26328.9	10310.7	16018.2
7131.0		8.3	1745.7	5377.0	3426.5	633.5	2793.0
3103.4	2919.0	141.7	30.0	12.7	31212.1	18492.3	12719.8
32722.6	4134.5	1944.9	24078.2	2565.0	44594.3	9745.1	34849.2
6547.7	386.7	76.8	1033.9	5050.3	18433.4	13208.3	5225.1
8772.9	1385.4	70.5	4823.1	2493.9	24482.3	10990.3	13492.0
2729.6		90.3	1812.7	826.6	1261.0	1261.0	
43436.3	3805.5	1487.7	27138.3	11004.8	29728.9	23115.7	6613.2
25362.5	245.4	278.6	14465.2	10373.3	5302.7	2189.3	3113.4
18215.8	173.2		9234.7	8807.9	226.0	181.0	45.0
1987.6			450.5	1537.1	842.2	505.6	336.6
18661.8	1550.0	1034.0	10437.7	5640.1	21734.1	7528.3	14205.8

C-1-16续表4

地 区	社会福利事业单位						其他社会福利支出
		社会福利院经费	儿童福利院经费	精神病人福利院经费	补贴安置农场经费	其他社会福利单位	
全 国	**1596132.9**	**735632.6**	**176155.4**	**198833.1**	**11810.5**	**473701.3**	**1185317.3**
中央级							17827.9
北 京	26273.5	9848.2	1104.6	6796.6		8524.1	105684.4
天 津	29009.1	2614.0	1296.1	4776.0	184.2	20138.8	5919.7
河 北	40069.3	9622.0	480.6		10.0	29956.7	24904.5
山 西	24783.4	15202.4	1363.7			8217.3	23968.4
内蒙古	44365.6	11895.6	3607.3	7456.8		21405.9	56127.4
辽 宁	35045.9	22778.2	2381.5			9886.2	10861.1
吉 林	25751.1	10434.7	1306.1	4907.0	2107.0	6996.3	5216.2
黑龙江	62826.0	28141.4	10469.9	16136.7	2973.6	5104.4	7465.9
上 海	83554.3	46726.4	9935.6	18599.7		8292.6	64476.5
江 苏	112082.1	60091.8	5876.6	28553.9	1076.2	16483.6	62113.1
浙 江	124530.0	42781.6	12737.2	4709.9	328.3	63973.0	56392.3
安 徽	42766.0	14288.7	9912.7	1491.2	341.0	16732.4	40910.3
福 建	63522.0	15580.7	3239.8	15847.6		28853.9	61388.9
江 西	20174.2	14683.2	632.9	1346.9		3511.2	11753.8
山 东	40442.5	15766.1	11289.6			13386.8	85492.1
河 南	57964.5	14909.1	9167.4	4965.0		28923.0	46751.0
湖 北	56160.2	37642.2	7533.6	2399.1		8585.3	24386.7
湖 南	79172.0	53382.1	4416.6	185.0	111.8	21076.5	46312.6
广 东	136065.3	83299.9	16548.1	19479.4		16737.9	73664.7
广 西	38980.0	12422.2	2646.3	7938.2	211.8	15761.5	39540.4
海 南	6424.7	3789.0	1014.8	733.5	100.0	787.4	15039.6
重 庆	49891.0	24105.9	9139.2	10054.2		6591.7	27821.7
四 川	132981.6	48741.2	12073.0	12855.6	5.0	59306.8	77385.5
贵 州	34961.0	6467.4	4621.0	8277.7	2563.2	13031.7	33522.2
云 南	23282.7	11186.9	2160.2	2998.4	1589.6	5347.6	21427.0
西 藏	8704.4	3470.8	3424.6			1809.0	2857.4
陕 西	39132.4	14771.0	12396.1	2180.7		9784.6	58540.4
甘 肃	54311.3	25696.6	3832.7	8031.9	208.8	16541.3	30851.7
青 海	8762.6	8416.4	177.6	85.0		83.6	16577.5
宁 夏	6083.8	2147.3	2335.3			1601.2	377.7
新 疆	88060.4	64729.6	9034.7	8027.1		6269.0	29758.7

单位：万元

社会救助	最低生活保障	城市最低生活保障	城市最低生活保障金	城市最低生活保障对象临时补助	农村最低生活保障	农村最低生活保障金	农村最低生活保障对象临时补助
24927885.6	**17024421.3**	**6879284.5**	**6602032.0**	**277252.5**	**10145136.8**	**9802378.3**	**342758.5**
218281.9	118765.3	80215.8	79411.2	804.6	38549.5	38402.0	147.5
292388.2	189504.7	122687.7	117969.3	4718.4	66817.0	62889.3	3927.7
855761.2	563254.3	181731.2	177160.7	4570.5	381523.1	374050.8	7472.3
688572.8	513536.8	221709.8	213016.4	8693.4	291827.0	277071.9	14755.1
814018.7	602749.3	281169.6	275514.6	5655.0	321579.7	313354.8	8224.9
727376.8	544306.3	352381.9	331171.2	21210.7	191924.4	172127.0	19797.4
601284.6	485998.9	325872.5	303992.0	21880.5	160126.4	150887.3	9239.1
1036529.0	782087.0	522770.4	479284.7	43485.7	259316.6	248639.2	10677.4
390198.3	170558.4	149860.4	144585.0	5275.4	20698.0	20249.1	448.9
936682.6	530334.0	140018.7	129540.8	10477.9	390315.3	367000.9	23314.4
616995.4	351042.9	63546.1	58894.8	4651.3	287496.8	272904.4	14592.4
1061699.3	679844.3	264900.8	259313.9	5586.9	414943.5	405437.7	9505.8
347573.2	177695.7	46581.1	44415.0	2166.1	131114.6	125228.3	5886.3
1124268.8	799481.1	366970.3	362447.9	4522.4	432510.8	428158.3	4352.5
1072954.8	694424.2	146029.5	136175.4	9854.1	548394.7	527022.1	21372.6
1256623.7	895787.6	293011.4	285935.6	7075.8	602776.2	591190.9	11585.3
1173591.3	684251.3	294591.9	261377.7	33214.2	389659.4	336692.8	52966.6
1397503.5	922124.9	423869.3	416281.6	7587.7	498255.6	487752.1	10503.5
1121026.4	617139.2	177732.2	162642.5	15089.7	439407.0	421165.1	18241.9
809762.8	522888.7	100007.7	99844.1	163.6	422881.0	421228.2	1652.8
121598.5	72964.9	29700.5	29609.0	91.5	43264.4	43002.1	262.3
651651.5	319909.9	165784.7	156619.2	9165.5	154125.2	140609.2	13516.0
1757959.3	1215364.5	491234.3	484439.1	6795.2	724130.2	705992.7	18137.5
995539.8	829745.7	164852.8	157668.4	7184.4	664892.9	645077.0	19815.9
1441506.2	1178350.6	428567.3	425535.6	3031.7	749783.3	746623.1	3160.2
115777.4	65617.4	30136.1	29976.4	159.7	35481.3	35274.3	207.0
880291.8	575121.4	221389.6	204802.1	16587.5	353731.8	332558.9	21172.9
1126099.3	921594.3	323073.1	321995.0	1078.1	598521.2	597715.5	805.7
240288.6	163765.3	78105.9	75034.3	3071.6	85659.4	81774.8	3884.6
240725.2	184033.2	62109.6	60501.7	1607.9	121923.6	118105.7	3817.9
813,354.70	652,179.20	328,672.30	316,876.80	11,795.50	323,506.90	314,192.80	9,314.10

C-1-16续表5

地 区	临时救助合计	临时救助	流浪乞讨人员救助	流浪乞讨人员救助单位经费	流浪乞讨人员救助经费	特困人员供养
全 国	**1310818.7**	**877282.8**	**433535.9**	**187384.6**	**246151.3**	**2373276.6**
中央级						
北 京	33326.5	10167.0	23159.5	5119.3	18040.2	7916.6
天 津	22653.0	19566.7	3086.3	1166.5	1919.8	15173.4
河 北	62652.2	50600.1	12052.1	7224.2	4827.9	107327.1
山 西	30272.6	21431.2	8841.4	2807.3	6034.1	56800.3
内蒙古	36299.5	30282.2	6017.3	3354.0	2663.3	53459.9
辽 宁	41002.6	26563.6	14439.0	5554.0	8885.0	59431.9
吉 林	16365.0	10422.3	5942.7	2947.3	2995.4	23303.3
黑龙江	39003.6	30017.9	8985.7	5638.7	3347.0	72370.6
上 海	44163.1	23848.3	20314.8	15641.8	4673.0	2414.6
江 苏	60871.8	35776.6	25095.2	13175.4	11919.8	139215.6
浙 江	57959.0	37546.8	20412.2	10138.4	10273.8	30420.7
安 徽	45802.2	27138.9	18663.3	5053.9	13609.4	149893.3
福 建	28135.4	17714.1	10421.3	4823.7	5597.6	49830.0
江 西	32489.7	22426.8	10062.9	2579.3	7483.6	84668.0
山 东	80985.3	62658.7	18326.6	6799.0	11527.6	108513.8
河 南	41441.0	18919.9	22521.1	10059.3	12461.8	165894.4
湖 北	65440.8	42273.8	23167.0	11676.6	11490.4	192706.7
湖 南	72154.8	45167.4	26987.4	7103.5	19883.9	177791.6
广 东	71540.0	24144.3	47395.7	24883.2	22512.5	187656.3
广 西	33047.4	16622.6	16424.8	7530.9	8893.9	92184.6
海 南	9795.0	3943.1	5851.9	2174.1	3677.8	14565.5
重 庆	70020.4	58337.0	11683.4	3277.1	8406.3	112782.4
四 川	55267.0	26989.6	28277.4	10102.5	18174.9	188820.8
贵 州	32687.9	22746.9	9941.0	3795.5	6145.5	25145.6
云 南	50761.4	44523.4	6238.0	2036.8	4201.2	66405.0
西 藏	3019.4	2628.3	391.1	225.9	165.2	4969.1
陕 西	56065.4	44615.4	11450.0	4576.1	6873.9	90542.6
甘 肃	38670.8	33009.4	5661.4	2536.8	3124.6	59096.3
青 海	25443.1	23689.5	1753.6	318.0	1435.6	8043.2
宁 夏	15131.8	13931.5	1200.3	388.6	811.7	7865.4
新 疆	38,351.00	29,579.50	8,771.50	4,676.90	4,094.60	18,068.00

单位：万元

城市特困人员救助供养	临时补助	农村特困人员救助供养	临时补助	其他社会救助	其他城市生活救助（含传统救济）	其他农村生活救助（含传统救济）
83869.9	**9101.2**	**2289406.7**	**188944.4**	**896058.2**	**403436.0**	**492622.2**
2247.9	108.2	5668.7	1177.3	29504.5	25649.5	3855.0
		15173.4	3752.1	17477.4	12673.2	4804.2
211.2	122.0	107115.9	3669.2	9439.1	2000.9	7438.2
348.8		56451.5	6411.8	8171.1	3463.2	4707.9
11992.2	20.0	41467.7	8.7	35303.3	11574.1	23729.2
3371.3	553.0	56060.6	4495.8	17338.0	12565.5	4772.5
2526.7	239.4	20776.6	2342.2	9269.9	4523.2	4746.7
3779.3	908.4	68591.3	2755.8	3912.1	2571.7	1340.4
		2414.6		132582.8	124668.8	7914.0
5024.6	960.0	134191.0	6421.5	53847.4	23527.0	30320.4
1237.8	18.7	29182.9	1128.6	53768.1	8789.2	44978.9
1739.1	42.0	148154.2	17312.6	19622.6	6018.7	13603.9
434.9	22.6	49395.1	4279.7	23008.2	8801.5	14206.7
10269.2	2011.7	74398.8	5097.4	34793.6	12858.2	21935.4
1139.3	55.7	107374.5	287.6	14097.2	8361.1	5736.1
61.3		165833.1	6393.0	20725.9	4362.1	16363.8
5509.4	492.4	187197.3	19962.3	61222.7	32414.9	28807.8
3504.4	756.8	174287.2	12364.8	59128.6	27411.9	31716.7
6033.9	640.9	181622.4	7617.1	15469.8	5066.4	10403.4
190.5	17.8	91994.1	7386.0	70301.2	3910.6	66390.6
1563.0		13002.5	2982.6	1490.6	962.3	528.3
13539.2	675.9	99243.2	2736.3	30202.8	14883.8	15319.0
263.8	110.8	188557.0	30797.3	59358.2	6787.1	52571.1
692.8	35.7	24452.8	575.2	10748.8	1697.9	9050.9
4290.1	699.9	62114.9	12773.4	24174.8	4396.2	19778.6
		4969.1	77.2	20771.6	10489.0	10282.6
2251.1	231.0	88291.5	8335.4	29479.2	11303.8	18175.4
		59096.3	10020.7	11940.2	2710.1	9230.1
		8043.2	2331.5	3735.2	1907.7	1827.5
223.9		7641.5	2327.0	2176.5	1979.1	197.4
1424.2	378.3	16643.8	3124.3	12996.8	5107.3	7889.5

C-1-16续表6

地 区	医疗救助	资助参加基本医疗保险	直接医疗救助	门诊救助	住院救助	优抚对象医疗补助
全 国	**3323310.8**	**633541.2**	**2327458.2**	**285219.1**	**2042239.1**	**362311.4**
中央级						
北 京	28769.0	6846.6	16550.4	6473.1	10077.3	5372.0
天 津	47579.7	9444.9	28416.2	10913.6	17502.6	9718.6
河 北	113088.5	26832.4	60815.1	6229.1	54586.0	25441.0
山 西	79792.0	16060.4	56292.6	3786.6	52506.0	7439.0
内蒙古	86206.7	12869.4	66999.5	5013.4	61986.1	6337.8
辽 宁	65298.0	16886.3	40744.0	5637.1	35106.9	7667.7
吉 林	66347.5	10179.4	51296.4	11188.7	40107.7	4871.7
黑龙江	139155.7	31380.0	102207.5	9706.5	92501.0	5568.2
上 海	40479.4	5038.0	33334.0	2116.9	31217.1	2107.4
江 苏	152413.8	27670.6	107519.7	19808.3	87711.4	17223.5
浙 江	123804.7	7842.0	100833.9	20171.0	80662.9	15128.8
安 徽	166536.9	49681.8	103017.4	12532.8	90484.6	13837.7
福 建	68903.9	12229.4	50497.0	12224.6	38272.4	6177.5
江 西	172836.4	25553.6	132620.5	19426.3	113194.2	14662.3
山 东	174934.3	33457.4	96885.2	7910.4	88974.8	44591.7
河 南	132774.8	30252.3	83777.8	3708.1	80069.7	18744.7
湖 北	169969.8	27904.6	127925.1	9573.0	118352.1	14140.1
湖 南	166303.6	33232.7	109444.6	22111.2	87333.4	23626.3
广 东	229221.1	41746.3	162531.8	15427.6	147104.2	24943.0
广 西	91340.9	16451.4	66796.8	2403.7	64393.1	8092.7
海 南	22782.5	4845.3	15280.8	696.7	14584.1	2656.4
重 庆	118736.0	19110.3	82688.9	19089.7	63599.2	16936.8
四 川	239148.8	56798.3	160024.9	23923.1	136101.8	22325.6
贵 州	97211.8	12797.3	76501.6	1287.9	75213.7	7912.9
云 南	121814.4	38777.9	66609.2	10224.0	56385.2	16427.3
西 藏	21399.9	1868.2	19399.9	1576.5	17823.4	131.8
陕 西	129083.2	9156.4	111147.0	8577.8	102569.2	8779.8
甘 肃	94797.7	18350.3	72944.3	3852.6	69091.7	3503.1
青 海	39301.8	9058.2	28282.0	1159.1	27122.9	1961.6
宁 夏	31518.3	3623.8	26740.7	3220.6	23520.1	1153.8
新 疆	91,759.7	17,595.7	69,333.4	5,249.1	64,084.3	4,830.6

单位：万元

自然灾害生活救助	生活救济费	紧急抢救、安置、转移灾民支出	救灾储备	自然灾害灾后重建补助	其他救助
1560797.1	**969337.3**	**89119.5**	**124186.7**	**269444.2**	**108709.4**
11959.1			11959.1		
2166.6	173.7	1529.1	104.1	166.5	193.2
798.7	35.7		763.0		
95409.7	69777.0	7814.3	1873.9	9541.6	6402.9
46600.5	38999.9	465.9	3823.6	1492.4	1818.7
57931.2	55199.5	419.0	1324.9	446.1	541.7
20020.9	13516.3	179.9	3087.7	1183.6	2053.4
23818.9	13495.5	5053.1	280.8	3680.2	1309.3
37201.1	33828.2	1679.2	354.0	102.0	1237.7
300.0					300.0
60223.8	20861.4	2577.0	2793.9	29272.1	4719.4
36151.4	15845.6	4118.5	8673.6	3319.2	4194.5
71623.3	45356.7	6035.1	1651.1	16650.6	1929.8
60913.0	21423.1	2268.1	1846.4	29401.7	5973.7
58311.4	38970.4	8666.0	561.2	5784.8	4329.0
15721.1	11874.7	13.7	2379.7	166.3	1286.7
46546.4	27475.2	1573.3	3548.5	9113.1	4836.3
146886.5	78500.5	13573.8	5146.0	40413.4	9252.8
106185.3	68530.7	9307.0	5531.1	12059.1	10757.4
37413.5	15610.2	1964.2	4710.8	11234.4	3893.9
48649.3	23190.1	1912.3	7133.1	13369.0	3044.8
5613.3	2472.4	509.9	237.2	1658.9	734.9
30766.1	21080.4	1984.5	4123.5	2610.9	966.8
81102.8	44916.7	1506.9	12977.6	18182.2	3519.4
91384.8	58744.9	4207.7	4973.9	15216.5	8241.8
79518.5	40473.0	1500.8	11835.2	19397.3	6312.2
29310.7	6448.7	4243.4	5325.5	7623.6	5669.5
43353.5	29877.1	1792.7	1059.0	4828.4	5796.3
81603.2	71639.6	444.0	4597.3	310.0	4612.3
28085.3	21725.8		5213.6	77.4	1068.5
16352.0	13348.0	150.0	490.9	491.5	1871.6
88875.2	65946.3	3630.1	5806.5	11651.4	1840.9

C-1-16续表7

地 区	民政管理事务	行政运行	一般行政管理事务	机关服务	拥军优属
全 国	**4417368.7**	**1124792.4**	**183322.8**	**29733.7**	**234839.6**
中央级	72228.7	9722.7	10442.5	3019.5	207.5
北 京	297806.9	80056.8	2786.4	2719.6	6827.5
天 津	242725.5	20466.0	16953.3	374.3	4270.5
河 北	110438.9	52953.9	5262.0	461.2	4400.9
山 西	66761.7	20455.2	2106.6	274.3	2811.6
内蒙古	78838.3	32120.3	3843.2	1392.0	3457.5
辽 宁	212865.3	29670.4	9355.7	738.0	7829.4
吉 林	70844.9	16639.9	1459.2	706.6	2216.3
黑龙江	53285.8	15433.2	2118.2	313.3	1885.4
上 海	165587.6	26017.8			18255.0
江 苏	270477.0	70031.2	8248.2	2412.5	24177.1
浙 江	237512.6	66712.9	10299.2	754.5	14838.9
安 徽	78991.8	23331.9	5142.9	1068.1	7189.9
福 建	97015.3	27771.7	3602.9	281.1	10006.5
江 西	60095.8	17239.8	4102.1	520.0	1923.8
山 东	235775.8	55042.2	11683.6	1637.4	19615.5
河 南	134205.9	39495.3	6912.6	3257.7	12208.3
湖 北	191293.5	45459.0	9235.6	1510.4	6443.8
湖 南	148386.3	46299.5	14121.6	1273.1	5159.5
广 东	370399.6	88986.9	11168.3	1842.1	25481.7
广 西	135101.3	35984.3	6668.4	670.2	10406.6
海 南	34771.5	5368.4	1612.5		4944.8
重 庆	117203.0	23446.9	3479.6	577.5	3812.5
四 川	238083.4	72730.4	8376.4	1272.6	8797.0
贵 州	120923.4	50116.5	3165.5	43.2	6270.4
云 南	182361.2	55118.9	5939.2	699.0	6018.3
西 藏	17863.3	9157.6	1001.8	2.0	623.5
陕 西	176337.7	28229.3	3504.5	502.0	4832.1
甘 肃	52041.4	19980.0	2543.1	833.1	1334.6
青 海	44203.7	6059.5	683.4	141.3	1259.0
宁 夏	34512.9	10551.2	2454.9		849.3
新 疆	68428.7	24142.8	5049.4	437.1	6484.9

单位：万元

老龄事务	民间组织管理	行政区划和地名管理	基层政权和社区建设	部队供应	其他民政管理事务支出
270368.8	**89441.1**	**152408.9**	**1225677.2**	**59923.2**	**1046861.0**
1516.5	20951.9	4436.9	414.5		21516.7
14263.2	2223.5	407.8	100857.5	129.4	87535.2
956.2	2290.4	37.3	171971.3	130.3	25275.9
1681.7	460.5	5267.4	12117.3	2330.4	25503.6
1847.7	178.7	4836.2	16099.4	907.5	17244.5
1465.3	358.5	4144.1	4223.8	1404.1	26429.5
2633.5	606.5	3429.0	126217.8	2527.1	29857.9
913.2	169.2	1454.4	24407.2	613.3	22265.6
1219.1	917.9	3522.0	14124.8	2019.0	11732.9
27963.6	7834.8	261.7	6148.4	1839.0	77267.3
25985.2	7975.2	7250.3	65458.4	1815.6	57123.3
24768.7	8941.0	6050.1	42519.5	5738.7	56889.1
4203.8	1406.3	3614.7	14184.6	1684.8	17164.8
6903.7	697.6	4193.4	13234.8	1150.2	29173.4
8071.3	1363.0	3672.1	8389.4	1380.2	13434.1
4977.1	4191.7	6250.8	76624.5	3605.0	52148.0
5626.1	1024.5	11559.0	26295.1	3255.9	24571.4
10465.7	808.6	8595.1	69621.0	3416.1	35738.2
7226.8	2737.8	9255.6	34445.6	1336.4	26530.4
13425.5	14841.7	9169.4	88177.5	4767.2	112539.3
10227.5	475.5	6087.8	30589.7	3469.2	30522.1
3956.3	317.3	1256.0	1710.9	536.8	15068.5
4811.7	668.1	4523.4	42835.1	908.5	32139.7
19126.4	4261.6	10979.2	62923.1	1792.9	47823.8
6248.5	202.5	4397.5	18612.5	1665.3	30201.5
47253.0	1611.5	6590.5	21870.9	2264.5	34995.4
547.1	22.0	2149.1	70.0	202.0	4088.2
4546.1	1297.1	5722.8	98358.8	7909.1	21435.9
2115.3	204.0	3233.8	999.2	350.5	20447.8
1615.8	64.0	3408.2	16731.0	76.0	14165.5
1248.0	230.5	2257.6	7677.5	5.0	9238.9
2559.2	107.7	4395.7	7766.1	693.2	16792.6

C-1-16续表8

地 区	行政事业单位离退休	地方离退休人员经费	离休人员离休金	退休人员退休金	退职人员退职金	离退休人员其他费用
全 国	**484177.0**	**121763.9**	**7210.0**	**96258.6**	**3208.9**	**15086.4**
中央级	5833.9					
北 京	60704.6	32493.6	80.5	27349.7	176.6	4886.8
天 津	3380.4	2847.5	38.0	2182.6	21.5	605.4
河 北	30949.2	6520.6	363.6	5202.8	125.5	828.7
山 西	8241.4	1636.2	144.5	1358.4	33.9	99.4
内蒙古	17677.1	2947.6	79.5	1963.0	859.6	45.5
辽 宁	21643.3	3180.1	418.6	2526.3	8.0	227.2
吉 林	7965.0	1159.0	62.9	774.2	45.6	276.3
黑龙江	14681.3	443.7	103.7	180.1		159.9
上 海	5664.3	1320.4	119.6	786.1		414.7
江 苏	27933.7	12258.3	1560.4	8055.0	456.2	2186.7
浙 江	16207.4	5537.5	351.0	4859.1	27.5	299.9
安 徽	18101.2	4357.1	587.8	3039.7	203.6	526.0
福 建	18164.1	8122.6	124.1	7360.6	142.4	495.5
江 西	10739.4	4961.8	337.9	4146.3	294.6	183.0
山 东	14901.2	3733.6	570.3	2897.8	16.1	249.4
河 南	22859.2	4824.6	601.3	2936.4	436.1	850.8
湖 北	22263.1	5785.8	269.2	4676.6	1.5	838.5
湖 南	7833.6	3617.2	242.1	3189.8	16.5	168.8
广 东	55450.5	2951.6	169.6	2529.7		252.3
广 西	17083.8	261.8		261.8		
海 南	2431.0	520.5	114.3	351.6		54.6
重 庆	13364.2	486.8	24.6	436.2		26.0
四 川	19253.2	4435.3	481.1	3600.7	77.5	276.0
贵 州	1680.9	1220.8	60.0	1055.9	3.7	101.2
云 南	16597.2	2441.4	37.4	1693.1		710.9
西 藏	1107.1	30.1				30.1
陕 西	7617.3	1206.4	113.9	991.8	20.0	80.7
甘 肃	6149.2	1221.7	120.0	962.1	25.9	113.7
青 海	1368.7	63.6				63.6
宁 夏	2342.1	216.6			216.6	
新 疆	3988.4	960.1	34.1	891.2		34.8

单位：万元

一次性抚恤金	行政单位离退休	事业单位离退休	离退休人员管理机构	其他行政事业单位离退休支出	其他
8051.6	**191801.1**	**137190.8**	**4178.6**	**29242.6**	**1522404.4**
	3904.4	1430.1	499.4		57315.2
2075.7	20247.1	3375.6	709.2	3879.1	186261.3
103.0	340.8	107.1		85.0	6425.0
235.4	11189.6	12907.2	45.0	286.8	4070.7
67.8	3424.9	2789.0		391.3	12561.5
33.6	7869.6	5939.6		920.3	48224.9
167.5	9120.3	8550.9	1.0	791.0	42048.2
57.1	2872.1	2511.8	0.2	1421.9	21074.9
159.9	4446.8	8119.5		1671.3	7809.9
311.6	1682.7	2617.9		43.3	37712.4
1267.0	9221.9	5593.8	8.5	851.2	123541.0
126.0	4672.5	4499.2	116.1	1382.1	51313.5
347.1	8752.1	4745.8	82.2	164.0	20180.0
308.4	5000.7	2942.0	38.7	2060.1	37350.7
104.2	3649.2	1984.8	38.4	105.2	38775.5
235.3	3218.8	7344.1		604.7	71703.8
673.3	9901.5	7513.6	85.5	534.0	52571.3
618.1	9431.5	5581.1	790.6	674.1	40558.6
134.5	3175.0	440.7		600.7	73314.3
42.8	22185.7	28234.3	1456.2	622.7	193507.8
	8157.9	8287.8	127.2	249.1	38615.8
	1600.7	54.4	2.4	253.0	19081.7
20.5	8715.1	1921.3		2241.0	18527.3
119.0	5655.8	2374.6		6787.5	48744.3
24.0	343.0	117.1			13460.4
704.3	10762.2	2351.6		1042.0	102866.8
	544.3	223.8		308.9	18361.7
80.7	3362.3	2899.6		149.0	15970.8
	3583.7	1039.7		304.1	28042.2
	755.4	100.7	178.0	271.0	15390.0
	1350.6	526.7		248.2	69890.8
34.8	2662.9	65.4		300.0	7132.1

C-1-17 社会服务事业费

地 区	优抚对象整体抚恤水平	定期抚恤水平	伤残抚恤	定期补助水平	在乡复退军人定期定量补助水平
全 国	**8030.9**	**16352.2**	**21224.3**	**3392.3**	**3025.7**
中央级					
北 京	30063.0	20291.0	20858.7	3770.1	3265.2
天 津	18295.2	26607.1	47225.6	7361.6	6893.3
河 北	6288.9	17409.5	19704.4	2837.7	2560.5
山 西	10712.7	14749.9	18273.6	3237.3	3346.8
内蒙古	18587.9	17992.5	17059.8	5128.2	5373.6
辽 宁	8761.2	19726.9	18608.4	2519.9	2760.1
吉 林	10355.4	16106.8	19829.3	2676.5	2587.4
黑龙江	12761.1	18779.3	18424.0	3784.0	3810.9
上 海	23746.2	12398.2	27433.8	4813.3	3904.3
江 苏	9669.9	16472.0	22917.9	3182.7	3230.0
浙 江	8960.9	26067.8	24742.6	3120.0	2743.1
安 徽	6326.4	14602.2	17132.5	3128.1	2922.2
福 建	7670.5	16340.2	17595.1	2915.0	2026.4
江 西	7933.6	16122.8	18293.4	3975.0	4541.7
山 东	8338.5	17519.4	24284.9	2842.5	2645.7
河 南	6591.0	15134.0	18235.9	2788.7	2316.6
湖 北	8003.2	15935.5	21196.3	3619.1	3256.2
湖 南	6120.8	14388.9	24952.8	2952.8	2528.0
广 东	9280.1	19222.2	28589.7	5407.7	4212.8
广 西	6584.4	19000.5	17993.2	3433.1	3011.4
海 南	10215.1	16383.3	24305.4	3687.6	3279.6
重 庆	7488.2	17526.3	19556.2	4276.2	3959.8
四 川	6589.1	15224.2	20503.5	3817.8	3423.4
贵 州	6979.0	14232.0	16118.1	3869.3	3188.7
云 南	7258.1	15197.8	22034.5	3058.6	2602.7
西 藏	28726.1	14008.8	21239.8	8406.3	8303.8
陕 西	10771.3	14753.4	17399.0	4128.5	3746.4
甘 肃	5055.8	15444.9	18048.7	2376.9	1625.5
青 海	11844.4	16446.3	10449.2	3201.8	2807.1
宁 夏	12041.4	38940.1	20091.5	3693.7	4104.9
新 疆	16535.4	15636.4	21407.3	7285.3	8125.1

总体支出水平

单位：元/人·年、元/个·年

在乡红军老战士定期定量补助费水平	红军失散人员定期定量补助水平	“参战”退伍军人生活补贴水平	“涉核”退伍军人生活补助水平	烈士纪念建筑物管理单位补助水平
47257.1	**21173.8**	**5612.9**	**6662.6**	**740394.0**
50000.0		8575.2	10685.5	50250.0
		10839.9	10476.9	1168444.4
		5899.3	6609.6	985687.5
46000.0	20000.0	5921.2	5643.2	889916.7
39250.0		7668.3	8518.5	1066375.0
		5980.6	6708.5	862447.4
36500.0		5411.2	7055.8	48033.3
42000.0	22000.0	5866.4	7184.2	530500.0
		12524.3	11377.9	8613222.2
	17000.0	7043.9	9244.2	822150.7
	23034.5	7310.0	7313.5	1149560.0
	18623.0	5800.1	6225.9	1956595.2
	20927.1	7668.7	10513.3	496428.6
48666.7	21407.4	7319.8	7907.2	245129.0
		5619.8	5690.2	905663.3
43500.0	21511.0	5494.4	5636.4	371258.1
43000.0	19490.6	5777.6	6115.0	413923.1
46000.0	21944.4	4159.1	9750.9	612945.5
	18500.0	7649.3	7405.5	1820379.3
	22832.3	6213.4	8829.3	1788050.0
	21250.0	4434.7	11298.3	4630000.0
		5187.8	8008.1	346000.0
44894.7	20757.9	5601.7	7436.9	235052.6
67000.0	20800.0	4862.3	6206.8	164428.6
	22666.7	3561.2	5694.4	233736.8
48888.9		6727.3		
45807.7	21159.1	5377.3	5558.4	554315.8
43200.0	19000.0	5087.6	6760.0	244600.0
		6030.5	4715.0	76666.7
246000.0	19000.0	5184.9	7719.3	85230.8
40666.7	20000.0	8280.0	6190.6	1014111.1

C-1-17续表1

地 区	荣誉军人康复医院补助水平	荣誉军人康复医院在院人员补助水平	复员军人疗养院补助水平	复员军人疗养院在院人员补助水平	复退军人精神病院补助水平
全 国	**24287454.5**	**151948.2**	**11029894.7**	**44332.8**	**15918662.7**
中央级					
北 京					
天 津			10440000.0	4643.5	23600000.0
河 北	92140000.0	277476.0	5575125.0	13166.2	40816000.0
山 西	1121000.0	77917.1	29881500.0	80573.2	20082000.0
内蒙古	7411000.0		314000.0	7053.1	11054500.0
辽 宁	9177000.0	89079.3	39817000.0	61390.3	2335500.0
吉 林	24519500.0				1668333.3
黑龙江	17398000.0	385833.3			6147000.0
上 海	18588000.0	172071.4			
江 苏	700000.0	114616.3	5646000.0	19947.0	43211000.0
浙 江	279349000.0	387850.6			25276000.0
安 徽	21072000.0	639548.4			32347000.0
福 建		2749.4			3566000.0
江 西	18235000.0	397959.5	480000.0	6211.0	100000.0
山 东	59726500.0	71873.4	23273857.1	68482.8	17732000.0
河 南	7538250.0	75020.7	6714000.0	20709.7	66619000.0
湖 北	36028000.0		612000.0	66209.3	22332500.0
湖 南	275333.3	10254.6	800000.0	28591.0	7349714.3
广 东	617000.0	29059.1	18179000.0	106044.7	10692777.8
广 西	36419000.0	144891.7	3808000.0	38142.5	41596000.0
海 南					
重 庆	2810000.0	39225.2			
四 川	46008800.0	323702.8	953000.0	10275.5	16600400.0
贵 州	6126000.0	9771.6			
云 南	3639000.0	354346.0			918000.0
西 藏					
陕 西	54494000.0	181787.4	6777333.3	46295.9	4819666.7
甘 肃					3907500.0
青 海					
宁 夏					
新 疆	4935000.0	1440000.0			369750.0

单位：元/个·年、元/人·年

复退军人精神病院在院人员补助水平	光荣院补助水平	光荣院在院人员补助水平	军队离休干部支出水平	军队退休干部支出水平	军队无军籍职工支出水平	孤儿补助水平
35229.3	**812460.6**	**10296.1**	**192934.8**	**131566.7**	**53058.3**	**12219.2**
	4216000.0	33464.4	132050.3	161393.1	59665.0	124086.4
10443.9	5641333.3	23775.8	127363.0	111117.0	63235.0	58141.6
39284.8	850193.3	7632.4	251487.6	154173.1	55186.8	9635.2
46435.2	993176.5	42159.3	236608.2	178997.2	43393.6	9084.4
20976.8	1114148.2	17387.7	197699.6	104962.8	46863.1	20465.8
2818.7	1322564.1	16924.7	265478.7	125259.4	53179.0	18601.8
	992920.0	5793.5	152882.1	95631.3	43608.0	8219.7
15588.5	1918750.0	7064.2	133085.6	73290.4	48533.6	8971.6
			126208.9	110171.9	64537.1	29265.9
39653.1	863333.3	12291.9	176415.4	143958.0	57463.1	22013.2
42913.8	490500.0	24783.8	196091.1	136728.0	59084.9	39500.4
21484.9	1341916.7	9727.7	148526.9	118110.5	44854.7	8501.4
6119.2	1135160.0	13434.8	188310.5	127074.8	50218.0	9917.3
4643.8	205798.9	1863.3	197553.9	103580.9	37417.8	15161.7
31883.9	892062.5	8555.8	183650.8	117936.8	62316.7	12635.5
73465.5	582720.9	7997.1	190260.3	119425.1	42062.9	7934.1
51863.0	1073435.5	12222.8	207711.5	123202.6	53980.5	9679.3
20737.0	932000.0	13637.1	140605.3	88079.2	40293.1	7602.0
16585.0	688666.7	17868.5	207553.0	125811.1	58104.1	14489.2
108424.0	305548.4	12426.6	190089.0	130112.2	48235.3	9786.7
	549222.2	20627.3	201689.7	101014.8	32850.5	26254.5
	2473285.7	24239.7	232292.9	112941.6	58381.2	18756.9
14114.7	596818.2	9355.6	213147.0	134412.6	43725.6	12516.9
	528555.6	9066.8	143789.2	117324.1	54638.5	8966.0
5203.4	1000000.0		70254.5	83200.0	36411.0	13510.1
				210800.9	75473.9	9747.8
12166.0	1114937.5	11394.1	216529.2	142993.7	48136.1	12461.0
50517.8	50000.0		158096.6	138560.0	44606.9	9003.2
			240000.0	148702.6	95759.7	12128.8
	27500.0	3024.9	57861.1	8933.8	30061.2	7541.2
815.8	306368.4	6773.4	995347.4	109368.0	54997.8	8497.7

C-1-17续表2

地 区	康复辅具机构(站)专项拨款支出水平	补贴火化场人员水平	补贴殡葬类单位补助水平	社会福利院补助水平	社会福利院在院人员生活费补助水平
全 国	**12228600.0**	**720.3**	**1214836.8**	**4586238.2**	**9094.1**
中央级					
北 京		1196.7	3665673.1	12310250.0	21774.1
天 津		161.1	11679740.7	8713333.3	3196.5
河 北	3500000.0	615.1	1304169.5	3103871.0	3046.0
山 西	4000000.0	7528.0	361661.3	7601200.0	16147.8
内蒙古		406.6	871310.1	2427673.5	4269.7
辽 宁		716.1	411456.8	4648612.2	9231.6
吉 林		285.1	1248514.9	1768593.2	3298.6
黑龙江		245.1	906748.2	5987531.9	7638.4
上 海			205726.0	21239272.7	6791.1
江 苏		651.4	1624164.7	9692225.8	8409.4
浙 江		1183.4	2299306.7	4503326.3	3930.7
安 徽	1420000.0	628.3	961761.6	2695981.1	15661.1
福 建		738.3	504407.4	2397030.8	14998.5
江 西	8477000.0	500.3	270206.9	1468320.0	2348.9
山 东		220.9	551238.4	6063884.6	5413.5
河 南	18875000.0	931.5	407679.3	2813037.7	8031.2
湖 北	23921500.0	225.2	2111144.7	3060341.5	10935.8
湖 南	4744000.0	769.2	1787936.7	6355011.9	23838.3
广 东	10180000.0	471.3	2662177.7	5590597.3	11132.8
广 西	31624000.0	1254.3	1651360.8	1365076.9	4236.0
海 南		1922.0	1745625.0	9472500.0	4785.9
重 庆		2405.3	1199981.1	8312379.3	4329.0
四 川		450.6	1249075.3	3637403.0	10998.8
贵 州	3867000.0	1432.0	414690.5	1220264.2	3562.4
云 南	13854000.0	1591.4	924109.6	2868435.9	6316.1
西 藏		13414.9			
陕 西	38055000.0	4002.0	575060.9	4615937.5	5086.2
甘 肃		1157.7	444771.4	6588871.8	4721.1
青 海	1732000.0	261.1	21428.6	9351555.6	14663.7
宁 夏		1313.9	62333.3	2684125.0	25694.2
新 疆	15500000.0	3932.3	1544108.7	9519058.8	5287.0

单位：元/个·年、元/人·年、元/人次

儿童福利院补助水平	儿童福利院在院人员生活费补助水平	精神病人福利院补助水平	精神病人福利院在院人员生活费补助水平	城市最低生活保障补助水平（不含春节补助）	农村最低生活保障补助水平（不含春节补助）	城市特困人员救助供养补助水平
3788288.2	**9352.3**	**13255540.0**	**9216.7**	**4460.1**	**2137.2**	**9259.7**
1104600.0	2099.9	67966000.0	37362.5	9698.3	8209.2	32960.4
6480500.0		47760000.0	9040.8	9694.7	6189.9	
961200.0	4377.4			3723.7	1974.3	7436.6
1704625.0	14061.5			4012.2	2337.7	13467.2
4509125.0	5011.5	14913600.0	406.2	5606.7	2778.9	9468.8
2381500.0	499.6			5340.4	2210.1	17087.2
1306100.0	4860.7	7010000.0	1663.3	4481.8	1917.8	6881.0
6979933.3	19826.6	23052428.6	35479.2	4313.4	2056.0	7310.1
33118666.7		61999000.0	7545.5	8594.7	5994.8	
4520461.5	5533.4	28553900.0	10191.1	5214.1	3339.7	16776.6
9797846.2	14700.2	23549500.0	811.4	5406.3	3823.8	6229.5
3197645.2	13957.5	4970666.7	2906.4	4765.9	2706.2	15500.0
2945272.7	10829.5	10565066.7	14961.7	5171.8	2713.6	3342.8
1265800.0	3057.6	6734500.0	2654.5	4046.6	2377.9	9042.2
8684307.7	2067.1			4413.0	2421.3	6222.3
5093000.0	14794.0	9930000.0	3955.4	3482.0	1802.3	1477.1
3139000.0	22854.2	11995500.0	1568.0	4727.5	2435.4	9200.7
2324526.3	8783.1	205555.6	462.5	3722.9	1680.5	10846.2
3848395.4	24022.9	64931333.3	17968.9	6387.1	2901.9	13246.8
1556647.1	12688.9	19845500.0	10024.0	4415.3	1449.7	3802.4
10148000.0				3929.3	2351.1	27517.6
15232000.0	2632.1	11171333.3	9648.7	4503.6	2383.9	11866.1
2414600.0	9239.0	6766105.3	3342.5	3601.9	1979.4	805.3
2009130.4	7964.7	3599000.0	4940.6	4401.8	2116.3	4018.6
939217.4	6982.0	9994666.7	3556.6	4744.9	1765.3	6166.6
6849200.0	2298.8			8360.2	1371.3	
11269181.8	8493.6	21807000.0	7385.4	4866.0	2550.8	8779.6
3193916.7	6099.1	26773000.0		4600.3	1840.8	
253714.3	1945.4	850000.0		4597.3	1585.3	
4670600.0	45057.4			4152.0	2797.3	15441.4
2053340.9	6342.9	8919000.0	4671.9	3643.9	1886.8	3648.1

C-1-17续表3

地 区	农村特困人员救助供养补助水平	流浪乞讨人员救助单位补助水平	救助流浪乞讨人员每次补助水平	临时救助户次补助水平	资助参加基本医疗保险补助水平
全 国	**4607.6**	**948302.6**	**737.4**	**1031.3**	**113.9**
中央级					
北 京	12670.3	2326954.6	549.9	4053.0	1023.3
天 津	13105.4	897307.7	1463.8	2241.6	399.3
河 北	4568.0	1444840.0	542.1	850.3	135.2
山 西	3751.1	338228.9	444.1	888.6	106.4
内蒙古	4802.3	860000.0	540.4	991.7	82.5
辽 宁	4133.5	841515.2	1393.0	908.5	178.0
吉 林	1861.2	589460.0	1155.5	826.3	161.4
黑龙江	5615.2	867492.3	1126.0	1561.7	131.1
上 海	9673.9	8232526.3	1936.7	642.1	516.0
江 苏	6779.0	1497204.6	851.7	881.9	202.9
浙 江	8967.5	1912905.7	1414.1	1014.2	485.9
安 徽	3615.1	1010780.0	1054.1	1519.6	143.5
福 建	6535.7	1121790.7	929.9	1598.4	192.7
江 西	3360.2	241056.1	1091.9	1740.1	122.2
山 东	5098.7	1152372.9	1125.9	2477.1	152.1
河 南	3458.6	1130258.4	736.6	761.6	85.5
湖 北	7531.9	884590.9	470.8	989.4	115.0
湖 南	4100.0	483231.3	301.4	643.9	94.9
广 东	7829.8	3362594.6	1065.8	1574.2	177.9
广 西	3418.1	809774.2	891.8	1852.2	95.2
海 南	4584.2	3105857.1	3537.0	1319.7	208.6
重 庆	5879.4	862394.7	1925.8	2582.0	122.8
四 川	3881.0	455067.6	1051.9	571.0	105.8
贵 州	2339.7	468580.3	646.7	1373.9	45.5
云 南	3579.5	268000.0	603.9	636.0	70.7
西 藏	3489.1	1129500.0	269.9	6980.9	383.1
陕 西	7058.1	502868.1	625.0	1331.4	123.8
甘 肃	5060.2	497411.8	1172.0	601.2	44.7
青 海	3364.5	795000.0	1097.6	2897.5	124.9
宁 夏	6442.0	277571.4	649.8	455.4	110.3
新 疆	3058.0	974354.2	653.3	886.7	133.0

单位：元/个·年、元/人·年、元/人次

直接医疗救助补助水平	门诊救助人次补助水平	住院救助人次补助水平	优抚对象医疗补助支出水平	救灾物资储备中心补助水平	老龄机构补助水平	军供站补助水平
863.3	**190.0**	**1709.1**	**885.5**	**4813438.0**	**1479041.6**	**1026082.2**
1749.4	914.9	4224.8	4211.4		10971692.3	44620.7
1254.4	659.4	2868.4	4223.6	3815000.0	735538.5	651500.0
1822.6	565.4	2442.4	1253.2	2677000.0	646807.7	685411.8
2377.3	802.9	2768.8	801.9	2731142.9	225329.3	907500.0
2087.9	947.7	2313.0	1899.7	4416333.3	814055.6	2340166.7
639.2	154.0	1294.1	1481.8	1625105.3	438916.7	935963.0
1055.6	728.7	1206.7	1114.4	702000.0	212372.1	139386.4
1570.1	382.6	2328.6	1007.5	590000.0	196629.0	1682500.0
1816.8	160.9	6011.5	1621.2		16449176.5	875714.3
307.4	72.6	1141.2	663.6	13969500.0	4640214.3	955579.0
360.2	93.9	1240.4	1721.4	14456000.0	4503400.0	2495087.0
1177.5	801.0	1259.5	579.4	8255500.0	1136162.2	401142.9
327.0	102.2	1099.4	880.8	9232000.0	1353666.7	676588.2
730.1	151.9	2104.3	1273.5	1870666.7	799138.6	920133.3
1169.9	169.4	2464.5	969.5	5949250.0	401379.0	1502083.3
1275.4	514.8	1369.1	652.8	5069285.7	907435.5	1017468.8
1302.2	646.8	1418.4	534.0	1390810.8	1868875.0	2627769.2
893.4	721.6	950.7	530.8	27655500.0	1953189.2	581043.5
1363.6	203.4	3393.8	1249.9	2617111.1	3356375.0	2648444.4
1122.2	71.3	2493.8	655.6	10190142.9	2272777.8	2040705.9
1328.7	96.1	3433.7	1682.1	1186000.0	5651857.1	2684000.0
228.7	65.2	926.8	716.9	20617500.0	2291285.7	211279.1
1024.7	570.8	1191.2	679.5	2317428.6	965979.8	640321.4
2037.3	99.3	3059.4	665.7	9947800.0	650885.4	1665300.0
904.9	626.4	984.2	1081.6	19725333.3	7746393.4	838703.7
3412.3	2807.2	3478.6	1725.1	53255000.0	5471000.0	2020000.0
2900.7	1374.8	3197.5	994.1	1765000.0	473552.1	4652411.8
2504.0	366.1	3713.0	910.9	2704294.1	232450.6	438125.0
1728.9	391.0	2025.0	2401.3	13034000.0	1154142.9	152000.0
2326.8	3369.5	2232.2	1783.9	545444.4	542608.7	25000.0
1903.1	388.0	2798.3	2707.4	14516250.0	115279.3	533230.8

C-1-18 中央专项基本

地 区	建设规模(平方米)	地方配套资金合计	中央对地方投资合计	养老 发改投资[2016]717号				养 发改	
				建设规模	小计	中央投资	地方投资	建设规模	小计
全 国	**2972988**	**429196**	**380000**	**2026588**	**525604**	**274450**	**251154**	**37000**	**9650**
北 京	14986	6852	869	14986	7721	869	6852		
天 津	15400	9086	864	15400	9950	864	9086		
河 北	152480	15443	17851	120432	25472	14792	10680		
山 西	84189	17728	11317	62020	20546	8463	12083		
内蒙古	96292	21277	12603	57305	22280	8495	13785		
辽 宁	82410	10758	11901	52876	13948	8735	5213		
吉 林	85303	16594	11606	63303	19131	8640	10491		
黑龙江	108151	22715	13115	73071	23300	8603	14697	2000	500
上 海									
江 苏	115034	34254	6737	81812	26515	4639	21876		
浙 江	93679	55415	7546	58959	27178	5611	21567		
安 徽	179037	24859	19999	109487	24844	14512	10332		
福 建	73909	7194	9545	49311	10975	6440	4535		
江 西	168129	10738	18226	116859	21619	13510	8109		
山 东	138265	29483	8897	94335	26030	6581	19449		
河 南	149177	12756	19933	109677	24930	15031	9899		
湖 北	155043	13743	18870	111151	23397	14439	8958		
湖 南	157694	24331	19230	116284	25836	14635	11201		
广 东	82326	18550	6241	51275	11263	4266	6997		
广 西	112449	7404	17164	91006	19159	14174	4985		
海 南	36180	4326	5659	33105	9235	5269	3966		
重 庆	65798	7025	11052	47014	12093	8159	3934		
四 川	158101	14126	22669	95301	24719	15797	8922		
贵 州	122890	11479	16614	84890	17537	11998	5539		
云 南	111770	10012	16710	66608	15667	11104	4563		
西 藏	22920	148	9553	16000	6950	6802	148		
陕 西	117351	4117	16396	70932	13898	11332	2566		
甘 肃	80835	3512	15087	55209	13540	11011	2529		
青 海	38490	4010	6986	28680	8391	5502	2889		
宁 夏	42080	5616	6868	35300	9930	5582	4348		
新 疆	71620	1445	13542	44000	9550	8595	955		
兵 团	41000	4200	6350					35000	9150

建设投资对账单

单位：平方米、万元

老 投资[2016]867号		儿童和精神卫生 发改投资[2016] 715号				殡葬 发改投资[2016]713号			
中央投资	地方投资	建设规模	小计	中央投资	地方投资	建设规模	小计	中央投资	地方投资
5550	**4100**	**447072**	**127105**	**50000**	**77105**	**462328**	**146837**	**50000**	**96837**
		6400	1940	480	1460	25648	5882	2579	3303
		11069	2918	1204	1714	11100	5581	1650	3931
		23487	6882	2138	4744	15500	4718	1970	2748
		14440	2427	1516	911	15094	6284	1650	4634
		19000	6800	1736	5064	3000	2269	1230	1039
300	200	14400	5702	1952	3750	18680	6328	2260	4068
		20200	9000	1238	7762	13022	5476	860	4616
		22000	22000	675	21325	12720	13783	1260	12523
		29250	5480	2327	3153	40300	14534	3160	11374
		14598	3914	1985	1929	10000	1850	1120	730
		16950	2745	2196	549	34320	4600	2520	2080
		22000	7500	1296	6204	21930	4850	1020	3830
		20000	3611	2382	1229	19500	4148	2520	1628
		18880	4602	2231	2371	25012	4614	2200	2414
		19030	3225	2195	1030	22380	14500	2400	12100
		16596	3540	1095	2445	14455	9988	880	9108
		6200	975	780	195	15243	4434	2210	2224
		3075	750	390	360				
		10600	2145	1373	772	8184	3839	1520	2319
		26600	7164	4292	2872	36200	4912	2580	2332
		19000	3556	2496	1060	19000	7000	2120	4880
		24042	5241	3026	2215	21120	5814	2580	3234
		3400	1500	1500		3520	1251	1251	
		22019	3765	2964	801	24400	2850	2100	750
		13626	2509	2006	503	12000	2550	2070	480
		6810	2005	1004	1001	3000	600	480	120
		6780	2104	936	1168		450	350	100
		13620	2405	2067	338	14000	3032	2880	152
5250	3900	3000	700	520	180	3000	700	580	120

C-1-19 社会服务事业基本

地 区	在建规模	使用彩票公益金项目规模	在建项目总投资	开工累计完成投资	本年计划投资
全 国	**30509336**	**11001071**	**8248484.7**	**4286565.4**	**2089494.5**
中央级	321766	141888	231021.2	88461.3	13020.0
北 京	462692	12798	347863.7	164215.5	87257.0
天 津	141327	141327	125049.6	46834.4	14953.0
河 北	701191	280470	149923.0	70777.4	53854.0
山 西	442874	70306	202781.7	34691.4	89116.3
内蒙古	721768	138324	188641.6	95216.0	24959.0
辽 宁	266229	140597	91156.8	69719.9	14327.9
吉 林	64176	17381	20395.4	6848.9	3685.0
黑龙江	35895	13107	10360.1	3791.3	690.0
上 海	65672		45382.9	21356.4	690.2
江 苏	2689897	409048	544922.2	323508.6	174791.5
浙 江	939001	408452	501581.0	222616.1	74434.3
安 徽	620436	174054	132146.4	74097.6	60796.9
福 建	537516	117696	212686.2	114239.6	38861.4
江 西	1100945	463926	243599.4	159286.7	104334.5
山 东	1630271	538695	667202.3	368943.3	126804.7
河 南	627486	145370	186374.5	71624.4	32562.6
湖 北	2147264	442492	575371.3	341914.7	115608.4
湖 南	1260128	480109	318251.2	152944.7	77356.4
广 东	1313698	667745	907014.2	387216.7	174595.8
广 西	1529366	781994	293758.4	157657.3	88395.7
海 南	524065	41188	51313.0	32017.7	20033.9
重 庆	1425396	750788	248340.2	168807.1	82464.9
四 川	911022	219716	292057.9	150404.6	71374.2
贵 州	2631346	416470	368385.3	220575.7	144529.4
云 南	1701140	184292	322983.9	176379.6	95552.2
西 藏			14350.0	8882.0	14201.0
陕 西	943382	209432	266428.4	180089.6	54432.7
甘 肃	3302560	2949395	251650.8	109562.1	70278.5
青 海	232271	39332	67754.9	52006.8	41481.7
宁 夏	473123	217749	163627.8	63280.8	40283.9
新 疆	745433	386930	206109.4	148597.2	83767.5

建设投资情况总表

单位：万元、平方米、张

本年实际完成投资	国家预算内投资	国内贷款	福利彩票公益金	其他	本年完工项目规模	未投入使用项目建设床位数
2457709.9	**843702.1**	**27000.7**	**683659.3**	**903347.8**	**12432269**	**343310**
22598.6	22598.6					
113076.4	59412.4		5983.0	47681.0	175745	4187
14907.3	0.0		14907.3	0.0	6117	500
50586.5	20869.5		19660.1	10056.9	275759	10643
24161.0	14933.3		7537.7	1690.0	75689	8085
63792.1	25620.7	1767.3	18596.4	17807.7	76775	8635
19341.9	5579.0		10871.6	2891.3	94180	4524
6848.9	2184.6		4664.3	0.0	21413	1329
3791.3	1958.3		220.0	1613.0	19179	584
15685.0	15040.6		625.6	18.8	32304	1917
185781.6	48820.8	2794.0	28205.6	105961.2	1918630	17032
92186.1	40838.2	300.0	21073.2	29974.7	161841	13017
60597.4	28167.0		7593.2	24837.2	202671	8270
68478.8	27885.0	6713.8	16648.9	17231.1	250178	6670
130722.8	34812.4	2880.0	41216.0	51814.4	775042	19006
131333.6	48514.7		35899.3	46919.6	748240	26274
42384.5	18875.7		17929.9	5578.9	194033	8501
196374.0	59860.3	4000.0	24077.3	108436.4	1339234	16716
92315.0	30638.1	100.0	25404.3	36172.6	647900	11638
174955.7	62997.1		33904.8	78053.8	354924	34709
97368.1	26465.0		46912.1	23991.0	541425	16539
20792.7	7271.4	695.3	2549.1	10276.9	106538	2061
100961.6	41490.8	96.0	37253.1	22121.7	684554	11785
103291.8	26394.8		38041.3	38855.7	278673	14863
157849.9	25730.0	6300.0	28770.6	97049.3	1588333	19496
108670.2	25807.8	242.0	41950.5	40669.9	720891	23826
8882.0	7582.0		1300.0	0.0	7334	529
73542.0	26195.8		16670.5	30675.7	304349	10623
65816.2	17904.6	1112.3	21385.2	25414.1	159645	8006
52006.8	27007.8		21344.0	3655.0	168617	5187
58781.5	9828.4		39829.0	9124.1	148077	15051
99828.6	32417.4		52635.4	14775.8	353979	13107

C-1-20 提供住宿的机构

地 区	在建规模	使用彩票公益金项目规模	在建项目总投资	开工累计完成投资	本年计划投资
全 国	**14069440.0**	**5342221.0**	**5150830.6**	**2600438.2**	**1339078.0**
中央级					
北 京	235492.0	12798.0	240604.2	101727.4	67557.0
天 津	27485.0	27485.0	22679.6	15479.6	3400.0
河 北	357623.0	146852.0	84611.4	43320.6	37499.6
山 西	393003.0	65083.0	176057.3	27841.3	86525.4
内蒙古	336549.0	86702.0	109669.9	65224.2	17984.0
辽 宁	178949.0	132241.0	65675.5	45746.8	12309.8
吉 林	41804.0	17381.0	12132.0	5159.2	2713.0
黑龙江	17579.0	9607.0	3752.1	3101.3	50.0
上 海	60686.0		43476.1	19629.1	332.6
江 苏	709585.0	200504.0	317886.4	200820.6	99158.7
浙 江	660166.0	316836.0	372340.1	150123.6	51765.4
安 徽	305298.0	42654.0	77054.4	37841.4	36666.9
福 建	369226.0	115846.0	160553.1	88560.4	28886.8
江 西	777350.0	412504.0	190122.0	122992.3	76815.1
山 东	1047598.0	412954.0	456778.6	228810.6	74806.7
河 南	469075.0	88724.0	115780.7	49351.2	22593.0
湖 北	1436755.0	179600.0	420418.5	248413.6	77245.7
湖 南	558849.0	192192.0	244005.8	125093.1	58483.4
广 东	1067464.0	623073.0	647558.3	250905.6	142813.6
广 西	797502.0	443485.0	160188.5	78455.7	49079.6
海 南	68655.0	19075.0	20702.4	13027.0	11102.5
重 庆	776912.0	514249.0	148643.5	104569.2	48551.2
四 川	497610.0	145304.0	171038.7	79725.3	28950.3
贵 州	673053.0	305818.0	137098.6	86949.9	57710.8
云 南	603494.0	105745.0	193570.4	95244.0	49578.1
西 藏			13200.0	8882.0	13200.0
陕 西	355622.0	113366.0	127310.3	86310.4	30349.0
甘 肃	317655.0	115580.0	113742.9	55111.3	51883.3
青 海	104571.0	34532.0	32472.9	21758.8	17746.7
宁 夏	387575.0	170926.0	130644.8	46152.9	27485.3
新 疆	436255.0	291105.0	141061.6	94109.8	55834.5

基本建设投资情况

单位：万元、平方米、张

本年实际完成投资	国家预算内投资	国内贷款	福利彩票公益金	其他	本年完工项目规模	未投入使用项目建设床位数
1583787.3	**539515.3**	**12333.6**	**472850.2**	**559088.2**	**6111572.0**	**334437.0**
60990.1	18995.3		5983.0	36011.8	106887.0	4187.0
3354.3			3354.3		6117.0	500.0
30635.9	12735.0		10088.7	7812.2	223916.0	10565.0
18893.0	12205.6		5767.4	920.0	75689.0	8075.0
44203.2	20811.5	1767.3	11190.3	10434.1	38947.0	8537.0
17348.5	5579.0		8958.6	2810.9	89840.0	4472.0
5159.2	925.9		4233.3		13169.0	1329.0
3101.3	1798.3		50.0	1253.0	17579.0	524.0
15327.4	15040.6		268.0	18.8	31630.0	1917.0
116956.9	31776.3	794.0	20157.7	64228.9	367054.0	15696.0
69883.0	34637.5	300.0	10091.8	24853.7	62130.0	13017.0
35986.9	15390.6		4979.8	15616.5	129311.0	8218.0
50719.1	18005.5	1960.0	14956.5	15797.1	213644.0	6656.0
99382.4	20471.4	1000.0	37973.2	39937.8	482902.0	17959.0
77090.5	30652.1		29386.2	17052.2	487689.0	24885.0
29224.8	9951.9		15857.3	3415.6	143950.0	8436.0
144924.5	54258.9	4000.0	13759.2	72906.4	959560.0	16219.0
71640.5	22031.1	100.0	21957.3	27552.1	294862.0	11440.0
143481.1	47040.6		30207.2	66233.3	274500.0	34649.0
53313.6	16997.6		26832.1	9483.9	345972.0	16027.0
11615.5	5921.0		1149.1	4545.4	68443.0	1824.0
54874.7	21193.8		27235.0	6445.9	387076.0	11373.0
56851.4	18348.4		10493.1	28009.9	109009.0	14719.0
72534.3	18017.4	1300.0	22912.2	30304.7	371825.0	18908.0
65223.0	20022.0		22157.2	23043.8	218853.0	22905.0
8882.0	7582.0		1300.0		7334.0	529.0
41601.0	18287.9		14136.0	9177.1	108198.0	10278.0
49229.4	11403.9	1112.3	11549.2	25164.0	88868.0	7981.0
21758.8	8106.8		12877.0	775.0	54817.0	5007.0
43753.3	5871.4		29568.7	8313.2	107241.0	14771.0
65847.7	15456.0		43420.8	6970.9	224560.0	12834.0

C-1-21 不提供住宿的机构

地 区	在建规模	使用彩票公益金项目规模	在建项目总投资	开工累计完成投资	本年计划投资
全 国	**3066779.0**	**861019.0**	**710593.8**	**474878.2**	**267547.7**
中央级					
北 京					
天 津					
河 北	185460.0	51389.0	26201.8	14102.6	10334.8
山 西	11742.0	4556.0	3347.0	2306.7	
内蒙古	31090.0	12640.0	6934.6	4651.2	1241.8
辽 宁	86319.0	7518.0	15857.3	14452.1	740.1
吉 林				196.7	
黑龙江	14816.0		5358.0	590.0	590.0
上 海					
江 苏	289546.0	135368.0	74355.8	42883.9	28092.8
浙 江	25758.0	21473.0	5024.6	2756.5	850.0
安 徽	126670.0	103800.0	19183.0	16428.4	13494.2
福 建	8219.0		3442.5	2167.1	473.0
江 西	134926.0	25732.0	18348.1	13145.1	10540.1
山 东	271427.0	87226.0	125615.7	79951.5	33261.0
河 南	43791.0	9090.0	21990.2	7573.1	5117.6
湖 北	185393.0	13333.0	29641.4	21610.6	9421.8
湖 南	231570.0	4554.0	24624.4	8855.7	5341.0
广 东	89527.0	25482.0	13822.9	8121.6	5829.0
广 西	320997.0	105645.0	42372.6	22161.6	17503.7
海 南	70169.0	22113.0	9661.3	7680.1	6777.0
重 庆	134075.0	51308.0	25525.3	18465.5	14242.3
四 川	81687.0	12200.0	17254.7	37859.7	10626.1
贵 州	205541.0	50285.0	65912.9	26720.2	25495.3
云 南	125578.0	45834.0	36724.7	20606.4	23179.8
西 藏					
陕 西	57818.0	9946.0	13819.9	10702.4	4099.9
甘 肃	65621.0	908.0	40349.1	39112.7	6035.1
青 海	77500.0		21446.0	17836.0	11640.0
宁 夏	71718.0	46823.0	20873.0	14908.0	12297.7
新 疆	119821.0	13796.0	22907.0	19032.8	10323.6

基本建设投资情况

单位：万元、平方米、张

本年实际完成投资	国家预算内投资	国内贷款	福利彩票公益金	其他	本年完工项目规模	未投入使用项目建设床位数
300423.7	**100049.1**	**1096.0**	**92322.7**	**106955.9**	**1476068.0**	**8873.0**
12687.8	5416.3		6831.5	440.0	38565.0	78.0
2306.7	533.7		1003.0	770.0		10.0
1316.9	464.8		406.2	445.9	14857.0	98.0
695.4			615.0	80.4	3560.0	52.0
196.7	196.7					
590.0	160.0		70.0	360.0	1600.0	60.0
24735.0	8746.3		5338.5	10650.2	168630.0	1336.0
556.1	141.6		414.5		2150.0	
16417.4	8470.6		1051.0	6895.8	24640.0	52.0
615.0	522.6		14.4	78.0	5260.0	14.0
13121.1	5003.0		1347.0	6771.1	134555.0	1047.0
32981.1	5282.6		3308.1	24390.4	85074.0	1389.0
5638.1	2903.0		580.8	2154.3	19895.0	65.0
13068.6	1612.4		5243.0	6213.2	140532.0	497.0
7368.5	3057.0		920.0	3391.5	85676.0	198.0
5601.8	1082.0		2432.9	2086.9	55824.0	60.0
16651.8	5020.6		5853.2	5778.0	101834.0	512.0
3681.3	799.8		1400.0	1481.5	2080.0	237.0
15854.5	7270.1	96.0	3590.6	4897.8	119615.0	412.0
34039.3	6501.5		20739.2	6798.6	70641.0	144.0
13819.0	3668.5	1000.0	4603.1	4547.4	66274.0	588.0
19764.2	3605.8		5932.0	10226.4	85638.0	921.0
6525.2	4380.3		679.3	1465.6	32045.0	345.0
6072.7	6020.7		40.0	12.0	54371.0	25.0
17836.0	7601.0		7365.0	2870.0	70000.0	180.0
14347.3	3777.0		10260.3	310.0	39036.0	280.0
13936.2	7811.2		2284.1	3840.9	53716.0	273.0

C-1-22 其他社会服务机构

地 区	在建规模	使用彩票公益金项目规模	在建项目总投资	开工累计完成投资	本年计划投资
全 国	**11583034.0**	**4048677.0**	**1568653.5**	**801063.7**	**329672.0**
中央级					
北 京	11200.0		18272.5	13488.1	5000.0
天 津	113842.0	113842.0	102370.0	31354.8	11553.0
河 北	100060.0	27561.0	31941.1	8080.9	4236.0
山 西	33127.0		19914.4	2070.4	1700.0
内蒙古	318192.0	11295.0	59243.1	14914.0	2587.4
辽 宁	780.0	780.0	9443.0	9463.0	1220.0
吉 林				521.0	
黑龙江	3500.0	3500.0	1250.0	50.0	50.0
上 海					
江 苏	1626524.0	28521.0	123929.0	65955.3	40200.0
浙 江	183302.0	10250.0	65259.0	40114.7	5008.7
安 徽	170448.0	18000.0	29290.5	16026.4	6745.0
福 建	73978.0		19798.8	14777.1	4473.6
江 西	132619.0	15690.0	14011.5	8892.5	7771.5
山 东	266829.0	26205.0	69496.0	44578.2	14195.0
河 南	98792.0	44056.0	44058.1	11719.2	2425.1
湖 北	443424.0	190000.0	99678.4	53804.3	23839.3
湖 南	469309.0	283283.0	49589.0	18908.9	13500.0
广 东	106930.0	5508.0	205597.7	98006.7	18342.6
广 西	155705.0	46209.0	32404.7	17235.6	9463.0
海 南	379011.0		19765.1	10760.0	1444.1
重 庆	482168.0	185141.0	60216.0	38651.0	15375.0
四 川	252553.0	6700.0	73068.5	5466.8	21608.0
贵 州	1688626.0	28767.0	157629.0	101944.3	60445.0
云 南	963568.0	32713.0	90511.2	58333.1	22674.3
西 藏					
陕 西	498182.0	72860.0	118364.0	80055.0	18097.0
甘 肃	2814733.0	2811267.0	1628.1	992.1	238.1
青 海	4600.0	4600.0	1100.0	600.0	600.0
宁 夏	13830.0		12110.0	2039.9	500.9
新 疆	177202.0	81929.0	38714.8	32260.4	16379.4

基本建设投资情况

单位：万元、平方米

本年实际完成投资					本年完工项目规模
	国家预算内投资	国内贷款	福利彩票公益金	其他	
360448.3	**98026.5**	**11271.1**	**57177.7**	**193973.0**	**4308880.0**
3086.3	2777.1			309.2	
11553.0			11553.0		
4787.5	2217.2		2503.3	67.0	10603.0
2070.4	1365.7		704.7		
8830.8	1448.4		1355.0	6027.4	14721.0
1240.0			1240.0		780.0
521.0	244.0		277.0		8244.0
50.0			50.0		
37607.2	5508.2	2000.0	1395.0	28704.0	1381837.0
6453.9	4217.1		1684.8	552.0	80081.0
4504.4	3198.5		78.0	1227.9	37700.0
11066.7	7706.9	2453.8		906.0	17678.0
8862.5	3123.0	1880.0	502.0	3357.5	129535.0
15635.0	11580.0		955.0	3100.0	133870.0
4596.7	4375.1		221.6		16840.0
31770.3	1020.0		1458.1	29292.2	201758.0
13219.0	5550.0		2460.0	5209.0	267182.0
18268.3	14054.7		333.4	3880.2	11837.0
9829.0	2436.9		3330.7	4061.4	24119.0
4945.3		695.3		4250.0	33335.0
25936.0	8816.5		6407.5	10712.0	171266.0
2209.3	1152.1			1057.2	32061.0
69628.3	3925.1	4000.0	100.0	61603.2	1112138.0
21486.9	1480.0	242.0	12712.1	7052.8	413400.0
23347.0	2890.0		556.0	19901.0	143626.0
992.1	480.0		274.0	238.1	766.0
600.0			600.0		3000.0
500.9				500.9	
16850.5	8460.0		6426.5	1964.0	62503.0

C-1-23 其他基本

地 区	在建规模	使用彩票公益金项目规模	在建项目总投资	开工累计完成投资	本年计划投资
全 国	**1790083**	**749154**	**818406.8**	**410185.3**	**153196.8**
中央级	321766	141888	231021.2	88461.3	13020.0
北 京	216000		88987.0	49000.0	14700.0
天 津					
河 北	58048	54668	7168.7	5273.3	1783.6
山 西	5002	667	3463.0	2473.0	890.9
内蒙古	35937	27687	12794.0	10426.6	3145.8
辽 宁	181	58	181.0	58.0	58.0
吉 林	22372		8263.4	972.0	972.0
黑龙江				50.0	
上 海	4986		1906.8	1727.3	357.6
江 苏	64242	44655	28751.0	13848.8	7340.0
浙 江	69775	59893	58957.3	29621.3	16810.2
安 徽	18020	9600	6618.5	3801.4	3890.8
福 建	86093	1850	28891.8	8735.0	5028.0
江 西	56050	10000	21117.8	14256.8	9207.8
山 东	44417	12310	15312.0	15603.0	4542.0
河 南	15828	3500	4545.5	2980.9	2426.9
湖 北	81692	59559	25633.0	18086.2	5101.6
湖 南	400	80	32.0	87.0	32.0
广 东	49777	13682	40035.3	30182.8	7610.6
广 西	255162	186655	58792.6	39804.4	12349.4
海 南	6230		1184.2	550.6	710.3
重 庆	32241	90	13955.4	7121.4	4296.4
四 川	79172	55512	30696.0	27352.8	10189.8
贵 州	64126	31600	7744.8	4961.3	878.3
云 南	8500		2177.6	2196.1	120.0
西 藏			1150.0		1001.0
陕 西	31760	13260	6934.2	3021.8	1886.8
甘 肃	104551	21640	95930.7	14346.0	12122.0
青 海	45600	200	12736.0	11812.0	11495.0
宁 夏				180.0	
新 疆	12155	100	3426.0	3194.2	1230.0

建设投资情况

单位：万元、平方米

本年实际完成投资	国家预算内投资	国内贷款	福利彩票公益金	其他	本年完工项目规模
213050.6	**106111.2**	**2300.0**	**61308.7**	**43330.7**	**535749**
22598.6	22598.6				
49000.0	37640.0			11360.0	68858
2475.3	501.0		236.6	1737.7	2675
890.9	828.3		62.6		
9441.2	2896.0		5644.9	900.3	8250
58.0			58.0		
972.0	818.0		154.0		
50.0			50.0		
357.6			357.6		674
6482.5	2790.0		1314.4	2378.1	1109
15293.1	1842.0		8882.1	4569.0	17480
3688.7	1107.3		1484.4	1097.0	11020
6078.0	1650.0	2300.0	1678.0	450.0	13596
9356.8	6215.0		1393.8	1748.0	28050
5627.0	1000.0		2250.0	2377.0	41607
2924.9	1645.7		1270.2	9.0	13348
6610.6	2969.0		3617.0	24.6	37384
87.0			67.0	20.0	180
7604.5	819.8		931.3	5853.4	12763
17573.7	2009.9		10896.1	4667.7	69500
550.6	550.6				2680
4296.4	4210.4		20.0	66.0	6597
10191.8	392.8		6809.0	2990.0	66962
1868.3	119.0		1155.3	594.0	38096
2196.1	700.0		1149.2	346.9	3000
2068.8	637.6		1299.2	132.0	20480
9522.0			9522.0		15640
11812.0	11300.0		502.0	10.0	40800
180.0	180.0				1800
3194.2	690.2		504.0	2000.0	13200

C-2-1 社会

地区	机构和设施数	工商登记	编制登记	民政登记	设施
全国	**423348**	**346**	**25028**	**49759**	**348215**
中央级	2		2		
北京	12643	15	683	1330	10615
天津	3282	3	96	284	2899
河北	38906	2	684	741	37479
山西	6240	1	687	367	5185
内蒙古	5013	3	526	405	4079
辽宁	8994	3	594	1644	6753
吉林	3347	6	1063	901	1377
黑龙江	4290	1	429	1056	2804
上海	6880	5	218	3655	3002
江苏	42837	22	1507	23096	18212
浙江	32049	24	937	3079	28009
安徽	9542	10	494	1222	7816
福建	6360	4	415	253	5688
江西	5460		1743	149	3568
山东	28195	17	962	3204	24012
河南	6379	2	1035	645	4697
湖北	16301	31	1818	609	13843
湖南	15647	2	1992	397	13256
广东	68480	56	1607	1545	65272
广西	14304	2	565	255	13482
海南	2667	3	46	262	2356
重庆	8656	22	583	683	7368
四川	24209	89	2697	1764	19659
贵州	24520	1	1111	224	23184
云南	3740	16	462	264	2998
西藏	93		19		74
陕西	7865	1	665	563	6636
甘肃	9941	3	417	229	9292
青海	1660		62	15	1583
宁夏	1404	1	132	257	1014
新疆	3442	1	777	661	2003

工作总表

单位：个、人

年末职工人数	女性	工商登记	编制登记	民政登记	设施
1856741	**765938**	**9172**	**282570**	**381389**	**1179965**
320	185		320		
61791	32943	611	11309	11756	38115
21081	12321	165	2361	5764	12778
94894	38236	73	12238	10583	71867
39073	14744	8	8617	3424	26949
26168	13019	48	5800	4444	15874
63862	36619	21	10088	13737	39887
31230	17163	122	12078	10431	8583
33351	15605	23	8337	7873	17006
73275	37045	392	7542	49902	15439
233862	80945	1032	20217	123222	89212
103410	44164	605	10738	16837	74296
52760	22737	169	6770	9815	35859
28161	11752	78	4269	2892	20853
25859	9326		10602	1415	13679
150577	63662	188	15161	32971	101386
46562	19636	52	13127	7226	26093
71059	31926	695	19150	6069	45085
63725	26665	145	16096	3518	43794
230525	86175	2674	19988	15647	192185
35319	15083	26	7751	4584	22952
13170	3787	325	986	1628	10229
35919	16631	531	5580	5954	23846
90210	34593	835	18672	12286	58278
108339	29989	21	9323	1704	97226
20044	8026	168	4584	2490	12747
2626	632		316		2310
37302	16261	87	7883	4851	24329
27423	9580	33	4181	1230	21939
5756	1813		922	81	4753
7888	4267	23	1664	1946	4255
21200	10408	22	5900	7109	8161

C-2-1续表1

地区	受教育程度		职业资格水平	
	大学专科人数	大学本科及以上人数	助理社会工作师人数	社会工作师人数
全国	**379398**	**219841**	**30385**	**18015**
中央级	80	240		2
北京	15134	14515	2816	1283
天津	5154	3848	996	319
河北	7687	4135	291	269
山西	8416	4361	811	624
内蒙古	7014	4561	713	369
辽宁	18184	13502	1299	836
吉林	6990	3638	443	371
黑龙江	8668	4061	738	334
上海	12908	6078	888	1812
江苏	41796	22368	3038	1590
浙江	20051	12746	1774	1011
安徽	11982	4355	878	410
福建	3572	2211	606	460
江西	3182	1233	227	132
山东	39639	23746	2777	1214
河南	9187	5166	562	452
湖北	14076	7199	679	479
湖南	14372	7578	1013	552
广东	44281	32666	5795	2824
广西	5897	3718	335	309
海南	1326	579	54	34
重庆	8791	5046	952	600
四川	21115	8657	1179	685
贵州	22317	7976	165	162
云南	3870	2512	150	128
西藏	301	190	24	3
陕西	8180	3682	392	259
甘肃	5359	3775	275	178
青海	1976	768	89	91
宁夏	1522	732	61	52
新疆	6371	3999	365	171

单位：人、人次、时

年龄结构				志愿服务	
35岁及以下人数	36岁至45岁人数	46岁至55岁人数	56岁及以上人数	志愿者服务人次数	志愿服务时间
547264	**707152**	**460972**	**141156**	**7150531**	**19411634.7**
215	50	38	17		
17928	21498	17673	4692	4565051	13094113.6
7079	6940	5593	1469	61166	98464.0
24226	34865	27528	8275	21174	68430.5
11338	14637	9284	3814	12448	51033.2
8386	10275	5702	1760	10814	22114.0
18663	24393	15089	5717	26655	47192.0
6880	13689	9953	708	23290	46578.0
9309	13717	7079	3246	32237	73656.0
18154	25258	22257	7606	36021	107112.0
63395	89699	62032	18736	345718	858538.5
28866	38041	26256	10253	227309	423164.0
13473	22010	13830	3441	89639	206262.0
8069	10240	6580	3222	128255	358763.0
5627	9598	7065	3569	5207	13945.7
51899	54542	35853	8283	689767	1576262.0
12909	19713	10220	3720	6650	22533.5
19180	28433	16452	6994	22684	38204.0
17480	25233	16878	4062	38881	122533.0
79716	88033	48396	14380	76197	256705.3
10311	11911	10284	2812	6026	16380.0
3273	4961	3812	1124	18442	31824.0
10035	12978	9912	2994	295144	706300.5
25807	36943	21516	5944	165312	518798.0
35796	42587	23921	6035	179083	416872.9
5819	8741	4330	1154	7937	44737.0
809	347	68	1402	23	65.0
10679	13893	10070	2660	24872	93236.0
10364	9945	5790	1324	2837	5605.0
2015	1848	947	942	518	1392.0
2177	3459	2054	173	5055	8737.0
7387	8675	4510	628	26119	82083.0

C-2-1续表2

地　区	企业会计制度财务指标			
	固定资产原价	营业收入	费用合计	营业利润
全　国	**368005.8**	**50135.5**	**3740915.4**	**-4753.5**
中央级				
北　京	59174.3	10963.9	75626.2	-1424.4
天　津	618.0	343.7	64894.8	-8.0
河　北	1816.0	306.0	27752.9	-0.9
山　西	10870.0	606.0	22108.6	-15.5
内蒙古	704.0	382.8	5970.8	-775.0
辽　宁	230.1	140.0	83238.4	25.0
吉　林	30.0	60.0	22433.7	
黑龙江	185.3	164.3	30152.6	9.5
上　海	2825.1	2596.7	160260.3	154.5
江　苏	53725.2	1460.0	798550.3	-1798.2
浙　江	63840.8	2919.0	2065376.5	26.0
安　徽	4466.0	1794.0	42535.3	-132.0
福　建	2134.2	476.4	15375.7	-11.0
江　西	675.0	81.5	16403.5	5.9
山　东	17038.0	3895.0	1314.2	287.0
河　南	320.0	236.0	62029.2	
湖　北	18129.2	1276.7	31092.0	22.3
湖　南	14861.0	664.0	28144.5	
广　东	32072.1	15712.2	13736.6	277.7
广　西	4103.5	1178.4	7892.5	-229.3
海　南	1512.2	1219.5	1668.0	-1860.7
重　庆	22002.0	2091.6	70592.0	330.7
四　川	35516.5	225.0	31258.4	-58.2
贵　州	1940.0	23.0	566.3	1.0
云　南	4146.0	58.0	8750.9	3.0
西　藏	4500.0			
陕　西	2629.3	1260.5	26401.6	416.1
甘　肃	638.0		392.1	
青　海				
宁　夏	6400.0		41.0	
新　疆	904.0	1.3	26356.5	1.0

单位：万元

事业单位会计制度财务指标			民间非营利组织会计制度财务指标		
固定资产原价	本年收入合计	本年支出合计	固定资产原价	本年收入合计	本年费用合计
8232854.2	**8341846.2**	**8037529.3**	**3785548.2**	**1515698.3**	**1326676.4**
30229.4	119533.4	98606.4			
400959.7	907723.2	851533.0	174315.5	71968.5	78312.9
135912.2	143492.5	132798.1	27120.7	33583.2	20287.3
359349.1	397819.6	369814.1	304928.6	26474.6	31175.1
177006.1	166239.8	153108.5	40273.5	5199.0	7359.1
185606.9	139190.2	136332.5	64203.7	14205.3	12405.2
343093.9	376418.2	438256.2	110016.4	29515.1	19223.3
165698.4	138465.8	129729.1	10672.9	9750.6	7501.4
217789.9	113412.0	109673.5	131017.5	90909.8	13339.5
266424.5	412957.8	383486.3	231515.6	423281.1	452074.7
687953.6	586905.0	571973.5	807657.0	282865.4	262244.1
380849.2	312931.4	294987.0	170839.3	105893.1	61446.6
166207.7	131588.4	125656.4	196299.8	38192.7	30100.0
93814.0	170801.0	149875.4	66542.8	5288.8	5292.0
220937.7	89034.1	82506.6	27297.0	6449.3	5951.5
525715.2	682361.4	686300.9	498377.4	144030.5	155273.1
219132.0	270700.5	275196.1	103492.3	18956.3	13569.7
517797.0	413373.3	405205.8	59484.9	16544.3	15491.2
503398.6	335981.9	305595.5	44334.6	52867.8	6384.1
613730.0	602243.5	585614.6	104158.3	40369.1	25687.8
172262.2	191436.1	186980.6	18642.9	8433.7	9500.1
33075.9	44870.6	43279.2	63308.6	1560.3	1439.6
120464.6	188271.6	171035.1	99841.0	32199.7	28648.2
593289.2	409777.5	398098.0	98746.3	20051.9	33413.1
196932.2	117273.3	111461.0	58224.3	4519.8	4144.0
186664.9	163311.9	151575.7	24947.4	1175.5	2379.1
21125.9	11496.7	11290.7			
312368.2	349740.8	352396.6	131381.5	9547.6	10114.0
121286.4	121600.5	110137.9	35973.1	2019.4	1366.7
29491.3	28596.5	31202.8	558.0	23.4	30.5
58141.1	45914.7	33839.5	19515.2	4382.2	1575.9
176147.2	158383.0	149982.7	61862.1	15440.3	10946.6

C-2-2 提供住宿的社会

地　区	单位数	按登记类型分				按床位	
		工商登记	编制登记	民政登记	一个机构多块牌子	0～99张	100～299张
全　国	**31912**	**324**	**18261**	**12341**	**986**	**17160**	**12059**
中央级	1		1				1
北　京	641	14	379	245	3	221	282
天　津	292	2	57	233		112	139
河　北	1142	2	513	601	26	570	421
山　西	696	1	383	303	9	480	190
内蒙古	784	2	417	353	12	446	278
辽　宁	1569	3	404	1133	29	969	472
吉　林	1386	6	745	619	16	951	377
黑龙江	970		271	697	2	587	278
上　海	677	4	55	616	2	220	349
江　苏	2476	22	1265	1157	32	937	1194
浙　江	1422	23	735	656	8	582	635
安　徽	1295	9	274	998	14	563	637
福　建	432	3	295	122	12	248	129
江　西	1631		1464	87	80	1004	575
山　东	2060	13	622	1418	7	776	1031
河　南	1306	1	744	544	17	792	456
湖　北	1881	28	1471	294	88	809	961
湖　南	1995	2	1721	181	91	1551	386
广　东	1643	56	1339	222	26	1092	404
广　西	616	2	349	182	83	445	139
海　南	66	3	30	19	14	44	15
重　庆	690	22	395	270	3	326	316
四　川	2953	85	2220	454	194	1539	1237
贵　州	1015	1	786	139	89	672	316
云　南	545	16	323	201	5	301	210
西　藏	16		16			5	6
陕　西	686		443	182	61	340	247
甘　肃	332	3	174	129	26	220	94
青　海	54		36	15	3	28	20
宁　夏	120	1	66	41	12	62	44
新　疆	520		268	230	22	268	220

服务机构总表

单位：个、人

数分		年末职工人数	其中：女性	工商登记	编办登记	民政登记	一个机构多块牌子
300～499张	500张以上						
1744	**949**	**409713**	**232549**	**8739**	**218827**	**174336**	**7811**
		185	130		185		
77	61	15746	9971	603	7587	7544	12
16	25	7325	4823	160	1970	5195	
94	57	20273	11506	73	10311	9706	183
20	6	9372	4073	8	6097	3166	101
40	20	8607	4377	6	4289	4270	42
83	45	18596	10991	21	8100	10081	394
38	20	15627	8769	122	7901	6927	677
63	42	13010	6332		7135	5871	4
73	35	25322	18807	315	3549	21428	30
235	110	36763	21370	1032	17972	17428	331
126	79	18551	11334	601	9131	8795	24
72	23	13224	6761	166	4214	8701	143
41	14	5979	3053	75	3471	2373	60
40	12	10563	4015		9253	870	440
184	69	30564	17088	156	11179	19166	63
36	22	16870	9123	9	10138	6525	198
59	52	20997	11724	626	16360	3411	600
35	23	17823	9328	145	14031	2521	1126
87	60	27516	17044	2674	17380	7198	264
20	12	10280	7085	26	5813	4073	368
1	6	1229	707	325	649	237	18
25	23	8429	4442	531	4148	3705	45
116	61	23021	11333	820	15926	4883	1392
19	8	6278	3034	21	4436	1305	516
20	14	5371	2919	168	3606	1557	40
3	2	270	196		270		
75	24	9523	4992		5879	3228	416
11	7	3573	1786	33	2564	883	93
1	5	850	485		741	81	28
10	4	1560	1025	23	1088	383	66
24	8	6416	3926		3454	2825	137

C-2-2续表1

地　区	受教育程度		职业资格水平		
	大学专科人数	大学本科及以上人数	助理社会工作师人数	社会工作师人数	35岁及以下人数
全　国	**80550**	**56045**	**6840**	**5676**	**110790**
中央级	71	114		2	138
北　京	2679	2774	256	200	3909
天　津	1490	977	273	94	1723
河　北	3324	2268	142	150	6573
山　西	1982	1500	43	121	3411
内蒙古	2022	1133	109	133	2058
辽　宁	4032	3608	180	248	3961
吉　林	1148	973	54	107	2563
黑龙江	3059	1596	329	180	3627
上　海	2039	1296	286	277	4754
江　苏	6777	4972	574	529	8754
浙　江	2540	2034	251	239	4294
安　徽	1988	1181	172	170	2801
福　建	1081	1053	145	165	1796
江　西	1347	629	99	74	2047
山　东	7533	5775	1328	816	10277
河　南	3713	2099	230	263	5401
湖　北	4349	2957	215	150	5435
湖　南	4203	2713	251	243	5207
广　东	4954	3890	718	451	6971
广　西	3073	1945	141	201	3730
海　南	237	179	19	19	498
重　庆	1672	1147	110	131	1843
四　川	6162	3150	359	267	7179
贵　州	1788	1135	75	83	1974
云　南	1386	1162	61	83	1739
西　藏	54	49	2		174
陕　西	2384	1448	106	103	3622
甘　肃	903	852	157	79	1302
青　海	311	200	11	5	409
宁　夏	380	316	31	38	514
新　疆	1869	920	113	55	2106

单位：人、人次、时

年龄结构			按人员性质		志愿服务	
36岁至45岁人数	46岁至55岁人数	56岁及以上人数	管理人员	专业技术技能人员	志愿者服务人次数	志愿服务时间
148907	**119157**	**30859**	**150867**	**258846**	**507302**	**1470907.3**
29	13	5	28	157		
5437	5067	1333	5183	10563	7992	19904.6
2439	2420	743	1859	5466	8507	17028.0
7824	4812	1064	5021	15252	5058	17017.0
3139	2274	548	3360	6012	3442	9014.0
3012	2698	839	3430	5177	339	1306.0
7238	6012	1385	8849	9747	2858	9124.0
5139	7571	354	7007	8620	1	
5222	3509	652	5823	7187	200	1600.0
8123	8652	3793	9128	16194	9567	23509.0
12117	11839	4053	8897	27866	121100	383117.0
5827	6214	2216	5616	12935	38883	76699.0
4764	4413	1246	6279	6945	14892	48743.0
2196	1509	478	2358	3621	22955	34522.0
4169	3648	699	5783	4780	2885	9371.0
11450	7239	1598	7415	23149	124413	301057.0
5971	4350	1148	6872	9998	4905	12482.0
8215	6025	1322	7941	13056	20519	34564.0
7486	4219	911	6664	11159	22114	83519.0
11059	7917	1569	10490	17026	34088	194641.5
3603	2352	595	2891	7389	2721	7053.0
401	269	61	432	797	345	130.0
2612	2995	979	4321	4108	13069	44589.7
8325	5755	1762	11392	11629	8647	16633.0
2600	1339	365	3967	2311	14019	36348.0
2219	1157	256	2300	3071	5007	35836.0
68	28		76	194	18	65.0
3230	2201	470	3629	5894	7009	19230.5
1332	784	155	1606	1967	1233	2728.0
271	137	33	253	597	518	1392.0
605	370	71	414	1146	2200	3400.0
2785	1369	156	1583	4833	7798	26284.0

C−2−2续表2

地　区	年末床位数	工商登记	编制登记	民政登记	一个机构多块牌子	年末收养人数	工商登记
全　国	**4140062**	**91655**	**2320489**	**1659138**	**68780**	**2363092**	**35641**
中央级	150		150			149	
北　京	143568	3858	83505	56062	143	81172	808
天　津	54539	2180	12248	40111		29688	192
河　北	169185	588	78179	87747	2671	76579	198
山　西	57848	26	28929	28172	721	30720	26
内蒙古	93132	364	45734	46232	802	45920	342
辽　宁	181253	299	74218	103283	3453	105423	183
吉　林	133521	549	69848	60447	2677	73498	154
黑龙江	135228		65211	69988	29	84895	
上　海	126141	1476	15266	108537	862	83208	362
江　苏	428412	6879	243075	174626	3832	219431	2402
浙　江	256728	10616	128224	117500	388	110530	5055
安　徽	163656	952	34940	126054	1710	86556	486
福　建	57146	704	32923	22538	981	25131	316
江　西	162739		149352	8078	5309	133001	
山　东	335122	4353	114455	215261	1053	194276	793
河　南	134463	40	74812	58610	1001	87034	34
湖　北	257488	12393	203339	36692	5064	156294	2483
湖　南	157761	1040	127082	24938	4701	103525	356
广　东	212206	21337	140982	47412	2475	92085	10696
广　西	52432	978	23209	24765	3480	30375	65
海　南	10512	4392	3249	2466	405	5666	3647
重　庆	92649	4305	52309	35557	478	57048	2263
四　川	359779	11951	275743	59875	12210	245474	3442
贵　州	86779	120	63246	18940	4473	46904	53
云　南	62567	1639	41676	18860	392	34841	1074
西　藏	10350		10350			4128	
陕　西	93149		59476	28589	5084	58155	
甘　肃	33166	371	20568	10477	1750	15433	126
青　海	7816		5834	1534	448	3514	
宁　夏	16463	245	9734	5627	857	9065	85
新　疆	54114		32623	20160	1331	33374	

单位：张、人天、人、人次

编制登记	民政登记	一个机构多块牌子	老年人	青壮年	少年儿童	年末在院(站)人天数
1491154	**854115**	**30686**	**1989483**	**117746**	**95852**	**577271777**
149			57	28	64	47998
61236	21645	24	32755	2659	1564	10802545
10198	20798		23249	1767	318	5451010
41792	40548	1141	68997	2284	1531	22468366
18427	13802	435	22876	2363	2871	6447186
22625	23818	220	39918	3174	1438	11103636
49825	53498	2163	78299	5006	3797	20048999
42013	30407	924	65142	5834	2270	18635903
41202	44246	12	75294	5381	1724	19476857
11281	71146	419	76317	4056	1956	24948225
143788	75085	1437	195011	8675	4621	56056025
55490	50049	77	101721	4201	2461	26391626
17085	69089	661	77361	1777	4077	23548880
15416	11003	267	17772	3448	1818	6854523
125698	4703	2635	120016	3680	6127	27250530
80288	119571	220	174731	2987	3046	54919215
52332	35893	421	70881	4039	5949	19305114
136117	18289	2299	133428	10652	4659	40253644
90949	11002	2403	83963	7387	6597	27119024
63264	21904	444	73254	5457	8120	25126496
14484	15268	1055	22261	3255	3316	7486262
1634	667	251	4995	85	309	390596
34032	20436	317	52581	2863	1342	16852957
207236	30832	4786	221341	13487	5138	62190920
38945	6199	2233	38800	3306	3515	11464034
24826	9380	92	26029	2121	1834	6174000
4128			863	3	2902	1042245
45113	14560	3527	48132	2940	2565	14053393
12613	4367	658	10586	696	2896	2561827
3149	438	74	1645	400	1295	748627
5954	2567	470	6788	872	514	1893603
19865	12905	1021	24420	2863	5218	6157511

C-2-2续表3

地 区	企业会计制度财务指标				事业
	固定资产原价	营业收入	费用合计	营业利润	固定资产原价
全 国	**338447.5**	**34165.8**	**14238.6**	**-4120.1**	**5898153.3**
中央级					12600.6
北 京	56227.0	8402.1	1801.5	-1097.5	224889.0
天 津	532.0	296.7	66.0		62320.9
河 北	1816.0	306.0	310.2	-0.9	265537.2
山 西	1830.0	30.0	16.0		127881.7
内蒙古	38.0	110.0	52.0	5.0	132053.8
辽 宁	230.1	140.0		25.0	241095.6
吉 林	30.0	60.0	60.0		124956.2
黑龙江					190136.1
上 海	242.0	245.0	1364.4	4.3	122454.4
江 苏	53725.2	1460.0	2172.6	-1798.2	526734.7
浙 江	63640.8	2919.0	556.1	26.0	260697.6
安 徽	3692.0	595.0	123.0	34.0	104342.3
福 建	2134.2	473.4	85.9	-11.0	77291.9
江 西	675.0	81.5	147.9	5.9	183970.7
山 东	13591.0	1228.0	1292.2	276.0	337416.8
河 南	40.0	50.0	49.0		135502.8
湖 北	17508.7	1217.8	532.0	12.0	400076.2
湖 南	14861.0	664.0	664.0		423027.1
广 东	30567.8	12201.7	1881.9	-17.5	452882.8
广 西	372.0	67.5	0.4		104060.8
海 南	1512.2	1219.5	1668.0	-1860.7	20230.5
重 庆	22002.0	2091.6	447.9	330.7	78848.2
四 川	35425.5	225.0	925.5	-58.2	471524.6
贵 州	1940.0	23.0	11.0	1.0	154088.0
云 南	4146.0	58.0	4.0	3.0	147968.4
西 藏	4500.0				20585.5
陕 西					228241.7
甘 肃	638.0		1.1		77617.3
青 海					18795.1
宁 夏	6400.0		3.0		43977.1
新 疆	131.0	1.0	3.0	1.0	126347.7

单位：万元

单位会计制度财务指标		民间非营利组织会计制度财务指标		
本年收入合计	本年支出合计	固定资产原价	本年收入合计	本年费用合计
5043189.8	**4860837.3**	**3087024.8**	**779705.2**	**677690.0**
1497.3	9283.3			
464549.9	315670.4	154471.3	57614.4	67634.2
111300.5	102842.0	26271.7	32318.3	18760.1
251623.8	229301.3	299413.6	24869.2	29247.1
113136.6	111860.8	38781.0	3452.1	6920.2
92451.1	89113.3	63083.8	13859.9	11974.8
275463.5	346206.3	91910.9	19826.7	16604.3
49306.1	47349.7	5145.7	6166.0	6156.0
97043.9	92571.5	127550.4	90057.9	9090.7
101577.7	92303.9	168675.6	170749.5	154102.7
445683.8	436243.0	520208.6	66299.4	68104.1
187078.2	181931.1	130733.6	39690.5	34639.2
78678.6	77606.3	175175.1	28351.1	28925.6
130983.9	111795.2	64470.1	3035.3	4568.2
56179.9	57936.2	22985.0	2000.6	1526.3
489380.1	493535.1	438252.7	102093.8	105856.2
158828.9	176798.7	101529.6	14754.8	11527.3
315317.4	308202.4	49657.9	10042.1	9376.9
243742.3	229116.4	32448.5	7164.0	4391.9
358181.1	355573.6	72958.8	14585.7	14375.2
114446.8	112151.8	17824.9	8242.3	9172.1
28199.2	26117.3	62941.0	1276.5	1152.6
67839.9	66624.6	95877.0	27362.4	23825.3
247934.7	239332.1	65210.2	11553.4	17069.5
54417.5	56221.0	50060.0	3890.0	3951.3
79310.1	70952.0	21655.6	1152.1	1559.0
3629.7	3378.1			
216164.9	222355.6	103729.4	7500.2	8080.8
96359.3	84063.4	29577.8	889.5	1049.5
15882.1	16140.7	458.0	23.4	30.3
25767.7	25164.5	18835.0	1221.8	1527.6
71233.3	73095.7	37132.0	9662.3	6491.0

C-2-3 养老服务

地区	单位数						
		工商登记	编制登记	民政登记	一个机构多块牌子	0～99张	100～299张
全　国	**28592**	**324**	**15735**	**12058**	**475**	**15065**	**11119**
中央级							
北　京	607	14	349	244		201	273
天　津	274	2	39	233		101	136
河　北	1054	2	451	585	16	513	393
山　西	578	1	284	291	2	388	168
内蒙古	714	2	359	343	10	402	258
辽　宁	1447	3	312	1106	26	885	439
吉　林	1301	6	666	619	10	902	353
黑龙江	840		173	667		503	242
上　海	649	4	28	615	2	202	345
江　苏	2343	22	1163	1155	3	863	1154
浙　江	1340	23	659	654	4	532	609
安　徽	1164	9	163	990	2	508	571
福　建	346	3	217	119	7	202	99
江　西	1497		1374	83	40	904	546
山　东	1959	13	525	1418	3	730	996
河　南	1148	1	610	528	9	694	409
湖　北	1684	28	1354	274	28	667	924
湖　南	1787	2	1577	169	39	1405	337
广　东	1491	56	1215	201	19	1022	339
广　西	480	2	260	177	41	345	110
海　南	55	3	21	18	13	40	8
重　庆	632	22	338	269	3	284	306
四　川	2573	85	2032	398	58	1277	1152
贵　州	870	1	678	138	53	577	276
云　南	412	16	203	192	1	220	163
西　藏	7		7			3	4
陕　西	569		333	182	54	254	224
甘　肃	249	3	107	122	17	165	70
青　海	36		23	12	1	22	11
宁　夏	92	1	52	35	4	42	38
新　疆	394		163	221	10	212	166

机构总表

单位：个、人

300～499张	500张以上	年末职工人数	女性	工商登记	编制登记	民政登记	一个机构多块牌子
1573	**835**	**338793**	**195552**	**8739**	**155939**	**170434**	**3681**
76	57	14446	9191	603	6335	7508	
14	23	6594	4501	160	1239	5195	
93	55	18788	10790	73	9020	9546	149
17	5	6361	3085	8	3289	3061	3
36	18	7158	3737	6	2894	4226	32
82	41	16628	10112	21	6333	9962	312
35	11	12864	7555	122	5663	6927	152
60	35	9572	5062		3883	5689	
72	30	23608	17681	315	1879	21384	30
223	103	33463	19419	1032	14858	17411	162
122	77	17142	10552	601	7765	8765	11
64	21	10849	5443	166	2070	8600	13
32	13	4182	2035	75	1727	2352	28
35	12	9312	3493		8213	838	261
167	66	27647	15456	156	8286	19166	39
28	17	12699	6927	9	6278	6300	112
49	44	16226	9036	626	12201	3211	188
27	18	13915	7255	145	10846	2409	515
75	55	21876	14089	2674	12669	6455	78
16	9	6895	4912	26	2727	4039	103
1	6	1089	654	325	521	227	16
24	18	7238	3811	531	2973	3689	45
95	49	15923	7371	820	10890	3646	567
14	3	4507	2136	21	2909	1266	311
18	11	3790	2129	168	2165	1452	5
		91	76		91		
71	20	7779	4251		4160	3228	391
8	6	2215	1092	33	1304	829	49
	3	374	191		301	69	4
8	4	1062	668	23	671	356	12
11	5	4500	2842		1779	2628	93

C-2-3续表1

地　区	受教育程度		职业资格水平		
	大学专科人数	大学本科及以上人数	助理社会工作师人数	社会工作师人数	35岁及以下人数
全　国	**57173**	**34793**	**5191**	**3969**	**82955**
中央级					
北　京	2340	2065	215	171	3457
天　津	1327	771	260	72	1465
河　北	3007	1772	128	130	6134
山　西	1263	897	29	89	1782
内蒙古	1478	673	87	83	1550
辽　宁	3416	2803	148	215	3322
吉　林	637	452	45	101	1805
黑龙江	1597	766	213	118	2148
上　海	1520	740	203	181	4018
江　苏	5864	3515	445	371	7542
浙　江	2168	1490	210	191	3808
安　徽	1297	699	111	116	2045
福　建	506	536	91	90	1020
江　西	929	399	69	57	1702
山　东	6647	4343	1177	664	9122
河　南	2020	1099	123	123	3738
湖　北	2912	1127	142	93	3408
湖　南	2802	1872	185	182	3751
广　东	3046	2350	455	283	4875
广　西	1938	863	89	141	2237
海　南	213	138	17	13	458
重　庆	1280	574	72	66	1330
四　川	3424	1355	272	149	3998
贵　州	1013	667	48	68	1345
云　南	891	632	37	41	1233
西　藏	4	5			59
陕　西	1764	1030	86	73	2966
甘　肃	546	471	133	54	795
青　海	90	69	5	4	159
宁　夏	205	163	14	11	321
新　疆	1029	457	82	19	1362

单位：人、人次、时

年龄结构			按人员性质分		志愿服务	
36岁至45岁人数	46岁至55岁人数	56岁及以上人数	管理人员	专业技术技能人员	志愿者服务人次数	志愿服务时间
125675	**103061**	**27102**	**126007**	**212786**	**446287**	**1315605.8**
5010	4723	1256	4606	9840	7985	19897.6
2268	2206	655	1623	4971	8307	16628.0
7260	4453	941	4611	14177	4813	16033.0
2422	1710	447	2788	3573	3337	8620.0
2626	2241	741	2883	4275	268	869.0
6620	5429	1257	7774	8854	2683	8996.0
3915	6923	221	5789	7075		0.0
4248	2664	512	4557	5015	200	1600.0
7620	8348	3622	8566	15042	7306	17394.0
11063	11006	3852	8189	25274	113789	366462.0
5351	5850	2133	5049	12093	28007	56651.0
3992	3760	1052	5085	5764	12528	40976.0
1680	1100	382	1702	2480	22935	34362.0
3721	3270	619	5096	4216	2489	7787.0
10618	6461	1446	6747	20900	104221	252010.0
4452	3516	993	5425	7274	2178	4725.0
6669	5055	1094	6847	9379	19940	33134.0
5949	3422	793	5326	8589	20750	77991.0
9056	6602	1343	8165	13711	33657	192359.5
2569	1648	441	2045	4850	2225	5710.0
359	221	51	364	725	345	130.0
2253	2727	928	3780	3458	10112	31780.7
6290	4387	1248	8796	7127	8360	16138.0
2001	917	244	3023	1484	7852	22002.0
1578	812	167	1643	2147	4724	34158.0
24	8		24	67		
2661	1772	380	2800	4979	6403	17555.0
850	465	105	1168	1047	1143	2548.0
122	82	11	149	225	17	90.0
397	289	55	328	734	2200	3400.0
2031	994	113	1059	3441	7513	25599.0

C-2-3续表2

地区	年末床位数	工商登记	编制登记	民政登记	一个机构多块牌子
全国	**3787751**	**91655**	**2019754**	**1634880**	**41462**
中央级					
北京	135692	3858	75972	55862	
天津	51425	2180	9134	40111	
河北	162189	588	73286	85863	2452
山西	51114	26	23257	27692	139
内蒙古	86253	364	39228	45916	745
辽宁	168727	299	62793	102722	2913
吉林	120214	549	58308	60447	910
黑龙江	121104		52599	68505	
上海	119009	1476	8204	108467	862
江苏	410441	6879	227695	174556	1311
浙江	247782	10616	119775	117344	47
安徽	149767	952	23191	125464	160
福建	47875	704	24138	22383	650
江西	154230		142706	7649	3875
山东	320724	4353	100691	215261	419
河南	118089	40	60199	57469	381
湖北	239052	12393	188324	35656	2679
湖南	140573	1040	113067	23701	2765
广东	189637	21337	121338	44984	1978
广西	41779	978	14944	24437	1420
海南	9954	4392	2691	2466	405
重庆	85511	4305	45221	35507	478
四川	319286	11951	249912	50611	6812
贵州	73966	120	52769	18920	2157
云南	51504	1639	31690	18061	114
西藏	1124		1124		
陕西	84430		50941	28589	4900
甘肃	26462	371	14705	10126	1260
青海	5112		3488	1304	320
宁夏	14035	245	8188	5080	522
新疆	40691		20176	19727	788

单位：张、人天、人

年在院总人天数	年末在院人数	女性	工商登记	编制登记	民政登记	一个机构多块牌子
537688683	**2198087**	**549323**	**35641**	**1298977**	**841084**	**22385**
10374987	77275	15565	808	54913	21554	
5139932	28131	12389	192	7141	20798	
21645152	73516	13232	198	32508	39691	1119
5634581	27525	3127	26	13906	13494	99
10208453	42788	7321	342	18597	23671	178
18776439	100792	20067	183	45409	53302	1898
17622749	68507	6639	154	37280	30407	666
17631539	78182	18047		35121	43061	
23559538	77734	47421	362	5877	71076	419
53561685	209694	57836	2402	131719	75055	518
25602694	107293	37570	5055	52217	49996	25
22134894	81012	18049	486	11724	68734	68
5501464	19873	5060	316	8517	10860	180
27023324	130338	35647		123275	4468	2595
53281938	187411	49855	793	66997	119571	50
17565580	79572	17187	34	43987	35205	346
38195897	146962	38021	2483	125023	17705	1751
25430882	95003	22664	356	82564	10412	1671
22830066	82707	36377	10696	51030	20625	356
6069497	24683	7698	65	9102	15064	452
391573	5625	2651	3647	1060	667	251
15836426	53634	12884	2263	30668	20386	317
56736655	225115	30772	3442	192218	26162	3293
10083108	41163	6310	53	33863	6199	1048
5517948	31101	5074	1074	20838	9151	38
219725	866	196		866		
13072563	54197	10067		36110	14560	3527
1940280	12292	2658	126	7372	4206	588
359698	1866	480		1571	245	50
1622600	7745	1320	85	5139	2189	332
4116816	25485	7139		12365	12570	550

C-2-3续表3

地区	在院人员按性质分			收养性机构年末在院人员	
	优抚对象	特困人员	自费人员	老人	青壮年
全 国	**71145**	**1084285**	**785087**	**1953536**	**72567**
中央级					
北 京	334	3109	31307	32740	2658
天 津	503	980	22099	23021	1151
河 北	3556	26145	35304	67352	1692
山 西	1803	13773	6994	22205	1289
内蒙古	1609	13762	24659	39557	1667
辽 宁	3004	25893	51468	77975	4769
吉 林	3987	26559	4503	63855	4034
黑龙江	3029	31425	33800	72859	2959
上 海	155	2142	74141	75547	2119
江 苏	7000	102561	83315	192411	5141
浙 江	633	23999	74009	101184	3730
安 徽	1459	54669	21183	76693	1316
福 建	615	3892	13488	16597	483
江 西	8586	103200	12846	119673	3434
山 东	5433	95555	73632	172852	1958
河 南	5692	44128	21481	69853	2550
湖 北	7157	97233	32543	131840	7393
湖 南	5594	62341	15436	82048	5452
广 东	1320	26379	44479	71388	3282
广 西	713	5105	16073	21170	860
海 南	93	713	4340	4995	85
重 庆	728	24276	27886	51637	1673
四 川	4425	185821	23675	212500	6758
贵 州	468	32503	4715	37884	912
云 南	271	19051	3503	25633	695
西 藏		278		863	3
陕 西	1763	35010	12615	47603	2419
甘 肃	272	7673	2762	10270	382
青 海	35	1254	353	1478	192
宁 夏	190	4266	913	6254	615
新 疆	718	10590	11565	23599	896

单位：张、人、人次、平方米

在院人数 按年龄分	在院人员按类型分			康复和医疗门诊 人次数	机构建筑 面积
少年儿童	自理 (完全自理)	介助 (半自理)	介护 (不能自理)		
39172	**1365087**	**437849**	**262339**	**7333752**	**78057803**
322	11749	10766	13205	228279	1881333
87	7181	7488	9590	183440	1106322
1323	45052	14330	10985	251532	4296640
2125	19127	3753	2739	45115	1469865
574	28341	9218	4239	36748	1776355
619	57376	16443	9544	110933	2509127
615	41790	17174	9540	62050	2427823
179	59583	10289	6125	37499	1570937
68	18916	26241	32577	275778	3328176
2487	120877	48365	30797	897117	8638849
1073	69697	22095	14195	834905	3642805
825	56885	16432	5517	86403	2723943
1036	8707	5101	4308	75685	1373110
5284	99454	24842	4095	34029	2863799
490	131313	31092	12895	541960	9205448
2936	55666	13104	6569	165838	2671297
2434	96287	30167	15213	544505	5037055
3644	60415	21287	9442	266491	3396760
4828	32273	21374	25851	1187467	4270571
1839	9748	6619	7502	114037	1013433
269	4564	220	565	8014	166601
324	42509	6611	4514	339257	1708932
2006	174632	37518	9114	477926	4711588
1790	32018	7252	1316	111522	1262172
290	16819	7300	2499	68271	938205
	815	22	29		21678
594	31660	13824	5132	166434	1815452
683	7929	2236	1170	56259	517465
22	1243	381	68	3535	120561
59	3790	2301	837	10023	469984
347	18671	4004	2167	112700	1121516

C-2-3续表4

地区	企业会计制度财务指标			
	固定资产原价	营业收入	费用合计	营业利润
全 国	**338447.5**	**34165.8**	**14238.6**	**-4120.1**
中央级				
北 京	56227.0	8402.1	1801.5	-1097.5
天 津	532.0	296.7	66.0	
河 北	1816.0	306.0	310.2	-0.9
山 西	1830.0	30.0	16.0	
内蒙古	38.0	110.0	52.0	5.0
辽 宁	230.1	140.0		25.0
吉 林	30.0	60.0	60.0	
黑龙江				
上 海	242.0	245.0	1364.4	4.3
江 苏	53725.2	1460.0	2172.6	-1798.2
浙 江	63640.8	2919.0	556.1	26.0
安 徽	3692.0	595.0	123.0	34.0
福 建	2134.2	473.4	85.9	-11.0
江 西	675.0	81.5	147.9	5.9
山 东	13591.0	1228.0	1292.2	276.0
河 南	40.0	50.0	49.0	
湖 北	17508.7	1217.8	532.0	12.0
湖 南	14861.0	664.0	664.0	
广 东	30567.8	12201.7	1881.9	-17.5
广 西	372.0	67.5	0.4	
海 南	1512.2	1219.5	1668.0	-1860.7
重 庆	22002.0	2091.6	447.9	330.7
四 川	35425.5	225.0	925.5	-58.2
贵 州	1940.0	23.0	11.0	1.0
云 南	4146.0	58.0	4.0	3.0
西 藏	4500.0			
陕 西				
甘 肃	638.0		1.1	
青 海				
宁 夏	6400.0		3.0	
新 疆	131.0	1.0	3.0	1.0

单位：万元

事业单位会计制度财务指标			民间非营利组织会计制度财务指标		
固定资产原价	本年收入合计	本年支出合计	固定资产原价	本年收入合计	本年费用合计
4636090.6	**3917754.8**	**3789531.4**	**2979802.6**	**771557.3**	**664475.6**
168440.7	428429.2	280131.7	154471.3	57614.4	67634.2
52486.8	88865.7	84899.5	26271.7	32318.3	18760.1
238623.5	231198.0	211862.3	298651.6	24490.5	28784.0
99409.5	91240.0	92229.1	37876.0	3321.1	6707.3
110316.3	61755.9	60961.0	61835.8	13679.2	11794.7
183180.3	256713.4	329692.9	91312.5	19703.1	16519.8
99147.6	29283.8	28518.7	5145.7	6166.0	6156.0
124440.0	63436.2	61033.3	125567.2	90057.9	6446.5
75964.5	49746.6	45818.9	168675.6	170749.5	154102.7
434608.7	353697.7	353979.9	520178.6	66293.4	68098.1
224125.1	147916.8	146223.9	130631.6	39538.5	34487.2
64936.1	58942.5	60670.7	174545.1	28306.1	28620.6
49437.8	92412.1	77665.7	64470.1	3035.3	4568.2
172603.0	49095.9	51902.8	22985.0	1952.6	1424.5
272165.7	421228.0	425708.0	438252.7	102093.8	105856.2
89978.1	114119.4	121066.2	92317.6	13753.6	10540.5
331793.4	232196.0	227255.3	48203.9	9627.9	9097.7
374168.1	188275.9	173733.6	32103.5	6966.0	4311.9
370854.1	281144.0	281263.0	71860.4	12906.0	14072.9
58854.0	54407.9	55025.5	17717.9	8209.0	9134.8
19226.1	26642.5	24589.8	3938.0	1276.5	1152.6
60087.2	35323.2	38523.1	95877.0	27362.4	23825.3
354318.9	139648.0	135176.4	36985.2	7917.9	9747.2
130090.1	31484.7	32976.2	49864.0	3890.0	3951.2
100049.7	59427.8	53938.3	21630.6	1152.1	1552.8
10930.6		338.3			
195318.8	192392.5	195932.9	103729.4	7500.2	8080.8
50985.1	75165.9	72197.2	28619.6	863.5	1005.1
10824.1	10467.6	11146.2	328.0	23.4	30.1
29570.0	19948.4	19622.6	18625.0	1126.8	1521.6
79156.7	33149.2	35448.4	37132.0	9662.3	6491.0

C-2-4 城市养老

地区	机构数	0～99张	100～299张	300～499张	500张以上
全 国	**8891**	**4251**	**3544**	**696**	**400**
中央级					
北 京	184	69	80	20	15
天 津	210	72	112	9	17
河 北	350	130	159	34	27
山 西	105	50	48	6	1
内蒙古	307	136	138	24	9
辽 宁	912	592	248	53	19
吉 林	620	426	168	20	6
黑龙江	608	407	163	28	10
上 海	429	161	214	41	13
江 苏	867	319	394	91	63
浙 江	386	110	185	48	43
安 徽	344	178	131	21	14
福 建	117	32	57	19	9
江 西	156	89	58	5	4
山 东	803	341	329	98	35
河 南	348	202	121	19	6
湖 北	268	125	118	9	16
湖 南	158	77	64	9	8
广 东	279	94	119	41	25
广 西	167	78	69	13	7
海 南	15	3	7		5
重 庆	293	126	142	16	9
四 川	345	181	128	21	15
贵 州	132	60	62	8	2
云 南	101	42	46	9	4
西 藏	2		2		
陕 西	126	33	60	24	9
甘 肃	47	17	24	3	3
青 海	7	3	2		2
宁 夏	19	4	9	4	2
新 疆	186	94	87	3	2

服务机构

单位：个、人

年末职工人数	女性	受教育程度：大学专科人数	受教育程度：大学本科及以上人数	职业资格水平：助理社会工作师人数	职业资格水平：社会工作师人数
150465	**96471**	**24414**	**11254**	**1958**	**1128**
6047	4119	800	413	84	75
5558	3944	988	481	235	33
7573	4576	1289	356	41	17
1691	980	252	126	5	14
3979	2326	647	227	62	27
9444	6020	1951	1382	55	78
6913	5318				
5354	3025	936	298	174	87
15115	11542	698	293	106	104
16851	10133	3424	1616	186	96
7092	4696	895	505	52	37
4403	2643	712	204	39	25
2387	1113	178	89	24	13
1482	610	149	39	4	5
13598	8330	3598	1914	313	171
5349	3301	773	298	68	55
3573	2353	606	193	11	6
2932	1736	630	372	16	21
9605	6443	1351	513	162	77
3857	2807	1161	403	24	56
636	379	103	81	6	11
4313	2607	776	295	28	20
3373	1800	642	290	74	9
1207	673	215	111	13	28
1418	820	350	224	13	9
37	32	3			
3101	1912	610	245	43	38
714	369	146	66	67	14
44	21	20	14		
213	139	23	15		1
2606	1704	488	191	53	1

C−2−4续表1

地 区	按人员性质分		年龄结构			
	管理人员	专业技术技能人员	35岁及以下人数	36岁至45岁人数	46岁至55岁人数	56岁及以上人数
全 国	**49042**	**101423**	**35422**	**53620**	**48144**	**13279**
中央级						
北 京	1231	4816	1194	1981	2196	676
天 津	1194	4364	1204	1887	1869	598
河 北	1962	5611	2436	2673	2032	432
山 西	687	1004	595	684	296	116
内蒙古	1560	2419	795	1432	1253	499
辽 宁	4309	5135	1672	3831	3211	730
吉 林	2558	4355		1407	5506	
黑龙江	2298	3056	1136	2383	1436	399
上 海	6870	8245	2579	4745	5480	2311
江 苏	3873	12978	4079	5510	5235	2027
浙 江	1778	5314	1652	2169	2434	837
安 徽	1662	2741	985	1574	1460	384
福 建	865	1522	581	986	580	240
江 西	723	759	318	781	309	74
山 东	3123	10475	4789	5021	3160	628
河 南	2120	3229	1268	1879	1611	591
湖 北	1408	2165	588	1257	1374	354
湖 南	757	2175	823	1235	691	183
广 东	2771	6834	2304	3819	2859	623
广 西	834	3023	1299	1395	867	296
海 南	174	462	324	187	99	26
重 庆	2004	2309	837	1387	1524	565
四 川	1486	1887	1028	1307	767	271
贵 州	639	568	321	484	277	125
云 南	397	1021	511	632	212	63
西 藏	4	33	28	9		
陕 西	896	2205	1233	1157	596	115
甘 肃	274	440	250	299	137	28
青 海	20	24	17	22	5	
宁 夏	62	151	54	76	57	26
新 疆	503	2103	522	1411	611	62

单位：人、人次、时、张、人天

志愿服务		年末床位数		年在院总人天数	年末在院人数	
志愿者服务人次数	志愿服务时间		光荣间床位			女性
161315	**477074.6**	**1359493**	**12901**	**166966909**	**680926**	**237919**
6983	16959.6	36305	750	4532482	15371	7641
7560	14990.0	37904	70	4442224	21084	11235
2138	8698.0	65709	700	8871921	29519	7286
1818	5355.0	12893	312	920801	6977	951
39	260.0	42973	86	4650676	22791	5335
1596	7641.0	95754	1166	10338947	49536	12359
		59548		8851900	29685	
		66529	410	7680138	41507	10271
		70538		15685617	49511	31515
53496	201279.0	163137	870	17869875	73294	24676
5957	12594.0	100072	1063	9515502	41237	16682
8177	26679.0	46609	313	5579829	20010	7721
1585	2335.0	24733	32	3413775	11538	2983
300	900.0	18050	987	2704441	11771	5449
53916	126456.0	133391	1440	17738462	64311	22824
242	406.0	40675	289	4966079	23970	7384
20	150.0	45483	1911	5089488	19542	7304
995	2846.0	24360	252	2853290	11878	4677
		63747	460	9095528	31614	17807
800	2155.0	23902	527	3464223	14021	4413
		7190	11	175765	4449	2349
3969	13513.0	40631	232	6956270	23489	7748
1737	2792.0	45342	158	4990867	20741	6367
1969	5755.0	17718	242	1096979	5053	1636
92	506.0	16019	34	903258	7046	1100
		357		96360	314	117
970	2855.0	26323	282	1801809	12997	5159
190	470.0	8272		421961	3371	1031
10	40.0	1569		41704	249	90
		5682	186	436391	2019	538
6756	21440.0	18078	118	1780347	12031	3271

C–2–4续表2

地　区	在院人员按性质分			在院人员按年龄分		
	优抚对象	特困人员	自费人员	老人	青壮年	少年儿童
全　国	**7189**	**84085**	**515972**	**666167**	**11045**	**3714**
中央级						
北　京	202	306	14216	14621	736	14
天　津	165	498	19810	20252	745	87
河　北	571	5840	22257	29091	235	193
山　西	111	855	4955	6945	11	21
内蒙古	151	1046	20823	22297	450	44
辽　宁	508	5030	41965	49078	445	13
吉　林				29685		
黑龙江	935	7946	26915	40479	925	103
上　海	67	472	48764	48773	738	
江　苏	1430	10733	55416	71710	1245	339
浙　江	176	4262	30858	39757	1381	99
安　徽	161	1948	16992	19796	81	133
福　建	32	245	11178	11499	21	18
江　西	327	8344	2782	11516	51	204
山　东	597	6999	56474	63775	494	42
河　南	457	3109	18810	23186	452	332
湖　北	244	1988	15031	18579	232	731
湖　南	216	2794	7570	11007	783	88
广　东	37	2964	26519	30365	817	432
广　西	116	643	11871	13760	172	89
海　南	14	16	4267	4449		
重　庆	67	1430	21775	23244	211	34
四　川	66	7315	9887	20204	258	279
贵　州	71	1411	3337	4758	105	190
云　南	89	2126	2014	6977	35	34
西　藏				314		
陕　西	259	2344	9949	12808	161	28
甘　肃	15	1019	2194	3307	4	60
青　海	2	89	158	249		
宁　夏	68	584	271	1950	69	
新　疆	35	1729	8914	11736	188	107

单位：人、人次、平方米

在院人员按类型分			康复和医疗门诊人次数	机构建筑面积
自理（完全自理）	介助（半自理）	介护（不能自理）		
377392	**163406**	**140128**	**1629667**	**30264173**
4019	4410	6942	137268	695310
5255	6634	9195	122871	867282
17599	5975	5945	38693	2175622
5253	1030	694	2406	361180
14527	5700	2564	6	840086
34346	9972	5218	26642	1328306
15407	8795	5483		898647
34108	3736	3663	1189	730251
10557	14704	24250	14778	1882600
34538	20721	18035	190081	4281223
25811	9441	5985	115755	1586655
10452	6576	2982	22183	765204
4965	3757	2816	13681	780762
8703	2188	880	5390	305826
44157	12503	7651	279711	4292538
13583	7120	3267	35250	992171
10587	5336	3619	20297	1089812
6072	3499	2307	30518	553054
9794	8095	13725	259339	1440674
5406	4142	4473	29189	433290
4005	118	326		104257
17830	3659	2000	143238	925589
13461	5524	1756	16355	721861
3089	1226	738	9459	233417
5307	1091	648	2327	249805
294	10	10		11500
5656	4411	2930	87337	631439
2292	529	550	12537	222671
212	28	9		42911
1116	527	376	1264	246307
8991	1949	1091	11903	573923

C-2-4续表3

地　区	企业会计制度财务指标				
	固定资产原价	营业收入	费用合计	营业利润	固定资产原价
全　国	**298273.4**	**30037.8**	**12311.7**	**-4449.3**	**681032.1**
中央级					
北　京	43049.7	5266.5	1465.9	-1147.4	39852.3
天　津	532.0	296.7	66.0		15549.5
河　北	1816.0	306.0	310.2	-0.9	42246.2
山　西	1830.0	30.0	16.0		13822.1
内蒙古	38.0	110.0	52.0	5.0	8710.4
辽　宁	230.0	140.0		25.0	23964.7
吉　林	30.0	60.0	60.0		
黑龙江					15317.3
上　海	115.0	215.0	1361.9		24444.6
江　苏	52745.2	1410.0	2172.6	-1798.2	83333.4
浙　江	63262.7	2838.9	487.2	26.0	64224.6
安　徽	3692.0	560.0	88.0	34.0	618.2
福　建	1564.2	449.4	85.9	-11.0	8405.5
江　西	657.0	50.0	90.0	5.0	21535.0
山　东	8391.0	526.0	406.8	5.4	40542.4
河　南	30.0	30.0	27.0		16271.8
湖　北	15806.5	1203.0	532.0	12.0	15804.0
湖　南	13860.0	664.0	664.0		125999.5
广　东	30445.2	12201.7	1876.7	-17.5	49300.2
广　西	372.0	67.5			225.0
海　南	1512.2	1219.5	1668.0	-1860.7	1813.2
重　庆	22002.0	2091.6	447.9	330.7	1836.7
四　川	19743.7	222.0	416.5	-58.7	13725.2
贵　州	1000.0	23.0	11.0	1.0	7243.4
云　南	4001.0	57.0	2.0	1.0	12819.8
西　藏	4500.0				1758.5
陕　西					8774.4
甘　肃	638.0		1.1		14682.4
青　海					1075.1
宁　夏	6400.0		3.0		4696.0
新　疆	10.0				2440.7

单位：万元

事业单位会计制度财务指标		民间非营利组织会计制度财务指标		
本年收入合计	本年支出合计	固定资产原价	本年收入合计	本年支出合计
185034.7	**179887.4**	**2118535.5**	**578955.5**	**473403.3**
12644.8	15330.2	75121.0	37566.3	47849.1
16526.6	15906.1	18166.5	28908.1	15062.1
10490.5	10088.3	207023.2	16189.2	18819.5
4249.3	5085.0	13913.6	1255.5	1317.8
1364.7	1309.8	54538.2	12021.5	10112.0
7856.1	8133.6	72630.0	16198.2	14015.9
		3030.0	6140.0	6140.0
1080.8	981.0	108736.4	88995.0	5564.3
5572.8	4911.7	54575.6	117278.1	106974.6
27169.1	25466.9	427496.1	48653.3	50666.5
18178.9	17014.4	88553.5	24896.5	21138.5
533.6	590.2	73089.8	14406.9	13790.1
1120.9	915.6	58633.4	2307.1	3329.8
1183.8	815.4	22224.0	1437.6	993.5
6418.2	6418.2	320751.4	64529.8	67226.4
2553.9	2757.3	65910.7	11548.5	8812.1
2912.9	2857.9	41414.9	8720.1	8409.1
8636.6	8495.2	23418.3	5896.7	3421.2
43476.4	38392.9	61696.5	10680.7	11660.5
78.0	17.1	16118.5	8014.3	8764.4
1182.8	1605.8	1938.0	1178.4	1024.5
814.1	812.3	94899.0	27197.1	23678.4
791.0	1489.3	20225.7	4827.6	6852.6
589.9	598.9	34869.0	3443.1	3541.8
1141.2	1292.8	5355.6	335.6	397.2
	338.3			
3659.1	3506.2	90847.2	5761.7	6223.1
1202.7	1185.7	23835.4	672.2	728.9
729.3	777.5	120.0	6.0	0.4
1512.4	1533.6	14648.0	471.1	667.3
1364.3	1260.2	24756.0	9419.3	6221.7

C−2−5 农村养老

地 区	单位数	0～99张	100～299张	300～499张	500张以上
全 国	**15398**	**8218**	**6433**	**550**	**197**
中央级					
北 京	267	91	134	26	16
天 津	37	14	17	3	3
河 北	435	169	195	48	23
山 西	293	184	100	7	2
内蒙古	308	211	84	8	5
辽 宁	399	243	147	6	3
吉 林	595	447	146	2	
黑龙江	139	54	52	18	15
上 海	197	40	118	26	13
江 苏	1271	425	707	116	23
浙 江	806	359	385	42	20
安 徽	706	268	395	40	3
福 建	88	81	6	1	
江 西	1048	639	391	14	4
山 东	953	255	626	53	19
河 南	594	338	251	2	3
湖 北	1128	402	701	19	6
湖 南	1331	1113	213	4	1
广 东	941	775	146	16	4
广 西	123	115	7	1	
海 南	19	18		1	
重 庆	300	149	150	1	
四 川	1925	923	936	48	18
贵 州	623	440	180	3	
云 南	224	127	90	4	3
西 藏	5	3	2		
陕 西	323	126	153	35	9
甘 肃	138	109	24	3	2
青 海	18	12	6		
宁 夏	57	26	27	2	2
新 疆	107	62	44	1	

服务机构

单位：个、人

年末职工人数	女性	受教育程度		职业资格水平	
		大学专科人数	大学本科及以上人数	助理社会工作师人数	社会工作师人数
112246	**55990**	**12895**	**3718**	**1296**	**833**
5348	3322	527	240	25	10
407	237	151	27	4	6
6424	3674	581	178	29	25
2479	1068	424	153	6	24
1706	712	265	57	7	5
3450	2120	383	173	3	3
3385	1468	368	167	23	83
1969	964	268	56	16	12
6845	4918	525	170	46	25
12098	6376	1293	346	66	37
6560	3556	585	117	88	83
4754	1801	168	50	17	13
386	168	24	17	1	2
4985	1644	293	4	22	6
10028	5147	1770	590	648	290
4301	2007	371	98	4	22
7585	3652	858	86	36	19
5688	2438	541	103	27	33
4973	2573	366	123	43	29
389	240	54	23		5
67	46	12	4		
1653	493	108	42	3	
8888	3470	1571	274	109	55
2066	795	409	263	6	24
1325	766	201	76	9	1
54	44	1	5		
2558	1301	418	163	13	4
609	274	167	64	31	7
135	42	27	10	2	4
438	266	28	14	4	
693	408	138	25	8	6

C-2-5续表1

地 区	按人员性质分		年龄结构			
	管理人员	专业技术技能人员	35岁及以下人数	36岁至45岁人数	46岁至55岁人数	56岁及以上人数
全 国	**47303**	**64943**	**24133**	**44058**	**34463**	**9592**
中央级						
北 京	1551	3797	1250	1943	1694	461
天 津	186	221	48	215	124	20
河 北	1353	5071	1983	2820	1369	252
山 西	1206	1273	602	876	790	211
内蒙古	673	1033	338	693	504	171
辽 宁	1837	1613	617	1455	1116	262
吉 林	2045	1340	1011	1416	873	85
黑龙江	1108	861	437	907	588	37
上 海	1367	5478	1120	2393	2333	999
江 苏	3056	9042	1981	4172	4406	1539
浙 江	2374	4186	1135	2097	2427	901
安 徽	2685	2069	653	1753	1776	572
福 建	198	188	34	145	165	42
江 西	2984	2001	652	1816	2092	425
山 东	2473	7555	3055	4283	2153	537
河 南	2175	2126	1285	1559	1188	269
湖 北	3601	3984	1471	3368	2292	454
湖 南	2913	2775	969	2843	1463	413
广 东	2249	2724	824	1825	1833	491
广 西	224	165	53	210	109	17
海 南	30	37	39	12	12	4
重 庆	1207	446	96	532	749	276
四 川	5550	3338	1652	3665	2744	827
贵 州	1632	434	679	1019	297	71
云 南	764	561	416	541	309	59
西 藏	20	34	31	15	8	
陕 西	1078	1480	946	872	615	125
甘 肃	363	246	160	224	179	46
青 海	68	67	49	46	39	1
宁 夏	139	299	103	173	141	21
新 疆	194	499	444	170	75	4

单位：人、人次、时、人天、张

志愿服务		年末床位数		年在院总人天数	年末在院人数	
志愿者服务人次数	志愿服务时间		光荣间床位			女性
145617	**480840.7**	**1799248**	**41119**	**301002373**	**1132253**	**229248**
959	2793.0	53120	40	5366892	17421	6525
225	550.0	7619		308816	2147	920
1925	6489.0	71982	1664	9962830	32450	4447
736	1113.0	26238	434	3201459	14198	1195
79	459.0	29825	359	3923956	13903	917
103	167.0	38345	503	5466194	23586	4438
		43343	2	6233078	28467	4392
		36496	1182	6926318	24299	4780
7210	17202.0	41326	5	6202509	23429	12851
29086	75875.0	207779	5569	32461992	115464	28523
7534	21897.0	116048	397	11897503	49744	14287
1994	5875.0	90141	2185	14905772	53857	8630
850	1025.0	5384	138	633170	2248	640
1200	3640.0	101767	7242	18870558	89800	24051
30060	73215.0	155022	6106	33756519	105503	25664
		58214	2568	10411597	43788	8087
11306	15530.0	142723	3530	27381030	98902	22747
14799	54537.0	85270	2469	17488226	62597	12238
21725	163919.0	72633	1095	7159945	25806	7554
		4380	360	737535	2704	673
300		876		76004	379	102
2950	8049.7	31604	77	6760484	23277	2088
5654	10377.0	233538	2119	46780296	182818	19206
1002	3600.0	47613	271	7920575	31595	3712
54	312.0	22990	888	3771034	15047	2868
		767		123365	552	79
3610	11252.0	46091	1381	9441013	32427	3865
191	554.0	10065	430	1020498	5326	1003
		1489		156976	764	191
1960	1960.0	6818	45	949489	3954	512
105	450.0	9742	60	706740	5801	2063

C-2-5续表2

地区	在院人员按性质分			在院人员按年龄分		
	优抚对象	特困人员	自费人员	老人	青壮年	少年儿童
全　国	**30643**	**890498**	**173621**	**1089819**	**34357**	**8077**
中央级						
北　京	19	1904	15160	16271	1103	47
天　津	57	81	2005	2137	10	
河　北	125	17017	11795	31684	726	40
山　西	210	11296	1476	12839	952	407
内蒙古	352	10169	2364	12904	788	211
辽　宁	1225	16384	5545	21782	1755	49
吉　林	2894	23328	898	25532	2580	355
黑龙江	1402	19169	2047	22869	1399	31
上　海	52	1447	20963	22132	1229	68
江　苏	4470	87142	22631	113010	1985	469
浙　江	293	17272	30975	48595	1104	45
安　徽	378	50282	2768	52961	728	168
福　建	36	880	1317	2229	5	14
江　西	2693	78671	5473	85524	2438	1838
山　东	3095	86179	16041	104696	708	99
河　南	3414	36461	2068	42248	1041	499
湖　北	3774	85234	8434	92118	5506	1278
湖　南	2069	52868	2142	60234	1855	508
广　东	448	16962	5029	25198	437	171
广　西	12	1570	1034	2601	86	17
海　南	20	296	63	377		2
重　庆	279	20868	1757	22468	749	60
四　川	2520	169605	7284	177139	5020	659
贵　州	48	28459	829	30818	142	635
云　南	82	13399	660	14466	481	100
西　藏		278		549	3	
陕　西	186	29396	2266	31403	958	66
甘　肃	204	4529	292	4990	211	125
青　海		719		744	17	3
宁　夏	87	3302	229	3660	285	9
新　疆	199	5331	76	5641	56	104

单位：人、人次、平方米

在院人员按类型分			康复和医疗门诊人次数	机构建筑面积
自理（完全自理）	介助（半自理）	介护（不能自理）		
852988	**215110**	**64155**	**1918357**	**33309208**
6956	5305	5160	37803	1002578
1475	497	175	14370	183368
22782	6422	3246	4452	1458014
11781	1711	706	5001	713079
10933	2166	804		553655
17632	4202	1752	11152	649682
19251	6072	3144	32537	949083
18195	4997	1107	11538	428074
7653	10165	5611	119899	1181128
82354	25408	7702	363293	3422330
36875	9139	3730	422604	1448152
43675	8914	1268	20829	1550789
1653	439	156	233	129039
70896	17248	1656	10349	1770813
83840	17305	4358	103255	4404922
38391	3953	1444	46993	1069402
72807	18614	7481	239913	2674058
46500	13365	2732	53881	1900154
15106	7903	2797	95451	1380993
1845	699	160	564	110518
377		2		28100
21260	1580	437	58964	430217
149930	27609	5279	129527	3178991
26137	5266	192	9820	784712
9027	5061	959	53743	442157
521	12	19		10178
23476	7616	1335	21220	829432
4217	903	206	41408	160143
541	195	28	292	59004
2195	1454	305	1143	179676
4707	890	204	8123	226768

C–2–5续表3

地 区	企业会计制度财务指标				
	固定资产原价	营业收入	费用合计	营业利润	固定资产原价
全 国	**40174.1**	**4128.0**	**1926.9**	**329.2**	**1718524.5**
中央级					
北 京	13177.3	3135.6	335.6	49.9	41778.0
天 津					
河 北					69715.1
山 西					11545.6
内蒙古					34091.6
辽 宁	0.1				31408.2
吉 林					50519.4
黑龙江					36890.1
上 海	127.0	30.0	2.5	4.3	
江 苏	980.0	50.0			199207.6
浙 江	378.1	80.1	68.9		76412.1
安 徽		35.0	35.0		19891.6
福 建	570.0	24.0			3680.7
江 西	18.0	31.5	57.9	0.9	91624.0
山 东	5200.0	702.0	885.4	270.6	64557.5
河 南	10.0	20.0	22.0		30321.1
湖 北	1702.2	14.8			156894.8
湖 南	1001.0				105014.4
广 东	122.6		5.2		137018.2
广 西			0.4		3697.6
海 南					8500.0
重 庆					24353.1
四 川	15681.8	3.0	509.0	0.5	210180.5
贵 州	940.0				93241.6
云 南	145.0	1.0	2.0	2.0	36004.4
西 藏					9172.1
陕 西					108653.2
甘 肃					10638.6
青 海					5202.4
宁 夏					14002.9
新 疆	121.0	1.0	3.0	1.0	34308.1

单位：万元

事业单位会计制度财务指标		民间非营利组织会计制度财务指标		
本年收入合计	本年支出合计	固定资产原价	本年收入合计	本年支出合计
291758.7	**365505.5**	**810152.1**	**185505.3**	**184981.5**
10804.6	8875.4	79350.3	20048.1	19785.1
		8105.2	3410.2	3698.0
15805.1	15712.5	91628.4	8301.3	9964.5
2225.8	2381.4	20309.4	2032.6	4220.1
6885.4	6320.6	7297.6	1657.7	1682.7
8379.3	87842.8	18682.5	3504.9	2503.9
10573.9	10658.5	2.0	10.0	10.0
5233.9	5114.5	14853.8	749.9	505.1
		114089.0	53419.2	47105.1
43700.6	48807.3	92183.5	17119.9	17359.4
20806.9	20216.0	40011.8	11382.4	11918.4
742.5	726.4	101255.3	13699.2	14790.5
463.3	468.1	5836.7	715.4	1225.6
12819.1	11351.6	373.0	116.0	56.8
15266.8	15266.8	116891.3	37486.0	38551.8
6212.1	5632.3	26073.9	2183.9	1710.4
29895.2	28366.6	1318.0	508.9	529.6
20122.3	19280.2	5177.2	893.3	876.7
19254.1	18269.6	3364.9	1731.0	1378.4
205.0	245.4	1599.4	194.7	370.4
160.5	160.5	2000.0	98.1	128.1
8011.6	7974.0	328.0	154.5	145.5
24020.6	22758.2	16759.5	3090.3	2894.6
4493.9	4482.5	5656.0	228.9	221.2
2680.8	2074.4	16189.0	814.5	1151.2
10008.2	9617.8	11432.2	1444.0	1617.2
10543.8	10566.7	4784.2	191.3	276.2
365.2	349.7	208.0	17.4	29.7
1676.0	1421.6	3070.0	222.7	202.3
402.2	564.1	1322.0	79.0	73.0

C-2-6 社会

地 区	单位数				
		0～99张	100～299张	300～499张	500张以上
全 国	**1604**	**502**	**698**	**235**	**169**
中央级					
北 京	8		4	2	2
天 津	3		3		
河 北	31	11	14	5	1
山 西	20	7	9	2	2
内蒙古	49	14	27	4	4
辽 宁	49	6	26	13	4
吉 林	59	10	32	12	5
黑龙江	47	9	18	11	9
上 海	22		13	5	4
江 苏	62	12	20	14	16
浙 江	95	17	33	32	13
安 徽	53	24	24	1	4
福 建	65	24	26	12	3
江 西	100	39	51	7	3
山 东	26	6	7	8	5
河 南	53	25	16	6	6
湖 北	123	17	72	14	20
湖 南	84	35	31	12	6
广 东	149	48	58	17	26
广 西	91	55	32	2	2
海 南	4	2	1		1
重 庆	29	1	13	6	9
四 川	134	34	64	22	14
贵 州	53	21	28	3	1
云 南	39	13	20	4	2
西 藏					
陕 西	32	13	7	10	2
甘 肃	39	16	20	2	1
青 海	9	6	2		1
宁 夏	8	5	1	2	
新 疆	68	32	26	7	3

福利院

单位：个、人

年末职工人数	女性	受教育程度		职业资格水平	
		大学专科人数	大学本科及以上人数	助理社会工作师人数	社会工作师人数
42634	**26660**	**9820**	**8552**	**1246**	**1208**
1029	645	341	363	14	16
136	73	49	44	5	2
1032	658	267	209	22	37
442	245	122	86	4	13
864	453	340	193	10	37
1952	1110	473	542	42	110
1710	467	185	244	20	9
1642	876	246	253	19	12
1609	1202	278	259	51	48
3006	2069	660	920	152	154
2511	1678	457	393	59	64
1065	715	224	235	39	44
805	460	184	170	48	50
1349	671	267	121	14	7
736	420	210	269	89	50
1112	637	295	215	39	31
3062	1979	752	332	64	46
2918	1924	831	688	97	82
5887	4316	894	1174	208	125
2116	1592	549	289	56	71
206	150	43	22	4	1
1077	605	291	201	34	44
2289	1351	591	378	55	63
770	437	229	170	28	12
524	314	149	173	8	24
904	437	280	234	20	20
511	263	142	104	17	19
156	112	33	21	3	0
358	237	146	101	7	9
856	564	292	149	18	8

C－2－6续表1

地 区	按人员性质分		年龄结构			
	管理人员	专业技术技能人员	35岁及以下人数	36岁至45岁人数	46岁至55岁人数	56岁及以上人数
全 国	**14983**	**27651**	**12765**	**16113**	**11529**	**2227**
中央级						
北 京	293	736	387	311	292	39
天 津	29	107	59	38	30	9
河 北	281	751	410	341	226	55
山 西	171	271	112	153	158	19
内蒙古	389	475	245	323	260	36
辽 宁	866	1086	503	765	589	95
吉 林	818	892	498	804	359	49
黑龙江	811	831	390	735	467	50
上 海	322	1287	298	470	531	310
江 苏	502	2504	1013	907	924	162
浙 江	715	1796	526	895	790	300
安 徽	444	621	256	437	327	45
福 建	285	520	211	317	216	61
江 西	625	724	352	582	385	30
山 东	208	528	243	243	193	57
河 南	385	727	522	345	205	40
湖 北	942	2120	869	1200	832	161
湖 南	713	2205	1121	938	756	103
广 东	2291	3596	1374	2801	1529	183
广 西	687	1429	755	758	505	98
海 南	29	177	44	91	66	5
重 庆	489	588	301	295	402	79
四 川	1101	1188	798	833	558	100
贵 州	459	311	223	328	192	27
云 南	206	318	174	227	116	7
西 藏						
陕 西	301	603	332	268	250	54
甘 肃	216	295	195	217	83	16
青 海	44	112	82	42	25	7
宁 夏	104	254	154	128	71	5
新 疆	257	599	318	321	192	25

单位：人、人次、时、张、人天

志愿服务		年末床位数		年在院总人天数	年末在院人数	
志愿者服务人次数	志愿服务时间		光荣间床位			女性
108311	**281245.5**	**371193**	**12790**	**55327062**	**199726**	**72288**
		3168	69	382599	2801	1371
		700		182930	460	116
23	90.0	5671	26	1070540	3460	794
75	150.0	3905		880368	2431	896
150	150.0	10001	109	1294170	4139	1008
224	428.0	12809	484	2263285	8043	2839
		14440	92	2127970	8392	1794
200	1600.0	14078	497	2824937	9445	2946
96	192.0	7095		1666302	4780	3055
30038	85621.0	26764	252	2983781	10547	4547
7100	10954.0	28957	448	3905341	14209	6251
2049	7825.0	7628	403	1304491	4021	1620
20500	31002.0	11811	755	1221048	3706	1317
481	1559.0	16059	950	2556719	12310	3064
8832	22283.0	8523	215	1157677	3655	1140
1734	3607.0	9977	1000	1647206	5209	1470
7089	12425.0	34847	2488	4510551	18583	6927
2182	10007.0	17047	812	3531151	11379	4495
11908	28278.5	44918	1364	6267064	20949	10705
1355	3412.0	9769	570	1556932	6131	2346
		680		112415	391	167
2379	8130.0	12373	299	2020344	6512	2986
877	2563.0	30375	449	4368748	15596	4862
3842	10588.0	6260	285	860155	3242	838
4521	33022.0	7342	80	825461	4449	1095
1275	2196.0	6938	574	1491457	4282	953
762	1524.0	5521	46	491942	2624	624
7	50.0	1835	90	160550	679	199
		1159	50	232261	945	268
612	3589.0	10543	383	1428667	6356	1595

C-2-6续表2

地 区	在院人员按性质分			在院人员按年龄分		
	优抚对象	特困人员	自费人员	老人	青壮年	少年儿童
全 国	**6818**	**94931**	**86496**	**150333**	**22979**	**26414**
中央级						
北 京	13	877	1907	1723	817	261
天 津		396	108	205	255	
河 北	10	2189	404	1980	410	1070
山 西	1	1300	337	600	263	1568
内蒙古	320	2504	1368	3406	416	317
辽 宁	211	4133	3218	5674	1870	499
吉 林	445	2755	3127	6785	1347	260
黑龙江	269	4213	4613	8765	635	45
上 海	22	223	4414	4628	152	
江 苏	629	4491	5193	6991	1890	1666
浙 江	66	2460	11543	12328	977	904
安 徽	92	2337	1412	3009	494	518
福 建	235	2625	817	2249	457	1000
江 西	330	8191	3458	9120	430	2760
山 东	196	2337	986	2727	584	344
河 南	370	3996	305	2218	920	2071
湖 北	979	8569	8128	16711	1484	388
湖 南	573	5659	4811	6476	1935	2968
广 东	344	6300	12568	14866	1869	4214
广 西	45	2861	2916	3805	593	1733
海 南		391		49	85	257
重 庆	90	1975	4293	5576	706	230
四 川	315	8627	6141	13273	1283	1040
贵 州	211	2396	234	1830	450	962
云 南	33	3526	829	4119	179	151
西 藏						
陕 西	592	3195	293	2524	1259	499
甘 肃	52	2112	276	1972	167	485
青 海	33	446	195	485	175	19
宁 夏	30	380	413	634	261	50
新 疆	312	3467	2189	5605	616	135

单位：人、人次、平方米

在院人员按类型分			康复和医疗门诊人次数	家庭寄养儿童数量	机构建筑面积
自理（完全自理）	介助（半自理）	介护（不能自理）			
97297	**48510**	**53919**	**1828809**	**6980**	**10744788**
716	1008	1077	49643	2	148303
98	178	184	2491	118	11900
1288	960	1212	14142	325	232548
662	538	1231	2072	1572	154592
2165	1138	836	29692	23	301789
3890	1863	2290	22209	106	370841
5707	1889	796	25233	89	449537
6564	1551	1330	24772	1	387343
706	1372	2702	141101		260892
3523	2153	4871	116390	253	826629
6739	3004	4466	100513	260	569490
2020	755	1246	14201	189	305658
1686	766	1254	58819	355	352264
7906	3005	1399	2785	431	444817
1808	1032	815	39051		294395
1967	1609	1633	24047	167	309334
9459	5376	3748	130863	141	983240
4921	2723	3735	61840	1104	564762
6684	5217	9048	491548	408	1299906
1987	1597	2547	70584	508	384552
85	94	212	7314	8	22427
3167	1338	2007	99768	323	307767
9888	3785	1923	83866	103	672872
2275	647	320	86691	53	160638
2459	1111	879	12201	20	223790
1935	1581	766	11161	86	233335
1420	803	401	2314	51	134151
490	158	31	3243		18646
479	313	153	7616		43501
4603	946	807	92639	284	274868

C-2-6续表3

地　区	事业单位会计制度财务指标		
	固定资产原价	本年收入合计	本年支出合计
全　国	**1283713.2**	**737413.1**	**723139.0**
中央级			
北　京	63314.0	35128.4	33260.4
天　津	3428.8	3147.2	2971.2
河　北	26278.1	13138.7	13155.6
山　西	29753.5	15101.8	14191.0
内蒙古	45974.5	14168.9	13699.3
辽　宁	57130.3	35464.8	35173.8
吉　林	42317.8	17245.2	16357.9
黑龙江	53333.7	18536.8	17719.8
上　海	50478.4	41692.3	38862.9
江　苏	105294.8	73741.9	71233.8
浙　江	61173.1	51635.2	50158.2
安　徽	22003.9	10990.5	11135.6
福　建	25674.2	18674.9	17526.1
江　西	36239.7	11411.4	10684.0
山　东	22248.7	25153.9	25153.9
河　南	16150.9	15599.6	14980.2
湖　北	91593.0	39740.6	40035.2
湖　南	88548.0	55424.8	53492.4
广　东	135081.2	95048.9	94057.3
广　西	37550.1	21481.4	22063.5
海　南	4275.7	2611.2	2811.7
重　庆	29471.3	21996.8	24614.6
四　川	89377.1	37271.6	35499.0
贵　州	20531.9	8359.4	9545.8
云　南	28099.3	6555.3	5558.6
西　藏			
陕　西	34337.4	17703.4	18365.8
甘　肃	18950.6	13074.4	12480.2
青　海	4055.1	2867.5	2744.4
宁　夏	9612.6	6190.8	6337.9
新　疆	31435.5	8255.5	9268.9

单位：万元

民间非营利组织会计制度财务指标		
固定资产原价	本年收入合计	本年费用合计
51115.0	**7096.5**	**6090.8**
3653.0	33.0	1169.4
2113.7	16.0	6.0
1977.0	313.0	377.1
11.0	52.2	23.0
499.0	520.2	72.2
2066.3	3259.6	1430.3
200.0	200.0	40.0
0.0	12.8	12.8
388.0	399.0	374.2
610.0	78.0	78.0
333.0	21.2	18.0
5471.0	398.9	159.0
3508.0	176.0	14.0
6799.0	494.3	1034.0
650.0	10.8	1.4
9339.0	218.0	188.2
86.0	2.0	4.4
1450.0	294.5	240.5
907.0	433.0	652.0
11054.0	164.0	196.3

C-2-7 光荣

地 区	单位数	0～99张	100～299张	300～499张	500张以上
全 国	**1040**	**817**	**192**	**25**	**6**
中央级					
北 京	10	8	2		
天 津	6	3	3		
河 北	119	95	17	4	3
山 西	85	78	6	1	
内蒙古	27	23	4		
辽 宁	39	23	15	1	
吉 林	25	19	6		
黑龙江	8	4	3	1	
上 海					
江 苏	9	8	1		
浙 江	12	11	1		
安 徽	24	8	14	2	
福 建	25	21	3		1
江 西	174	124	42	8	
山 东	16	7	9		
河 南	43	36	6		1
湖 北	62	34	23	5	
湖 南	108	89	18	1	
广 东	42	39	3		
广 西	62	61	1		
海 南	9	9			
重 庆	7	6	1		
四 川	44	36	5	2	1
贵 州	45	42	3		
云 南	1	1			
西 藏					
陕 西	16	14	2		
甘 肃	1	1			
青 海					
宁 夏	2	2			
新 疆	19	15	4		

院

单位：个、人

年末职工人数	女性	受教育程度		职业资格水平	
		大学专科人数	大学本科及以上人数	助理社会工作师人数	社会工作师人数
9308	**4381**	**2267**	**1004**	**168**	**143**
176	81	46	67	5	
143	82	68	36	4	16
1552	781	288	80	10	4
746	303	240	88	3	18
292	122	107	57	1	1
468	240	160	147	27	5
431	95	84	41	2	9
143	56	17	6	2	
86	57	13	14	4	1
46	25	23	8	1	2
224	124	56	36	8	10
156	89	30	27	3	7
1047	327	80	23	27	26
159	96	49	24	9	6
431	230	110	18	3	0
870	486	266	82	14	5
899	424	221	100	28	16
354	211	64	31	11	8
247	138	59	25	3	1
59	26	14	2		
41	20	19	20	1	
251	120	92	32	1	5
193	89	86	19		2
6	1	3	1		1
133	75	45	7	1	
8	3	2			
4	4				
143	76	25	13		

C−2−7续表1

地　区	按人员性质分		年龄结构		
	管理人员	专业技术技能人员	35岁及以下人数	36岁至45岁人数	46岁至55岁人数
全　国	**4025**	**5283**	**2569**	**4101**	**2258**
中央级					
北　京	96	80	39	57	63
天　津	84	59	38	59	44
河　北	361	1191	490	728	286
山　西	300	446	193	359	158
内蒙古	102	190	76	106	104
辽　宁	227	241	154	201	93
吉　林	242	189	121	198	105
黑龙江	58	85	54	70	19
上　海					
江　苏	24	62	15	34	20
浙　江	18	28	5	21	17
安　徽	70	154	46	101	62
福　建	65	91	38	70	43
江　西	637	410	233	434	316
山　东	39	120	72	56	28
河　南	173	258	149	195	76
湖　北	357	513	219	398	221
湖　南	362	537	233	391	237
广　东	180	174	109	138	99
广　西	130	117	58	103	75
海　南	39	20	9	23	21
重　庆	27	14	14	14	13
四　川	155	96	73	119	43
贵　州	145	48	44	103	43
云　南	1	5	2	2	2
西　藏					
陕　西	89	44	49	54	24
甘　肃	8			1	7
青　海					
宁　夏	2	2	1		2
新　疆	34	109	35	66	37

单位：人、人次、人天、张、时

56岁及以上人数	志愿服务		年末床位数		年在院总人天数
	志愿者服务人次数	志愿服务时间		光荣间床位	
380	**17021**	**40130**	**74558**	**28479**	**10830734**
17	27	111	660	594	46377
2	300	600	670	460	120250
48	717	746	10288	2965	1227022
36	524	1276	3754	1866	441453
6			1699	671	324136
20	760	760	3284	1266	427871
7			2283	135	409448
			898	571	177121
17	134	553	470	265	84540
3	4500	6450	555	154	37761
15	218	387	2816	1518	329779
5			1713	634	189472
64	263	846	15653	5715	2802537
3	4303	11934	1290	0	195089
11	52	240	3030	1341	403746
32	1408	4746	7250	3167	1041713
38	1724	6501	7047	3281	1198223
8	5	10	1647	544	164274
11	70	143	2187	916	230985
6	45	130	329	127	26047
	814	2088	400	103	54058
16	42	172	3736	1332	392716
3	971	1949	1132	205	134256
	36	208	80		10800
6	68	160	709	415	157960
0			20		260
0					
1			25	15	3620
5	40	120	933	219	199220

C-2-7续表2

地区	年末在院人数	女性	在院人员按性质分 优抚对象	特困人员	自费人员
全国	**41652**	**7305**	**21902**	**13806**	**5233**
中央级					
北京	127	28	100	22	24
天津	352	105	123	5	118
河北	3680	421	2324	1014	259
山西	1603	43	1248	314	57
内蒙古	931	61	752	43	104
辽宁	1490	293	754	272	412
吉林	1660	453	648	476	478
黑龙江	692	50	369	97	225
上海					
江苏	290	78	263	2	32
浙江	124		63		
安徽	915	70	811	102	11
福建	524	85	294	142	94
江西	13747	2909	4793	7889	918
山东	630	62	630		
河南	1883	126	1212	532	149
湖北	4389	950	2115	1442	744
湖南	3941	810	2640	751	600
广东	616	92	336	153	77
广西	768	164	467	31	189
海南	130	33	59	10	10
重庆	189	12	178	2	9
四川	1324	144	988	178	195
贵州	484	79	119	217	142
云南	30	11	21		
西藏					
陕西	463	14	425	36	
甘肃	14		1	13	
青海					
宁夏	10	2	5		
新疆	646	210	164	63	386

单位：人、人次、平方米

在院人员按年龄分			在院人员按类型分			康复和医疗门诊人次数	机构建筑面积
老人	青壮年	少年儿童	自理(完全自理)	介助(半自理)	介护(不能自理)		
40004	**904**	**744**	**31832**	**7678**	**2142**	**124163**	**2413713**
125	2		58	43	26	3565	35142
351	1		163	153	36	1950	28772
3582	82	16	2731	715	234	14995	344898
1566	8	29	1221	316	66	4547	164814
926	3	2	715	191	25		64594
1196	236	58	1068	259	163	19246	81532
1553	107		1225	318	117	4280	70556
692			662	5	25		22269
286	2	2	221	64	5	1080	42590
99		25	57	53	14	777	13153
908	1	6	738	156	21	4884	88215
520		4	386	121	17	571	43365
13037	242	468	11400	2213	134	497	301500
630			504	110	16	1672	46543
1842	15	26	1419	317	147	13013	206416
4277	81	31	3231	809	349	28060	203903
3900	13	28	2787	838	316	7065	302515
589	16	11	435	114	67	439	90693
768			445	181	142	1204	64912
120		10	97	8	25	700	11817
188	1		156	27	6	7945	13865
1313	5	6	975	300	49	4253	69504
425	56	3	415	53	16	2977	15090
25		5	21	3	6		500
459	4		332	92	39	408	54701
1		13		1	13		500
10				7	3		500
616	29	1	370	211	65	35	30854

C–2–7续表3

地 区	事业单位会计制度财务指标		
	固定资产原价	本年收入合计	本年支出合计
全 国	**190691.8**	**73825.4**	**75470.2**
中央级			
北 京	7908.0	4370.9	4200.3
天 津	3885.2	3218.7	3244.5
河 北	32294.7	10406.9	10426.3
山 西	12496.8	8083.7	8327.0
内蒙古	8415.1	3937.5	4326.4
辽 宁	14250.2	4981.5	5296.0
吉 林	3769.5	1464.7	1502.3
黑龙江	4694.6	1383.2	1397.0
上 海			
江 苏	3814.8	779.7	779.7
浙 江	533.6	844.0	752.3
安 徽	9270.5	2748.5	2921.5
福 建	2260.2	1553.0	1625.7
江 西	16274.0	3058.2	3072.1
山 东	2604.8	1420.1	1420.1
河 南	4921.8	1739.9	1717.5
湖 北	22037.6	6916.7	6798.1
湖 南	19312.6	6594.9	6326.2
广 东	5199.8	3009.8	2961.2
广 西	4135.7	1020.5	1056.1
海 南	784.4	274.4	250.3
重 庆	1636.0	1037.5	1037.5
四 川	4688.7	2186.9	1927.3
贵 州	283.0	37.6	37.6
云 南	100.0		
西 藏			
陕 西	1544.0	2045.3	2045.3
甘 肃	107.2	90.0	90.0
青 海			
宁 夏	3.0		
新 疆	3466.0	621.3	1931.9

单位：万元

民间非营利组织会计制度财务指标		
固定资产原价	本年收入合计	本年费用合计
1808.1	**488.0**	**502.4**
17.0	35.0	35.0
9.8	21.0	20.4
424.7	101.5	102.5
127.0	84.0	84.0
60.0	34.5	34.5
1.0	50.0	
50.0	30.0	30.0
130.0	15.0	16.5
988.6	117.0	179.5

C-2-8 荣誉军人

地　区	单位数	编制登记	一个机构多块牌子	0～99张	100～299张	300～499张	500张以上
全　国	**44**	**41**	**3**	**12**	**17**	**9**	**6**
中央级							
北　京							
天　津							
河　北	1	1			1		
山　西	5	5		3	2		
内蒙古	1	1			1		
辽　宁	1	1				1	
吉　林	2	2			1	1	
黑龙江	1	1				1	
上　海	1	1		1			
江　苏	1	1			1		
浙　江	1	1					1
安　徽	1	1			1		
福　建	1	1			1		
江　西	1	1					1
山　东	2	2				2	
河　南	4	4		2	1	1	
湖　北	1	1					1
湖　南	3	2	1		1		2
广　东	2	2			2		
广　西	1	1			1		
海　南							
重　庆	3	3		2		1	
四　川	5	3	2	1	2	1	1
贵　州	3	3		2	1		
云　南	1	1			1		
西　藏							
陕　西	1	1				1	
甘　肃							
青　海							
宁　夏							
新　疆	1	1		1			

康复疗养院

单位：个、人

年末职工人数	女性	受教育程度		职业资格水平		按人员性质分	
		大学专科人数	大学本科及以上人数	助理社会工作师人数	社会工作师人数	管理人员	专业技术技能人员
5916	**3394**	**1546**	**2382**	**41**	**76**	**968**	**4948**
212	110	36	133	4	1	61	151
215	105	22	38	1	4	34	181
70	36	18	36	1	4	17	53
159	87	29	58		3	21	138
425	207					126	299
126	28					28	98
39	19	19	18		4	7	32
264	190	82	105		3	53	211
722	512	137	390		1	11	711
129	56	41	57		1	19	110
54	29	18	21	2	1	2	52
289	176	76	163	2	9	17	272
553	280	69	361	5	15	138	415
465	281	137	148		2	37	428
332	182	78	163	4	3	26	306
531	324	210	259	2	3	74	457
221	123	92	99	7	17	95	126
45	21	21	20	5	2	8	37
154	86	86	16	6	2	53	101
437	289	193	155	1	1	37	400
152	95	41	56			63	89
101	48	35	24	1		18	83
192	92	91	49			17	175
29	18	15	13			6	23

C-2-8续表1

地 区	年龄结构				志愿服务	
	35岁及以下人数	36岁至45岁人数	46岁至55岁人数	56岁及以上人数	志愿者服务人次数	志愿服务时间
全 国	**2331**	**1601**	**1583**	**401**	**426**	**852**
中央级						
北 京						
天 津						
河 北	83	57	48	24		
山 西	60	82	66	7		
内蒙古	21	19	23	7		
辽 宁	32	62	55	10		
吉 林	175	90	80	80		
黑龙江	43	47	36			
上 海	21	12	4	2		
江 苏	157	38	47	22		
浙 江	454	102	91	75	426	852
安 徽	44	27	43	15		
福 建	20	16	11	7		
江 西	103	43	128	15		
山 东	200	169	151	33		
河 南	103	148	197	17		
湖 北	79	136	94	23		
湖 南	246	178	99	8		
广 东	60	91	64	6		
广 西	5	16	21	3		
海 南						
重 庆	82	25	39	8		
四 川	224	104	97	12		
贵 州	34	36	73	9		
云 南	34	32	33	2		
西 藏						
陕 西	48	65	68	11		
甘 肃						
青 海						
宁 夏						
新 疆	3	6	15	5		

单位：人、人次、张、人天、时

年末床位数	光荣间床位	年在院总人天数	年末在院人数	女性	在院人员按性质分 优抚对象	特困人员	自费人员
11113	**1841**	**1831938**	**6308**	**1819**	**2047**	**602**	**2579**
200		72000	200	67	71		129
485	109	72019	214	37	115	8	91
100	23	7180	19		19		
493	72	60155	148	35	72		76
600		350	300				
440		19710	54		54		
50	50	5110	14		14		
220	40	65334	191		19	172	
690	30	244999	673	350	35	5	633
200		11315	31	8	17		
250	100	38500	100	35	18		82
750		80000	628	89	393	20	215
800		127970	193	31	96		97
685	144	95482	296	87	146	30	149
528	200	160312	216	89	35		181
1537	240	343550	1261	412	96	231	263
487	35	35019	285	140	30		225
230	20	70014	189	98	17		63
503	190	45270	167	50	114	1	52
1110	298	169299	696	193	512	96	103
305	32	69514	212	45	19	20	173
100	58	1850	46		46		
300	200	36621	167	53	101	19	47
50		365	8		8		

C-2-8续表2

地区	在院人员按年龄分			在院人员按类型分		
	老人	青壮年	少年儿童	自理(完全自理)	介助(半自理)	介护(不能自理)
全国	**3965**	**2161**	**182**	**2402**	**2361**	**1545**
中央级						
北京						
天津						
河北	195	5		28	93	79
山西	76	38	100	106	108	
内蒙古	9	10			9	10
辽宁	88	60			46	102
吉林	300			200	100	
黑龙江	54			54		
上海	14					14
江苏	181	10			10	181
浙江	405	268		215	458	
安徽	19	12			31	
福建	100			17	18	65
江西	351	273	4	489	113	26
山东	163	30		164	19	10
河南	186	102	8	166	85	45
湖北	125	85	6	168	32	16
湖南	373	846	42	90	824	347
广东	262	23		48	30	207
广西	180	9		9		180
海南						
重庆	161	6		96	7	64
四川	482	192	22	359	231	106
贵州	53	159		102	60	50
云南	46			5	34	7
西藏						
陕西	141	26		86	45	36
甘肃						
青海						
宁夏						
新疆	1	7			8	

单位：万元

康复和医疗门诊人次数	机构建筑面积	事业单位会计制度财务指标		
		固定资产原价	本年收入合计	本年支出合计
1194538.0	**932107.0**	**259846.2**	**178103.3**	**189244.3**
53257.0	5000.0	5417.0	4653.0	4632.0
14766.0	44431.0	2613.4	6363.8	5982.8
7050.0	11363.0	3855.2	1658.5	1532.9
10000.0	42448.0	7513.8	3561.7	3304.9
	60000.0	2540.9		
	3000.0	560.0	575.0	575.0
	3556.0	1041.5	2481.5	2044.3
108372.0	47676.0	10752.1	7128.3	8755.8
195256.0	25355.0	14381.0	27668.0	31467.0
24306.0	14077.0	5497.0	4946.0	5075.0
2381.0	67680.0	2469.2	1673.7	1547.6
15008.0	40043.0	4145.6	6721.7	12636.4
39367.0	81100.0	87816.4	16165.1	16635.8
46535.0	64223.0	10674.0	4016.9	9789.5
125372.0	72042.0	29873.0	18822.1	15872.0
110535.0	68275.0	13288.2	16461.3	14929.4
123862.0	31500.0	13257.7	13125.9	13269.5
12440.0	15239.0	5287.5	3806.9	5232.0
29342.0	31494.0	2790.1	3463.2	4084.7
234877.0	66510.0	19132.6	19975.1	19663.3
2575.0	68315.0	5563.3	4424.9	3938.7
	21953.0	1868.4	4565.8	1717.5
39237.0	31724.0	7807.5	5837.6	5449.4
	15,103	1,700.8	7.3	1,108.8

C-2-9 复员军人

地 区	单位数	0～99张	100～299张	300～499张	500张以上	年末职工人数	女性
全 国	**38**	**13**	**15**	**6**	**4**	**3029**	**1674**
中央级							
北 京							
天 津	1			1		109	59
河 北	8	2	4	1	1	853	506
山 西	2	1		1		283	161
内蒙古	1		1			5	2
辽 宁	1				1	236	106
吉 林							
黑龙江							
上 海							
江 苏	4	3	1			83	42
浙 江							
安 徽							
福 建							
江 西	2	1	1			11	4
山 东	7	2	3	1	1	866	486
河 南	2		1		1	70	36
湖 北	1		1			7	3
湖 南	1		1			110	35
广 东	2		2			145	75
广 西	1	1				16	9
海 南							
重 庆							
四 川	2	1		1		42	28
贵 州							
云 南							
西 藏							
陕 西	3	2		1		193	122
甘 肃							
青 海							
宁 夏							
新 疆							

疗养院

单位：个、人

受教育程度		职业资格水平		按人员性质分	
大学专科人数	大学本科及以上人数	助理社会工作师人数	社会工作师人数	管理人员	专业技术技能人员
922	**1453**	**45**	**83**	**551**	**2478**
18	52		1	17	92
212	436	4	14	103	750
38	179	3	3	84	199
				3	2
73	83	5	3	74	162
37	19	3	12	12	71
1	1			5	6
307	440	23	39	131	735
14	20			36	34
4				7	
60	45			15	95
58	69	4	9	34	111
4	6			7	9
29	6			6	36
67	97	3	2	17	176

C-2-9续表1

地区	年龄结构				志愿服务	
	35岁及以下人数	36岁至45岁人数	46岁至55岁人数	56岁及以上人数	志愿者服务人次数	志愿服务时间
全国	**1113**	**846**	**833**	**237**	**2091**	**6160**
中央级						
北京						
天津	51	6	44	8		
河北	261	284	232	76		
山西	88	100	79	16		
内蒙古			5			
辽宁	42	56	123	15		
吉林						
黑龙江						
上海						
江苏	22	24	24	13	430	1170
浙江						
安徽						
福建						
江西	1	5	5			
山东	368	208	213	77	1601	4670
河南	37	12	15	6		
湖北	4	3				
湖南	65	40	5			
广东	30	64	47	4		
广西	7	1	6	2		
海南						
重庆						
四川	18	15	9		37	176
贵州						
云南					18	104
西藏						
陕西	119	28	26	20	5	40
甘肃						
青海						
宁夏						
新疆						

单位：张、人天、人、人次、时

年末床位数		年在院总人天数	年末在院人数		在院人员按性质分		
	光荣间床位			女性	优抚对象	特困人员	自费人员
7469	**1117**	**1499847**	**4410**	**744**	**2546**	**363**	**1186**
300		78840	216	13	158		58
1673	343	423490	1058	217	455	85	460
450		112635	196	5	118		78
120	21	5175	15		15		
560		202066	560	103	234	74	252
340	193	79946	253	12	189	21	43
180		7052	135	85	50	85	
1595		280918	1008	134	819	40	34
710	115	33945	193	33	93		
150	45	1720	35	4	10		25
100		10213	88	32		38	50
339	100	96581	228	79	125		61
56		8000	56	4	56		
330	50	29234	89		24		65
566	250	130032	280	23	200	20	60

C-2-9续表2

地区	在院人员按年龄分			在院人员按类型分		
	老人	青壮年	少年儿童	自理（完全自理）	介助（半自理）	介护（不能自理）
全国	**3248**	**1121**	**41**	**3176**	**784**	**450**
中央级						
北京						
天津	76	140		190	26	
河北	820	234	4	624	165	269
山西	179	17		104	50	42
内蒙古	15			1	14	
辽宁	157	403		440	101	19
吉林						
黑龙江						
上海						
江苏	233	9	11	241	9	3
浙江						
安徽						
福建						
江西	125		10	60	75	
山东	861	142	5	840	123	45
河南	173	20		140	20	33
湖北	30	5		35		
湖南	58	20	10	45	38	5
广东	108	120		206	15	7
广西	56			56		
海南						
重庆						
四川	89			19	69	1
贵州						
云南						
西藏						
陕西	268	11	1	175	79	26
甘肃						
青海						
宁夏						
新疆						

单位：人、人次、平方米、万元

康复和医疗门诊人次数	机构建筑面积	事业单位会计制度财务指标		
		固定资产原价	本年收入合计	本年支出合计
638218.0	**393814.0**	**128207.0**	**82019.3**	**84803.5**
41758.0	15000.0	9725.7	733.6	1134.0
125993.0	80558.0	33978.9	22689.0	22683.3
16323.0	31769.0	18132.7	6363.8	5125.6
	4869.0	529.8	40.0	40.0
21684.0	36318.0	12468.5	5661.8	5892.4
117901.0	18401.0	3881.0	2217.6	2235.8
	800.0	341.0	254.6	142.0
78904.0	85950.0	20518.3	26354.6	30257.7
	29751.0	1400.8	1172.7	1169.6
	14000.0	284.0	88.8	79.9
2652.0	8000.0	900.0	760.0	760.0
216828.0	26805.0	9149.8	8673.7	8588.1
56.0	4922.0	686.9	845.4	841.5
9048.0	1850.0	126.0	56.0	31.0
7071.0	34821.0	16083.6	6107.7	5822.6

C-2-10 军休

地 区	单位数	0～99张	100～299张	300～499张
全 国	**1577**	**1252**	**220**	**52**
中央级				
北 京	138	33	53	28
天 津	17	12	1	1
河 北	110	106	3	1
山 西	68	65	3	
内蒙古	21	18	3	
辽 宁	46	21	3	8
吉 林				
黑龙江	37	29	6	1
上 海				
江 苏	129	96	30	2
浙 江	40	35	5	
安 徽	36	30	6	
福 建	50	44	6	
江 西	16	12	3	1
山 东	152	119	22	5
河 南	104	91	13	
湖 北	101	89	9	2
湖 南	102	91	9	1
广 东	76	66	9	1
广 西	35	35		
海 南	8	8		
重 庆				
四 川	118	101	17	
贵 州	14	12	2	
云 南	46	37	6	1
西 藏				
陕 西	68	66	2	
甘 肃	24	22	2	
青 海	2	1	1	
宁 夏	6	5	1	
新 疆	13	8	5	

所

单位：个、人

500张以上	年末职工人数	女性	受教育程度	
			大学专科人数	大学本科及以上人数
53	**15195**	**6982**	**5309**	**6430**
24	1846	1024	626	982
3	241	106	53	131
	1142	485	334	380
	505	223	165	227
	242	86	101	103
14	919	429	347	418
1	338	113	130	153
1	1075	552	355	495
	211	85	71	77
	274	104	96	117
	394	176	72	212
	149	61	63	48
6	1707	697	644	745
	971	435	320	302
1	797	381	348	271
1	837	374	309	305
	691	348	221	341
	225	105	90	97
	121	53	41	29
	643	313	306	220
	119	47	33	48
2	416	180	153	134
	698	312	253	235
	373	183	89	237
	39	16	10	24
	49	22	8	33
	173	72	71	66

C−2−10续表1

地　区	职业资格水平		按人员性质分	
	助理社会工作师人数	社会工作师人数	管理人员	专业技术技能人员
全　国	**437**	**498**	**9135**	**6060**
中央级				
北　京	87	70	1435	411
天　津	12	14	113	128
河　北	18	32	490	652
山　西	7	13	306	199
内蒙古	6	9	139	103
辽　宁	16	13	440	479
吉　林				
黑龙江	2	7	254	84
上　海				
江　苏	34	68	669	406
浙　江	10	4	153	58
安　徽	8	23	205	69
福　建	13	17	287	107
江　西		4	105	44
山　东	90	93	635	1072
河　南	9	13	499	472
湖　北	13	14	506	291
湖　南	15	27	492	345
广　东	20	18	545	146
广　西	1	6	155	70
海　南	7	1	92	29
重　庆				
四　川	32	16	461	182
贵　州	1	2	85	34
云　南	6	6	257	159
西　藏				
陕　西	6	9	402	296
甘　肃	18	14	307	66
青　海			17	22
宁　夏	3	1	21	28
新　疆	3	4	65	108

单位：人、人次、时

年龄结构				志愿服务	
35岁及以下人数	36岁至45岁人数	46岁至55岁人数	56岁及以上人数	志愿者服务人次数	志愿服务时间
4622	**5336**	**4251**	**986**	**11506**	**29303**
587	718	478	63	16	34
65	63	95	18	222	488
471	357	260	54	10	10
132	168	163	42	184	726
75	53	92	22		
302	250	242	125		
88	106	118	26		
275	378	350	72	605	1964
36	67	91	17	2490	3904
61	100	92	21	90	210
136	146	85	27		
43	60	35	11	245	842
395	638	563	111	5509	13452
374	314	224	59	150	472
178	307	242	70	117	283
294	324	171	48	1050	4100
174	318	171	28	19	152
60	86	65	14		
42	46	23	10		
205	247	169	22	13	58
44	31	35	9	68	110
96	144	140	36	3	6
239	217	193	49	475	1052
190	109	59	15		
11	12	13	3		
9	20	18	2	240	1440
40	57	64	12		

C-2-10续表2

地 区	执行事业单位会计制度		
	固定资产原价	本年收入合计	本年支出合计
全 国	**374075.8**	**2369600.3**	**2171481.5**
中央级			
北 京	15588.4	365480.5	218465.4
天 津	19897.6	65239.6	61643.7
河 北	28693.5	154014.8	135164.3
山 西	11045.4	48851.8	51136.3
内蒙古	8739.7	33700.9	33732.0
辽 宁	36444.6	190808.2	184049.4
吉 林			
黑龙江	13644.3	36626.5	35246.0
上 海			
江 苏	28325.0	198960.5	196700.6
浙 江	7400.7	28783.8	26616.0
安 徽	7654.9	38981.4	40222.0
福 建	6948.0	68926.3	55582.6
江 西	2443.7	13647.1	13201.3
山 东	33877.6	330449.3	330555.5
河 南	10237.7	82824.3	85019.8
湖 北	15307.0	133819.7	133245.6
湖 南	21105.4	80276.0	70450.2
广 东	21847.2	98555.2	105724.4
广 西	7271.2	26970.7	25569.9
海 南	3852.8	22413.6	19761.5
重 庆			
四 川	17088.8	55346.8	53808.3
贵 州	3226.9	13579.0	14372.7
云 南	21157.8	44484.7	43295.0
西 藏			
陕 西	18118.7	147031.2	151125.8
甘 肃	6606.3	50255.0	47875
青 海	491.5	6505.6	7274.6
宁 夏	1255.5	10569.2	10329.5
新 疆	5805.6	22498.6	21314.5

单位：万元、户、人

机构内的户数	分散安置户数	年末机构管理军休干部人数	分散安置人数	本年发放离退休金
164677	**45615**	**181316**	**48504**	**1653252.2**
42439	2373	44096	2541	183998.5
4232	1671	5372	1500	36535.8
6666	6341	10249	7100	116695.9
3389	1805	3876	1970	37943.6
1535	1018	2075	1085	23816.8
17482	13	17675	246	121125.5
		3		
2663	327	2750	565	33615.7
11731	2995	12936	3281	164640.4
1460	152	1447	141	17078.7
2373	631	2943	765	31315.2
3984	1519	3628	1871	48753.7
1771	54	1982	35	7504.1
20103	5632	18707	6596	226618.6
4798	1614	5879	1646	62995.1
8071	3271	8189	2894	99409.9
5212	585	5044	1185	53995.1
5866	3887	7432	4223	78601.7
1255	503	1311	497	17443.2
879	546	809	533	14507.2
4855	808	4673	822	45964.6
938	486	1103	526	15109.9
4973	1379	5014	531	37007.9
3503	5065	8626	5045	110547.3
2584	2363	3288	2331	42082.1
219	145	321	147	5003.2
351	19	828	11	8203.1
1345	413	1060	417	12739.4

C-2-11 智障与精神疾病

地 区	单位数	单位数按登记类型分			单位数按床位数量分	
		编制登记	民政登记	一个机构多块牌子	0～99张	100～299张
全 国	**244**	**221**	**4**	**19**	**41**	**83**
中央级						
北 京	1	1			1	
天 津	2	2				
河 北	2	2				
山 西	8	8				6
内蒙古	7	7				4
辽 宁	3	3			2	1
吉 林	14	10		4	3	1
黑龙江	8	8				1
上 海	3	3				
江 苏	11	11				3
浙 江	3	3				1
安 徽	4	4			2	1
福 建	17	17			1	8
江 西	3	2		1	2	
山 东	12	12				4
河 南	6	6			2	1
湖 北	12	12				2
湖 南	17	15		2	2	7
广 东	12	12			1	6
广 西	8	8				2
海 南						
重 庆	9	9			5	1
四 川	26	21		5	6	7
贵 州	27	22		5	13	8
云 南	5	5				3
西 藏						
陕 西	4	4				2
甘 肃	5	5				4
青 海	1	1				1
宁 夏	1			1		
新 疆	13	8	4	1	1	9

服务机构总表

单位：个、人

		年末职工人数		年末职工人数按登记类型分		受教育程度	
300～499张	500张以上		女性	编制登记	民政登记	大学专科人数	大学本科及以上人数
55	**65**	**28095**	**16260**	**27057**	**179**	**9051**	**9692**
		173	140	173		60	68
1	1	364	165	364		65	69
	2	522	281	522		86	260
1	1	2094	640	2094		391	377
2	1	534	278	534		209	192
		98	63	98		18	11
2	8	1414	719	951		174	214
1	6	1202	478	1202		256	407
1	2	541	363	541		175	178
3	5	1717	1105	1717		472	849
1	1	160	104	160		20	76
	1	458	320	458		183	145
7	1	1164	733	1164		407	271
1		152	97	152		64	50
8		1708	1072	1708		493	912
2	1	1024	617	1024		371	482
4	6	2742	1698	2742		735	1409
3	5	1889	1252	1643		679	522
3	2	1568	885	1568		618	545
3	3	1752	1234	1752		702	582
	3	482	250	482		161	198
5	8	3289	1941	3225		1509	984
2	4	776	436	690		370	166
	2	379	223	379		142	162
1	1	360	169	360		130	116
1		394	241	394		83	182
		223	159	223		121	70
1		122	76	122		48	28
2	1	794	521	615	179	309	167

C-2-11续表1

地 区	职业资格水平		按人员性质分		年龄	
	助理社会工作师人数	社会工作师人数	管理人员	专业技术技能人员	35岁及以下人数	36岁至45岁人数
全 国	**382**	**298**	**4790**	**23305**	**12876**	**8059**
中央级						
北 京			10	163	52	78
天 津	3		92	272	114	72
河 北	4	6	71	451	147	182
山 西	3	7	129	1965	1356	407
内蒙古	3	10	85	449	182	139
辽 宁	1		95	3	22	46
吉 林	2		520	894	398	632
黑龙江	68	6	367	835	451	340
上 海	18	12	122	419	267	103
江 苏	26	28	147	1570	665	504
浙 江	2	5	27	133	62	35
安 徽	1	1	111	347	234	116
福 建	20	19	186	978	577	314
江 西	5	7	49	103	54	43
山 东	63	51	240	1468	718	433
河 南	7	23	105	919	408	331
湖 北	18	16	287	2455	1382	733
湖 南	15	12	316	1573	764	684
广 东	53	22	257	1311	658	571
广 西	11	14	183	1569	941	428
海 南						
重 庆	7	15	92	390	189	157
四 川	20	16	658	2631	1983	696
贵 州	3	3	237	539	235	286
云 南	3	3	117	262	171	119
西 藏						
陕 西	5	4	62	298	126	86
甘 肃	1	4	56	338	182	139
青 海			53	170	136	55
宁 夏	5	9	9	113	53	56
新 疆	15	5	107	687	349	274

单位：人、人次、时、张

结构		志愿服务		年末床位数	光荣间床位	床位按登记类型分	
46岁至55岁人数	56岁及以上人数	志愿者服务人次数	志愿服务时间			编制登记	民政登记
5892	**1268**	**13668**	**29950**	**81951**	**1726**	**81618**	**333**
39	4			150		150	
124	54			957		957	
148	45			1129		1129	
289	42	2	2	1970	280	1970	
173	40			2110	27	2110	
25	5	100		390	25	390	
340	44			5500		5500	
359	52			4702		4702	
108	63	1471	2943	1800		1800	
448	100	1480	3160	6456	10	6456	
59	4	6100	12200	1200		1200	
61	47	120	545	865		865	
219	54			4402	67	4402	
45	10	132	528	410		410	
468	89	3030	7000	3617		3617	
247	38	101	300	1926	2	1926	
524	103			5806	252	5806	
395	46			4671	224	4671	
282	57	14	70	4594	5	4594	
310	73	50	300	3604	218	3604	
111	25	485	1582	2381		2381	
483	127	50	100	11433	9	11433	
195	60	200	401	3804	77	3804	
72	17	18	104	2031		2031	
123	25	30	30	1260	360	1260	
66	7			1051	110	1051	
16	16			260		260	
13				450		450	
150	21	285	685	3022	60	2689	333

C-2-11续表2

地区	年在院总人天数	年末在院人数		在院人数按登记类型分	
			女性	编制登记	民政登记
全国	**20547541**	**67751**	**19377**	**67446**	**305**
中央级					
北京	47820	30	14	30	
天津	300760	844	226	844	
河北	349569	979	175	979	
山西	554205	1653	200	1653	
内蒙古	569778	1708	486	1708	
辽宁	100190	322	63	322	
吉林	793136	3087	722	3087	
黑龙江	1157231	3593	992	3593	
上海	614873	1678	478	1678	
江苏	1652185	5571	1552	5571	
浙江	271385	749	287	749	
安徽	230647	682	111	682	
福建	1054108	3994	1063	3994	
江西	77987	354	5	354	
山东	753195	2931	458	2931	
河南	613538	1812	614	1812	
湖北	1369192	4531	1671	4531	
湖南	977168	3673	1171	3673	
广东	1355850	4076	1092	4076	
广西	1086540	3432	1073	3432	
海南					
重庆	664164	2141	714	2141	
四川	3340844	10622	3642	10622	
贵州	765293	2877	743	2877	
云南	318885	1454	408	1454	
西藏					
陕西	327906	1048	292	1048	
甘肃	167970	463	160	463	
青海	78840	216	98	216	
宁夏	126317	428	190	428	
新疆	827965	2803	677	2498	305

单位：人天、人

在院人员按性质分			在院人员按年龄分		
优抚对象	特困人员	自费人员	老人	青壮年	少年儿童
10151	**18629**	**26611**	**23668**	**42649**	**1434**
		4	15	1	14
157	260	403	228	616	
566	90	323	448	529	2
550	331	762	550	1074	29
126	367	1046	231	1471	6
69	164	89	112	210	
663	1189	342	1287	1800	
93	2600	650	1164	2408	21
46	113	903	535	1143	
906	2310	2072	2293	3267	11
97	47	422	335	409	5
334	43	189	273	405	4
371	960	2132	1005	2965	24
18	131	205	108	246	
1503	245	754	1879	1029	23
279	142	1168	283	1482	47
833	958	2268	1109	3249	173
558	617	1585	1366	1795	512
724	1129	1027	1799	2073	204
261	516	2004	1023	2386	23
61	657	1404	944	1190	7
853	2417	4163	3897	6586	139
52	724	714	721	2036	120
141	738	96	281	1173	
436	332	295	519	521	8
90	283	44	141	314	8
175	18	23	155	57	4
30	221	177	156	257	15
159	1027	1347	811	1957	35

C-2-11续表3

地区	在院人员按类型分			康复和医疗门诊人次数
	自理（完全自理）	介助（半自理）	介护（不能自理）	
全国	**35226**	**24660**	**7865**	**3502960**
中央级				
北京	5	7	18	17389
天津	797	47		72016
河北	488	461	30	71548
山西	1076	533	44	68127
内蒙古	971	636	101	72680
辽宁	268	31	23	
吉林	1535	1460	92	90294
黑龙江	1711	1142	740	466124
上海	690	988		7213
江苏	3139	1928	504	167103
浙江	466	210	73	
安徽	538	98	46	77629
福建	2447	1180	367	376268
江西	152	185	17	
山东	2250	506	175	75855
河南	531	526	755	269614
湖北	2318	1939	274	523221
湖南	1561	1285	827	250648
广东	1776	1727	573	103415
广西	1370	1556	506	243519
海南				
重庆	1169	721	251	57103
四川	4612	4214	1796	258187
贵州	2012	665	200	36914
云南	541	791	122	19809
西藏				
陕西	712	265	71	29579
甘肃	211	205	47	84556
青海	211	5		88
宁夏	73	257	98	7560
新疆	1596	1092	115	56501

单位：人、人次、平方米、万元

机构建筑面积	事业单位会计制度财务指标		
	固定资产原价	本年收入合计	本年支出合计
3370955	**595925.7**	**718319.8**	**662103.8**
7993	6537.6	13209.8	12820.3
11677	8317.5	15508.1	11535.4
32318	20780.3	12749.8	10832.9
156406	26510.9	20032.8	17803.9
77922	5243.5	21324.6	19440.2
8750	103.0	424.9	414.9
112067	14363.9	14501.7	13373.8
144574	29892.7	15920.2	20383.3
83562	19039.0	24458.6	19491.1
214501	68523.0	72286.9	61042.5
47000	9269.6	11600.0	10339.5
26380	5305.5	3074.7	3164.9
172125	19429.0	32025.5	27872.8
22516	3128.0	3184.7	3153.2
181636	35850.7	46069.0	46069.0
96266	15801.5	27645.2	26232.7
249916	53279.9	68250.4	64427.5
131358	24662.4	43815.1	42142.4
326509	32958.5	42149.4	40188.5
390086	32399.5	42929.3	41242.5
94440	9314.9	17001.7	16823.6
315130	76175.0	91647.0	86500.8
121233	9612.7	12940.2	13711.1
97853	21099.1	8354.1	6513.3
74237	13578.7	8420.5	10142.1
26071	6335	14366	6025.3
16830	4563.1	4256.5	3926.2
6200	1022.3	2413.0	2334.5
125399	22829.1	27760.0	24155.6

C-2-12 福利类

地区	单位数	编制登记	一个机构多块牌子	0～99张	100～299张	300～499张	500张以上
全国	**150**	**142**	**8**	**33**	**47**	**27**	**43**
中央级							
北京	1	1		1			
天津	1	1					1
河北							
山西	1	1			1		
内蒙古	5	5			3	2	
辽宁	1	1		1			
吉林	7	7		1			6
黑龙江	7	7				1	6
上海	3	3				1	2
江苏	10	10			3	3	4
浙江	2	2				1	1
安徽	3	3		2	1		
福建	15	15		1	7	6	1
江西	2	1	1	1		1	
山东							
河南	5	5		2	1	2	
湖北	2	2			1		1
湖南	9	8	1	2	5		2
广东	3	3		1	1		1
广西	4	4			1	1	2
海南							
重庆	9	9		5	1		3
四川	19	16	3	5	4	4	6
贵州	23	22	1	10	8	2	3
云南	3	3			1		2
西藏							
陕西	1	1					1
甘肃	3	3			3		
青海	1	1			1		
宁夏	1		1			1	
新疆	9	8	1	1	5	2	1

精神病院和医院

单位：个、人

年末职工人数	女性	受教育程度		职业资格水平		按人员性质分	
		大学专科人数	大学本科及以上人数	助理社会工作师人数	社会工作师人数	管理人员	专业技术技能人员
15079	**8902**	**5332**	**4925**	**191**	**150**	**2821**	**12258**
173	140	60	68			10	163
247	108	65	69	3		2	245
85	44	33	28	1	1	24	61
338	163	145	93	3	8	67	271
3	2					1	2
842	414	167	204	1		247	595
1136	444	232	392	68	6	358	778
541	363	175	178	18	12	122	419
1448	941	437	672	26	25	131	1317
78	49	8	36			19	59
237	173	118	53		1	75	162
1040	654	352	254	18	18	180	860
148	96	61	50	5	7	48	100
719	434	299	310	5	10	92	627
352	184	131	72			56	296
927	621	291	231	1	5	169	758
654	420	209	329	1	2	36	618
906	625	304	359	5	4	81	825
482	250	161	198	7	15	92	390
2498	1431	1180	749	11	12	503	1995
690	385	326	149	3	3	228	462
260	156	100	114	2	2	88	172
129	51	26	72	5	3	26	103
186	125	46	24	1	2	21	165
223	159	121	70			53	170
122	76	48	28	5	9	9	113
615	394	237	123	2	5	83	532

C–2–12续表1

地 区	年龄结构				志愿服务	
	35岁及以下人数	36岁至45岁人数	46岁至55岁人数	56岁及以上人数	志愿者服务人次数	志愿服务时间
全 国	**6656**	**4463**	**3172**	**788**	**4147**	**9848**
中央级						
北 京	52	78	39	4		
天 津	75	65	70	37		
河 北						
山 西	16	29	38	2		
内蒙古	98	91	119	30		
辽 宁	1	1	1			
吉 林	247	339	225	31		
黑龙江	437	319	328	52		
上 海	267	103	108	63	1471	2943
江 苏	599	404	364	81	1480	3160
浙 江	35	19	21	3		
安 徽	141	40	25	31	120	545
福 建	497	290	209	44		
江 西	52	41	45	10	132	528
山 东						
河 南	345	213	132	29	101	300
湖 北	52	124	105	71		
湖 南	351	356	192	28		
广 东	274	266	102	12		
广 西	508	208	157	33	50	300
海 南						
重 庆	189	157	111	25	485	1582
四 川	1542	549	325	82		
贵 州	216	244	173	57	190	386
云 南	117	75	53	15	18	104
西 藏						
陕 西	66	26	28	9		
甘 肃	32	109	41	4		
青 海	136	55	16	16		
宁 夏	53	56	13			
新 疆	258	206	132	19		

单位：张、人天、人、人次、时

年末床位数		年在院总人天数	年末在院人数		在院人员按性质分		
	光荣间床位			女性	优抚对象	特困人员	自费人员
53373	**383**	**12916810**	**43645**	**13262**	**2613**	**14722**	**16879**
150		47820	30	14			4
657		232505	657	216		260	373
230		12190	228	55	2	145	83
1358	7	325305	1039	307	90	341	608
50		1000	50	10		50	
4820		705531	2744	670	323	1186	342
4416		1124591	3497	907	25	2580	600
1800		614873	1678	478	46	113	903
5334	10	1315003	4450	1084	618	2243	1391
910		165535	459	232	60	47	254
265		37927	154	56	6	43	104
3806	67	857626	3451	909	345	795	1819
360		70127	329			124	205
1326	2	433809	1212	447		142	779
880		139665	395	41		20	301
2096	15	394597	1616	631	138	229	865
2014		626268	1795	554	79	511	256
2024		585042	1936	700	33	245	1104
2381		664164	2141	714	61	657	1404
8561	5	2378482	7897	2978	256	1845	3348
3804	77	765293	2877	743	52	724	714
1631		191500	1080	324	61	640	8
650	200	140606	458	163	50	298	110
451		120450	330	128	32	218	34
260		78840	216	98	175	18	23
450		126317	428	190	30	221	177
2689		761744	2498	613	131	1027	1070

C-2-12续表2

地　区	在院人员按年龄分			在院人员按类型分		
	老人	青壮年	少年儿童	自理（完全自理）	介助（半自理）	介护（不能自理）
全　国	**14492**	**28357**	**796**	**21674**	**16232**	**5739**
中央级						
北　京	15	1	14	5	7	18
天　津	172	485		657		
河　北						
山　西	39	171	18	155	68	5
内蒙古	194	839	6	334	606	99
辽　宁	50			50		
吉　林	1235	1509		1192	1460	92
黑龙江	1094	2386	17	1681	1114	702
上　海	535	1143		690	988	
江　苏	1874	2570	6	2460	1568	422
浙　江	168	286	5	209	182	68
安　徽	92	58	4	70	48	36
福　建	779	2648	24	2157	1028	266
江　西	104	225		127	185	17
山　东						
河　南	83	1082	47	131	394	687
湖　北	369	26			329	66
湖　南	446	881	289	800	486	330
广　东	988	775	32	928	651	216
广　西	601	1328	7	898	727	311
海　南						
重　庆	944	1190	7	1169	721	251
四　川	2670	5094	133	3105	3202	1590
贵　州	721	2036	120	2012	665	200
云　南	193	887		521	443	116
西　藏						
陕　西	86	364	8	399	30	29
甘　肃	45	277	8	172	125	33
青　海	155	57	4	211	5	
宁　夏	156	257	15	73	257	98
新　疆	684	1782	32	1468	943	87

单位：人、人次、平方米、万元

康复和医疗门诊人次数	机构建筑面积	事业单位会计制度财务指标		
		固定资产原价	本年收入合计	本年支出合计
1918301	**2136773**	**329656.5**	**443082.7**	**406040.1**
17389	7993	6537.6	13209.8	12820.3
38632	2000	2504.7	12461.2	8596.9
451	8262	773.6	2376.3	2376.3
28321	66458	2713.8	14883.8	13961.4
	500	3.0	10.0	
90294	96400	13954.3	14099.7	12971.8
457430	126074	29892.7	15920.2	19110.2
7213	83562	19039.0	24458.6	19491.1
62677	172209	45582.0	57686.9	50332.1
	25500	7000.0	8323.5	6864.7
17870	8700	1048.2	3074.7	3164.9
358213	136058	18108.1	29010.0	24851.8
	21316	3108.0	3184.7	3153.2
227407	69530	9471.9	17891.8	18351.0
19230	34035	561.0	1305.0	1336.0
66287	42930	9516.0	20104.2	19898.6
65799	246023	16511.3	25356.4	24367.8
91104	310162	14397.4	24335.6	23149.0
57103	94440	9314.9	17001.7	16823.6
195735	237907	56670.5	73844.1	69202.3
36914	121233	9612.7	12940.2	13711.1
13739	41423	18349.1	5689.1	4767.3
	28154	3779.3	2616.3	3787.2
8593	19575	2792.9	8869.4	2535.2
88	16830	4563.1	4256.5	3926.2
7560	6200	1022.3	2413.0	2334.5
50252	113299	22829.1	27760.0	24155.6

C-2-13 复退军人

地区	单位数	0～99张	100～299张	300～499张	500张以上	年末职工人数	女性
全国	**94**	**8**	**36**	**28**	**22**	**13016**	**7358**
中央级							
北京							
天津	1			1		117	57
河北	2				2	522	281
山西	7		5	1	1	2009	596
内蒙古	2		1		1	196	115
辽宁	2	1	1			95	61
吉林	7	2	1	2	2	572	305
黑龙江	1		1			66	34
上海							
江苏	1				1	269	164
浙江	1		1			82	55
安徽	1				1	221	147
福建	2		1	1		124	79
江西	1	1				4	1
山东	12		4	8		1708	1072
河南	1				1	305	183
湖北	10		1	4	5	2390	1514
湖南	8		2	3	3	962	631
广东	9		5	3	1	914	465
广西	4		1	2	1	846	609
海南							
重庆							
四川	7	1	3	1	2	791	510
贵州	4	3			1	86	51
云南	2		2			119	67
西藏							
陕西	3		2	1		231	118
甘肃	2		1	1		208	116
青海							
宁夏							
新疆	4		4			179	127

精神病院

单位：个、人

受教育程度		职业资格水平		按人员性质分	
大学专科人数	大学本科及以上人数	助理社会工作师人数	社会工作师人数	管理人员	专业技术技能人员
3719	**4767**	**191**	**148**	**1969**	**11047**
				90	27
86	260	4	6	71	451
358	349	2	6	105	1904
64	99		2	18	178
18	11	1		94	1
7	10	1		273	299
24	15			9	57
35	177		3	16	253
12	40	2	5	8	74
65	92	1		36	185
55	17	2	1	6	118
3				1	3
493	912	63	51	240	1468
72	172	2	13	13	292
604	1337	18	16	231	2159
388	291	14	7	147	815
409	216	52	20	221	693
398	223	6	10	102	744
329	235	9	4	155	636
44	17			9	77
42	48	1	1	29	90
104	44		1	36	195
37	158		2	35	173
72	44	13		24	155

C−2−13续表1

地　区	年龄结构				志愿服务	
	35岁及以下人数	36岁至45岁人数	46岁至55岁人数	56岁及以上人数	志愿者服务人次数	志愿服务时间
全　国	**6220**	**3596**	**2720**	**480**	**9521**	**20102**
中央级						
北　京						
天　津	39	7	54	17		
河　北	147	182	148	45		
山　西	1340	378	251	40	2	2
内蒙古	84	48	54	10		
辽　宁	21	45	24	5		
吉　林	151	293	115	13		
黑龙江	14	21	31			
上　海						
江　苏	66	100	84	19		
浙　江	27	16	38	1	6100	12200
安　徽	93	76	36	16		
福　建	80	24	10	10		
江　西	2	2				
山　东	718	433	468	89	3030	7000
河　南	63	118	115	9		
湖　北	1330	609	419	32		
湖　南	413	328	203	18		
广　东	384	305	180	45	14	70
广　西	433	220	153	40		
海　南						
重　庆						
四　川	441	147	158	45	50	100
贵　州	19	42	22	3	10	15
云　南	54	44	19	2		
西　藏						
陕　西	60	60	95	16	30	30
甘　肃	150	30	25	3		
青　海						
宁　夏						
新　疆	91	68	18	2	285	685

单位：人、人次、时、张、人天

年末床位数	光荣间床位	年在院总人天数	年末在院人数	女性	在院人员按性质分 优抚对象	特困人员	自费人员
31371	**1454**	**7803833**	**25083**	**6485**	**7681**	**4146**	**9984**
300		68255	187	10	157		30
1129		349569	979	175	566	90	323
1740	280	542015	1425	145	548	186	679
752	20	244473	669	179	36	26	438
340	25	99190	272	53	69	114	89
2130		87605	343	52	340	3	
286		32640	96	85	68	20	50
1122		337182	1121	468	288	67	681
290		105850	290	55	37		168
600		192720	528	55	328		85
596		196482	543	154	26	165	313
50		7860	25	5	18	7	
3617		753195	2931	458	1503	245	754
600		179729	600	167	279		389
4926	252	1229527	4136	1630	833	938	1967
3175	209	604471	2356	743	465	545	835
2580	5	729582	2281	538	645	618	771
1580	218	501498	1496	373	228	271	900
3074	115	1030617	2912	694	695	623	861
541		82947	491	137		31	91
400		127385	374	84	80	98	88
610	160	187300	590	129	386	34	185
600	110	47520	133	32	58	65	10
333	60	66221	305	64	28		277

C-2-13续表2

地 区	在院人员按年龄分			在院人员按类型分		
	老人	青壮年	少年儿童	自理 (完全自理)	介助 (半自理)	介护 (不能自理)
全 国	**9622**	**14823**	**638**	**14168**	**8684**	**2231**
中央级						
北 京						
天 津	56	131		140	47	
河 北	448	529	2	488	461	30
山 西	511	903	11	921	465	39
内蒙古	37	632		637	30	2
辽 宁	62	210		218	31	23
吉 林	52	291		343		
黑龙江	70	22	4	30	28	38
上 海						
江 苏	419	697	5	679	360	82
浙 江	167	123		257	28	5
安 徽	181	347		468	50	10
福 建	226	317		290	152	101
江 西	4	21		25		
山 东	1879	1029	23	2250	506	175
河 南	200	400		400	132	68
湖 北	740	3223	173	2318	1610	208
湖 南	1113	1020	223	897	864	595
广 东	811	1298	172	848	1076	357
广 西	422	1058	16	472	829	195
海 南						
重 庆						
四 川	1340	1566	6	1586	1113	213
贵 州	140	351		401	90	
云 南	88	286		20	348	6
西 藏						
陕 西	433	157		313	235	42
甘 肃	96	37		39	80	14
青 海						
宁 夏						
新 疆	127	175	3	128	149	28

单位：人、人次、平方米、万元

康复和医疗门诊人次数	机构建筑面积	事业单位会计制度财务指标		
		固定资产原价	本年收入合计	本年支出合计
1610457	**1246336**	**266269.2**	**275237.1**	**256063.7**
33384	9677	5812.8	3046.9	2938.5
71548	32318	20780.3	12749.8	10832.9
67676	148144	25737.3	17656.5	15427.6
44359	11464	2529.7	6440.8	5478.8
	8250	100.0	414.9	414.9
	26821	409.6	402.0	402.0
8694	18500			1273.1
104426	42292	22941.0	14600.0	10710.4
	21500	2269.6	3276.5	3474.8
59759	17680	4257.3		
18055	36067	1320.9	3015.5	3021.0
	1200	20.0		
75855	181636	35850.7	46069.0	46069.0
42207	26736	6329.6	9753.4	7881.7
503991	215881	52718.9	66945.4	63091.5
197954	89428	15146.4	23710.9	22243.8
37616	80486	16447.2	16793.0	15820.7
152415	79924	18002.1	18593.7	18093.5
65657	77223	19504.5	17802.9	17298.5
9000				
6070	56430	2750.0	2665.0	1746.0
29579	46083	9799.4	5804.2	6354.9
75963	6496	3541.9	5496.7	3490.1
6249	12100			

C-2-14 儿童服务

地区	单位数	单位数按登记类型分			单位数按床位数量分	
		编制登记	民政登记	一个机构多块牌子	0～99张	100～299张
全　国	**705**	**377**	**35**	**293**	**376**	**232**
中央级						
北　京	12	10	1	1	5	5
天　津	2	2				1
河　北	5	3	2		3	2
山　西	13	5	2	6	10	3
内蒙古	8	7	1		1	5
辽　宁	12	9	1	2	7	2
吉　林	10	8		2	3	5
黑龙江	16	16			1	13
上　海	4	3	1		3	
江　苏	32	11		21	18	9
浙　江	13	10		3	3	7
安　徽	36	27		9	12	18
福　建	11	6	3	2	5	4
江　西	16	7		9	11	3
山　东	17	14		3	3	4
河　南	22	17	2	3	11	7
湖　北	72	18		54	58	8
湖　南	53	20	2	31	38	10
广　东	46	27	14	5	23	18
广　西	43	7	1	35	31	11
海　南	1	1				1
重　庆	6	5	1		2	2
四　川	99	26		73	73	18
贵　州	29	16		13	12	14
云　南	28	22	2	4	12	14
西　藏	5	5				
陕　西	13	11		2	4	6
甘　肃	18	12	1	5	6	9
青　海	8	5	1	2	3	2
宁　夏	10	4		6	8	1
新　疆	45	43		2	10	30

机构总表

单位：个、人

		年末职工人数		年末职工人数按登记类型分		
300～499张	500张以上		女性	编制登记	民政登记	一个机构多块牌子
66	**31**	**14466**	**9683**	**11435**	**801**	**2230**
1	1	526	372	488	36	2
1		128	85	128		
		36	14	20	16	
		174	91	67	12	95
1	1	339	182	336	3	
1	2	593	367	503	9	81
1	1	371	179	309		62
1	1	438	276	438		
	1	409	337	365	44	
4	1	632	455	494		138
2	1	498	370	487		11
5	1	839	550	727		112
2		153	107	114	21	18
2		196	111	119		77
7	3	470	324	449		21
2	2	917	775	869	18	30
5	1	765	501	382		383
5		668	340	335	49	284
5		1737	1213	1165	515	57
1		870	648	630	14	226
		11	11	11		
	2	300	229	284	16	
6	2	912	552	527		385
2	1	272	170	204		68
1	1	287	188	232	20	35
3	2	150	115	150		
1	2	263	149	255		8
2	1	444	270	395	18	31
1	2	181	118	147	10	24
1		264	220	212		52
3	2	623	364	593		30

C-2-14续表1

地　区	受教育程度		职业资格水平		按人员性质分	
	大学专科人数	大学本科及以上人数	助理社会工作师人数	社会工作师人数	管理人员	专业技术技能人员
全　国	**4533**	**4355**	**508**	**651**	**4654**	**9812**
中央级						
北　京	159	259	13	18	133	393
天　津	37	70	8	14	42	86
河　北	1				15	21
山　西	41	62	5	12	51	123
内蒙古	127	106	13	30	101	238
辽　宁	156	381	9	6	151	442
吉　林	52	60		2	91	280
黑龙江	164	125	4	25	250	188
上　海	120	169	31	52	72	337
江　苏	176	260	56	63	113	519
浙　江	123	223	20	20	107	391
安　徽	218	164	33	26	479	360
福　建	58	62	10	19	87	66
江　西	68	26	8	1	87	109
山　东	137	224	41	42	129	341
河　南	515	143	7	30	165	752
湖　北	261	213	30	26	257	508
湖　南	213	96	20	18	257	411
广　东	441	317	71	59	564	1173
广　西	202	226	21	22	179	691
海　南					10	1
重　庆	78	185	17	32	90	210
四　川	328	249	16	34	480	432
贵　州	102	106	13	6	171	101
云　南	64	127	6	22	119	168
西　藏	39	37	2		45	105
陕　西	77	107	8	13	106	157
甘　肃	109	84	18	13	109	335
青　海	68	42	4	1	28	153
宁　夏	91	84	12	18	27	237
新　疆	308	148	12	27	139	484

单位：人、人次、时

年龄结构				志愿服务	
35岁及以下人数	36岁至45岁人数	46岁至55岁人数	56岁及以上人数	志愿者服务人次数	志愿服务时间
5957	**5080**	**2955**	**474**	**26601**	**67875**
183	162	156	25	7	7
63	35	22	8		
10	12	11	3		
39	80	46	9		
187	80	61	11		
278	142	150	23		
127	124	75	45		
178	159	84	17		
232	92	61	24		
259	177	171	25	4010	8745
209	149	127	13	530	1070
281	291	240	27	1405	5385
51	57	43	2		
73	62	58	3	132	528
231	145	75	19	13179	32303
303	468	139	7	2358	6782
253	289	185	38	226	600
242	278	129	19	46	151
755	646	296	40		
364	320	162	24	120	200
3	5	3			
191	60	41	8	20	20
332	336	206	38	77	193
137	83	42	10	3837	10060
114	128	38	7	54	312
108	28	14		18	65
104	90	64	5	81	152
193	160	83	8		
93	65	20	3	501	1302
116	100	41	7		
248	257	112	6		

C-2-14续表2

地 区	事业单位会计制度财务指标			民间非营利组织会计制度财务指标		
	固定资产原价	本年收入合计	本年支出合计	固定资产原价	本年收入合计	本年费用合计
全 国	**431292.6**	**287756.6**	**276746.6**	**8415.7**	**5718.7**	**3206.9**
中央级						
北 京	18248.7	20756.9	20802.4	100.0	351.0	425.0
天 津	891.2	5901.3	5598.2			
河 北	201.0	356.2	356.2	286.8	53.6	21.0
山 西	408.5	665.8	649.8	260.0		34.0
内蒙古	13618.4	7006.4	6516.1	200.0	30.0	30.0
辽 宁	46772.0	12488.5	12233.7	100.0	86.3	86.3
吉 林	8284.8	3937.7	3894.6			
黑龙江	24217.4	15131.3	8829.4			
上 海	18173.6	16535.3	16262.8	2.7	272.0	281.8
江 苏	11828.3	15954.7	17427.3			
浙 江	14614.7	19424.7	19321.0			
安 徽	22402.4	13915.6	11017.1			
福 建	3682.5	4108.5	3803.0	11.2	1618.6	131.6
江 西	1833.7	1528.2	918.7			
山 东	19576.5	17130.3	16805.3			
河 南	17140.0	9414.6	9029.1	312.0	75.0	14.0
湖 北	11806.3	9956.0	11676.2			
湖 南	19480.4	8824.8	9744.4	835.0	330.0	10.0
广 东	32841.0	24920.1	24786.7	5636.0	2832.8	2041.7
广 西	6929.8	10132.3	9292.6	90.0	18.1	81.5
海 南	460.0	95.0	92.6			
重 庆	8122.7	13743.9	9546.1	20.0	20.0	20.0
四 川	28768.8	12708.1	13416.5			
贵 州	9021.5	3963.2	3687.2			
云 南	15663.6	5630.8	5075.2	450.0	16.3	15.0
西 藏	8904.9	3309.7	2719.8			
陕 西	15534.9	13286.1	14217.8			
甘 肃	17697.7	5526.6	4402.9	12.0	15.0	15.0
青 海	2934.0	349.8	347.1	100.0		
宁 夏	12657.5	2960.3	2940.4			
新 疆	18575.8	8093.9	11336.4			

单位：张、人

为儿童提供服务机构床位数	按登记类型分			为儿童提供服务机构年末收养人数			按登记类型分		
	编制登记	民政登记	一个机构多块牌子		女性	儿童	编制登记	民政登记	一个机构多块牌子
100097	**78307**	**3401**	**18389**	**54627**	**20002**	**54627**	**46748**	**2222**	**5657**
1910	1660	200	50	1228	461	1228	1119	91	18
668	668			231	129	231	231		
534	284	250		199	44	199	104	95	
1188	470	140	578	683	289	683	256	91	336
1633	1601	32		858	293	858	835	23	
4254	3744	50	460	3176	1212	3176	2892	19	265
3127	2810		317	1655	110	1655	1397		258
3708	3708			1524	557	1524	1524		
2091	2021	70		1868	756	1868	1798	70	
4290	2418		1872	2116	936	2116	1657		459
2575	2284		291	1383	543	1383	1331		52
6017	4693		1324	3248	1249	3248	2659		589
1504	1130	155	219	756	281	756	558	143	55
1682	1085		597	843	66	843	816		27
5406	4782		624	2533	1084	2533	2363		170
4042	3702	210	130	2897	1142	2897	2671	210	16
4886	2616		2270	2021	953	2021	1497		524
4485	3062	541	882	2416	1219	2416	1906	284	226
5656	4203	1223	230	2784	1179	2784	1915	811	58
3184	1110	160	1914	1453	640	1453	772	130	551
40	40			40	23	40	40		
2499	2449	50		1011	417	1011	961	50	
8135	4456		3679	2953	1112	2953	2119		834
3861	2531		1330	1602	609	1602	1087		515
3330	2882	170	278	1544	237	1544	1356	134	54
3123	3123			2902	1228	2902	2902		
2945	2903		42	1963	782	1963	1963		
3581	3106	100	375	2205	882	2205	2132	41	32
1828	1650	50	128	1269	83	1269	1215	30	24
840	520		320	440	195	440	310		130
7075	6596		479	4826	1291	4826	4362		464

C-2-15 儿童

地　区	单位数	0～99张	100～299张	300～499张	500张以上	年末职工人数	女性
全　国	**465**	**164**	**206**	**64**	**31**	**12770**	**8977**
中央级							
北　京	10	4	4	1	1	479	354
天　津	2		1	1		128	85
河　北	5	3	2			36	14
山　西	8	5	3			118	78
内蒙古	8	1	5	1	1	339	182
辽　宁	10	5	2	1	2	572	361
吉　林	10	3	5	1	1	371	179
黑龙江	15	1	12	1	1	430	270
上　海	3	2			1	345	280
江　苏	13	2	6	4	1	564	427
浙　江	13	3	7	2	1	498	370
安　徽	31	10	15	5	1	800	536
福　建	11	5	4	2		153	107
江　西	5	2	1	2		101	79
山　东	13		3	7	3	441	311
河　南	18	8	6	2	2	858	748
湖　北	24	14	5	4	1	495	381
湖　南	19	7	7	5		343	217
广　东	43	22	17	4		1617	1166
广　西	17	8	8	1		712	576
海　南	1		1			11	11
重　庆	6	2	2		2	300	229
四　川	50	26	16	6	2	713	479
贵　州	23	6	14	2	1	232	153
云　南	23	7	14	1	1	270	177
西　藏	5			3	2	150	115
陕　西	11	2	6	1	2	255	147
甘　肃	12	1	8	2	1	397	253
青　海	7	2	2	1	2	177	116
宁　夏	5	3	1	1		247	212
新　疆	44	10	29	3	2	618	364

收养机构

单位：个、人

受教育程度		职业资格水平		按人员性质分		年龄结构	
大学专科人数	大学本科及以上人数	助理社会工作师人数	社会工作师人数	管理人员	专业技术技能人员	35岁及以下人数	36岁至45岁人数
3868	**3913**	**448**	**589**	**3752**	**9018**	**5344**	**4403**
149	222	10	14	86	393	169	146
37	70	8	14	42	86	63	35
1				15	21	10	12
26	49	5	11	39	79	27	56
127	106	13	30	101	238	187	80
143	373	9	6	135	437	274	136
52	60		2	91	280	127	124
164	117	4	25	247	183	175	154
91	151	27	48	59	286	202	68
139	248	50	60	85	479	229	148
123	223	20	20	107	391	209	149
206	148	33	25	451	349	273	278
58	62	10	19	87	66	51	57
12	12	1	1	22	79	32	25
130	218	40	41	124	317	219	132
480	128	5	26	148	710	276	442
156	156	21	20	120	375	162	183
78	43	11	7	106	237	135	130
416	288	59	47	506	1111	689	611
155	163	18	14	83	629	314	258
				10	1	3	5
78	185	17	32	90	210	191	60
245	199	16	30	341	372	260	245
80	93	13	4	134	98	122	75
57	121	6	21	105	165	109	123
39	37	2		45	105	108	28
76	103	8	13	104	151	100	86
92	75	14	13	90	307	179	145
68	42	4	1	24	153	91	65
86	74	12	18	17	230	111	91
304	147	12	27	138	480	247	256

C-2-15续表1

地区	年龄结构		志愿服务		年末床位数	年在院总人天数	年末在院人数	
	46岁至55岁人数	56岁及以上人数	志愿者服务人次数	志愿服务时间				女性
全　国	**2640**	**383**	**26107**	**66679**	**89624**	**15704985**	**52906**	**19030**
中央级								
北　京	145	19	7	7	1460	426375	1190	425
天　津	22	8			668	17190	231	129
河　北	11	3			534	61870	199	44
山　西	31	4			1000	216615	682	289
内蒙古	61	11			1633	300582	858	293
辽　宁	139	23			4174	1139755	3175	1212
吉　林	75	45			3127	220021	1655	110
黑龙江	84	17			3608	504884	1504	537
上　海	56	19			1991	398580	1818	739
江　苏	165	22	3981	8653	3265	641357	2075	921
浙　江	127	13	530	1070	2575	511119	1383	543
安　徽	224	25	1405	5385	5453	1029215	3126	1201
福　建	43	2			1504	271825	756	281
江　西	44		132	528	965	88336	771	38
山　东	71	19	13031	31921	5122	909385	2509	1071
河　南	133	7	2358	6782	3657	916496	2889	1142
湖　北	134	16	40	180	3376	625466	1803	759
湖　南	72	6	35	49	3218	606275	2124	1142
广　东	281	36			5308	900129	2628	1118
广　西	128	12			2220	306033	1300	574
海　南	3				40	365	40	23
重　庆	41	8	20	20	2499	352367	1011	417
四　川	177	31	77	193	6879	867640	2904	1070
贵　州	30	5	3837	10060	3627	522565	1584	608
云　南	33	5	54	312	3141	331491	1544	237
西　藏	14		18	65	3123	822465	2902	1228
陕　西	64	5	81	152	2903	666565	1963	782
甘　肃	67	6			2996	423101	1757	528
青　海	18	3	501	1302	1800	269426	1269	83
宁　夏	38	7			693	145085	430	195
新　疆	109	6			7065	1212407	4826	1291

单位：人、人次、时、张、人天、平方米

家庭寄养儿童数量	机构建筑面积	事业单位会计制度财务指标			民间非营利组织会计制度财务指标		
		固定资产原价	本年收入合计	本年支出合计	固定资产原价	本年收入合计	本年费用合计
11553	**2623734**	**412057.3**	**276770.2**	**266352.0**	**8415.7**	**5718.7**	**3206.9**
469	96152	17582.4	18351.5	18635.6	100.0	351.0	425.0
371	12712	891.2	5901.3	5598.2			
98	7881	201.0	356.2	356.2	286.8	53.6	21.0
60	11632	408.5	662.8	646.8	260.0		34.0
12	50625	13618.4	7006.4	6516.1	200.0	30.0	30.0
213	104012	46769.0	12472.3	12217.5	100.0	86.3	86.3
25	228979	8284.8	3937.7	3894.6			
71	110616	22974.1	14866.5	8517.0			
1059	35036	17696.6	15054.3	14786.8	2.7	272.0	281.8
285	97161	11828.3	15954.7	17427.0			
507	59083	14614.7	19424.7	19321.0			
168	174830	22402.4	13915.6	11017.1			
668	27648	3682.5	4108.5	3803.0	11.2	1618.6	131.6
	11180	1833.7	1367.6	908.7			
444	154473	19055.4	16501.8	16176.8			
464	235653	17067.0	9384.6	8999.1	312.0	75.0	14.0
420	59701	11718.3	9882.0	11602.2			
997	70155	11647.3	6457.4	7382.6	835.0	330.0	10.0
193	154189	25458.0	21674.5	21763.4	5636.0	2832.8	2041.7
273	44232	6919.8	10132.3	9292.6	90.0	18.1	81.5
	2100	460.0	95.0	92.6			
	125400	8122.7	13743.9	9546.1	20.0	20.0	20.0
262	106788	28676.8	12637.9	13325.1			
271	69960	8966.5	3945.3	3669.3			
1199	102677	15648.4	5508.3	4988.2	450.0	16.3	15.0
2	56400	8904.9	3309.7	2719.8			
121	90787	15534.9	13286.1	14217.8			
42	105700	17672.7	5519.3	4396.6	12.0	15.0	15.0
	13194	2934.0	349.8	347.1	100.0		
112	32459	11924.5	2950.3	2930.4			
2747	172319	18558.5	8011.9	11256.7			

C-2-16 未成年人

地　区	单位数					年末职工人数	
		0～99张	100～299张	300～499张	500张以上		女性
全　国	**240**	**212**	**26**	**2**		**1696**	**706**
中央级							
北　京	2	1	1			47	18
天　津							
河　北							
山　西	5	5				56	13
内蒙古							
辽　宁	2	2				21	6
吉　林							
黑龙江	1		1			8	6
上　海	1	1				64	57
江　苏	19	16	3			68	28
浙　江							
安　徽	5	2	3			39	14
福　建							
江　西	11	9	2			95	32
山　东	4	3	1			29	13
河　南	4	3	1			59	27
湖　北	48	44	3	1		270	120
湖　南	34	31	3			325	123
广　东	3	1	1	1		120	47
广　西	26	23	3			158	72
海　南							
重　庆							
四　川	49	47	2			199	73
贵　州	6	6				40	17
云　南	5	5				17	11
西　藏							
陕　西	2	2				8	2
甘　肃	6	5	1			47	17
青　海	1	1				4	2
宁　夏	5	5				17	8
新　疆	1		1			5	

救助保护中心

单位：个、人

受教育程度		职业资格水平		按人员性质分		年龄结构	
大学专科人数	大学本科及以上人数	助理社会工作师人数	社会工作师人数	管理人员	专业技术技能人员	35岁及以下人数	36岁至45岁人数
665	**442**	**60**	**62**	**902**	**794**	**613**	**677**
10	37	3	4	47		14	16
15	13		1	12	44	12	24
13	8			16	5	4	6
	8			3	5	3	5
29	18	4	4	13	51	30	24
37	12	6	3	28	40	30	29
12	16		1	28	11	8	13
56	14	7		65	30	41	37
7	6	1	1	5	24	12	13
35	15	2	4	17	42	27	26
105	57	9	6	137	133	91	106
135	53	9	11	151	174	107	148
25	29	12	12	58	62	66	35
47	63	3	8	96	62	50	62
83	50		4	139	60	72	91
22	13		2	37	3	15	8
7	6		1	14	3	5	5
1	4			2	6	4	4
17	9	4		19	28	14	15
				4		2	
5	10			10	7	5	9
4	1			1	4	1	1

C-2-16续表1

地 区	年龄结构		志愿服务		本年在站救助人次数	
	46岁至55岁人数	56岁及以上人数	志愿者服务人次数	志愿服务时间		从其他站转入的
全 国	**315**	**91**	**494**	**1196**	**51554**	**4340**
中央级						
北 京	11	6			350	
天 津						
河 北						
山 西	15	5			399	
内蒙古						
辽 宁	11				338	
吉 林						
黑龙江					20	
上 海	5	5			38	
江 苏	6	3	29	92	2240	349
浙 江						
安 徽	16	2			343	69
福 建						
江 西	14	3			2036	109
山 东	4		148	382	378	1
河 南	6				678	45
湖 北	51	22	186	420	2923	195
湖 南	57	13	11	102	22687	1324
广 东	15	4			642	610
广 西	34	12	120	200	2214	121
海 南					1183	
重 庆						
四 川	29	7			10346	970
贵 州	12	5			639	356
云 南	5	2			36	2
西 藏						
陕 西					34	
甘 肃	16	2			494	
青 海	2				117	
宁 夏	3				3214	189
新 疆	3				205	

单位：人、人次、时、张

女性	肢体残疾人	智障及精神病人	救治的危重病人	跨省接送	床位数
5709	**2730**	**2888**	**312**	**1579**	**10473**
				61	450
6					188
20	77	77	2		80
					100
12					100
308	521	137		450	1025
120	11	10	1	46	564
209	346	2		397	717
154	10		1	41	284
54	2	2		15	385
116	128	61	8	188	1510
3161	1190	2161	127	71	1267
180	3	115		154	348
267	218	89	11	71	964
757	202	175	56	10	1256
313	10	32	102	34	234
8	7		2		189
3		2		1	42
20	4	24	2	25	585
					28
1	1	1		15	147
					10

C-2-16续表2

地区	年末在站人数	女性	本年在站人天数	本年不在站救助人次数	在站滞留三个月以上人数	残疾人人数
全国	**1721**	**972**	**197428**	**3872**	**368**	**168**
中央级						
北京	38	36	9393		1	
天津						
河北				2192		
山西	1		233			
内蒙古						
辽宁	1		987	5	1	
吉林						
黑龙江	20	20	400	2		
上海	50	17	17663			
江苏	41	15	20206		36	11
浙江						
安徽	122	48	6054	37	32	6
福建				200		
江西	72	28	6201		60	21
山东	24	13	8730	202	2	
河南	8		827	248	1	
湖北	218	194	12782	219	15	11
湖南	292	77	16918	476	22	3
广东	156	61	55923	94	115	91
广西	153	66	8969	1	44	18
海南				145		
重庆						
四川	49	42	27364	16	23	2
贵州	18	1	2525	5	6	
云南			30			
西藏						
陕西						
甘肃	448	354	513			
青海				30		
宁夏	10		1710		10	5
新疆						

单位：张、人、人天、人次、万元

事业单位会计制度财务指标		
固定资产原价	本年收入合计	本年支出合计
19235.3	**10986.4**	**10394.6**
666.3	2405.4	2166.8
	3.0	3.0
3.0	16.2	16.2
1243.3	264.8	312.4
477.0	1481.0	1476.0
		0.3
	160.6	10.0
521.1	628.5	628.5
73.0	30.0	30.0
88.0	74.0	74.0
7833.1	2367.4	2361.8
7383.0	3245.6	3023.3
10.0		
92.0	70.2	91.4
55.0	17.9	17.9
15.2	122.5	87.0
25.0	7.3	6.3
733.0	10.0	10.0
17.3	82.0	79.7

C-2-17 其他提供住宿的

地区	单位数	单位数按登记类型分			单位数按	
		编制登记	民政登记	一个机构多块牌子	0～99张	100～299张
全 国	**2371**	**1931**	**244**	**196**	**1865**	**408**
中央级	1	1				1
北 京	21	19		2	14	3
天 津	14	14			11	2
河 北	81	57	14	10	61	19
山 西	97	86	10	1	86	9
内蒙古	55	44	9	2	46	8
辽 宁	107	80	26	1	83	21
吉 林	61	61			50	11
黑龙江	106	74	30	2	87	17
上 海	21	21			15	4
江 苏	90	80	2	8	66	18
浙 江	66	63	2	1	52	11
安 徽	91	80	8	3	67	20
福 建	58	55		3	48	10
江 西	115	81	4	30	95	16
山 东	72	71		1	53	16
河 南	130	111	14	5	98	24
湖 北	113	87	20	6	88	21
湖 南	138	110	10	18	115	22
广 东	94	85	7	2	52	32
广 西	85	74	4	7	76	7
海 南	10	8	1	1	6	4
重 庆	43	43			39	2
四 川	255	143	56	56	190	48
贵 州	89	70	1	18	74	12
云 南	100	93	7		78	20
西 藏	4	4			3	1
陕 西	100	95		5	90	7
甘 肃	60	50	6	4	55	5
青 海	9	7	2		5	4
宁 夏	17	10	6	1	12	5
新 疆	68	54	5	9	50	8

社会服务机构总表

单位：个、人

床位数量分		年末职工人数		年末职工人数按登记类型分		
300～499张	500张以上		女性	编制登记	民政登记	一个机构多块牌子
72	**18**	**28359**	**11054**	**24396**	**2922**	**1041**
		185	130	185		
1	3	601	268	591		10
	1	239	72	239		
1		927	421	749	144	34
2		743	257	647	93	3
1		576	180	525	41	10
	2	1277	449	1166	110	1
		978	316	978		
1		1798	516	1612	182	4
	2	764	426	764		
6	1	951	391	903	17	31
3		751	308	719	30	2
4		1078	448	959	101	18
		480	178	466		14
4		903	314	769	32	102
3		739	236	736		3
4	2	2230	804	1967	207	56
2	1	1264	489	1035	200	29
1		1351	481	1207	63	81
5	3	2335	857	1978	228	129
2		763	291	704	20	39
		129	42	117	10	2
2		409	152	409		
14	2	2897	1469	1284	1237	376
3		723	292	633	39	51
2		915	379	830	85	
		29	5	29		
2	1	1121	423	1104		17
		520	183	471	36	13
		72	17	70	2	
		112	61	83	27	2
9		499	199	467	18	14

C−2−17续表1

地　区	受教育程度		职业资格水平		按人员性质分	
	大学专科人数	大学本科及以上人数	助理社会工作师人数	社会工作师人数	管理人员	专业技术技能人员
全　国	**9793**	**7205**	**759**	**758**	**15416**	**12943**
中央级	71	114		2	28	157
北　京	120	382	28	11	434	167
天　津	61	67	2	8	102	137
河　北	230	236	10	14	324	603
山　西	287	164	6	13	392	351
内蒙古	208	162	6	10	361	215
辽　宁	442	413	22	27	829	448
吉　林	285	247	7	4	607	371
黑龙江	1042	298	44	31	649	1149
上　海	224	209	34	32	368	396
江　苏	265	348	47	67	448	503
浙　江	229	245	19	23	433	318
安　徽	290	173	27	27	604	474
福　建	110	184	24	37	383	97
江　西	286	154	17	9	551	352
山　东	256	296	47	59	299	440
河　南	807	375	93	87	1177	1053
湖　北	441	208	25	15	550	714
湖　南	509	223	31	31	765	586
广　东	849	678	139	87	1504	831
广　西	231	274	20	24	484	279
海　南	24	41	2	6	58	71
重　庆	153	190	14	18	359	50
四　川	901	562	51	68	1458	1439
贵　州	303	196	11	6	536	187
云　南	289	241	15	17	421	494
西　藏	11	7			7	22
陕　西	413	195	7	13	661	460
甘　肃	165	115	5	8	273	247
青　海	32	19	2		23	49
宁　夏	36	41			50	62
新　疆	223	148	4	4	278	221

单位：人、人次、时、张

年龄结构				志愿服务	
35岁及以下人数	36岁至45岁人数	46岁至55岁人数	56岁及以上人数	志愿者服务人次数	志愿服务时间
9002	**10093**	**7249**	**2015**	**20746**	**57476.5**
138	29	13	5		
217	187	149	48		
81	64	68	26	200	400.0
282	370	200	75	245	984.0
234	230	229	50	103	392.0
139	167	223	47	71	437.0
339	430	408	100	75	128.0
233	468	233	44	1	
850	475	402	71		
237	308	135	84	790	3172.0
288	373	214	76	1821	4750.0
215	292	178	66	4246	6778.0
241	365	352	120	839	1837.0
148	145	147	40	20	160.0
218	343	275	67	132	528.0
206	254	235	44	3983	9744.0
952	720	448	110	268	675.0
392	524	261	87	353	830.0
450	575	273	53	1318	5377.0
683	786	737	129	417	2212.0
188	286	232	57	326	843.0
37	37	45	10		
133	142	116	18	2452	11207.0
866	1003	679	349	160	202.0
257	230	185	51	2130	3885.0
221	394	235	65	211	1262.0
7	16	6			
426	393	242	60	495	1493.5
132	183	170	35	90	180.0
21	29	19	3		
24	52	27	9		
147	223	113	16		

C-2-17续表2

地　区	年末床位数	编制登记	民政登记	一个机构多块牌子	年在院（站）总人天数	女性
全　国	**167470**	**140810**	**20524**	**6136**	**9711896**	**4960**
中央级	150	150				
北　京	5816	5723		93	1203827	587
天　津	1489	1489			19353	117
河　北	5333	3480	1634	219	233182	148
山　西	3576	3232	340	4	238510	75
内蒙古	3136	2795	284	57	128360	21
辽　宁	7882	7291	511	80	229430	61
吉　林	3230	3230			22957	47
黑龙江	5714	4202	1483	29	50457	40
上　海	3241	3241			340932	334
江　苏	7225	6506	70	649	589685	520
浙　江	5171	4965	156	50	369390	205
安　徽	7007	6191	590	226	504099	144
福　建	3365	3253		112	187563	91
江　西	6417	5151	429	837	390818	46
山　东	5375	5365		10	523596	144
河　南	10406	8985	931	490	485937	516
湖　北	7744	6593	1036	115	751536	570
湖　南	7432	6282	696	454	607753	204
广　东	12319	10847	1205	267	861715	296
广　西	3865	3551	168	146	308188	200
海　南	518	518			49166	
重　庆	2258	2258			200436	36
四　川	20723	9942	9264	1517	542608	143
贵　州	4607	4142	20	445	132026	85
云　南	5702	5073	629		331870	78
西　藏	6103	6103			3134	
陕　西	4514	4372		142	174463	85
甘　肃	2072	1706	251	115	59005	101
青　海	616	436	180		10765	
宁　夏	1138	576	547	15	15351	14
新　疆	3326	3162	100	64	145784	52

单位：人天、万元

事业单位会计制度财务指标			民间非营利组织会计制度财务指标		
固定资产原价	本年收入合计	本年支出合计	固定资产原价	本年收入合计	本年费用合计
565654.6	**506390.1**	**523445.3**	**107222.2**	**8147.9**	**13214.4**
12600.6	1497.3	9283.3			
36937.1	33839.2	31899.0			
2391.3	7715.0	7637.4			
13192.4	16583.7	17662.9	762.0	378.7	463.1
11245.1	9207.8	9496.1	905.0	131.0	212.9
8974.9	8983.3	9399.5	1248.0	180.7	180.1
24774.7	20444.0	18398.5	598.4	123.6	84.5
9475.3	8696.7	8568.3			
17878.8	7010.3	7436.6	1983.2		2644.2
27306.5	27784.3	28716.2			
35324.4	26941.5	26905.3	30.0	6.0	6.0
22911.0	29044.6	24931.2	102.0	152.0	152.0
22380.9	13150.0	13822.5	630.0	45.0	305.0
10757.4	11528.7	11124.1			
12554.0	8723.5	7812.3		48.0	101.8
24820.3	18879.1	18879.1			
22728.9	21454.8	33397.9	9212.0	1001.2	986.8
27827.8	22879.3	23072.0	1454.0	414.2	279.2
16665.3	21558.4	21833.7	345.0	198.0	80.0
65303.8	73923.3	71845.2	1098.4	1679.7	302.3
13886.6	18282.2	17939.2	107.0	33.3	37.3
2256.5	4322.3	5378.0	59003.0		
8480.5	12412.3	12292.3			
32527.3	21409.8	23097.5	28225.0	3635.5	7322.3
11960.6	11438.4	12854.6	196.0		0.1
20665.7	13360.1	13140.3	25.0		6.2
835.4	320.0	564.6			
20058.0	16531.5	16934.3			
12693.9	5788.7	5467.7	958.2	26.0	
702.0	1726.2	1660.7	130.0		
2125.4	2087.8	2027.7	210.0	95.0	
13412.2	8866.0	9967.3			

C-2-18 生活无着人员

地　区	单位数	0～99张	100～299张	300～499张	500张以上	年末职工人数	女性
全　国	**1736**	**1464**	**233**	**26**	**13**	**17344**	**5982**
中央级							
北　京	20	14	3		3	560	254
天　津	13	11	1		1	218	69
河　北	50	44	6			404	121
山　西	78	69	7	2		539	187
内蒙古	39	34	4	1		414	108
辽　宁	64	47	16		1	829	251
吉　林	50	43	7			722	241
黑龙江	64	58	6			647	189
上　海	18	15	2		1	336	120
江　苏	69	54	12	3		716	278
浙　江	53	46	7			528	174
安　徽	45	31	11	3		440	142
福　建	43	36	7			335	114
江　西	96	84	10	2		585	188
山　东	55	43	10	2		499	149
河　南	85	68	13	3	1	1102	385
湖　北	84	68	14	1	1	860	306
湖　南	113	97	16			1014	329
广　东	71	42	23	3	3	1740	569
广　西	67	64	3			484	175
海　南	7	4	3			87	29
重　庆	38	35	2	1		347	127
四　川	173	154	18		1	1202	442
[illegible]	75	64	10	1		423	170
[illegible]	[illegible]	65	6			462	161
[illegible]	[illegible]	1	1			23	4
[illegible]	[illegible]	81	5	2	1	980	368
[illegible]	[illegible]	43	2			380	149
[illegible]	[illegible]	2	1			34	8
[illegible]	[illegible]	7	2			72	36
[illegible]	[illegible]	40	5	2		362	139

救助管理站

单位：个、人

受教育程度		职业资格水平		按人员性质分	
大学专科人数	大学本科及以上人数	助理社会工作师人数	社会工作师人数	管理人员	专业技术技能人员
6174	**5235**	**530**	**604**	**10754**	**6590**
115	355	28	11	412	148
60	53	2	8	87	131
131	114	8	13	171	233
221	140	5	12	315	224
148	124	6	9	275	139
318	283	11	24	561	268
198	198	4	2	447	275
263	151	6	4	426	221
129	173	18	30	292	44
224	285	45	61	366	350
188	203	16	21	341	187
144	136	16	18	284	156
78	154	22	35	266	69
189	120	17	7	366	219
176	211	35	47	192	307
374	253	15	39	552	550
318	156	23	13	404	456
432	164	28	29	581	433
659	522	120	73	1252	488
128	187	12	22	324	160
18	30	2	6	42	45
130	159	12	18	303	44
480	328	43	61	848	354
183	135	10	5	312	111
153	169	10	12	243	219
7	5			3	20
360	167	7	13	581	399
143	92	4	8	211	169
22	7	2		9	25
20	35			41	31
165	126	3	3	247	115

C-2-18续表1

地 区	年龄结构				志愿服务	
	35岁及以下人数	36岁至45岁人数	46岁至55岁人数	56岁及以上人数	志愿者服务人次数	志愿服务时间
全 国	**5634**	**6358**	**4254**	**1098**	**18656**	**50843**
中央级						
北 京	211	168	141	40		
天 津	72	62	65	19	200	400
河 北	137	150	78	39	99	334
山 西	200	165	139	35	103	392
内蒙古	96	103	180	35	60	360
辽 宁	250	266	248	65	22	42
吉 林	192	333	168	29	1	
黑龙江	190	228	196	33		
上 海	127	82	74	53	352	784
江 苏	247	272	145	52	1767	4631
浙 江	151	220	106	51	4216	6745
安 徽	137	154	117	32	559	1163
福 建	130	110	67	28	20	160
江 西	162	244	135	44		
山 东	160	176	132	31	3983	9744
河 南	452	361	221	68	124	397
湖 北	277	358	162	63	320	724
湖 南	375	444	163	32	1318	5377
广 东	454	614	561	111	417	2212
广 西	130	191	126	37	326	843
海 南	25	26	28	8		
重 庆	108	119	105	15	2134	10321
四 川	424	454	282	42	160	202
贵 州	167	148	88	20	1717	3153
云 南	131	209	105	17	211	1262
西 藏	4	13	6			
陕 西	390	336	202	52	485	1474
甘 肃	109	139	105	27	62	124
青 海	7	12	12	3		
宁 夏	14	34	17	7		
新 疆	105	167	80	10		

单位：人、人次、时

本年在站救助人次数	从其他站转入的	女性	未成年人	老年人	肢体残疾人
2835371	**114125**	**461794**	**111603**	**258039**	**108478**
327716	3518	93678	5403	8750	1725
12994	36	912	485	760	260
50532	1231	9861	3962	7612	2355
120361	925	8771	5267	5746	3264
30358	8704	5624	1068	3147	3558
61649	1456	6100	2804	8478	2174
25186	2468	4186	882	5454	2329
27326	1959	3477	935	3999	1655
22360	65	3998	1090	2414	583
135845	9685	22504	3837	15561	3078
67431	655	10815	2047	6373	1678
93391	7942	12001	5307	10088	4870
42567	1003	3792	1024	3346	1567
64606	5056	5037	2269	6128	2114
82566	3226	13221	4733	6394	3722
125340	4299	23752	4330	18352	3382
220380	6736	23898	4777	19537	7636
605227	7375	112558	13869	49458	19895
169000	12371	16752	5559	11358	6715
74451	2504	11104	1849	4309	1123
7555	47	820	124	1607	120
37509	1950	6022	1290	6342	1538
149637	16085	27982	10331	21995	12126
63171	4577	8775	5781	3456	3008
57839	3566	7340	17012	6936	3524
3286			157	10	
101398	2868	7805	2519	9302	3507
23553	2849	4417	1114	3820	1827
8803	114	1417	3	189	3270
8000	182	678	290	489	239
15334	673	4497	1485	6629	5636

C-2-18续表2

地 区					床位数
	智障及精神病人	救治的危重病人	自主返乡	跨省接送	
全 国	**425100**	**18557**	**744371**	**74528**	**102471**
中央级					
北 京	6204	563	12980	3136	5467
天 津	2280	11	7329	122	1289
河 北	5323	1537	18289	1651	2438
山 西	6854	189	19103	651	2701
内蒙古	5560	323	9457	943	1852
辽 宁	4407	341	15370	1389	5318
吉 林	2161	400	7938	2433	2220
黑龙江	1615	251	7115	1297	2231
上 海	1674	227	11167	554	2042
江 苏	10676	799	85901	8922	4590
浙 江	12157	298	23868	2114	3008
安 徽	11867	373	26388	3988	4043
福 建	1554	176	31414	642	2003
江 西	4488	66	18551	2084	4639
山 东	12592	386	22906	4322	3700
河 南	21520	1514	22501	2172	5715
湖 北	40118	3579	44153	7990	4927
湖 南	209453	935	78150	5077	5412
广 东	8634	3330	90764	3309	7339
广 西	11724	220	16016	1738	2339
海 南	717	21	5828	275	468
重 庆	3196	313	24553	1516	1762
四 川	18858	1342	55961	8600	7379
贵 州	4262	277	28755	1960	3267
云 南	3279	89	12734	849	2027
西 藏					6082
陕 西	5489	704	27246	3021	4019
甘 肃	1826	55	12116	2185	1407
青 海	5213		353		180
宁 夏	251	7	1578	59	541
新 疆	1148	231	5887	1529	2066

单位：人、张、人天

成年人床位数	儿童床位数	年末在站人数	女性	儿童	本年在站人天数
82649	**19822**	**26773**	**4960**	**4304**	**8426155**
4654	813	2639	587	464	1203827
1081	208	482	117	160	19353
1767	671	618	148	158	230950
2017	684	635	75	102	238480
1429	423	205	21	13	98424
3917	1401	791	61	52	178270
1542	678	249	47	19	22777
1890	341	311	40	54	39507
1835	207	879	334	58	340932
3765	825	1469	520	215	533312
2423	585	841	205	104	293590
3024	1019	1163	144	250	373862
1291	712	336	91	25	106279
3915	724	1231	46	72	274418
2860	840	1401	144	319	380373
4010	1705	1932	516	573	456379
3874	1053	2196	570	191	733606
4704	708	1719	204	225	544818
5689	1650	2019	296	414	806817
1960	379	733	200	141	246447
394	74	1		1	49166
1277	485	262	36	67	173253
6017	1362	1682	143	224	529558
2653	614	726	85	83	122191
1746	281	374	78	117	129834
6082		340			3134
3425	594	937	85	128	136988
1121	286	298	101	21	55925
180					8550
494	47	74	14	2	15351
1613	453	230	52	52	79784

C-2-18续表3

地 区	本年不在站救助人次数	在站滞留三个月以上人数	残疾人人数	未成年人人数
全 国	**447424**	**19662**	**8343**	**1045**
中央级				
北 京		2636	5	9
天 津	121	6	5	1
河 北	36338	622	136	72
山 西	15106	648	435	45
内蒙古	18930	374	49	3
辽 宁	1790	206	155	5
吉 林	738	59	24	
黑龙江	2376	47	19	3
上 海	1731	818	362	43
江 苏	1875	1300	497	35
浙 江	5223	823	213	34
安 徽	35336	875	382	15
福 建	17432	295	218	17
江 西	1893	82	69	7
山 东	19240	904	735	19
河 南	42909	1431	903	56
湖 北	20545	1236	680	33
湖 南	31374	2512	1472	26
广 东	41490	1752	775	453
广 西	23069	722	361	47
海 南	1515			
重 庆	6142	378	178	29
四 川	12789	700	224	23
贵 州	31216	289	70	10
云 南	11696	192	42	25
西 藏	2834			
陕 西	8558	553	230	28
甘 肃	2614	53	48	2
青 海	4130	55		
宁 夏	1278	37	35	
新 疆	47136	57	21	5

单位：人次、万元

事业单位会计制度财务指标		
固定资产原价	本年收入合计	本年支出合计
330810.2	**387031.5**	**390989.8**
5275.1	31685.2	29983.0
1765.9	6689.6	6828.5
7260.0	9263.9	11413.0
9692.3	8009.8	8318.1
6099.3	6619.1	7203.5
13734.4	14607.3	14533.7
6315.4	7113.8	7005.7
6292.8	4454.1	5111.1
18029.2	16947.1	17985.1
23549.7	23197.0	23112.0
10222.8	20907.9	18884.5
10682.6	10404.2	11068.9
6014.8	9090.9	8670.4
6148.0	6352.4	5850.8
14996.4	13926.3	13926.3
10145.7	13805.1	12927.2
24631.2	17964.3	18228.6
11949.1	18731.9	18337.7
49074.6	63955.7	62509.8
8009.1	11304.9	11348.0
1712.1	2860.6	3943.1
7157.1	10641.2	10560.5
20265.4	17478.2	18859.1
6596.9	5409.0	7008.1
9509.7	7462.7	7715.1
85.4		244.6
16248.7	14465.7	14871.5
10094.2	4488.0	4029.7
228.1	918.0	939.5
1398.1	1641.8	1760.7
7626.1	6635.8	7812.0

C-2-19 军

地　区	单位数					年末职工人数	女性
		0～99张	100～299张	300～499张	500张以上		
全　国	**315**	**187**	**97**	**22**	**9**	**4977**	**1953**
中央级							
北　京	1			1		41	14
天　津	1		1			21	3
河　北	9	7	2			94	28
山　西	6	4	2			102	39
内蒙古	5	3	2			95	26
辽　宁	12	8	3		1	211	70
吉　林	11	7	4			256	75
黑龙江	11	4	6		1	169	70
上　海	1		1			40	13
江　苏	16	10	5	1		199	89
浙　江	10	5	3	2		119	52
安　徽	34	26	7	1		473	252
福　建	11	8	3			95	48
江　西	14	8	4	2		278	106
山　东	17	10	6	1		240	87
河　南	24	13	9		2	587	210
湖　北	9	4	3	1	1	204	64
湖　南	13	9	3	1		250	119
广　东	13	6	4	1	2	237	107
广　西	13	7	4	2		232	92
海　南	2	2				32	9
重　庆	5	4		1		62	25
四　川	14	7	2	4	1	197	63
贵　州	8	4	2	2		95	36
云　南	21	9	11	1		286	142
西　藏	1	1				5	1
陕　西	10	8	2			112	47
甘　肃	8	6	2			98	24
青　海	4	2	2			36	9
宁　夏	1		1			10	2
新　疆	10	5	3	1	1	101	31

供站

单位：个、人

受教育程度		职业资格水平		按人员性质分	
大学专科人数	大学本科及以上人数	助理社会工作师人数	社会工作师人数	管理人员	专业技术技能人员
1563	**1166**	**66**	**61**	**2717**	**2260**
5	27			22	19
1	14			15	6
21	47	2	1	53	41
50	24	1	1	47	55
37	23		1	71	24
81	59	3	2	128	83
87	49	3	2	160	96
75	47	2	4	106	63
11	9	2		35	5
36	58	1	6	72	127
40	42	3	2	73	46
114	19	8	1	199	274
26	17	1	2	67	28
86	34		2	175	103
80	85	12	12	107	133
161	111	7	10	320	267
75	49	2	2	87	117
60	55	1	2	149	101
94	89	7	6	165	72
80	79	5	2	148	84
2	5			12	20
23	31	2		56	6
83	50	2	1	102	95
28	22		1	75	20
78	46	1		133	153
3	2			3	2
49	19			51	61
22	16	1		47	51
10	12			12	24
6	4			2	8
39	22		1	25	76

C-2-19续表

地　区	年龄结构				志愿服务	
	35岁及以下人数	36岁至45岁人数	46岁至55岁人数	56岁及以上人数	志愿者服务人次数	志愿服务时间
全　国	**1063**	**1865**	**1655**	**394**	**1337**	**3308**
中央级						
北　京	6	19	8	8		
天　津	9	2	3	7		
河　北	30	26	28	10		
山　西	17	48	29	8		
内蒙古	21	48	22	4	11	77
辽　宁	39	82	68	22		
吉　林	41	135	65	15		
黑龙江	29	81	52	7		
上　海	7	6	9	18		
江　苏	23	90	63	23	54	119
浙　江	17	37	51	14		
安　徽	60	170	196	47	280	674
福　建	12	25	48	10		
江　西	54	88	116	20	132	528
山　东	46	78	103	13		
河　南	192	208	156	31	144	278
湖　北	47	74	61	22	12	60
湖　南	56	95	80	19		
广　东	50	84	90	13		
广　西	51	84	77	20		
海　南	7	9	15	1		
重　庆	25	23	11	3	318	886
四　川	40	72	69	16		
贵　州	34	29	24	8	348	610
云　南	36	133	99	18		
西　藏	2	3				
陕　西	36	46	27	3	10	20
甘　肃	21	27	44	6	28	56
青　海	14	15	7			
宁　夏	1	2	5	2		
新　疆	40	26	29	6		

单位：人、万元、张、人次、人天

事业单位会计制度财务指标			床位数	接待人次数		本年在站人天数
固定资产原价	本年收入合计	本年支出合计			接待军队人次数	
188481.7	**93753.8**	**101040.0**	**37089**	**4034297**	**3067083**	**1285741**
31662.0	2154.0	1916.0	349	142500	142500	
625.4	1025.4	808.9	200	21734	21734	
3430.5	3729.2	2918.0	442	95736	66845	2232
792.8	1198.0	1172.0	445	50543	38564	30
2766.0	2157.7	1989.5	459	52005	52005	29936
3406.1	1769.4	1827.5	1443	42048	36491	51160
3159.9	1582.9	1562.6	1010	90781	54858	180
7499.6	2556.2	2325.5	1700	35113	24780	10950
2417.3	2158.4	2043.1	179	41982	15501	
11124.7	3657.5	3713.3	1662	202800	88109	56373
12688.2	7906.7	5837.7	1522	241698	149159	75800
11317.8	2665.8	2673.6	2268	170810	125820	130237
3204.3	1331.3	1359.6	1177	97573	91885	81284
6406.0	2361.1	1951.5	1349	134717	71482	116400
9823.9	4952.8	4952.8	1675	189262	189262	143223
12168.7	6428.5	19219.7	3062	408365	213366	29558
3196.6	4915.0	4843.4	1781	104657	98355	17930
4657.2	2822.5	3496.0	1208	270908	216336	62935
16179.2	9967.6	9335.4	3478	233702	220999	54898
5728.5	6534.3	6175.4	1338	97536	85576	61741
544.4	1461.7	1434.9	50	18946	18946	
1323.4	1771.1	1731.8	496	104987	102417	27183
11640.6	3750.0	3738.1	3715	280996	278790	13050
1337.5	3061.4	2721.3	1129	110372	93937	9835
8965.9	5099.0	4743.5	2746	335640	168488	202036
	320.0	320.0	1	30000	30000	
2930.5	1690.4	1687.4	445	112283	112268	37475
2521.7	1241.5	1398.0	334	134713	95836	3080
473.9	808.2	721.2	256	84365	84349	2215
727.0	446.0	267.0	10			
5762.1	2230.2	2155.3	1160	97525	78425	66000

C-2-20 其他提供住宿的

地 区	单位数					年末职工人数	
		0～99张	100～299张	300～499张	500张以上		女性
全 国	**320**	**214**	**78**	**24**	**4**	**6038**	**3119**
中央级	1		1			185	130
北 京							
天 津							
河 北	22	10	11	1		429	272
山 西	13	13				102	31
内蒙古	11	9	2			67	46
辽 宁	31	28	2		1	237	128
吉 林							
黑龙江	31	25	5	1		982	257
上 海	2		1		1	388	293
江 苏	5	2	1	2		36	24
浙 江	3	1	1	1		104	82
安 徽	12	10	2			165	54
福 建	4	4				50	16
江 西	5	3	2			40	20
山 东							
河 南	21	17	2	1	1	541	209
湖 北	20	16	4			200	119
湖 南	12	9	3			87	33
广 东	10	4	5	1		358	181
广 西	5	5				47	24
海 南	1		1			10	4
重 庆							
四 川	68	29	28	10	1	1498	964
贵 州	6	6				205	86
云 南	8	4	3	1		167	76
西 藏	1	1				1	
陕 西	1	1				29	8
甘 肃	7	6	1			42	10
青 海	2	1	1			2	
宁 夏	7	5	2			30	23
新 疆	11	5		6		36	29

社会服务机构

单位：个、人

受教育程度		职业资格水平		按人员性质分	
大学专科人数	大学本科及以上人数	助理社会工作师人数	社会工作师人数	管理人员	专业技术技能人员
2056	**804**	**163**	**93**	**1945**	**4093**
71	114		2	28	157
78	75			100	329
16				30	72
23	15			15	52
43	71	8	1	140	97
704	100	36	23	117	865
84	27	14	2	41	347
5	5	1		10	26
1				19	85
32	18	3	8	121	44
6	13	1		50	
11				10	30
272	11	71	38	305	236
48	3			59	141
17	4	2		35	52
96	67	12	8	87	271
23	8	3		12	35
4	6			4	6
338	184	6	6	508	990
92	39	1		149	56
58	26	4	5	45	122
1				1	
4	9			29	
	7			15	27
				2	
10	2			7	23
19		1		6	30

C−2−20续表1

地 区	年龄结构				志愿服务	
	35岁及以下人数	36岁至45岁人数	46岁至55岁人数	56岁及以上人数	志愿者服务人次数	志愿服务时间
全 国	**2305**	**1870**	**1340**	**523**	**753**	**3326**
中央级	138	29	13	5		
北 京						
天 津						
河 北	115	194	94	26	146	650
山 西	17	17	61	7		
内蒙古	22	16	21	8		
辽 宁	50	82	92	13	53	86
吉 林						
黑龙江	631	166	154	31		
上 海	103	220	52	13	438	2388
江 苏	18	11	6	1		
浙 江	47	35	21	1	30	33
安 徽	44	41	39	41		
福 建	6	10	32	2		
江 西	2	11	24	3		
山 东						
河 南	308	151	71	11		
湖 北	68	92	38	2	21	46
湖 南	19	36	30	2		
广 东	179	88	86	5		
广 西	7	11	29			
海 南	5	2	2	1		
重 庆						
四 川	402	477	328	291		
贵 州	56	53	73	23	65	123
云 南	54	52	31	30		
西 藏	1					
陕 西		11	13	5		
甘 肃	2	17	21	2		
青 海		2				
宁 夏	9	16	5			
新 疆	2	30	4			

单位：人、人次、时、张、人天

年末床位数		年在院总人天数	年末在院人数		在院人员按性质分		
	光荣间床位			女性	优抚对象	特困人员	自费人员
27910	**421**	**3387286**	**14877**	**4039**	**168**	**3770**	**7949**
150		47998	149	78			149
2453	49	429124	1267	312	7	169	960
430	40	47631	224				110
825		27983	361			22	134
1121		50536	342	85	15	135	101
1783	114	186518	1285	108		19	659
1020		375234	1049	433		686	363
973		217015	581	229		294	267
641		8016	264	51	44		206
696		157832	451	82	4	66	278
185		32625	172	47		172	
429		62900	235	75			
1629	23	217025	821	194	22	246	368
1036		74172	584	107		285	58
812	5	89028	415	80	3	212	131
1502	41	52106	499	131	7	71	136
188		26000	74	51		55	23
9629	146	1183021	4915	1597	64	1043	3399
211	3	11750	45	31	1	11	33
929		11221	368	120		273	95
20		55	20				
50		30	10				
331		36095	175	5	1	11	163
180		41131	163	85			
587		440	378	138			316
100		1800	30				

C−2−20续表2

地区	在院人员按年龄分			在院人员按类型分		
	老人	青壮年	少年儿童	自理（完全自理）	介助（半自理）	介护（不能自理）
全国	**11833**	**1999**	**619**	**7510**	**3369**	**3572**
中央级	57	28	64	32	106	11
北京						
天津						
河北	1197	63	7	644	423	200
山西	121		34	145	7	3
内蒙古	130	36		103	50	13
辽宁	212	27	2	121	101	19
吉林						
黑龙江	1271	14		916	189	180
上海	235	794	20	42	262	745
江苏	307	267	7	110	58	413
浙江	202	62		205	54	5
安徽	395	56		204	228	19
福建	170		2	154	17	1
江西	235			200	20	15
山东						
河南	745	7	69	503	144	174
湖北	479	10	31	444	62	14
湖南	356	34	25	261	110	44
广东	67	102	304	105	60	308
广西	68	9	1	47	30	1
海南						
重庆						
四川	4831	69	40	2621	1197	1122
贵州	55	7	3	45		20
云南	115	253		61	95	212
西藏						
陕西	10			10		
甘肃	175			155	6	14
青海	12	151		163		
宁夏	378			189	150	39
新疆	10	10	10	30		

单位：人、人次、平方米

康复和医疗门诊人次数	机构建筑面积	事业单位会计制度财务指标			民间非营利组织会计制度财务指标		
		固定资产原价	本年收入合计	本年支出合计	固定资产原价	本年收入合计	本年费用合计
97667	**860819**	**46362.7**	**25604.8**	**31415.5**	**107222.2**	**8147.9**	**13214.4**
4135	30000	12600.6	1497.3	9283.3			
2987	64148	2501.9	3590.6	3331.9	762.0	378.7	463.1
	15198	760.0		6.0	905.0	131.0	212.9
	10338	109.6	206.5	206.5	1248.0	180.7	180.1
652	33455	7634.2	4067.3	2037.3	598.4	123.6	84.5
	31779	4086.4			1983.2		2644.2
829	30403	6860.0	8678.8	8688.0			
16147	34300	650.0	87.0	80.0	30.0	6.0	6.0
435	2999		230.0	209.0	102.0	152.0	152.0
1600	31698	380.5	80.0	80.0	630.0	45.0	305.0
62	27616	1538.3	1106.5	1094.1			
	21050		10.0	10.0		48.0	101.8
895	130886	414.5	1221.2	1251.0	9212.0	1001.2	986.8
754	12206				1454.0	414.2	279.2
153	17769	59.0	4.0		345.0	198.0	80.0
63900	9648	50.0			1098.4	1679.7	302.3
	17020	149.0	443.0	415.8	107.0	33.3	37.3
	100000				59003.0		
5060	120449	621.3	181.6	500.3	28225.0	3635.5	7322.3
	17500	4026.2	2968.0	3125.2	196.0		0.1
	42173	2190.1	798.4	681.7	25.0		6.2
	1000	750.0					
	1000	878.8	375.4	375.4			
58	14624	78.0	59.2	40.0	958.2	26.0	44.4
	23500				130.0		0.2
	12460	0.3			210.0	95.0	6.0
	7600	24.0					

C-2-21 不提供住宿的社会

地 区	机构和设施数	工商登记	编制登记	民政登记	设施
全 国	**391436**	**22**	**6767**	**37418**	**347229**
中央级	1		1		
北 京	12002	1	304	1085	10612
天 津	2990	1	39	51	2899
河 北	37764		171	140	37453
山 西	5544		304	64	5176
内蒙古	4229	1	109	52	4067
辽 宁	7425		190	511	6724
吉 林	1961		318	282	1361
黑龙江	3320	1	158	359	2802
上 海	6203	1	163	3039	3000
江 苏	40361		242	21939	18180
浙 江	30627	1	202	2423	28001
安 徽	8247	1	220	224	7802
福 建	5928	1	120	131	5676
江 西	3829		279	62	3488
山 东	26135	4	340	1786	24005
河 南	5073	1	291	101	4680
湖 北	14420	3	347	315	13755
湖 南	13652		271	216	13165
广 东	66837		268	1323	65246
广 西	13688		216	73	13399
海 南	2601		16	243	2342
重 庆	7966		188	413	7365
四 川	21256	4	477	1310	19465
贵 州	23505		325	85	23095
云 南	3195		139	63	2993
西 藏	77		3		74
陕 西	7179	1	222	381	6575
甘 肃	9609		243	100	9266
青 海	1606		26		1580
宁 夏	1284		66	216	1002
新 疆	2922	1	509	431	1981

服务机构和设施总表

单位：个、人

年末职工人数	女性	工商登记	编制登记	民政登记	设施
1447028	**533389**	**433**	**63743**	**207053**	**1172154**
135	55		135		
46045	22972	8	3722	4212	38103
13756	7498	5	391	569	12778
74621	26730		1927	877	71684
29701	10671		2520	258	26848
17561	8642	42	1511	174	15832
45266	25628		1988	3656	39493
15603	8394		4177	3504	7906
20341	9273	23	1202	2002	17002
47953	18238	77	3993	28474	15409
197099	59575		2245	105794	88881
84859	32830	4	1607	8042	74272
39536	15976	3	2556	1114	35716
22182	8699	3	798	519	20793
15296	5311		1349	545	13239
120013	46574	32	3982	13805	101323
29692	10513	43	2989	701	25895
50062	20202	69	2790	2658	44485
45902	17337		2065	997	42668
203009	69131		2608	8449	191921
25039	7998		1938	511	22584
11941	3080		337	1391	10211
27490	12189		1432	2249	23801
67189	23260	15	2746	7403	56886
102061	26955		4887	399	96710
14673	5107		978	933	12707
2356	436		46		2310
27779	11269	87	2004	1623	23913
23850	7794		1617	347	21846
4906	1328		181		4725
6328	3242		576	1563	4189
14784	6482	22	2446	4284	8024

C-2-21续表1

地 区	受教育程度		职业资格水平	
	大学专科人数	大学本科及以上人数	助理社会工作师人数	社会工作师人数
全 国	**298848**	**163796**	**23545**	**12339**
中央级	9	126		
北 京	12455	11741	2560	1083
天 津	3664	2871	723	225
河 北	4363	1867	149	119
山 西	6434	2861	768	503
内蒙古	4992	3428	604	236
辽 宁	14152	9894	1119	588
吉 林	5842	2665	389	264
黑龙江	5609	2465	409	154
上 海	10869	4782	602	1535
江 苏	35019	17396	2464	1061
浙 江	17511	10712	1523	772
安 徽	9994	3174	706	240
福 建	2491	1158	461	295
江 西	1835	604	128	58
山 东	32106	17971	1449	398
河 南	5474	3067	332	189
湖 北	9727	4242	464	329
湖 南	10169	4865	762	309
广 东	39327	28776	5077	2373
广 西	2824	1773	194	108
海 南	1089	400	35	15
重 庆	7119	3899	842	469
四 川	14953	5507	820	418
贵 州	20529	6841	90	79
云 南	2484	1350	89	45
西 藏	247	141	22	3
陕 西	5796	2234	286	156
甘 肃	4456	2923	118	99
青 海	1665	568	78	86
宁 夏	1142	416	30	14
新 疆	4502	3079	252	116

单位：人、人次、时

年龄结构				志愿服务	
35岁及以下人数	36岁至45岁人数	46岁至55岁人数	56岁及以上人数	志愿者服务人次数	志愿服务时间
436474	**558245**	**341815**	**110297**	**6643229**	**17940727**
77	21	25	12		
14019	16061	12606	3359	4557059	13074209
5356	4501	3173	726	52659	81436
17653	27041	22716	7211	16116	51414
7927	11498	7010	3266	9006	42019
6328	7263	3004	921	10475	20808
14702	17155	9077	4332	23797	38068
4317	8550	2382	354	23289	46578
5682	8495	3570	2594	32037	72056
13400	17135	13605	3813	26454	83603
54641	77582	50193	14683	224618	475422
24572	32214	20042	8037	188426	346465
10672	17246	9417	2195	74747	157519
6273	8044	5071	2744	105300	324241
3580	5429	3417	2870	2322	4575
41622	43092	28614	6685	565354	1275205
7508	13742	5870	2572	1745	10052
13745	20218	10427	5672	2165	3640
12273	17747	12659	3151	16767	39014
72745	76974	40479	12811	42109	62064
6581	8308	7932	2217	3305	9327
2775	4560	3543	1063	18097	31694
8192	10366	6917	2015	282075	661711
18628	28618	15761	4182	156665	502165
33822	39987	22582	5670	165064	380525
4080	6522	3173	898	2930	8901
635	279	40	1402	5	
7057	10663	7869	2190	17863	74006
9062	8613	5006	1169	1604	2877
1606	1577	810	909		
1663	2854	1684	102	2855	5337
5281	5890	3141	472	18321	55799

C-2-21续表2

地区	企业会计制度财务指标				
	固定资产原价	营业收入	费用合计	营业利润	固定资产原价
全　国	**8608.2**	**4647.2**	**3726676.8**	**-180.9**	**2003890.7**
中央级					17628.8
北　京	8.0	11.7	73824.7		170795.6
天　津	86.0	47.0	64828.8	-8.0	71825.4
河　北			27442.7		86551.9
山　西			22092.6		39432.1
内蒙古	666.0	272.8	5918.8	-780.0	47453.8
辽　宁			83238.4		88263.9
吉　林			22373.7		34426.8
黑龙江	185.3	164.3	30152.6	9.5	21361.0
上　海	2583.1	2351.7	158895.9	150.2	125940.9
江　苏			796377.7		137669.2
浙　江	200.0		2064820.4		109928.8
安　徽	300.0	220.0	42412.3		51182.8
福　建		3.0	15289.8		10507.3
江　西			16255.6		30819.0
山　东	186.0	71.0	22.0	21.0	173302.0
河　南	280.0	186.0	61980.2		73483.5
湖　北	620.5	58.9	30560.0	10.3	93089.6
湖　南			27480.5		68422.4
广　东			11854.7		111772.6
广　西			7892.1		60192.3
海　南					11133.3
重　庆			70144.1		34459.3
四　川	91.0		30332.9		101499.2
贵　州			555.3		36247.3
云　南			8746.9		29186.8
西　藏					455.0
陕　西	2629.3	1260.5	26401.6	416.1	67877.8
甘　肃			391.0		33574.9
青　海					10468.1
宁　夏			38.0		12765.9
新　疆	773.0	0.3	26353.5		42173.4

单位：万元

事业单位会计制度财务指标		民间非营利组织会计制度财务指标		
本年收入合计	本年支出合计	固定资产原价	本年收入合计	本年支出合计
2911624.9	**2785702.2**	**686816.4**	**721672.3**	**632263.5**
118036.1	89323.1			
411488.1	505879.6	19744.2	14003.1	10253.7
25502.4	23127.6	849.0	1264.9	1527.2
136931.9	129099.8	5228.2	1173.1	1443.9
45093.4	32929.6	1215.5	1615.9	192.0
40120.0	40015.7	910.1	134.7	220.3
86347.4	77516.2	17580.8	9478.5	2448.2
82045.9	75373.7	5527.2	3584.6	1345.4
11914.0	11990.9	3467.1	851.9	1604.6
294433.0	273197.3	62837.3	252107.0	297690.2
118024.2	112618.5	287448.4	216560.0	194134.0
104945.3	94171.4	40105.7	66050.6	26655.4
42505.6	36981.2	21124.7	9796.6	869.4
30726.2	29409.8	2061.5	634.9	592.2
26501.8	18719.6	4312.0	4400.7	4323.4
179055.0	178839.5	59992.7	41916.7	49396.9
98066.5	85470.2	1650.7	3125.3	1041.6
80091.6	78774.8	9767.0	6088.0	5835.1
73507.7	58141.4	11050.1	45175.8	1902.2
180106.7	167531.2	25563.5	21270.9	8968.6
65684.4	63480.8	728.0	140.0	209.2
13810.8	13218.8	315.0	283.8	287.0
109790.5	93850.0	3944.0	4817.3	4802.9
144364.6	139906.8	33406.1	4863.0	9021.3
57446.8	48231.9	8164.3	629.8	192.6
76539.1	72908.6	2841.8	7.1	798.9
7867.0	7668.0			
119110.2	115169.5	27652.1	2047.4	2033.2
20753.2	22044.8	6383.3	1088.9	257.8
11796.4	14122.6			
18505.2	6914.3	680.2	3065.4	42.3
80513.9	69075.0	22265.9	5496.4	4174.0

C-2-22 社区服务

地区	机构和设施数	工商登记	编制登记	民政登记	设施	农村
全国	**386186**	**14**	**1619**	**37324**	**347229**	**208298**
中央级						
北京	11913	1	215	1085	10612	5120
天津	2952		3	50	2899	1087
河北	37598		14	131	37453	33707
山西	5294		54	64	5176	3317
内蒙古	4159		40	52	4067	1269
辽宁	7259		27	508	6724	1571
吉林	1735		92	282	1361	578
黑龙江	3185		25	358	2802	440
上海	6129		105	3024	3000	390
江苏	40137		21	21936	18180	16705
浙江	30454	1	45	2407	28001	19883
安徽	8086	1	88	195	7802	3288
福建	5818		11	131	5676	2424
江西	3564		16	60	3488	519
山东	25872	4	78	1785	24005	13160
河南	4812		31	101	4680	2135
湖北	14152	2	81	314	13755	5874
湖南	13402		21	216	13165	7558
广东	66677		112	1319	65246	29756
广西	13476		4	73	13399	11321
海南	2584			242	2342	2091
重庆	7853		75	413	7365	3883
四川	20802	4	23	1310	19465	9813
贵州	23285		106	84	23095	18272
云南	3071		15	63	2993	1263
西藏	74				74	69
陕西	6975		20	380	6575	4161
甘肃	9413		49	98	9266	6990
青海	1580				1580	988
宁夏	1215		1	212	1002	511
新疆	2660	1	247	431	1981	155

机构和设施总表

单位：个、人

年末职工人数	女性	受教育程度：大学专科人数	受教育程度：大学本科及以上人数	职业资格水平：助理社会工作师人数	职业资格水平：社会工作师人数
1402814	**514423**	**283834**	**148489**	**22811**	**11483**
44889	22446	12111	11053	2530	1039
13381	7330	3579	2653	719	219
72943	26010	3896	1370	126	78
27758	9778	5692	2250	741	467
16798	8299	4710	3090	577	205
43563	24924	13628	9043	1109	573
12810	7582	5051	1978	345	251
19409	8859	5293	2101	403	143
46761	17630	10527	4209	562	1490
195052	58727	34405	16699	2395	980
83573	32167	17114	10190	1510	742
38117	15335	9490	2768	676	215
21437	8379	2278	913	450	278
14095	4855	1419	399	113	43
117142	45502	31099	16739	1408	310
26959	9352	4539	2433	281	106
47785	19198	8850	3608	452	316
44076	16573	9515	4412	749	270
201392	68430	38866	28149	4977	2322
23114	7057	2122	1138	159	87
11601	2939	1011	341	33	10
26551	11749	6798	3350	798	458
64617	22007	13872	4689	794	378
100221	26172	19685	6122	79	70
13826	4743	2194	1020	72	33
2310	409	222	131	22	3
25891	10405	5127	1669	271	138
22624	7319	4189	2595	112	87
4725	1239	1618	510	78	85
5780	3066	909	232	26	7
13614	5942	4025	2635	244	80

C-2-22续表1

地 区	年龄结构				志愿
	35岁及以下人数	36岁至45岁人数	46岁至55岁人数	56岁及以上人数	志愿者服务人次数
全 国	**419187**	**542298**	**332798**	**108334**	**5675513**
中央级					
北 京	13658	15657	12281	3293	4055221
天 津	5213	4387	3078	703	52149
河 北	16975	26451	22393	7124	14057
山 西	7163	10796	6605	3194	954
内蒙古	6008	6988	2861	896	10332
辽 宁	14082	16633	8657	4191	23653
吉 林	3239	7293	2007	271	
黑龙江	5404	8122	3328	2555	361
上 海	12993	16775	13315	3678	26078
江 苏	53877	76868	49720	14587	219436
浙 江	24000	31787	19810	7982	177210
安 徽	10019	16779	9158	2155	42468
福 建	6053	7775	4860	2699	118
江 西	3244	4921	3130	2800	578
山 东	40610	42088	27910	6534	547445
河 南	6297	12798	5360	2504	1465
湖 北	12987	19287	9980	5531	569
湖 南	11511	17048	12359	3086	11422
广 东	72075	76454	40117	12746	4860
广 西	5790	7566	7592	2165	2200
海 南	2629	4430	3494	1048	17790
重 庆	7822	10032	6719	1978	277588
四 川	17457	27791	15298	4071	5092
贵 州	32900	39362	22322	5637	152323
云 南	3796	6208	2962	860	2711
西 藏	618	254	36	1402	5
陕 西	6243	10006	7525	2117	14248
甘 肃	8592	8187	4729	1116	1462
青 海	1525	1524	771	901	
宁 夏	1440	2643	1584	88	2853
新 疆	4967	5388	2837	422	10865

单位：人、人次、时、张

服务	床位数合计	日间照料床位数		留宿照料床位数	
志愿服务时间			农村		农村
15477984	**3228448**	**1415600**	**876807**	**1812848**	**1200037**
11876705	10415	5722	2366	4693	748
80361	12487	6482	3564	6005	4992
44452	284319	185415	167256	98904	77885
2809	57695	39867	29391	17828	14094
20464	132692	18896	3854	113796	109912
37880	43517	21683	9311	21834	10703
	5003	4099	223	904	1
387	72677	21568	4285	51109	12343
82405	18443	2402	3	16041	1560
459278	224622	147247	66747	77375	21959
317541	300925	164950	120246	135975	61062
117413	208744	19282	7323	189462	152939
336	83332	20606	10464	62726	34891
831	34163	12753	8281	21410	17734
1228677	356214	161159	105632	195055	120232
9137	231495	60899	38272	170596	129707
1427	92806	56178	21966	36628	11911
27607	114650	48044	32442	66606	48100
15458	145173	83578	36996	61595	28823
5155	121600	21077	18858	100523	94890
30815	8634	3102	1046	5532	3899
647093	95221	30418	14297	64803	56405
18934	199191	62713	26325	136478	78766
352084	101329	53852	33557	47477	39518
8519	60098	17777	6913	42321	21531
	2467	1993	1780	474	394
58527	67339	37852	30123	29487	21991
2553	106166	87913	64814	18253	13297
	16300	7067	3974	9233	5219
5329	4517	2702	1358	1815	1737
25809	16214	8304	5140	7910	2794

C-2-22续表2

地区	年末收养人数合计	日间照料人数	农村	留宿照料人数	农村
全国	**1079129**	**351681**	**236057**	**727448**	**518049**
中央级					
北京	3483	1922	1088	1561	283
天津	1279	405	205	874	863
河北	55690	31906	29852	23784	15749
山西	24594	17950	13102	6644	5720
内蒙古	72942	4916	881	68026	69506
辽宁	7499	2086	843	5413	3431
吉林	537	514	57	23	1
黑龙江	31117	6575	2514	24542	7206
上海	1104	1104			
江苏	41490	24884	14484	16606	5023
浙江	62392	19403	14745	42989	11754
安徽	62390	1283	3	61107	51579
福建	14229	3495	410	10734	5662
江西	15100	6673	6392	8427	7644
山东	181954	74532	48176	107422	63015
河南	127784	26186	21687	101598	79874
湖北	25226	12315	4989	12911	4939
湖南	53933	22905	16585	31028	22679
广东	26734	17932	9802	8802	3815
广西	45664	9312	8706	36352	35077
海南	2583	668	102	1915	1520
重庆	64577	20801	9601	43776	38800
四川	65730	9482	6040	56248	39632
贵州	21983	5507	3847	16476	14254
云南	17695	2776	1416	14919	10231
西藏	1172	1165	993	7	7
陕西	27894	11982	10294	15912	13459
甘肃	10165	7217	5133	2948	1997
青海	3159	500	48	2659	1511
宁夏	949	384	214	565	561
新疆	8081	4901	3848	3180	2257

单位：人、人次、人天、个、平方米

本年收养照料人天数	老年人活动人次数	社区服务志愿者组织数	注册社区志愿者人数	城镇便民、利民服务网点数	机构建筑面积
70588501	**20719403**	**116335**	**3390450**	**86927**	**115902434**
283968	1442212	15158	947103	2244	1643039
		88		2914	1131619
5627916	546479	3661	3517	592	7557998
67695	124752	412	10920	65	1749120
15349039	851393	2560	13049	381	3229563
57130	7639	1427	42790	3924	2746202
35770	174	375			671181
64427	93827	15		97	1404571
218779	3044	2713	128239	141	1412881
1535529	3585138	6524	152968	13716	11706284
106226	1255348	23242	16136	2001	8059187
3394467	71568	1104	47636	5989	3617517
361747	11686	494	1162	381	1792174
23263	41986	503	1950	375	1022379
20324988	7504548	11335	51058	12244	16372390
2308663	109345	190	8236	121	4555989
109120	244674	354	449	2571	3637317
2604623	68149	1102	7368	2513	4482164
411474	853010	2394	434230	2150	11790250
3063178	684823	125		320	2892702
730	13000	11	126	19	517442
8330952	2540608	35242	601705	9794	2978588
2267853	322501	964	34128	5553	6899829
339560	2167	2716	6023	14599	5944185
915657	32970	3	40	21	1886104
62780					367460
2709332	207064	3206	879557	1835	2135951
	3382	1	20	884	1737154
			40		491052
1450				2	308885
12185	97916	416	2000	1481	1161257

C-2-22续表3

地 区	企业会计制度财务指标			
	固定资产原价	营业收入	费用合计	营业利润
全 国	**2155.0**	**323.0**	**98.2**	**30.7**
中央级				
北 京	8.0	11.7		
天 津				
河 北				
山 西				
内蒙古				
辽 宁				
吉 林				
黑龙江				
上 海				
江 苏				
浙 江	200.0			
安 徽	300.0	220.0	62.0	
福 建				
江 西				
山 东	186.0	71.0	22.0	21.0
河 南				
湖 北	597.0	20.0	7.5	9.7
湖 南				
广 东				
广 西				
海 南				
重 庆				
四 川	91.0			
贵 州				
云 南				
西 藏				
陕 西				
甘 肃				
青 海				
宁 夏				
新 疆	773.0	0.3	6.7	

单位：万元

事业单位会计制度财务指标			民间非营利组织会计制度财务指标		
固定资产原价	本年收入合计	本年支出合计	固定资产原价	本年收入合计	本年费用合计
117825.6	**174309.2**	**158281.0**	**598078.1**	**633360.4**	**630720.5**
41870.0	51095.7	52398.7	19723.9	13964.8	10253.7
249.3	427.5	382.7	849.0	1264.3	1527.2
4749.0	1575.3	1518.0	5226.2	1173.1	1443.9
3163.5	687.0	687.0	180.0	239.0	192.0
659.0	615.0	615.0	910.1	134.7	220.3
658.1	457.3	463.1	3799.5	1560.0	2448.2
976.2	6077.2	6076.2	2487.9	863.5	1345.4
505.0	453.5	481.6	3467.1	851.9	1604.6
11486.3	56949.1	43894.8	62168.6	246223.4	296508.5
1197.7	3490.3	3430.7	277513.3	209992.5	194134.0
1789.2	2453.5	2801.0	11206.9	32738.2	26485.3
2150.3	1454.1	1275.0	5256.3	861.8	808.2
33.0	245.0	240.0	982.0	559.1	592.2
340.0	79.4	79.4	4252.0	4357.0	4323.4
11470.8	4488.3	4542.9	59992.7	41916.7	49396.9
1959.0	437.4	437.4	1383.7	972.3	1041.6
8615.6	2773.2	2731.4	9466.0	5531.5	5835.1
2789.4	519.1	405.5	3001.6	31956.5	1772.2
7669.3	9434.9	10012.8	25563.5	21270.9	8968.6
227.6	19.0	19.0	727.0	140.0	209.2
			315.0	283.8	287.0
2872.5	2600.0	2600.0	3944.0	4817.3	4802.9
276.6	111.2	124.5	33406.1	4863.0	9021.3
5719.9	20499.4	15006.0	8152.3	569.8	192.6
912.3	38.1	59.7	2841.8	7.1	798.9
1513.4	6853.1	7172.1	27652.1	2047.4	2033.2
95.0	18.0	18.0	3125.0	139.6	257.8
	96.5	85.4	504.0	17.8	42.3
3877.6	361.1	723.1	19980.5	4043.4	4174.0

C-2-23 社区服务

地区	机构和设施数	工商登记	编制登记	民政登记	设施	农村
全国	**809**	**2**	**201**	**115**	**491**	**27**
中央级						
北京	17		17			
天津	10		3	4	3	
河北	20		4	4	12	2
山西	26		6	2	18	
内蒙古	2		1		1	
辽宁	26		3	3	20	
吉林	13		4		9	2
黑龙江	31		5	2	24	
上海	7		5	2		
江苏	58		15	21	22	1
浙江	26		9	10	7	2
安徽	42	1	17	3	21	1
福建	25		6	5	14	
江西	46		2	4	40	3
山东	113	1	23	14	75	
河南	35		10	7	18	1
湖北	31		17		14	1
湖南	54		12	1	41	5
广东	28		12	4	12	1
广西	5		2		3	
海南						
	2				2	
重庆	12		2	2	8	
四川	63		7	8	48	1
贵州	16			1	15	1
云南	7			1	6	
西藏						
陕西	54		13	6	35	
甘肃	20		1	2	17	6
青海						
宁夏	2		1	1		
新疆	18		4	8	6	

指导中心

单位：个、人

年末职工人数	女性	受教育程度		职业资格水平	
		大学专科人数	大学本科及以上人数	助理社会工作师人数	社会工作师人数
7831	**3435**	**2139**	**1722**	**331**	**150**
467	276	87	178	67	18
60	28	10	32		
290	178	60	22		4
133	29	21	23	2	2
9	5	6	1		
196	97	70	86	2	3
52	24	17	13		2
255	151	107	112	3	4
92	64	22	66	4	9
514	254	129	121	33	9
1098	154	89	76	6	5
433	151	58	35	97	8
132	72	17	26	4	9
249	146	66	27	5	1
1759	842	740	463	22	26
255	129	74	26	15	6
229	130	62	45	19	4
343	145	106	50	14	5
173	86	41	79	13	19
19	13	12	3		1
4	1	3			1
32	14	9	12		
296	119	98	63	8	3
83	31	23	7	1	2
64	37	19	39	3	
346	144	135	51	12	6
70	27	12	11		
44	18				
134	70	46	55	1	3

C-2-23续表1

地区	年龄结构				志愿服务	
	35岁及以下人数	36岁至45岁人数	46岁至55岁人数	56岁及以上人数	志愿者服务人次数	志愿服务时间
全 国	**2693**	**3545**	**1324**	**269**	**180317**	**604335**
中央级						
北 京	107	169	177	14	136726	506629
天 津	19	18	21	2	14	56
河 北	111	124	52	3	5898	15409
山 西	37	43	39	14		
内蒙古	1	6	2			
辽 宁	50	98	45	3		
吉 林	14	24	12	2		
黑龙江	96	102	40	17		
上 海	42	32	15	3	9478	18956
江 苏	179	211	89	35	988	1602
浙 江	167	864	59	8	134	392
安 徽	164	202	52	15	2276	2620
福 建	40	69	19	4		
江 西	62	132	35	20		
山 东	899	608	200	52	22697	52584
河 南	120	101	34			
湖 北	56	107	55	11		
湖 南	111	141	81	10	87	532
广 东	66	69	27	11		
广 西	5	11	3			
海 南						
		3	1			
重 庆	7	15	10		42	229
四 川	85	104	92	15	25	57
贵 州	39	28	16		267	541
云 南	14	31	15	4		
西 藏						
陕 西	116	127	81	22	1440	4108
甘 肃	32	30	8		235	570
青 海						
宁 夏	4	20	20			
新 疆	50	56	24	4	10	50

单位：人、人次、时、张

床位数合计	日间照料床位数	农村	留宿照料床位数	农村	年末收养人数合计	日间照料人数	农村	留宿照料人数	农村
19791	**14697**	**5707**	**5094**	**1081**	**3425**	**1887**	**579**	**1538**	**344**
2070	420		1650		854	160		694	
209	209								
1798	832	700	966	900	600	320	280	280	280
169	119		50		40	16		24	
60	60								
343	337		6		10	10			
599	589	130	10						
290	239		51		54	22		32	
340	338		2		46	46			
4295	4294	4199	1						
500	380		120	20	16	3		13	2
115	91		24		14			14	
1204	1054	140	150	62	199	129	90	70	62
1390	1085		305		708	519		189	
780	450	6	330		191	101	6	90	
236	154		82						
541	421	30	120	25	238	190	30	48	
205	152	42	53	2	54	54			
20	20								
325	105		220		33	23		10	
1381	1221		160		30	24		6	
262	116	61	146	50					
229	130		99		18	13		5	
1235	730		505		127	64		63	
1167	1125	377	42	22	193	193	173		
28	26	22	2						

C-2-23续表2

地 区	本年收养照料人天数	老年人活动人次数	社区服务志愿者组织数	注册社区志愿者人数	机构建筑面积
全 国	**272640**	**288317**	**14074**	**570842**	**949064**
中央级					
北 京	194910	78170	8205	408053	104968
天 津			20		10604
河 北	310	28520	3500	3500	25760
山 西	1420	211			10806
内蒙古					5241
辽 宁					94724
吉 林					7054
黑龙江					42042
上 海			1051	76317	6035
江 苏	7744	920	197	135	83931
浙 江					22810
安 徽		5304	1	14	20745
福 建			46		15092
江 西	735				27955
山 东	60190	25944	280	1725	216535
河 南		20			12688
湖 北					47882
湖 南	5280				52519
广 东		126995	530	79272	18433
广 西					3658
海 南					400
重 庆	1090	6354	31	622	13910
四 川		237	36	626	21600
贵 州					9930
云 南					6178
西 藏					
陕 西	961	15110	175	558	49254
甘 肃		532	1	20	13280
青 海					
宁 夏					200
新 疆			1		4830

单位：人、人次、人天、个、平方米

事业单位会计制度财务指标			民间非营利组织会计制度财务指标		
固定资产原价	本年收入合计	本年支出合计	固定资产原价	本年收入合计	本年费用合计
66154.8	**58134.5**	**57192.6**	**9924.5**	**5273.2**	**3200.5**
28897.3	28479.0	27869.6			
249.3	427.5	382.7	127.8	179.7	690.4
80.0	635.3	553.5	238.7	101.5	270.6
49.5	36.0	36.0	3.0	24.0	2.0
25.0	154.0	154.0			
54.0	279.3	284.3	108.0	10.2	10.8
11.2	4174.8	4173.8			
235.0	180.5	180.5	6.0		15.0
5125.3	3689.7	3671.7	39.4	195.0	195.0
593.8	3208.0	3155.2	849.4	438.9	662.6
1498.5	1288.3	1324.1	960.9	2960.2	73.0
895.4	533.5	447.8	12.0	26.0	3.0
5.0	204.0	204.0	44.0	54.8	70.9
	61.0	61.0	238.0	33.0	80.0
10673.3	2203.6	2203.6	4768.0	915.9	915.9
34.0	154.2	154.2	83.0	154.0	80.7
7591.7	2305.5	2263.7			
2777.4	481.1	395.5	3.0	2.0	2.0
5313.7	2506.8	2506.8	142.0	2.0	47.0
22.6	5.0	5.0			
262.0	34.5	34.5	5.0	7.0	7.0
216.0	104.2	117.5	208.7	68.3	27.2
			5.0	5.0	0.1
			5.0		0.1
1309.8	6805.2	6805.2	252.5	39.5	27.6
	2.0	2.0	1605.0	56.0	0.3
	96.5	85.4	10.0		
235.0	85.0	121.0	210.1	0.2	19.3

C-2-24 社区服务

地 区	机构和设施数	工商登记	编制登记	民政登记	设施
全 国	**23493**	**7**	**893**	**2068**	**20525**
中央级					
北 京	198	1	183		14
天 津	289			32	257
河 北	452			5	447
山 西	645		22	38	585
内蒙古	852		38	2	812
辽 宁	838		21	17	800
吉 林	623		12	48	563
黑龙江	586		13	10	563
上 海	260		89	84	87
江 苏	2777		2	1019	1756
浙 江	2965		21	216	2728
安 徽	1234		20	9	1205
福 建	224		5	7	212
江 西	383		14	1	368
山 东	1371	3	55	87	1226
河 南	696		11	4	681
湖 北	633	2	18	105	508
湖 南	601		1	5	595
广 东	1843		82	50	1711
广 西	175				175
海 南	57			11	46
重 庆	339		11		328
四 川	1707	1	16	35	1655
贵 州	1543		97	2	1444
云 南	117		1	12	104
西 藏					
陕 西	475		6	1	468
甘 肃	862		46	5	811
青 海	30				30
宁 夏	66			15	51
新 疆	652		109	248	295

中心

单位：个、人

农村	为居民提供便民办事服务	为居民提供活动场所服务	为居民提供养老等服务	农村	为居民提供便民信息服务
8182	**16837**	**4525**	**3224**	**1462**	**2978**
17	159	60	13		76
82	207	78	4		21
84	190	120	129	35	21
279	449	82	105	38	9
67	703	211	18	2	123
182	533	90	149	45	104
390	592	28	38		21
117	443	178	34		50
12	214	21	2		23
1075	1538	566	754	271	178
2159	1622	602	714	619	57
628	819	135	197	101	174
50	124	52	47	5	8
69	266	76	8		36
460	1079	541	446	137	665
152	502	80	108	51	35
81	415	181	25	1	56
142	563	104	32	1	492
326	1519	217	44	32	155
15	96	32	1		46
	51	2	4		
60	282	134	3		80
218	1467	210	122	19	291
721	1398	291	85	28	150
29	79	10	31	14	8
205	354	114	2		5
525	606	127	105	62	48
16	15	10			6
7	64	2	2		9
14	488	171	2	1	31

C-2-24续表1

地　区	年末职工人数	女性	受教育程度		职业资格水平	
			大学专科人数	大学本科及以上人数	助理社会工作师人数	社会工作师人数
全　国	**145570**	**57295**	**39570**	**22031**	**3443**	**1868**
中央级						
北　京	2081	1203	507	836	33	29
天　津	1526	859	454	245	124	16
河　北	1847	955	398	202	8	11
山　西	3550	1244	653	328	21	12
内蒙古	5022	2656	1628	1044	193	64
辽　宁	6182	3259	2056	1687	96	40
吉　林	2797	1386	764	377	29	74
黑龙江	4613	1876	1766	592	57	25
上　海	5258	2693	1832	1380	221	147
江　苏	25780	5224	6933	1129	295	129
浙　江	10807	4513	2904	1441	488	145
安　徽	6927	2840	1860	861	111	35
福　建	1214	500	222	119	34	16
江　西	1505	702	290	59	36	14
山　东	9391	3841	3143	2193	71	18
河　南	4667	1816	1043	464	22	33
湖　北	3601	1418	797	244	33	28
湖　南	3355	1536	956	429	71	26
广　东	11499	5736	3124	3953	1285	838
广　西	863	284	122	61	6	
海　南	600	99	50	18		
重　庆	1934	833	559	302	9	12
四　川	6985	2321	1660	486	88	70
贵　州	11305	3835	2856	1918	7	10
云　南	900	326	140	89	2	3
西　藏						
陕　西	2296	774	481	149	13	5
甘　肃	3344	1922	970	687	45	23
青　海	169	66	49	32	7	6
宁　夏	777	466	61	44	1	3
新　疆	4775	2112	1292	662	37	36

单位：人、人次、时

年龄结构				志愿服务	
35岁及以下人数	36岁至45岁人数	46岁至55岁人数	56岁及以上人数	志愿者服务人次数	志愿服务时间
51997	**57337**	**27787**	**8449**	**2003221**	**5524912**
496	773	663	149	1786016	5072784
472	683	286	85	49880	75905
632	781	381	53	1874	3112
1111	1588	686	165	350	900
2004	2128	699	191	2444	4996
2210	2258	1323	391	627	1376
811	1800	174	12		
1369	1786	1274	184	2	16
2260	1502	1033	463	4216	6497
9723	10149	4176	1732	5654	14092
2387	4367	2964	1089	39475	67640
2106	3014	1528	279	4863	16839
323	578	275	38		
447	618	385	55	20	60
4180	3522	1408	281	30749	75538
1645	1890	616	516	21	27
1272	1330	812	187	12	36
929	1547	647	232	3547	7354
5965	3720	1482	332	260	520
388	307	138	30		
183	261	111	45		
536	866	485	47	37524	91647
2129	3052	979	825	2104	2180
4166	4187	2304	648	25544	61791
247	362	250	41	60	60
722	799	555	220	837	4523
1518	1248	530	48	276	756
77	52	38	2		
98	179	486	14	382	588
1591	1990	1099	95	6484	15676

C-2-24续表2

地区	床位数合计	日间照料床位数		留宿照料床位数		年末收养人数合计	日间照料人数
			农村		农村		
全　国	**139087**	**94299**	**31751**	**44788**	**16127**	**24131**	**15837**
中央级							
北　京	616	567	39	49		165	160
天　津	2487	2217	836	270			
河　北	2426	2073	962	353	153	49	39
山　西	4319	2887	916	1432	435	833	802
内蒙古	1908	1674	48	234	172	315	188
辽　宁	4212	2150	432	2062	985	700	303
吉　林	917	855		62		163	163
黑龙江	6153	3705	490	2448	2	4999	2779
上　海	2003	2003				919	919
江　苏	12338	9623	2725	2715	1258	1670	735
浙　江	25201	21479	13320	3722	1671	1040	839
安　徽	20859	8255	2677	12604	6046	1394	1028
福　建	574	288	80	286	46		
江　西	1031	1013	223	18		195	195
山　东	6051	5199	1639	852	209	3464	2821
河　南	9705	5268	321	4437	706	3941	1800
湖　北	1650	1093	132	557	128	218	118
湖　南	2071	1355	232	716	224	424	346
广　东	12865	7704	1572	5161	2998	805	792
广　西	38	30		8	1	18	18
海　南	372	78		294			
重　庆	1644	1119	58	525	22	994	743
四　川	7011	4073	205	2938	21	290	249
贵　州	5356	3988	2562	1368	558	1066	442
云　南	1098	594	240	504	40	21	
西　藏							
陕　西	833	515	278	318	183	154	87
甘　肃	4047	3707	1573	340	115	108	103
青　海	330	315	145	15			
宁　夏	57	57				3	3
新　疆	915	415	46	500	154	183	165

单位：张、人、人次、人天、个、平方米

农村	留宿照料人数	农村	本年收养照料人天数	老年人活动人次数	社区服务志愿者组织数	注册社区志愿者人数	机构建筑面积
2993	**8294**	**2025**	**913435**	**2477607**	**42250**	**632941**	**9352575**
14	5		11938	785017	3690	319775	138794
					43		153321
24	10	10		7050	56		128592
172	31	30			389	10920	192239
	127	110	52387	260306	228	8118	617384
93	397	354			235	340	438069
			35770	174	375		135918
378	2220			29424			211265
			218279	2724	1608	48609	130109
239	935	725	28468	86924	413	17405	1099097
273	201	66	4606	98821	874	15317	1085219
	366	47	12000	13099	103	29629	367160
					129	75	92279
152			12605	5600	266	1935	116310
1174	643	131	399389	903797	2389	18404	899956
76	2141	79	1780	4996	29		413828
42	100	100		20948	129		220095
5	78		913	3890	96		254559
29	13	2	43	36955	235	1172	560709
			730	22009			45177
							11600
48	251	20	119892	98647	29515	101542	211224
20	41			15104	164	20273	425937
204	624	301		682	668	1844	510943
	21						69871
40	67	43	14635	2280	339	36281	170333
10	5						234751
							8012
							31006
	18	7		79160	277	1302	378818

C-2-24续表3

地区	企业会计制度财务指标				
	固定资产原价	营业收入	费用合计	营业利润	固定资产原价
全国	**612.0**	**62.7**	**13.5**	**30.7**	**32984.2**
中央级					
北京	8.0	11.7			12584.7
天津					
河北					
山西					1011.0
内蒙古					633.0
辽宁					9.0
吉林					33.0
黑龙江					40.0
上海					6056.0
江苏					488.9
浙江					19.8
安徽					161.0
福建					28.0
江西					340.0
山东	6.0	31.0	6.0	21.0	797.5
河南					1267.0
湖北	597.0	20.0	7.5	9.7	774.7
湖南					
广东					594.6
广西					
海南					
重庆					224.5
四川	1.0				60.6
贵州					5656.5
云南					5.0
西藏					
陕西					203.6
甘肃					74.0
青海					
宁夏					
新疆					1921.8

单位：万元

事业单位会计制度财务指标		民间非营利组织会计制度财务指标		
本年收入合计	本年支出合计	固定资产原价	本年收入合计	本年支出合计
106732.6	**91439.4**	**36678.7**	**20820.1**	**21295.4**
21806.8	23762.4			
		269.5	115.8	137.9
		59.0	2.0	0.1
261.0	261.0	108.0	215.0	180.0
460.0	460.0	6.0	7.8	8.3
25.0	25.0	48.2	81.0	107.2
190.4	190.4	77.0	24.0	45.3
23.0	51.1	18.0	3.0	35.2
53163.0	40162.5	647.6	2679.4	2346.5
87.3	80.5	14209.5	9207.0	9404.7
968.9	1015.1	954.3	1224.7	946.7
381.1	381.1	1970.0	16.0	126.5
41.0	36.0	16.2	25.0	23.9
18.4	18.4	8.0		2.0
2284.7	2339.3	1980.7	2836.7	2859.5
159.0	159.0	194.0	98.0	98.8
226.6	226.6	654.0	953.2	1040.0
28.0		72.2	96.5	99.0
5710.6	6335.6	818.0	1134.0	1031.9
		95.0		6.0
337.5	337.5			
7.0	7.0	290.0	104.6	227.7
20458.4	15003.0	12.0	7.3	3.7
		7.0	2.0	199.4
45.9	364.9	2.0	3.0	4.0
16.0	16.0	52.0	4.0	1.8
		150.0		
33.0	207.0	13960.5	1980.1	2359.3

C-2-25 社区

地 区	机构和设施数	工商登记	编制登记	民政登记	设施	农村
全 国	**137533**	**1**	**330**	**8843**	**128359**	**71756**
中央级						
北 京	6430				6430	3676
天 津	1894				1894	567
河 北	2124		2	4	2118	363
山 西	1836		21	9	1806	916
内蒙古	1013			7	1006	24
辽 宁	3822			2	3820	558
吉 林	1070		76	234	760	186
黑龙江	1376		4	3	1369	109
上 海	2786		3	150	2633	338
江 苏	15586			6399	9187	8513
浙 江	12136		9	308	11819	9414
安 徽	3155		21	12	3122	967
福 建	2971			24	2947	960
江 西	1045				1045	100
山 东	9712			393	9319	5020
河 南	875			1	874	150
湖 北	4381		46	23	4312	1012
湖 南	3657		6	14	3637	982
广 东	20097			329	19768	14416
广 西	1509			17	1492	280
海 南	2296			229	2067	1945
重 庆	2345			5	2340	403
四 川	8939			166	8773	4237
贵 州	18126				18126	14709
云 南	1416		8	12	1396	362
西 藏						
陕 西	2436		1	222	2213	550
甘 肃	1834			6	1828	685
青 海	444				444	47
宁 夏	763			187	576	263
新 疆	1459	1	133	87	1238	4

服务站

单位：个、人

为居民提供便民办事服务	为居民提供活动场所服务	为居民提供养老等服务	农村	为居民提供便民信息服务	年末职工人数	女性
97481	**32224**	**15452**	**7965**	**24931**	**556093**	**218737**
5285	2921	415	57	2649	28285	14462
1244	571	23	1	234	9070	5529
1100	118	942	147	14	8050	4046
1079	380	269	236	153	10115	3655
679	251	2	1	129	5682	3141
2813	211	528	138	488	24177	15577
1038		9		27	9827	6077
781	347	49	28	206	6370	3628
1395	999	13		382	13133	7080
8043	2003	6122	3934	1848	68387	22742
8955	1869	785	613	953	31088	11204
2500	352	31	5	405	14600	6377
2119	384	501	70	256	12016	5207
652	258	12		123	3567	1328
7739	5033	2534	1011	4546	43244	18427
679	86	11	4	100	3955	1622
3249	775	203	85	458	17046	6653
2965	926	397	101	2560	15767	7175
12582	6868	350	299	1483	59893	18277
746	280	31	1	514	8515	3312
1840	214	54	31	257	9805	2599
1767	750	144	38	245	11899	6248
6845	1029	532	360	3082	27973	9683
15653	4201	1079	692	2820	77897	19205
1180	101	36	16	129	7950	2705
1786	459	87	1	210	11506	5378
1006	464	223	83	154	4502	1804
324	53			70	1545	697
541	147	70	13	27	3703	2057
896	174			409	6526	2842

C-2-25续表1

地区	受教育程度		职业资格水平		年龄	
	大学专科人数	大学本科及以上人数	助理社会工作师人数	社会工作师人数	35岁及以下人数	36岁至45岁人数
全国	**127391**	**57974**	**9542**	**4021**	**173254**	**218505**
中央级						
北京	7527	6126	2054	812	7631	10141
天津	2738	2072	582	187	4133	2668
河北	1633	553	8	8	2917	3005
山西	1944	804	262	163	2531	3974
内蒙古	1797	1405	197	102	2323	2222
辽宁	9124	5441	676	333	8219	8888
吉林	4233	1527	316	175	2361	5410
黑龙江	2024	795	124	61	2627	2835
上海	1713	804	226	89	1468	5583
江苏	13546	6117	1123	394	17757	25878
浙江	5885	2808	382	231	10491	10875
安徽	4432	1072	176	44	4295	7041
福建	1549	563	337	181	4307	4640
江西	414	51	5	15	1020	1737
山东	13235	5794	298	78	15700	16044
河南	1116	341	9	1	1507	1445
湖北	3803	1263	90	45	5035	7631
湖南	4142	1734	286	114	4852	5268
广东	8456	5963	801	241	17920	24573
广西	1477	733	76	22	3786	2705
海南	936	319	25	6	2321	3925
重庆	4387	1965	647	324	4594	4494
四川	6932	1922	354	155	8324	11870
贵州	14891	3617	39	28	25188	31245
云南	1472	485	12	4	2544	3488
西藏						
陕西	3369	1126	224	111	3462	4321
甘肃	1379	744	10	11	1890	1637
青海	586	251	57	57	712	572
宁夏	593	157	25	4	908	1903
新疆	2058	1422	121	25	2431	2487

单位：人、人次、张、时

结构		志愿服务		床位数合计	
46岁至55岁人数	56岁及以上人数	志愿者服务人次数	志愿服务时间		日间照料床位数
129261	**35073**	**3244874**	**8698925**	**311098**	**263904**
8266	2247	2130957	6293737	2497	2445
1995	274	1255	2400	2626	2281
1830	298	1384	3775	7518	6438
2372	1238	600	1900	6668	6612
925	212	5038	9738	372	300
4079	2991	23001	36456	8810	7224
1800	256			3463	2631
726	182	355	355	4440	3818
4691	1391	6717	49610	291	291
19768	4984	140522	294086	72204	67721
6730	2992	133231	233087	46741	40524
2952	312	23774	48858	5295	3217
2423	646			8368	7799
674	136	545	715	883	833
8608	2892	390740	844864	27719	25359
695	308	18	21	1682	1212
3237	1143	67	156	15550	10785
4705	942	5549	14142	5246	4063
14012	3388	3640	11098	22632	17678
1768	256			278	218
2592	967	17790	30815	1285	654
2375	436	219628	484387	5050	4291
6688	1091	2272	14776	15785	11081
17465	3999	123057	276874	28093	22187
1588	330	2211	7269	3045	2294
3058	665	5844	25824	3648	2262
824	151	117	148	7626	7006
224	37			1192	1192
844	48	2471	4741	912	852
1347	261	4091	9093	1179	636

C-2-25续表2

地区				年末收养人数合计		
	农村	留宿照料床位数	农村		日间照料人数	农村
全　国	**123964**	**47194**	**21311**	**62818**	**54960**	**29127**
中央级						
北　京	833	52		404	404	163
天　津	1289	345		17	17	17
河　北	446	1080	1	868	660	
山　西	5375	56	40	3466	3466	3049
内蒙古		72	45	25	25	
辽　宁	3169	1586	370	197	155	
吉　林	93	832	1	374	351	57
黑龙江	491	622	471	516	290	84
上　海				181	181	
江　苏	34889	4483	2012	15858	15461	10567
浙　江	29289	6217	5039	4686	4544	2727
安　徽	696	2078	850	260	80	
福　建	3618	569	140	723	556	148
江　西	23	50		43	43	
山　东	7914	2360	1345	11482	10329	2811
河　南	77	470	22	185	85	18
湖　北	2387	4765	833	4246	3398	1444
湖　南	847	1183	284	1328	1094	447
广　东	8867	4954	1384	6988	6136	5267
广　西	7	60	35	42	42	3
海　南	449	631	410	172	70	44
重　庆	393	759	73	3311	2902	344
四　川	3248	4704	2383	1766	1241	355
贵　州	15643	5906	4745	4309	2371	1388
云　南	421	751	176	32	32	
西　藏						
陕　西	553	1386	241	824	566	19
甘　肃	2601	620	366	486	432	175
青　海	60					
宁　夏	279	60	38	11	11	
新　疆	7	543	7	18	18	

单位：人、个、人次、张、平方米

留宿照料人数	农村	本年收养照料人天数	老年人活动人次数	社区服务志愿者组织数	注册社区志愿者人数	城镇便民、利民服务网点数	机构建筑面积
7858	**3702**	**3001520**	**5566395**	**28273**	**1918946**	**86927**	**35728366**
		19600	579025	3263	219275	2244	828293
				25		2914	653281
208		2082	27926	90		592	1296941
		3667	93073			65	333793
			347299	2254	1557	381	312627
42			7579	1188	42190	3924	1152612
23	1						511955
226	160			15		97	363560
		500	320	34	1884	141	622002
397	289	632973	2659382	4844	122172	13716	5012218
142	97	49836	109540	382	521	2001	2927973
180	150	6205	51428	967	15150	5989	896369
167	23	214425	3110	243	1077	381	529648
		9923	36386	237	15	375	200558
1153	590	1368493	943186	3369	17941	12244	4392053
100			2140	19		121	498051
848	440	53940	25746	195	139	2571	1297520
234	86	88396	25157	948	56	2513	773009
852	263	72941	2580	432	195270	2150	2781909
		11680		5		320	286402
102				11	126	19	380717
409	36	415921	522729	4373	490093	9794	907827
525	129		68607	691	11918	5553	2270515
1938	1328		679	2014	4056	14599	4187186
						21	522799
258	62	50938	42207	2539	794863	1835	710041
54	48					884	329521
							129828
						2	188171
			18296	135	643	1481	430987

C-2-25续表3

地　区	企业会计制度财务指标			
	固定资产原价	营业收入	费用合计	固定资产原价
全　国	**773.0**	**0.3**	**6.7**	**5157.9**
中央级				
北　京				
天　津				
河　北				10.0
山　西				2100.0
内蒙古				
辽　宁				
吉　林				932.0
黑龙江				
上　海				1.0
江　苏				
浙　江				14.9
安　徽				95.0
福　建				
江　西				
山　东				
河　南				
湖　北				249.2
湖　南				12.0
广　东				
广　西				
海　南				
重　庆				
四　川				
贵　州				
云　南				23.0
西　藏				
陕　西				
甘　肃				
青　海				
宁　夏				
新　疆	773.0	0.3	6.7	1720.8

单位：万元

事业单位会计制度财务指标		民间非营利组织会计制度财务指标		
本年收入合计	本年支出合计	固定资产原价	本年收入合计	本年支出合计
2816.7	**2912.6**	**176256.1**	**119346.7**	**105705.5**
16.0	16.0	2.2	2.0	8.5
378.0	378.0	18.0		
			0.1	0.2
		5.0	39.0	36.9
1712.0	1712.0	2410.9	839.5	1300.1
20.0	20.0	12.0	6.0	3.3
87.6	54.0	12034.7	12561.5	9187.5
		125012.9	82788.5	73468.9
17.4	5.9	599.1	12640.6	9331.9
96.5	76.5	293.2	24.0	56.3
		27.0	35.1	53.3
		23592.3	7007.1	7080.3
		30.0	2.0	2.0
241.1	241.1	116.0	28.0	69.0
		297.4	233.5	243.6
		2580.7	195.5	573.7
		3.0		
		210.0	283.8	281.0
		168.2	125.4	125.4
		1991.5	113.7	1173.3
3.0	12.0	353.0		459.8
2.0	2.0	2735.0	916.6	721.1
		6.0		100.6
		214.0	11.0	11.0
243.1	395.1	3544.0	1493.8	1417.8

C-2-26 社区养老

地区	机构和设施数	民政登记	设施	农村	年末职工人数	女性
全　国	**34924**	**4288**	**30636**	**21809**	**156252**	**56416**
中央级						
北　京	22	1	21	14	173	102
天　津	122		122	116	478	145
河　北	1152	20	1132	350	5061	2328
山　西	1499	1	1498	1333	7647	2776
内蒙古	892	11	881	151	2837	1269
辽　宁	267	62	205	108	2244	840
吉　林						
黑龙江	663	286	377	102	4484	1759
上　海	69	10	59	6	640	213
江　苏	4669	2740	1929	3072	24763	8875
浙　江	4437	322	4115	3126	13086	5404
安　徽	1301	8	1293	1081	7258	2315
福　建	1088	13	1075	706	4231	1388
江　西	334	22	312	224	2883	554
山　东	1450	238	1212	778	12038	4895
河　南	1675	33	1642	1258	11973	3618
湖　北	1759	105	1654	733	5720	2953
湖　南	1717	5	1712	1099	6031	1621
广　东	1768	12	1756	1319	9154	3703
广　西	1184	20	1164	944	2499	882
海　南	56		56	24	173	37
重　庆	865	19	846	611	3131	1537
四　川	3676	250	3426	1750	11489	4119
贵　州	1386	41	1345	1076	3879	1187
云　南	1098	15	1083	619	3613	1279
西　藏	74		74	69	2310	409
陕　西	410	32	378	288	1667	759
甘　肃	750	3	747	590	3811	624
青　海	255		255	124	1822	340
宁　夏	71	2	69	35	194	83
新　疆	215	17	198	103	963	402

单位：个、人

受教育程度		职业资格水平		年龄结构			
大学专科人数	大学本科及以上人数	助理社会工作师人数	社会工作师人数	35岁及以下人数	36岁至45岁人数	46岁至55岁人数	56岁及以上人数
21028	**11903**	**2856**	**1082**	**34096**	**57486**	**43977**	**20693**
22	26	6	9	36	56	64	17
100	60	6	3	18	277	131	52
553	206	62	14	1036	2071	1459	495
1702	653	284	183	2031	2891	1924	801
625	146	28	15	798	1268	538	233
180	143	168	86	350	691	700	503
768	244	157	37	777	2026	984	697
303	122	3	1	306	178	109	47
3461	1657	277	134	6833	9194	6874	1862
1440	798	161	97	2274	4140	4571	2101
593	188	164	41	1026	2673	2578	981
272	92	53	54	751	1277	1391	812
216	109	23	9	346	593	742	1202
1941	1609	353	48	2293	4235	4920	590
1251	1122	181	36	1774	6080	2789	1330
731	433	43	62	1122	2111	2019	468
1021	889	268	21	1427	2416	1815	373
1099	1122	224	32	1764	2636	1980	2774
112	49	15	29	247	953	880	419
10	3	8	3	46	102	23	2
326	149	14	19	574	1031	1219	307
1818	804	176	73	3013	4589	2878	1009
654	277	22	23	1197	1353	798	531
422	274	35	18	732	1651	817	413
222	131	22	3	618	254	36	1402
224	32	4	1	395	566	587	119
216	202	27	13	1498	1263	704	346
463	145	6	12	414	372	251	785
13				50	117	15	12
270	218	66	6	350	422	181	10

C-2-26续表1

地区	志愿服务		床位数合计	社区日间照料床位数	
	志愿者服务人次数	志愿服务时间			农村
全国	**104466**	**249862**	**1535425**	**373178**	**209340**
中央级					
北京	1522	3555	1950	2	
天津	500	1000	6674	1284	1084
河北	966	3906	55754	16548	9260
山西	4	9	31410	17856	14655
内蒙古	2850	5730	23942	13623	1448
辽宁	5	8	17776	6662	2986
吉林					
黑龙江	4	16	51648	11323	3007
上海	318	428	16027		
江苏	56395	116940	82445	38699	20715
浙江	3189	13902	141023	45657	30779
安徽	3991	9515	151453	4003	2008
福建	82	264	51583	4307	3457
江西	13	56	30487	9337	7795
山东	27088	67255	147142	15562	8249
河南	1426	9089	202043	45686	33178
湖北	388	854	34760	15896	2880
湖南	781	2557	62034	11299	6507
广东			52769	27530	16441
广西	57	130	31775	2628	1142
海南			2697	1412	407
重庆	1154	3010	41257	4467	3104
四川	569	1723	141211	25042	11835
贵州	1778	5326	47326	14785	5858
云南	230	980	44059	11120	4439
西藏	5		2467	1993	1780
陕西	952	3360	19607	3077	1446
甘肃	199	249	21660	15840	10371
青海			10974	1951	302
宁夏			839	431	100
新疆			10633	5158	4107

单位：人、人次、时、张

社区留宿收养床位数	农村	年末收养人数合计	社区日间照料人数	农村	社区留宿收养床位数	农村
1162247	**746613**	**592320**	**99872**	**67952**	**492448**	**334140**
1948	688	431			431	272
5390	4992	1262	388	188	874	863
39206	24072	17553	2022	961	15531	8668
13554	11776	14041	8221	6772	5820	5087
10319	7053	7679	4336	845	3343	2961
11114	4607	3432	1071	418	2361	1043
40325	6558	20355	2969	1863	17386	3354
16027	1560					
43746	12907	16606	4591	2946	12015	2743
95366	46197	28518	5292	4167	23226	10262
147450	126714	53587	35		53552	45593
47276	27740	9492	243	243	9249	4652
21150	17672	14579	6223	6085	8356	7582
131580	71546	84251	7167	3536	77084	39240
156357	122312	117549	22216	19860	95333	76464
18864	4163	11727	3237	456	8490	1936
50735	36247	29959	5415	2482	24544	17521
25239	18297	8498	4246	2086	4252	1598
29147	24398	12530	902	435	11628	10416
1285	1033	936	339		597	465
36790	33722	28272	2593	1711	25679	23758
116169	72521	56827	5456	3785	51371	37264
32541	27580	14297	2196	1829	12101	10971
32939	17580	14527	1877	685	12650	8613
474	394	1172	1165	993	7	7
16530	11900	12012	1618	1164	10394	8560
5820	4451	2500	1561	689	939	439
9023	5038	3109	450		2659	1511
408	386	183	136		47	47
5475	2509	6436	3907	3753	2529	2250

C-2-26续表2

地　区	本年收养照料人天数	老年人活动人次数	社区服务志愿者组织数	注册社区志愿者人数	机构建筑面积
全　国	**31007016**	**5951930**	**26858**	**45325**	**24924548**
中央级					
北　京	57520				25830
天　津					117800
河　北	980808	219285			1223959
山　西	61983				904189
内蒙古	1750488	232481	78	3374	326891
辽　宁	32400				480664
吉　林					
黑龙江	64427	64403			495821
上　海					234929
江　苏	648852	583910	542	5096	1619271
浙　江	44634	1021958	21960	177	1647683
安　徽	3117840	7	10	2485	1433165
福　建	133232	8196	26	10	728127
江　西					429393
山　东	9017965	1967946	3643	5379	3157730
河　南	2290863	99819	142	8236	2344655
湖　北	27350	44715	30	310	689343
湖　南	1629539	32000	14	6682	1363418
广　东	254459	684400	23	535	716654
广　西	540849	208102			609704
海　南	365	13000			63129
重　庆	4669412	645595	311	4966	726408
四　川	2108188	70988	40	719	2458769
贵　州	339560	736	20	48	725495
云　南	915657	32970	2		1001072
西　藏	62780				367460
陕　西	2245800	21419	17	7268	284946
甘　肃					217067
青　海				40	257758
宁　夏					20090
新　疆	12045				253128

单位：人天、人次、人、平方米、万元

民间非营利组织会计制度财务指标		
固定资产原价	本年收入合计	本年费用合计
96386.9	**63916.2**	**38367.3**
4.8	49.1	55.0
4537.3	58.3	161.3
4.0		
188.1	2.0	53.3
603.5	471.0	647.5
2895.5	754.4	1323.2
22.4	526.4	514.7
31814.6	14538.9	12359.6
1789.2	4664.7	6131.3
838.0	30.0	45.5
472.0	70.0	61.5
89.0	330.0	84.4
7197.0	4975.9	8975.1
683.0	256.7	281.5
6572.0	3513.2	3915.7
360.0	30299.2	315.2
37.0		10.0
372.7	22.5	72.5
623.0	298.4	299.4
7392.1	2319.3	2487.0
2785.3	190.0	68.9
2386.8	5.0	12.1
24018.8	339.0	443.1
35.0	4.0	0.6
60.0	3.0	18.7
605.8	195.2	30.2

C-2-27 社区互助型

地区	单位数	农村	年末职工人数	女性
全 国	**76374**	**70857**	**147596**	**46606**
中央级				
北 京	226	170	680	292
天 津				
河 北	33141	32646	55668	17761
山 西	383	321	1961	548
内蒙古	1050	1026	1522	268
辽 宁	254	253	545	187
吉 林				
黑龙江	59	57	239	54
上 海				
江 苏	374	216	1938	820
浙 江	465	239	898	445
安 徽	134	76	593	309
福 建	1278	654	2134	529
江 西				
山 东	5805	5216	21288	7212
河 南	291	268	434	116
湖 北	4213	3362	9870	4060
湖 南	5524	4977	12755	3838
广 东	74	67	148	124
广 西	10197	10049	9405	1794
海 南	3	3	5	1
重 庆	1761	1416	2761	938
四 川	2119	1638	4513	1273
贵 州	1851	1638	5185	1346
云 南	71	59	93	33
西 藏				
陕 西	3139	2857	8498	2873
甘 肃	2933	2664	4880	1482
青 海	839	801	1170	129
宁 夏	162	161	358	149
新 疆	28	23	55	25

养老设施

单位：个、人

受教育程度		职业资格水平		年龄结构
大学专科人数	大学本科及以上人数	助理社会工作师人数	社会工作师人数	35岁及以下人数
13885	**5203**	**341**	**328**	**35050**
206	76			164
1044	290	13	7	11793
366	79	35	4	522
120	52	8		230
105	13	8	6	120
16	102			26
181	45	9	5	233
22	5	2	1	295
136	41	16	15	183
105	34		3	452
3833	2041	67	19	8256
21	22			46
1078	275	120	134	2587
2210	966	39	83	2611
				62
122	87	1	6	779
1				1
620	177	2	5	692
730	210	8	5	938
808	184	2		1330
1				5
830	290	3	9	1319
719	123	6	18	1878
517	82	2	8	311
75				182
19	9			35

C−2−27续表1

地　区	年龄结构			志愿
	36岁至45岁人数	46岁至55岁人数	56岁及以上人数	志愿者服务人次数
全　国	**55085**	**42961**	**14303**	**51336**
中央级				
北　京	280	198	38	
天　津				
河　北	19520	18156	6199	3915
山　西	669	467	303	
内蒙古	687	341	219	
辽　宁	228	170	27	20
吉　林				
黑龙江	152	58	3	
上　海				
江　苏	810	753	142	538
浙　江	312	205	92	
安　徽	199	172	33	221
福　建	909	293	430	
江　西				
山　东	7193	4729	1110	37236
河　南	208	123	57	
湖　北	3916	2320	1047	
湖　南	5432	3570	1070	760
广　东	74	12		
广　西	2955	4394	1276	2143
海　南	2	2		
重　庆	1122	767	180	673
四　川	1859	1166	550	
贵　州	2091	1382	382	890
云　南	68	14	6	
西　藏				
陕　西	3607	2668	904	4940
甘　肃	2131	720	151	
青　海	522	256	77	
宁　夏	121	23	7	
新　疆	18	2		

单位：人次、张、人 、时

服务					
志愿服务时间	床位数合计	日间照料床位数	农村	留宿照料床位数	农村
147871	**771184**	**435282**	**392265**	**335902**	**313149**
	1821	1821	1349		
18195	207256	156307	154716	50949	49977
	5969	5864	4717	105	105
	105799	2631	2358	103168	102642
40	1164	1023	1023	141	111
	2129	155	155	1974	1914
1892	3703	2215	1392	1488	813
	5189	4169	3541	1020	53
732	3055	1061	271	1994	1634
	16015	3901	2242	12114	6208
93504	140921	89780	81621	51141	44979
	2276	2125	1865	151	76
	27236	22775	15419	4461	3578
1520	36846	27021	23959	9825	9006
	1216	1216	1036		
5025	89023	17850	17702	71173	70442
	9			9	9
1973	13005	7062	4524	5943	5727
	14781	11485	8767	3296	1528
5177	16639	11739	8742	4900	4301
	485	481	303	4	4
19813	31589	25926	23307	5663	5312
	39118	33769	28586	5349	3696
	3788	3607	3467	181	181
	1616	763	743	853	853
	536	536	460		

C-2-27续表2

地　区	年末收养人数合计	日间照料人数	农村	留宿照料人数	农村
全　国	**260101**	**121822**	**110621**	**138279**	**134554**
中央级					
北　京	1178	1178	900		
天　津					
河　北	34217	28419	28203	5798	5780
山　西	2786	2786	2103		
内蒙古	64645	89	36	64556	66435
辽　宁	257	257	257		
吉　林					
黑龙江	1223	52	52	1171	1111
上　海					
江　苏	566	165	102	401	218
浙　江	217			217	
安　徽	1268	82	3	1186	1069
福　建	1037	50	19	987	987
江　西					
山　东	63996	39957	37342	24039	21137
河　南	172	97	22	75	
湖　北	5457	5271	3047	186	86
湖　南	19321	14569	13067	4752	4375
广　东	503	503	433		
广　西	32970	8272	8266	24698	24657
海　南					
重　庆	9370	5259	3475	4111	4056
四　川	4220	2119	1640	2101	860
贵　州	992	467	403	525	475
云　南	120	120	112		
西　藏					
陕　西	11266	9124	8611	2142	2001
甘　肃	3710	2890	2452	820	793
青　海	48	48	48		
宁　夏	562	48	28	514	514
新　疆					

单位：人、人次、人天、个、平方米

本年收养照料人天数	老年人活动人次数	社区服务志愿者组织数	注册社区志愿者人数	机构建筑面积
29185496	**3730993**	**1350**	**44402**	**17500760**
				70498
4636621	257837	15	17	4501785
585				88566
13546164	7587			1852463
11100				32560
				22956
58995	4546			74747
				103691
207687	230			63078
9998				218031
5299233	2095400	625	3312	3613572
				75131
23600	53830			772279
814314	4708	6	57	1447562
5030				23130
2503629	454087			1878058
				300
1512151	560555	569	379	419797
159531	166903			487921
	37	14	75	367848
				22941
396858	125273	121	40562	771616
				456320
				92489
				33058
				10363

C-2-28 其他社区服务

地区	机构和设施数	工商登记	编制登记	民政登记	设施	农村	年末职工人数	女性
全国	**113053**	**4**	**195**	**22010**	**90844**	**35667**	**389472**	**131934**
中央级								
北京	5020		15	1084	3921	1243	13203	6111
天津	637			14	623	322	2247	769
河北	709		8	98	603	262	2027	742
山西	905		5	14	886	468	4352	1526
内蒙古	350		1	32	317	1	1726	960
辽宁	2052		3	424	1625	470	10219	4964
吉林	29				29		134	95
黑龙江	470		3	57	410	55	3448	1391
上海	3007		8	2778	221	34	27638	7580
江苏	16673		4	11757	4912	3828	73670	20812
浙江	10425	1	6	1551	8867	4943	26596	10447
安徽	2220		30	163	2027	535	8306	3343
福建	232			82	150	54	1710	683
江西	1756			33	1723	123	5891	2125
山东	7421			1053	6368	1686	29422	10285
河南	1240		10	56	1174	306	5675	2051
湖北	3135			81	3054	685	11319	3984
湖南	1849		2	191	1656	353	5825	2258
广东	42867		18	924	41925	13627	120525	40504
广西	406		2	36	368	33	1813	772
海南	170			2	168	119	1014	202
重庆	2531		62	387	2082	1393	6794	2179
四川	4298	3		851	3444	1969	13361	4492
贵州	363		9	40	314	127	1872	568
云南	362		6	23	333	194	1206	363
西藏								
陕西	461			119	342	261	1578	477
甘肃	3014		2	82	2930	2520	6017	1460
青海	12				12		19	7
宁夏	151			7	144	45	704	293
新疆	288		1	71	216	11	1161	491

机构和设施

单位：个、人

受教育程度		职业资格水平		年龄结构			
大学专科人数	大学本科及以上人数	助理社会工作师人数	社会工作师人数	35岁及以下人数	36岁至45岁人数	46岁至55岁人数	56岁及以上人数
79821	**49656**	**6298**	**4034**	**122097**	**150340**	**87488**	**29547**
3762	3811	370	171	5224	4238	2913	828
277	244	7	13	571	741	645	290
208	97	35	34	486	950	515	76
1006	363	137	103	931	1631	1117	673
534	442	151	24	652	677	356	41
2093	1673	159	105	3133	4470	2340	276
37	61			53	59	21	1
612	256	62	16	509	1221	246	1472
6657	1837	108	1244	8917	9480	7467	1774
10155	7630	658	309	19152	30626	18060	5832
6774	5062	471	263	8386	11229	5281	1700
2411	571	112	72	2245	3650	1876	535
113	79	22	15	180	302	459	769
433	153	44	4	1369	1841	1294	1387
8207	4639	597	121	9282	10486	8045	1609
1034	458	54	30	1205	3074	1103	293
2379	1348	147	43	2915	4192	1537	2675
1080	344	71	21	1581	2244	1541	459
26146	17032	2654	1192	46298	45382	22604	6241
277	205	61	29	585	635	409	184
11	1			78	137	765	34
897	745	126	98	1419	2504	1863	1008
2634	1204	160	72	2968	6317	3495	581
453	119	8	7	980	458	357	77
140	133	20	8	254	608	278	66
88	21	15	6	229	586	576	187
893	828	24	22	1776	1878	1943	420
3		6	2	11	6	2	
167	31			198	303	196	7
340	269	19	10	510	415	184	52

C-2-28续表1

地区	志愿服务		床位数合计	日间照料床位数		留宿照料床位数
	志愿者服务人次数	志愿服务时间			农村	
全国	**91299**	**252080**	**451863**	**234240**	**113780**	**217623**
中央级						
北京			1461	467	145	994
天津	500	1000	491	491	355	
河北	20	55	9567	3217	1172	6350
山西			9160	6529	3728	2631
内蒙古			611	608		3
辽宁			11212	4287	1701	6925
吉林			24	24		
黑龙江			8017	2328	142	5689
上海	5349	6914	122	108	3	14
江苏	15339	30666	53592	28651	7026	24941
浙江	1181	2520	78476	48827	39118	29649
安徽	7343	38849	27582	2366	1671	25216
福建	36	72	6677	4220	1067	2457
江西			558	516	100	42
山东	38935	94932	32991	24174	6209	8817
河南			15009	6158	2825	8851
湖北	102	381	13374	5475	1148	7899
湖南	698	1502	7912	3885	867	4027
广东	960	3840	55486	29298	9038	26188
广西			486	351	7	135
海南			4251	938	190	3313
重庆	18567	65847	33940	13374	6218	20566
四川	122	198	19022	9811	2270	9211
贵州	787	2375	3653	1037	691	2616
云南	210	210	11182	3158	1510	8024
西藏						
陕西	235	899	10427	5342	4539	5085
甘肃	635	830	32548	26466	21306	6082
青海			16	2		14
宁夏			1093	599	236	494
新疆	280	990	2923	1533	498	1390

单位：人、人次、时、张

农村	年末收养人数合计	日间照料人数	农村	留宿照料人数	农村
101756	**136334**	**57303**	**24785**	**79031**	**43284**
60	451	20	11	431	11
2782	2403	446	384	1957	1011
1738	3428	2659	1006	769	603
	278	278			
4630	2903	290	75	2613	2034
3398	3970	463	137	3507	2581
	4	4			
4969	6744	3886	630	2858	1048
8102	27931	8728	7578	19203	1329
17675	5865	55		5810	4718
757	2963	2646		317	
	84	83	65	1	
2153	18053	13739	3313	4314	1917
6591	5746	1887	1705	3859	3331
3209	3578	291		3287	2377
2314	2663	1291	554	1372	697
6142	9886	6201	1987	3685	1952
14	104	78	2	26	4
2447	1475	259	58	1216	1055
16861	22597	9281	4023	13316	10930
2313	2597	393	240	2204	1379
2284	1319	31	23	1288	1179
3731	2977	734	619	2243	1618
4355	3511	523	460	2988	2793
4647	3168	2038	1634	1130	717
	2	2			
460	190	186	186	4	
124	1444	811	95	633	

C-2-28续表2

地　区	本年收养照料人天数	老年人活动人次数	社区服务志愿者组织数	注册社区志愿者人数	机构建筑面积
全　国	**6208394**	**2704161**	**3530**	**177994**	**27447121**
中央级					
北　京					474656
天　津					196613
河　北	8095	5861			380961
山　西	40	31468	23		219527
内蒙古		3720			114957
辽　宁	13630	60	4	260	547573
吉　林					16254
黑龙江					268927
上　海			20	1429	419806
江　苏	158497	249456	528	8160	3817020
浙　江	7150	25029	26	121	2271811
安　徽	50735	1500	23	358	837000
福　建	4092	380	50		208997
江　西					248163
山　东	4179718	1568275	1029	4297	4092544
河　南	16020	2370			1211636
湖　北	4230	99435			610198
湖　南	66181	2394	38	573	591097
广　东	79001	2080	1174	157981	7689415
广　西	6290	625	120		69703
海　南	365				61296
重　庆	1612486	706728	443	4103	699422
四　川	134	662	33	592	1235087
贵　州		33			142783
云　南			1	40	263243
西　藏					
陕　西	140	775	15	25	149761
甘　肃		2850			486215
青　海					2965
宁　夏	1450				36360
新　疆	140	460	3	55	83131

单位：人、人次、人天、个、平方米、万元

事业单位会计制度财务指标			民间非营利组织会计制度财务指标		
固定资产原价	本年收入合计	本年支出合计	固定资产原价	本年收入合计	本年费用合计
13528.7	**6625.4**	**6736.4**	**278831.9**	**424004.2**	**462151.8**
388	809.9	766.7	19719.1	13915.7	10198.7
			451.7	968.8	698.9
4659	924	948.5	389	1009.3	1003.4
3	12	12	47		10
1	1	1	716	124.8	158.5
595.1	153	153.8	3034.8	958.8	1645.8
230	230	230	535.6	88.5	227.9
304	8.8	6.6	49424.5	230261.1	284264.8
115	195	195	105626.9	103019.2	98238.2
256	178.9	455.9	6903.4	11248	10002.4
998.9	443	369.6	2143.1	765.8	576.9
			422.8	374.2	382.6
			3917	3994	4157
			22454.7	26181.1	29566.1
658	124.2	124.2	393.7	461.6	578.6
			2124	1037.1	810.4
	10	10	2269	1325.3	1112.4
1761	1217.5	1170.4	21985.8	19939.4	7306
205	14	14	351.3	117.5	136.7
			10		
2386	2228	2228	3147.8	4386.5	4371.1
			23523.8	2257.1	5106.1
63.4	41	3	5350	367.5	119.9
884.3	35.1	47.7	90	0.1	127.5
			643.8	749.3	837.4
21			1427	75.6	154.5
			70	3.8	12.6
			1660.1	374.1	347.4

C-2-29 老龄事业

地区	机构数（编办登记）	年末职工人数	女性	受教育 大学专科人数
全国	**1828**	**8400**	**3707**	**2947**
中央级				
北京	13	142	68	20
天津	13	51	28	14
河北	26	84	36	27
山西	82	398	171	194
内蒙古	18	74	35	24
辽宁	60	252	136	84
吉林	43	178	83	70
黑龙江	62	273	129	96
上海	17	166	97	39
江苏	56	243	118	69
浙江	55	227	111	60
安徽	37	117	35	31
福建	51	151	62	54
江西	101	345	119	146
山东	124	901	288	320
河南	62	261	108	91
湖北	56	249	107	112
湖南	37	132	63	65
广东	40	205	86	47
广西	45	158	83	64
海南	7	232	97	29
重庆	21	95	56	35
四川	198	684	313	269
贵州	96	370	180	161
云南	61	337	151	114
西藏	1	2	2	2
陕西	96	728	333	258
甘肃	91	482	192	101
青海	14	25	11	8
宁夏	23	102	36	38
新疆	222	736	373	305

机构情况

单位：个、人

程度	职业资格水平		年龄结构	
大学本科及以上人数	助理社会工作师人数	社会工作师人数	35岁及以下人数	36岁至45岁人数
3142	**87**	**129**	**2170**	**3159**
120	4	5	32	58
33		2	17	12
29	3	1	23	38
78	5	8	126	155
46	1	5	18	29
114	3		74	71
40	3	1	43	65
108	2		56	100
109	6	15	52	51
100	5	8	65	77
98	4		61	84
60	1	1	30	35
63	1	1	23	48
57	1	6	89	129
429	5	13	208	340
65	5	7	101	108
79		1	57	94
27	2	1	37	54
118	4	10	62	70
62	3	3	28	50
18			112	91
45	2	5	20	27
278	4	10	148	256
161	2	1	72	146
136	7	5	73	126
232	7	1	253	265
104	2		103	199
1			5	11
54	1	1	21	34
278	4	18	161	336

C–2–29续表

地　区	年龄结构		志愿服务	
	46岁至55岁人数	56岁及以上人数	志愿者服务人次数	志愿服务时间
全　国	**2497**	**574**	**878334**	**2263995**
中央级				
北　京	40	12	501806	1197440
天　津	21	1	300	600
河　北	17	6	94	318
山　西	95	22	438	522
内蒙古	24	3	143	344
辽　宁	79	28	18	33
吉　林	55	15	23289	46578
黑龙江	97	20	19675	39663
上　海	53	10		
江　苏	82	19	1356	4981
浙　江	66	16	11116	28324
安　徽	40	12	31157	38042
福　建	69	11	105104	323690
江　西	88	39	1100	2100
山　东	290	63	3784	10870
河　南	43	9	18	96
湖　北	76	22	1175	1505
湖　南	36	5	4814	9847
广　东	61	12	1394	3584
广　西	66	14	335	1840
海　南	16	13	307	879
重　庆	41	7	3878	12475
四　川	221	59	151294	482935
贵　州	133	19	4819	12577
云　南	108	30	2	8
西　藏	2			
陕　西	170	40	3338	14482
甘　肃	154	26	122	264
青　海	7	2		
宁　夏	43	4	2	8
新　疆	204	35	7456	29990

单位：万元、人、人次、时

事业单位会计制度财务指标		
固定资产原价	本年收入合计	本年费用合计
80606.9	**299318.0**	**283171.9**
569.9	29899.0	16213.6
143.2	4579.0	3213.5
168.2	1333.9	1346.7
650.2	4240.8	4172.4
238.9	1365.7	1343.0
612.8	5860.6	4527.0
685.1	4105.6	4235.8
2915.7	2947.3	3765.6
5517.3	73493.9	73288.0
7693.2	6354.4	6298.0
3357.3	11519.1	11491.4
364.8	2899.3	2903.8
654.6	8485.8	8177.9
918.6	2376.7	2475.1
5780.3	19053.6	19071.5
332.5	1762.8	2476.2
1528.0	4147.4	4162.6
402.9	1505.9	1560.1
15925.3	26610.4	26563.5
637.6	4395.7	4897.7
87.5	203.0	321.9
2168.0	2921.3	2991.5
6665.1	17135.9	15004.3
2015.8	9643.7	10147.6
10937.4	8695.4	8508.5
2.0		
2850.3	32076.4	32402.5
1976.0	2578.2	2545.1
89.2	78.3	137.3
848.6	2429.0	1873.4
3870.6	6619.9	7056.4

C-2-30 居家养老

地区	老龄人口情况						老年维权	
	60岁及以上老年人口数	65岁及以上老年人口数	80岁及以上老年人口数	100岁及以上老年人口数	纯老年人家庭人口数	老龄系统接待来信来访次数	老年法律援助中心	涉老案件数
全　国	**229323177**	**152031382**	**30882234**	**71556**	**31540376**	**406310**	**19309**	**58611**
中央级								
北　京	3352174	2280051	593653	958	556136	54819	278	5209
天　津	2438980	1567534	359359	337	311591	28622	176	4266
河　北	11574182	7817782	1386671	2152	957153	4955	401	514
山　西	4702326	3127610	597807	939	577628	7221	596	1210
内蒙古	3919323	2506050	440344	355	615067	3773	154	567
辽　宁	8306700	5397709	1039979	1598	1942267	14312	1913	2049
吉　林	5627960	3530010	665813	892	939498	831	38	105
黑龙江	5624807	3983926	672842	954	1558059	3747	494	1204
上　海	4567920	2917696	792958	2833	1069984	41482	17	3814
江　苏	16729062	11537428	2425835	5599	3124215	38599	1372	3477
浙　江	10306111	6789316	1615523	2365	2435138	34913	333	4061
安　徽	11470780	7938744	1671386	3817	1278620	8457	559	1525
福　建	5408168	3466237	871992	1968	911609	5473	1375	2732
江　西	6658610	3948042	850267	1270	258582	5893	343	491
山　东	18672379	11790148	2203924	4971	3903069	7195	2088	2343
河　南	14002561	9363482	2060041	6492	1165759	5133	1023	869
湖　北	10356388	6702973	1201039	2195	869870	11317	572	1290
湖　南	12085047	8363782	1793224	2516	2078597	20726	314	1831
广　东	12976536	8410033	2078138	7585	763320	10761	816	588
广　西	8378261	5650986	1193234	6568	580213	11217	242	971
海　南	1019408	816358	239046	2124	47922	1974	7	154
重　庆	7047363	4766613	1003856	1509	1282817	5432	404	5960
四　川	17922011	12257538	2195115	5256	1850117	33711	1627	3768
贵　州	5606240	3781887	592514	1227	342500	5803	913	550
云　南	6236442	3946735	847321	1596	717689	8409	1238	5533
西　藏	210109	161830	29308	92	1365	560		
陕　西	5941462	3931005	710240	1037	621788	12111	500	1790
甘　肃	3979463	2567774	386039	450	312935	7256	492	345
青　海	724957	508362	83241	157	82612			
宁　夏	847588	465986	52433	87	46616	4211	67	237
新　疆	2629859	1737755	229092	1657	337640	7397	957	1158

服务情况

单位：个、人、张

老龄事业发展情况								
	老年活动设施			老年福利			老年医疗护理机构	
维权协调组织数	老年活动站/中心/室数	老年人参与人数	年末活动人次数	享受高龄补贴的老年人数	享受护理补贴的老年人数	享受养老服务补贴的老年人数	老年医院数	床位数
70305	**358580**	**42838649**	**193959349**	**23553913**	**404967**	**2829303**	**3004**	**138374**
8264	6613	824498	5237467	371015	11468	244698	17	2407
1508	2033	337008	589854	20207	3551	12300	32	1746
1140	13762	935317	5200703	984199	3607	35566	119	3044
2231	18497	1039920	3249997	304423	160	58714	51	1403
162	1981	272009	2602665	370875	1373	8650	9	720
1869	6182	870967	1845231	102947	5078	11483	16	627
672	1557	84170	200652	6667	2397	6678	17	262
886	4187	537665	2898078	174369	15646	12687	280	4187
712	6266	343234	26613737	1639401	35009	176728	40	5406
6116	20052	4297994	59740098	2258107	83924	215220	300	29904
3682	32615	7125670	16665012	1134141	22647	171223	44	6282
2192	8023	1358461	3622704	1489879	16391	92793	44	7126
2112	16301	1808201	3463916	559137	19479	66492	44	3165
3515	14178	1016215	1590090	477507	622	548	78	1511
3714	55105	2714206	4414634	1346824	20618	176779	80	10401
2785	32053	1337235	2049379	417638	1900	12768	165	4863
2659	10651	1970627	13806286	1040324	5599	13755	115	6052
899	8914	1114258	1639500	240173	12636	104985	121	5741
1619	14467	2309896	5463887	2696666	20621	20945	73	6817
1684	6389	1096612	2153810	994775	6882	2525	49	5432
93	879	324398	421498	169827	1382	3149	2	50
2963	7573	2050252	3308425	330402	7158	27849	17	1752
9607	29384	4244762	14177321	1774008	67760	1111176	551	15881
2533	4452	694656	1894017	498793	15981	185757	173	3481
2755	15537	2175447	6778459	863392	1361	19700	38	3112
	5	1831	1941	18583	3219			
2088	6948	894871	1467782	2589550	7023	22131	135	3714
1145	3847	451730	623004	155960	4474	7525	383	2157
	579	90843	135084	312348		6061		
330	794	99871	259956	21450	456	71	1	12
370	8756	415825	1844162	190326	6545	347	10	1119

C-2-30续表

地　区	老龄事业							
	老年医疗护理机构			老年人协会个数	参加人数	村、居老年人协会	参加人数	乡、街道老年人协会
	老年临终关怀医院数	床位数	年底在院人数					
全　国	**1660**	**31939**	**15053**	**426112**	**45902065**	**347142**	**35984904**	**33519**
中央级								
北　京	4	307	173	5612	367419	5217	313518	183
天　津	1	30	22	3381	389080	3167	343650	193
河　北	53	535	30	16925	740565	13420	578117	1081
山　西	67	4669	295	14237	860444	13087	725926	613
内蒙古				1348	178952	898	99980	299
辽　宁	6	830	100	9802	1077418	7744	887982	1129
吉　林				1631	61517	812	47284	70
黑龙江	43	1209	480	6595	629316	4349	424180	1154
上　海	22	206	123	2793	272106	2618	247648	164
江　苏	68	8290	5556	18829	3794710	16623	3065750	1266
浙　江	3	466	457	30682	6931056	27092	6516012	901
安　徽	8	206	112	13041	1451404	11586	1171654	1085
福　建	33	1798	958	15551	2250262	14188	2028983	771
江　西	6	287	204	19295	1244624	8184	831489	921
山　东	18	1670	908	68665	2174389	55537	1437495	8216
河　南	16	424	325	17480	1140633	13001	767406	1121
湖　北	1100	492	321	18496	2066101	15092	1471329	1284
湖　南	63	1729	677	13061	2059511	11437	1616253	1122
广　东	24	2847	1080	15514	2379100	12556	1973070	1336
广　西	3	200	146	9177	1629522	7768	1184342	837
海　南				693	126779	532	72391	127
重　庆	2	75	30	10095	2225267	8451	1345692	1152
四　川	87	4200	2296	44621	5874670	39913	4245472	4100
贵　州	17	82	42	15183	1170174	13479	849646	1252
云　南	4	49	36	16965	2572723	9594	1633045	1390
西　藏				6	1647			
陕　西	11	1138	492	20352	1404052	17220	1503252	555
甘　肃	1	200	190	10097	515585	8898	431265	616
青　海				254	23605	229	8459	13
宁　夏				839	68213	709	51678	102
新　疆				4892	221221	3741	111936	466

单位：人、人次、张、个、万元

发展情况

参加人数	县、市老年人协会	参加人数	老年基金会	事业投入经费	其他老年社团组织	参加人数	老年学校 老年学校个数	在校人数
6945182	**5478**	**3038491**	**1274**	**28190**	**38482**	**4202115**	**53913**	**7102437**
38843	4	1073	2	4	5894	531036	2203	209456
45860	6	2263			4103	127822	641	141963
150691	96	112629	3	23	159	126344	229	35500
104410	96	28601	2	28	79	28555	2362	93091
33597	131	38842			208	8840	62	14069
162475	169	18940	17	3	2760	75242	1034	98948
28145	6	16400	1	5	131	22508	329	29686
176431	228	23033	1		133	13702	285	33875
45786	10	4225	14	4940	9	705	679	502587
597714	227	101258	7	10370	8593	578019	3806	1221964
311129	32	443148	263	2132	819	142557	11816	877648
219319	176	56234	1	9	760	83709	2858	257979
171658	73	89803	216	4386	773	293718	11119	930784
404554	305	128227	13	106	1437	98008	1135	231511
325673	431	235474	6	280	3001	109344	1259	268277
135033	262	28766			191	21578	2299	157978
443138	948	195925	3	164	507	219267	982	214720
311283	147	250013	6	471	705	277252	488	81791
234448	388	102337	493	1938	2244	170710	465	106625
291756	111	77468	3	77	882	80922	586	83259
34994	26	18924	1	162	13	4042	7	3366
530365	302	310989	5	224	971	505798	1761	263427
1346537	457	397119	10	227	1558	398706	2561	616303
264206	203	69606	1	7	1297	109440	1677	172916
296587	457	223986	96	595	472	65436	2284	338909
	5	713						
101418	68	17474	4	206	438	69766	275	65384
63683	37	8672	2	2	160	34382	47	12525
13304	4	3156	94	1824	87	1558	100	891
21459	16	4213			26	879	16	1682
40686	57	28980	10	7	72	2270	548	35323

C-2-31 民政部门直属

地区	单位数	工商登记	编办登记	年末职工人数	#女性	#残疾职工	#女残疾职工
全 国	**25**	**8**	**17**	**1425**	**463**	**94**	**19**
中央级							
北 京	1		1	94	27	7	
天 津	1	1		5		2	
河 北	1		1	17	4	2	1
山 西	1		1	81	29	2	
内蒙古	1	1		42	10	2	
辽 宁							
吉 林							
黑龙江	1	1		23	6	8	2
上 海	1	1		77	30	2	
江 苏	1		1	155	53	1	
浙 江							
安 徽	1		1	10	10	2	1
福 建	1	1		3	2	1	
江 西	1		1	28	7	14	
山 东	1		1	116	30	4	
河 南	2	1	1	123	38	13	2
湖 北	2	1	1	136	35	3	2
湖 南	1		1	95	33	3	1
广 东	2		2	74	18	8	2
广 西	1		1	87	35	3	2
海 南							
重 庆							
四 川							
贵 州	1		1	56	20	2	1
云 南	1		1	74	33	5	1
西 藏							
陕 西	1	1		87	24	9	3
甘 肃							
青 海	1		1	10	3		
宁 夏							
新 疆	1		1	32	16	1	1

康复辅具机构

单位：个、人

受教育程度		受教育程度		年龄结构			
大学专科人数	大学本科及以上人数	助理社会工作师人数	社会工作师人数	35岁及以下人数	36岁至45岁人数	46岁至55岁人数	56岁及以上人数
429	**307**	**33**	**33**	**435**	**410**	**449**	**131**
27	29		1	43	21	21	9
						5	
3	5			5	4	4	4
16	29		2	18	24	35	4
18	6	1		16	11	11	4
5				13	5	4	1
13	7			5	35	27	10
80	15	2	1	87	40	20	8
2			1	2	4	4	
					2	1	
5	2	1		1	6	15	6
27	22			10	31	65	10
28	26	5	13	59	27	30	7
32	22		1	37	31	48	20
57	35	1	1	32	28	25	10
13	27	14	6	15	19	29	11
21	19	5	6	29	31	18	9
12	24	1		16	24	15	1
33	9	1	1	29	9	34	2
27	17	2		7	40	30	10
1	9			3	2	5	
9	4			8	16	3	5

C-2-31续表

地　区	企业会计制度财务指标			
	固定资产原价	本年收入合计	本年支出合计	营业利润
全　国	**27403.3**	**15646.7**	**8338.0**	**-664.1**
中央级				
北　京	2939.3	2550.1	1047.3	-326.9
天　津	86.0	47.0	19.2	-8.0
河　北				
山　西	9040.0	576.0	125.5	-15.5
内蒙古	666.0	272.8	442.0	-780.0
辽　宁				
吉　林				
黑龙江	185.3	164.3	39.5	9.5
上　海	2583.1	2351.7	1015.6	150.2
江　苏				
浙　江				
安　徽	474.0	979.0	394.0	-166.0
福　建		3.0	3.0	
江　西				
山　东	3261.0	2596.0	1383.0	-10.0
河　南	280.0	186.0	186.0	
湖　北	23.5	38.9	18.3	0.6
湖　南				
广　东	1504.3	3510.5	2355.8	295.2
广　西	3731.5	1110.9	949.1	-229.3
海　南				
重　庆				
四　川				
贵　州				
云　南				
西　藏				
陕　西	2629.3	1260.5	359.7	416.1
甘　肃				
青　海				
宁　夏				
新　疆				

单位：万元

事业单位会计制度财务指标		
固定资产原价	本年收入合计	本年费用合计
17659.0	**28402.8**	**23948.7**
84.0	245.0	237.0
5816.5	5815.6	5839.0
542.7	1740.6	950.3
4455.8	3629.0	2934.0
1409.0	5220.9	4179.6
1274.0	5966.0	4793.0
1483.0	2402.6	1732.7
1135.0	1853.7	1761.8
	140.0	216.2
1459.0	1389.4	1305.1

C-2-32 残疾人教育

地　区	残疾人就业服务机构（个）	残疾人就业人数（万人）	省市县乡残联实有人员（人）
全　国	**2811**	**896.1**	**113013**
北　京	17	9.3	1274
天　津	20	8.3	956
河　北	187	61.0	5628
山　西	120	28.5	4509
内蒙古	80	23.4	3195
辽　宁	115	28.9	4107
吉　林	69	18.1	3042
黑龙江	124	22.1	3258
上　海	18	9.3	1077
江　苏	111	46.2	4973
浙　江	102	26.9	4732
安　徽	99	53.2	3646
福　建	94	20.6	2577
江　西	87	33.4	4016
山　东	135	54.4	6240
河　南	163	40.6	8116
湖　北	107	39.7	3414
湖　南	133	38.6	4999
广　东	133	27.3	7555
广　西	120	31.3	3365
海　南	19	3.0	728
重　庆	39	24.8	1968
四　川	134	86.2	9090
贵　州	82	31.1	3122
云　南	138	45.3	3723
西　藏	2	1.8	286
陕　西	120	26.3	4148
甘　肃	98	26.1	4058
青　海	29	4.1	1213
宁　夏	21	5.5	777
新　疆	84	17.3	2887
兵　团	10	2.4	113
黑龙江垦区	1	1.1	221

指标解释：

1.残疾人就业服务机构：指截止到本年度12月31日，省（自治区、直辖市）、地（州、盟）、市（地市级市、县级市）、县（旗）、市辖区各级残联所建的残疾人就业服务机构数。

2.残疾人就业人数：指截止到本年度12月31日持证残疾人分不同就业形式（包括集中就业、按比例就业、个体就业、辅助性就业、公益性岗位就业、农村种养殖、灵活就业。）的就业总人数。

就业情况

高等院校录取残疾考生（人）	接收托养服务残疾人（万人）	农村贫困残疾人危房改造（户）
11534	**104.2**	**82126**
227	12.3	499
142	3.6	658
309	2.0	2341
283	0.2	13
294	1.3	17532
341	2.9	2804
449	0.6	102
242	0.8	1706
99	3.2	203
606	6.2	921
651	25.4	2296
536	1.5	8071
288	2.6	4220
335	0.8	1995
743	6.1	1273
866	1.6	4713
358	2.3	280
466	2.4	10049
570	3.6	2106
279	3.6	3173
108	1.8	35
276	3.1	5136
505	4.1	3879
500	0.8	315
636	2.6	1774
30	0.1	25
290	2.2	361
483	1.6	2024
92	0.3	1026
128	0.6	0
328	3.2	2535
60	0.8	61
14	0.1	0

3.高等院校录取残疾考生：指本年度高等特殊教育院校和普通高等院校录取的残疾考生数。

4.接收托养服务残疾人：指本年度接受机构托养和居家托养的智力、精神、无生活自理能力、长期需要专人照料或护理的残疾人数。

5.农村贫困残疾人危房改造：指本年度完成危房改造的农村贫困残疾人户数。

C-2-33 孤儿和

地　区	孤儿数	集中供养孤儿	社会散居孤儿	收养登记合计	中国公民收养登记
全　国	**460450**	**87502**	**372948**	**18736**	**15965**
中央级					
北　京	2071	1660	411	140	96
天　津	805	552	253	62	20
河　北	16479	2163	14316	255	219
山　西	12850	2688	10162	244	102
内蒙古	5185	1182	4003	197	102
辽　宁	7233	3165	4068	183	160
吉　林	5106	1491	3615	23	7
黑龙江	7286	1369	5917	69	45
上　海	1824	1726	98	306	246
江　苏	16510	3269	13241	1721	1561
浙　江	4235	2196	2039	2483	2403
安　徽	27250	3216	24034	737	654
福　建	5504	1871	3633	1076	1008
江　西	21358	5342	16016	284	167
山　东	17360	2862	14498	1982	1841
河　南	34032	4855	29177	717	259
湖　北	19284	3067	16217	695	614
湖　南	37274	4950	32324	706	630
广　东	35807	8860	26947	1436	1080
广　西	21888	2385	19503	1757	1594
海　南	1548	336	1212	86	86
重　庆	5404	1374	4030	247	208
四　川	28878	3991	24887	1001	949
贵　州	20232	2801	17431	253	168
云　南	24176	1820	22356	1255	1171
西　藏	5967	5967		13	13
陕　西	11569	2569	9000	387	207
甘　肃	18828	2593	16235	86	48
青　海	15771	1778	13993	49	45
宁　夏	6646	439	6207	37	26
新　疆	22090	4965	17125	249	236

家庭收养

单位：人、件

香港居民	澳门居民	台湾居民	华　侨	外国人收养登记	协议解除收养关系登记	#中国公民
77	**3**	**26**	**25**	**2771**	**562**	**531**
			1	44	1	1
2				42	5	5
				36	10	10
1				142		
				95	1	1
			1	23	1	1
				16		
1		2		24	6	6
		1	2	60	5	5
1				160	45	45
		1	14	80	72	72
				83		
8		7		68	6	5
				117	34	34
3		1	1	141	4	4
			2	458	30	30
3		1		81	6	6
				76	40	40
50	3	3	3	356	12	11
2		7		163	117	117
2						
3		1		39	20	20
1		1	1	52	72	72
				85	4	4
				84	1	1
		1		180	45	17
				38		
				4	3	3
				11		
				13	22	21

C-2-34 被收养的

地区	被收养人合计	女性	残疾儿童	社会福利机构抚养的儿童	#被外国人收养
全　国	**18736**	**12586**	**2554**	**8884**	**2490**
中央级					
北　京	140	70	49	49	43
天　津	62	30	36	59	41
河　北	255	139	52	124	36
山　西	244	113	34	192	140
内蒙古	197	97	22	111	95
辽　宁	183	96	21	65	22
吉　林	23	4		22	16
黑龙江	69	26	15	22	14
上　海	306	242	61	175	59
江　苏	1721	1153	274	877	160
浙　江	2483	1933	27	1501	
安　徽	737	481	9	312	83
福　建	1076	833	68	467	66
江　西	284	207	110	184	115
山　东	1982	1187	164	675	141
河　南	717	343	474	565	458
湖　北	695	457	85	220	
湖　南	706	471	76	305	76
广　东	1436	1016	339	1019	356
广　西	1757	1438	162	818	151
海　南	86	69		49	
重　庆	247	153	36	68	38
四　川	1001	560	56	394	50
贵　州	253	185	71	123	84
云　南	1255	847	64	129	
西　藏	13			12	
陕　西	387	198	174	220	180
甘　肃	86	46	37	55	38
青　海	49	23	6	4	4
宁　夏	37	25	11	17	11
新　疆	249	144	21	51	13

儿童情况

单位：人

社会孤儿数		近亲属抚养人数		生父母有特殊困难无力抚养人数		其他	
	#被外国人收养		#被外国人收养		#被外国人收养		#被外国人收养
4696	**244**	**1076**	**7**	**601**	**8**	**3479**	**22**
64		3		3		21	1
		1	1	1		1	
57		26		4		44	
13		18		7	2	14	
9		20		39		18	
81		13		2	1	22	
						1	
10		14	2	8	3	15	5
80		14		1		36	1
298		125		19		402	
692	68	86		3		201	12
281		32		16		96	
326		44	2	7		232	
50		12	2	1		37	
604		21		14		668	
31		62		29		30	
217	80	70		62		126	1
175		71		27		128	
186		108		20		103	
458	12	70		49		362	
17		2		9		9	
78		21		11		69	1
220		116		143	1	128	1
36	1	3		16		75	
573	83	38		56	1	459	
1							
45		20		36		66	
18		7				6	
8		22		2		13	
11						9	
57		37		16		88	

C-2-35 救助、低保

地 区	单位数	编办登记	民政登记	年末职工人数	女性	受教育 大学专科人数
全 国	**949**	**946**	**3**	**8005**	**3589**	**2771**
中央级						
北 京	16	16		131	71	29
天 津	1	1		8	5	
河 北	6	6		39	23	8
山 西	89	89		750	366	282
内蒙古	23	23		253	139	83
辽 宁	14	14		105	44	22
吉 林	68	68		1064	319	221
黑龙江	31	31		266	132	78
上 海	7	6	1	89	51	15
江 苏	8	8		25	9	2
浙 江	15	15		74	46	17
安 徽	23	23		95	34	32
福 建	19	19		68	40	18
江 西	63	63		397	182	146
山 东	11	10	1	61	31	16
河 南	47	47		379	177	135
湖 北	71	71		646	305	278
湖 南	69	69		603	232	237
广 东	4	4		38	23	2
广 西	107	107		576	314	195
海 南	3	2	1	17	11	6
重 庆	36	36		293	163	80
四 川	63	63		346	153	130
贵 州	68	68		1015	434	510
云 南	19	19		85	38	24
西 藏						
陕 西	29	29		299	149	125
甘 肃	21	21		166	54	31
青 海	1	1		2	2	
宁 夏	13	13		102	37	42
新 疆	4	4		13	5	7

服务机构

单位：个、人

程度	职业资格水平		年龄结构	
大学本科及以上人数	助理社会工作师人数	社会工作师人数	35岁及以下人数	36岁至45岁人数
3310	**163**	**173**	**3818**	**3192**
97	6	5	58	45
8		2	8	
7		1	18	14
299	18	16	362	268
145	22	16	105	107
60		5	34	40
312	12	9	483	492
136	1	4	84	127
62	14	6	50	32
15	3	1	12	9
41	2	10	35	26
51	5	4	37	43
38	6	10	38	24
90	11	9	141	202
41	1	7	31	25
116	1	5	230	103
233	8	8	232	309
168	5	15	278	237
36	4		24	6
318	3	3	256	253
10		1	3	8
205	16	4	157	103
132	10	18	161	149
400	6	6	640	311
54	1		38	46
112	5	3	171	97
76		2	108	39
				2
42	2	3	23	64
6	1		1	11

C−2−35续表

地　区	年龄结构		志愿服务	
	46岁至55岁人数	56岁及以上人数	志愿者服务人次数	志愿服务时间
全　国	**886**	**109**	**3169**	**7577**
中央级				
北　京	24	4	30	60
天　津				
河　北	7			
山　西	111	9	6	19
内蒙古	37	4		
辽　宁	15	16		
吉　林	83	6		
黑龙江	50	5		
上　海	6	1		
江　苏	4		23	60
浙　江	10	3		
安　徽	13	2	96	
福　建	6			
江　西	46	8	33	221
山　东	5			
河　南	42	4	83	274
湖　北	93	12	57	126
湖　南	70	18	142	392
广　东	7	1		
广　西	66	1	120	800
海　南	6			
重　庆	31	2	267	840
四　川	31	5	125	126
贵　州	64		2060	4173
云　南	1		1	2
西　藏				
陕　西	27	4	116	454
甘　肃	17	2	10	30
青　海				
宁　夏	13	2		
新　疆	1			

单位：万元、人、人次、时

事业单位会计制度财务指标		
固定资产原价	本年收入合计	本年支出合计
28354.1	**98626.1**	**99741.5**
250.5	17504.5	17426.3
407.2	667.2	697.6
28.9	96.3	84.5
1546.2	3297.2	3381.9
415.7	1979.2	1988.9
94.4	651.3	644.3
884.4	4943.7	5241.5
897.5	789.4	815.4
418.4	13463.5	13487.0
15.1	148.6	148.5
208.9	1112.2	1131.6
197.4	713.0	767.4
78.8	422.6	468.6
444.0	1236.0	1209.6
66.3	401.6	401.6
1230.0	1467.7	1541.8
11912.0	6898.4	7057.0
1651.6	7323.5	6289.2
960.8	1745.6	1876.9
2408.2	12099.9	12319.4
36.9	977.5	1021.4
972.9	4384.3	4388.9
489.6	2440.2	2793.3
1446.1	3673.4	3895.1
39.0	7964.6	8169.6
521.6	1793.4	1839.6
422.2	148.5	302.5
	3.8	3.8
140.5	242.0	336.3
169.0	37.0	12.0

C-2-36 城市最低

地　区	城市最低生活保障人数	按人员性质分类					
		#女　性	#残疾人	#重度残疾人	老年人	成年人	按
							在职人员
全　国	**14802422**	**6435570**	**1564792**	**75609**	**2579514**	**9508534**	**226764**
中央级							
北　京	81882	35824	18178		13140	47690	4625
天　津	121684	61158	20050	15788	18348	75611	3466
河　北	475772	214272	39551	4377	77296	297869	7471
山　西	530928	232104	43901	390	62590	326737	10776
内蒙古	491401	242063	74495	7140	68630	381373	1028
辽　宁	620121	258030	107798	295	81126	399852	5941
吉　林	678281	326550	79602		60771	575533	290
黑龙江	1111158	499790	132359	563	112275	851528	7400
上　海	168225	62359	29843		5340	127065	11408
江　苏	248442	111469	33581	410	68555	137563	3400
浙　江	108937	39971	32221	5280	25156	63142	2545
安　徽	544104	233187	69672	1	167946	299232	4967
福　建	85879	35546	17207	388	20924	52218	1087
江　西	895682	351387	121355	3715	182587	526273	23212
山　东	308575	130883	30181	9901	53007	206389	9124
河　南	821176	323303	56154	730	189625	489660	8378
湖　北	552887	261462	41381	36	104437	388594	46357
湖　南	1118173	460866	89999	1240	269274	658779	8738
广　东	254644	94815	35458	227	63130	139542	6478
广　西	226134	90303	21887	8668	52706	139633	2741
海　南	75354	33211	8452	105	9176	52693	1128
重　庆	347765	158073	63206		41601	233282	601
四　川	1344965	507207	192133	8626	301757	815077	14622
贵　州	358188	148790	26941	2747	60137	225345	5152
云　南	896829	435193	24516	28	209106	582811	5236
西　藏	35856	15373	2378	204	8299	20959	3585
陕　西	420888	205921	21740	2	35787	239338	2894
甘　肃	699949	289055	34034	20	64356	461607	5139
青　海	163213	85053	7367	562	22547	107378	2235
宁　夏	145716	63235	12426		14859	93682	1195
新　疆	869614	429117	76726	4166	115026	492079	15545

生活保障

单位：人、户

年龄分类				城市最低生活保障户数
灵活就业	登记失业	无就业条件	未成年人	
3043739	**2529273**	**3708758**	**2714374**	**8553041**
9851	20773	12441	21052	48802
7134	36832	28179	27725	74543
93843	66560	129995	100607	273883
153561	49626	112774	141601	280134
189375	68293	122677	41398	304482
79487	162121	152303	139143	372927
111294	459993	3956	41977	454143
107911	182303	553914	147355	674024
2047	51597	62013	35820	118379
21434	30772	81957	42324	141682
13757	19264	27576	20639	75735
100318	50962	142985	76926	344490
15095	10636	25400	12737	54017
197322	159833	145906	186822	431927
77322	73139	46804	49179	172849
141202	136137	203943	141891	512972
178781	66611	96845	59856	340349
119317	192426	338298	190120	662452
53948	22340	56776	51972	132521
84490	27836	24566	33795	121741
5862	4222	41481	13485	36227
105042	43177	84462	72882	214749
261026	191949	347480	228131	819361
75540	34565	110088	72706	202678
452664	67810	57101	104912	591769
5796	3581	7997	6598	20590
103598	69050	63796	145763	210320
126272	125925	204271	173986	294272
19819	6637	78687	33288	81027
37416	18674	36397	37175	77071
93215	75629	307690	262509	412925

C-2-37 农村最低

地　区	农村最低生活保障人数	纳入扶贫建档立卡对象	按人员性质分类		
			女　性	残疾人	重度残疾人
全　国	**45864626**	**380473**	**17741561**	**4902056**	**380473**
中央级					
北　京	46779		18876	16582	
天　津	101600	14290	41613	19202	14290
河　北	1894573	44366	697601	192567	44366
山　西	1185256	1138	456764	139339	1138
内蒙古	1127626	17997	557109	158053	17997
辽　宁	778820	1971	285120	104146	1971
吉　林	786780	1	383496	486734	1
黑龙江	1209362	1247	568167	77919	1247
上　海	33778		17219	11059	
江　苏	1098910	367	435737	114727	367
浙　江	713704	30345	273241	203422	30345
安　徽	1498194	264	611985	221804	264
福　建	461493	4736	186463	78853	4736
江　西	1800571	11119	612152	319718	11119
山　东	2176628	102476	815103	238949	102476
河　南	3280238	2475	1097961	293953	2475
湖　北	1382491	424	625038	180139	424
湖　南	2902350	2328	1021681	293870	2328
广　东	1451361	55	458198	147772	55
广　西	2905689	91409	1108178	177337	91409
海　南	182906		82224	16096	
重　庆	589830		266702	89820	
四　川	3566780	33055	1087353	592631	33055
贵　州	3048113	19649	1093273	200060	19649
云　南	4229418	73	1897645	134303	73
西　藏	257236	159	107202	10855	159
陕　西	1303725		567146	119239	
甘　肃	3247111	108	1237541	108131	108
青　海	515836	421	228525	12904	421
宁　夏	422218		146023	40949	
新　疆	1665250		756225	100923	

生活保障

单位：人、户

按人员年龄分类					农村最低生活保障户数
老年人	成年人	有劳动条件	无劳动条件	未成年人	
18588539	**22152115**	**1114429**	**1051362**	**5123972**	**26352666**
19755	21510		1	5514	28925
29771	54761			17068	49188
1113577	673191	95934	118350	107805	1375141
694214	436136	1	2	54906	913568
698157	402084	53304	56612	27385	872911
366160	358339	489	2861	54321	533570
463136	294561		4521	29083	607785
636854	519117		11698	53391	800027
12438	19663		136	1677	27326
436774	534750	2391	2467	127386	592108
269485	367295	615	5982	76924	466070
655494	711192	447	690	131508	871247
139439	262689		6	59365	242437
548391	980286	19644	16666	271894	875272
1273833	770885	376481	430583	131910	1608429
1780682	1277103	11172	17362	222453	2629574
518664	731943			131884	807755
1306386	1370346	1307	3629	225618	1778908
449548	684422	1026	2579	317391	606658
891821	1415914	386311	192265	597954	1019010
39322	106471			37113	78339
106133	394118			89579	313426
1646309	1561495	89278	156963	358976	2243946
1054330	1503469	69641	25959	490314	1450352
1460921	2370326		1	398171	2514310
97880	105969	5968	1978	53387	87061
435493	732146	2	4	136086	585493
712729	2052336	418	47	482046	1082349
82550	307484			125802	153834
142259	251173			28786	324065
506034	880941			278275	813582

C−2−38 特困人员

地 区	城市特困人员救助供养				
		女 性	残疾人	老年人	未成年人
全 国	**90575**	**15258**	**26486**	**63600**	**5367**
中央级					
北 京	682	182	326	480	11
天 津	3	1		2	1
河 北	284	65	101	204	4
山 西	259	16	94	166	10
内蒙古	12665	1339	5700	7792	121
辽 宁	1973	420	960	1118	49
吉 林	3672	447	1032	1808	99
黑龙江	5170	1034	3058	2555	69
上 海					
江 苏	2995	506	401	2749	5
浙 江	1987	555	668	1656	109
安 徽	1122	189	97	970	76
福 建	1301	304	288	952	75
江 西	11357	2114	2400	6719	2496
山 东	1831	338	748	1253	58
河 南	415	87	182	249	3
湖 北	5988	1250	1428	4764	49
湖 南	3231	408	290	3011	6
广 东	4555	1016	1120	3803	70
广 西	501	100	73	451	32
海 南	568	133	17	457	19
重 庆	11410	971	2327	9456	101
四 川	3276	1101	320	2218	935
贵 州	1724	183	211	1450	151
云 南	6957	1372	2436	5526	400
西 藏					
陕 西	2564	410	1069	1807	158
甘 肃					
青 海	36	10	19	27	
宁 夏	145	29	89	51	1
新 疆	3904	678	1032	1906	259

救助供养

单位：人

全自理	半护理	全护理	集中供养	分散供养
56870	**24611**	**9094**	**28147**	**62428**
626	27	29	119	563
1	2			3
177	96	11	105	179
185	74	0	36	223
7342	3501	1822	3631	9034
848	729	396	892	1081
2630	882	160	531	3141
1908	2448	814	1633	3537
2201	640	154	774	2221
585	734	668	1898	89
855	220	47	411	711
937	219	145	237	1064
7527	2733	1097	3818	7539
1168	479	184	442	1389
141	147	127	119	296
3671	1378	939	3204	2784
1812	797	622	829	2402
3016	924	615	601	3954
482	13	6	71	430
289	227	52	277	291
9409	1823	178	3289	8121
732	2391	153	560	2716
1200	505	19	726	998
5504	1296	157	2601	4356
1776	644	144	299	2265
10	26			36
60	71	14	64	81
1778	1585	541	980	2924

C-2-38续表

地　区	农村特困人员救助供养	女　性	残疾人	老年人	未成年人
全　国	**4968767**	**761561**	**945800**	**4229782**	**141005**
中央级					
北　京	4474	358	2430	3660	19
天　津	11578	1076	2616	10075	47
河　北	234490	17248	42886	205612	2373
山　西	150494	11513	44141	108967	4686
内蒙古	86349	5351	25319	65479	470
辽　宁	135624	14030	28868	114937	2382
吉　林	111633	17896	41364	71028	1743
黑龙江	122152	22153	44714	87649	1695
上　海	2496	390	629	2124	11
江　苏	197951	27596	22383	187320	2184
浙　江	32543	4485	3800	30965	150
安　徽	409816	59203	55079	372891	5383
福　建	75578	9888	20949	58439	2167
江　西	221412	63051	33279	191622	15113
山　东	210594	32907	20470	202392	1717
河　南	479484	71208	61043	438584	10195
湖　北	248538	37172	54529	213630	1141
湖　南	425093	74140	84918	355327	14514
广　东	231963	33965	34523	209987	8435
广　西	269142	41389	37042	244696	10371
海　南	28364	7325	1972	28110	468
重　庆	168798	14354	29201	148565	1580
四　川	485843	57860	91882	411346	12444
贵　州	104514	18244	16532	81266	13175
云　南	173528	43221	56087	118211	14364
西　藏	14242	3704	629	5439	623
陕　西	125092	18004	38064	97126	3754
甘　肃	116787	21021	27428	96486	2304
青　海	23906	7871	4854	18275	2701
宁　夏	11862	2759	3621	9160	237
新　疆	54427	22179	14548	40414	4559

单位：人

全自理	半护理	全护理	集中供养	分散供养
3795533	**944971**	**228263**	**1396560**	**3572207**
4070	299	105	1711	2763
8549	2428	601	1073	10505
164465	53779	16246	38359	196131
113708	28553	8233	19844	130650
64119	16124	6106	10816	75533
98090	31042	6492	27447	108177
90181	18045	3407	21193	90440
83809	34271	4072	29196	92956
1513	762	221	1017	1479
160924	31461	5566	70762	127189
23970	7011	1562	31237	1306
324676	70681	14459	122079	287737
63207	10266	2105	8382	67196
160973	50711	9728	125390	96022
169911	32476	8207	123262	87332
391603	70382	17499	108239	371245
173365	58584	16589	51154	197384
290229	100150	34714	83699	341394
189724	34790	7449	22980	208983
245445	18879	4818	22523	246619
23752	1699	2913	2483	25881
139618	23172	6008	58567	110231
372985	95365	17493	256150	229693
85797	13454	5263	47155	57359
126746	38302	8480	28482	145046
9337	3933	972	9655	4587
87642	28492	8958	44045	81047
68736	45828	2223	9080	107707
14759	6472	2675	5113	18793
6952	3805	1105	3302	8560
36678	13755	3994	12165	42262

C-2-39 医疗救助

地 区	资助参加基本医疗保险人数	重点救助对象	民政部门直接救助人次数
全 国	**55604175**	**5939375**	**26961185**
中央级			
北 京	66909		94607
天 津	236536	207731	226537
河 北	1984983	281143	333674
山 西	1509982	5597	236796
内蒙古	1559631	188400	320896
辽 宁	948462	194	637412
吉 林	630705	149134	485938
黑龙江	2393574		650948
上 海	97632	18	183475
江 苏	1364106	134130	3498117
浙 江	161378	8898	2799561
安 徽	3461357	169994	874851
福 建	634669	9560	1544235
江 西	2091712	105516	1816576
山 东	2200170	731818	828131
河 南	3539301	72533	656877
湖 北	2426720	2206144	982385
湖 南	3500700	254775	1225036
广 东	2346902	15769	1191976
广 西	1727855	138222	595218
海 南	232332	23915	115008
重 庆	1555873		3615445
四 川	5366451	264893	1561706
贵 州	2814051	778255	375514
云 南	5481548	102932	736094
西 藏	48760		56853
陕 西	739900	2204	383176
甘 肃	4104566	36719	291316
青 海	725426	9049	163582
宁 夏	328571	24235	114927
新 疆	1323413	17597	364318

和临时救助

单位：人、户、万元、人次

住院救助人次			门诊救助人次		
	重点救助对象	重特大疾病医疗救助对象		重点救助对象	重特大疾病医疗救助对象
11949234	**1197534**	**444787**	**15011951**	**2541233**	**188416**
23853	1493	7058	70754	1655	277
61019	51681	2841	165518	143001	
223492	20339	9382	110182	5796	311
189632	1427	1245	47164		
267996	68207	21699	52900	30998	2102
271287	21631	4779	366125	13846	50480
332388	45757	6044	153550	23815	2944
397236		1170	253712		370
51929	34		131546		
768623	13538	3310	2729494	13807	
650305	9112	1082	2149256	131692	3579
718392	255	16	156459	19917	2909
348123	11967	17356	1196112	19072	1628
537913	12971	13406	1278663	74291	13218
361030	163223	16468	467101	35145	14140
584853	13827	2476	72024	1578065	2053
834386	490535	176390	147999	115557	31744
918607	103297	71664	306429	31270	16655
433454	11943	2603	758522	21353	5270
258213	18019	2463	337005	1683	157
42473	1922	2462	72535	16522	5072
686262	13413	9815	2929183	81786	27108
1142612	97335	48669	419094	32500	4687
245848	818	2327	129666	118600	22
572883	14178	14350	163211	19711	639
51237	285	2	5616	10	
320784	763	41	62392		295
186081	473	79	105235		
133938	971	40	29644	3094	
105369		2542	9558		
229016	8120	3008	135302	8047	2756

C-2-39续表

地区	传统救济	临时救助户次	按属地分类	
			本地户籍	非本地户籍
全国	**602181**	**8506993**	**8263275**	**243718**
中央级				
北京	28	25085	25073	12
天津	3	87291	87243	48
河北	6124	595107	586018	9089
山西	6751	241172	237944	3228
内蒙古	20453	305347	291024	14323
辽宁	7699	292404	273355	19049
吉林	1040	126130	115264	10866
黑龙江	824	192208	189966	2242
上海	15	371434	367208	4226
江苏	47218	405685	378270	27415
浙江	2353	370201	360888	9313
安徽	43236	178588	176707	1881
福建	3746	110825	110275	550
江西	38402	128881	126379	2502
山东	520	252954	248638	4316
河南	23947	248430	241427	7003
湖北	19058	427289	414875	12414
湖南	98087	701500	676112	25388
广东	1636	153380	144794	8586
广西	112853	89747	86746	3001
海南	86	29880	28583	1297
重庆	13156	225940	221417	4523
四川	58871	472661	462343	10318
贵州	21314	165561	130226	35335
云南	37429	700068	693559	6509
西藏		3765	3517	248
陕西	2679	335101	329957	5144
甘肃	29340	549076	547988	1088
青海	323	81758	81365	393
宁夏	3403	305925	302329	3596
新疆	1587	333600	323785	9815

单位：人、人次

按对象分类		
低保人员	特困人员	其他
3692111	**1966602**	**2848280**
16956	1162	6967
41161	7871	38259
175658	257391	162058
63100	90619	87453
162155	75241	67951
241610	32922	17872
92480	26341	7309
95076	37718	59414
283370	9272	78792
166043	113848	125794
107816	75121	187264
91216	47898	39474
24198	28379	58248
84708	25885	18288
100869	64698	87387
125247	72763	50420
142046	89539	195704
335673	159155	206672
68346	40574	44460
36697	16117	36933
6373	4277	19230
99982	45572	80386
229502	82630	160529
54723	22228	88610
170184	107832	422052
1751	867	1147
107334	98621	129146
216929	193122	139025
39061	27442	15255
123908	44145	137872
187939	67352	78309

C-2-40 救灾储

地区	单位数	年末职工人数		受教育程度		职业资
			女性	大学专科人数	大学本科及以上人数	助理社会工作师人数
全　国	**258**	**1258**	**414**	**440**	**537**	**19**
中央级						
北　京						
天　津	2	27	10	7	17	3
河　北	7	40	8	12	10	
山　西	14	73	21	35	25	
内蒙古	3	20	6	6	7	
辽　宁	19	121	47	60	50	1
吉　林	4	33	11	7	3	
黑龙江	6	33	9	9	17	
上　海	1	1				
江　苏	2	7	4		5	
浙　江	6	8			3	
安　徽	2	14	5	7	7	
福　建	2	15	7	1	13	1
江　西	3	6	2	2		
山　东	4	32	9	8	24	
河　南	7	65	14	15	43	1
湖　北	37	115	51	41	37	
湖　南	2	7	1		5	
广　东	18	114	44	43	54	3
广　西	7	48	24	23	22	2
海　南	2	12	4	4	8	
重　庆	2	8	1	1	4	1
四　川	56	198	62	75	76	2
贵　州	5	28	3	13	14	1
云　南	6	55	23	10	35	4
西　藏	1	4		3		
陕　西	6	60	17	18	17	
甘　肃	17	47	15	11	21	
青　海	4	13	3	3	9	
宁　夏	9	29	10	16	4	
新　疆	4	25	3	10	7	

备机构

单位：个、人、人次、时

格水平	年龄结构				志愿服务	
社会工作师人数	35岁及以下人数	36岁至45岁人数	46岁至55岁人数	56岁及以上人数	志愿者服务人次数	志愿服务时间
38	**445**	**493**	**263**	**57**	**404**	**794**
	12	10	4	1	10	75
3	12	11	14	3		
1	15	38	14	6		
2	3	10	7			
1	45	40	26	10	21	23
	13	14	6			
	12	10	10	1		
				1		
1	4	1	2		5	40
2		4	1	3		
1	4	5	3	2	6	44
2	8	5	2			
		3	3			
3	7	11	11	3		
1	23	22	19	1	57	171
1	32	59	19	5	165	250
	3	3	1			
3	45	41	24	4		
	6	24	15	3		
	7	4	1			
	3	3	1	1		
6	88	77	32	1	134	146
	12	13	2	1	6	45
5	34	13	8			
	2	2				
2	20	23	14	3		
	19	17	10	1		
	6	3	2	2		
	6	15	6	2		
4	4	12	6	3		

C-2-40续表

地　区	事业单位会计制度财务指标			总建筑面积
	固定资产原价	本年收入合计	本年支出合计	
全　国	**113361.4**	**41210.2**	**41618.1**	**808730.0**
中央级				
北　京				
天　津	1523.8	912.5	1022.1	10466.0
河　北	942.4	2321.4	2316.9	19409.7
山　西	875.5	2063.0	2223.5	17374.1
内蒙古	1603.2	576.7	815.1	38133.7
辽　宁	3852.5	2376.2	2428.5	51925.7
吉　林	1026.8	316.3	278.5	
黑龙江	934.4	774.8	507.8	4524.7
上　海				2000.0
江　苏	455.2	2415.6	2645.3	7057.0
浙　江	24.0	29.0	28.0	250.0
安　徽	2089.8	156.6	257.9	7020.0
福　建	69.2	487.2	458.8	12500.0
江　西	24.0		5.8	232.0
山　东	3208.8	3883.3	3871.4	12865.0
河　南	2494.7	216.7	218.4	18625.0
湖　北	2956.7	2887.4	2912.5	68259.8
湖　南	276.3	2.0	2.0	19500.0
广　东	9237.7	4466.6	4205.1	32043.0
广　西	3200.4	1709.6	1621.1	12150.0
海　南	1033.0	301.7	303.2	4055.0
重　庆	2148.7	1550.7	1149.3	3796.0
四　川	46816.1	1952.9	2229.1	162180.1
贵　州	230.5	859.5	233.3	6200.0
云　南	3405.5	734.1	729.4	45867.0
西　藏	30.0			8675.0
陕　西	6071.7	6323.9	2590.2	49728.0
甘　肃	2132.0	770.5	907.8	53824.1
青　海	6150.9	630.5	3187.1	30255.9
宁　夏	6871.6	1588.5	740.0	93298.2
新　疆	3676.0	903.0	3730.0	16515.0

单位：万元、平方米、顶

库房建筑面积	空余库房建筑面积	租用库房面积	仓储物资种类			
			单帐篷	#中央储备	棉帐篷	#中央储备
682920.4	**50321.0**	**34220.0**	**426356.0**	**155835.0**	**236302.0**	**55809.0**
9420.0	60.0		7934.0	4850.0	13022.0	7516.0
18859.7	4100.0		1640.0		1486.0	
22946.0	440.0	9580.0	14038.0		8498.0	
29783.3	2806.0		1966.0		3280.0	
44787.0		1800.0	5494.0	222.0	2024.0	1066.0
3924.7			170.0			
2000.0			120.0			
6732.0			2515.0			
250.0			30.0			
6700.0			11859.0	8059.0	412.0	412.0
12650.0		250.0	17237.0	15500.0	700.0	700.0
109.0			400.0			
12500.0	5000.0		7670.0	3380.0	2175.0	
16097.0	950.0	2186.0	9262.0	62.0	5.0	5.0
41788.0	2870.0	9740.0	25773.0	18935.0	6626.0	5885.0
17500.0	300.0		16503.0	15085.0	2000.0	2000.0
28109.0	1390.0	5041.0	10783.0			
9976.0	250.0	700.0	16382.0	14214.0	408.0	
3723.3		1523.0	6385.0			
3796.0			2307.0			
127209.0	22769.0	3400.0	158416.0	34694.0	23021.0	3866.0
5000.0	1000.0		653.0	150.0		
36187.4	3000.0		19331.0	4739.0		
2323.0	1562.0				720.0	
49408.0	360.0		34590.0	9109.0	8782.0	7064.0
40693.9	3264.0		26553.0	10806.0	17125.0	12606.0
29182.9			5305.0	5245.0	24468.0	5789.0
89015.2	200.0		12274.0	19.0	111076.0	
12250.0			10766.0	10766.0	10474.0	8900.0

C-2-41 民政部门

地区	直接接收捐赠情况			间接接收
	捐赠款数额	捐赠衣被合计	捐赠其他物资价值	捐赠款数额
全国	**402815.1**	**6638.3**	**73795.0**	**58645.3**
中央级				
北京	91256.8	110.8	15196.5	
天津	550.8	0.1		36.8
河北	21955.8	817.3	856.0	121.4
山西	2461.5	0.8	29.2	31.0
内蒙古	271.5	3.0	9155.4	
辽宁	319.7		61.0	
吉林	728.4			
黑龙江	909.2	420.0	8.6	
上海	5342.0	37.8	355.0	1656.3
江苏	173977.7	1530.6	5903.0	45047.9
浙江	831.8	1.6	255.5	770.2
安徽	1739.5		21.2	23.0
福建	5076.0		20.8	
江西	21356.7	149.3	34913.5	333.5
山东	6194.3			
河南	6845.1	9.1		129.5
湖北	8811.7	0.7	2544.2	172.3
湖南	68.4	0.2	14.8	258.0
广东	14042.1	84.6	771.2	6138.8
广西	149.0	74.2	37.6	89.0
海南	567.1	0.3		
重庆	13000.2		1572.6	1774.2
四川	15655.2	701.2	456.1	865.1
贵州	5966.4	2.2	667.5	81.6
云南	1032.4	2685.6	731.0	1036.7
西藏	450.9			
陕西	743.3		46.0	45.0
甘肃	350.7	1.4	1.2	
青海	621.6			26.0
宁夏	28.0			9.0
新疆	1511.3	7.5	177.1	

接收的社会捐赠

单位：万元、万件、人次、个

捐赠情况		受益人次数	社会捐赠接收工作站、点数		
捐赠衣被合计	捐赠其他物资价值			社会捐赠接收工作站数	慈善超市数
488.0	**14483.2**	**11657700**	**28904**	**12899**	**8966**
		6369943	1574	111	152
		18304	697	447	37
	2.5	433658	655	537	50
		47527	604	366	90
	9805.1	19021	376	7	138
		17123	895	685	159
		28395	256	85	100
		10665	934	324	579
0.5	600.0	1814	3426	229	154
279.8	2932.6	2047826	3329	1316	1617
		18362	298	121	153
190.0		1553	318	222	94
		13391	804	316	471
0.2	20.0	221158	284	180	51
		52135	2319	1245	797
14.0		85234	750	462	65
		119994	643	446	281
	27.6	59204	1642	620	809
		1003247	905	671	154
		185344	1149	639	282
		1700	38	13	7
0.3	942.5	476532	1783	997	658
2.4	2.9	248921	2577	1180	1465
	80.0	137412	1042	604	256
0.3	25.0	16729	125	110	16
			82	57	7
		8579	408	185	43
		1198	293	210	84
		82	42	27	10
			154	77	93
0.5	45.0	12649	502	410	94

C-2-42 福利彩票发

地 区	单位数	编制登记	民政登记	年末职工人数	女性	受教育程度	
						大学专科人数	大学本科及以上人数
全 国	**788**	**697**	**91**	**11858**	**5222**	**4144**	**3858**
中央级	1	1		135	55	9	126
北 京	17	17		136	59	47	79
天 津	10	9	1	102	44	14	69
河 北	20	11	9	343	170	96	93
山 西	12	12		281	143	100	110
内蒙古	16	16		260	112	117	78
辽 宁	18	15	3	422	174	160	207
吉 林	48	48		556	105	76	89
黑龙江	18	17	1	159	66	53	44
上 海	17	3	14	235	126	66	85
江 苏	78	75	3	895	380	281	344
浙 江	59	43	16	676	349	264	199
安 徽	48	19	29	745	380	298	210
福 建	10	10		334	129	94	81
江 西	33	31	2	117	37	40	11
山 东	18	18		778	326	276	349
河 南	42	42		583	242	229	179
湖 北	46	45	1	439	221	178	132
湖 南	75	75		519	216	147	150
广 东	62	58	4	866	386	273	271
广 西	28	28		747	343	284	97
海 南	3	3		51	20	22	18
重 庆	1	1		167	43	35	115
四 川	7	7		803	454	396	226
贵 州	13	12	1	262	112	94	100
云 南	12	12		114	48	51	28
西 藏	1	1		40	25	20	10
陕 西	27	26	1	287	128	104	90
甘 肃	17	15	2	247	121	63	82
青 海	2	2		100	56	28	36
宁 夏	10	6	4	246	70	125	77
新 疆	19	19		213	82	104	73

行机构情况

单位：个、人、人次、时

职业资格水平		年龄结构				志愿服务	
助理社会工作师人数	社会工作师人数	35岁及以下人数	36岁至45岁人数	46岁至55岁人数	56岁及以上人数	志愿者服务人次数	志愿服务时间
178	**153**	**6202**	**3833**	**1544**	**279**	**1383**	**4205**
		77	21	25	12		
3	4	56	46	29	5	2	4
	1	46	37	15	4		
1	6	185	114	38	6		
1	1	153	83	42	3		
1	1	143	77	34	6		
	1	218	123	66	15		
5	1	252	241	49	14		
2	7	71	64	21	3	1	6
1		84	90	31	30		
36	28	429	315	122	29	763	2300
5	9	367	221	74	14		
12	5	470	192	75	8	80	240
1		114	127	77	16		
2		44	44	24	5	111	423
18	21	399	253	101	25		
24	5	290	198	87	8	86	261
1		206	165	62	6	52	81
1	14	269	178	64	8	102	367
45	20	446	278	127	15	1	
11	4	366	279	92	10		
2	4	17	15	19			
1		95	47	23	2		
2		618	131	44	10		
1	2	158	78	22	4	88	186
1		47	49	14	4		
		15	23	2			
	6	160	79	41	7	97	338
1		131	80	32	4		
	1	49	32	18	1		
	1	151	73	20	2		
	11	76	80	54	3		

C-2-42续表

地　区	事业单位会计制度财务指标		
	固定资产原价	本年收入合计	本年支出合计
全　国	**826389.4**	**1190937.9**	**1002794.9**
中央级	17628.8	118036.1	89323.1
北　京	15578.5	25286.9	17339.9
天　津	17839.9	13045.7	12479.4
河　北	36388.6	60243.7	54768.3
山　西	17613.0	25820.6	14017.4
内蒙古	38842.4	26556.2	24966.9
辽　宁	59258.7	36581.7	27938.3
吉　林	14303.9	29648.9	21877.1
黑龙江	10962.4	4939.0	4992.5
上　海	23658.0	18382.8	18065.5
江　苏	84101.8	80011.0	75289.8
浙　江	53702.8	53147.7	41634.7
安　徽	16327.6	20946.4	15194.8
福　建	5032.4	17418.4	16439.0
江　西	19208.4	16998.9	8511.0
山　东	83798.5	89950.8	89674.7
河　南	34568.6	76919.7	65295.2
湖　北	30855.9	50603.3	49821.5
湖　南	36787.9	50344.9	38234.3
广　东	48502.1	96881.3	91318.0
广　西	30005.2	23176.9	23098.2
海　南	8561.2	6316.5	6960.7
重　庆	12244.1	37309.4	20974.9
四　川	2440.5	42569.3	43462.1
贵　州	17968.6	19787.5	16480.7
云　南	8615.9	53211.8	48899.6
西　藏	423.0	7867.0	7668.0
陕　西	40828.7	24278.8	22898.8
甘　肃	19617.3	14150.1	14350.3
青　海	3520.7	7446.5	7171.5
宁　夏	4411.3	13640.1	3585.0
新　疆	12792.7	29420.0	10063.7

单位：万元

民间非营利组织会计制度财务指标		
固定资产原价	本年收入合计	本年费用合计
88738.3	**88311.9**	**1543.0**
20.3	38.3	
	0.6	
2.0		
1035.5	1376.9	
13781.3	7918.5	
3039.3	2721.1	
668.7	5883.6	1181.7
9935.1	6567.5	
28898.8	33312.4	170.1
15868.4	8934.8	61.2
1079.5	75.8	
60.0	43.7	
267.0	2153.0	
301.0	556.5	
8048.5	13219.3	130.0
1.0		
12.0	60.0	
3258.3	949.3	
176.2	3047.6	
2285.4	1453.0	

C-2-43 优抚对象享受

地区	抚恤、补助优抚对象总人数	在院集中供养人数	定期抚恤人数合计	烈属	城市
全国	**8748016**	**67549**	**219574**	**124950**	**29318**
中央级					
北京	45044	91	1512	371	178
天津	46278	98	794	309	129
河北	581850	2312	10382	4635	811
山西	179482	2034	5946	3540	366
内蒙古	50259	685	1589	699	343
辽宁	213620	2146	5361	1986	568
吉林	120689	2466	3951	2120	1125
黑龙江	116407	1078	3543	2042	963
上海	39362	84	5231	4250	3775
江苏	469764	3816	12979	5675	850
浙江	306861	235	4426	2137	525
安徽	458250	2021	7923	4004	1007
福建	185980	932	6849	5053	629
江西	294185	4136	17837	15641	2173
山东	841128	7475	19456	9139	1323
河南	737344	6991	12384	5543	1174
湖北	441551	3044	20767	15167	2013
湖南	794183	5887	19108	11534	2774
广东	422033	693	6437	4005	1766
广西	289185	511	3811	2423	369
海南	26429	2480	2108	1822	305
重庆	253368	895	4224	2042	749
四川	846258	12254	20431	9358	1758
贵州	228416	212	3026	1583	426
云南	321886	198	5663	3021	648
西藏	3308	542	1371	1144	1032
陕西	247598	2199	7623	3704	657
甘肃	126654	1469	2095	621	165
青海	14350	96	484	221	76
宁夏	12484	28	434	185	77
新疆	33810	441	1829	976	564

定期抚恤、补助情况

单位：人

农　村	因公牺牲军人遗属	城　市	农　村	病故军人遗属	城　市	农　村
95632	**38725**	**10821**	**27904**	**55899**	**17681**	**38218**
193	155	85	70	986	721	265
180	132	46	86	353	241	112
3824	2328	548	1780	3419	908	2511
3174	962	205	757	1444	343	1101
356	408	186	222	482	253	229
1418	1076	363	713	2299	706	1593
995	639	377	262	1192	683	509
1079	622	297	325	879	411	468
475	142	116	26	839	690	149
4825	1880	467	1413	5424	842	4582
1612	919	224	695	1370	485	885
2997	1644	479	1165	2275	700	1575
4424	852	166	686	944	272	672
13468	1009	263	746	1187	355	832
7816	4036	839	3197	6281	1778	4503
4369	3123	819	2304	3718	1151	2567
13154	3405	512	2893	2195	611	1584
8760	3296	1042	2254	4278	1333	2945
2239	864	483	381	1568	791	777
2054	466	107	359	922	232	690
1517	122	75	47	164	71	93
1293	872	294	578	1310	482	828
7600	5292	1403	3889	5781	1654	4127
1157	526	152	374	917	252	665
2373	920	234	686	1722	584	1138
112	122	98	24	105	60	45
3047	1644	443	1201	2275	510	1765
456	649	155	494	825	174	651
145	83	32	51	180	86	94
108	118	54	64	131	67	64
412	419	257	162	434	235	199

C-2-43续表

地　区	定期补助人数合计	在乡退伍红军老战士	在乡西路红军老战士	红军失散人员	在乡复员军人
全　国	**7813467**	**55**	**50**	**2060**	**636698**
中央级					
北　京	31669	1			2529
天　津	38218				1621
河　北	529185				21455
山　西	152390	4		1	15101
内蒙古	37070	4			5564
辽　宁	181994				16830
吉　林	98863	2			13285
黑龙江	99087	1		2	19583
上　海	27105				1848
江　苏	409788			1	35250
浙　江	279837			29	16284
安　徽	418495			183	24271
福　建	167226			96	12198
江　西	256546	2	4	918	20608
山　东	730256				49883
河　南	666267	2		137	36411
湖　北	389752	1		53	25762
湖　南	727239	1		144	84956
广　东	390895			4	16296
广　西	274996			161	22590
海　南	22173			8	3531
重　庆	229162				16810
四　川	767580	4	34	223	88606
贵　州	210991	1		5	21339
云　南	298420			3	22443
西　藏	640	3	6		46
陕　西	218574	26		88	25544
甘　肃	114173	2	3	2	7174
青　海	10571				1021
宁　夏	10126		1	1	1544
新　疆	24179	1	2	1	6315

单位：人

抗　日	带病回乡退伍军人	60岁以上农村籍退伍军人	参战退役人员	参试退役人员	部分60周岁以上烈士子女(含错杀被平反人员子女)	其　他
19321	**1127704**	**4055748**	**1362905**	**179705**	**239617**	**208925**
154	1631	21409	3147	830	1907	215
92	11579	15654	7543	65	1238	518
2920	48109	355316	49142	18740	29641	6782
1255	24403	80193	9019	6933	12886	3850
140	9400	18178	1396	135	921	1472
216	12846	113924	5913	4010	2857	25614
266	10899	67853	3337	1182	1812	493
445	9208	61218	4762	543	1737	2033
22	551	21645	2371	606		84
3449	46750	237593	32746	4464	15016	37968
134	16398	214441	24248	2364	1694	4379
811	130924	206641	30759	11230	7080	7407
21	9577	105424	29278	302	6405	3946
181	41458	88865	40188	2553	54355	7595
4300	85702	473059	67971	14675	38966	
1399	81264	407706	89565	25860	17954	7368
841	96833	183095	63224	7983	11849	952
357	147751	299975	172415	8253	11175	2569
275	26622	170496	151010	8045	2523	15899
58	3113	95573	87875	3309	3478	58897
478	1014	9082	7715	238	435	150
29	64365	88653	51262	5185	1451	1436
237	179798	333250	130591	17878	7221	9975
36	12878	89902	86167	237	354	108
39	20917	101233	150547	36	2515	726
	59	481	11		12	22
750	24078	98902	41387	21649	2957	3943
136	4055	78062	15889	6679	874	1433
1	1292	6024	788	1207	121	118
19	561	4999	1114	285	71	1550
260	3669	6902	1525	4229	112	1423

C-2-44 伤残人员和

地区	伤残人员合计	按伤残等						
		一级				二级		
			因战	因公	因病		因战	因公
全国	**714975**	**3332**	**820**	**2256**	**256**	**2316**	**295**	**1587**
中央级								
北京	11863	43	2	37	4	41	2	30
天津	7266	32		31	1	20	1	17
河北	42283	156	8	129	19	94	11	60
山西	21146	82	13	66	3	37	6	24
内蒙古	11600	55	6	47	2	22	2	14
辽宁	26265	140	24	110	6	97	19	62
吉林	17875	132	20	101	11	78	24	39
黑龙江	13777	58	14	40	4	45	2	37
上海	7026	22	3	18	1	18	1	16
江苏	46997	183	46	115	22	138	26	89
浙江	22598	52	8	39	5	97		50
安徽	31832	151	35	98	18	58	8	35
福建	11905	50	3	43	4	32	3	20
江西	19802	104	28	66	10	183	7	153
山东	91416	281	61	201	19	287	11	236
河南	58693	272	48	189	35	215	28	143
湖北	31032	173	50	107	16	84	6	60
湖南	47836	332	154	166	12	238	54	160
广东	24701	106	19	73	14	42	4	21
广西	10378	37	16	19	2	29	8	15
海南	2148	9	2	6	1	5	2	1
重庆	19982	114	45	57	12	36	5	21
四川	58247	247	66	170	11	189	19	150
贵州	14399	107	33	72	2	44	15	23
云南	17803	119	41	68	10	79	12	29
西藏	1297	7	4	3		4	3	1
陕西	21401	143	57	80	6	45	12	28
甘肃	10386	62	9	49	4	18		17
青海	3295	19	3	16		3		3
宁夏	1924	6		6		3		3
新疆	7802	38	2	34	2	35	4	30

优抚对象医疗保障情况

单位：人

级分类

因 病	三 级	因 战	因 公	因 病	四 级	因 战	因 公	因 病
434	**15574**	**3500**	**9831**	**2243**	**12989**	**1565**	**7415**	**4009**
9	188	23	129	36	146	21	89	36
2	109	23	67	19	81	14	51	16
23	706	117	441	148	627	80	266	281
7	399	111	224	64	272	38	137	97
6	163	21	116	26	123	14	54	55
16	541	130	353	58	292	71	139	82
15	603	166	321	116	616	156	270	190
6	245	37	172	36	282	12	89	181
1	109	18	72	19	107	10	52	45
23	1272	461	703	108	1018	128	598	292
47	449	36	262	151	402	15	153	234
15	641	156	412	73	345	55	220	70
9	164	17	127	20	146	10	82	54
23	345	61	175	109	625	30	203	392
40	2878	615	2026	237	2339	148	1963	228
44	965	199	503	263	1803	201	717	885
18	656	101	432	123	537	47	306	184
24	1257	321	780	156	883	185	554	144
17	428	108	263	57	253	50	129	74
6	182	58	100	24	77	20	42	15
2	46	16	26	4	24	5	12	7
10	415	68	299	48	328	38	209	81
20	1217	237	842	138	870	114	609	147
6	277	88	165	24	121	15	87	19
38	415	150	159	106	259	46	86	127
	33	9	24		15	2	13	
5	395	95	264	36	105	13	64	28
1	199	24	141	34	117	8	80	29
	52	9	40	3	22	4	15	3
	40	6	29	5	32	4	26	2
1	185	19	164	2	122	11	100	11

C-2-44续表1

地区	按伤残							
	五级	因战	因公	因病	六级	因战	因公	因病
全国	**47933**	**11566**	**23764**	**12603**	**158725**	**30246**	**88605**	**39874**
中央级								
北京	491	81	343	67	1872	283	1333	256
天津	519	63	241	215	1452	206	926	320
河北	3005	485	1264	1256	10070	1331	5158	3581
山西	1404	455	675	274	4404	1126	2345	933
内蒙古	592	84	416	92	3061	280	2290	491
辽宁	1695	484	982	229	5471	1273	3357	841
吉林	2160	551	1410	199	5246	1100	3601	545
黑龙江	978	331	443	204	3025	958	1415	652
上海	359	79	187	93	1159	207	659	293
江苏	3332	971	1313	1048	11896	2823	6314	2759
浙江	1226	193	476	557	4520	428	2173	1919
安徽	1848	490	913	445	7416	1401	3843	2172
福建	1160	116	380	664	3368	292	1280	1796
江西	1408	225	618	565	4060	694	2022	1344
山东	5681	1694	3164	823	23370	4972	14234	4164
河南	4569	751	1899	1919	13897	2145	7744	4008
湖北	1771	278	971	522	6405	827	3486	2092
湖南	3667	1112	1851	704	10182	2371	5498	2313
广东	1469	358	598	513	4669	1017	2443	1209
广西	673	237	344	92	1838	564	858	416
海南	141	46	67	28	443	130	210	103
重庆	1107	282	624	201	3704	684	2176	844
四川	3655	920	1847	888	12059	2254	6660	3145
贵州	764	293	375	96	2389	611	1282	496
云南	1037	394	421	222	2979	757	1491	731
西藏	93	16	77		201	49	145	7
陕西	1523	346	671	506	4952	874	2463	1615
甘肃	668	88	479	101	1983	204	1220	559
青海	210	29	172	9	540	100	389	51
宁夏	99	14	68	17	441	59	322	60
新疆	629	100	475	54	1653	226	1268	159

单位：人

等级分类								
七级	因战	因公	八级	因战	因公	九级	因战	因公
206274	**41955**	**164319**	**202400**	**47162**	**155238**	**38678**	**1441**	**37237**
3612	558	3054	4004	607	3397	962	15	947
1999	241	1758	2205	305	1900	463	12	451
11909	1925	9984	12038	1961	10077	2323	33	2290
6444	1676	4768	5921	1441	4480	858	20	838
3425	373	3052	3174	411	2763	659	6	653
7665	2010	5655	8073	2352	5721	1325	39	1286
3739	632	3107	3144	561	2583	1131	10	1121
4299	1753	2546	4199	1920	2279	448	11	437
1982	331	1651	2564	443	2121	431	18	413
12827	3122	9705	12840	3436	9404	2022	109	1913
5599	671	4928	8589	889	7700	1110	16	1094
9116	1775	7341	8922	2013	6909	1899	57	1842
2765	433	2332	3147	571	2576	745	10	735
5536	874	4662	5879	1077	4802	1082	61	1021
27529	6103	21426	21532	5742	15790	4695	105	4590
15608	2563	13045	14258	2523	11735	3771	142	3629
9236	1304	7932	9032	1509	7523	1928	48	1880
13792	3245	10547	13566	3596	9970	2520	189	2331
6584	1498	5086	8436	2425	6011	1561	79	1482
3027	921	2106	3376	1226	2150	745	35	710
552	166	386	624	191	433	220	25	195
6711	1082	5629	5847	1349	4498	1038	34	1004
17903	3536	14367	16993	4050	12943	2666	136	2530
4563	1069	3494	4829	1568	3261	708	33	675
5385	1532	3853	6017	2152	3865	919	43	876
377	93	284	335	91	244	182	37	145
6780	1455	5325	6346	1545	4801	700	61	639
3407	339	3068	3103	409	2694	534	16	518
1190	155	1035	880	175	705	218	7	211
512	98	414	604	118	486	117	5	112
2201	422	1779	1923	506	1417	698	29	669

C-2-44续表2

单位：人

地区	按伤残等级分类			按人员种类分类				优抚对象享受医疗保障人数
	十级	因战	因公	残疾军人	伤残国家机关工作人员	伤残人民警察	伤残民兵民工	
全国	**26754**	**1213**	**25541**	**658081**	**30868**	**21775**	**4251**	**4091568**
中央级								
北京	504	8	496	10662	412	754	35	12756
天津	386	7	379	6397	145	694	30	23010
河北	1355	29	1326	39949	1398	728	208	203012
山西	1325	38	1287	20204	648	204	90	92767
内蒙古	326	9	317	8628	1929	905	138	33363
辽宁	966	28	938	22958	1308	1697	302	51746
吉林	1026	16	1010	13058	2433	2242	142	43715
黑龙江	198	8	190	12765	476	474	62	55267
上海	275	12	263	6441	127	447	11	12999
江苏	1469	63	1406	45178	930	756	133	259555
浙江	554	17	537	21879	399	187	133	87885
安徽	1436	44	1392	29245	1777	639	171	238810
福建	328	6	322	11226	327	213	139	70132
江西	580	43	537	18455	774	484	89	115131
山东	2824	68	2756	88097	1679	1329	311	459962
河南	3335	138	3197	55608	1819	1113	153	287165
湖北	1210	61	1149	29171	998	781	82	264798
湖南	1399	134	1265	42504	3328	1920	84	445098
广东	1153	77	1076	23759	451	443	48	199553
广西	394	46	348	9334	387	192	465	123446
海南	84	8	76	1870	95	45	138	15792
重庆	682	31	651	18543	756	616	67	236262
四川	2448	124	2324	53788	2501	1587	371	328562
贵州	597	71	526	12938	874	541	46	118872
云南	594	57	537	15762	827	790	424	151887
西藏	50	21	29	658	341	232	66	764
陕西	412	29	383	20129	898	269	105	88321
甘肃	295	6	289	9586	464	299	37	38459
青海	161	5	156	2408	536	281	70	8169
宁夏	70		70	1557	195	137	35	6468
新疆	318	9	309	5324	1636	776	66	17842

C-2-45 优待和烈士褒扬

单位：户、万元、人、处

地 区	优待				烈士褒扬	
	优待优抚对象户数	优待军属户数	优待总金额	固定优待军属总额	本年新增享受烈士待遇的人数	零散烈士纪念设施
全 国	**3043916**	**826332**	**1713321.6**	**841350.4**	**150**	**11815**
中央级						
北 京	11809	6705	20721.9	19979.1		544
天 津	9639	4399	14192.5	6342.8	1	4
河 北	186919	44721	115426.7	52382.0	3	1418
山 西	82351	18273	58870.0	31536.2	8	1236
内蒙古	23553	11613	37191.6	14314.4	1	111
辽 宁	54353	14445	24579.0	8661.9		90
吉 林	8834	1839	6622.1	2949.0	4	430
黑龙江	37811	11594	22146.3	7534.3	5	35
上 海	23793	6628	35958.8	13078.2	2	1
江 苏	220213	46739	138080.5	55031.6	6	586
浙 江	120202	38966	106021.2	53005.8	12	229
安 徽	136261	40951	72611.4	31076.1	8	316
福 建	80931	12299	43966.7	12383.6	6	253
江 西	72265	28876	31890.9	11799.1	2	531
山 东	449849	91664	215392.5	135494.1	28	614
河 南	222592	87280	132722.2	91951.1	4	336
湖 北	238758	32442	142825.0	38438.3	3	612
湖 南	247908	61089	63915.7	27040.4	18	365
广 东	84698	32367	64717.6	26374.4	7	1293
广 西	170427	33698	57255.7	21163.1	2	646
海 南	7844	1934	5598.6	2202.0	1	98
重 庆	201094	25395	41337.4	14812.2	2	360
四 川	197032	78128	117610.4	53778.3	3	699
贵 州	40902	24296	25514.1	18365.1	4	369
云 南	39838	20643	17747.2	7382.1	6	207
西 藏	323	101	687.5	556.4	1	
陕 西	28912	28531	78616.3	76561.2	13	364
甘 肃	15067	10956	4981.3	2703.4		9
青 海	3700	918	3022.1	833.9		24
宁 夏	2515	887	1179.5	406.2		4
新 疆	23523	7955	11918.9	3214.1		31

C-2-46 接收军队

地　区	本年接收人员合计	军队离退休干部	离　休	地方离退休干部	离　休	军队退休士官	军队无军籍职工
全　国	**11053**	**8080**	**209**	**549**	**49**	**465**	**1959**
中央级							
北　京	1795	1685	1	10		13	87
天　津	379	207	17	41	2	22	109
河　北	1037	456	44	291	4	34	256
山　西	86	28	4	13		18	27
内蒙古	84	73	2			3	8
辽　宁	723	648	56			18	57
吉　林	192	144	3	1		18	29
黑龙江	346	242	2			3	101
上　海	737	737	4				
江　苏	525	406	8			12	107
浙　江	127	57	3			26	44
安　徽	340	166	34	68	15	34	72
福　建	181	121	7	9		1	50
江　西	204	50	4	43	1	5	106
山　东	458	314				91	53
河　南	287	166	4	33	27	48	40
湖　北	289	264		8		17	
湖　南	118	99	3	4		10	5
广　东	376	248	7	8		2	118
广　西	56	37		10		9	
海　南	64	48				2	14
重　庆	160	87				8	65
四　川	353	322	1	4		24	3
贵　州	57	40		1		5	11
云　南	201	179	4			20	2
西　藏	1173	707					466
陕　西	394	363				7	24
甘　肃	98	83		5		7	3
青　海	51	51					
宁　夏	36	35				1	
新　疆	126	17	1			7	102

离退休、退职人员

单位：人

本年实有人数合计	军队离退休干部		地方离退休干部		军队退休士官	军队无军籍职工	军队离退休干部服务站
		离　休		离　休			
375389	**220709**	**17475**	**24089**	**930**	**7296**	**123295**	**429**
76531	47434	1771	5605	10	578	22914	11
7844	5147	416	734	4	82	1881	
17513	9825	845	1290	60	958	5440	24
5611	2548	365	275	25	270	2518	9
4231	2595	263	325	9	84	1227	11
33407	22321	1527	1014	116	303	9769	22
8290	4854	263	338	11	1	3097	1
5696	3644	257	43	2	77	1932	13
12483	8210	517	110	4	13	4150	7
21641	13127	1158	1963	139	274	6277	4
7856	4338	593	1060	15	78	2380	10
5402	3252	577	510	93	229	1411	66
7622	3671	409	2817	12	65	1069	3
4242	1259	334	1312	43	187	1484	2
24911	16885	2016	642	86	1360	6024	8
11989	6983	753	821	126	623	3562	16
14600	7620	811	1190	52	245	5545	4
12624	5460	750	1564	30	229	5371	19
16615	8336	707	311	10	64	7904	12
3337	1985	146	44		50	1258	13
2511	828	29	71	7	13	1599	2
5934	3736	140	107	2	155	1936	10
16471	9694	653	813	15	516	5448	13
2296	1339	166	206	6	18	733	42
12030	6912	723	334	5	100	4684	93
1099	657				1	441	
16330	10146	771	233	32	248	5703	8
6692	2860	238	202	11	262	3368	
1874	738	28			50	1086	1
1028	645	36			56	327	1
6679	3660	213	155	5	107	2757	4

C−2−47 军队离退休

地 区	单位数	年末职工人数		受教育程度		职业资
			女性	大学专科人数	大学本科及以上人数	助理社会工作师人数
全 国	**269**	**3848**	**1741**	**1243**	**1957**	**116**
中央级						
北 京	28	376	187	92	246	13
天 津	1	41	26	10	31	1
河 北	25	377	196	129	139	9
山 西	4	38	17	7	22	
内蒙古	1	21	11	5	16	
辽 宁	15	479	166	95	298	4
吉 林	33	598	206	298	182	20
黑龙江	1	5	2	5		
上 海	20	357	183	104	207	16
江 苏	3	21	12	4	10	
浙 江	13	151	83	29	111	
安 徽	8	58	22	24	18	2
福 建	6	46	22	10	21	1
江 西	1	3	1	2		
山 东	7	154	56	39	92	6
河 南	8	95	49	49	29	4
湖 北	4	57	17	5	43	
湖 南	10	56	29	14	27	
广 东	5	88	40	21	59	8
广 西	4	62	32	10	52	2
海 南						
重 庆	38	327	153	152	154	24
四 川	14	144	97	64	51	2
贵 州	2	5	3	2	3	
云 南	6	93	49	30	53	1
西 藏						
陕 西	7	73	30	17	49	
甘 肃						
青 海	1	19	11			
宁 夏	1	27	14			1
新 疆	3	77	27	26	44	2

人员管理中心

单位：个、人、人次、时

格水平	年龄结构				志愿服务	
社会工作师人数	35岁及以下人数	36岁至45岁人数	46岁至55岁人数	56岁及以上人数	志愿者服务人次数	志愿服务时间
119	**1409**	**1348**	**881**	**210**	**1510**	**5092**
24	106	134	127	9		
1	25	10	4	2		
9	184	130	58	5	861	3389
3	14	11	9	4		
4	12	3	5	1		
3	157	140	140	42	80	100
2	185	293	76	44		
	2	3				
17	146	87	92	32		
5	7	10	4			
4	63	39	41	8		
1	18	17	18	5		
	15	14	14	3		
	1	2				
14	63	50	38	3	232	515
9	19	44	26	6		
	17	26	13	1		
5	16	30	9	1	12	40
8	29	32	25	2		
2	26	23	12	1		
2	87	125	91	24	268	877
	48	46	39	11		
	3	2			22	46
1	44	33	15	1		
1	54	12	6	1	35	125
	17	1		1		
2	14	9	4			
2	37	22	15	3		

C-2-47续表

地区	事业单位会计制度财务指标		
	固定资产原价	本年收入合计	本年支出合计
全　国	**194069.2**	**889872.9**	**996136.8**
中央级			
北　京	70760.4	279756.6	396234.6
天　津	500.0	426.0	426.0
河　北	12445.5	52055.4	50297.8
山　西	741.7	2629.6	2722.0
内蒙古	146.7	7505.7	8305.6
辽　宁	10118.4	34482.5	34532.7
吉　林	9029.0	34105.0	34896.4
黑龙江	9.0	120.0	120.0
上　海	10336.2	118992.1	111868.7
江　苏	520.0	103.5	76.6
浙　江	5211.0	32046.8	32416.9
安　徽	3011.5	10890.1	11938.2
福　建	1014.0	1186.6	965.6
江　西	3.0	2.0	9.0
山　东	6257.9	35196.1	35196.1
河　南	6415.4	5648.7	5059.2
湖　北	13790.1	2037.3	1463.7
湖　南	1446.0	4697.6	3677.9
广　东	11312.1	24428.2	20334.0
广　西	5610.7	17957.5	17412.6
海　南			
重　庆	8836.5	59524.1	60494.6
四　川	3401.0	75639.8	71653.5
贵　州	1.8	35.0	32.6
云　南	2288.7	3599.1	4331.1
西　藏			
陕　西	578.5	44108.4	44558.1
甘　肃			
青　海	166.0	3181.8	3091.2
宁　夏		114.8	62.3
新　疆	10118.1	39402.6	43959.8

单位：人、万元

年末机构管理军休干部人数	分散安置人数	本年发放离退休金
7485	**4906**	**111015**
		9434
119	119	1770
561	561	7128
35		1848
376	376	9579
91	91	109
55	55	79
		943
		2133
442	442	354
		3793
3564	1020	34549
		14
174	174	2818
2068	2068	36463

C-2-48 军队离退休

地区	单位数	年末职工人数		受教育程度		职业资格水平		年龄	
			女性	大学专科人数	大学本科及以上人数	助理社会工作师人数	社会工作师人数	35岁及以下人数	36岁至45岁人数
全国	**24**	**400**	**176**	**186**	**170**	**6**	**7**	**94**	**140**
中央级									
北京	10	236	100	112	102	3	3	53	89
天津	1	11	3		11			4	1
河北	1	3		3				2	
山西									
内蒙古									
辽宁	2	14	5	5	8			3	7
吉林									
黑龙江									
上海	2	50	29	14	30	2	4	20	13
江苏	3	38	17	17	11	1		4	12
浙江									
安徽									
福建									
江西	1	13	8	9	3				2
山东									
河南									
湖北									
湖南	1	4	2	1	1			1	2
广东									
广西									
海南	1	18	7	14	2			6	8
重庆									
四川	2	13	5	11	2			1	6
贵州									
云南									
西藏									
陕西									
甘肃									
青海									
宁夏									
新疆									

人员活动中心

单位：个、人、人次、时、万元

结构		志愿服务		事业单位会计制度财务指标		
46岁至55岁人数	56岁及以上人数	志愿者服务人次数	志愿服务时间	固定资产原价	收入合计	支出合计
135.0	**31.0**	**162.0**	**474.0**	**87789.5**	**21799.8**	**19579.6**
76.0	18.0			29776.0	6050.6	4062.9
4.0	2.0			40202.9	2442.5	1957.1
1.0				654.0	201.0	199.0
4.0		6.0	6.0	6743.3	1217.8	1217.8
16.0	1.0	156.0	468.0	5584.9	4368.9	3277.3
20.0	2.0			3490.1	2511.0	2086.5
8.0	3.0			263.2	355.2	2769.2
1.0				706.7	80.0	80.0
2.0	2.0			180.0	4505.0	3864.0
3.0	3.0			188.4	67.8	65.8

C-2-49 烈士纪念

地区	单位数	年末职工人数		受教育程度		职业资
			女性	大学专科人数	大学本科及以上人数	助理社会工作师人数
全国	**1109**	**9020**	**3654**	**2854**	**2026**	**132**
中央级						
北京	4	41	14	17	15	1
天津	9	130	52	40	49	
河北	80	775	283	189	214	10
山西	48	322	146	108	48	3
内蒙古	8	93	30	29	40	2
辽宁	38	310	132	98	114	2
吉林	30	364	88	119	61	4
黑龙江	16	173	70	70	59	1
上海	9	217	92	91	73	1
江苏	73	663	255	161	197	22
浙江	25	150	74	27	70	2
安徽	42	380	155	110	60	10
福建	21	128	58	36	29	1
江西	62	292	100	66	42	
山东	98	829	332	321	275	11
河南	93	1227	533	388	176	11
湖北	52	635	268	231	88	3
湖南	55	410	188	133	40	4
广东	29	232	104	62	62	22
广西	20	247	110	105	65	9
海南	1	10	2	3	3	
重庆	15	49	24	18	26	
四川	114	384	169	136	53	6
贵州	35	104	31	52	17	
云南	19	89	22	28	15	2
西藏						
陕西	38	354	183	120	48	1
甘肃	50	284	93	61	45	3
青海	3	12	3	7	3	
宁夏	13	42	9	12	7	
新疆	9	74	34	16	32	1

建筑物管理机构

单位：个、人、人次、时

格水平	年龄结构				志愿服务	
社会工作师人数	35岁及以下人数	36岁至45岁人数	46岁至55岁人数	56岁及以上人数	志愿者服务人次数	志愿服务时间
204	**2714**	**3372**	**2362**	**572**	**82754**	**180606**
2	13	11	8	9		
	31	44	42	13	200	400
21	249	279	184	63	1104	3255
5	76	123	99	24	7608	38669
3	23	38	25	7		
5	89	101	90	30	19	26
	102	152	106	4		
	40	64	60	9	12000	32000
3	50	52	65	50	220	730
37	156	250	219	38	3035	8763
5	46	53	40	11	100	600
12	92	171	106	11	940	1780
4	22	49	42	15	78	215
	60	120	103	9	500	1000
30	294	294	194	47	13893	35144
43	489	442	263	33	36	113
2	177	247	136	75	147	251
3	126	167	94	23	275	761
4	49	74	89	20	35854	43022
3	80	82	71	14	650	1532
	1	4	5			
	8	29	11	1	74	426
6	107	162	93	22	20	24
	21	51	24	8	5746	11414
	19	38	31	1	216	372
5	149	141	56	8	29	80
10	109	91	64	20	10	30
	1	2	7	2		
	8	16	14	4		
1	27	25	21	1		

C-2-49续表

地区	事业单位会计制度财务指标		
	固定资产原价	本年收入合计	本年支出合计
全　国	**537835.6**	**167148.0**	**160429.7**
中央级			
北　京	11990.3	1894.8	2203.6
天　津	10959.1	3002.0	2949.2
河　北	31091.3	18859.9	18331.6
山　西	14842.0	6355.2	5725.4
内蒙古	5547.9	1521.5	1981.2
辽　宁	6925.7	4720.0	5764.5
吉　林	7521.4	2849.2	2768.2
黑龙江	5137.0	1890.0	1308.0
上　海	68939.8	8782.7	9316.0
江　苏	34379.6	17174.2	16804.1
浙　江	45635.6	4637.0	4667.8
安　徽	27041.4	5446.1	4644.1
福　建	3625.3	2480.6	2659.9
江　西	9075.1	3713.0	2710.2
山　东	62719.4	26081.3	26081.3
河　南	22027.5	7984.5	7508.0
湖　北	22022.3	5523.7	6446.5
湖　南	23087.6	3068.7	3099.4
广　东	18165.3	16539.7	13220.9
广　西	18102.6	6325.8	4112.8
海　南	1234.7	1507.1	747.6
重　庆	5216.6	1500.7	1250.8
四　川	41221.9	4447.5	4574.2
贵　州	7381.6	545.7	703.9
云　南	1853.0	442.3	448.9
西　藏			
陕　西	15513.6	3676.2	3708.2
甘　肃	9332.4	3087.9	3921.1
青　海	541.3	315.5	315.5
宁　夏	493.9	394.3	231.9
新　疆	6210.4	2380.9	2224.9

单位：万元、平方米、个、人次

管理单位占地面积	烈士纪念建筑物面积	烈士纪念建筑物数	纪念馆(陈列馆)个数	藏品数	参观人次数	本机构管理的其他烈士纪念园地数
41674038.2	**4907531.4**	**8572**	**1237**	**216091**	**71098517**	**396**
68916.0	25665.0	39	5	1054	555000	6
339913.3	43191.3	35	13	1662	1216860	1
3408847.3	272299.9	523	83	38209	4101604	24
1233829.0	308242.5	128	44	3524	1219406	12
388623.0	42830.0	34	12	423	444180	1
1762953.0	244287.0	393	26	15925	2192281	8
597358.0	29066.0	401	27	5787	1028413	5
369705.1	69174.8	350	14	5096	648723	1
356750.0	38704.7	50	14	2640	1661995	5
2764844.5	487271.0	393	103	20447	8808497	5
1029137.1	76674.3	110	30	6579	1697349	1
3851749.8	256639.0	806	196	5710	4742288	5
777106.0	61269.7	148	20	1465	3319979	24
534946.8	94403.0	856	42	6425	898191	74
5207886.6	431723.7	661	139	30003	8964680	8
2430745.5	225723.2	898	90	10033	3966772	7
2568220.7	220513.5	315	104	17475	3365355	68
1147333.9	410904.9	124	22	3462	1605237	1
1258411.0	97508.2	241	12	2059	5191985	7
2278146.9	173269.9	60	10	2229	1777432	6
338532.0	147107.0	77	20	856	410666	25
200675.0	56849.0	114	18	2759	2247575	36
5412530.0	475661.3	1074	77	9889	3519634	11
794598.0	261011.0	224	13	422	1623286	19
514187.9	102109.7	75	12	2150	561768	6
507378.0	101284.0	78	32	4998	1706718	3
596730.0	76508.0	222	34	2532	2497965	20
89945.2	20480.0	25	6	10800	340000	4
206975.6	40879.6	76	9	859	130250	3
637063.0	16280.2	42	10	619	654428	

C-2-50 自然灾害损失

地 区	人口受灾情况				农作物
	受灾人口	死亡人口	失踪人口	紧急转移安置人口	受灾面积
合 计	**18911.7**	**1432**	**274**	**910.1**	**26220.7**
北 京	24.8			2.7	34.7
天 津	14.5			0.1	24
河 北	1428.2	193	89	46.4	1447.2
山 西	648.8	27	3	6.5	503.7
内蒙古	596.2	17	1	1.1	3629.9
辽 宁	156.5	3		7.2	581.9
吉 林	259.9			5.2	748.2
黑龙江	589.1	4		0.1	4223.7
上 海	0.5	1			3.1
江 苏	237.7	101		14	301.1
浙 江	436.9	60	16	53.6	456
安 徽	1487.8	35	1	119.3	1341.2
福 建	562.3	181	25	128.9	386.7
江 西	805.1	43	2	73.4	786.1
山 东	544.2	6		0.8	552.2
河 南	712.2	44	10	10.2	519.3
湖 北	2331	117	16	171.8	2741.2
湖 南	1660.1	48	4	77.5	1375.5
广 东	618.5	48	4	33.4	630.7
广 西	301.6	54	10	9.3	301
海 南	457.3	13	9	63.9	509.3
重 庆	371.8	56	5	8.8	190.4
四 川	741.7	68	14	10.9	410.6
贵 州	661.7	103	12	30.9	330.7
云 南	1168.7	105	26	6	868.5
西 藏	45.6	7	17	8.1	14.5
陕 西	543.9	25		3.7	632.9
甘 肃	997.8	7	1	0.7	1343.3
青 海	124.4	15		5	134.7
宁 夏	186.1	3		0.6	390.4
新 疆	138.7	47	8	9.1	313.6
兵 团	58.1	1	1	0.9	494.4

情况总表

单位：万人次、人、千公顷、万间、亿元

受灾情况		房屋倒损情况			直接经济损失
成灾面积	绝收面积	倒塌房屋	严重损坏房屋	一般损坏房屋	
13670.3	**2902.2**	**52.1**	**77.8**	**256.2**	**5032.91**
26.4	6.6	0.1	0.1	0.6	16.7
21.4	0.1			1.6	3.6
561.8	118.3	10.4	12.5	31	618.85
206.8	32.3	3	4.3	15.9	109
2277.5	547.5		0.3	1.3	179.8
122.7	18.7	0.1	1	4.8	45.85
456.8	90.4	0.1	0.9	0.9	98.7
2663.7	264.1		0.1	0.8	160.4
2.2	0.6				0.2
66.5	7.3	1.9	1.6	5.1	120.87
171.8	19.5	0.4	0.6	2	167.3
557.6	409.3	5.2	5.9	11.4	564
193.7	51.3	3.1	3.1	12.7	473.52
393.6	72.5	1.2	0.9	4.4	106
228.3	34.7	0.2	0.6	2.5	72.6
238.4	63.1	4.2	3.5	6.3	124.6
1505.6	368.8	7.9	9.9	17.9	837.7
582.2	96	4.2	6.1	22.9	265.5
187.7	38.9	0.7	0.8	0.7	146.87
92.3	11.6	0.8	1.1	4.9	28.5
98.3	30.9	0.2	0.3	0.5	79.25
119.4	24.2	1.1	1.5	4.2	47.9
242.1	60.9	0.8	2	10.2	77.5
170.3	51.7	1.8	4.6	20.6	173.3
437.2	107	0.9	4.2	26.2	141
10.8	6.7	1.5	2.4	4.9	33
364.6	70.1	0.2	0.7	3.3	78.4
814.9	131.9	0.2	0.7	3.2	91.3
109.7	9.8	0.2	3.1	17	32.1
239.5	62.3	0	0.2	0.9	17.4
237.2	55.1	1.6	4.6	16.6	71.4
269.3	40	0.1	0.2	0.9	49.8

C-2-51 旱灾

地区	人口受灾情况		
	受灾人口	因旱需生活救助人口	因旱饮水困难需救助人口
合 计	**3057.2**	**639.1**	**234.6**
北 京			
天 津			
河 北	27.1	0.1	
山 西	75.1	2.3	0.3
内蒙古	410.8	173.7	62.8
辽 宁			
吉 林	171.3	20	
黑龙江	384.9	80.4	
上 海			
江 苏	30.8		
浙 江			
安 徽	111.4	2.4	1.6
福 建			
江 西	49.3	5.2	2.4
山 东	113.4	11.7	4.9
河 南	206.9	3.4	0.9
湖 北	164.7	53.7	38.4
湖 南	1.9	1.6	1.5
广 东			
广 西	12.7	1.2	0.5
海 南			
重 庆	68.3	14	12.5
四 川	176	36.8	12.7
贵 州	15.8	7.9	7.6
云 南	3.5		
西 藏	0.4	0.4	
陕 西	239.8	20.9	16
甘 肃	638.2	145.3	39.6
青 海	35.9	0.6	0.6
宁 夏	116.4	57.4	32.2
新 疆	1.7		
兵 团	0.9	0.1	0.1

损失情况

单位：万人次、千公顷、万头、亿元

农作物受灾情况			损失情况	
受灾面积	成灾面积	绝收面积	饮水困难大牲畜	直接经济损失
9872.7	**6130.8**	**1018.3**	**582.5**	**418.1**
216.7	20.8	0.7		0.4
77	43.6	4.4		4.2
2770.5	1957.9	489.4	518.8	139.2
401	48.6	5.3		
524.3	336.9	52.3		42.2
2955	2166.2	172.3		111.6
134.3	10.1			1.4
179.5	127.4	17.6		14.2
35.3	30.2	6.5		3
211.6	85.3	15.3	0.6	8
173.3	73.7	18.9	3.6	5.4
341.9	157.9	39	17.1	14.1
11.6	4.8	0.4		
34.6	20.2	1.2		0.2
15.5	4.4	1.3		
47.2	30	5.5	7.8	4.7
113	67.6	15	1	5.7
6.6	3.3	0.8	0.4	0.5
47.7	15.2	1.9		0.1
0.8			1.7	
240.1	110.6	22.5	1.1	10.4
998.2	594.5	99.9	6.1	41.2
38.3	27.7		7.2	3.7
279.2	174.6	46.9	17.1	6.5
2.8	2.8	0.9		0.2
16.7	16.5	0.3		1.2

C-2-52 洪涝和地质

地 区	人员受灾情况				农作物
	受灾人口	死亡人口	失踪人口	紧急转移安置人口	受灾面积
合 计	**9954.9**	**968**	**214**	**604.2**	**8531.4**
北 京	13.6			2.7	16.1
天 津	14.3			0.1	23.6
河 北	1112	187	89	43.7	953.5
山 西	283.8	21	3	6.4	256.5
内蒙古	76.1	9	1	0.5	256.2
辽 宁	78.2			7.2	95.8
吉 林	26.1			0.2	70.7
黑龙江	52	1		0.1	283.8
上 海					
江 苏	62.1				92.6
浙 江	59.5	8	1	3.2	75.8
安 徽	1277.7	34	1	119.2	1107.2
福 建	84.4	51	2	9.8	50
江 西	661.7	33	2	70.6	416.6
山 东	154.2	1		0.4	105.6
河 南	316.9	32	9	10.1	206.8
湖 北	2080.5	110	16	171.6	1870.2
湖 南	1525.8	40	4	76	1142.5
广 东	156	35	4	8.2	73.2
广 西	130.8	31	8	3.8	85.8
海 南					
重 庆	271.5	50	5	8.6	127.7
四 川	327.6	58	14	9.6	138.7
贵 州	385.2	95	12	29.2	197.6
云 南	460.1	80	25	4.7	225.5
西 藏	28.8	2	8	5.3	12.9
陕 西	99.2	24		3.1	98.3
甘 肃	86.9	7	1	0.6	104.3
青 海	10.9	11		0.2	13.5
宁 夏	7.2	3		0.6	11.7
新 疆	88	44	8	7.8	170.6
兵 团	23.8	1	1	0.7	248.1

灾害损失情况

单位：万人次、人、千公顷、万间、亿元

受灾情况		房屋倒损情况			直接经济损失
成灾面积	绝收面积	倒塌房屋	严重损坏房屋	一般损坏房屋	
4338	**1297.3**	**44.1**	**59.7**	**155.8**	**3134.4**
13.2	1.5	0.1	0.1	0.6	11.7
21.2	0.1			1.6	2.5
372.1	103.3	10.2	12.3	28.5	580.5
78.1	16.6	2.9	4.1	12.1	70.8
61.3	14.7		0.1	0.7	13.6
57.4	9.7	0.1	0.5	1.4	33.9
42.8	8.8		0.2	0.2	4.4
65.4	8.7		0.1	0.3	11.4
44.3	4.9			0.1	4.6
36.1	5.6	0.1	0.1	0.4	24.1
405	390.8	5.2	5.8	11	546.2
29.4	6.5	0.2	0.1	3.2	38.4
263.9	55.1	1.1	0.7	3.9	91.3
59.2	6.1	0.1	0.1	0.3	7.6
125.4	38.4	4.1	3.3	5.8	108.1
1229.5	319.2	7.9	9.5	15.6	816.1
482.9	84.7	4	5.7	18.9	256.6
33.4	5.2	0.4	0.5	0.3	25.2
49.2	7.5	0.5	0.3	1	14.3
78.4	17.3	1.1	1.4	3.6	41.3
82.7	23.9	0.7	1.6	6.2	55.4
107.5	31.8	1.7	3.9	9.6	160.4
143.2	39.4	0.8	2.2	12	81.3
10.3	6.4	0.7	1.6	2.1	14.2
62.1	16.5	0.2	0.6	2.6	25.3
74.4	19	0.2	0.6	1.4	21.1
9.2	1.5	0.1	0.1	0.2	6.2
10.6	3.7		0.2	0.7	3.9
122.3	30	1.6	3.9	11	44
167.5	20.4	0.1	0.1	0.5	20

C-2-53 风雹灾害

地区	人口受灾情况				农作物
	受灾人口（万人次）	死亡人口（人）	失踪人口（人）	紧急转移安置人口	受灾面积
合计	**2728.1**	**251**	**6**	**26.3**	**2908**
北京	11.2				18.6
天津	0.2				0.4
河北	279.1	6		2.7	261.6
山西	269.9	4		0.1	104.5
内蒙古	103.6	8		0.6	418.7
辽宁	37.4	2			39.4
吉林	17.3				61.3
黑龙江	74	3			210.9
上海	0	1			
江苏	136.4	101		14	70.1
浙江	1				0.4
安徽	42.8	1			35.2
福建	1.7	4		0.1	1.5
江西	76.5	8		2.3	35.2
山东	245.2	3		0.4	208.5
河南	187.9	12	1	0.1	139.1
湖北	42.7	7		0.2	36.9
湖南	91	7		1.3	45.3
广东	3.2	8		0.2	2.3
广西	76	18	2	2.3	51.2
海南	0.8	6	3		0.5
重庆	5.8	4		0.2	1.8
四川	101.6	7		0.2	71.7
贵州	232.2	8		0.5	111.1
云南	199.8	23		0.2	158.1
西藏	0.6	5			0.5
陕西	200			0.6	286.8
甘肃	147.6			0.1	76.7
青海	48.5	4		0.1	66.5
宁夏	31.2				33.3
新疆	33.6	1		0.1	138.6
兵团	29.3				221.3

损失情况

单位：万人次、人、千公顷、万间、亿元

受灾情况		房屋倒损情况			直接经济损失
成灾面积	绝收面积	倒塌房屋	严重损坏房屋	一般损坏房屋	
1424.2	**268.8**	**3.5**	**7.6**	**60.2**	**463.9**
13.2	5.1				5
0.2					0.3
156.7	13.1	0.2	0.2	2.5	27.9
70.9	11.2	0.1	0.1	2.7	32.9
96.2	23.1		0.2	0.6	22.8
10	3.2		0.5	3.4	9.1
40.9	8.1			0.1	3.5
150.7	20			0.5	12.2
11.3	2.1	1.9	1.6	5	114.2
0.4				0.1	0.1
10	0.1		0.1	0.4	2.1
1.3	0.2	0.1	0.1	0.5	0.7
10	3.8	0.1	0.2	0.5	10.6
78.7	12.1	0.1	0.5	2.2	36.2
39.3	5.8	0.1	0.2	0.5	10.8
20.3	5.5		0.3	2.1	3.2
21.9	5.4	0.2	0.4	3.8	8.2
1.5	0.3	0.1	0	0.1	0.9
4.9	1.7	0.2	0.7	3.5	8.5
0.2	0.1				0.4
0.9	0.2		0.1	0.4	0.6
43.9	12.9	0.1	0.4	3.3	10
52.6	18.5	0.1	0.7	10.7	11
94.5	25.5	0.1	1	8.5	21
0.4	0.2				0.1
187.8	30		0.1	0.7	42.1
39.1	6.2		0.1	0.6	16.9
60.6	8.3	0.1	0.1	7.2	6.5
13.3	3.3			0.2	6
111.4	23.5			0.1	12.4
81.1	19.3				27.7

C-2-54 台风灾害

地区	人口受灾情况				农作物
	受灾人口(万人次)	死亡人口(人)	失踪人口(人)	紧急转移安置人口	受灾面积
合计	**1721.2**	**174**	**24**	**260.6**	**2023.5**
北京					
天津					
河北					
山西					
内蒙古					
辽宁	40.9				45.7
吉林	31.2			5	73.1
黑龙江	72.8				673.5
上海	0.5				3.1
江苏					
浙江	250.4	46	3	43.5	113.6
安徽					
福建	468.1	120	20	119	179.3
江西	12.9			0.5	8.2
山东					
河南					
湖北					
湖南	5.1			0.1	2.8
广东	295.4			24.2	406.7
广西	58.5	2		3	35.2
海南	456.5	5		63.9	459.4
重庆					
四川					
贵州	7.1			1.1	3.5
云南	21.8	1	1	0.3	19.4
西藏					
陕西					
甘肃					
青海					
宁夏					
新疆					
兵团					

注：台风灾害损失包含台风风暴潮。

损失情况

单位：万人次、人、千公顷、万间、亿元

受灾情况		房屋倒损情况			直接经济损失
成灾面积	绝收面积	倒塌房屋	严重损坏房屋	一般损坏房屋	
598	**145.1**	**3.7**	**4.9**	**13.2**	**766.4**
6.7	0.5				2.4
25.6	12.9	0.1	0.7	0.6	46.7
184.7	48.5				23.1
2.2	0.6				0.2
					0
57.7	9.5	0.3	0.5	1.5	113
0	0	0	0	0	0
83.6	19.2	2.8	2.9	9	433.7
6.2	0.4				0.8
1.2	0.6			0.1	0.3
128.5	19.4	0.2	0.3	0.3	59.4
12.2	1	0.1	0.1	0.1	3.8
77.3	26.6	0.2	0.3	0.5	76.7
2.5	0.4			0.2	0.6
9.6	5.5		0.1	0.9	5.7

C-2-55 地震灾害

地　区	人口受灾情况				农作物
	受灾人口（万人次）	死亡人口（人）	失踪人口（人）	紧急转移安置人口	受灾面积
合　计	**50.9**	**1**		**9.9**	**0.1**
北　京					
天　津					
河　北					
山　西	1				
内蒙古					
辽　宁					
吉　林					
黑龙江					
上　海					
江　苏					
浙　江					
安　徽					
福　建					
江　西					
山　东					
河　南					
湖　北					
湖　南					
广　东					
广　西	2.6			0.2	0.1
海　南					
重　庆	0.3				
四　川	3.6			1	
贵　州	0				
云　南	9.2			0.8	
西　藏	7.3			1.8	
陕　西					
甘　肃	1.6				
青　海	13			4.7	
宁　夏					
新　疆	10.5	1		1.2	
兵　团	1.8	0		0.2	

损失情况

单位：万人次、人、千公顷、万间、亿元

受灾情况		房屋倒损情况			直接经济损失
成灾面积	绝收面积	倒塌房屋	严重损坏房屋	一般损坏房屋	
		0.1	**5.4**	**25.2**	**55.6**
			0.1	1.1	0.3
				0.3	1
				0.2	0.1
				0.5	0.9
			0.9	4.6	4.3
		0.1	0.7	1.8	17.9
				1.2	1.8
			2.9	9.6	15
			0.7	5.5	14
			0.1	0.4	0.3

C-2-56 低温冷冻和

地区	人口受灾情况				农作物
	受灾人口（万人次）	死亡人口（人）	失踪人口（人）	紧急转移安置人口	受灾面积
合计	**1399.4**	**3**	**9**	**9.1**	**2885**
北京					
天津					
河北	10				15.4
山西	19				65.7
内蒙古	5.7				184.5
辽宁					
吉林	14				18.8
黑龙江	5.4				100.5
上海					
江苏	8.4				4.1
浙江	126			6.9	266.2
安徽	55.9			0.1	19.3
福建	8.1				155.9
江西	4.7				290.8
山东	31.4				26.5
河南	0.5				0.1
湖北	43.1				492.2
湖南	36.3			0.1	173.3
广东	163.9			0.8	148.5
广西	21				94.1
海南					33.9
重庆	25.9	2			13.7
四川	132.9			0.1	87.2
贵州	21.4			0.1	11.9
云南	474.3				417.8
西藏	8.5		9	1	0.3
陕西	4.9				7.7
甘肃	123.5				164.1
青海	16.1				16.4
宁夏	31.3				66.2
新疆	4.9	1			1.6
兵团	2.3				8.3

雪灾损失情况

单位：万人次、人、千公顷、万间、亿元

受灾情况		房屋倒损情况			直接经济损失
成灾面积	绝收面积	倒塌房屋	严重损坏房屋	一般损坏房屋	
1179.3	**172.7**	**0.7**	**0.2**	**1.8**	**178.6**
12.2	1.2				0.7
14.2	0.1				0.8
162.1	20.3				4.2
10.6	8.3				1.9
96.7	14.6				2.1
0.8	0.3				0.3
77.6	4.4				30.1
15.2	0.8				1.5
79.4	25.4				0.7
83.3	6.7				0.3
5.1	1.2				18.4
					0.3
97.9	5.1		0.1	0.2	4.3
71.4	4.9			0.1	0.4
24.3	14				61
5.8	0.2				0.7
16.4	2.9				
10.1	1.2				1.2
47.9	9.1			0.2	5.5
4.4	0.2			0.1	0.8
174.7	34.7			0.2	28.6
0.1	0.1	0.7	0.1	1	0.8
4.1	1.1				0.6
106.9	6.8				10.3
12.2					0.7
41	8.4				1
0.7	0.7				0.8
4.2					0.6

C-2-57 海洋灾害

地 区	人口受灾情况				农作物
	受灾人口（万人次）	死亡人口（人）	失踪人口（人）	紧急转移安置人口	受灾面积
合 计		**15**	**21**		
北 京					
天 津					
河 北					
山 西					
内蒙古					
辽 宁					
吉 林					
黑龙江					
上 海					
江 苏					
浙 江		5	12		
安 徽					
福 建		4	3		
江 西					
山 东					
河 南					
湖 北					
湖 南					
广 东		4			
广 西					
海 南		2	6		
重 庆					
四 川					
贵 州					
云 南					
西 藏					
陕 西					
甘 肃					
青 海					
宁 夏					
新 疆					
兵 团					

注：海洋灾害损失包括温带风暴潮、海浪、海冰、海岸侵蚀。

损失情况

单位：万人次、人、千公顷、万间、亿元

受灾情况		房屋倒损情况			直接经济损失
成灾面积	绝收面积	倒塌房屋	严重损坏房屋	一般损坏房屋	
					15.91
					0.8
					9.35
					0.45
					0.37
					0.02
					2.4
					0.37
					2.15

C-2-58 森林火灾

地区	人口受灾情况				农作物
	受灾人口（万人次）	死亡人口（人）	失踪人口（人）	紧急转移安置人口	受灾面积
合计		**20**			
北京					
天津					
河北					
山西		2			
内蒙古					
辽宁		1			
吉林					
黑龙江					
上海					
江苏					
浙江		1			
安徽					
福建		2			
江西		2			
山东		2			
河南					
湖北					
湖南		1			
广东		1			
广西		3			
海南					
重庆					
四川		3			
贵州					
云南		1			
西藏					
陕西		1			
甘肃					
青海					
宁夏					
新疆					
兵团					

损失情况

单位：万人次、人、千公顷、万间、亿元

受灾情况		房屋倒损情况			直接经济损失
成灾面积	绝收面积	倒塌房屋	严重损坏房屋	一般损坏房屋	

C-3-1 成员组

地区	单位数	年末职工人数	女性	受教育程度		职业资
				大学专科人数	大学本科及以上人数	助理社会工作师人数
全国	**1364883**	**10429986**	**3101106**	**1559066**	**1162696**	**50045**
中央级	2339	37879	16567	73	27799	583
北京	17749	206566	72254	38210	101507	4154
天津	10433	64506	29684	16497	18374	1041
河北	73970	592972	198400	49777	33220	1983
山西	43463	263089	75952	37094	12541	364
内蒙古	27076	161746	50083	34673	14487	589
辽宁	36806	268040	93871	52473	35343	1324
吉林	21871	100711	28542	14750	4480	980
黑龙江	27221	216961	77465	23938	11774	568
上海	20024	219180	52306	66469	21308	1521
江苏	105650	679780	191874	126796	87099	8388
浙江	79523	530209	161643	105137	63010	3223
安徽	43686	356391	97120	67017	48909	2764
福建	42893	346395	79484	34566	28326	939
江西	36297	278760	75718	30792	11599	1218
山东	126911	707082	186926	129764	88722	3527
河南	80902	470055	137117	67979	37570	962
湖北	57952	450439	140520	79319	32991	1052
湖南	59554	377443	124689	72675	45028	734
广东	85891	740177	259941	136974	133019	6211
广西	40135	429013	102147	45482	27726	1016
海南	9354	72967	22945	9654	7494	3
重庆	27322	225739	97025	50215	46098	3031
四川	92516	763207	248636	82856	89994	1599
贵州	30236	270537	67425	33289	41985	219
云南	36851	536978	185440	44456	29513	615
西藏	6094	37126	9596	2075	1425	3
陕西	43642	381245	98105	42322	25041	726
甘肃	40149	309484	44839	27191	12726	311
青海	8280	44283	10340	4146	1371	46
宁夏	8540	94528	21619	8088	7164	114
新疆	21553	196498	42833	24319	15053	237

织总表

单位：个、人、人次、时

格水平	年龄结构				志愿服务	
社会工作师人数	35岁及以下人数	36岁至45岁人数	46岁至55岁人数	56岁及以上人数	志愿者服务人次数	志愿服务时间
35666	**3193360**	**3986949**	**2337538**	**912139**	**2126625**	**5725722**
8766	10128	14519	8329	4903		
1779	51340	51010	89245	14971	780	4700
319	15260	21710	21419	6117	13796	34414
2376	151692	284735	122180	34365	32142	130584
611	81832	92652	63374	25231	4106	9961
427	49381	60083	39313	12969	19581	49040
559	73932	96209	56841	41058	46240	60739
682	22983	60106	11994	5628		
705	75903	81919	45309	13830	163315	512466
1828	69428	72641	50546	26565	23027	67927
2911	191942	247269	171836	68733	279915	736570
1871	158827	201037	110840	59505	139985	419297
882	105366	138342	84429	28254	124114	329907
692	85058	116777	90385	54175	6770	11536
283	89405	123059	50259	16037	1298	3894
1449	200660	305957	155567	44898	283661	725999
497	163954	178661	92959	34481	5096	5333
418	154839	150384	115826	29390	3132	8030
1060	137948	146829	69764	22902	20064	54257
3181	326369	229044	135073	49691	13433	35211
634	108111	161532	111931	47439	660	1263
97	23770	31178	13862	4157	13	
1644	85976	73015	47864	18884	582145	1399236
776	250180	301416	135333	76278	91323	292733
85	75322	113566	60210	21439	198821	575195
149	153643	186837	116771	79727	5020	6780
6	9466	14374	9391	3895	1	
429	99676	134553	114662	32354	30652	63146
179	84167	116080	91003	18234	1743	2297
29	11598	20886	9392	2407	4949	9987
63	22475	56633	11681	3739	1	
279	52729	103936	29950	9883	30842	175222

C-3-1续表

地区	企业会计制度财务指标				执行
	固定资产原价	营业收入	费用合计	营业利润	固定资产原价
全　国	**2163749.6**	**532835.1**	**19085.9**	**17234.2**	**3357236.3**
中央级					
北　京	1795783.1	523749.7	19072.9	19270.6	427009.9
天　津					
河　北					3357.5
山　西					274366.5
内蒙古	11468.6				27103.8
辽　宁	65.0				14937.9
吉　林	14048.5				14048.5
黑龙江	16987.4	3.0			17031.4
上　海	41173.4	8937.0		-2039.0	266458.0
江　苏	182222.8				485302.3
浙　江	38452.0				381388.9
安　徽					44872.9
福　建	1821.0				8834.2
江　西	8048.7				75165.1
山　东					
河　南					4824.0
湖　北					179256.4
湖　南	9858.5				9894.5
广　东	22854.4	123.4	12.0	2.6	674248.5
广　西					
海　南					11208.9
重　庆					62614.2
四　川	2117.5				20425.8
贵　州					62.4
云　南					295551.2
西　藏	670.0				10371.8
陕　西					
甘　肃	10.0				1408.3
青　海	3541.0				3576.4
宁　夏	190.5				656.0
新　疆	14437.2	22.0	1.0		43261.0

单位：万元

事业单位会计制度财务指标		民间非营利组织会计制度财务指标		
本年收入合计	本年支出合计	固定资产原价	本年收入合计	本年支出合计
1743008.3	**1533918.8**	**32551843.2**	**27962880.3**	**26561717.9**
		887180.2	6543650.1	5290020.4
250426.7	306608.3	3483212.3	1420744.1	1217297.7
		139771.6	180653.4	237927.9
1427.2	1427.2	1368431.7	584059.8	1538996.7
56498.8	56453.7	389250.3	210325.2	206163.1
19727.3	22086.9	130810.9	87238.1	91613.0
5814.2	7914.0	254756.2	713116.5	562295.4
2050.8	1807.6	37556.9	30757.4	31864.7
2277.3	2315.1	206870.1	90752.5	176182.4
272580.8	151735.6	881077.6	2954491.7	2598204.8
201972.1	115282.4	2243192.6	2836445.9	2693398.0
151342.5	105346.7	2155080.7	1710422.2	1436936.5
11948.6	11687.2	1265662.0	591873.3	598761.8
25314.3	25089.1	297145.4	250990.4	280565.4
58032.9	56607.4	364508.5	287695.2	705017.2
		819331.4	1130725.4	1129605.3
4500.0	4414.4	546522.8	240269.9	233742.3
84646.3	84181.8	685372.2	516987.3	499668.2
19826.3	19655.7	632732.7	1124205.5	694519.2
441203.9	416892.4	10505186.4	2686431.0	2552365.0
		197348.0	109331.7	95851.0
6920.3	6797.0	57786.7	291344.2	61075.9
30361.3	30194.9	674644.3	636973.0	551249.3
22446.1	37074.1	2058781.2	1778967.3	1874212.6
147.0	112.0	156468.5	248964.6	255212.8
63749.2	57756.6	662766.2	289839.1	340682.5
342.1	342.1	13668.2	3619.7	3457.0
		1065988.6	181376.4	299219.0
		148243.9	72528.4	73122.5
723.0	723.0	57320.0	69480.9	70763.5
373.0	373.0	66410.3	49031.1	103298.7
8356.3	11040.6	98764.8	39589.0	58428.1

C-3-2 社会组

地区	单位数	年末职工人数		受教育程度		职业资格水平	
			女性	大学专科人数	大学本科及以上人数	助理社会工作师人数	社会工作师人数
全国	**702405**	**7636579**	**2330770**	**1419690**	**1105238**	**27824**	**27126**
中央级	2339	37879	16567	73	27799	583	8766
北京	10754	171206	53893	33819	98580	1100	554
天津	5062	41502	18856	14065	16625	132	83
河北	20916	394701	161959	47279	32454	1622	2188
山西	13004	149528	48812	32355	10037	111	194
内蒙古	13664	109199	32510	30157	13010	432	392
辽宁	21039	195579	63423	46563	33388	48	65
吉林	10669	64290	15671	14248	4098	843	620
黑龙江	14401	158491	57120	22130	10782	245	588
上海	14181	191235	35577	63708	19506	390	1315
江苏	84094	568288	157336	115405	81799	3411	1473
浙江	47536	404450	125403	101331	60400	1386	1003
安徽	25708	277980	73899	58977	46908	1623	502
福建	26154	275716	61669	30848	27419	586	510
江西	15813	200149	55473	28784	10646	857	249
山东	45963	379249	91063	106293	76291	3043	1196
河南	29328	255285	92576	58801	35127	696	380
湖北	28498	330597	103311	72723	30956	604	268
湖南	30361	268942	92874	70568	44080	469	989
广东	59455	609387	223365	129061	130121	4253	2431
广西	23928	347863	82195	44030	27454	915	588
海南	6293	55745	18736	7590	7264	2	89
重庆	16199	167962	75476	39917	42995	1863	1066
四川	39448	550764	195959	79414	88695	903	583
贵州	11848	182832	47202	31534	41223	152	66
云南	22552	464420	169758	43357	29287	542	128
西藏	627	12664	4789	1313	1182	1	2
陕西	20758	291200	76648	40022	24350	540	364
甘肃	22763	241013	32012	27167	12254	283	171
青海	3658	24991	6054	3308	987	40	27
宁夏	5751	81340	16628	7301	6990	26	56
新疆	9641	132132	23956	17549	12531	123	220

织总表

单位：个、人、人次、时

年龄结构				志愿服务	
35岁及以下人数	36岁至45岁人数	46岁至55岁人数	56岁及以上人数	志愿者服务人次数	志愿服务时间
2617288	**2792428**	**1535080**	**691783**	**423713**	**1129627**
10128	14519	8329	4903		
43798	39651	76868	10889		
8338	15002	14845	3317	1150	2300
119569	202678	55295	17159	9059	37016
59268	49654	28215	12391	297	1204
37677	38708	24513	8301	1605	4746
57019	68932	35679	33949	558	1123
21562	27559	10216	4953		
64461	49540	32720	11770	34	106
63437	64445	41312	22041		
164129	204067	138883	61209	75571	165625
131454	148149	73990	50857	62525	112402
91058	101454	62217	23251	39156	89718
71548	82840	70495	50833	2380	6933
74915	79234	33541	12459	6	24
130010	160647	67701	20891	115004	305436
121173	85899	32104	16109	231	468
131001	99774	77613	22209	1076	2190
114798	94677	42737	16730	3377	10144
302582	183107	88930	34768	8003	28254
95490	133375	81257	37741	660	1263
20851	23750	8415	2729		
70225	51726	30982	15029	45427	144603
204912	212471	76198	57183	1125	1794
53951	78929	35457	14495	5198	16879
134805	155906	97899	75810	3870	4110
5373	4475	2163	653		
85516	98745	83821	23118	26328	49382
69511	81824	75210	14468	351	642
7165	12544	3932	1350		
19327	51176	7601	3236		
32237	76971	15942	6982	20722	143266

C-3-2续表

地 区	行政执法	行政处罚数	并处罚款	(1) 警告	(2) 限期（责令）停止活动	(3) 撤销登记	取缔非法社会组织
全 国	**2363**	**2347**	**2**	**501**	**53**	**1793**	**16**
中央级							
北 京	195	189		37	11	141	6
天 津	39	33		4	3	26	6
河 北	127	127				127	
山 西	13	13				13	
内蒙古	17	17				17	
辽 宁							
吉 林							
黑龙江							
上 海	8	8				8	
江 苏	81	80		46	20	14	1
浙 江	17	17		9		8	
安 徽	54	54				54	
福 建							
江 西							
山 东	866	866		319		547	
河 南	36	34				34	2
湖 北	23	23		2		21	
湖 南	2	2				2	
广 东	186	185		75	6	104	1
广 西	20	20				20	
海 南							
重 庆	83	83		6	8	69	
四 川	121	121				121	
贵 州	15	15				15	
云 南							
西 藏							
陕 西	361	361				361	
甘 肃							
青 海							
宁 夏							
新 疆	99	99	2	3	5	91	

单位：起、个、万元

当年新登记数	当年年检单位数	被认定的慈善组织	民间非营利组织会计制度财务指标		
			固定资产原价	本年收入合计	本年费用合计
70309	**358309**	**708**	**27399933.5**	**27476139.0**	**26327743.4**
35	1822	96	887180.2	6543650.1	5290020.4
1144	1772	325	1264163.7	1420744.1	1217297.7
349	1411		109871.6	180653.4	237927.9
2290	12439	6	1292277.9	584059.8	1538996.7
1411	3510	1	285430.1	187279.1	197535.2
1996	5468	10	119257.3	81950.4	90561.5
1437	5933	24	212684.9	700067.2	548451.5
470	909	1	22941.4	28706.6	31849.6
1153	5145	17	188602.4	88463.2	175917.1
1098	11663	20	300192.8	2944866.6	2596163.6
9841	57631	10	1873940.6	2773078.5	2674071.4
4602	23689	20	1208046.4	1455938.8	1349711.5
2208	15765		1162686.3	580660.3	587940.5
2284	16841	21	272522.3	240416.0	276927.4
883	9643		343100.8	274415.3	696022.5
6170	33839	22	819331.4	1130725.4	1129605.3
2809	14124	13	546522.8	240269.9	233742.3
2045	11126	6	550939.7	506605.9	491658.5
2595	12576	30	620811.7	1114882.0	693042.2
5972	36602	14	10328276.4	2671125.0	2513711.0
2494	6261		184981.0	107820.4	94512.7
777	1531	11	57722.7	291344.2	61075.9
1143	10241	15	618828.5	620912.6	547695.7
3827	16671	1	2026442.6	1769393.7	1867496.2
1294	3598	1	156267.7	248964.6	255212.8
2022	20046	26	530256.7	276798.9	327479.9
34	468		13610.2	3619.7	3457.0
1714	11021	5	1065988.6	181376.4	299219.0
4385	1324	3	145490.3	72528.4	72377.5
272	1709		41140.9	66267.4	68053.9
701	895		65818.3	49031.1	103298.7
854	2636	10	84605.3	39524.0	56710.3

C-3-3 社会

地 区	单位数	年末职工人数		受教育程度		职业资
			女性	大学专科人数	大学本科及以上人数	助理社会工作师人数
全 国	**335932**	**3959949**	**909587**	**521874**	**456993**	**8741**
中央级	1985	32507	14514		27158	583
北 京	4267	83494	12924	9280	65720	222
天 津	2153	13482	4579	3370	7116	7
河 北	10181	232645	95213	15746	10412	320
山 西	6520	66737	16598	13528	3313	22
内蒙古	7362	65029	15756	19559	6669	373
辽 宁	7851	83604	13173	12833	11322	10
吉 林	5448	36225	5413	4707	1600	536
黑龙江	5959	103415	38809	9804	5628	24
上 海	4007	32356	4780	14664	4647	182
江 苏	34952	219191	54622	47347	21411	1301
浙 江	22266	149337	34978	38849	20884	471
安 徽	12504	118677	15062	16029	10101	1356
福 建	16380	193319	27853	17758	8390	207
江 西	8180	109189	20848	16598	4755	20
山 东	17380	133537	25526	34164	27082	687
河 南	9587	56709	14441	11181	5160	190
湖 北	12272	181008	46387	28828	9233	96
湖 南	13973	124124	30537	24871	17694	37
广 东	27077	207502	32913	24719	54404	352
广 西	12999	234820	32101	19644	14312	313
海 南	2693	24445	4423	3983	4613	
重 庆	7472	48244	9673	8288	7935	335
四 川	19355	311510	90133	25666	34446	328
贵 州	6785	127486	22755	17485	30413	26
云 南	14973	390199	137040	29785	13295	125
西 藏	571	12274	4665	1250	1119	1
陕 西	11200	178632	36030	19055	11548	325
甘 肃	17827	207855	22163	17967	7596	200
青 海	2156	15364	3948	1598	525	13
宁 夏	3792	68137	10164	3813	2121	25
新 疆	5805	98896	11566	9505	6371	54

团体

单位：个、人、人次、时

格水平	年龄结构				志愿服务	
社会工作师人数	35岁及以下人数	36岁至45岁人数	46岁至55岁人数	56岁及以上人数	志愿者服务人次数	志愿服务时间
13751	**992407**	**1530557**	**967367**	**469618**	**231789**	**637236**
8766	8197	12912	7343	4055		
169	7419	19967	53235	2873		
9	1125	2951	8525	881	300	600
96	40225	149871	32072	10477	1565	5286
56	17232	25654	16960	6891	15	19
308	18696	23005	16358	6970	898	3236
12	13646	28407	16473	25078	275	583
280	12612	14981	6552	2080		
36	47252	28797	20035	7331	24	32
370	7967	10083	7440	6866		
397	45826	73363	63525	36477	35776	81484
526	32542	59321	41135	16339	52461	93684
335	26235	50116	28519	13807	10068	20695
167	32508	58136	56766	45909	1465	5128
15	36728	40057	23509	8895		
300	39967	52513	29783	11274	49066	138180
100	20108	22379	9670	4552	148	296
89	66606	52821	53222	8359	355	974
15	38016	47862	26273	11973	1105	3010
232	61031	74700	47056	24715	7949	28054
518	44013	94481	63079	33247	660	1263
87	8433	10836	3693	1483		
371	10535	16214	12833	8662	19578	61040
135	97777	113872	49479	50382	295	525
23	27214	61734	26927	11611	2172	4857
56	96261	129495	90673	73770	3280	3280
2	5170	4360	2103	641		
78	35247	59679	67582	16124	23918	44168
21	56409	72075	66828	12543	331	642
3	4237	7048	3143	936		
51	15047	45720	5391	1979		
128	18126	67147	11185	2438	20085	140200

C-3-3续表1

地 区	社会组织负责人	女性	按活动区域分 中央级社团	省级社团	地级社团
全 国	**738205**	**126590**	**1985**	**30493**	**82554**
中央级	24439	8222	1985		
北 京	71455	17383		1904	
天 津	5517	393		972	
河 北	18132	2170		1036	3044
山 西	9952	873		743	2039
内蒙古	13858	2161		765	2696
辽 宁	14800	4654		835	3433
吉 林	8137	766		763	1924
黑龙江	9408	1252		1072	2401
上 海	20456	4293		1284	
江 苏	52260	8684		1076	6199
浙 江	46468	8556		1179	5052
安 徽	17462	2131		1053	3881
福 建	18588	3011		1237	3625
江 西	13314	1882		864	2457
山 东	52710	10513		930	6091
河 南	15177	3010		1005	3423
湖 北	32203	5170		966	3477
湖 南	28866	5144		952	4141
广 东	60098	7139		1894	9726
广 西	19090	2732		918	2720
海 南	8071	904		1038	519
重 庆	25839	4148		1046	
四 川	35749	6077		1339	4351
贵 州	35372	3126		801	1524
云 南	18663	2752		964	2951
西 藏	841	85		247	113
陕 西	26531	5301		952	2042
甘 肃	18426	2367		579	1691
青 海	2476	245		555	507
宁 夏	3084	58		718	747
新 疆	10763	1388		806	1780

单位：人、个

县级社团	当年新增单位数	当年年检单位数	被认定的慈善组织数	行业性社团
220900	**28602**	**167266**	**156**	**41382**
	21	1488	1	401
2363	368	568		110
1181	65	356		268
6101	893	6932	5	1672
3738	635	1597	1	741
3901	1031	3011	8	1450
3583	334	2500	23	2064
2761	182	585	1	284
2486	392	2062	14	534
2723	114	3736		106
27677	2882	23531	3	2919
16035	1747	10882		1842
7570	858	7863		1490
11518	1263	11204	3	2646
4859	367	4953		589
10359	1825	13498	17	5627
5159	665	4408	11	824
7829	783	5005	5	1385
8880	1065	5147	26	2047
15457	2342	16533	2	1987
9361	781	3390		567
1136	316	736	1	422
6426	396	4873	3	1221
13665	1483	6895	1	2413
4460	650	1794	1	1041
11058	1351	13315	18	1122
211	33	435		110
8206	1021	5466		968
15557	3808	1045	3	2421
1094	135	1311		401
2327	455	589		375
3219	341	1558	9	1335

C-3-3续表2

地　区	社会组织					
	科技与研究	生态环境	教育	卫生	社会服务	文化
全　国	**16356**	**6466**	**9581**	**9067**	**48089**	**34966**
中央级	60	6	37	25	27	57
北　京	377	68	154	172	528	392
天　津	198	28	111	65	345	191
河　北	492	176	297	478	1306	1112
山　西	464	131	149	127	950	933
内蒙古	404	127	345	172	790	1090
辽　宁	259	188	221	309	808	736
吉　林	145	59	166	127	1225	446
黑龙江	238	94	205	254	1125	821
上　海	645	54	145	179	539	348
江　苏	1360	443	726	801	9251	3892
浙　江	1387	537	752	631	2325	2204
安　徽	684	215	284	334	2170	1399
福　建	467	362	834	420	2932	2059
江　西	259	199	321	393	1066	883
山　东	1034	253	386	455	2240	2433
河　南	717	225	357	256	1117	1016
湖　北	760	194	274	402	1492	1219
湖　南	642	336	562	427	1691	1439
广　东	1668	300	735	527	3639	2971
广　西	545	109	218	160	2326	883
海　南	287	24	61	43	227	400
重　庆	428	103	242	174	580	619
四　川	658	564	680	671	2715	2008
贵　州	238	93	165	156	840	733
云　南	393	248	315	446	1555	1499
西　藏	20	14	12	21	193	94
陕　西	556	128	220	205	1112	1427
甘　肃	169	899	164	237	1659	893
青　海	102	115	137	134	247	150
宁　夏	170	50	182	69	404	213
新　疆	530	124	124	197	665	406

单位：个

按行业分类

体育	法律	工商业服务	宗教	农业及农村发展	职业及从业组织	其他
25440	**3238**	**37604**	**4878**	**61113**	**20149**	**58985**
18	5	1538	4	9	3	196
283	63	709	43	561	150	767
156	43	359	24	105	85	443
795	94	1204	205	1525	685	1812
729	81	510	110	608	347	1381
734	72	879	77	1054	415	1203
538	99	943	138	939	515	2158
290	96	224	64	567	179	1860
556	73	512	92	756	536	697
381	44	830	68	64	236	474
4221	454	3279	359	3110	1620	5436
1897	232	3996	362	2006	2096	3841
1082	131	1255	215	2117	932	1686
1112	150	1450	334	2042	1161	3057
663	99	852	156	994	650	1645
1425	166	2240	234	3501	1352	1661
801	115	1358	225	1142	731	1527
959	135	1626	189	1941	613	2468
977	186	1508	238	2246	1221	2500
2232	89	3602	255	1458	1144	8457
509	52	795	94	4036	541	2731
249	5	470	13	419	136	359
477	35	988	96	2419	431	880
1382	180	1626	325	3802	1343	3401
456	52	913	119	1297	619	1104
879	226	1259	317	4562	786	2488
20	9	45	7	105	7	24
509	49	1036	178	4290	421	1069
298	50	410	183	10442	729	1694
316	17	74	29	333	39	463
163	50	217	30	1322	126	796
333	86	897	95	1341	300	707

C-3-3续表3

地　区	行政执法	行政处罚数	并处罚款	(1) 警告	(2) 限期（责令）停止活动	(3) 撤销登记	取缔非法社会组织
全　国	**1565**	**1556**	**2**	**265**	**29**	**1262**	**9**
中央级							
北　京	180	174		27	11	136	6
天　津	15	13		3		10	2
河　北	117	117				117	
山　西	13	13				13	
内蒙古	15	15				15	
辽　宁							
吉　林							
黑龙江							
上　海							
江　苏	21	21		14		7	
浙　江	9	9		5		4	
安　徽	33	33				33	
福　建							
江　西							
山　东	475	475		173		302	
河　南	15	15				15	
湖　北	23	23		2		21	
湖　南	1	1				1	
广　东	89	88		36	5	47	1
广　西	20	20				20	
海　南							
重　庆	64	64		5	8	51	
四　川	65	65				65	
贵　州	5	5				5	
云　南							
西　藏							
陕　西	309	309				309	
甘　肃							
青　海							
宁　夏							
新　疆	96	96	2		5	91	

单位：起、万元

民间非营利组织会计制度财务指标		
固定资产原价	本年收入合计	本年费用合计
3492013.0	**6113593.0**	**6788587.7**
759588.6	1880124.2	1307793.7
277646.0	425506.4	225166.7
14879.6	56605.0	51126.0
66988.7	77959.4	996926.7
70250.3	51923.1	36589.4
20975.3	29224.7	31072.9
19875.4	97134.2	118926.9
5754.2	8315.0	12162.9
20860.1	67270.1	96783.2
22775.0	458383.3	355933.4
515406.9	420307.3	557079.4
146304.3	353019.6	310791.5
116621.0	88067.2	95676.3
36386.0	84256.2	93186.5
76270.9	34648.8	452307.2
125735.3	321210.1	319996.8
35789.5	30730.6	30319.6
70582.7	146441.7	142560.1
163271.6	170453.2	153422.4
356193.7	687898.3	688883.5
49042.8	19271.9	20284.7
10835.6	2081.5	2740.0
55200.9	126147.7	130729.6
124442.6	187575.7	186949.8
33362.2	47822.1	44424.8
74976.8	47361.9	67672.6
10985.9	506.0	881.2
86412.7	67987.4	131633.8
67264.5	46951.1	43188.2
9827.3	54716.4	50352.5
13687.0	11229.4	11655.6
33819.6	12463.5	21369.8

C－3－4 基金

地　区	单位数	年末职工人数		受教育程度		职业资
			女性	大学专科人数	大学本科及以上人数	助理社会工作师人数
全　国	**5559**	**30876**	**9101**	**5929**	**10564**	**466**
中央级	245	3797	1352			
北　京	515	5000	2750	914	4086	324
天　津	69	242	126	62	148	
河　北	85	288	108	94	169	3
山　西	73	406	40	10		
内蒙古	122	235	33	24	35	
辽　宁	92	338	97	114	206	
吉　林	81	103	23			
黑龙江	96	144	3	1	2	
上　海	335	1546	8	1101	318	
江　苏	608	2420	613	228	239	15
浙　江	511	1411	472	525	572	7
安　徽	112	410	39	25	58	
福　建	256	1435	231	131	98	12
江　西	64	298	64	173	100	
山　东	135	539	114	254	180	21
河　南	125	421	50	218	167	
湖　北	132	1082	206	369	472	2
湖　南	249	1404	179	332	781	2
广　东	804	4769	1308	388	1067	29
广　西	71	648	209	138	40	1
海　南	80	501	68	72	158	
重　庆	76	474	143	146	251	15
四　川	153	546	271	121	315	1
贵　州	51	321	120		318	
云　南	98	272	102	79	164	15
西　藏	14	25			18	
陕　西	101	580	59	53	80	18
甘　肃	68	582	153	137	186	
青　海	29	58				
宁　夏	67	338	151	101	218	1
新　疆	42	243	9	119	118	

会

单位：个、人、人次、时

格水平	年龄结构				志愿服务	
社会工作师人数	35岁及以下人数	36岁至45岁人数	46岁至55岁人数	56岁及以上人数	志愿者服务人次数	志愿服务时间
186	**10522**	**8018**	**8298**	**4038**	**1785**	**6091**
	1406	1131	770	490		
29	2537	1	2119	343		
	74	80	32	56		
4	98	86	57	47		
	197	66	74	69	260	1045
	106	93	31	5		
1	78	95	78	87		
	89	14				
5	1	2	141			
45	585	464	230	267		
11	793	612	696	319	140	289
8	521	539	250	101	261	493
	19	197	99	95		
	220	326	468	421	500	1000
	61	221	16			
6	223	257	35	24	294	911
1	57	43	144	177		
2	246	392	297	147		
1	297	376	444	287		
23	1783	1409	1062	515	25	200
1	118	283	195	52		
2	87	109	238	67		
36	98	220	83	73	305	2153
	193	142	120	91		
	78	80	94	69		
5	65	94	74	39		
		9	14	2		
5	134	166	154	126		
1	220	200	134	28		
	7	34	17			
	79	168	59	32		
	52	109	73	9		

C-3-4续表1

地　区	社会组织负责人数	女性	按性质分	
			公募基金会	非公募基金会
全　国	**11902**	**2504**	**1730**	**3791**
中央级	868	6	93	114
北　京	3053	836	94	421
天　津	242	63	21	48
河　北	74	26	16	69
山　西	115	6	29	44
内蒙古	131	5	95	27
辽　宁	106	23	45	47
吉　林	61	12	24	57
黑龙江	50	20	43	53
上　海	855	270	57	278
江　苏	683	49	220	388
浙　江	636	104	158	353
安　徽	106	2	22	90
福　建	285	48	40	216
江　西	184	34	24	40
山　东	172	27	46	89
河　南	407	60	42	83
湖　北	943	185	24	108
湖　南	1146	152	128	121
广　东	481	321	183	621
广　西	100	30	26	45
海　南	294	52	21	59
重　庆	246	41	27	49
四　川	127	15	63	90
贵　州	80	9	30	21
云　南	107	5	43	55
西　藏	23	8	9	5
陕　西	140	75	30	71
甘　肃	41	5	15	53
青　海	29		16	13
宁　夏	67	14	25	42
新　疆	50	1	21	21

单位：人、个

涉外基金会	境外基金代表机构	当年登记单位数	当年年检单位数	被认定的慈善组织数
9	**29**	**749**	**3821**	**520**
9	29	6	244	95
		128	238	325
			69	
		22	60	
		8		
		14	81	1
		8	77	1
			61	
		10	48	3
		65	260	20
		66	431	7
		74	368	9
		9	87	
		36	144	17
		13	64	
		14	16	5
		6	101	
		26	93	1
		26	195	3
		127	595	8
		15	65	
		13	51	
		12	64	12
		6	125	
		5		
		11	87	8
			14	
		12	74	5
		9		
			29	
		8	42	
			38	

C-3-4续表2

地　区	社会组织					
	科技与研究	生态环境	教育	卫生	社会服务	文化
全　国	**230**	**61**	**1320**	**140**	**1819**	**258**
中央级	1		1		2	
北　京	24	10	75	33	283	54
天　津	2		22	2	29	5
河　北	1		7	2	2	
山　西			27	3	2	10
内蒙古	1	1	8	3	98	3
辽　宁	2		33		44	2
吉　林		2	22	1	46	1
黑龙江	2	6	22	7	48	2
上　海	14	7	69	21	175	24
江　苏	3	3	163	12	207	24
浙　江	10		193	10	144	23
安　徽	3	3	26	2	45	5
福　建		3	112	8	78	6
江　西			13		37	
山　东	4	2	34	7	29	14
河　南			16	1	4	6
湖　北		5	57	1	42	6
湖　南	3		139	1	15	10
广　东	147	5	56	9	246	11
广　西	1		16	6	36	1
海　南	1	3	25	2	12	13
重　庆	2		30	2	27	3
四　川	4		57	2	30	4
贵　州	1		9		30	
云　南		5	23	2	6	8
西　藏		1	4	1	1	4
陕　西	1		25	2	13	12
甘　肃	2	2	19		29	4
青　海		3	4		7	3
宁　夏	1		11		48	
新　疆			2		4	

单位：个

按行业分类

体育	法律	工商业服务	宗教	农业及农村发展	职业及从业组织	国际及涉外组织	其他
35	**39**	**43**	**36**	**71**	**22**	**30**	**1260**
		8				29	9
4	3			3			26
2		1	1				5
			3				70
							31
1		2		2			3
1	1	6			1		2
	8	1					
2	2	1	1	1	1		1
3		9	2		2		9
3	3	2	6	27	4		151
5	1	1	3	21			100
1	1	1			7		18
		5	1	3			40
	1		3	1			9
2	1	2		1			39
1							97
2	4		1	3			11
2	1		5	1	3		69
3	2	1	1	1			322
		1		1			9
	4	1	4	3			12
	1	1	2		2		6
2	2			1	1		50
1							10
	1		1				52
	2						1
	1		1	1			45
				1	1		10
			1			1	10
							7
							36

C-3-4续表3

地　区	行政执法	行政处罚数	(1) 警告	(2) 限期（责令）停止活动	(3) 撤销登记
全　国	**15**	**15**	**4**		**11**
中央级					
北　京					
天　津					
河　北					
山　西					
内蒙古					
辽　宁					
吉　林					
黑龙江					
上　海					
江　苏					
浙　江	**7**	**7**	**4**		**3**
安　徽					
福　建					
江　西					
山　东					
河　南					
湖　北					
湖　南					
广　东	**8**	**8**			**8**
广　西					
海　南					
重　庆					
四　川					
贵　州					
云　南					
西　藏					
陕　西					
甘　肃					
青　海					
宁　夏					
新　疆					

单位：起、万元

民间非营利组织会计制度财务指标		
固定资产原价	本年收入合计	本年费用合计
722643.4	**7824365.4**	**5387268.4**
85259.0	4500890.7	3842135.4
9800.1	263075.9	15716.8
7773.8	45743.3	22302.6
1554.7	15631.8	833.2
1432.0	9421.0	11108.0
1654.0	639.3	179.7
3384.2	37466.6	26145.6
328.7	500.0	1007.9
240.0	225.0	506.0
	370854.2	238529.2
7624.3	760883.9	434264.1
10989.6	145700.5	109816.3
2523.8	1653.0	420.7
30290.0	31627.0	27324.6
1140.0	15008.0	11569.4
1498.4	5877.6	5561.8
135.0	1114.9	156.6
1837.0	63119.9	35292.5
21557.3	486955.0	107735.7
28902.7	710013.8	187726.3
1585.2	1175.6	476.7
1600.0	4000.0	1200.0
71683.0	56923.8	49196.7
6627.9	99162.9	72871.7
385.1	134872.1	143432.0
569.0	18271.2	15145.5
801.3	2339.1	1989.5
393582.7	18042.4	1163.4
32.0	20.0	17.8
285.0	8155.7	5680.4
16127.6	14761.2	15426.3
11440.0	240.0	2336.0

C-3-5 民办

地 区	单位数	年末职工人数		受教育程度		职业资
			女性	大学专科人数	大学本科及以上人数	助理社会工作师人数
全 国	**360914**	**3645754**	**1412082**	**891887**	**637681**	**18617**
中央级	109	1575	701	73	641	
北 京	5972	82712	38219	23625	28774	554
天 津	2840	27778	14151	10633	9361	125
河 北	10650	161768	66638	31439	21873	1299
山 西	6411	82385	32174	18817	6724	89
内蒙古	6180	43935	16721	10574	6306	59
辽 宁	13096	111637	50153	33616	21860	38
吉 林	5140	27962	10235	9541	2498	307
黑龙江	8346	54932	18308	12325	5152	221
上 海	9839	157333	30789	47943	14541	208
江 苏	48534	346677	102101	67830	60149	2095
浙 江	24759	253702	89953	61957	38944	908
安 徽	13092	158893	58798	42923	36749	267
福 建	9518	80962	33585	12959	18931	367
江 西	7569	90662	34561	12013	5791	837
山 东	28448	245173	65423	71875	49029	2335
河 南	19616	198155	78085	47402	29800	506
湖 北	16094	148507	56718	43526	21251	506
湖 南	16139	143414	62158	45365	25605	430
广 东	31574	397116	189144	103954	74650	3872
广 西	10858	112395	49885	24248	13102	601
海 南	3520	30799	14245	3535	2493	2
重 庆	8651	119244	65660	31483	34809	1513
四 川	19940	238708	105555	53627	53934	574
贵 州	5012	55025	24327	14049	10492	126
云 南	7481	73949	32616	13493	15828	402
西 藏	42	365	124	63	45	
陕 西	9457	111988	40559	20914	12722	197
甘 肃	4868	32576	9696	9063	4472	83
青 海	1473	9569	2106	1710	462	27
宁 夏	1892	12865	6313	3387	4651	
新 疆	3794	32993	12381	7925	6042	69

非企业

单位：个、人、人次、时

格水平	年龄结构				志愿服务	
社会工作师人数	35岁及以下人数	36岁至45岁人数	46岁至55岁人数	56岁及以上人数	志愿者服务人次数	志愿服务时间
13189	**1614359**	**1253853**	**559415**	**218127**	**190139**	**486300.5**
	525	476	216	358		
356	33842	19683	21514	7673		
74	7139	11971	6288	2380	850	1700.0
2088	79246	52721	23166	6635	7494	31730.0
138	41839	23934	11181	5431	22	140.0
84	18875	15610	8124	1326	707	1510.0
52	43295	40430	19128	8784	283	540.0
340	8861	12564	3664	2873		
547	17208	20741	12544	4439	10	74.0
900	54885	53898	33642	14908		
1065	117510	130092	74662	24413	39655	83852.0
469	98391	88289	32605	34417	9803	18225.0
167	64804	51141	33599	9349	29088	69023.0
343	38820	24378	13261	4503	415	805.0
234	38126	38956	10016	3564	6	24.0
890	89820	107877	37883	9593	65644	166345.0
279	101008	63477	22290	11380	83	171.5
177	64149	46561	24094	13703	721	1216.0
973	76485	46439	16020	4470	2272	7134.0
2176	239768	106998	40812	9538	29	
69	51359	38611	17983	4442		
	12331	12805	4484	1179		
659	59592	35292	18066	6294	25544	81410.0
448	106942	98457	26599	6710	830	1269.0
43	26659	17115	8436	2815	3026	12022.0
67	38479	26317	7152	2001	590	830.0
	203	106	46	10		
281	50135	38900	16085	6868	2410	5214.0
149	12882	9549	8248	1897	20	
24	2921	5462	772	414		
5	4201	5288	2151	1225		
92	14059	9715	4684	4535	637	3066.0

C-3-5续表1

地　区	社会组织负责人	女性	按性质分 法人	合伙
全　国	**516173**	**179975**	**291207**	**8679**
中央级	101	64	107	1
北　京	16590	7581	5888	12
天　津	3472	1446	2778	7
河　北	14496	3661	6909	387
山　西	8025	1884	5903	98
内蒙古	8367	2955	4750	209
辽　宁	17088	6280	10920	148
吉　林	6076	1810	3051	22
黑龙江	11907	6009	5012	175
上　海	26466	11623	8726	12
江　苏	53145	14973	42978	770
浙　江	32160	12061	20983	478
安　徽	16485	5057	10020	463
福　建	9309	3247	8040	340
江　西	11084	3246	5017	231
山　东	61896	18741	22541	1043
河　南	28288	11658	14292	1127
湖　北	24703	7021	13619	417
湖　南	23757	7900	11340	498
广　东	36749	12986	28841	145
广　西	11611	5118	7649	212
海　南	5896	1700	3002	285
重　庆	19498	8690	7829	76
四　川	28294	11153	16409	493
贵　州	6774	2024	2705	300
云　南	8033	2673	5390	240
西　藏	29	8	30	2
陕　西	12066	3955	6561	201
甘　肃	4871	1282	3533	157
青　海	2000	547	1383	10
宁　夏	1997	334	1462	41
新　疆	4940	2288	3539	79

单位：人、个

个体	当年登记单位数	当年年检单位数	被认定的慈善组织数
61028	**40958**	**187222**	**32**
1	8	90	
72	648	966	
55	284	986	
3354	1375	5447	1
410	768	1913	
1221	951	2376	1
2028	1095	3356	
2067	288	263	
3159	751	3035	
1101	919	7667	
4786	6893	33669	
3298	2781	12439	11
2609	1341	7815	
1138	985	5493	1
2321	503	4626	
4864	4331	20325	
4197	2138	9615	2
2058	1236	6028	
4301	1504	7234	1
2588	3503	19474	4
2997	1698	2806	
233	448	744	10
746	735	5304	
3038	2338	9651	
2007	639	1804	
1851	660	6644	
10	1	19	
2695	681	5481	
1178	568	279	
80	137	369	
389	238	264	
176	513	1040	1

C-3-5续表2

地区	社会组织					
	科技与研究	生态环境	教育	卫生	社会服务	文化
全国	**17693**	**444**	**199007**	**25452**	**54043**	**18067**
中央级	25		8	6	26	19
北京	458	8	2993	367	1323	289
天津	69		1553	229	541	112
河北	567		6072	2014	943	289
山西	548	14	4144	328	607	328
内蒙古	469	8	3623	262	621	270
辽宁	307	12	8192	1584	1555	277
吉林	181		3231	242	1046	142
黑龙江	646	8	5128	222	1308	196
上海	450	24	3146	189	3291	690
江苏	925	55	9804	2507	21798	2951
浙江	1513	46	13540	927	3428	1497
安徽	606	11	7006	2208	1739	478
福建	547	12	6517	436	467	603
江西	274	2	5571	522	278	228
山东	3591	16	11588	2743	3249	2738
河南	1066	18	13130	2572	970	515
湖北	723	109	7741	1077	1504	1196
湖南	373	10	12696	892	612	650
广东	1560	31	20555	748	3469	1722
广西	235	5	9175	231	437	246
海南	186		2378	458	158	177
重庆	157		6124	118	697	116
四川	553	14	13201	1503	1561	624
贵州	196	4	3500	473	338	104
云南	274	4	5464	465	437	220
西藏	3	11	21		2	2
陕西	540	8	6047	1122	635	509
甘肃	393	3	2620	512	308	421
青海	31		790	79	126	158
宁夏	80	11	1058	57	167	149
新疆	147		2391	359	402	151

单位：个

按行业分类

体育	法律	工商业服务	宗教	农业及农村发展	职业及从业组织	国际及涉外组织	其他
16627	**617**	**3459**	**102**	**1311**	**418**	**7**	**23667**
	1	12				3	9
347	21	19	1	17	9		120
257		24	1		3		51
427	5	29	5	17	12		270
286	2	13	2	15	6		118
382	8	196	6	18	13		304
506	11	35	8	3	13		593
201	3	9	1	6	1		77
607	2	11	3	6	2		207
664	34	226		48	11	4	1062
2565	249	768	7	205	56		6644
1278	17	238	5	48	38		2184
488	1	66	12	84	4		389
500	2	94	4	5	14		317
251	3	21	1	11	3		404
2109	119	420	9	38	58		1770
893	5	50	3	4	5		385
438	47	274	7	659	71		2248
348	2	92	4	2	2		456
1170	6	179	4	7	26		2097
389	1	24	1	3	1		110
94		14		1			54
395	2	66	1	24	12		939
566	33	414	5	56	5		1405
175	1	16	3	9	8		185
380	3	33	3	4	3		191
	1						2
243	32	42		7	4		268
205	4	33	6	10	28		325
68		5		1	1		214
163		26		2	3		176
232	2	10		1	6		93

C-3-5续表3

地　区	行政执法	行政处罚数	(1) 警告	(2) 限期（责令）停止活动	(3) 撤销登记	取缔非法社会组织
全　国	**783**	**776**	**232**	**24**	**520**	**7**
中央级						
北　京	15	15	10		5	
天　津	24	20	1	3	16	4
河　北	10	10			10	
山　西						
内蒙古	2	2			2	
辽　宁						
吉　林						
黑龙江						
上　海	8	8			8	
江　苏	60	59	32	20	7	1
浙　江	1	1			1	
安　徽	21	21			21	
福　建						
江　西						
山　东	391	391	146		245	
河　南	21	19			19	2
湖　北						
湖　南	1	1			1	
广　东	89	89	39	1	49	
广　西						
海　南						
重　庆	19	19	1		18	
四　川	56	56			56	
贵　州	10	10			10	
云　南						
西　藏						
陕　西	52	52			52	
甘　肃						
青　海						
宁　夏						
新　疆	3	3	3			

单位：起、万元

民间非营利组织会计制度财务指标		
固定资产原价	本年收入合计	本年费用合计
23185277.1	**13538180.6**	**14151887.3**
42332.6	162635.2	140091.3
976717.6	732161.8	976414.2
87218.2	78305.1	164499.3
1223734.5	490468.6	541236.8
213747.8	125935.0	149837.8
96628.0	52086.4	59308.9
189425.3	565466.4	403379.0
16858.5	19891.6	18678.8
167502.3	20968.1	78627.9
277417.8	2115629.1	2001701.0
1350909.4	1591887.3	1682727.9
1050752.5	957218.7	929103.7
1043541.5	490940.1	491843.5
205846.3	124532.8	156416.3
265689.9	224758.5	232145.9
692097.7	803637.7	804046.7
510598.3	208424.4	203266.1
478520.0	297044.3	313805.9
435982.8	457473.8	431884.1
9943180.0	1273212.9	1637101.2
134353.0	87372.9	73751.3
45287.1	285262.7	57135.9
491944.6	437841.1	367769.4
1895372.1	1482655.1	1607674.7
122520.4	66270.4	67356.0
454710.9	211165.8	244661.8
1823.0	774.6	586.3
585993.2	95346.6	166421.8
78193.8	25557.3	29171.5
31028.6	3395.3	12021.0
36003.7	23040.5	76216.8
39345.7	26820.5	33004.5

C-3-6 自治组

地 区	单位数	居民1000户以下	居民1000户－3000户	居民3000户以上	社区居委会（村委会）成员	#中共党员
全 国	**662478**	**466679**	**157942**	**37857**	**2793407**	**1584403**
中央级						
北 京	6995	4244	2230	521	35360	20531
天 津	5371	3646	1432	293	23004	8975
河 北	53054	42261	9332	1461	198271	94640
山 西	30459	24843	4696	920	113561	46784
内蒙古	13412	9121	3713	578	52547	26535
辽 宁	15767	7904	5720	2143	72461	39626
吉 林	11202	6643	3409	1150	36421	3745
黑龙江	12820	6497	5057	1266	58470	26665
上 海	5843	2219	3304	320	27945	14341
江 苏	21556	8891	9786	2879	111492	73106
浙 江	31987	23508	7446	1033	125759	58587
安 徽	17978	7500	7883	2595	78411	51463
福 建	16739	12213	3966	560	70679	28288
江 西	20484	12443	7191	850	78611	28604
山 东	80948	66477	11926	2545	327833	269074
河 南	51574	34477	14413	2684	214770	116349
湖 北	29454	20532	6783	2139	119842	82269
湖 南	29193	20185	6966	2042	108501	69954
广 东	26436	16207	7600	2629	130790	87688
广 西	16207	10832	4576	799	81150	53956
海 南	3061	2442	450	169	17222	12776
重 庆	11123	6077	3945	1101	57777	35864
四 川	53068	39913	10015	3140	212443	114080
贵 州	18388	15236	2516	636	87705	41452
云 南	14299	9524	4118	657	72558	48480
西 藏	5467	5409	57	1	24462	16674
陕 西	22884	18599	3320	965	90045	43587
甘 肃	17386	13933	2841	612	68471	28860
青 海	4622	3717	366	539	19292	7291
宁 夏	2789	2021	572	196	13188	7858
新 疆	11912	9165	2313	434	64366	26301

织总表

单位：个、人

				受教育程度	
#女性	社区居委会（村委会）主任	#主任、书记“一肩挑”	#女性	大学专科人数	大学本科及以上人数
770336	**660716**	**227208**	**99321**	**139376**	**57458**
18361	6993	4085	2141	4391	2927
10828	5275	1827	1081	2432	1749
36441	52961	9303	5770	2498	766
27140	30349	10958	2967	4739	2504
17573	13391	1903	1955	4516	1477
30448	15734	7060	4303	5910	1955
12871	11135	3766	2319	502	382
20345	12786	2579	3699	1808	992
16729	5790	1309	3162	2761	1802
34538	21485	5660	5084	11391	5300
36240	31787	2399	3493	3806	2610
23221	17902	3604	2747	8040	2001
17815	16703	1067	1900	3718	907
20245	20410	1872	3880	2008	953
95863	80948	60507	13427	23471	12431
44541	51393	21446	4602	9178	2443
37209	29413	24515	2902	6596	2035
31815	29152	12962	4119	2107	948
36576	26343	18470	3674	7913	2898
19952	16186	4148	1714	1452	272
4209	3059	2762	261	2064	230
21549	11117	734	1994	10298	3103
52677	52906	4230	9273	3442	1299
20223	18299	1468	2828	1755	762
15682	14242	5854	1612	1099	226
4807	5465	1628	876	762	243
21457	22884	1720	1714	2300	691
12827	17335	1680	2479	24	472
4286	4617	1210	564	838	384
4991	2779	1381	556	787	174
18877	11877	5101	2225	6770	2522

C-3-6续表1

地 区	职业资格水平		年龄结构				志愿
	助理社会工作师人数	社会工作师人数	35岁及以下人数	36岁至45岁人数	46岁至55岁人数	56岁及以上人数	志愿者服务人次数
全 国	**22221**	**8540**	**576072**	**1194521**	**802458**	**220356**	**1702912**
中央级							
北 京	3054	1225	7542	11359	12377	4082	780
天 津	909	236	6922	6708	6574	2800	12646
河 北	361	188	32123	82057	66885	17206	23083
山 西	253	417	22564	42998	35159	12840	3809
内蒙古	157	35	11704	21375	14800	4668	17976
辽 宁	1276	494	16913	27277	21162	7109	45682
吉 林	137	62	1421	32547	1778	675	
黑龙江	323	117	11442	32379	12589	2060	163281
上 海	1131	513	5991	8196	9234	4524	23027
江 苏	4977	1438	27813	43202	32953	7524	204344
浙 江	1837	868	27373	52888	36850	8648	77460
安 徽	1141	380	14308	36888	22212	5003	84958
福 建	353	182	13510	33937	19890	3342	4390
江 西	361	34	14490	43825	16718	3578	1292
山 东	484	253	70650	145310	87866	24007	168657
河 南	266	117	42781	92762	60855	18372	4865
湖 北	448	150	23838	50610	38213	7181	2056
湖 南	265	71	23150	52152	27027	6172	16687
广 东	1958	750	23787	45937	46143	14923	5430
广 西	101	46	12621	28157	30674	9698	
海 南	1	8	2919	7428	5447	1428	13
重 庆	1168	578	15751	21289	16882	3855	536718
四 川	696	193	45268	88945	59135	19095	90198
贵 州	67	19	21371	34637	24753	6944	193623
云 南	73	21	18838	30931	18872	3917	1150
西 藏	2	4	4093	9899	7228	3242	1
陕 西	186	65	14160	35808	30841	9236	4324
甘 肃	28	8	14656	34256	15793	3766	1392
青 海	6	2	4433	8342	5460	1057	4949
宁 夏	88	7	3148	5457	4080	503	1
新 疆	114	59	20492	26965	14008	2901	10120

单位：个、人、人次、时

服务	居民(村民)小组	当年完成选举的居(村)委会数	当年完成选举的居(村)选民登记总数			
志愿服务时间				本届登记选民数	参加投票人数	委托投票人数
4596095	**5898833**	**97274**	**171337751**	**103966549**	**87955417**	**7768379**
4700	67977	3633	3308317	2669951	2179118	364901
32114	83070	2285	2468445	665449	597632	365141
93568	335628	799	1495738	215630	178536	7010
8757	109986	4063	2880893	1325305	1105326	79369
44294	76508	428	695504	344943	136631	57
59616	214708	5586	10234233	6406162	5369604	319887
	71983	3217	3598078	1043609	857721	17889
512360	151267	3139	10380583	4499291	3113344	53895
67927	304803	567	2008185	44482	41348	2038
570945	313338	13915	36712617	29860300	24547428	3143089
306895	241875	3363	4952471	1276184	1231106	65363
240189	302372	1853	5929279	1644471	1602349	201651
4603	178807					
3870	158078	813	1731069	1131995	1121826	9035
420563	534578					
4865	361027					
5840	222070					
44113	462638					
6957	253306					
	270013					
	27328	2158	3892239	3012332	2834889	115225
1254633	97871	11075	21710971	19098416	15830508	1895757
290939	406078	17134	20681024	6454201	5673037	252972
558316	185739	7943	15172318	11771061	10395049	622437
2670	161539	5959	13900192	7351970	6447129	182414
	15386	2455	731014	717506	660798	5099
13764	128953	1127	1195492	1069168	977623	19155
1655	89431	4457	6136729	2974285	2795723	41691
9987	13757	254	302415			
	17186	362	433597	226452	137971	2060
31956	41533	689	786348	163386	120721	2244

C-3-6续表2

地区	企业会计制度财务指标				事业
	固定资产原价	营业收入	费用合计	营业利润	固定资产原价
全国	**2163749.6**	**532835.1**	**166572.5**	**17234.2**	**3357236.3**
中央级					
北京	1795783.1	523749.7	162245.5	19270.6	427009.9
天津					
河北					3357.5
山西					274366.5
内蒙古	11468.6				27103.8
辽宁	65.0		1.0		14937.9
吉林	14048.5				14048.5
黑龙江	16987.4	3.0	96.9		17031.4
上海	41173.4	8937.0	3806.1	-2039.0	266458.0
江苏	182222.8				485302.3
浙江	38452.0				381388.9
安徽					44872.9
福建	1821.0				8834.2
江西	8048.7				75165.1
山东					
河南					4824.0
湖北					179256.4
湖南	9858.5				9894.5
广东	22854.4	123.4	422.0	2.6	674248.5
广西					
海南					11208.9
重庆					62614.2
四川	2117.5				20425.8
贵州					62.4
云南					295551.2
西藏	670.0				10371.8
陕西					
甘肃	10.0				1408.3
青海	3541.0				3576.4
宁夏	190.5				656.0
新疆	14437.2	22.0	1.0		43261.0

单位：万元

单位会计制度财务指标		民间非营利组织会计制度财务指标		
本年收入合计	本年支出合计	固定资产原价	本年收入合计	本年支出合计
1743008.3	**1533918.8**	**5151909.7**	**486741.3**	**233974.5**
250426.7	306608.3	2219048.6		
		29900.0		
1427.2	1427.2	76153.8		
56498.8	56453.7	103820.2	23046.1	8627.9
19727.3	22086.9	11553.6	5287.7	1051.5
5814.2	7914.0	42071.3	13049.3	13843.9
2050.8	1807.6	14615.5	2050.8	15.1
2277.3	2315.1	18267.7	2289.3	265.3
272580.8	151735.6	580884.8	9625.1	2041.2
201972.1	115282.4	369252.0	63367.4	19326.6
151342.5	105346.7	947034.3	254483.4	87225.0
11948.6	11687.2	102975.7	11213.0	10821.3
25314.3	25089.1	24623.1	10574.4	3638.0
58032.9	56607.4	21407.7	13279.9	8994.7
4500.0	4414.4			
84646.3	84181.8	134432.5	10381.4	8009.7
19826.3	19655.7	11921.0	9323.5	1477.0
441203.9	416892.4	176910.0	15306.0	38654.0
		12367.0	1511.3	1338.3
6920.3	6797.0	64.0		
30361.3	30194.9	55815.8	16060.4	3553.6
22446.1	37074.1	32338.6	9573.6	6716.4
147.0	112.0	200.8		
63749.2	57756.6	132509.5	13040.2	13202.6
342.1	342.1	58.0		
		2753.6		745.0
723.0	723.0	16179.1	3213.5	2709.6
373.0	373.0	592.0		
8356.3	11040.6	14159.5	65.0	1717.8

C-3-7 村民

地 区	单位数	居民1000户以下	居民1000户–3000户	居民3000户以上	社区居委会（村委会）成员
全 国	**559186**	**425511**	**113044**	**20631**	**2253181**
中央级					
北 京	3941	3574	347	20	14406
天 津	3681	3231	413	37	12177
河 北	48860	40470	7434	956	176885
山 西	28106	24120	3381	605	102511
内蒙古	11078	8394	2486	198	40849
辽 宁	11555	7144	3665	746	46430
吉 林	9327	6103	2439	785	29220
黑龙江	9050	5289	3266	495	40400
上 海	1590	1002	539	49	6227
江 苏	14477	6733	6181	1563	72466
浙 江	27568	21548	5573	447	104936
安 徽	14586	6568	6135	1883	60571
福 建	14407	11075	3015	317	58391
江 西	17046	10660	5786	600	64779
山 东	74217	62530	9889	1798	295254
河 南	46831	32332	12623	1876	190540
湖 北	25064	18855	5053	1156	97548
湖 南	23955	17646	4998	1311	85348
广 东	19734	14090	4630	1014	92008
广 西	14276	10171	3706	399	69190
海 南	2552	2173	305	74	14050
重 庆	8064	5170	2644	250	38948
四 川	45945	36337	7756	1852	180482
贵 州	14619	12750	1535	334	67206
云 南	11971	8625	3110	236	58690
西 藏	5259	5243	15	1	23156
陕 西	20277	17331	2407	539	76864
甘 肃	16027	13369	2227	431	61707
青 海	4146	3468	184	494	16898
宁 夏	2275	1896	340	39	9966
新 疆	8702	7614	962	126	45078

委员会

单位：个、人

#中共党员	#女性	社区居委会（村委会）主任	#主任、书记“一肩挑”	#女性
1292486	**507312**	**557902**	**186373**	**58572**
10395	4255	3941	2299	378
4856	2724	3635	712	100
84896	25504	48794	8002	4154
42753	21500	28002	9943	2015
20923	10086	11062	1080	706
26233	11794	11532	3986	1491
2165	9373	9266	2799	1401
19929	8541	9023	1389	1354
4561	2188	1584	416	492
48528	17098	14450	3331	2432
46712	26062	27403	1403	1892
40643	15094	14515	2725	1669
23031	12560	14379	812	1137
23721	14096	16990	1266	2686
244648	84978	74217	55866	10989
105120	34100	46659	19642	3015
67048	25992	25041	21153	1215
54991	22468	23931	10454	2536
62732	19382	19675	13604	1490
47215	14258	14258	3594	1056
10696	3009	2550	2283	165
24154	11771	8064	246	872
96054	41278	45846	3211	7215
31440	12589	14550	966	1568
39593	11182	11927	5021	1084
15567	4415	5257	1556	841
36987	15252	20277	1202	868
26095	9891	15983	1289	1943
6245	3034	4142	1021	394
6000	2551	2267	989	196
18555	10287	8682	4113	1218

C–3–7续表1

地　区	受教育程度		职业资格水平	
	大学专科人数	大学本科及以上人数	助理社会工作师人数	社会工作师人数
全　国	**81326.0**	**27819.0**	**3434.0**	**1272.0**
中央级				
北　京	1801.0	493.0	96.0	14.0
天　津	291.0	25.0	1.0	3.0
河　北	1521.0	229.0	116.0	33.0
山　西	2910.0	1635.0	68.0	223.0
内蒙古	2108.0	572.0	1.0	14.0
辽　宁	3193.0	566.0	45.0	18.0
吉　林	156.0	96.0	6.0	
黑龙江	202.0	15.0	109.0	39.0
上　海	491.0	289.0	86.0	30.0
江　苏	6472.0	2291.0	1345.0	268.0
浙　江	1788.0	1154.0	172.0	91.0
安　徽	4477.0	949.0	135.0	39.0
福　建	2369.0	484.0	50.0	10.0
江　西	996.0	711.0	12.0	8.0
山　东	20606.0	10377.0	201.0	121.0
河　南	7546.0	1855.0	69.0	43.0
湖　北	3221.0	826.0	26.0	5.0
湖　南	1163.0	564.0	28.0	19.0
广　东	3329.0	452.0	519.0	180.0
广　西	728.0	65.0	9.0	12.0
海　南	1298.0	48.0		3.0
重　庆	5114.0	710.0	92.0	19.0
四　川	2108.0	792.0	146.0	35.0
贵　州	774.0	185.0	14.0	8.0
云　南	683.0	85.0	13.0	7.0
西　藏	643.0	199.0	2.0	4.0
陕　西	885.0	96.0	20.0	5.0
甘　肃	5.0	377.0	1.0	5.0
青　海	619.0	270.0		1.0
宁　夏	76.0	21.0	35.0	1.0
新　疆	3753.0	1388.0	17.0	14.0

单位：人、人次、时

年龄结构				志愿服务	
35岁及以下人数	36岁至45岁人数	46岁至55岁人数	56岁及以上人数	志愿者服务人次数	志愿服务时间
421981.0	**970933.0**	**672702.0**	**187565.0**	**858900.0**	**2321120.6**
1013.0	4336.0	6699.0	2358.0	100.0	800.0
2151.0	3744.0	4382.0	1900.0	11741.0	30754.0
25393.0	73360.0	61992.0	16140.0	18688.0	77378.0
19365.0	38190.0	32804.0	12152.0	206.0	317.0
7786.0	16293.0	12445.0	4325.0	1052.0	2710.0
7039.0	17292.0	16027.0	6072.0	1855.0	3875.0
496.0	26928.0	1287.0	509.0		
6638.0	22761.0	9425.0	1576.0	29.0	160.0
1508.0	2144.0	2068.0	507.0	17451.0	51465.0
16663.0	28217.0	22400.0	5186.0	91899.0	320556.0
20859.0	44374.0	31953.0	7750.0	49312.0	187174.0
9372.0	29168.0	17790.0	4241.0	37149.0	103107.0
10541.0	28551.0	16569.0	2730.0	3270.0	3438.0
11215.0	36293.0	14107.0	3164.0	3.0	6.0
62528.0	130884.0	79842.0	22000.0	140614.0	351541.0
35667.0	82245.0	55540.0	17088.0	4865.0	4865.0
18218.0	41033.0	32072.0	6225.0	12.0	36.0
16810.0	41386.0	22071.0	5081.0	3893.0	8679.0
13683.0	30613.0	35530.0	12182.0	5229.0	6692.0
9255.0	23767.0	27440.0	8728.0		
1989.0	6239.0	4594.0	1228.0	13.0	
8887.0	14543.0	12615.0	2903.0	260986.0	547593.0
36666.0	75542.0	51296.0	16978.0	60530.0	221617.0
16241.0	26936.0	18931.0	5098.0	139289.0	373463.6
15636.0	25179.0	15041.0	2834.0	1130.0	2640.0
3649.0	9497.0	6939.0	3071.0	1.0	
10973.0	30522.0	27087.0	8282.0	3299.0	10612.0
12658.0	30942.0	14602.0	3505.0	1334.0	1655.0
3528.0	7180.0	5212.0	978.0	4949.0	9987.0
2031.0	3921.0	3542.0	472.0	1.0	
13523.0	18853.0	10400.0	2302.0		

C−3−7续表2

地 区	当年完成选举的村委会数	当年完成选举的村选民登记数	本届登记选民数	参加投票人数	委托投票人数
全 国	**77011**	**120575159**	**73754381**	**64400407**	**6406161**
中央级					
北 京	3272	2749967	2650133	2164685	362765
天 津	2029	2120394	603115	541531	328676
河 北	721	1469924	209736	173651	4061
山 西	3858	2782352	1269899	1069454	79200
内蒙古	106	260470	285	251	
辽 宁	4963	8332957	6061071	5056573	319798
吉 林	2634	2831603	928702	817278	14827
黑龙江	1291	4954907	473471	490393	42709
上 海	39	341306	38528	35882	1550
江 苏	9310	24183472	20761909	17626893	2637727
浙 江	2981	3993612	873225	865058	32676
安 徽	1383	4109530	1420468	1406296	197328
福 建					
江 西	598	1394292	922995	917588	
山 东					
河 南					
湖 北					
湖 南					
广 东					
广 西					
海 南	1719	2791514	2319912	2234770	93165
重 庆	8060	13221840	11517292	9766716	1371656
四 川	15346	17265990	5308197	4655792	228714
贵 州	6465	11570415	9045447	8047353	502429
云 南	4923	9933616	5579823	5009265	145369
西 藏	2394	693293	679785	626664	5089
陕 西	101	162756	153842	139373	1096
甘 肃	3890	4686148	2739238	2572695	34416
青 海	197	251263			
宁 夏	307	129661	127870	113861	2060
新 疆	424	343877	69438	68385	850

单位：个、人、次

经推举产生的村民代表数	女性	当年召开村民会议次数	当年召开村民代表会议的次数	自然村	村委会小组数
8742713	**1334484**	**371556**	**609730**	**1842421**	**4478489**
101901	33766	6726	18637	3941	27211
26794	3689	237	643	3132	22202
52842	14170	1570	4932	61574	297125
83612	12101	5226	9403	40887	98197
25772	2792	1558	2993	39185	53622
269267	37105	2047	3423	26502	84184
88394	4522	1413	2058	13595	48408
773553	2716	142	236	17749	100144
1355	530	57	110	1293	23955
443436	93251	8792	33686	63532	203518
130978	45235	34752	17088	82367	188642
547579	214630	1305	3298	132156	255424
		62	62	66425	151086
48685				112976	141233
1864513	459473	187139	365166	94272	459181
				149433	327680
				87100	178396
				108476	393892
		3138	6345	138661	203444
190	35	484	542	155738	232175
55369	14613	1264	4237	16667	23600
309005	77830	43875	38438	5991	67622
2507296	71209	11727	16094	84015	345927
284838	46452	31209	46450	83720	144292
781352	165043	8748	3734	118785	140102
60185	7149			12498	14305
3482	256	18120	28722	51884	113222
191876	24555	1681	2936	46380	79156
50772	126			6461	12940
12556	1730	253	466	7432	14144
27111	1506	31	31	9594	33460

C-3-7续表3

地 区	企业会计制度财务指标				
	固定资产原价	营业收入	费用合计	营业利润	固定资产原价
全 国	**1960899.0**	**532798.2**	**166565.5**	**17234.2**	**2272647.1**
中央级					
北 京	1795783.1	523749.7	162245.5	19270.6	364540.0
天 津					
河 北					2363.0
山 西					254759.8
内蒙古	8615.0				18111.2
辽 宁	16.0		1.0		13870.7
吉 林	13767.5				13767.5
黑龙江	16144.4		90.9		16181.9
上 海	41040.9	8937.0	3806.1	-2039.0	245673.4
江 苏	7749.5				203775.9
浙 江	30564.0				329966.6
安 徽					36326.4
福 建	1821.0				1821.0
江 西	6884.9				65015.2
山 东					
河 南					4331.2
湖 北					109659.5
湖 南	4569.5				4557.5
广 东	20857.4	111.5	422.0	2.6	318053.8
广 西					
海 南					9150.1
重 庆					35568.0
四 川	1942.0				15267.0
贵 州					26.8
云 南					189080.7
西 藏					271.8
陕 西					
甘 肃	10.0				1396.6
青 海	3367.8				3399.2
宁 夏	48.0				592.0
新 疆	7718.0				15120.3

单位：万元

事业单位会计制度财务指标		民间非营利组织会计制度财务指标		
本年收入合计	本年支出合计	固定资产原价	本年收入合计	本年支出合计
1091203.8	**928407.7**	**4825100.1**	**398199.3**	**187865.2**
159954.3	217030.4	2219048.6		
		29900.0		
833.0	833.0	76153.8		
50460.5	48514.0	97240.3	20872.2	7781.7
14437.4	16665.1	8165.0	3913.4	545.0
4607.2	6264.8	37051.7	10637.9	11704.3
1781.5	1541.5	14334.5	1781.5	12.1
1640.7	1682.7	17424.7	1651.7	
258798.9	139589.3	579548.9	8889.8	1059.2
101357.1	50724.2	193119.5	26381.5	5660.4
112856.5	68299.1	936067.1	247274.9	85201.0
9233.2	8992.3	78887.4	7961.0	7921.3
7934.6	7935.6	23035.9	7835.0	2106.8
24540.7	23316.0	20090.9	10634.2	5721.6
3616.8	3552.6			
64728.0	64183.4	132352.3	9667.8	7594.8
4348.8	4402.5	6340.0	5129.4	1157.6
193289.9	184623.9	162474.2	5116.6	31741.4
		11770.2	1351.9	1128.5
5920.8	5843.8	64.0		
13735.4	13717.5	50651.8	13360.3	2705.4
15811.6	22930.2	31200.3	8773.9	6162.6
67.0	57.0	200.8		
38556.4	35160.2	70902.1	3983.6	4916.9
342.1	342.1	58.0		
		2727.6		720.0
582.0	582.0	15089.0	2982.7	2573.2
250.5	250.5	592.0		
1518.9	1374.0	10609.5		1451.4

C-3-8 社区

地　区	单位数	居民1000户以下	居民1000户－3000户	居民3000户以上	社区居委会（村委会）成员	#中共党员
全　国	**103292**	**41168**	**44898**	**17226**	**540226**	**291917**
中央级						
北　京	3054	670	1883	501	20954	10136
天　津	1690	415	1019	256	10827	4119
河　北	4194	1791	1898	505	21386	9744
山　西	2353	723	1315	315	11050	4031
内蒙古	2334	727	1227	380	11698	5612
辽　宁	4212	760	2055	1397	26031	13393
吉　林	1875	540	970	365	7201	1580
黑龙江	3770	1208	1791	771	18070	6736
上　海	4253	1217	2765	271	21718	9780
江　苏	7079	2158	3605	1316	39026	24578
浙　江	4419	1960	1873	586	20823	11875
安　徽	3392	932	1748	712	17840	10820
福　建	2332	1138	951	243	12288	5257
江　西	3438	1783	1405	250	13832	4883
山　东	6731	3947	2037	747	32579	24426
河　南	4743	2145	1790	808	24230	11229
湖　北	4390	1677	1730	983	22294	15221
湖　南	5238	2539	1968	731	23153	14963
广　东	6702	2117	2970	1615	38782	24956
广　西	1931	661	870	400	11960	6741
海　南	509	269	145	95	3172	2080
重　庆	3059	907	1301	851	18829	11710
四　川	7123	3576	2259	1288	31961	18026
贵　州	3769	2486	981	302	20499	10012
云　南	2328	899	1008	421	13868	8887
西　藏	208	166	42		1306	1107
陕　西	2607	1268	913	426	13181	6600
甘　肃	1359	564	614	181	6764	2765
青　海	476	249	182	45	2394	1046
宁　夏	514	125	232	157	3222	1858
新　疆	3210	1551	1351	308	19288	7746

居委会

单位：个、人

#女性	社区居委会（村委会）主任	#主任、书记“一肩挑”	#女性	受教育程度	
				大学专科人数	大学本科及以上人数
263024	**102814**	**40835**	**40749**	**58050**	**29639**
14106	3052	1786	1763	2590	2434
8104	1640	1115	981	2141	1724
10937	4167	1301	1616	977	537
5640	2347	1015	952	1829	869
7487	2329	823	1249	2408	905
18654	4202	3074	2812	2717	1389
3498	1869	967	918	346	286
11804	3763	1190	2345	1606	977
14541	4206	893	2670	2270	1513
17440	7035	2329	2652	4919	3009
10178	4384	996	1601	2018	1456
8127	3387	879	1078	3563	1052
5255	2324	255	763	1349	423
6149	3420	606	1194	1012	242
10885	6731	4641	2438	2865	2054
10441	4734	1804	1587	1632	588
11217	4372	3362	1687	3375	1209
9347	5221	2508	1583	944	384
17194	6668	4866	2184	4584	2446
5694	1928	554	658	724	207
1200	509	479	96	766	182
9778	3053	488	1122	5184	2393
11399	7060	1019	2058	1334	507
7634	3749	502	1260	981	577
4500	2315	833	528	416	141
392	208	72	35	119	44
6205	2607	518	846	1415	595
2936	1352	391	536	19	95
1252	475	189	170	219	114
2440	512	392	360	711	153
8590	3195	988	1007	3017	1134

C-3-8续表1

地 区	职业资格水平		年龄结构				志愿
	助理社会工作师人数	社会工作师人数	35岁及以下人数	36岁至45岁人数	46岁至55岁人数	56岁及以上人数	志愿者服务人次数
全 国	**18787**	**7268**	**154091**	**223588**	**129756**	**32791**	**844012**
中央级							
北 京	2958	1211	6529	7023	5678	1724	680
天 津	908	233	4771	2964	2192	900	905
河 北	245	155	6730	8697	4893	1066	4395
山 西	185	194	3199	4808	2355	688	3603
内蒙古	156	21	3918	5082	2355	343	16924
辽 宁	1231	476	9874	9985	5135	1037	43827
吉 林	131	62	925	5619	491	166	
黑龙江	214	78	4804	9618	3164	484	163252
上 海	1045	483	4483	6052	7166	4017	5576
江 苏	3632	1170	11150	14985	10553	2338	112445
浙 江	1665	777	6514	8514	4897	898	28148
安 徽	1006	341	4936	7720	4422	762	47809
福 建	303	172	2969	5386	3321	612	1120
江 西	349	26	3275	7532	2611	414	1289
山 东	283	132	8122	14426	8024	2007	28043
河 南	197	74	7114	10517	5315	1284	
湖 北	422	145	5620	9577	6141	956	2044
湖 南	237	52	6340	10766	4956	1091	12794
广 东	1439	570	10104	15324	10613	2741	201
广 西	92	34	3366	4390	3234	970	
海 南	1	5	930	1189	853	200	
重 庆	1076	559	6864	6746	4267	952	275732
四 川	550	158	8602	13403	7839	2117	29668
贵 州	53	11	5130	7701	5822	1846	54334
云 南	60	14	3202	5752	3831	1083	20
西 藏			444	402	289	171	
陕 西	166	60	3187	5286	3754	954	1025
甘 肃	27	3	1998	3314	1191	261	58
青 海	6	1	905	1162	248	79	
宁 夏	53	6	1117	1536	538	31	
新 疆	97	45	6969	8112	3608	599	10120

单位：人、人次、时

服务	当年完成选举的居(村)委会数	当年完成选举的居(村)选民登记总数				居委会小组数
志愿服务时间			本届登记选民数	参加投票人数	委托投票人数	
2274975	**20263**	**50762592**	**30212168**	**23555010**	**1362218**	**1420344**
3900	361	558350	19818	14433	2136	40766
1360	256	348051	62334	56101	36465	60868
16190	78	25814	5894	4885	2949	38503
8440	205	98541	55406	35872	169	11789
41584	322	435034	344658	136380	57	22886
55741	623	1901276	345091	313031	89	130524
	583	766475	114907	40443	3062	23575
512200	1848	5425676	4025820	2622951	11186	51123
16462	528	1666879	5954	5466	488	280848
250389	4605	12529145	9098391	6920535	505362	109820
119721	382	958859	402959	366048	32687	53233
137082	470	1819749	224003	196053	4323	46948
1165						27721
3864	215	336777	209000	204238	9035	16845
69022						75397
						33347
5804						43674
35434						68746
265						49862
						37838
	439	1100725	692420	600119	22060	3728
707040	3015	8489131	7581124	6063792	524101	30249
69322	1788	3415034	1146004	1017245	24258	60151
184852	1478	3601903	2725614	2347696	120008	41447
30	1036	3966576	1772147	1437864	37045	21437
	61	37721	37721	34134	10	1081
3152	1026	1032736	915326	838250	18059	15731
	567	1450581	235047	223028	7275	10275
	57	51152				817
	55	303936	98582	24110		3042
31956	265	442471	93948	52336	1394	8073

C-3-8续表2

地 区	企业会计制度财务指标			事业
	固定资产原价	营业收入	费用合计	固定资产原价
全 国	**202850.6**	**36.9**	**7.0**	**1084589.2**
中央级				
北 京				62469.9
天 津				
河 北				994.5
山 西				19606.7
内蒙古	2853.6			8992.6
辽 宁	49.0			1067.2
吉 林	281.0			281.0
黑龙江	843.0	3.0	6.0	849.5
上 海	132.5			20784.6
江 苏	174473.3			281526.4
浙 江	7888.0			51422.3
安 徽				8546.5
福 建				7013.2
江 西	1163.8			10149.9
山 东				
河 南				492.8
湖 北				69596.9
湖 南	5289.0			5337.0
广 东	1997.0	11.9		356194.7
广 西				
海 南				2058.8
重 庆				27046.2
四 川	175.5			5158.8
贵 州				35.6
云 南				106470.5
西 藏	670.0			10100.0
陕 西				
甘 肃				11.7
青 海	173.2			177.2
宁 夏	142.5			64.0
新 疆	6719.2	22.0	1.0	28140.7

单位：万元

单位会计制度财务指标		民间非营利组织会计制度财务指标		
本年收入合计	本年支出合计	固定资产原价	本年收入合计	本年支出合计
651804.5	**605511.1**	**326809.6**	**88542.0**	**46109.3**
90472.4	89577.9			
594.2	594.2			
6038.3	7939.7	6579.9	2173.9	846.2
5289.9	5421.8	3388.6	1374.3	506.5
1207.0	1649.2	5019.6	2411.4	2139.6
269.3	266.1	281.0	269.3	3.0
636.6	632.4	843.0	637.6	265.3
13781.9	12146.3	1335.9	735.3	982.0
100615.0	64558.2	176132.5	36985.9	13666.2
38486.0	37047.6	10967.2	7208.5	2024.0
2715.4	2694.9	24088.3	3252.0	2900.0
17379.7	17153.5	1587.2	2739.4	1531.2
33492.2	33291.4	1316.8	2645.7	3273.1
883.2	861.8			
19918.3	19998.4	2080.2	713.6	414.9
15477.5	15253.2	5581.0	4194.1	319.4
247914.0	232268.5	14435.8	10189.4	6912.6
		596.8	159.4	209.8
999.5	953.2			
16625.9	16477.4	5164.0	2700.1	848.2
6634.5	14143.9	1138.3	799.7	553.8
80.0	55.0			
25192.8	22596.4	61607.4	9056.6	8285.7
		26.0		25.0
141.0	141.0	1090.1	230.8	136.4
122.5	122.5			
6837.4	9666.6	3550.0	65.0	266.4

C-3-9 其他社会服务

地区	单位数				年末职工人数		受教育程度	
		工商登记	编制登记	民政登记		女性	大学专科人数	大学本科及以上人数
全国	**5559**	**839**	**4200**	**401**	**89960**	**29517**	**25479**	**11984**
中央级								
北京	63	4	59		1868	640	422	530
天津	41	2	33		909	281	209	350
河北	219	5	208	2	3650	1001	758	330
山西	119	17	89	5	1324	480	395	304
内蒙古	159	27	127	4	2139	611	706	293
辽宁	510	38	250	215	6117	1958	1885	1099
吉林	199	36	161	1	4794	1254	1734	463
黑龙江	172	18	148	3	3255	1010	1069	464
上海	90	55	35		3593	1511	729	447
江苏	330	56	235	22	4899	1617	1497	824
浙江	274	65	196	9	3945	1000	998	572
安徽	192	27	147	10	3105	1032	776	268
福建	162	30	129	3	2877	840	453	235
江西	182	8	162	6	1887	592	368	82
山东	267	19	236	11	4263	1330	1545	798
河南	268	29	237	2	5978	1944	1752	555
湖北	254	24	220	7	4176	1572	1525	446
湖南	257	37	212	5	3281	1165	1258	457
广东	302	53	235	11	7271	2047	1627	863
广西	154	29	124	1	2261	874	753	409
海南	19	7	9	1	282	58	48	28
重庆	160	36	97	12	2262	929	688	391
四川	371	52	296	11	4849	1808	1347	502
贵州	136	60	71	5	3595	1357	839	301
云南	171	11	152		1427	393	474	220
西藏	2		2		30	6	3	8
陕西	161	33	122	6	2884	1060	730	350
甘肃	126	21	91	14	1235	442	225	171
青海	21	10	8	3	129	30	39	9
宁夏	69	18	39	6	512	214	168	79
新疆	109	12	70	26	1163	461	459	136

机构总表

单位：个、人、人次、时

职业资格水平		年龄结构				志愿服务	
助理社会工作师人数	社会工作师人数	35岁及以下人数	36岁至45岁人数	46岁至55岁人数	56岁及以上人数	志愿者服务人次数	志愿服务时间
917	**940**	**28808**	**34244**	**20718**	**839**	**4200**	**520**
14	15	670	562	480	4	59	
3	2	276	235	250	2	33	6
12	24	1237	1475	733	5	208	6
8	11	493	497	254	17	89	13
10	16	588	810	588	27	127	5
82	195	1919	2219	1519	38	250	222
9	9	1304	1667	1289	36	161	2
17	16	766	1428	828	18	148	6
13	25	1007	1122	988	55	35	
110	84	1356	1880	1283	56	235	39
43	49	1045	1396	1114	65	196	13
84	49	993	1217	739	27	147	18
38	46	855	1166	671	30	129	3
22	21	590	853	367	8	162	12
53	68	1531	1634	857	19	236	12
61	42	2690	2189	902	29	237	2
49	43	1359	1672	909	24	220	10
27	23	1313	1260	593	37	212	8
115	55	2211	2890	1743	53	235	14
35	23	836	820	467	29	124	1
2		69	102	86	7	9	3
25	27	718	871	514	36	97	27
44	39	1466	2007	1111	52	296	23
2	9	1145	1530	717	60	71	5
18	18	503	547	199	11	152	8
		13	9	6		2	
4	14	880	1060	777	33	122	6
2	4	471	412	303	21	91	14
		37	62	28	10	8	3
12	13	81	172	170	18	39	12
3		386	480	233	12	70	27

C-3-9续表

地 区	企业会计制度财务指标				事业
	固定资产原价	营业收入	费用合计	营业利润	固定资产原价
全 国	**966064.0**	**1085109.8**	**276085.8**	**215804.0**	**1894378.9**
中央级					
北 京	25463.9	59255.5	20477.4	15737.6	95305.1
天 津	5980.2	5653.2	1610.2	2493.8	39811.5
河 北	4070.2	4592.6	2980.8	-301.6	79292.2
山 西	15370.0	3114.1	1495.1	-512.1	33375.6
内蒙古	15309.6	5346.6	3413.2	98.3	34058.2
辽 宁	42501.9	26683.3	13996.5	2608.3	104242.6
吉 林	22933.8	2585.1	998.7	-57.0	75475.0
黑龙江	17901.7	10777.8	6197.2	902.0	64916.6
上 海	257792.3	474979.2	74300.9	120038.2	6735.2
江 苏	38962.6	61415.9	11088.1	34299.7	185950.4
浙 江	28095.8	53321.5	14672.6	10350.2	104495.6
安 徽	16651.1	11315.3	3835.5	1593.2	53712.3
福 建	58824.7	23112.4	11448.9	1133.1	42299.9
江 西	10452.5	4272.9	1424.5	320.9	68803.9
山 东	7108.9	4828.3	1944.6	479.1	101569.9
河 南	21104.1	8549.2	3609.0	876.1	50078.0
湖 北	13885.3	18895.4	7959.6	2244.7	91119.6
湖 南	30936.4	7961.5	3410.2	518.8	59725.1
广 东	51031.9	36093.2	14911.6	4959.2	240077.6
广 西	34184.4	80659.7	9639.8	3025.1	48513.1
海 南	17653.5	4182.0	2661.2	333.0	8109.7
重 庆	33760.3	26060.6	11163.6	2546.9	34709.1
四 川	64606.9	60179.5	19389.9	4332.9	111248.3
贵 州	79242.2	50471.5	21337.7	4396.0	37745.8
云 南	13239.5	6177.5	1931.1	912.0	38408.1
西 藏	367.2				1867.0
陕 西	16295.2	22776.3	8528.7	919.0	27643.6
甘 肃	6647.6	7236.5	1112.1	1513.2	28520.7
青 海	1013.3	30.0	30.0		1498.1
宁 夏	5817.0	1411.7	246.4	-1.8	2159.4
新 疆	8860.0	3171.5	270.7	45.2	22911.7

单位：万元

单位会计制度财务指标		民间非营利组织会计制度财务指标		
本年收入合计	本年支出合计	固定资产原价	本年收入合计	本年支出合计
1512340.8	**1398034.8**	**72605.2**	**22245.0**	**20400.3**
125525.3	119424.2			
79842.2	56630.8	157.5	176.3	151.3
42930.6	40908.6	150.0	12.0	8.0
22266.4	22141.4	801.8	10.2	1.9
21106.7	20745.4	446.0	28.4	36.4
88294.0	81468.7	8267.6	2775.9	2552.1
17507.7	18876.6	7.0	3.0	8.0
45486.7	40161.1	261.0	30.1	82.4
12502.1	12355.8			
139814.1	132687.3	9295.9	6286.1	4394.0
114537.6	102671.9	561.4	1529.5	875.0
45612.8	43183.8	3000.7	1310.9	1150.7
33100.3	30012.9	634.0	2.0	45.0
17358.3	18622.4	2059.5	74.0	1925.1
80956.4	80978.3	4093.0	1749.4	1749.4
30735.0	30259.3	10.0	2.0	2.0
94367.8	80091.2	1117.0	677.1	522.1
64016.4	53233.0	551.0	587.0	511.0
190734.7	174317.8	1915.0	366.9	133.1
35343.8	36839.3			
5599.2	6654.4	0.1		
46170.5	43653.1	15353.4	2365.8	2543.8
59112.8	56247.6	13932.1	2342.1	2472.0
7521.3	9206.4	3463.0	1276.0	404.1
15835.7	15124.1	70.9	27.7	36.5
610.0	617.0			
35247.9	32775.8	533.0	49.2	33.0
13665.7	12584.3	1528.7	323.3	106.4
794.9	799.9	587.0	44.0	48.4
3947.4	3267.4	2125.6	87.8	484.8
21796.5	21495.0	1683.0	108.3	123.8

C-3-10 婚姻登记

地区	单位数	编制登记	民政登记	年末职工人数	女性	受教育程度：大学专科人数	受教育程度：大学本科及以上人数
全国	**1393**	**1274**	**119**	**8502**	**5629**	**3337**	**2601**
中央级							
北京	11	11		105	86	17	82
天津	14	8	6	191	106	51	127
河北	42	38	4	403	246	101	58
山西	57	49	8	262	177	120	79
内蒙古	30	29	1	146	93	72	53
辽宁	105	98	7	710	492	267	296
吉林	65	64	1	475	297	122	95
黑龙江	33	30	3	232	154	93	50
上海	17	17		166	116	50	90
江苏	81	64	17	530	374	201	182
浙江	49	45	4	246	185	92	121
安徽	41	33	8	265	165	124	62
福建	27	27		83	54	29	32
江西	66	60	6	263	188	83	19
山东	95	94	1	778	505	343	298
河南	31	31		275	190	97	42
湖北	95	92	3	594	433	296	143
湖南	99	96	3	598	354	292	119
广东	60	57	3	424	282	194	135
广西	57	57		229	160	104	75
海南	3	1	2	24	11	2	8
重庆	54	39	15	335	191	104	144
四川	92	80	12	452	289	210	106
贵州	10	10		31	22	14	11
云南	25	17	8	97	62	29	25
西藏							
陕西	46	46		307	211	123	79
甘肃	56	56		182	106	57	35
青海							
宁夏	15	9	6	38	33	21	9
新疆	17	16	1	61	47	29	26

服务机构总表

单位：个、人、人次、时、处

职业资格水平		年龄结构				志愿服务		办理婚姻登记事务的处数
助理社会工作师人数	社会工作师人数	35岁及以下人数	36岁至45岁人数	46岁至55岁人数	56岁及以上人数	志愿者服务人次数	志愿服务时间	
173	**204**	**3780**	**3410**	**1204**	**108**	**12185**	**27858**	**4863**
4	4	57	35	13		4	4	16
1		80	44	53	14	206	547	17
	8	191	176	32	4	210	690	194
4	3	125	104	32	1			134
		40	72	33	1			119
15	20	309	285	104	12	11	17	179
3	3	195	173	100	7			68
2		108	102	20	2			196
4	12	72	64	23	7			21
22	22	278	184	57	11	273	576	109
14	14	112	101	31	2	3932	6809	107
10	13	122	97	45	1	566	1281	113
7	6	39	39	4	1			123
3	4	106	126	30	1			112
15	30	346	307	117	8	3224	7846	168
2	2	146	94	33	2	24	88	194
18	10	240	251	98	5	72	115	111
10	7	310	220	64	4	171	604	148
13	11	197	159	64	4	829	917	293
2	1	67	116	43	3			134
		9	15					177
12	17	132	145	56	2	1211	4894	82
7	8	185	197	61	9	124	160	444
		15	13	3		1198	2950	526
5	5	37	54	6				174
								136
	2	143	124	38	2	130	360	160
		91	60	27	4			146
								182
	2	13	18	6	1			101
		15	35	11				179

C-3-10续表

地区	事业单位会计制度财务指标		
	固定资产原价	本年收入合计	本年支出合计
全国	**77450.0**	**80903.0**	**73119.9**
中央级			
北京	491.3	2209.6	2198.2
天津	750.3	18418.7	17101.5
河北	361.6	1400.3	1404.6
山西	198.7	643.8	692.3
内蒙古	364.7	843.2	923.4
辽宁	2244.6	3692.4	3943.5
吉林	577.8	1396.1	1396.8
黑龙江	1213.9	1244.6	1319.9
上海	1987.6	5928.9	5816.5
江苏	1117.9	4146.0	4177.3
浙江	1235.8	2589.1	2919.8
安徽	971.7	1234.5	1219.1
福建	269.2	675.3	622.1
江西	50598.7	402.6	454.7
山东	3485.1	5353.2	5375.1
河南	277.4	489.7	445.0
湖北	1485.2	3657.0	3681.6
湖南	1720.1	15510.8	7055.4
广东	2003.0	3229.2	3441.0
广西	585.0	836.3	911.4
海南	28.4		96.7
重庆	1962.7	3150.4	3177.5
四川	2113.9	1430.1	1482.6
贵州	113.5	48.4	55.4
云南	199.7	290.5	1036.3
西藏			
陕西	468.2	1873.5	1866.6
甘肃	328.4	99.1	108.3
青海			
宁夏	136.9	14.6	25.0
新疆	158.7	95.1	172.3

单位：万元

民间非营利组织会计制度财务指标		
固定资产原价	本年收入合计	本年费用合计
1198.4	**1794.6**	**1470.0**
157.5	176.3	151.3
1.8	10.2	1.9
	10.0	10.0
1.0	57.6	9.5
5.0	3.0	8.0
15.0	11.6	28.7
126.7	531.5	360.2
129.0	223.0	115.2
110.7	87.9	57.2
17.5	38.0	17.3
10.3	206.4	206.4
15.0	60.6	50.6
51.0	3.0	1.0
12.0	54.2	7.0
0.1		
392.4	189.5	202.0
68.5	97.1	196.4
70.9	27.7	36.5
9.0	2.0	5.8
5.0	5.0	5.0

C-3-11 结婚登

地 区	登记结婚件数	登记结婚人数	按居住		
			内地居民登记结婚件数	内地居民登记结婚人数	涉外及华侨、港澳台居民登记结婚件数
全 国	**11428216**	**22856432**	**11386050**	**22770310**	**42166**
中央级					
北 京	166207	332414	165195	330390	1012
天 津	98164	196328	97848	195696	316
河 北	551896	1103792	550919	1101838	977
山 西	300121	600242	299966	599932	155
内蒙古	198392	396784	198191	396382	201
辽 宁	312562	625124	310900	621800	1662
吉 林	221505	443010	220749	441498	756
黑龙江	306307	612614	304778	609556	1529
上 海	125215	250430	123531	247062	1684
江 苏	716111	1432222	714705	1429410	1406
浙 江	366823	733646	363896	727792	2927
安 徽	713361	1426722	711977	1423954	1384
福 建	314648	629296	309569	619138	5079
江 西	302014	604028	300907	601814	1107
山 东	670678	1341356	669587	1339174	1091
河 南	968979	1937958	968087	1936174	892
湖 北	513823	1027646	512629	1025258	1194
湖 南	499373	998746	497770	995540	1603
广 东	786123	1572246	777990	1556826	8133
广 西	393951	787902	391762	783524	2189
海 南	78255	156510	77730	155460	525
重 庆	278527	557054	277882	555764	645
四 川	727118	1454236	725628	1451256	1490
贵 州	453162	906324	452777	905554	385
云 南	446076	892152	443130	886268	2946
西 藏	30055	60110	30044	57650	11
陕 西	332406	664812	331860	663720	546
甘 肃	219095	438190	218951	437902	144
青 海	61187	122374	61167	122334	20
宁 夏	62028	124056	61983	123760	45
新 疆	214054	428108	213942	427884	112

记服务

单位：对、人

地分类

内地居民	#女 性	香港居民	澳门居民	台湾居民	华 侨	外国人
40809	**26367**	**5364**	**1305**	**7177**	**5127**	**24550**
919	645	57	6	125	18	899
308	226	10		45	5	264
976	276	10	7	71	10	880
154	2306	45	35	49	17	10
200	124	5	2	32	4	159
1653	1294	37	12	177	88	1357
747	509	14	14	102	31	604
1527	978	26	14	183	312	996
1533	1100	95	16	312	36	1376
1390	1056	54	14	420	20	914
2071	1146	39	9	218	2288	1229
1383	505	25	7	220	21	1112
5023	3036	1182	108	1368	770	1707
1107	414	45	13	218	23	808
1024	663	82	9	138	24	905
891	559	26	18	248	14	587
1193	873	113	31	340	13	698
1600	1211	144	58	625	32	747
8077	5368	2802	809	780	1272	2526
2189	866	136	40	308	45	1660
523	409	167	11	218	12	119
643	517	61	16	203	11	356
1485	1057	100	30	402	33	930
385	282	34	13	125	11	202
2944	427	22	4	83	5	2834
11	5	1	1		2	7
543	310	18	4	116	7	404
143	95	8	2	34	2	99
20	6	1		3	1	15
35	21	3	1	7		44
112	83	2	1	7		102

C-3-11续表

地区	按婚姻状况分类			
	初婚人数	再婚人数	#女性	#恢复结婚件数
全国	**19132566**	**3723866**	**1950215**	**473905**
中央级				
北京	200750	131664	64185	22282
天津	161474	34854	17357	16023
河北	851411	252381	137026	313
山西	530845	69397	37974	6943
内蒙古	280929	115855	63865	17159
辽宁	554958	70166	35715	27482
吉林	395931	47079	23706	20978
黑龙江	522071	90543	46531	28564
上海	159162	91268	45320	20340
江苏	1162847	269375	139073	46357
浙江	605781	127865	65408	13195
安徽	1141695	285027	149119	39537
福建	539946	89350	46971	501
江西	508278	95750	50732	13401
山东	995075	346281	183520	1610
河南	1850977	86981	44042	41399
湖北	971991	55655	28727	6914
湖南	786720	212026	114854	16702
广东	1365312	206934	99589	33170
广西	674702	113200	64054	8841
海南	140883	15627	7942	1688
重庆	380608	176446	92677	15586
四川	1093585	360651	194176	33747
贵州	866973	39351	19877	11368
云南	744088	148064	74314	1329
西藏	57556	2554	757	6
陕西	544943	119869	66039	12670
甘肃	425510	12680	6541	3121
青海	108285	14089	7408	32
宁夏	102977	21079	11346	2453
新疆	406303	21805	11370	10194

单位：对、人

按年龄分类				
20～24岁	25～29岁	30～34岁	35～39岁	40岁及以上
5523560	**8722990**	**2930063**	**1606326**	**4073493**
21823	131703	71047	40945	66896
31602	78295	37983	19448	29000
354407	417655	125335	66690	139705
166794	233317	60024	33021	107086
73790	162569	57319	29918	73188
94733	241673	98548	56149	134021
70461	155955	65334	39863	111397
91744	183161	85482	57385	194842
18272	90749	49426	28144	63839
312668	523310	133374	83723	379147
131708	318670	100190	48857	134221
408540	479682	126145	89677	322678
136169	281545	83570	35030	92982
175245	233559	68429	40093	86702
280593	633220	179906	87953	159684
522989	749452	210709	145827	308981
230535	420687	125568	62473	188383
220364	436726	144355	68068	129233
431319	655385	228708	99803	157031
191565	291790	142970	63607	97970
37945	54474	23676	11063	29352
157671	180705	69499	34164	115015
406453	486418	176593	100575	284197
241104	268869	118078	79376	198897
230713	267523	115157	74329	204430
17326	21656	10189	5546	5393
157114	305958	85223	35728	80789
131162	183729	48289	20120	54890
28371	46894	16325	9541	21243
34874	43015	13550	8670	23947
115506	144646	59062	30540	78354

C-3-12 离婚登

地 区	总 计	民政部门合计			
			内地居民登记离婚	涉外及华侨、港澳台居民登记离婚	
					#外国人
全 国	**4158211**	**3486257**	**3479942**	**6315**	**2894**
北 京	105805	97583	97327	256	190
天 津	65220	60164	60087	77	60
河 北	220153	179332	179260	72	49
山 西	76520	58962	58945	17	0
内蒙古	98364	79024	78996	28	14
辽 宁	160101	136114	135865	249	179
吉 林	129229	116755	116648	107	73
黑龙江	187192	164660	164468	192	103
上 海	82558	74350	73845	505	307
江 苏	261305	219687	219427	260	139
浙 江	147096	122870	122483	387	192
安 徽	217237	185039	184915	124	74
福 建	96338	80169	79323	846	244
江 西	102139	86405	86290	115	57
山 东	254506	201101	200958	143	87
河 南	277458	239324	239210	114	48
湖 北	183118	160236	160041	195	78
湖 南	193452	164083	163844	239	79
广 东	211858	186406	185025	1381	403
广 西	112768	92691	92514	177	82
海 南	16631	13139	13050	89	15
重 庆	139029	122072	121931	141	61
四 川	296234	255173	254928	245	107
贵 州	121041	92896	92836	60	21
云 南	119305	95481	95285	196	168
西 藏	3484	2848	2848	0	0
陕 西	101433	78588	78526	62	38
甘 肃	50325	33451	33433	18	9
青 海	15164	9939	9937	2	2
宁 夏	19544	14641	14634	7	6
新 疆	93575	63,074	63,063.00	11	9

说明：全国的含有军事。

记服务

单位：件(对)、人

法院部门合计	离婚		收案	维持	
	判决离婚	调解离婚		判决不离	调解不离
671954	**218735**	**453219**	**1381673**	**297673**	**53593**
8222	2779	5443	18299	3639	145
5056	1658	3398	13225	3395	903
40821	12964	27857	84864	19220	1081
17558	6220	11338	38401	7583	3416
19340	6774	12566	36153	2847	1260
23987	8300	15687	50029	9597	1133
12474	5405	7069	24147	3803	434
22532	6410	16122	37153	2392	432
8208	2537	5671	17662	4082	234
41618	10796	30822	97089	25530	4079
24226	7621	16605	51199	13271	1588
32198	8977	23221	71696	18599	1461
16169	7477	8692	34518	8920	477
15734	6106	9628	37190	9703	1843
53405	20078	33327	117863	29645	6616
38134	13767	24367	87411	24307	1597
22882	7180	15702	47994	13804	857
29369	10773	18596	62038	17818	1632
25452	10960	14492	51265	12070	702
20077	8294	11783	37632	8798	1104
3492	1292	2200	6279	1009	725
16957	5971	10986	33519	7854	744
41061	12193	28868	78152	16800	3215
28145	7993	20152	49237	7032	1500
23824	6925	16899	43826	5767	2875
636	90	546	915	28	79
22845	6319	16526	49716	7576	5555
16874	5388	11486	37357	7220	2283
5225	1276	3949	10425	957	861
4903	1525	3378	11804	2279	778
30501	4681	25820	44548	2117	3984

C-3-13 殡葬服务

地 区	单位数	工商登记	编制登记	民政登记	年末职工人数	女性	受教育程度	
							大学专科人数	大学本科及以上人数
全 国	**4166**	**839**	**2926**	**401**	**81458**	**23888**	**22142**	**9383**
中央级								
北 京	52	4	48		1763	554	405	448
天 津	27	2	25		718	175	158	223
河 北	177	5	170	2	3247	755	657	272
山 西	62	17	40	5	1062	303	275	225
内蒙古	129	27	98	4	1993	518	634	240
辽 宁	405	38	152	215	5407	1466	1618	803
吉 林	134	36	97	1	4319	957	1612	368
黑龙江	139	18	118	3	3023	856	976	414
上 海	73	55	18		3427	1395	679	357
江 苏	249	56	171	22	4369	1243	1296	642
浙 江	225	65	151	9	3699	815	906	451
安 徽	151	27	114	10	2840	867	652	206
福 建	135	30	102	3	2794	786	424	203
江 西	116	8	102	6	1624	404	285	63
山 东	172	19	142	11	3485	825	1202	500
河 南	237	29	206	2	5703	1754	1655	513
湖 北	159	24	128	7	3582	1139	1229	303
湖 南	158	37	116	5	2683	811	966	338
广 东	242	53	178	11	6847	1765	1433	728
广 西	97	29	67	1	2032	714	649	334
海 南	16	7	8	1	258	47	46	20
重 庆	106	36	58	12	1927	738	584	247
四 川	279	52	216	11	4397	1519	1137	396
贵 州	126	60	61	5	3564	1335	825	290
云 南	146	11	135		1330	331	445	195
西 藏	2		2		30	6	3	8
陕 西	115	33	76	6	2577	849	607	271
甘 肃	70	21	35	14	1053	336	168	136
青 海	21	10	8	3	129	30	39	9
宁 夏	54	18	30	6	474	181	147	70
新 疆	92	12	54	26	1102	414	430	110

机构总表

单位：个、人、人次、时

职业资格水平		年龄结构				志愿服务	
助理社会工作师人数	社会工作师人数	35岁及以下人数	36岁至45岁人数	46岁至55岁人数	56岁及以上人数	志愿者服务人次数	志愿服务时间
744	**736**	**25028**	**30834**	**19514**	**6082**	**12022**	**37718**
10	11	613	527	467	156	87	87
2	2	196	191	197	134	200	400
12	16	1046	1299	701	201	293	869
4	8	368	393	222	79		
10	16	548	738	555	152		
67	175	1610	1934	1415	448	112	198
6	6	1109	1494	1189	527		
15	16	658	1326	808	231	1	6
9	13	935	1058	965	469	2099	10890
88	62	1078	1696	1226	369	2348	4942
29	35	933	1295	1083	388	771	1801
74	36	871	1120	694	155	2507	6587
31	40	816	1127	667	184	10	20
19	17	484	727	337	76	234	856
38	38	1185	1327	740	233		
59	40	2544	2095	869	195	224	677
31	33	1119	1421	811	231	172	386
17	16	1003	1040	529	111	200	770
102	44	2014	2731	1679	423	98	392
33	22	769	704	424	135		
2		60	87	86	25		
13	10	586	726	458	157	439	959
37	31	1281	1810	1050	256	25	79
2	9	1130	1517	714	203	1704	6158
13	13	466	493	193	178	7	20
		13	9	6	2		
4	12	737	936	739	165	258	734
2	4	380	352	276	45		
		37	62	28	2		
12	11	68	154	164	88	75	525
3		371	445	222	64	158	362

C-3-13续表1

地 区	火化炉数	全年遗体火化数	国际运尸数	外国人	港澳台	侨民
全 国	**6206**	**4718141**	**360**	**184**	**151**	**2**
中央级						
北 京	82	101254				
天 津	67	69717				
河 北	390	183188				
山 西	63	23574				
内蒙古	165	70953	1		1	
辽 宁	359	288147				
吉 林	171	100690				
黑龙江	263	163444				
上 海	96	128439	98	65	10	
江 苏	543	525061				
浙 江	360	318387	1	1		
安 徽	270	278751				
福 建	226	202363				
江 西	197	80584				
山 东	518	611920				
河 南	322	138793				
湖 北	328	221952				
湖 南	161	90234				
广 东	432	473186	260	118	140	2
广 西	104	82200				
海 南	6	3296				
重 庆	128	76882				
四 川	309	216293				
贵 州	169	92236				
云 南	227	69061				
西 藏	6	940				
陕 西	99	57760				
甘 肃	54	18911				
青 海	31	6932				
宁 夏	12	3848				
新 疆	48	19145				

单位：具、个、台

穴位数	#本年销售穴位数	安葬数	#本年安葬数	节地生态安葬数
15570132	**613939**	**10907556**	**652251**	**604507**
739363	15353	598295	21109	2987
188562	5248	198728	6676	7931
395201	6569	148554	12399	4064
131104	3808	66150	4110	29
336852	34940	261552	24434	341
837370	67575	531771	40242	2203
23435	1191	15409	3978	1791
260423	17148	268311	31354	1821
2011419	72879	1401510	49410	345
1576563	87524	1397562	60219	44609
1229919	32615	993313	32613	10931
480562	17060	378967	33063	12883
283344	13274	207198	16533	5457
175210	7272	69093	11409	6307
253808	7227	210956	36204	199013
293252	8140	184702	9191	364
1056702	23050	727235	38854	2108
408028	20564	224237	27076	16090
1027989	27835	644542	26369	221452
378223	15469	229221	15876	25288
75352	2408	46526	2536	4200
666676	15822	358813	17800	16080
1258765	43622	812681	45344	2301
544827	23342	215061	28883	216
246533	8497	103012	17204	11023
441947	15094	410403	17370	274
171540	8547	150746	8900	4359
5359	1368	2597	322	20
43990	5195	26968	5067	
27814	5303	23443	7706	20

C-3-13续表2

地 区	企业会计制度财务指标				事业
	固定资产原价	营业收入	费用合计	营业利润	固定资产原价
全 国	**966064.0**	**1085109.8**	**276085.8**	**215804.0**	**1816928.9**
中央级					
北 京	25463.9	59255.5	20477.4	15737.6	94813.8
天 津	5980.2	5653.2	1610.2	2493.8	39061.2
河 北	4070.2	4592.6	2980.8	-301.6	78930.6
山 西	15370.0	3114.1	1495.1	-512.1	33176.9
内蒙古	15309.6	5346.6	3413.2	98.3	33693.5
辽 宁	42501.9	26683.3	13996.5	2608.3	101998.0
吉 林	22933.8	2585.1	998.7	-57.0	74897.2
黑龙江	17901.7	10777.8	6197.2	902.0	63702.7
上 海	257792.3	474979.2	74300.9	120038.2	4747.6
江 苏	38962.6	61415.9	11088.1	34299.7	184832.5
浙 江	28095.8	53321.5	14672.6	10350.2	103259.8
安 徽	16651.1	11315.3	3835.5	1593.2	52740.6
福 建	58824.7	23112.4	11448.9	1133.1	42030.7
江 西	10452.5	4272.9	1424.5	320.9	18205.2
山 东	7108.9	4828.3	1944.6	479.1	98084.8
河 南	21104.1	8549.2	3609.0	876.1	49800.6
湖 北	13885.3	18895.4	7959.6	2244.7	89634.4
湖 南	30936.4	7961.5	3410.2	518.8	58005.0
广 东	51031.9	36093.2	14911.6	4959.2	238074.6
广 西	34184.4	80659.7	9639.8	3025.1	47928.1
海 南	17653.5	4182.0	2661.2	333.0	8081.3
重 庆	33760.3	26060.6	11163.6	2546.9	32746.4
四 川	64606.9	60179.5	19389.9	4332.9	109134.4
贵 州	79242.2	50471.5	21337.7	4396.0	37632.3
云 南	13239.5	6177.5	1931.1	912.0	38208.4
西 藏	367.2				1867.0
陕 西	16295.2	22776.3	8528.7	919.0	27175.4
甘 肃	6647.6	7236.5	1112.1	1513.2	28192.3
青 海	1013.3	30.0	30.0		1498.1
宁 夏	5817.0	1411.7	246.4	-1.8	2022.5
新 疆	8860.0	3171.5	270.7	45.2	22753.0

单位：万元

单位会计制度财务指标		民间非营利组织会计制度财务指标		
本年收入合计	本年支出合计	固定资产原价	本年收入合计	本年支出合计
1431437.8	**1324914.9**	**71406.8**	**20450.4**	**18930.3**
123315.7	117226.0			
61423.5	39529.3			
41530.3	39504.0	150.0	12.0	8.0
21622.6	21449.1	800.0		
20263.5	19822.0	446.0	18.4	26.4
84601.6	77525.2	8266.6	2718.3	2542.6
16111.6	17479.8	2.0		
44242.1	38841.2	246.0	18.5	53.7
6573.2	6539.3			
135668.1	128510.0	9169.2	5754.6	4033.8
111948.5	99752.1	432.4	1306.5	759.8
44378.3	41964.7	2890.0	1223.0	1093.5
32425.0	29390.8	634.0	2.0	45.0
16955.7	18167.7	2042.0	36.0	1907.8
75603.2	75603.2	4082.7	1543.0	1543.0
30245.3	29814.3	10.0	2.0	2.0
90710.8	76409.6	1102.0	616.5	471.5
48505.6	46177.6	500.0	584.0	510.0
187505.5	170876.8	1903.0	312.7	126.1
34507.5	35927.9			
5599.2	6557.7			
43020.1	40475.6	14961.0	2176.3	2341.8
57682.7	54765.0	13863.6	2245.0	2275.6
7472.9	9151.0	3463.0	1276.0	404.1
15545.2	14087.8			
610.0	617.0			
33374.4	30909.2	533.0	49.2	33.0
13566.6	12476.0	1528.7	323.3	106.4
794.9	799.9	587.0	44.0	48.4
3932.8	3242.4	2116.6	85.8	479.0
21701.4	21322.7	1678.0	103.3	118.8

C-3-14 殡仪

地区	单位数	年末职工人数		受教育程度		职业资
			女性	大学专科人数	大学本科及以上人数	助理社会工作师人数
全国	**1775**	**46682**	**12179**	**13615**	**5280**	**456**
中央级						
北京	12	567	134	188	130	1
天津	10	401	87	94	99	2
河北	155	2759	595	536	229	12
山西	26	386	90	86	96	4
内蒙古	68	1161	294	393	127	3
辽宁	79	2662	716	775	326	23
吉林	47	1951	290	1180	234	6
黑龙江	95	2421	705	784	334	14
上海	15	1086	305	316	176	3
江苏	93	2893	719	827	443	56
浙江	77	2188	444	642	249	23
安徽	69	2110	610	476	151	64
福建	62	1898	503	218	96	20
江西	86	1315	329	199	34	8
山东	123	2849	596	1012	409	29
河南	114	3530	992	1056	267	34
湖北	78	2435	778	854	183	21
湖南	65	1394	396	502	180	6
广东	88	4053	933	883	466	74
广西	32	990	310	343	163	19
海南	2	58	11	13	10	
重庆	37	891	314	318	136	4
四川	88	1927	542	521	178	15
贵州	56	1919	675	430	143	
云南	77	764	165	283	110	2
西藏	2	30	6	3	8	
陕西	44	1060	303	386	169	3
甘肃	26	438	146	75	98	1
青海	11	67	15	32	9	
宁夏	8	105	48	73	11	9
新疆	30	374	128	117	16	

馆

单位：个、人、人次、时

格水平	年龄结构				志愿服务	
社会工作师人数	35岁及以下人数	36岁至45岁人数	46岁至55岁人数	56岁及以上人数	志愿者服务人次数	志愿服务时间
308	**14706**	**17985**	**10780**	**3211**	**8647**	**26995**
2	171	150	180	66	52	52
	125	78	111	87	100	200
13	884	1146	591	138	285	837
8	94	151	110	31		
4	296	444	331	90		
17	820	1026	592	224	49	92
4	389	656	527	379		
15	525	1035	673	188	1	6
7	419	307	236	124	1999	10690
39	772	1077	814	230	1960	3326
23	583	834	595	176	301	774
28	665	832	510	103	1606	4162
26	554	749	472	123		
2	370	591	292	62	234	856
29	935	1102	614	198		
11	1671	1242	522	95	116	320
8	740	975	565	155	160	350
2	511	525	298	60	155	610
21	1162	1662	983	246	98	392
13	403	314	203	70		
	19	16	22	1		
10	295	351	195	50	255	592
14	564	857	408	98		
1	631	888	333	67	1192	3546
2	332	277	124	31	7	20
	13	9	6	2		
6	383	379	250	48	40	170
3	215	119	81	23		
	28	25	13	1		
	1	16	57	31		
	136	152	72	14	37	

C-3-14续表1

地区	火化炉数	全年遗体火化数	国际运尸数	外国人	港澳台	侨民
全国	**6206**	**4718141**	**360**	**184**	**151**	**2**
中央级						
北京	82	101254				
天津	67	69717				
河北	390	183188				
山西	63	23574				
内蒙古	165	70953	1		1	
辽宁	359	288147				
吉林	171	100690				
黑龙江	263	163444				
上海	96	128439	98	65	10	
江苏	543	525061				
浙江	360	318387	1	1		
安徽	270	278751				
福建	226	202363				
江西	197	80584				
山东	518	611920				
河南	322	138793				
湖北	328	221952				
湖南	161	90234				
广东	432	473186	260	118	140	2
广西	104	82200				
海南	6	3296				
重庆	128	76882				
四川	309	216293				
贵州	169	92236				
云南	227	69061				
西藏	6	940				
陕西	99	57760				
甘肃	54	18911				
青海	31	6932				
宁夏	12	3848				
新疆	48	19145				

单位：具、个、台

穴位数	#本年销售穴位数	安葬数	#本年安葬数	节地生态安葬数
2558533	**102907**	**1726561**	**222993**	**478693**
10785	136	9459	142	
38406	1807	9692	1729	
193299	2704	53456	7224	4053
883	110	755	103	21
154253	14940	138441	16834	341
15994	1548	42949	10818	
2489	135	4198	2866	1791
120280	2951	151381	12983	1821
120897	3141	110467	7119	4064
141952	3953	109148	4393	7420
114900	4147	65419	18838	11435
137947	6266	107699	9563	5322
154869	6213	54811	10087	5475
76213	630	88054	29467	170435
54845	2415	37395	2486	30
152977	7653	112953	19586	109
173666	6200	117811	9991	12238
125749	1905	89231	4772	220326
5912	1482	4342	2518	20880
119876	3598	72775	5321	1939
97835	10370	87657	10594	78
211299	9548	28817	15254	91
140221	4838	54505	12442	7798
151945	1836	141930	1605	
24448	1759	20003	1796	3006
				20
6089	291	1701	291	
10504	2331	11512	4171	

C-3-14续表2

地区	企业会计制度财务指标				事业
	固定资产原价	营业收入	费用合计	营业利润	固定资产原价
全国	**363273.5**	**181405.8**	**63675.1**	**17433.6**	**1467007.8**
中央级					
北京					56754.9
天津					22314.1
河北	338.0	471.0	384.4	-60.0	72577.1
山西	670.0	53.0	41.0	18.0	31900.1
内蒙古	5165.7	1607.6	1716.4	-86.7	31374.2
辽宁	11297.1	6621.5	4208.3	34.7	87291.4
吉林	19125.4	1107.6	147.2	0.6	64013.5
黑龙江	8799.3	1905.0	1321.5	146.7	55838.1
上海	92607.8	81585.6	19384.4	12425.4	3972.0
江苏	6780.7	2711.3	503.5	621.2	162923.8
浙江	4837.5	4185.5	1382.4	491.4	94356.7
安徽	3484.3	1941.6	852.7	121.0	38924.6
福建	50088.5	13211.0	7989.3	-326.5	35288.6
江西	8710.2	2092.2	668.3	202.9	16672.6
山东					88453.0
河南	4519.1	885.4	323.6	102.5	45591.6
湖北	2490.1	295.9	320.6	-3.0	61546.3
湖南	9074.0	1829.2	1200.5	20.9	30678.4
广东	5911.8	2324.1	1762.1	72.9	212989.1
广西	15997.4	3338.1	1909.3	-45.0	40402.3
海南	116.0	1836.8	910.2	63.5	
重庆	10808.1	3203.6	1981.9	18.7	27841.7
四川	32538.3	28808.4	6836.4	2180.0	67190.4
贵州	55517.6	19343.4	9573.0	1429.8	35146.0
云南	3820.0	50.0			36012.9
西藏	367.2				1867.0
陕西	2840.0	348.0	69.1	4.6	20304.4
甘肃					19549.8
青海	733.3				1221.0
宁夏	20.0				530.0
新疆	6616.1	1650.0	189.0		3482.2

单位：万元

单位会计制度财务指标		民间非营利组织会计制度财务指标		
本年收入合计	本年支出合计	固定资产原价	本年收入合计	本年支出合计
985770.2	**938659.5**	**38340.0**	**8583.0**	**10029.1**
40988.3	38302.3			
15241.7	17211.5			
33359.7	33306.1	150.0	12.0	8.0
14623.3	15060.7			
16459.9	15925.1	433.0	18.4	23.4
63060.8	58009.8	1840.5	368.6	121.0
10750.4	11015.1	2.0		
36019.4	31126.7	200.0	18.5	0.3
1634.0	1634.0			
98969.7	97521.8	6082.7	3716.3	3348.5
91648.5	82563.6			
32242.5	32058.9	2720.0	1106.0	1024.1
22738.1	21177.6	634.0		45.0
16087.3	17286.9	1992.0	36.0	1882.8
66230.0	66230.0	1648.5	857.3	857.3
22597.7	22749.5			
56896.2	51502.2	1030.0	600.0	455.0
33526.3	31765.8	500.0	500.0	500.0
149635.2	136518.3	625.0	80.0	48.0
24467.5	25435.2			
933.8	706.8			
37603.1	32744.3	13726.0	1053.0	1045.0
37860.7	37342.9	700.0		60.0
6282.0	7192.8	1302.0	29.0	2.1
13955.2	12495.7			
610.0	617.0			
26994.2	27567.1	313.0	29.0	19.2
10305.2	9345.9	903.7	37.8	18.2
725.5	725.5	587.0	44.0	48.4
63.0	213.0	2096.6	75.8	474.0
3261.0	3307.4	854.0	1.3	48.8

C-3-15 公

地区	单位数	年末职工人数		受教育程度		职业资
			女性	大学专科人数	大学本科及以上人数	助理社会工作师人数
全国	**1386**	**26314**	**9455**	**5551**	**2417**	**187**
中央级						
北京	34	1112	382	203	266	9
天津	6	147	50	20	45	
河北	13	393	133	91	34	
山西	25	601	189	154	112	
内蒙古	24	550	161	155	73	3
辽宁	274	2344	629	681	345	36
吉林	45	1918	608	242	95	
黑龙江	32	477	110	130	34	1
上海	49	2297	1073	348	156	5
江苏	110	1204	442	391	124	20
浙江	81	1115	276	116	75	
安徽	57	648	229	152	41	9
福建	19	365	156	69	29	1
江西	5	132	44	41	21	8
山东	38	541	197	162	79	9
河南	42	1043	401	258	78	2
湖北	56	831	272	222	79	5
湖南	44	800	319	243	69	10
广东	70	1859	630	282	119	15
广西	30	714	314	207	99	8
海南	8	148	29	22	3	2
重庆	38	806	324	189	47	8
四川	119	2036	830	419	163	21
贵州	31	1350	598	260	83	1
云南	23	348	103	73	19	8
西藏						
陕西	39	1251	466	132	50	1
甘肃	31	519	157	67	22	
青海	8	54	13	3		
宁夏	20	275	113	43	13	3
新疆	15	436	207	176	44	2

墓

单位：个、人、人次、时

格水平	年龄结构				志愿服务	
社会工作师人数	35岁及以下人数	36岁至45岁人数	46岁至55岁人数	56岁及以上人数	志愿者服务人次数	志愿服务时间
290	**7508**	**9370**	**7029**	**2407**	**2555**	**8256**
6	401	354	272	85	26	26
	30	58	41	18		
3	119	124	89	61	8	32
	252	213	91	45		
	168	177	163	42		
143	689	733	719	203	51	84
2	654	618	555	91		
1	101	234	105	37		
	503	735	723	336	100	200
14	238	495	349	122	350	1556
1	199	320	403	193	460	966
7	195	249	157	47	797	2071
	106	148	80	31		
15	53	59	14	6		
9	223	185	103	30		
14	328	437	203	75	41	123
20	270	325	178	58	12	36
10	292	295	172	41	40	150
3	555	677	493	134		
5	268	268	141	37		
	28	49	49	22		
	241	258	225	82	43	84
16	589	765	538	144	23	72
5	357	523	340	130	419	2358
8	60	112	39	137		
1	252	459	437	103	144	376
	125	199	179	16		
	7	33	13	1		
7	43	96	83	53		
	162	172	75	27	41	122

C-3-15续表

地 区	企业会计制度财务指标				事业单位会计制度财务指标		
	固定资产原价	本年收入合计	本年支出合计	营业利润	固定资产原价	本年收入合计	本年费用合计
全 国	**590336.6**	**899717.3**	**209516.2**	**197964.1**	**211837.4**	**289705.9**	**252125.7**
中央级							
北 京	25463.9	59255.5	20477.4	15737.6	35545.4	70637.5	71802.5
天 津	5980.2	5653.2	1610.2	2493.8	8515.4	15142.8	10232.4
河 北	3732.2	4121.6	2596.4	-241.6	2782.2	6930.9	4922.5
山 西	14700.0	3061.1	1454.1	-530.1	1071.4	5901.1	5287.0
内蒙古	9605.9	3689.0	1684.8	180.0	531.8	2012.6	1980.2
辽 宁	31204.3	20061.8	9788.2	2573.6	13652.1	18158.0	16069.3
吉 林	3125.7	1112.9	580.3	-101.4	931.4	3066.6	3222.5
黑龙江	8524.4	8122.8	4114.9	565.3	5428.9	7211.5	6255.2
上 海	165184.5	393393.6	54916.5	107612.8			
江 苏	32176.9	58698.6	10584.6	33678.5	20331.0	33429.1	27799.2
浙 江	23217.0	48886.4	13251.9	9829.5	5408.1	10475.3	7335.2
安 徽	13166.8	9373.7	2982.8	1472.2	8387.1	11101.2	8658.7
福 建	8062.2	8889.5	3007.1	1337.0	391.5	2916.0	1592.1
江 西	1542.3	2180.7	756.2	118.0	525.0	310.0	310.0
山 东	7108.9	4828.3	1944.6	479.1	8859.1	8779.0	8779.0
河 南	16585.0	7663.8	3285.4	773.6	3302.4	4265.7	3717.9
湖 北	11395.2	18599.5	7639.0	2247.7	18422.7	28757.9	19800.3
湖 南	15158.4	5765.3	1693.7	497.9	11676.1	5766.1	5662.6
广 东	45084.1	33678.1	13069.5	4886.3	13079.4	19281.5	17188.0
广 西	18187.0	77321.6	7730.5	3070.1	2371.3	4875.6	5220.4
海 南	17527.5	2345.2	1751.0	269.5	311.0	1018.0	189.5
重 庆	22752.2	22857.0	9181.7	2528.2	775.2	2267.5	4462.9
四 川	31662.0	31259.5	12441.0	2164.2	36298.9	16655.9	14249.8
贵 州	22757.2	30442.6	11173.2	2946.9	899.0	30.1	870.1
云 南	9419.5	6127.5	1931.1	912.0	579.9	132.4	110.2
西 藏							
陕 西	13455.2	22428.3	8459.6	914.4	2181.5	4398.3	1361.3
甘 肃	6218.0	7206.5	1091.1	1506.2	8257.3	2084.1	1984.1
青 海	280.0	30.0	30.0		20.0	30.0	30.0
宁 夏	5732.0	1363.7	232.4	-1.8	1002.3	2913.2	1880.8
新 疆	1328.1	1300.0	57.0	44.6	300.0	1158.0	1152.0

单位：万元

民间非营利组织会计制度财务指标			穴位数	#本年销售穴位数	安葬数	#本年安葬数	节地生态安葬数
固定资产原价	本年收入合计	本年费用合计					
20957.6	**8606.9**	**6346.9**	**13011599**	**511032**	**9180995**	**429258**	**125814**
			728578	15217	588836	20967	2987
			150156	3441	189036	4947	7931
			201902	3865	95098	5175	11
800.0			130221	3698	65395	4007	8
13.0		3.0	182599	20000	123111	7600	
6426.1	2329.7	2401.6	821376	66027	488822	29424	2203
			20946	1056	11211	1112	
46.0		53.4	140143	14197	116930	18371	
			2011419	72879	1401510	49410	345
2775.5	590.6	243.8	1455666	84383	1287095	53100	40545
347.4	1086.5	524.8	1087967	28662	884165	28220	3511
170.0	102.0	63.0	365662	12913	313548	14225	1448
	2.0		145397	7008	99499	6970	135
50.0		25.0	20341	1059	14282	1322	832
2300.0	205.7	205.7	177595	6597	122902	6737	28578
			238407	5725	147307	6705	334
43.0	14.0	14.0	903725	15397	614282	19268	1999
	84.0	10.0	234362	14364	106426	17085	3852
1278.0	232.7	78.1	902240	25930	555311	21597	1126
			372311	13987	224879	13358	4408
			75352	2408	46526	2536	4200
490.0	841.0	841.0	546800	12224	286038	12479	14141
3163.6	1469.0	1315.6	1160930	33252	725024	34750	2223
2161.0	1247.0	402.0	333528	13794	186244	13629	125
			106312	3659	48507	4762	3225
120.0	5.2	4.8	290002	13258	268473	15765	274
600.0	285.5	86.1	147092	6788	130743	7104	1353
			5359	1368	2597	322	
20.0	10.0	5.0	37901	4904	25267	4776	
154.0	102.0	70.0	17310	2972	11931	3535	20

C-3-16 殡葬管

地区	单位数	年末职工人数		受教育程度		职业资
			女性	大学专科人数	大学本科及以上人数	助理社会工作师人数
全国	**1005**	**8462**	**2254**	**2976**	**1686**	**101**
中央级						
北京	6	84	38	14	52	
天津	11	170	38	44	79	
河北	9	95	27	30	9	
山西	11	75	24	35	17	
内蒙古	37	282	63	86	40	4
辽宁	52	401	121	162	132	8
吉林	42	450	59	190	39	
黑龙江	12	125	41	62	46	
上海	9	44	17	15	25	1
江苏	46	272	82	78	75	12
浙江	67	396	95	148	127	6
安徽	25	82	28	24	14	1
福建	54	531	127	137	78	10
江西	25	177	31	45	8	3
山东	11	95	32	28	12	
河南	81	1130	361	341	168	23
湖北	25	316	89	153	41	5
湖南	49	489	96	221	89	1
广东	84	935	202	268	143	13
广西	35	328	90	99	72	6
海南	6	52	7	11	7	
重庆	31	230	100	77	64	1
四川	72	434	147	197	55	1
贵州	39	295	62	135	64	1
云南	46	218	63	89	66	3
西藏						
陕西	32	266	80	89	52	
甘肃	13	96	33	26	16	1
青海	2	8	2	4		
宁夏	26	94	20	31	46	
新疆	47	292	79	137	50	1

理机构

单位：个、人、人次、时

格水平	年龄结构				志愿服务	
社会工作师人数	35岁及以下人数	36岁至45岁人数	46岁至55岁人数	56岁及以上人数	志愿者服务人次数	志愿服务时间
138	**2814**	**3479**	**1705**	**464**	**820**	**2467**
3	41	23	15	5	9	9
2	41	55	45	29	100	200
	43	29	21	2		
	22	29	21	3		
12	84	117	61	20		
15	101	175	104	21	12	22
	66	220	107	57		
	32	57	30	6		
6	13	16	6	9		
9	68	124	63	17	38	60
11	151	141	85	19	10	61
1	11	39	27	5	104	354
14	156	230	115	30	10	20
	61	77	31	8		
	27	40	23	5		
15	545	416	144	25	67	234
5	109	121	68	18		
4	200	220	59	10	5	10
20	297	392	203	43		
4	98	122	80	28		
	13	22	15	2		
	50	117	38	25	141	283
1	128	188	104	14	2	7
3	142	106	41	6	93	254
3	74	104	30	10		
5	102	98	52	14	74	188
1	40	34	16	6		
	2	4	2			
4	24	42	24	4	75	525
	73	121	75	23	80	240

C-3-16续表

地区	企业会计制度财务指标				事业
	固定资产原价	营业收入	费用合计	营业利润	固定资产原价
全 国	**12454.0**	**3987.0**	**2895.0**	**406.0**	**138083.7**
中央级					
北 京					2513.5
天 津					8231.7
河 北					3571.3
山 西					205.4
内蒙古	538.0	50.0	12.0	5.0	1787.5
辽 宁	1.0				1054.5
吉 林	683.0	365.0	271.0	44.0	9952.3
黑龙江	578.0	750.0	761.0	190.0	2435.7
上 海					775.6
江 苏	5.0	6.0			1577.7
浙 江	41.0	250.0	38.0	29.0	3495.0
安 徽					5428.9
福 建	674.0	1012.0	453.0	123.0	6350.6
江 西	200.0				1007.6
山 东					772.7
河 南					906.6
湖 北					9665.4
湖 南	6704.0	367.0	516.0		15650.5
广 东	36.0	91.0	80.0		12006.1
广 西					5154.5
海 南	10.0				7770.3
重 庆	200.0				4129.5
四 川	407.0	112.0	113.0	-11.0	5645.1
贵 州	967.0	686.0	592.0	19.0	1587.3
云 南					1615.6
西 藏					
陕 西					4689.5
甘 肃	430.0	30.0	21.0	7.0	385.2
青 海					257.1
宁 夏	65.0	48.0	14.0		490.2
新 疆	916.0	222.0	25.0	1.0	18970.8

单位：万元

单位会计制度财务指标		民间非营利组织会计制度财务指标		
本年收入合计	本年支出合计	固定资产原价	本年收入合计	本年支出合计
155961.7	**134129.7**	**12109.2**	**3260.5**	**2554.3**
11689.9	7121.2			
31039.0	12085.4			
1239.7	1275.4			
1098.2	1101.4			
1791.0	1916.7			
3382.8	3446.1		20.0	20.0
2294.6	3242.2			
1011.2	1459.3			
4939.2	4905.3			
3269.3	3189.0	311.0	1447.7	441.5
9824.7	9853.3	85.0	220.0	235.0
1034.6	1247.1		15.0	6.4
6770.9	6621.1			
558.4	570.8			
594.2	594.2	134.2	480.0	480.0
3381.9	3346.9	10.0	2.0	2.0
5056.7	5107.1	29.0	2.5	2.5
9213.2	8749.2			
18588.8	17170.5			
5164.4	5272.3			
3647.4	5661.4			
3149.5	3268.4	745.0	282.3	455.8
3166.1	3172.3	10000.0	776.0	900.0
1160.8	1088.1			
1457.6	1481.9			
1981.9	1980.8	100.0	15.0	9.0
1177.3	1146.0	25.0		2.1
39.4	44.4			
956.6	1148.6			
17282.4	16863.3	670.0		

C-4-1 其他

地 区	单位数	编制登记	年末职工人数	女性	受教育程度 大学专科人数	大学本科及以上人数
全 国	**1987**	**1987**	**16197**	**7490**	**4114**	**6923**
中央级	29	29	1413	714	168	1199
北 京	73	73	890	408	184	598
天 津	21	21	185	97	48	121
河 北	35	35	710	419	159	119
山 西	77	77	518	249	123	147
内蒙古	21	21	226	90	80	108
辽 宁	105	105	800	329	221	374
吉 林	26	26	207	81	57	31
黑龙江	27	27	234	106	80	75
上 海	40	40	414	229	90	281
江 苏	68	68	537	257	145	240
浙 江	156	156	776	358	164	386
安 徽	25	25	151	59	53	40
福 建	48	48	241	119	52	151
江 西	392	392	1385	489	299	250
山 东	52	52	436	208	104	176
河 南	126	126	1564	720	408	657
湖 北	84	84	732	333	211	260
湖 南	97	97	807	386	224	239
广 东	37	37	435	225	125	221
广 西	73	73	799	361	285	242
海 南	8	8	69	25	30	25
重 庆	21	21	131	45	41	64
四 川	135	135	948	463	273	434
贵 州	76	76	502	207	147	175
云 南	29	29	188	68	61	57
西 藏						
陕 西	39	39	381	202	104	66
甘 肃	31	31	230	76	64	73
青 海	3	3	15	9	5	10
宁 夏	8	8	62	22	16	18
新 疆	25	25	211	136	93	86

事业单位

单位：个、人、人次、时

职业资格水平		年龄结构				志愿服务	
助理社会工作师人数	社会工作师人数	35岁及以下人数	36岁至45岁人数	46岁至55岁人数	56岁及以上人数	志愿者服务人次数	志愿服务时间
362	**494**	**5703**	**5666**	**3831**	**997**	**9052**	**23376**
20	41	605	401	313	94		
19	36	315	277	231	67		
7	9	45	70	54	16	300	600
17	17	288	227	176	19	680	2930
5	19	105	207	165	41		
	8	84	79	52	11		
1	9	255	311	153	81		
23	2	92	71	29	15		
19	2	107	82	40	5		
18	53	143	141	98	32		
22	34	153	219	141	24	594	1877
15	68	269	244	219	44	3908	7174
8	3	24	64	58	5	122	256
6	23	89	84	61	7	18	72
31	15	425	708	224	28	701	2795
8	13	158	136	109	33	1848	5195
40	21	588	484	376	116	126	450
9	17	238	254	175	65	107	171
7	15	271	279	186	71	160	750
6	14	176	144	87	28		
27	22	300	259	191	49		
6	1	26	21	17	5		
1	1	31	56	38	6	100	200
32	27	416	292	193	47		
9	9	158	158	164	22	235	556
1	5	75	68	33	12		
1		144	140	80	17	111	288
2	4	60	67	87	16	42	62
		7	4	4			
	1	7	20	24	11		
2	5	49	99	53	10		

C-4-1续表

地 区	事业单位会计制度财务指标			
	固定资产原价	本年收入合计	本年支出合计	营业利润
全 国	**21811.9**	**22606.5**	**10727.6**	**1074.8**
中央级	13537.6	17960.0	7752.9	-5.5
北 京	195.1	1643.1	394.4	489.9
天 津				
河 北				
山 西	3.2	1.0	1.0	
内蒙古				
辽 宁				
吉 林	1.0			
黑龙江				
上 海				
江 苏	48.4	993.7	451.1	668.0
浙 江	1394.3	81.7	521.9	-200.0
安 徽	883.0	50.0	81.0	-4.0
福 建				
江 西	827.8	103.7	88.6	
山 东				
河 南				
湖 北				
湖 南				
广 东				
广 西	2878.8	330.3	482.9	-153.4
海 南				
重 庆				
四 川	2006.7	1443.0	953.8	279.8
贵 州				
云 南				
西 藏				
陕 西				
甘 肃				
青 海				
宁 夏	15.0			
新 疆	21.0			

单位：万元

民间非营利组织会计制度财务指标		
固定资产原价	本年收入合计	本年费用合计
1198.4	**1794.6**	**1470.0**
157.5	176.3	151.3
1.8	10.2	1.9
	10.0	10.0
1.0	57.6	9.5
5.0	3.0	8.0
15.0	11.6	28.7
126.7	531.5	360.2
129.0	223.0	115.2
110.7	87.9	57.2
17.5	38.0	17.3
10.3	206.4	206.4
15.0	60.6	50.6
51.0	3.0	1.0
12.0	54.2	7.0
0.1		
392.4	189.5	202.0
68.5	97.1	196.4
70.9	27.7	36.5
9.0	2.0	5.8
5.0	5.0	5.0

06

附 录

2017

《中国民政统计年鉴-2016》勘误

1.第98页，第1行，2015年社会服务社会工作师“44480”修改为“45248”，助理社会工作师“52104”修改为“59043”；第2 行，2015年社会工作师“12931”修改为“13699”，助理社会工作师“19588”修改为“20902”。

2.第99页，第1行，2015年不提供住宿的社会服务机构社会工作师“8470”修改为“9238”，助理社会工作师“14964”修改为“16278”；第99页，第3行，增加一行，分别为768、845、−9.1、1314、1870、−29.7。

3.第106页，倒数第1行，“52.4”修改为“68.4”，“29.1”修改为“68.5”。

4.第141页，社会工作师，2015年“11912”修改为“13699”；第141页，助理社会工作师，2015年“60379”修改为“59403”、“19272”修改为“20902”、“38342”修改为“37006”。

5.第152页，“十二五”时期，“135.2”修改为“137”、2014年“24.36”修改为“25”、2015年“30.2”修改为“32”。

6.第153页，倒数第2行、“1.96”修改为“2”、“0.2”修改为“2”。

7.第279页，内容与第280页，及281页第一列内容重复。